The Matrix of Race

Second Edition

Sara Miller McCune founded SAGE Publishing in 1965 to support the dissemination of usable knowledge and educate a global community. SAGE publishes more than 1000 journals and over 600 new books each year, spanning a wide range of subject areas. Our growing selection of library products includes archives, data, case studies and video. SAGE remains majority owned by our founder and after her lifetime will become owned by a charitable trust that secures the company's continued independence.

Los Angeles | London | New Delhi | Singapore | Washington DC | Melbourne

The Matrix of Race

Social Construction, Intersectionality, and Inequality

Second Edition

Rodney D. Coates

Miami University of Ohio

Abby L. Ferber

University of Colorado, Colorado Springs

David L. Brunsma

Virginia Tech

Los Angeles | London | New Delhi
Singapore | Washington DC | Melbourne

FOR INFORMATION:

SAGE Publications, Inc.
2455 Teller Road
Thousand Oaks, California 91320
E-mail: order@sagepub.com

SAGE Publications Ltd.
1 Oliver's Yard
55 City Road
London, EC1Y 1SP
United Kingdom

SAGE Publications India Pvt. Ltd.
B 1/I 1 Mohan Cooperative Industrial Area
Mathura Road, New Delhi 110 044
India

SAGE Publications Asia-Pacific Pte. Ltd.
18 Cross Street #10-10/11/12
China Square Central
Singapore 048423

Printed in Canada

ISBN 978-1-5443-5497-2

Acquisitions Editors: Jeff Lasser

Content Development Editor: Tara Slagle

Product Associate: Tiara Beatty

Typesetter: diacriTech

Proofreader: Jennifer Grubba

Cover Designer: Scott Van Atta

Marketing Manager: Jennifer Jones

BRIEF CONTENTS

DETAILED CONTENTS

PREFACE

OUR STORIES

We (Dave, Abby, and Rodney) have studied, researched, published, and taught in the fields of race and ethnic studies, critical race theory, and pedagogy collectively for over 75 years. In that time, we have seen how the field of race and ethnic studies has morphed into critical race and ethnic studies. We have seen how social movements, activism, and political processes have not only shaped our discussions but shaped how we view the world. In the process, we have learned that race and ethnicity are not static, but dynamic. This dynamism is based upon the observation that we can change not only the parameters of race and ethnicity, but also the structures, practices, and policies as well. As active agents, we can and must be aware if we are to make these changes substantive, informed, and inclusive. For this to happen, we must all be willing to engage. The first step of engagement is to tell our stories. It is our stories that define not only our realities but ourselves. As we retell these and other stories, we construct the building blocks that give value and meaning to and for our lives. These stories help us to understand each other and provide bridges that link us into the fabric of our communities and societies. Our stories are important, they tell of not only our past but can point to a different future. They are therefore our legacy and our hope. The story of race has shaped our nation, both our past and present, but it need not shape our future. Race is deeply personal for each one of us, yet, as sociologists, we have learned much more about ourselves by situating our own lives within a broader context. We hope to help you do the same. We are all situated somewhere in the matrix, so this text is about each of us. We are all in this together. We begin with our own stories.

Rodney

My grandfather was a sharecropper from Yazoo, Mississippi. In 1917, he arrived in East St. Louis, Illinois, a city with a robust industrial base that benefited significantly from World War I, and where much of the mostly White labor force was either in the military or on strike. Many Black men were migrating to East St. Louis at the time, looking for work.

White organized labor, fearful of losing job security, became hostile and targeted the new arrivals. On May 28, at a White union meeting, rumors began circulating that Black men were forcibly seducing and raping White women. A mob of more than 3,000 White men left this meeting and began beating random Black men on the street. The violence claimed the life of a 14-year-old boy, his mother was scalped, and 244 buildings were destroyed—all before the governor called in the National Guard. Rumors continued to circulate, and Blacks were selectively attacked by roving groups of White vigilantes.

But it wasn't over. On July 1, 1917, a Black man attacked a White man. The retaliatory response by Whites was massive, and an entire section of the Black community was destroyed while the police and fire departments refused to respond. My grandfather said that "blood ran like water through the streets." Many residents were lynched, and the entire Black section of the city was burned. No Whites have ever been charged with or convicted of any of these crimes. For the next 50 years, segregation maintained an uneasy peace in this troubled city.

Racial segregation, not only in housing but also in hospitals, dictated that I could not be born in the city where my parents resided (East St. Louis, Illinois), because the only hospital that would allow Negro women access was in St. Louis, Missouri. I grew up in a segregated city and went to all-Black elementary, middle, and high schools. Since mainstream educational institutions tended not to hire Black professionals, many of my English, math, and science teachers had advanced degrees, so I received the equivalent of a private education. Given my Blackness and the presumption that I would be a laborer and not a scholar, I also was equally trained in carpentry and sheet metal work. A system designed to keep the races separate provided an outstanding education—one that I was more than ready to take advantage of during the height of the civil rights movement.

The landmark U.S. Supreme Court decision in *Brown v. Board of Education* (1954) had desegregated the schools, and suddenly places like Southern Illinois University, the University of Illinois, and the University of Chicago were open to someone like me, a kid from a city that would soon become defined as a ghetto. As Blacks asserted their rights and the courts supported them, more doors opened to Blacks, and many Whites began to flee to the suburbs. This White flight, and the loss of business and industries, served to create ghettos where just a few short years before there had been thriving urban centers. I eventually obtained a bachelor's degree, two master's degrees, and a PhD from some of the best educational institutions in this country. My story has sensitized me to the ways in which race, class, and gender are intertwined in the great American narrative. I specialize in critical pedagogy, critical race theory, race and ethnic relations, stratification, human rights and social justice, educational sociology, political processes, urban sociology, political sociology, and public sociology.

Abby

I was raised to not recognize my whiteness. Instead, throughout my childhood, my Jewish and gender identity felt much more salient. Growing up in a White, Jewish, upper-middle-class suburb of Cleveland, Ohio (one of the most segregated U.S. cities), I was taught about the Nazi Holocaust, the Inquisition, and the long history of pogroms. My elementary school building was bombed and anti-Semitic epithets were scrawled on the walls. The message I internalized was that Jews were the universal scapegoat, and even when they were fully assimilated and successful, their safety was never secure. I learned that my own sense of identity was less important than how others saw me.

The whitening of my ancestors is part of the story of race. My great-grandmother, Anna, whom I am named for, fled her small Russian village when she was 16 years old to avoid an arranged marriage. Her parents disowned her, and never spoke to her again. She immigrated to the United States, and years later learned that her family had been killed in Nazi concentration camps. Her husband, my great-grandfather, learned the same story about his own family. Successive generations have experienced anti-semitic incidents.

Yet, I have always been the beneficiary of White privilege, *every single day*. I have never had to worry about being pulled over by police, not getting a job, or not being able to rent or purchase a home because of my race. I did not have to teach my daughter how to behave around the police for her own safety. As Jews became defined as White, my grandparents were able to take out loans and start a small business, and my parents both attended college.

As a graduate student, I learned I was a White, heterosexual, upper middle class, and temporarily able-bodied, Jewish woman. My dissertation research on the organized White supremacist movement made my White privilege much more visible and real to me, ironically, because these White supremacists believe I am not White. Studying this movement was surreal as I spent my days immersed in writings that proclaimed I was not White, while simultaneously being steeped in White privilege. I recognized that I felt safe and protected *because* of my Whiteness.

I contribute to the construction and reproduction of White privilege and White supremacy whether I intend to or not. Rather than experiencing guilt or shame, I work to be a part of the solution. I feel the urgency of the many issues we examine here, and hope White readers will as well.

Dave

I was born in Des Moines, Iowa, to a Puerto Rican mother and a largely unknown White father. My mother and her brothers and sisters had been adopted and raised by my solidly White, privileged, Christian grandparents in mostly White neighborhoods. While there were some variations in the degree of Puerto Rican identity felt among my family members, by and large they were White. I too was raised White. I have come to embrace my Puerto Rican identity, but I did not really know about it until the stories and structures of my life were already quite fully built along White lines.

As I grew up, although I delved into critical literatures, music, and film outside the scope of public school and family, it was expected that I would be White—talk White, dress White, and, ultimately, think and live White. I was also destined to reproduce the structures of White privilege and racism, despite the fact that I could see them then, and can see them even more clearly now. My life as a White American preordained my complacency and tacit agreement with the exploitative racial contract in White America, even while I fully disagreed with it.

I went to a Mennonite college that preaches a kind of liberation theology, from which many go on to serve in missionary or "development" capacities all around the world—with good intentions but often ending up as color-blind extensions of American (or Jesus) imperialism. There were few people of color there, or in graduate school. Meanwhile, my critical, social justice lenses were becoming more sharply focused. I am still learning to "see" myself, my story, my place in the matrix; this is an important step in seeing others deeply as well. My research is focused on (multi)racial identity, race and ethnicity, human rights, sociology of education, and the sociology of culture. I use these now to work to reclaim those stories that have been ignored, to lay bare the structures of White racism, and to help rewrite the stories toward racial justice.

Now, we encourage you to join us.

ROAD MAP OF THE MATRIX

Chapter 1: Race and the Social Construction of Difference

The Matrix of Race provides a lens by which we can critically evaluate and understand how race, intertwined with such things as class, gender, sexuality, ethnicity across history, geography, and institutional structures produces a racialized system and hierarchy favoring some, particularly European Americans, at the expense of others, particularly Native Americans, Asian Americans, African Americans, and Hispanic Americans. History, the reality of our shared past, reflects a series of choices. These choices, once made, often take on a life of their own, but we should always remember that they were and continue to be choices. Nothing demonstrates the accuracy of this assessment than the particular set of choices that served to shape our nation having to do with race. Social scientists and geneticists alike have come to understand that race and racial categorizations are uniquely social creations that have been purposefully constructed. Specific rewards, privileges, and sanctions have been used to support and legitimate race. White supremacy and privilege, systemic racial oppression and segregation, racially motivated hate crimes and criminal sanctions are deeply rooted in our Nation's history. Racial inequity permeates every part of our lives: schools, housing, medicine, workplaces, our criminal justice and political systems all continue to reproduce racial inequity and drastically different opportunities, experiences, and life outcomes based on race. Our goal in this book is to provide you with historical perspectives, theoretical frameworks, and diverse views of race and racial ideologies so that you can intelligently participate and contribute to dialogues and practices that will ultimately dismantle race and racial structures.

Chapter 2: The Shaping of a Nation: The Social Construction of Race in America

The next chapter will explore the shaping of our Nation. It will highlight the patterns, practices, and realities created through the shaping of our nation were a set of choices that established the racial templates for the matrix of race. These racial templates, varying across the different colonial systems, account for the different racial trajectories that came into being. In this chapter we will see how the decisions by French and Spanish colonial powers decided to establish settler colonies that precluded the initial immigration of European women. Within these colonial situations there was an increased likelihood that marriage unions would form with women from various indigenous tribal groups and imported Africans. These choices meant that the racial structures created were more likely to be more diverse and fluid. Creolization, reflecting multiracial family structures, were the obvious outcomes. The racial hierarchies that developed tended to reflect these decisions, as gradations of skin tone favoring lighter skinned individuals and groups were accorded higher status. Alternatively, within the English colonies, where the decision was to colonize, English women were encouraged to immigrate. Within these structures, more rigid racial rules were established that discouraged interracial unions. These rules were particularly aimed at preserving the rights and inheritance of children born of European unions, while delegitimizing the children of interracial ones. Racial hierarchies based upon the presumption of Whitehite purity resulted. As a consequence, we see the creation of intersectional identities. These identities, favoring either skin tone or presumed White purity, by definition asserted the primacy of White males and the secondary status of females, regardless of color. Within the more rigid cluster of English colonies, White women were deemed more attractive and desirable than lower status women of color. Alternatively, within either the French or Spanish colonies, biracial and multiracial females with lighter skin tones were perceived as more attractive and higher status.

Chapter 3: The Social Construction and Regulation of Families

As we broaden our understanding of what counts as a family, we must reassess historical narratives that have excluded certain family formations. Researchers are not exempt from the prejudices and assumptions of the broader culture. As family researcher Stephen Marks (2000, 611) reflects: "Most family scholars continue to be White, heterosexual, married persons such as myself. The research published . . . reflects the interests of those who do the studies." However, as more and more research is conducted by scholars previously excluded—men and women of color, White women, LGBTQ+ people, and working-class people, for example—the kinds of subjects that are being studied, the questions that are being asked, and the concealed stories and voices of resistance that are being brought in are changing the field. As Marks goes on, "These scholars have challenged their exclusion." Family structure is embedded in the wider social structure defined by race, class, and gender. In fact, historically what constituted family and kin, who could become a family, and who were "illegitimate" continues to reflect our racial designations and problems. Thus, we see broadening recognition and research on a wide array of family formations and experiences. At the same time, we need to cultivate more curious citizens who will ask the unasked questions and challenge narratives that distort the realities we see all around us.

Chapter 4: Work and Wealth Inequality

The workplace and the economy, like other institutions, are structured by, and actively reproduce, racial inequality. Historical inequality, occupational segregation, discrimination, inequitable application of social policy, immigration policy, and economic restructuring are some of the significant factors contributing to racial inequality in the workplace and the economy. While the impact of income inequality on families today should not be underestimated, it is essential that we also understand the concept of wealth inequality. Wealth inequality reveals the lasting impact of our history of state-sponsored racism. These factors are concealed by stock stories that blame individuals or cultures for their own lack of economic success. Finding solutions that will work is not the primary problem we face, however; rather, the problem is changing attitudes. Our stock stories about American meritocracy and color blindness must be challenged.

How do we explain the fact that the intersections of race, class, and gender are so fundamental to the shaping of inequality, power, and privilege—yet members of the dominant group so firmly assert that race no longer matters and that the gender revolution is over? There is increased recognition of "diversity in American society," and yet there is also a persistent belief among privileged groups that race does not matter. This belief keeps people blind to the continuing differences in power and privilege that characterize U.S. society, making it difficult to generate public support for programs designed to reduce inequality.

Chapter 5: Health, Medicine, and Healthcare

Today's disparities among racial and ethnic groups in health and mortality are evidence of the historical and ongoing effects of structural racism. Racial disparities exist in healthcare access, disease prevention, identification of disease, treatment, care coordination, outcomes, patient satisfaction, and more. Today's health disparities have been significantly shaped by historical patterns of White privilege and White supremacy. Modern medicine displaced traditional methods of healing in many cultures and played a central role in the construction of racial classifications and corresponding notions of difference. History is replete with examples of resistance to health inequities. African Americans developed their own healthcare systems in response to their exclusion from segregated institutions.

The matrix perspective highlights various social factors contributing to racial health inequity and inequality, including stress, social relationships, socioeconomic factors, residential segregation, environmental factors, and mistrust, as well as the interactions of race, class, gender, age, and more. The field of social epidemiology highlights the relationships among race, class, and health, and explains the "epidemiological paradox" of better *overall* health among Asians and Latinos, racial groups with significant numbers of immigrants.

Disenfranchised groups have created many organizations to address and act as advocates for their health needs. Urban Indian health organizations and a wide array of health organizations founded by women of color place these groups' health needs within the broader context of social and institutional factors shaped by a history of racism. These organizations argue that health disparities cannot be remedied without broader structural changes. Organizations started and run by women of color and disabled women have fought for a more inclusive understanding of women's reproductive health needs.

Chapter 6: Education

Schools and institutions can liberate or oppress, and their roles are still debated today, as the matrix of race still matters in education and vice versa. The institution of education in the United States has been shaped by decisions, definitions, and declarations about differences. In this chapter we will explore the history of U.S. public education and its expressed and concealed functions, and we will reflect on who gets an education and why. Regardless of type or level of schooling, the institution of education in the United States has almost always been the site of conflict, debate, and confrontation over access, meanings of education, and what is taught, why, and to whom (as well as whose knowledge counts as knowledge worth having). This conflict is often between dominant (White, male, upper-class, heterosexual) groups and Blacks, Latinos, women, poor and working-class families, sexual minorities, and those with physical and mental disabilities. To understand current educational realities, we must first understand the formative moments in the shaping of the matrix of education. The institution of education is both vital and complex. While some see education as a solution for inequalities of all sorts, others see the education system as rife with inequalities—especially for those who are not White or affluent. Educational opportunities are not the same for all. In this chapter, we examine how educational segregation is woven into the fabric of the United States, how different educations are creating different identities, and the important role of the matrix of race in this reality.

Chapter 7: Crime and Deviance

Race, gender, and class disparities are represented in who gets defined as either criminal or deviant. Historically these differentials can be traced to the slave codes, immigration policy, and the development of reservations for Native Americans. Taken together, these practices, policies, and laws account for the racially differentiated criminal justice system. Whiteness was created as a means of assuring that the racial state would be preserved. Laws were created to fortify this structure at the expense of people of color. Contemporary trends in scholarship on crime and deviance highlight the racial, gendered, and class differentials in how justice is administered across the United States. These disparities are observed throughout the justice system, in differential policing, racial profiling, and differential sentencing and incarceration rates.

The matrix of crime and deviance starts by recognizing that the assumptions about crime and deviance are intended to ensure that race, gender, and class differentials are preserved. The matrix informs us that certain socially defined people and groups (reflecting the interactions of race, class, and gender) situated in particular spaces and places are more apt to be labeled deviant than others. It also informs us that the nexus of various spaces interacts with social identities to produce different types and definitions of deviance. As we consider the various dimensions of the matrix lens, space and place help us to understand that crime and deviance are situationally and contextually specific. Therefore, urban areas produce different types of deviance possibilities than do corporate spaces. Hate crimes, which constitute a particular type of deviance, are utilized as means of social control. Among the outcomes of the linking of national and corporate policies around crime and deviance have been the militarization of the police and the creation of the prison-industrial complex. These policies have called for increased surveillance, criminalization, and incarceration of the members of designated racial and ethnic groups. Ultimately, this process also accounts for the fact that Blacks, Hispanics, and the poor are more likely to receive the death penalty.

Chapter 8: Power, Politics, and Identities

The U.S. electorate is made up of various identity groups that reflect the matrix of race, class, gender, and region. These identities do not share equally in political outcomes, as witnessed by the significant number of Black and Hispanic felons who have been disenfranchised in recent years. Gender cannot be ignored, as we see how it interacts with race, education, and class, which helps to explain some recent political outcomes. One of these is that Black women, and women in general, are more likely to vote than their male counterparts but less likely to hold political office.

Resource scarcity often underlies political struggles, and political systems come into being to regulate conflicts over these resources. In the process, differences associated with race, class, gender, and geography often become politicized. Our application of the matrix allows us to see how these political processes have played out over time, producing both de jure and de facto outcomes that have unique impacts.

Millennials may change the very course of this country as they become the largest generation and as they become more economically viable and politically active. More diverse than any preceding generation, and with a strong understanding of the effective use of social media, millennials have a huge potential for bringing about political change. The question is not if they will create change, but when and what forms these changes will take.

Chapter 9: Sports and the American Dream

The matrix, with its focus on intersectional differences, helps fill the gaps in our understanding of how sport and athleticism create institutions that have differential impacts on racial, class, and gendered groups within U.S. society. The perspective anticipates that geographic and social locations, identities across time, and agency provide necessary insights into how this process operates. Institutional analysis demonstrates that sport and sporting events produce medial and cultural products. Through these processes race, class, and gender interactions are manifested. Space and place concerns within the matrix approach highlight the importance of geographical and historical spaces that affect social identities within sport. Identities are constantly affected by sports as they legitimate, modify, and re-create racial hegemonies. Finally, both agency and resistance have been demonstrated by multiple individuals and groups who have utilized their status within sport to transform both sport and the nation. An examination of U.S. sport through time reveals many concealed stories. Native Americans, long before European colonization, were active creators of sport and games. Most of these were directly associated with the needs of hunting and gathering communities. Consequently, stick games, racing, hunting, and archery were frequently vital parts of youth socialization. Industrialization served to transform the U.S. sport landscape as it drew an increasingly large number of immigrants and others into the urban centers. One of the significant outcomes of this transformation was the rise in team sports. From the early 19th century, elite sport clubs catering to White ethnics were established throughout the Northeast. Baseball and other team sports were soon to follow.

Chapter 10: The Military, War, and Terrorism

The contemporary U.S. military accounts for 16% of the total U.S. budget, which represents a third of all moneys spent globally on defense. Although it is predominantly male, White, and young, the U.S. military is one of the most diverse institutions in the nation. Race, gender, and age differences occur across all the branches. Younger recruits tend to join the Marine Corps, while the Air Force attracts older recruits. Women are underrepresented in all branches, but they are most likely to enlist in the Air Force. Close to a third of all enlisted personnel are members of racial minority groups. While racial minorities constitute 23.4% of those eligible to enlist, they make up 32.9% of enlisted ranks. Middle- and upper-class individuals are least likely to be found among enlisted personnel. Clear gender differences are evident across the various services. Women of color are more likely to serve in either the Army or the Navy than in other military branches. Immigrants continue to join the military as a means of becoming naturalized citizens. Our military institutions, the most diverse institutions in the nation, hold the key to the effective and efficient use of all our human resources. Encouraging all citizens to serve in, participate with, and provide oversight of our military institutions can be the greatest deterrent to abuses, the greatest safeguard to peace, and the most effective weapon against terrorism. Wars are more likely to occur where lawlessness, hopelessness, and helplessness prevail. The most likely to suffer are those most vulnerable, regardless of whether they are in the United States or abroad. In such situations it is difficult to determine who is right or wrong, evil or good. In reality, none of these terms make any sense in the face of devastated lives, pain, and suffering. We should realize that during our own Revolutionary War, we were the extremists, the terrorists, and the discontents.

Chapter 11: Media

All of the different forms of media have a role in the construction of difference in our lives. Media not only transmits, but it also reproduces our values, ideas, ways of being, and histories. The exciting thing about media is also the daunting thing about media – it is always morphing and shifting as it always morphs and shifts us. Every ethnic group that ventured upon these shores brought with them a range of symbolic communications that told their stories, captured their identities, and projected their values. We look at several approaches to understanding the *whys* and *hows* of media development, as well as how mediated realities reproduce and/or challenge the racial status quo through the information and messages it deploys throughout society. One approach has been to focus on the shape of the media form and the kinds of relationships it encourages, since media is an extension of ourselves and our communities, perhaps the medium, itself, is the message. Often the media and its messages are expressions of the dominant class and the ruling relations of its power—in order to secure that power, dominant messages and controlling images are esigned to etch themselves into the psyche and consciousness, and effectively internally and cognitively colonize a population.

The media are embedded within our society and our relations in a variety of ways; yet, these ways are more or less enhanced and effective depending on our exposure to and our engagement with those forms of media. Whether books and magazines, news, advertising, or film, our position within the matrix affects how we choose (and are able) to engage with those media. The matrix not only impacts individual use and interpretation of these mediated forms, but our positions in the matrix also determines who writes, produces, distributes, and markets such messages and information to which communities, and, with which desires (e.g., profit, power, empowerment, etc.). In order to make media an effective tool of liberation and community organization, we need to develop our media literacy and learn how to harness it in order to create a more just world for all. This is done through hard work, study, and practicing critical media literacy skills. Many minority and racialized groups who have learned how to harness the power of media are using that power to create social movements to effect change for themselves, and ultimately, for all.

Chapter 12: Transforming the Matrix, Transforming the Future

Emerging and transforming stories are all around us, if we learn how to recognize them, acknowledge them, and celebrate as well as amplify them. Doing so will help remake the matrix of race to one that is more inclusive and validating for everyone. Recognizing that some stories serve the status quo, that the stock stories often are only so because they are repeated the most, ingrained within our dominant institutions, and, therefore, wrapped up with power and privilege is crucial to building a new future. Understanding the past and its stories, both those dominant ones and those concealed ones, and why, will help us move forward in strength as a society. This also involves recognizing the connections between the global, the regional, the national, and the local.

When people band together in common desire to affect change, to fight for rights, to amplify and raise their experiences, their stories, their hopes and dreams in a society that has squashed and made them invisible, these are social movements for social justice. People can also band together to attempt to reclaim their oppression over others, pass legislation that supports only a small echelon of society (e.g., White men), and otherwise push against those crying out for social justice—these are social movements of backlash, designed to further bolster structures of oppression and power. The #BlackLivesMatter movement is an excellent example of social movements for social justice and the White supremacist movement, in all its various guises, is a good example of movements against social justice. It is important to understand the power of social movements and compare those organized for racial justice and those designed to maintain the racial status quo in order to work to transform the matrix.

Transforming the matrix where the dizzying variation of experience can come together to create a society that works for all involves recognizing that we are all implicated in the matrix of race—it connects (and works to separate) all of us, it affects each and every one of our lives, identities, communities, and opportunities. As such, we all have a part to play in understanding and then working to change the matrix of race. Activism for racial justice and the involvement of allies in the fight for racial justice is crucial. Equally crucial is to understand the differences between activism and allyship and evaluate your own engagement in transforming the matrix of race. We are all in this together and it will take us, each one, to work to change the matrix.

ACKNOWLEDGMENTS

RODNEY'S ACKNOWLEDGMENTS

I honor the ancestors of all races, ethnicities, genders, and periods who not only survived but also challenged, transformed, and thrived in spite of the racial matrix. I stand on the shoulders of these giants. There are many whose names, input, and insights go unmentioned here, but not forgotten. Throughout my life I have been blessed to have a continual stream of teachers, mentors, colleagues, and heroes who refused to let me be mediocre. So I must thank Clifford Harper, Judith Blau, William J. Wilson, Eduardo Bonilla-Silva, Darnell Hawkins, Douglas Parker, Corey W. Dolgan, Joe Feagin, Al Long, and C. Lee Harrington for always being there. Where would I be without the constant support, love, and companionship of my family? I could not, nor would I want to, make it without you, Sherrill, Angela, Chris, and Avery. And to the hundreds of students who read, studied, asked critical questions about, and reflected on multiple drafts of these chapters—you have my thanks and sympathies. Some of those early drafts were truly murder. My coauthors, Abby and David, what can I say, no words, no tributes can equal your devotion and faith in this project. Thanks, my friends.

ABBY'S ACKNOWLEDGMENTS

I was honored and humbled when Rodney Coates invited me to join this project. I have learned and grown, both personally and professionally, working with Rodney and David. None of us expected that we would still be writing this text in 2017, and it is due to Rodney's persistence and brilliant leadership that we have continued on this journey. I am incredibly grateful for the many colleagues and mentors who have touched my life and strengthened and supported both my professional and personal growth. A few of the people I want to especially acknowledge are Donald Cunnigen, Joe Feagin, Andrea Herrera, Elizabeth Higginbotham, Michael Kimmel, Peggy McIntosh, Eddie Moore Jr., Wanda Rushing, and Diane Wysocki. Personally, I dedicate this book to the late Joan Acker, Miriam Johnson, and Sandra Morgen. When I was a graduate student at the University of Oregon, each of these faculty mentors changed the course of my life as a scholar/teacher, along with Mary Romero, Rose Brewer, and John Lie. I am grateful for my teammates and coconspirators at the Matrix Center (and especially the Knapsack Institute), who have contributed to building the matrix model over the past 18 years; to the many folks I have had the honor of building relationships with in my service to the White Privilege Conference and the Privilege Institute; and to the many people who have invested their time and passion in creating, nurturing, and growing Sociologists for Women in Society. I do not take for granted the gift of this wide community of social justice activists and academics, both those who have preceded me and those I work and grow beside. Finally, and most important, I thank my husband, Joel, and daughter, Sydney, for their patience, support, and boundless love. I love you more than words can tell.

DAVID'S ACKNOWLEDGMENTS

I would like to thank my longtime brother Rodney Coates for reaching out to me in the summer of 2011 to ask if I wanted to join him in creating a unique, critical, and intersectional race textbook. Our early discussions centered on changing the way we teach race and ethnicity to undergraduate students and inspired this textbook. I was equally enthralled when Abby Ferber agreed to join us on this journey. The journey has been a long one, with many twists and turns. Along the way several people have been there to lean on, to discuss with, to commiserate with, and to bounce ideas off of. No list is ever complete, but I would like to acknowledge my deeply supportive partner, Rachel, and my three wonderful children, Karina, Thomas, and Henry—I love you all more than you will ever know. I also must acknowledge the following people for their support along the way: David Embrick, Jennifer Wyse, James Michael Thomas, John Ryan, Sarah Ovink, Jaber Gubrium, Ellington Graves, Minjeong Kim, Petra Rivera-Rideau, Kerry Ann Rockquemore, Slade Lellock, Nate Chapman, Hephzibah Strmic-Pawl, Megan Nanney, Carson Byrd, and Anthony Peguero. All of these people, and many, many graduate students and undergraduate students, have heard me discuss "the textbook" that I am writing—well, here it is. I also want to thank my inspirations, among many: Gloria Anzaldúa, Charles Mills, Patricia Hill Collins, Immortal Technique, Eduardo Bonilla-Silva, Lauryn Hill, Michael Omi, Paulo Freire, Joey Sprague, J. R. R. Tolkien, and my grandfather, Wilbur Nachtigall.

FROM ALL THREE AUTHORS

Jointly, we thank the SAGE crew—Jeff Lasser, Jessica Carlisle, and a host of others—thanks for being there, pushing us, and walking with us down this path. We would also like to thank the reviewers who contributed their many suggestions, critiques, and insights that helped us write *The Matrix of Race*:

Thea S. Alvarado, Pasadena City College
Steven L. Arxer, University of North Texas at Dallas
Celeste Atkins, Cochise College
Laura Barnes, Lenoir Community College
Joyce Bell, University of Pittsburgh
Michelle Bentz, Central Community College, Nebraska
Jacqueline Bergdahl, Wright State University
Latrica Best, University of Louisville
Devonia Cage, University of Memphis
Elizabeth E. Chute, Carroll College
James A. Curiel, Norfolk State University
Melanie Deffendall, Delgado Community College

Sherry Edwards, University of North Carolina at Pembroke

David G. Embrick, Loyola University Chicago

Katherine Everhart, Northern Arizona University

Amy Foerster, Pace University

Joan Gettert Gilbreth, Nebraska Wesleyan University

Robert W. Greene, Marquette University

Denise A. Isom, California Polytechnic State University San Luis Obispo

Shanae Jefferies, University of North Texas

Shelly Jeffy, University of North Carolina Greensboro

Hortencia Jimenez, Hartnell College

Gary Jones, University of Winchester

Tony S. Jugé, Pasadena City College

Henry Kim, Wheaton College

Jeanne E. Kimpel, Hofstra University

Phil Lewis, Queens College

David Luke, University of Kentucky

Ying Ma, Austin Peay State University

Keith Mann, Cardinal Stritch University

Lynda Mercer, University of Louisville

Dan Monti, Saint Louis University

Sarah Morrison, Lindenwood University

Kaitlyne A. Motl, University of Kentucky

Zabedia Nazim, Wilfrid Laurier University

Mytoan Nguyen-Akbar, University of Washington

Godpower O. Okereke, Texas A&M University Texarkana

Mary Kay Park, Biola University

Chavella T. Pittman, Dominican University

Jennifer Pizio, Mercy College

Janis Prince, Saint Leo University

Allan Rachlin, Franklin Pierce University

Heather Rodriguez, Central Connecticut State University

Penny J. Rosenthal, Minnesota State University, Mankato

Enrique Salmon, California State University East Bay

Allison Sinanan, Stockton University

Don Stewart, College of Southern Nevada

Mary Frances Stuck, State University of New York Oswego

Paul Sturgis, William Woods University

Rita Takahashi, San Francisco State University

Michelle Tellez, Northern Arizona University

Santos Torres Jr., California State University, Sacramento

Kathryn Tillman, Florida State University

Gerald Titchener, Des Moines Area Community College

Catherine Turcotte, Colby-Sawyer College
Curt Van Guison, St. Charles Community College
Michelle Dusseau, University of Central Florida
Giselle C. Greenidge, University of North Texas
Jeanne Kimpel, Hofstra University
Brenda Savage, Louisiana Tech University
LaToya Tavernier, Framingham State University
Jennifer Weiner, Fisher College
John W. Anderson Jr., Ball State University
Brian L. Rich, Transylvania University
Lori Waite, Tennessee Wesleyan University

PART I

INTRODUCTION TO RACE AND THE SOCIAL MATRIX

1 RACE AND THE SOCIAL CONSTRUCTION OF DIFFERENCE

Black Lives Matter and other protests make us aware of racial inequities and point to solutions.

Credit: Ira L. Black/Corbis via Getty Images

LEARNING OBJECTIVES

1.1 Explain how the concept of race is socially constructed.

1.2 Summarize the operation of racism.

1.3 Analyze the relationship between social contexts and race.

In June of 2020, the deaths of African Americans at the hands of police triggered widespread social protests in every state, and around the globe. These racially motivated deaths, both recently and over the past decade, have not been isolated incidents. People around the world are recognizing that they are part of the larger historical, systemic oppression of African Americans and other people of color in a nation founded on White supremacy.

There are overwhelming problems that will not be changed quickly, and they are not new to us. In 1968, the Kerner Commission, as it became known, released their now infamous report declaring that the country was "moving toward two societies, one Black, one White—separate and unequal." The report identified actions to address institutionalized racism and change the path we were on. Unfortunately, few people heeded their warning. Now, more than half a century later, we find we are back in the same place. Former mayor of New Orleans Mitch Landrieu writes: "We cannot continue to go over, under or around the issue of race. We have to go through it." (2020).

THE SOCIAL CONSTRUCTION OF RACE

History, the reality of our shared past, reflects a series of choices. These choices, once made, often take on a life of their own, but we should always remember that they were and continue to be choices. Nothing better demonstrates the accuracy of this assessment than the particular set of choices that served to shape our nation on questions of race.

Since human genes have changed, or mutated, over time, we must question if race is either natural or static. If race were indeed a fact of nature, it would be simple to identify who falls into which racial category, and we would expect racial categories to remain static across history and societies. Differences in physical features, such as skin color, hair color, eye color, and height, exist both within and between groups. Physical features can vary even within families. However, these differences are not due to an underlying biological basis of race. There is more biological variation within our so-called racial groups than there is between them. Race must derive from human interventions. These interventions reflect the social construction of race.

As a consequence, what social scientists and geneticists alike have come to understand is that race and any categorizations based on it are uniquely social creations that have been purposefully constructed. Specific rewards, privileges, and sanctions have been used to support and legitimate race. The systematic distribution of these rewards, privileges, and sanctions across populations through time has produced and reproduced social hierarchies that reflect our racial categorizations. We collectively refer to these systematic processes as the **social construction of race**.

Defining Terms

The term **race** refers to a social and cultural system by which we categorize people based on presumed biological differences. While the term has biological overtones, it has virtually nothing to do with biology and everything to do with society. Race exists as a system by which we, as a nation, have categorized various population groups. With these classifications have come a whole series of stereotypes, presumed attributes, behaviors, attitudes, and identities.

The very idea of race requires us to actively engage it, grant it its powers, and facilitate its presence throughout our society. We do all this through our various accepted societal rules and social structures. Institutions are both **norms** (or rules that govern behavior within society) and

Skin color exists along a continuum. Attempts to divide this range into a limited number of boxes is part of the construction of race.

Credit: iStock.com/LeoPatrizi

sustained social structures that serve to regulate our most basic roles and tasks such as family, politics, military, criminal justice, economy, health, and more.

Race operating both within and across these various institutions constitutes what we call a system. When this system of race operates to deny rewards, apply sanctions, and otherwise discriminate against some while rewarding others, we call such a system **systemic racism**. We recognize that systems of race do not operate alone, but in tandem with other systems such as sexuality and gender, class, ability, and age. These are the realities that shape our identities within and across institutions.

When we talk about race, and other major **identity** terminology (i.e., referring to specific socially constructed groups), we often reduce the idea to two opposites. Binary constructs typically present race, and other major categories, as two opposing realms:

- White/Black
- female/male
- gay/straight
- rich/poor
- young/old

These kinds of binary constructs oversimplify the realities of these various identities, and obscure and confound the multitude of identities that do not exist along this binary continuum. This is yet another reason why we utilize a matrix approach.

Our approach to all of these identities, while recognizing the multiple ways in which our various identities intersect, focuses on race. This primacy is more to facilitate our discussions, rather than an indication of the importance of race over any of the other categories. That being said, we recognize that if we were to start from a different identity category, our analysis would be different.

During our exploration of race, we will think about how race intersects with several identities, including but not limited to:

- **Gender**: A broad range of identities that reflect both social and cultural differences which include female, male, transgender, gender-neutral, nonbinary, agender, pangender, genderqueer, two-spirit, third-gender, some combination of all of these, or none of these.

- **Sexuality**: How a person identifies, who they are attracted to, how they define their sexual feelings, thoughts, and behaviors toward others, and how they conceive of themselves.

- **Class**: A set of categories that reflect wealth, occupation, and income. This identity defines an individual's economic position within society.

- **Ethnicity**: A designation that identifies a social group that shares a common cultural or national tradition.

Finally, we would like to comment on the terms we have elected to use in this book. We have decided to capitalize all racial and ethnic identity groups. Thus White, Black, Hispanic, Native American, Latinx, and Asian, are all capitalized. We also recognize the distinctions between various Hispanic, Latinx groups and have struggled to be honest in the representation of that distinction. Part of the dilemma is that while Hispanic makes reference to a language group, Latinx makes reference to geographical groups. Making this even more complex, not all Latinx are Hispanic and not all Hispanics are Latinx. Then there are the various distinctions such as Latino/Latina and Latinx, which reflects both political and normative conventions that are continually in flux.

We have therefore decided to avoid presuming that one size fits all and have tried to use terms that reflect the specific identity that we are referencing. Therefore, when we are talking about the language group, both pan-ethnic and multiracial, as used by the U.S. Census, we use the broader term Hispanic. Alternatively, when we are referring to a specific group who originates from or identifies with a particular geographical area within Latin America, we use the designation Latinx. Similarly, when we are talking about those from Mexico, Cuba, Puerto Rico, or the Caribbean, we use explicit designations. We also respect the terminology used by the authors of specific research that we discuss.

Constructing Race in the United States

In Chapter 2, we will discuss the extent to which the construction of race in the United States follows the pattern of European settler colonialism and imperialism. For now, we present a brief explanation of how racial categorizations became significant within the United States.

So, what does this racially constructed system look like in the contemporary United States? Try this exercise: First, create a list of the racial groups in the United States. Then, write down your estimate of the percentage of the U.S. population that is accounted for by each group.

When we ask our students to attempt this exercise, the answers we get are varied. Some list four races; some list ten. Some include Hispanics/Latinx, and some do not. Some include Middle Easterners, while some do not. Some include a category for multiracial identity. Race is something we assume we all know when we see it, but we may in fact be "seeing" different things. Race cannot be reduced to physical features like skin color—in fact, while skin tone is often the first item we "check off" on our racial checklist, we then move to other social and visual clues.

The United States Census

The U.S. Constitution requires that a counting of the nation's population be conducted every 10 years—a national census (see Figure 1.1). The purposes and uses of the census have both changed and expanded across the years. The census was originally necessary to

Each of us is part of a racial story that begins early in our lives, a racial story that has also been written long before we were born.

Credit: MBI/Alamy

FIGURE 1.1 ■ Census Categories Have Changed Over Time

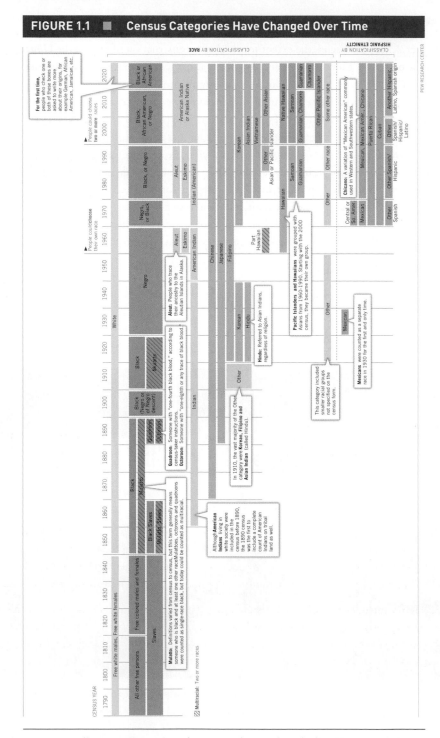

Source: https://www.pewresearch.org/wp-content/uploads/2020/02/PH_15.06.11_MultiRacial-Timeline.pdf

determine voting representation, including the numbers of representatives states could elect to Congress, the allocation of federal and state funds, and more. Over time, the census categories of race and other cultural and language groups have changed to reflect the nation's evolving population as well as, importantly, the political interests and power relations of the time.

What have we discovered? Race is a social construction that artificially divides people into distinct groups based on characteristics such as physical appearance, ancestry, culture, ethnic classification, and the social, economic, and political needs, desires, and relations of a society at a given historical moment (Adams, Bell, and Griffin 1997; Ferrante and Brown 2001). The U.S. Census Bureau, for instance, currently recognizes five racial categories, along with a "some other race" option (which was added in 2020 in response to public pressure). The five categories are as follows (derived from U.S. Census 2020):

1. *American Indian or Alaska Native* includes individuals that identify with the original population groups of North and South America (to include Central America) and who continue to maintain tribal affiliation or community. It includes such groups as Navajo Nation, Blackfeet Tribe, Mayan, Aztec, Native Village of Barrow Inupiat Traditional Government, and Nome Eskimo Community.

2. *Asian* category refers to all individuals who identify with one or more nationalities or ethnic groups deriving from the Far East, Southeast Asia, or the Indian subcontinent. It includes, but is not limited to, those who identify as Chinese, Filipino, Asian Indian, Vietnamese, Korean, and Japanese. Others included in this category are Pakistani, Cambodian, Hmong, Thai, Bengali, Mien, and others.

3. *Black or African American* includes all individuals who derive from or identify with one or more nationalities or ethnic groups that originate from any Black racial groups of Africa. This group includes African Americans, Jamaicans, Haitians, Nigerians, Ethiopians, and Somalis. It may also include those from Ghanaian, South African, Barbadian, Kenyan, Liberian, and Bahamian backgrounds.

4. *Native Hawaiian or other Pacific Islander* includes all individuals that identify or originate from nationalities or ethnic groups from Hawaii, Guam, Samoa, or other Pacific Islands. This category also includes, but is not limited to, Native Hawaiian, Chamorro, Tongan, Fijian, Chuukese, Pohnpeian, Saipanese, and Yapese.

5. *White* includes all individuals that identify with one or more nationalities or ethnic groups originating in Europe, the Middle East, or North Africa. These groups may include, but are not limited to, German, Irish, English, Italian, Lebanese, Egyptian, Polish, French, Iranian, Slavic, Cajun, and Chaldean.

Not only have our official designations for race and ethnic groups differed over time, but how people identify themselves has also shown a great deal of variability. For example, from the

2000 census to that of 2010, almost 10 million U.S. residents changed how they identified their race when asked by the Census Bureau (Linshi 2014). This clearly demonstrates the fluidity of racial identity.

Future Race and Ethnic Demographics

What will our country look like in the next 50 years? Projections of population growth indicate that minorities (including Hispanics, Blacks, Asian Americans, and Native Hawaiians and other Pacific Islanders) will make up slightly more than 50% of the U.S. population. The most significant changes will be seen in the reduced numbers of Whites and the almost doubling of the numbers of Hispanics and other minorities. We often read headlines predicting that Whites will become a minority. However, these are misleading. Whites will still be the single largest group in the United States, constituting 49.4% of the population in 2060 (Figure 1.2). The United States will become a minority-majority nation, which means that the total of all minority groups combined will make up the majority of the population. We may see little change in the dynamics of power and race relations, however, as the proportion of Whites will still be nearly twice that of any individual minority group.

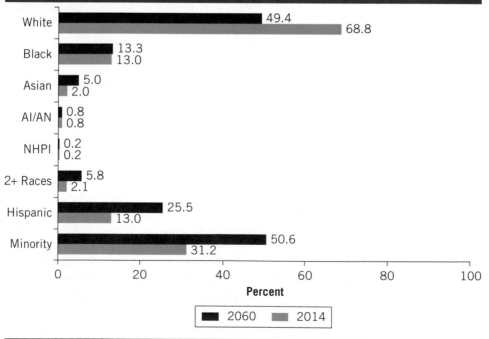

FIGURE 1.2 ■ Population Growth Projections Over the Next Fifty Years Predict a Minority-Majority Nation

Source: U.S. Census Bureau, "Projections of the Size and Composition of the U.S. Population 2014-2060," Population Estimates and Projections, Current Population Reports, March 2015.

Critical Thinking

1. Explain why biology does not explain race. Why are simple, binary constructions of identity problematic?

2. History has shown that race and ethnicity are socially constructed. What do current trends suggest about how these social constructions may change in the future?

3. Can you trace your roots? What different racial and ethnic groups are in your family tree? What does this say about how we define racial and ethnic groups?

THE OPERATION OF RACISM

We have examined what race is, how it is constructed, and how it reproduced. We now shift our focus to the concept and operation of racism.

Prejudice and Discrimination

Anyone can be the victim of prejudice. **Prejudice** is a judgment of an individual or group, often based on race, ethnicity, religion, gender, class, or other social identities. It is often shaped by, and also leads to, the promotion of **stereotypes,** which are assumptions or generalizations applied to an entire group. Even seemingly positive stereotypes put people in boxes, like the myth of Asian Americans as the "model minority," which includes the stereotype that all Asian Americans are gifted in math and science. How might this stereotype affect Asian American students who are not doing well in school? How does it prevent us from seeing the poverty that specific Asian American groups, such as the Hmong, Cambodians, and Thais, are more likely to experience (Takei and Sakamoto 2011)?

Prejudices and stereotypes are beliefs that often provide foundations for action in the form of **discrimination**—that is, the differential allocation of goods, resources, and services, and the limitation of access to full participation in society, based on an individual's membership in a particular social category (Adams et al. 1997). Prejudices and stereotypes exist in the realm of beliefs, and when these beliefs guide the ways in which we treat each other, they produce discrimination. Anyone can be the victim of prejudice, stereotyping, or discrimination, including White people, and for a wide variety of reasons, such as clothing, appearance, accent, and membership in clubs or gangs. Put simply, discrimination is prejudice plus power.

Prejudice, stereotypes, and discrimination are probably what first come to mind when we think about racism. But the study of racism goes far beyond these. Like sexism, racism is a system of oppression. **Oppression** is more than simply individual beliefs and actions—it involves the systematic devaluing, undermining, marginalizing, and disadvantaging of certain social identity groups in contrast to a privileged norm (Ferber and Samuels 2010). Oppression is based on membership in socially constructed identity categories; it is *not* based on individual characteristics.

One sociologist describes racial oppression as a birdcage: an interlocking network of institutional barriers that prevents escape (Frye 2007). Alternatively, others point out the systemic racism. This view posits that core racist realities, values, and ideologies are manifested in all of the major institutions within society (Feagin 2001). Throughout this text we will demonstrate how race exists both historically and contextually as an ongoing form of inequality that pervades every major social institution, including education, employment, government, healthcare, family, criminal justice, sports, and leisure.

The Contours of Racism

Racism is a system of oppression by which those groups with relatively more social power subordinate members of targeted racial groups who have relatively little social power. This subordination is supported by individual actions, cultural values, and norms embedded in stock stories, as well as in the institutional structures and practices of society (National Education Association 2015). It is inscribed in codes of conduct, legal sanctions, and organizational rules and practices. Specifically, racism is the subordination of people of color by those who consider themselves White; by implication, the practice of racism defines Whites as superior and all non-Whites as inferior.

There are specific sets of responses typically associated with race:

- *Racial prejudice, or racial prejudgments*, reflect not only our fears but also our ignorance of racialized others and those that appear to racially identify like ourselves.

- *Racial identifications* are a set of attitudes, cultural and normative values, and presumed shared histories that establish group boundaries. These group boundaries are enforced by people both within and external to the group.

- *Racial boundary enforcements* are structural or institutional mechanisms that serve to preserve those boundaries, such as segregation (Frankenberg et al., 2017); marriage (Samuel and Whitehead, 2015); laws, police, and the courts (Steinmetz et al., 2017); and economics (Balibar and Wallerstein, 1991; Marable, 2016).

- *Bigotry (intolerance toward those who are different from ourselves) and discrimination*, deriving their power from institutions, are the mechanisms by which racial hierarchies are developed and preserved.

Racism is systemic. It is not about isolated individual actions; individual actions take place within a broader, systemic, cross-institutional context. People of color may themselves harbor prejudices and discriminate on the basis of race; however, without the larger social and historical context of systemic differences in power, these individual actions do not constitute racism. While this may seem counterintuitive, keep in mind that we are looking at racism from a sociological perspective, focusing on the importance of social context, research, and group experience, rather than on individual behavior. Individual experiences of race and racism will vary. We find it less important to focus on "racists" than on the social matrix of racism in which we live. Additionally, while White people do not experience racism, they may face oppression based on sexual orientation, class, or other social identities.

Racism in the United States is directed primarily against Blacks, Asian Americans, Latinx, and Native Americans. Some argue that the hatred and discrimination faced by Muslims should also be classified as racism, and that they are becoming a racialized group. Racism is the basis of conflict and violence in societies throughout the world, and the forms it takes are varied. Racism is practiced by Whites against Blacks, "Coloreds," and Indians in South Africa; by Islamic Arabs against Black Christians in the Sudan; by East Indians against Blacks in Guyana; by those of Spanish descent against those of African and Indian descent in Brazil and Paraguay; by White "Aryans" against Jews and Romani in Germany; by the Japanese against the Eta, or Burakumin, in Japan; and by Whites against Africans, Sikhs, Muslims, and Hindus in Great Britain. Racism can take many forms, and it changes over time.

Formal and Informal Racism

Formal or overt racism occurs when discriminatory practices and behaviors are sanctioned by the official rules, codes, or laws of an organization, institution, or society. Many of the most obvious forms of racism are no longer legal or openly accepted in U.S. society. Such racist practices as slavery, or the harsh set of laws that came into being in the aftermath of the Civil War that stripped the newly freed slaves of their rights, or the act of Congress that stripped Native Americans of their land rights and forced them to relocate onto reservations, are now condemned (but also too conveniently forgotten). Debate is ongoing regarding whether or not other practices—such as immigration policy, the display of the Confederate flag, and the use of American Indian sports mascots—are racist in intent or impact.

Informal or covert racism is subtle in its application, and often ignored or misdiagnosed. It acts informally in that it is assumed to be part of the natural, legitimate, and normal workings of society and its institutions. Thus, when we discuss student learning outcomes we may talk about poor motivation, inadequate schools, or broken homes. We ignore that these characteristics are also typically associated with poor Black and Latinx neighborhoods (Coates 2011). Recent work has helped us to understand the many ways that these subtle forms of racism are manifested.

Implicit Bias

Implicit biases are unconscious attitudes or stereotypes that affect how we perceive others, and their and our actions and decisions. It was not until 1998 that we began researching and documenting degrees and forms of bias. Almost all of us possess various form of bias. They reflect not our conscious values, but rather the cultural and social messages about race that we have unconsciously learned (Greenwald, McGhee, and Schwartz 1998). Implicit bias tests can provide a snapshot of those unconscious, learned beliefs, which can impact our behavior in ways we are not aware of.

Bias, prejudice, and discrimination are learned as part of the social environment that we live in. Therefore, despite the laws, expressed attitudes, and programs aimed at effecting change, we continually discover the problem shaping our everyday lives.

Tests have been developed to not only measure but track our attitudes and beliefs about other identities. These tests, called implicit bias or association tests, can also be mapped across the country, revealing geographical differences and a more nuanced variability.

The expression of implicit bias is a function of both the individual and certain situations that "encourage discrimination more than others, largely independently of the individual decision makers passing through those contexts" (Vuletich and Payne 2019, 859). In order to understand the basis of implicit bias, we must understand the situational context of the actions. Scholar Allan Johnson (2012) describes these as "paths of least resistance." He argues that most of the time, we follow the paths of least resistance, the patterns and processes that are already established within institutions. It makes sense; most of us do not want to make waves. He argues that to change people's behaviors, we need to alter the paths of least resistance. Rather than changing the attitudes of the majority of people within an institution, the rules of the game need to be changed. Individuals will then begin following a new playbook in order to succeed, whether at school, work, or in any organization.

White Privilege

When we study racism, we most often study the experiences of marginalized and oppressed groups. However, everyone's life is shaped by race. Privilege is the flip side of oppression—it involves the systemic favoring, valuing, validating, and inclusion of certain social identities over others. Whiteness is a privileged status. **White privilege** refers to how all Whites collectively benefit not only as individuals but as a group.

To be White is to have greater access to rewards and valued resources simply because of group membership. Because they exist in relationship to each other, oppression and privilege operate hand in hand; one cannot exist without the other. Just like oppression, privilege is based on group membership, not individual factors. We do not choose to be the recipients of oppression or privilege, and we cannot opt out of either one. A White person driving down the street cannot ask the police to pull her over because of her race. Experiences of racism can affect some people and not others independent of their desires and behaviors.

Making Whiteness visible by acknowledging privilege allows us to examine the ways in which all White people, not just those we identify as "racist," benefit from their racial categorization. Accepting the fact that we live in a society that is immersed in systems of oppression can be difficult, because it means that despite our best intentions, we all participate in perpetuating inequality. In fact, privilege is usually invisible to the people who experience it until it is pointed out. The reality is that White people do not need to think about race very often. Their **social location**—how a group or individual is represented across various social institutions that reflect privilege, status, and power—becomes both invisible and the assumed norm.

Research on White privilege has grown over the past three decades, along with the interdisciplinary subfield of **Whiteness studies**. Works by literary theorists, legal scholars, anthropologists, historians, psychologists, and sociologists alike have contributed to this burgeoning field (Brodkin 1998; Case 2013; Jacobson 1998; Haney López 2006; Moore, Penick-Parks, and Michael 2015; Morrison 1992). However, people of color have been writing about White privilege for a long time. Discussions of White privilege are found in the works of writers such as W. E. B. Du Bois, Anna Julia Cooper, and Ida B. Wells.

Peggy McIntosh's (1988) classic article "White Privilege and Male Privilege" was one of the first attempts by a White person to document the unearned advantages that Whites experience on a daily basis. For example, White privilege means being able to assume that most of the people you or your children study with in school will be of the same race; being able to go shopping without being followed around in the store; never being called a credit to your race; and being able to find "flesh-colored" bandages to match your skin color. McIntosh also identifies a second type of privilege that gives one group power over another. This conferred dominance legitimates privileges that no one should have in a society that values social justice and equity, such as the right to "own" another human being.

Most of us are the beneficiaries of at least one form of privilege, and often many more. Recognizing this often leads people to feel guilt and shame. However, privilege is derived from group membership; it is not the result of anything we have done as individuals. We are born into these systems of privilege and oppression; we did not create them. Once we become aware of them, though, we must be accountable and work to create change. We can choose whether to acknowledge privilege as it operates in our lives, and whether to use it as a means of creating social change. As scholar Shelly Tochluk (2008, 249–50) notes, this requires that we "begin with personal investigation. If we are going to take a stand, we need to feel prepared to deal with our own sense of discomfort and potential resistance or rejection from others."

Color Blindness

Many people claim **color blindness** in regard to race and ethnicity—that is, they assert that they do not see race or ethnicity, only humans—and the idea of color blindness informs many of our most prevalent stock stories today. According to this ideology, if we were all to embrace a color-blind attitude and just stop "seeing" race, race and its issues would finally become relics of the past. This approach argues that we should treat people simply as human beings, rather than as racialized beings (Plaut 2010). In fact, White people in the United States generally believe that "we have achieved racial equality," and about half believe that African Americans are doing as well as, or even better than, Whites (Bush 2011, 4). But pretending race does not exist is not the same as creating equality.

As we have learned, a new form of racism has shifted the more overt forms of racism to the more covert forms (those racial discrimination/actions that are often hidden or subtle that serve to marginalize racialized individuals or groups). One of the leading elements of these more subtle forms of racism are associated with **microaggressions**, the verbal and nonverbal behaviors that insult persons or groups that can be both intentional and unintentional. This new racism is much less overt, avoiding the use of blatantly racist terminology. Sociologist Eduardo Bonilla-Silva (2018) has labeled this ideology **color-blind racism**. According to Bonilla-Silva, color-blind ideology has four components:

- *Abstract liberalism*: Abstract concepts of equal opportunity, rationality, free choice, and individualism are used to argue that discrimination is no longer a problem, and any individual who works hard can succeed.

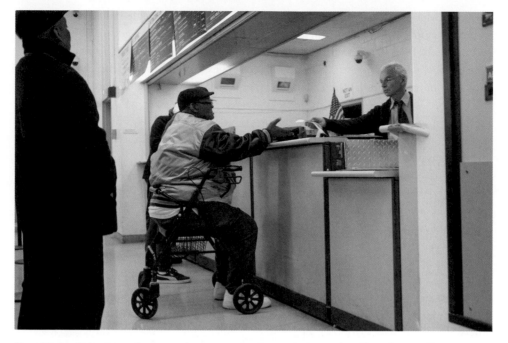

The subtle insults known as microaggressions are common in everyday interactions, like at the post office, even when things seem fine on the surface.

Credit: Education Images/UIG via Getty Images

- *Naturalization*: Ongoing inequality is reframed as the result of natural processes rather than social relations. Segregation is explained, for example, as the result of people's natural inclination to live near others of the same race.

- *Cultural racism:* It is claimed that inherent cultural differences serve to separate racialized groups.

- *Minimization of racism:* It is argued that we now have a fairly level playing field, everyone has equal opportunities to succeed, and racism is no longer a real problem.

While many embrace color blindness as nonracist, by ignoring the extent to which race still shapes people's life chances and opportunities, this view actually reinforces and reproduces the subtle and institutional racial inequality that shapes our lives. Throughout this text, we will examine the extent to which racial inequality is still pervasive, as well as many stock stories in circulation today that make it difficult for us to see this reality. We will challenge those stories by exploring concealed and resistance stories, and by considering the possibilities for constructing transformative stories.

Color-blind ideology leads to the conclusion that we've done all we can in regard to racial inequality. Many Whites invoke the election of Barack Obama to the presidency as confirmation of their assumptions of a color-blind nation (Bonilla-Silva 2018; Cunnigen and Bruce 2010). The concealed story revealed by sociology, however, is that racial inequality has been and remains entrenched in the United States.

Credit: Saul Loeb/AFP/Getty Images

Critical Thinking

1. What are some of the ways that race operates?

2. Racism is dynamic across geographic and social places and across historical periods. Consider some recent events either in the news or at your university: How do they reflect these dynamic processes? (*Hint:* Do you believe that the same types of events would have taken place, say, 50 years ago?)

3. Consider some common stereotypes about athletes, academics, or other professionals. Can you identify any racial stereotypes about which groups might be better at certain sports, disciplines, or professions? What might account for the prevalence of these stereotypes? Do you believe that those stereotypes have changed over time, or that they differ geographically? Would they be similar to those in, say, England or Nigeria? What may account for either the similarities or the differences you observe?

4. At your institution are there any student groups that appear to have greater access to rewards and resources than other groups do? If so, what might account for their privilege?

THE SOCIAL MATRIX OF RACE

Diversity is a process, not an event, and inclusion is an action, not a slogan. Many of you have likely heard both these words—diversity and inclusion—often. Many public organizations offer multiple "diverse" and "inclusive" events. These programs, which frequently face resistance, have traditionally focused on recognizing and appreciating diversity and creating a climate where marginalized individuals feel included and welcome. Yet as hard fought as many of these programs have been, they are frequently limited. Our intention is not to blame or shame anyone.

Our goal is to do more than superficially examine diversity and inclusion. We want to give you the tools to understand why, how, and under what circumstances our diverse society has come into being. In the process, we hope to help you alter both the conversations around race and the structures that preserve the hierarchies that differentially reward and punish individuals solely due to classifications of race, gender, class, and sexual orientation.

We focus particularly on race and the way it shapes our identities, society, and its institutions, and prospects for change. But we also examine race within the context of gender, class, and other social identities that interact with one another and reflect the way we live as social beings.

For example, college-educated women of color between the ages of 18 and 26 are more likely to have different experiences within political, economic, educational, or sport institutions than, say, older White males with only a high school education. Therefore, within the matrix, using the lens of race, in this example we would be concerned with how the intersections of gender, class, and age impact one's ability to obtain an education, participate in political campaigns, or participate in sport.

A number of scholars have embraced the image of racial identity as a matrix (Case 2013; Collins 2000; Ferber, O'Reilly

A camera has several lenses and potentially filters. Imagine that the camera is the matrix, the framework for our realities. Depending on what lens, or identity (race, gender, etc.), we use as our vantage point, our subject will look different. Different types of filters, or intersections, highlight differences in perceptions, actions, and outcomes.

Credit: Borges Samuel/Alamy

Herrera, and Samuels 2009). Generally, a **matrix** is the surrounding environment in which something (e.g., a value, cell, or human) originates, develops, and grows. The concept of a matrix captures the basic sociological understanding that contexts—social, cultural, economic, historical, and otherwise—matter. Figure 1.3 is our visual representation of the social matrix of race, depicting the intersecting worlds of identity, social institutions, and cultural and historical contexts, connecting with one another on the micro and macro levels.

In this text we center the concepts and experiences of race within the context of our many shifting social identities and systems of inequality. As we learned earlier, our social identities are the ways in which our group memberships, in such categories as race, class, and gender, help define our sense of self. While we often assume a concrete or single group identity, the reality is that identity is seldom so simple. For example, while many of us identify as being White, Black, Hispanic, Asian, or Native American, few of us are racially or ethnically homogeneous. Consequently, how we derive our racial identity is actually a result of both historical and contemporary social constructions.

The same can be said regarding our social status, class, gender, and other identities. We also recognize that these identities interact in ways that produce extremely nuanced and complex, dynamic identities. The third ring of the social matrix of race consists of the social institutions in which we live and interact. **Social institutions** are patterned, structured sets of roles and behaviors centered on the performance of important social tasks within any given society. These institutions help order and facilitate social interactions. That being so, many of our activities happen within social institutions such as marriage and family, education, sports, the military, and the economy. In Figure 1.3 we have included only the social institutions we examine in this text; this is not an exhaustive list. Finally, all of these systems are shaped by place and time.

To support an understanding of race within the context of a social matrix, in the following sections we introduce the five key insights about race that we will develop throughout this text (see Table 1.1).

Race Is Inherently Social

We have already introduced the argument that race is a social construction. As race theorists Matthew Desmond and Mustafa Emirbayer (2010, 51) put it, "You do not come into this world African or European or Asian; rather, this world comes into you." If races are constructed, it makes sense then to ask: When does this happen, and why? The creation of "races" occurred at a specific point in time to advance specific relations of inequality. The classifications were invented by those they were created to serve, not by those who came to be defined as "Others" by Whites. We will examine this history in Chapter 2.

We have already demonstrated the range of ways that reveal to us the constructed nature of race. In the next chapter, we will discuss at length the idea that race and racial meanings are constructed through narrative, and the many different stories we tell about race. Here, we will discuss the other three dimensions of this Social Matrix.

FIGURE 1.3 ■ Race Intersects with Cultural and Historical Context, Social Institutions, and Other Identities

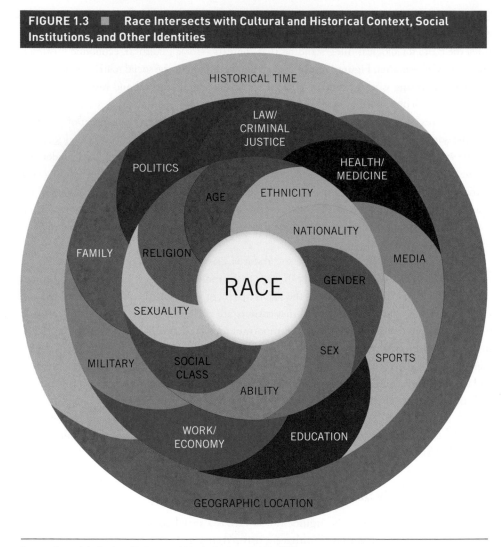

Source: Copyright Rodney D. Coates, Abby L. Ferber, and David Brunsma.

Race Is a Narrative

Too many people believe that **diversity**, the amount of social variability within a specific social context, is a binary construct. Diversity is actually a multilevel, multidimensional, multidirectional highway with many on- and off-ramps. We are not either/or; our realities are more complex than us/them. This journey starts by understanding that race, as part of our collective stories, is a kind of narrative.

As we have established, race is not real; it is a fiction with very real consequences. Because it is fictional, scholars across many disciplines have used the language of storytelling to discuss race. For example, perhaps one of the most dominant stories we hear today is that race is a taboo

TABLE 1.1 ■ Five Key Insights about Race	
Race is inherently social.	Race has no biological basis, and it varies both cross-culturally and historically.
Race is a narrative.	We learn narrative story lines that we draw on to interpret what we see and experience, and these stories become embedded in our minds as truth, closing off other ways of seeing and sense making.
Racial identity is relational and intersectional.	Our racial identity is defined in our relationships to others, based on interactions with them and our reactions to our experiences and socialization. Further, our racial identity is shaped by, and experienced in the context of, our other social identities, such as gender, class, sexuality, ability, and age.
Race is institutional and structural.	Independently and together, various institutional structures, including family, school, community, and religion, influence our actions and beliefs about race.
We are active agents in the matrix.	We move among a variety of social institutions, and as we do, we contribute to their reproduction. We make choices every day, often unconsciously, that either maintain or subvert racial power dynamics and inequality.

topic. When children ask their parents about racial differences, they are often hushed and told not to talk about such things in public. Perhaps the most significant racial narrative is the story that races exist in nature. We have just shown that this is not true. Yet until we are taught otherwise, most of us go through life assuming that biological racial differences exist. This is the power of narrative in our lives as social beings.

In her important book *Storytelling for Social Justice* (2010), educator and activist Lee Anne Bell provides a model for analyzing stories about race. She argues that there are essentially four different kinds of stories that we encounter in our lives: stock stories, concealed stories, resistance stories, and transforming stories.

- **Stock stories**: "Stock stories are the tales told by the dominant group," but they are often embraced by those whose oppression they reinforce (Bell 2010, 23). They inform and organize the practices of social institutions and are encoded in law, public policy, public space, history, and culture. Stock stories are shaped by the White racial frame.

- **Concealed stories**: We can always find concealed stories if we look closely enough. These consist of the data and voices that stock stories ignore, and they often convey a very different understanding of identity and inequity. In the case of concealed stories, "we explore such questions as: What are the stories about race and racism that we don't hear? Why don't we hear them? How are such stories lost/left out? How do we recover these stories? What do these stories show us about racism that stock stories do not?" (24).

- **Resistance stories**: Narratives that directly challenge stock stories are resistance stories. They speak of defying domination and actively struggling for racial justice and social change. "Guiding questions for discovering/uncovering resistance stories include: What stories exist (historical or contemporary) that serve as examples of resistance? What role does resistance play in challenging the stock stories about racism? What can we learn about antiracist action and perseverance against the odds by looking at these stories?" (25).

- **Transforming stories**: Once we examine concealed and resistance stories, we can use them to write transforming stories that guide our actions as we work toward a more just society. "Guiding questions include: What would it look like if we transformed the stock stories? What can we draw from resistance stories to create new stories about what ought to be? What kinds of stories can support our ability to speak out and act where instances of racism occur?" (26).

Racial Identity Is Relational and Intersectional

As philosopher Elizabeth Spelman (1988) points out, we often think about our various identities—race, gender, sexuality, class, ability—as though they are connected like a necklace made of pop beads. But unlike the beads of the necklace, our separate identities cannot just be popped apart. They intersect and shape each other; they are relational and intersectional (Crenshaw 1991).

The **relational aspects of race** are demonstrated by the fact that categories of race are often defined in opposition to each other (for example, to be White means one is not Black, Asian, or Native American) and according to where they fall along the continuum of hierarchy. We also construct and reconstruct racial meanings and views through our relationships with others—whether of the same race or of a different race. Our first knowledge of race usually comes from our relationships with our immediate family members. We develop a sense of our own racialized self, and many come to discover, through their relationships with others, that their ascribed racial identity is different from their self-identification. Through these interactions, people often expect multiracial people to choose one identity, or even tell them that their own self-definition is wrong. President Obama often spoke about his White mother who raised him, but that he still saw himself as Black, because he was Black to the rest of the world.

Our cross-racial interactions with each other frequently have the effect of disrupting some of our stereotypes about the other. For example, because we live such segregated lives, for many students, college is the first time they really experience diversity and spend time with people from different racial groups. Race is also relational in its intersections with other social identities, such as gender and class.

Intersectional theories argue that race, gender, and other salient social identities are intertwined and inseparable, and cannot be comprehended on their own. Sociologist Ivy Ken offers a useful metaphor. If we think about race as sugar, gender as flour, and class as baking soda, what happens when we mix them and a few other ingredients together? If we are lucky, we end up with cookies; we "produce something new—something that would not exist if that mixing had not occurred" (Ken 2008, 156). When these ingredients are combined, they are changed in the process.

David J. Connor (2006), a special education teacher in New York City, provides an example. He wondered why his classes were filled overwhelmingly with African American and Latino males despite the fact that learning disabilities occur across class, race, and gender. Connor found that he needed an intersectional perspective to understand: "I noticed that the label [learning disabled] signified different outcomes for different people. What seemed to be a beneficial category of disability to middle-class, White students, by triggering various supports and services—served to disadvantage Black and/or Latinx urban youngsters, who were more likely to be placed in restrictive, segregated settings" (154). Here, race, class, and dis/ability intersect to produce different consequences for differently situated youth.

As this example demonstrates, sources of oppression are related, and interrelated, in varied ways. There is no single formula for understanding how they work together. We are all shaped by all of these significant constructs, whether they privilege us or contribute to our oppression; we all experience specific configurations of race, class, and gender that affect our subjectivities, opportunities, and life chances.

Although its name is new, intersectional theory has a long history. Early theorists like Maria Stewart, Sojourner Truth, Frederick Douglass, Ida B. Wells, and Anna Julia Cooper struggled with the ways race divided the women's suffrage movement, and the ways gender inequity limited Black women's participation in the antislavery movement. Decades later, women of color waged battles for full inclusion within the civil rights and women's movements. African American sociologists like Belinda Robnett (1999) and Bernice McNair Barnett (1995) have examined the ways in which the foundational leadership activities of Black women in many civil rights organizations have been ignored or written out of history (becoming concealed stories). Vicki Ruiz (1999) has examined similar dynamics in her research on the work of Chicanas in the Chicano movement. We can find many resistance stories in the lives of women of color who have refused to direct their energies toward just one form of oppression, arguing that their lives are shaped by their race and their gender simultaneously.

An intersectional approach does not require that we always examine every form of inequity, and it certainly does not suggest that it is merely a result of adding categories. Instead, we need to recognize that intersectionality permeates every subject we study, and that even when we choose to focus on a single system of inequality, such as race, we must bring an intersectional lens to the work so we are inclusive of everyone in the group, people of every gender, gender identity, sexual identity, class, and more. If not, we will end up with only a limited picture of the experiences and dynamics of race.

Over the past few decades, research involving explicitly intersectional analysis has accelerated. Sociologists and others have examined the ways our various social locations intersect and interact in shaping our lives and society at every level. These represent interconnected axes of oppression and privilege that shape all of our lived experiences (Collins 2000).

Race Is Institutional and Structural

To say that race is institutional is to recognize that it operates alongside and in tandem with our dominant social institutions. For instance, education is a social institution in which there are roles (e.g., teachers and students) and expected behaviors (e.g., teaching and learning) that come together as a social structure to educate. But schools also contribute to other important social tasks, including socialization and social control (with differential impact on students based on race and other social identities) (Spade and Ballantine 2011).

Our institutional focus reflects our view that while race is often described in its outcomes such as bigotry, prejudice, and other biased behaviors and reactions, these behaviors and reactions operate within specific social and structural settings. Institutional structures normalize racial boundaries through various laws, codes of conduct (both implicit and explicit), and other boundary maintenance mechanisms.

Boundaries

How we define the other, in relation to ourselves, is essentially a means of establishing boundaries. Us/them, family/non-family, citizen/foreigner, as well as all of our racial, ethnic, gender, class, age, and sexual categories are essentially boundaries. **Boundaries** are socially constructed and contentious social spaces which are used to identify "others." Once established, we often forget that these boundaries and the identities they define are social constructions and appear to be fixed and unmoving. The reality is that identities are constantly in flux, hence the constant conflict associated with maintaining their boundedness. Racial classifications are types of boundaries.

Racial Classifications

Anthropologist Audrey Smedley (2007) has identified some of the key features of our dominant racial narrative. From this worldview, racial classifications are constructed as follows:

1. They are exclusive, discrete classifications.

2. They involve visible physical differences that reflect inherent internal ones (such as intelligence, disposition, morals).

3. They are inherited.

4. They are unchanging, determined by nature and/or God.

5. They are valued differently and ranked hierarchically (in terms of superiority, beauty, degree of civilization, capacity for moral reasoning, and more).

This narrative makes clear that the ideology of race privileges some groups by dividing people into artificial, hierarchical categories to justify inequitable access to resources.

Racial Framing

The ideology of race is part of what Joe Feagin (2010) identifies as the "White racial frame." In societies characterized by racial hierarchies, **racial frames** are constructed from the ideological justifications, processes, procedures, and institutions that define and structure society. According to Feagin (2010, 10–11), a racial frame consists of the following:

1. racial stereotypes (a beliefs aspect)

2. racial narratives and interpretations (integrating cognitive aspects)

3. racial images (a visual aspect) and language accents (an auditory aspect)

4. racialized emotions (a "feelings" aspect)

5. inclinations to discriminatory action

The repetition of the White racial frame over generations, in fact, since the founding of the United States, is the key to its power. When the same messages are repeated over and over, they appear to be part of our social being; they become "natural" to us.

This means that efforts to eliminate racial structures must do more than attack the racial attitudes and behaviors associated with bigotry, prejudice, and discrimination. While such work is admirable, the racialized structural components of institutions require structural transformations to effectively reduce or eliminate racial outcomes. These structural transformations, often fueled by both individual efforts but also social movements, will also be evidenced throughout this course.

We Are Active Agents in the Matrix

While constructs of race and ethnicity shape us, we also shape them. Once we realize that race is socially constructed, it follows that we recognize our role as active agents in reconstructing it—through our actions and through the stories we construct that inform our actions (Markus and Moya 2010, 4). Emphasizing the concept of agency is also essential to creating social change. If race is something we *do,* then we can begin to do it differently.

Agency

Agency is the ability of an individual to effect change, to make choices, to act independently. Some individuals, because of their social, economic, or political status, might have more formal agency than others. Such formal agency, deriving from their position, allows them access to greater resources and a greater range of choices. The principal purposes and outcomes of discrimination, prejudice, and exploitation are to reduce the choices available to some individuals and groups based on arbitrary, socially defined characteristics such as race, gender, or sexuality. Consequently, such individuals and groups become creative in the use of informal agency. Rule norm breaking, failure to comply, sabotage, and more characterize **informal agency**. Many examples of informal agency have occurred throughout our history.

- During slavery there were frequent reports of slaves breaking tools and sabotage, as well as enslaved people running away and engaging in openly hostile actions.

- Throughout history, many immigrants have disregarded national borders.

- LGBTQ individuals have used "outing" as a means of highlighting the discrimination and problems faced by their members.

- Activists, even those locked up in prisons, have individually utilized hunger strikes as a means of effectively getting the attention of wider audiences.

Individual agency demonstrates that regardless of levels of isolation, resources, and status, individuals can and do effect change both within their individual circumstances and within the wider society for themselves and others. It is because we, too, embrace the concept of agency that we have written this text. We hope to make visible the stock stories that perpetuate racial inequality, and to examine the ways in which those narratives govern the operations of organizations and institutions. All of us, as individuals, play a role in reproducing or subverting the dominant narratives, whether we choose to or not. While we inherit stories about race that help us to explain the world around us, we can also seek out alternative stories. All of us, as individuals, play a role in the reproduction of institutional structures, from our workplaces to our places of worship to our schools and our homes.

Social Movements

Social movements are forms of collective actions, either informal or within formal organizations, which aim to alter our specific structures, institutions, practices, or behaviors, or our society as a whole. Social movements may use a variety of tactics or strategies to accomplish these goals. These tactics can range from things as simple as holding a candlelight vigil to more coordinated activities that make specific demands and force specific responses from authorities.

Contemporary social movements (including #BlackLivesMatter, #MeToo, #TimesUp, #DACA, #MuslimBan) have become increasingly popular with the advent of social media and the internet. They have fostered activism associated with labor, civil rights (for example, among

Social movements define our realities and redefine our identities.

Credit: Samuel Corum/Getty Images

Blacks, Hispanics, Native Americans, immigrants, women, and LGBTQ people), peace, counterculture, and White supremacy.

We shall see throughout this book that both agency and social movements have been vital as transformative processes throughout our history. In fact, agency and social movements provide us hope for the future, and are central to understanding and embracing our collective and individual stories.

Writing Our Own Stories: Asking the Hard Questions

Each of the key insights that inform our framework is essential. Racial attitudes and racialized social structures need to be examined in relationship to one another. For example, many scholars have argued that economic insecurity and resource scarcity often fan the flames of race prejudice. Critical knowledge is gained when we understand how dominant discourses and ideology preserve and perpetuate the status quo. Understanding how these dominant discourses are framed and how they are buttressed by our institutional practices, policies, and mechanisms allows us to see not only how these patterns are replicated and reproduced but also how they can be replaced (Bush 2011, 37).

This knowledge also helps us understand our own place in the matrix. The enduring stock story of the United States as a meritocracy makes it difficult for us to see inequality as institutionalized (McNamee and Miller 2014). The news and entertainment media bombard us with color-blind "depictions of race relations that suggest that discriminatory racial barriers have been dismantled" (Gallagher 2009, 548). It's no wonder that individuals often experience some cognitive dissonance when confronted with the concept of privilege. We often turn to our familiar stock stories to explain how we feel, countering with responses like "The United States is a meritocracy!" or "Racism is a thing of the past!" Table 1.2 lists some common responses, informed by our stock stories, to learning about privilege (Ferber and Samuels 2010). Do you share any of these feelings?

While our stock stories serve the interests of the dominant group, they are perceived as natural, normal, and the way of the world. It is easy to forget that these stories were created at specific moments to justify specific sets of interactions. Race, as part of our structured social system, has become realized as residential segregation, differential educational outcomes, income gaps, racially stratified training and occupational outcomes, social stigmas, and restrictions on social relationships (Smedley 2007, 21–22).

It is only through a deliberate process of critical inquiry that we can deconstruct these seemingly normal relationships to reveal the intentional and unintentional processes of construction and their underlying context. Critical sociological inquiry into the creation and maintenance of difference helps make the familiar strange, the natural unnatural, and the obvious not so obvious, and, in a world where things are often not what they seem, it allows us to see more clearly and deeply.

As we learn to understand ourselves and others, we can break down the divisions between us and build a foundation for transformative stories and new relationships. Our goal is not only to share information and knowledge about the dynamics of race and racism but also to connect this knowledge with our individual lives.

TABLE 1.2 ■ Feeling Race: Understanding Privilege

"I don't feel privileged, my life is hard too!"	This is an example of minimizing or denying privilege (Johnson 2006). We often focus on our oppressed identities as a means of ignoring our privilege.
"My family didn't own slaves!"	As historians have documented, "Into the mid-nineteenth century, the majority of Whites—in the elites and among ordinary folk—either participated directly in slavery or in the trade around slavery, or did not object to those who did so" (Feagin 2001, 15). The economies of many northern cities were based almost entirely on the slave trade, and generations of Whites have reaped "undeserved enrichment" from the forced labor of slaves, the cheap labor of other minority group members, and the land and resources taken, often violently, from Native Americans and Mexicans. These practices contribute directly to today's tremendous racial wealth gap.
"I treat everyone the same!"	This type of response shifts the focus to prejudiced and bigoted individuals and allows us to ignore systemic oppression and privilege, and our own role in their reproduction.
"Anyone could succeed if they would just try harder!"	This adherence to the myth of meritocracy attributes the failures of an individual solely to that individual, without considering systemic inequalities that create an unfair system. It is a form of blaming the victim (Johnson 2006).
"We need to move on! If we would just stop talking about it, it wouldn't be such a big problem!"	Systemic inequalities exist and ignoring them will not make them go away. As Justice Harry Blackmun stated in his opinion in the U.S. Supreme Court case of *University of California v. Bakke* (1978), "In order to get beyond racism, we must first take account of race. There is no other way" (para. 14).
"Stop being so sensitive! I didn't mean it."	Speaking in a derogatory manner about a person or group of people based on social group memberships can have a devastating impact (Sue 2010). Disconnecting our own language or actions minimizes the indiscretion and sends the message that anyone who challenges the language or behavior is simply being overly sensitive.
"I am just one person; I can't change anything!"	Seeing ourselves as incapable of creating change is a means of excusing ourselves from accepting any responsibility and denies agency.

WHAT IS YOUR STORY?

Before we begin our learning journey, let's start by examining ourselves. The action continuum shown in Figure 1.4 encourages us to consider our current beliefs and actions around oppression and privilege. Our focus here is on race and racism. This is a personal exercise; be honest. Do not feel ashamed or proud of where you place yourself. Simply acknowledge where you feel you fit. Keep in mind that this is not a straight line moving directly from one

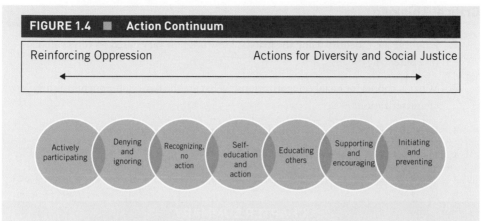

FIGURE 1.4 ■ Action Continuum

Reinforcing Oppression   Actions for Diversity and Social Justice

Actively participating — Denying and ignoring — Recognizing, no action — Self-education and action — Educating others — Supporting and encouraging — Initiating and preventing

end to the other. We all move back and forth, and may jump from one stage to another, over the course of our lives, and in our daily experiences. Save your response so you can reflect back on your position throughout the course.

- **Actively participating:** Telling derogatory jokes, putting down people from targeted groups, intentionally avoiding targeted group members, discriminating against targeted group members, verbally or physically harassing targeted group members.

- **Denying:** Enabling discrimination and injustice by denying that targeted group members are oppressed; not actively discriminating or oppressing, but by denying that oppression exists, contributing to its reproduction.

- **Recognizing, no action:** Aware of oppressive actions by self or others and their harmful effects but taking no action to stop this behavior. This inaction is the result of fear, lack of information, and confusion about what to do. Experiences discomfort at the contradiction between awareness and action.

- **Educating self and taking action:** Aware of oppression and injustice, recognizes oppressive actions of self and others and takes action to stop them. Taking actions to learn more about oppression and privilege, and the life experiences affected by unjust social relations by reading, attending workshops, seminars, cultural events, participating in discussions, joining organizations or groups that oppose injustice, attending social actions and change events.

- **Educating others:** Moving beyond only educating self to questions and dialogue with others. Rather than only intervening against prejudice and discrimination, also engaging people in discussion to educate.

- **Supporting, encouraging:** Supporting others who speak out against injustice or who are working to be more inclusive of targeted group members by backing up others who speak out, forming an allies' group, joining a coalition group, and so on.

- **Initiating, preventing:** Working to change individual and institutional actions and policies that discriminate against targeted group members, planning educational programs or other events, working for passage of legislation that protects excluded groups from discrimination, being explicit about making sure members of historically marginalized groups are full participants in organization or group. Working to create change in organizations and other spheres of influence. (Adapted from Adams, Bell, and Griffin 2007)

Critical Thinking

1. Examine your identity using the matrix. How might it vary based on time and place (the outer ring)?

2. What accounts for racial categorizations? What are the basic components of this characterization?

3. Explain the different types of stories and their relevance to the matrix.

4. Describe the types of actions you can take to foster change.

CHAPTER SUMMARY

1.1 Explain how the concept of race is socially constructed.

History, the reality of our shared past, reflects a series of choices. These choices, once made, often take on a life of their own, but we should always remember that they were and continue to be choices. There is more biological variation within our so-called racial groups than there is between them. Race must derive from human interventions. These interventions reflect the social construction of race. Our approach to all of these identities, while recognizing the multiple ways in which our various identities intersect, focuses on race. This primacy is more to facilitate our discussions, rather than an indication of the importance of race over any of the other categories. That being said, we recognize that if we were to use a different identity, our analysis would be different.

1.2 Summarize the operation of racism.

Racism is a system of oppression by which those groups with relatively more social power subordinate members of targeted racial groups who have relatively little social power. This subordination is supported by individual actions, cultural values, and norms embedded in stock stories, as well as in the institutional structures and practices of society. Racism in the United States is directed primarily against Blacks, Asian Americans, Latinx, and Native Americans. Some argue that the hatred and discrimination faced by Muslims should also be classified as racism, and that they are becoming a racialized group. Bias, prejudice, and discrimination are learned as part of the social environment that we live in. Therefore, despite the laws, expressed attitudes, and programs aimed at change, we continually discover the problem shaping our everyday lives

1.3 Analyze the relationship between social contexts and race.

We focus particularly on race and the way it shapes our identities, society and its institutions, and prospects for change. But we also examine race within the context of gender, class, and other social identities that interact with one another and reflect the way we live as social beings. Our institutional focus reflects our view that while race is often described in its outcomes such as bigotry, prejudice, and other biased behaviors and reactions, these behaviors and reactions operate within specific social and structural settings. Institutional structures serve to normalize racial boundaries through various laws, codes of conduct (both implicit and explicit), and other boundary maintenance mechanisms. There are essentially four different kinds of stories that we encounter in our lives: stock stories, concealed stories, resistance stories, and transforming stories.

KEY TERMS

Agency

Boundaries

Class

Color blind racism

Color blindness

Discrimination

Diversity

Ethnicity

Formal racism

Gender

Identity

Implicit bias

Informal agency

Informal racism

Intersectional theories

Matrix

Microaggressions

Norms

Oppression

Prejudice

Race

Racial frames

Racism

Relational aspects of race

Sexuality

Social institutions

Social location

Stereotypes

Systemic racism

White privilege

Whiteness studies

REFERENCES

Adams, Maurianne, Lee Anne Bell, and Pat Griffin, eds. 2007. *Teaching for Diversity and Social Justice: A Sourcebook.* New York: Routledge.

Balibar, Etienne and Immanuel Wallerstein. 1991. *Race, Nation, and Class: Ambiguous Identities.* London: Verso.

Barnett, Bernice McNair. 1995. "Black Women's Collectivist Movement Organizations: Their Struggles during the 'Doldrums.'" In *Feminist Organizations: Harvest of the New Women's Movement,* edited by Myra Marx Ferree and Patricia Yancey Martin. Philadelphia: Temple University Press.

Bell, Lee Anne. 2010. *Storytelling for Social Justice: Connecting Narrative and the Arts in Antiracist Teaching.* New York: Routledge.

Bonilla-Silva, Eduardo. 2018. *Racism without Racists: Color-Blind Racism and the Persistence of Racial Inequality in the United States.* 3rd ed. Lanham, MD: Rowman & Littlefield.

Brodkin, Karen. 1998. *How Jews Became White Folks and What That Says about Race in America.* New Brunswick, NJ: Rutgers University Press.

Bush, Melanie E. L. 2011. *Everyday Forms of Whiteness: Understanding Race in a "Post-racial" World.* 2nd ed. Lanham, MD: Rowman & Littlefield.

Case, Kim. 2013. *Deconstructing Privilege: Teaching and Learning as Allies in the Classroom.* New York: Routledge.

Coates, Rodney D. 2011. "Covert Racism: An Introduction." In *Covert Racism: Theories, Institutions, and Experiences,* edited by Rodney D. Coates. Leiden, Netherlands: Brill.

Collins, Patricia Hill. 2000. *Black Feminist Thought: Knowledge, Consciousness, and the Politics of Empowerment.* 2nd ed. New York: Routledge.

Connor, David J. 2006. "Michael's Story: 'I Get into Such Trouble Just by Walking': Narrative Knowing and Life at the Intersections of Learning Disability, Race, and Class." *Equity & Excellence in Education* 39, no. 2: 154–65.

Crenshaw, Kimberlé. 1991. "Mapping the Margins: Intersectionality, Identity Politics, and Violence against Women of Color." *Stanford Law Review* 43, no. 6: 1241–99.

Desmond, Matthew, and Mustafa Emirbayer. 2010. *Racial Domination, Racial Progress: The Sociology of Race in America*. New York: McGraw-Hill.

Feagin, J. R. 2001. *Racist America: Roots, Current Realities, and Future Reparations*. New York: Routledge.

Feagin, J. 2010. *The White Racial Frame: Centuries of Racial Framing and Counter-framing*. New York: Routledge.

Ferber, Abby L., Christina M. Jiménez, Andrea O'Reilly Herrera, and Dena R. Samuels. 2009. *The Matrix Reader: Examining the Dynamics of Oppression and Privilege*. Boston: McGraw Hill.

Ferber, Abby L., and Dena R. Samuels. 2010. "Oppression without Bigots." SWS Factsheet, Sociologists for Women in Society. Accessed April 4, 2017. https://www.socwomen.org/wp-content/uploads/2010/05/fact_3-2010-oppression.pdf.

Ferrante, Joan, and Prince Brown Jr. 2001. *The Social Construction of Race and Ethnicity in the United States*. 2nd ed. Upper Saddle River, NJ: Prentice Hall.

Frankenberg, E., Siegel-Hawley, G., Diem, S. 2017. "Segregation by District Boundary Line: The Fragmentation of Memphis-Area Schools." *Educational Researcher,* 46(8), 449–463.

Frye, Marilyn. 2007. *The Politics of Reality: Essays in Feminist Theory*. Berkeley, CA: Crossing Press.

Gallagher, Charles. 2009. "Color-Blinded America or How the Media and Politics Have Made Racism and Racial Inequality Yesterday's Social Problem." In *The Matrix Reader: Examining the Dynamics of Oppression and Privilege,* edited by Abby L. Ferber, Christina M. Jiménez, Andrea O'Reilly Herrera, and Dena R. Samuels, 548–51. Boston: McGraw-Hill.

Haney López, Ian. 2006. *White by Law: The Legal Construction of Race*. Rev. ed. New York: New York University Press.

Jacobson, Matthew Frye. 1998. *Whiteness of a Different Color: European Immigrants and the Alchemy of Race*. Cambridge, MA: Harvard University Press.

Johnson, Allan G. 2006. *Privilege, Power, and Difference*. 2nd ed. Boston: McGraw-Hill.

Ken, Ivy. 2008. "Beyond the Intersection: A New Culinary Metaphor for Race-Class-Gender Studies." *Sociological Theory* 26, 152–72.

Landrieu, Mitch. 2020."The Price We Have Paid for Not Confronting Racism." *The New York Times*. Accessed online at https://www.nytimes.com/2020/06/03/opinion/george-floyd-protest-racism.html)

Linshi, Jack. 2014. "10 Million Americans Switched Their Race or Ethnicity for the Census." *Time,* August 7. Accessed April 7, 2017. http://time.com/3087649/census-race-ethnicity-report.

Marable, Manning. 2016. *Beyond Black and White: From Civil Rights to Barack Obama*. London: Verso.

Markus, Hazel Rose, and Paula M. L. Moya. 2010. *Doing Race: 21 Essays for the 21st Century*. New York: W. W. Norton.

McIntosh, Peggy. 1988. "White Privilege and Male Privilege: A Personal Account of Coming to See Correspondences through Work in Women's Studies." Working Paper 189, Wellesley College Center for Research on Women.

McNamee, Stephen, and Robert K. Miller Jr. 2014. *The Meritocracy Myth*. 3rd ed. Lanham, MD: Rowman & Littlefield.

Moore, Eddie, Jr., Marguerite W. Penick-Parks, and Ali Michael, eds., 2015. *Everyday White People Confront Racial and Social Injustice: 15 Stories*. Sterling, VA: Stylus.

Morrison, Toni. 1992. *Playing in the Dark: Whiteness and the Literary Imagination*. New York: Vintage Books.

National Education Association. 2015. "Ensuring Safe Schools for All Students." Accessed August 3, 2015. http://www.nea.org/tools/30437.htm.

Perry, Samuel L., and Andrew L. Whitehead. 2015. "Christian nationalism and white racial boundaries: examining whites' opposition to interracial marriage." *Ethnic and Racial Studies* 38(10): 1671–1689. DOI: 10.1080/01419870.2015.1015584

Plaut, Victoria C. 2010. "Diversity Science: Why and How Difference Makes a Difference." *Psychological Inquiry* 21, no. 2: 77–99. doi:10.1080/10478401003676501.

Robnett, Belinda. 1999. *How Long? How Long? African-American Women in the Struggle for Civil Rights.* Oxford: Oxford University Press.

Ruiz, Vicki L. 1999. *From Out of the Shadows: Mexican Women in Twentieth-Century America.* Oxford: Oxford University Press.

Smedley, Audrey. 2007. *Race in North America: Origin and Evolution of a Worldview*. 3rd ed. Boulder, CO: Westview Press.

Spade, Joan Z., and Jeanne H. Ballantine. 2011. *Schools and Society: A Sociological Approach to Education*. Thousand Oaks, CA: Sage.

Spelman, Elizabeth V. 1988. *Inessential Woman: Problems of Exclusion in Feminist Thought*. Boston: Beacon Press.

Steinmetz, K. F., Schaefer, B. P., and Henderson, H. 2017. "Wicked overseers: American policing and colonialism." *Sociology of Race and Ethnicity* 3(1): 68–81. DOI: 10.1177/2332649216665639

Sue, Derald Wing. 2010. *Microaggressions in Everyday Life: Race, Gender, and Sexual Orientation.* Hoboken, NJ: John Wiley.

Takei, Isao, and Arthur Sakamoto. 2011. "Poverty among Asian Americans in the 21st Century." *Sociological Perspectives* 54, no. 2: 251–76.

Tochluk, Shelly. 2008. *Witnessing Whiteness: First Steps toward an Antiracist Practice and Culture.* Lanham, MD: Rowman & Littlefield.

U.S. Census. 2020. "Questions asked on the form." Accessed online at URL: https://2020census.gov/en/about-questions.html?cid=23759: 2020%20census%20questions:sem.ga:p:dm:en:&utm_source=sem.ga&utm_medium=p&utm_campaign=dm:en&utm_content=23759&utm_term=2020%20census%20questions questions:sem.ga questions:sem.ga

Vuletich, H. A., Payne, B. K. 2019.Stability and Change in Implicit Bias. *Psychological Science* 30(6): 854–862. doi:10.1177/0956797619844270

2

THE SHAPING OF A NATION

The Social Construction of Race in America

The COVID-19 pandemic has negatively impacted immigrants as well as minority racial and ethnic populations, underscoring social and economic precarity.

Credit: Alejandra Villa Loarca/Newsday RM via Getty Images

LEARNING OBJECTIVES

2.1 Explain how recent events have affected how we experience race.

2.2 Describe the Americas before Columbus.

2.3 Identify patterns of Spanish, French, and British colonialism in the Americas.

The recent crisis around the COVID-19 pandemic has demonstrated, once again, the centrality of immigrants in the United States. Many essential workers are immigrants, and they were on the frontline of our efforts to combat this virus. They were restocking our grocery shelves, caring for those in hospice centers, picking our strawberries, and working in the factories that provide food and goods (Lowrey 2020). Immigrants, as well as other racial minorities, were also more likely to be in economically precarious situations as businesses shut down and social distancing was enforced. Some became targets for hate and discrimination, and they were also more likely to be excluded from benefiting from the Congressional stimulus, the series of tax rebates and incentives used to help stimulate the economy and save corporations and individuals/families from financial ruin (Chishti and Bolter 2020).

The United States is a "nation of immigrants," whose very entrance is adorned with a statue which proclaims, "give me your poor, your tired, your huddled masses, yearning to breathe free." Non-European groups that are categorized according to race have historically had greater difficulties entering, remaining in, and succeeding in the United States. The history of these difficulties reveals a set of choices which instituted race as an integral feature in the shaping of our nation. These choices, once made, often take on a life of their own, but we should always remember that they were and continue to be choices. Nothing demonstrates the accuracy of this assessment than the particular set of choices that served to shape our nation having to do with race. In this chapter we shall examine these choices as we explore the shaping of a nation and the social construction of race in America.

RACE TODAY: ADAPTING AND EVOLVING

Anti-Asian racism has escalated since the initial outbreak of the coronavirus pandemic in January of 2020. TikTok, a popular social media platform among high schoolers, often highlighted both racist and misleading videos about coronavirus, and on Twitter you can find racist memes that blamed the outbreak of the virus on Asian American eating habits. Asian American and Pacific Islanders have been targeted, threatened, and harassed. Incidents include statements from public officials calling COVID-19 the "Chinese virus" and other terms that sought to make the Asian and Pacific Islander communities scapegoats. Equally troubling were the spread of extremist views that continued the long-standing anti-Semitic and xenophobic conspiracies accusing both Jews and Chinese of creating, spreading, and profiting from the virus (Cassen 2020). To some extent, the targeting of Chinese Americans reflects the changing demographics and other social forces.

Changing Demographics and Social Forces

The United States is a nation of immigrants that has historically been defined by racial and ethnic diversity. The U.S. immigrant population, while at record highs, is still below many other countries in the world. In 2017, the 44 million foreign-born persons living in the U.S. comprised just 13% of the population. Although impressive, 25 other nations and territories had a higher percentage of immigrants in the same year:

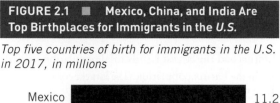

FIGURE 2.1 ■ Mexico, China, and India Are Top Birthplaces for Immigrants in the *U.S.*

Top five countries of birth for immigrants in the U.S. in 2017, in millions

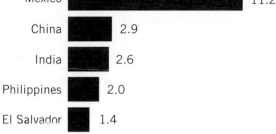

Mexico 11.2
China 2.9
India 2.6
Philippines 2.0
El Salvador 1.4

Note: China includes Taiwan and Hong Kong.

Source: Pew Research Center tabulations of 2017 American Community Survey (1% IPUMS), https://www.pewresearch.org/fact-tank/2019/06/17/key-findings-about-u-s-immigrants/.

- Australia (29%)

- New Zealand (23%)

- Canada (21%) (Cilluffo and Cohn 2019)

Forty percent of the world's migrants live in either the U.S. or Europe. For most of the 20th century, immigrants to the United States mostly came from Europe, with the greatest numbers hailing from Germany or Italy. Between 1890 and 1919, almost 90% of migrants to the U.S. came from Europe. Today, only 9% of the migrant population was born in the European Union, Norway, or Switzerland (Lopez 2016). Figure 2.1 shows the top three birthplaces for immigrants in the United States (Radford 2017).

Increasing Diversity

American diversity has increased over the past few years as racial and ethnic groups are growing faster than their White counterparts. Asian and mixed-race persons are the two fastest-growing segments of the U.S. population, with both groups growing by 3 percentage points. The non-Hispanic White population is the only group which is experiencing a decline. In 2018, the White population accounted for just over 60% of the U.S. population. The second largest group was Hispanic or Latinx, who now represent a little over 18%. Blacks or African Americans accounted for 13.5%, Asians almost 6%, and Native Americans were 1.3% of the population. Those citing two or more races now constitute 2.7% of our population (Census 2018).

While the country as a whole has grown more diverse, some areas of the United States are more diverse than others.

- Whereas California had the largest Latinx total population in 2016, Texas had the largest increase in the Latinx population. The largest concentration of Latinx was in New Mexico (48.5%).

- Alternatively, California had the largest White population, while Texas had the largest numeric increase of Whites. The largest concentration of Whites (as a percentage of the total population) is Maine (95.5%).

- While New York had a larger Black or African American population than any other state (3.8 million), the largest increase in this population went to Texas. The District of Columbia has the highest concentration of Blacks (49.4%).

- California has the largest Asian population and the largest American Indian or Alaska Native population of any state (152,400 and 1.1 million, respectively). Alaska accounts for the largest concentration of American Indians or Alaska Natives, while Hawaii has the largest concentration of Asians (Census 2017).

But diversity is just one dimension of understanding changing social forces. The other factor has to do with the amount of actual change that is taking place. Consequently, while one sixth of the country remained completely White through the 2000 census, over the past years these same areas (particularly in northern New England and much of the Midwest) have seen increasing population shifts. The majority of Americans (60% or 190 million) live in urban areas which are magnets for diversity. Many cities in the Southeast, for example in Georgia and the Carolinas, are seeing a growing Latinx population joining the more established Black and White communities.

The most diverse cities in the United States, such as Boston, Seattle, and Orlando, have almost 60 million people (slightly less than one sixth of our country's population). This is in part due to immigration.

Understanding Immigration

People report choosing to immigrate for a variety of reasons, including:

- seeking economic opportunities (52%)

- fleeing violence and insecurity (18%)

- reuniting with family (2%)

But the decision to immigrate is often not simple, as more than a quarter (28%) cite multiple reasons (Meyer and Taft-Morales 2019).

Over the past decade, migration to the United States from Central America has been associated with so-called **pull factors**, such as economic and educational opportunities, and the desire to reunify families. These factors are not isolated from what is happening in the host countries. For these countries, **push factors**—such as weak institutions, corrupt government officials, chronic unemployment and poverty, rising levels of crime and illicit drugs—increase insecurity and erode confidence in governmental institutions (Wilson 2019).

While immigrants decide to leave their home countries to settle somewhere else, **refugees** are forced to leave their country to avoid war, persecution, or natural disaster (UNHCR 2020). They often have sufficient reason to believe that they will be targeted because of their race, religion, nationality, political opinion, or membership in a specific social group. Often they cannot return home or are afraid of reprisals if they do.

During the early to mid-1990s, an average of 116,000 refugees, many from the former Soviet Union, entered the U.S. each year. From 2008 to 2017, an average of 67,000 refugees annually entered our country. Over half of these refugees came from Asia, with many from Iraq and Burma (formerly Myanmar). Since 1980, 55% of all refugees have come from Asia.

By the end of 2018, 70.8 million persons were forced to relocate worldwide as a consequence of persecution, conflict, violence, or human rights violations. With an increase of 2.3 million forcibly displaced persons over the previous year, this constituted a record high (USA for UNHCR 2020).

For most of the past 40 years, the U.S. led the world in refugee resettlement, but since 2017, it has trailed (Figure 2.2) (Krogstad 2019).

In 2019 the United States capped the number of refugees at 30,000, and for fiscal year 2020, a maximum of 18,000 refugees were to be admitted. This would be the lowest level of refugees

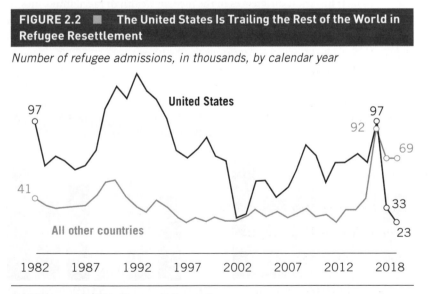

FIGURE 2.2 ■ The United States Is Trailing the Rest of the World in Refugee Resettlement

Number of refugee admissions, in thousands, by calendar year

Note: Figures rounded to the nearest thousand.

Source: Pew Research Center of United Nations High Commissioner for Refugees data, accessed June 12, 2019. https://www.pewresearch.org/fact-tank/2019/10/07/key-facts-about-refugees-to-the-u-s/.

resettling in the U.S. in a single year since 1980, when Congress first created the resettlement program (Krogstad 2019).

In the early 1990s the United States became one of the first nations to grant refugee status to LGBTQ+ refugees and asylum seekers due to persecution targeting sexual orientation or gender identity in their home countries. Over the past few years, these policies are being reversed as countless numbers of LGBTQ migrants are refused asylum. Most impacted may be those coming from countries such as El Salvador, Honduras, and Guatemala in Central America, where sexual and gender-based violence is highest (Washington Post Editorial Board 2018).

Our diverse landscape has already begun to influence our nation in both obvious and very subtle ways. These differences, as we will see in future chapters, will have a profound impact on all of our institutions.

Revising the Experience of Work, Gender, and Race

Today, women are driving the new labor trends in the U.S., where most new hires are minorities between the ages of 25 and 54 (Figure 2.3). Most of these new hires are women of color. Hispanic women between the ages of 25 and 54 are leading the surge. Since 2007 (at the beginning of our last recession), Hispanic female employment rates have increased 2.2%. The employment rates of Black women also grew. Other winners in the labor market were Black men and White women. But despite these increases in employment rates, the highest income earners, which are the richest 1%, were heavily represented by Whites and males (Smialek 2019).

It is also important to note that stable jobs for women of color do not always lead to wealth accumulation. In fact, historical differences in the median wealth of racial minorities continue to be a reality. This reality is brought home when we consider that the wealth gaps between non-Hispanic White households is over $150,000 more than the median of either non-Hispanic Black or Hispanic households (Dettling, Hsu, Jacobs, et al., 2017).

Wage disparities affect all women, but Hispanic, African American, American Indian, Native Hawaiian, and other Native American women are the lowest paid. For the women in

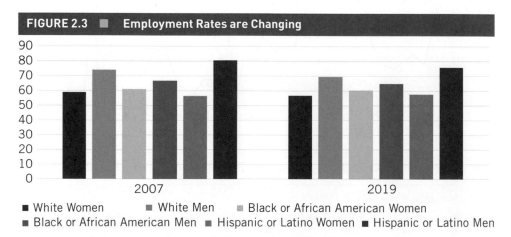

FIGURE 2.3 ■ Employment Rates are Changing

Legend:
- White Women
- White Men
- Black or African American Women
- Black or African American Men
- Hispanic or Latino Women
- Hispanic or Latino Men

Source: Data from U.S. Bureau of Labor Statistics, Current Population Survey.

these groups, however, the gender gap—the difference between their wages and those of men in the same groups—is not as great as the gap for White non-Hispanic women, who experience the largest gender gap. Closer examination reveals that among all groups, Hispanic women, followed by African American women, have the largest earning gap when compared to White men (Hegewisch and Hartmann 2019).

The Evolving Narrative of Popular Culture

Two popular book series, J. K. Rowling's *Harry Potter* series and Stephenie Meyer's *Twilight* saga, demonstrate how race, class, and gender issues prevail even in fictional universes (Moje, Young, Readence, and Moore 2000; Strommen and Mates 2004). Some of the allure of the *Twilight* series might be that it weaves together concerns about sex, race, and class as the human protagonist violates norms and falls in love with a vampire. The story suggests that our society can overcome both racism and sexism in this fictionalized world where vampires, werewolves, and humans get along and battle for gender equality (Wilson 2011). Unfortunately, this fictionalized social reality is just that—fictionalized (Bonilla-Silva 2008). Other popular books feature worlds where race, power, oppression, and liberation are clearly etched into the narratives. Take the case of the *Harry Potter* books, which present a strikingly racialized narrative where the world is divided among the "pure-blood" wizarding families; the "halfbloods," or wizards born of non-wizarding families, and the "Muggles," or non-magical humans.

If children are our future, then the worlds that they live in and the dreams they are allowed to experience are in many ways structured by print and other media. In 2016, just 12% of all children's books printed in the U.S. were written by racial minorities (See Figure 2.4). This is especially important since 39% of all Americans identify with a minority group. These limitations are even more troubling when we realize that, even when minorities are represented in children's books, these books are often written by non-minorities. This gap is especially true for Black characters (Ro 2019).

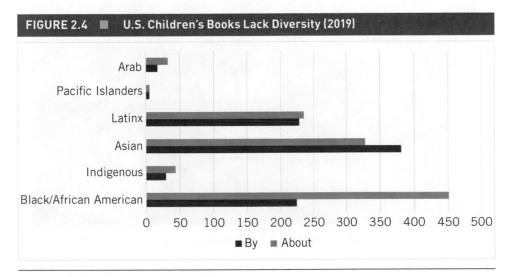

FIGURE 2.4 ■ U.S. Children's Books Lack Diversity (2019)

Source: Data from Cooperative Children's Book Center.

The Impact of Social Media and Technology

In our digital age, slurs, assaults, bigotry, and prejudice across gender, class, and social groups can spread beyond geographical borders due to the existence of social media. Most people between the ages of 18 and 29 years old are active on some form of social media (Smith and Anderson 2018). In fact, universities across the nation are discovering that the digital age has opened a new door for racist, sexist, homophobic, and other forms of bigotry. Consequently, rather than challenging the racial status quo, the online world has ultimately reproduced it.

After being challenged by activist groups like Women, Action and the Media, The Everyday Sexism Project, and representatives from historically marginalized groups (Jewish, Muslim, and LGBT communities), Facebook decided to take direct action to combat toxic messages, images, and texts. In 2018, Facebook launched an algorithm designed to limit toxic content from its platform. This algorithm screens words, representations, and content that are deemed hateful, cruel, insensitive, or prejudiced (Brenner 2018). Unfortunately, there is some evidence that the algorithm actually increases divisiveness by targeting Black, Hispanic, and other minority users in the U.S. (Seetharaman and Horwitz 2020).

We are a nation of immigrants. While English is the dominant language, more than 300 other languages are spoken here (Shin and Kominski 2010). In fact, the United States has no official language. Examining the nation's story helps us understand why.

Immigrants increase racial and ethnic diversity in the United States.

Credit: John Moore/Getty Images

Critical Thinking

1. Why do current demographic shifts define us as a nation? How might these changes differ across different geographical areas?

2. How do demographic shifts affect various social institutions?

3. How might future demographic changes affect different areas and institutions? How can social media become an instrument of change?

4. How will the demographic evolution affect you? Are you ready for the changes that are coming?

CONCEALED STORIES: INDIGENOUS PEOPLES IN THE AMERICAS BEFORE COLUMBUS

As a nation, we rely on certain stories to bind us together, the most central of which has to do with the founding and discovery of our country—our own "stock story":

In fourteen hundred and ninety-two, Columbus sailed the ocean blue.

According to this story, a brave and daring Christopher Columbus set off from Europe with three ships to find a shorter route to Asia. Columbus, often portrayed as a scientific and astronomical genius, proved not only that the world is round but also that its circumnavigation was feasible.

Recent historical revisions have challenged this story, suggesting that this "discovery" was more like an invasion. Though vastly outnumbered by the natives of the Americas, the Europeans benefited greatly from "guns, germs, and steel"—the superior weaponry and disease-causing microbes they brought from Europe that allowed them to impose their wills on the indigenous Americans (Diamond 1999).

The Earliest Americans

Prior to Columbus, Native Americans inhabited the Americas. From the Abenakis of Maine to the Zunis of New Mexico, Native Americans are descendants from an even earlier group of immigrants to the Americas. These Asian immigrants were the first Americans, arriving more than 20,000 years ago. There is a good chance that they came via two different routes:

1. People on foot, traversing the glacial land bridge between Siberia and Alaska, were mostly hunters and gatherers who followed the mastodon and long-horned bison, and might have been responsible for their eventual extinction.

2. Fishers and hunters utilizing boats from the Pacific Islands allowed the currents to guide them to these shores. (Arnaiz-Villena et al., 2010)

Many of the early Native American communities were urban, with populations reaching the tens of thousands. Archaeologists and anthropologists have identified several towns, with temples and evidence of a priestly class, along with nobles, merchants, and artisans, demonstrating highly stratified, hierarchical, and technologically sophisticated civilizations.

A Rich History

Hundreds of years before Columbus, North America was home to millions of people and hundreds of population groups, tribes, and linguistic and cultural systems. These people called themselves Iroquois, Lakota, Apache, and hundreds of other names.

Native Americans typically gave specific names to each feature of a river or mountain. Many of these names are still in use today.

Credit: MPI/Archive Photos/Getty Images

In the Northeast, the Iroquois and the Algonquin, two major language and cultural groups, occupied a region now known as the Northeastern Woodlands. The Algonquin controlled two major areas, one encompassing the Great Lakes and the other near the Atlantic Ocean. Several tribes constituted the Algonquin. The Wampanoag were the first tribe in this region encountered by the Europeans. Both the Illini and the Potawatomi occupied the Illinois region. The League of the Iroquois, formed as early as 1090, comprised five tribes who lived in the areas today known as New York State and the Southeastern Woodlands (which stretched from the Atlantic Ocean to the Mississippi River and from the Gulf of Mexico to the Ohio River). The largest northern groups in the confederation were the Cherokee, the Chickasaw, and the Creek. The southern regions were dominated by the Natchez, Biloxi, and Seminole—known as the Mound Builders (Lord and Burke 1991).

Many geographical place names help identify the first peoples of the Americas. More than half of U.S. state names are representative of the original inhabitants of those areas, including:

- Michigan, from the Allegany language, meaning "big water"

- Minnesota, from the Siouan language, meaning "water that reflects the sky"

- Missouri, from the Siouan language, meaning "water flowing along"

- Ohio, from the Iroquois language, meaning "good river"

Some state names reflect the dominance of particular tribes, such as Massachusetts, Connecticut, Illinois, and the Dakotas. While Native Americans rarely gave a single name to an entire river or mountain, they typically gave names to specific features, such as the mouth or bend of a particular river. We have many of these names still with us today, such as Potomac (Iroquois, meaning "the place to which tribute is brought") or Allegheny (Iroquois derived from *Monongahela,* which means "falling banks").

Their histories are reflected in the many names they gave this land—such as the Lakota and Mohawk's Anowarkowa (Turtle Island), the Powhatan's Tsenacommacah (densely inhabited area), and the Shawnee's Kantukee (the great meadow, or the dark and bloody ground). They lived in teepees and huts, cities and villages; they built burial mounds, temples, and multistory buildings. And they routinely and systematically planted and harvested more than 100 kinds of crops (including tomatoes, quinoa, and peaches) using crop-rotation techniques and an understanding of the importance of seasonal flooding for the enrichment of nutrient-poor soil (Mann 2005).

In their farming, these original Americans added charcoal and broken pottery to the tropical red clays—an agricultural method recognized today. Skilled at metallurgy, they examined metals for their malleability and toughness (Mendoza 1997).

The earliest Americans hunted buffalo, boar, turkey, rabbit, and deer. Their diet also included perch, catfish, oysters, and salmon. They mastered carving, weaving, tanning, and pot making. Not only did they develop highly sophisticated artistry in jewelry, weaving, and textiles, but they also created pictorial art on cave walls and rocks. Their works are displayed in some of the finest museums across the world today. These peoples had highly developed written, oral, and symbolic languages; math and calendar systems; religions; political systems; and constitutions. Their civilizations were hundreds of years older than the oldest European nation, richer than we will ever know, and more varied than has ever been captured in the stock stories of "cowboys and Indians."

These Native Americans were neither brutes nor savages, neither pagans nor infidels. They were not prototypical environmentalists or solitary figures in contest with the forces of progress—they were humans, with all of the creative and marvelous social inventions we have come to recognize as human, such as democratic governance and constitutional bodies, federations and confederations, family and community. They had both philosophies and mythologies, prophecies and paradigms, educational systems, and beliefs about the cosmos, hopes and dreams. They had wars and civil unrest, and military, political, civil, and religious leaders.

They bartered and traded and had many types of coinage and economies. Ultimately, they lived full, expansive, rich, and complete lives long before Columbus and the Europeans discovered them and entered their matrix to create a new one.

Critical Thinking

1. In what ways does historical revision recast Columbus's voyage from that of a discovery to that of an invasion?

2. How do our geographical place names reflect our indigenous past?

3. Explain why stereotypical representations of Native Americans fail to capture their complexities.

COLONIALISM: THE SHAPING OF OUR STORIED PAST

European colonization of the Americas actually began in the 10th and 11th centuries, when Viking sailors explored what is currently Canada. In their explorations, they settled Greenland, sailed up the Arctic region of North America, and engaged in violent conflict with several indigenous populations. More extensive European colonization began in 1492, when Spanish ships captained by Christopher Columbus inadvertently landed on the northern tip of Cuba. In all instances, colonial adventures were particularly nationalistic, as evidenced by the names of Nueva Española, Nouvelle-France, and New England. Settlement of this so-called New World centered on transplanting, cloning, and grafting European institutions into the Americas. These particularities were aggravated by competition over control of land, ports, raw resources, and native peoples.

The Basics of Colonialism

Colonialism is a set of hierarchical relationships in which groups are defined culturally, ethnically, and/or racially, and these relationships serve to guarantee the political, social, and economic interests of the dominant group (Barrera 1976, 3). Under the guise of advancing the "kingdom of God," the Spanish, French, and English pursuit of colonies was more closely aligned with greed and desire for fame.

Religious ideology was used to justify wars of aggression, exploitation, subjugation, extermination, enslavement, and colonization. The structures, ideologies, and actions that form patterns of colonialism shape groups' interrelated experiences in profound ways—the realities behind colonialism are complex, and usually structurally and culturally catastrophic for the colonized. We can view colonialism through three primary lenses:

1. As a structure of domination subjugating one group of people to another across political entities

2. As "internal" or "domestic" colonialism, a similar structure occurring within a given nation-state, typically against socially marked groups

3. As a "colonialism of the mind," wherein the colonized are institutionally, pedagogically, linguistically, and cognitively conquered by the colonizer

The colonies that developed within the Americas are best classified as settler colonies. **Settler colonies** are distinguished by the colonizing nation's control of political, economic, social, and cultural mechanisms in the colonies, which creates a colonial elite. The European elite who migrated to the settler colonies in the Americas were intent on settlement, creation of a self-sustaining independent political/economic system, and domination of both geography and indigenous populations. Even while settler colonies maintained dependency relationships with their respective European nations, they nevertheless achieved significant autonomy (Stasiulis and Yuval-Davis 1995).

European settlements and population dynamics varied considerably both across different European groups and compared with those established by Native Americans. Pre-Columbian population estimates suggest that Native Americans were generally distributed throughout the Americas, with most occupying the areas that are now Mexico and Central America (47%), followed by South America (35%) and the Caribbean (10%). The remainder were scattered across what would become the United States and Canada. The first groups of colonizers, the Spanish and Portuguese, settled in the most densely populated areas. Later colonizing efforts by both the French and the English created settlements in the less densely populated areas, primarily in North America and Canada (Figure 2.5). Such dynamics produced very different sets of opportunities and issues for both the colonizers and the colonized.

Spanish Colonialism (1492)

We must be willing to confront the history of the Americas in terms that are more complex and nuanced than those often provided by simple historical accounts. At no time were the colonies ever fully independent of, or politically isolated from, what was happening in Europe or among the various Native American nations. In 1492, when Columbus stumbled on a set of islands off

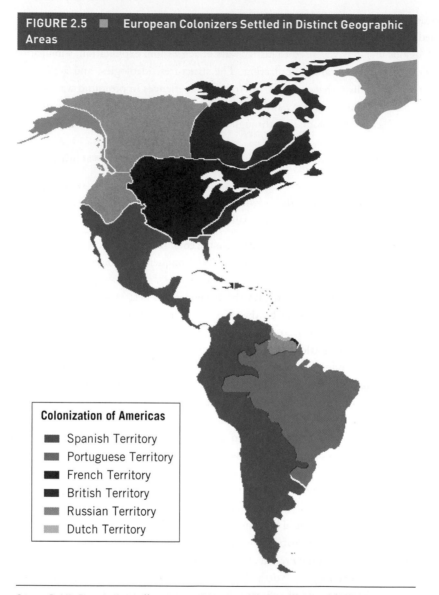

FIGURE 2.5 ■ **European Colonizers Settled in Distinct Geographic Areas**

Colonization of Americas

- Spanish Territory
- Portuguese Territory
- French Territory
- British Territory
- Russian Territory
- Dutch Territory

Source: Public Domain, https://commons.wikimedia.org/w/index.php?curid=3546356.

the coast of Florida, he named them Hispana, the Latin name for Spain. Despite the fact that this land was home to a significant population, Columbus declared it *terra nullius* (empty land), revealing much about how explorers and, later, colonists saw themselves in relation to others and the world around them.

Constructing a Racial Ideology

The Spanish encountered a significantly different people with specific cultural, political, and gender systems. Native American gender systems varied across tribal groups. Gender relations within the Taino tribes, for example, were both egalitarian and nonexclusive. Women were able to own property and often served as ritual leaders and organized most of the subsistence work (Deagan and Cruxent 2002, 31–32; Deagan 2004).

By 1570, the Spanish colonies were utilizing two racial distinctions:

1. *Spanish-born or -descended:* This group consisted of those born in either Spain or the colonies and included both those of mixed heritage and those considered "purebloods."

2. *Native-born or -descended:* This group consisted of all Native Americans, who were considered vassals of the king.

Each of these groups had different rights, obligations, and privileges. Natives, under Spanish laws, were obliged to provide labor for both government and private enterprises deemed vital to colonial interests, and to pay special poll taxes or tributes. While these laws were intended to create two distinct classes, the flexible laws of both marriage and residence allowed many Native Americans to adopt European-style dress and "pass" as purebloods (Jackson 2006, 902).

The Catholic Church, notably through the Spanish Inquisition and the Franciscan order, used purity certifications to impose barriers on some Spaniards who sought to immigrate to the Americas. The church would use these same purity levels to label both Africans and Native Americans as "New Christians" and mark both as "impure" (Martinez 2004, 483). Any offspring of interracial unions involving New Christians would thus be less valued. Put simply, Blacks, Native Americans, and others could be redeemed and baptized, but they still could not mix with "purebloods."

Grounded in vague notions of purity and supposed biological differences, these rules would later become the basis for the **racial caste system**, a permanent hierarchy based on race that developed in Spanish America (Martinez 2008). These laws also reveal the centrality of gender relations to the construction of culture and race. In order to distinguish one culture from another and define one as superior, societies must maintain borders. These borders are inscribed onto women's bodies and then policed by regulating sexual relationships. The bodies and wombs of White women were considered sacred—they were the only source of future generations of Whites (Martinez 2008, 483–84). European men, on the other hand, maintained for themselves access to all women's bodies.

Concealed Story: Columbus Encounters a New People/World

If you have ever tasted barbecue, smoked tobacco, paddled a canoe, slept on a hammock, or watched a hurricane cross the ocean, then you should thank the Taíno, the Indians who invented these words long before Christopher Columbus "discovered" this new people in this new world (Poole 2011).

As we look back to 1492, one thing is perfectly clear. Columbus did not "discover" the Americas. Columbus, itinerant trader, was obsessed with finding the more expeditious western sea route to Cathay (China), India, and the mythical spice and gold islands of Asia. Columbus began his voyage when he left Spain in August of 1492 (History.com editors 2020). Columbus was granted "the Capitulations of Santé Fe" by Ferdinand and Isabella, the Catholic monarchs of Castile. As an admiral, all lands he "discovered" would be acquired in the name of Spain. Further, he would rule on behalf of the monarchs, able to "hear and dispatch all civil and criminal proceedings pertaining to the said offices of the admiralty, viceroyalty and governorship." Accordingly, Columbus and his heirs would receive 10% of all "removable assets" discovered in the new lands, including but not limited to gold, silver, pearls, precious stones, and, apparently, slaves. Further, the act called for the creation of a crown monopoly which would control all "removable assets" (Stone 1975). Ironically, these "capitulations" established the conditions which would lead to the absolute capitulation and genocide of the indigenous populations of the Americas.

The ill-fated voyage of capitulation reached shore when Columbus's flagship went aground on Christmas Day, 1492. Claiming this land for Spain, Columbus then dismantled the ship and used the timber to build Fort Navidad (or Christmas Fort). Whatever rights to this land might have been held by the actual owners, the Taínos, were set aside as this became the first Spanish settlement in this "New World" (Maclean 2008). Columbus first describes the natives as being docile and easily controlled. In fact, the evidence suggests that he was a tyrant, who routinely visited cruelty on the native Taínos and also on other Spaniards. However, the extremes of cruelty, which included rape, torture, genocide, and slavery, were reserved for the indigenous population (Lane 2015). In less than 30 years, by 1519, a full third of the Native population had died as a result of smallpox. Some estimate this number to be closer to 85% (Poole 2011). These sets of choices, for choices they certainly were, became the deciding moments that shaped us as a nation.

The Slave System

Columbus was the first to employ slavery in the colonies. Two days after he "discovered" America, Columbus wrote in his journal that with 50 men he could order "the entire population be taken to Castile, or held captive."

On his second voyage in December 1494, Columbus captured 1,500 Taínos on the island of Hispaniola and selected 550 of "the best males and females" to be presented to the Spanish queen, Isabella, and sold in the slave markets of Seville, Spain (Beal 2008, 60). Impressed with the industrious and gentle islanders, Columbus quickly began seizing their land and enslaving them to work in his mines. He also precipitated the sexual slavery of girls as young as 9 and 10. Columbus remarked in his log, "A hundred castellanoes are as easily obtained for a woman or a farm, and it is very general and there are plenty of dealers who go about looking for girls; those from nine to ten are now in demand" (Kasum 2016).

In 1525 a total of 5,271 slaves appeared on the notarial records of Seville; almost 400 were listed as Blacks or mulattoes (Phillips 1985, 161).

The Spanish colonies were considered lenient with regard to racial classification, for multiple reasons:

Black slaves were the major source of labor on sugar plantations in Spanish America, particularly after Native American populations were decimated.

Credit: Art by William Clark, 1823

- The colonial laws accorded protections to Native Americans and to slaves.

- Slaves' rights were protected by both judicial and ecclesiastical authority.

- Spanish slave laws were derived from Roman legal traditions.

- Manumission (the freeing of slaves) did not require prior approval from the crown.

- Slaves could purchase their own freedom.

- Slaves had legal recourse through the Spanish courts, even for grievances against their masters. (Parise 2008, 13–14)

Ultimately, the supply of Native American labor in the Spanish colonies was decimated by continual warfare, disease, and sheer overwork. Under the licensing system established by King Ferdinand in 1513, an estimated 75,000 to 90,000 African slaves were sent to Spanish America by 1600. This figure would more than triple by the end of the 17th century, accounting for approximately 350,000 enslaved Africans (Landers 1997, 85). With these massive increases in the labor force, the Spanish colonies shifted to plantation economies, which also fundamentally altered Spanish slavery. Blacks began to outnumber Whites in Hispaniola and Mexico by an estimated ratio of 10 to 1 by the early to mid-16th century. Many of the medieval slave protections were stripped away, and Spanish officials' worst nightmares were realized as slave insurrections repeatedly threatened one colonial settlement after another.

French Colonialism (1534)

New France, the first site colonized by France in North America, was created by the 1534 expedition headed by Jacques Cartier along the Saint Lawrence River in what is now Quebec. Cartier's explorations allowed France to claim the land that would later become Canada. The French sought gold along the Saint Lawrence River, but settled for fishing and fur trading instead. And it was here, in 1608, that Quebec was established as the first French colony (Greer 1997, 6).

The French attempted to colonize a large chunk of the Americas with an extremely small and mostly male colonial force. The fact that the Frenchmen were outnumbered and unable to establish cultural dominance and stable communities helps explain their eventual failure.

Among financiers and merchants, the French colonial expansion into the Americas was conceived of as a business venture, and profits were often seen as more important than colonial development. Officially, the primary goal of these ventures was the Christianization of the natives, but it was not until after the first successful settlements were established that this royal rhetoric was given serious consideration. The thrust of the efforts, inspired by the fur trade, provided the motivation to integrate the indigenous population into the French colonial policy, as governors and foreign missionaries were determined to save the "savages" (Belmessous 2005).

Labor Crisis and Slavery

The French, like the Spanish, soon discovered that Native American slaves could not provide sufficient labor. As the plantations and economies expanded, so did labor needs. French colonies like Louisiana encountered labor crises as they attempted to shift their economies to tobacco and sugar production. On May 1, 1689, King Louis XIV gave royal approval for the trade and use of Africans as slaves. Twenty years later, in 1709, slavery was declared legal in New France.

The first groups of imported slaves came from both France and Africa between 1717 and 1720. The group from France consisted of more than 1,400 White men and women who had been convicted as thieves and deported to New France. Riots by these French slaves caused a sudden halt to this form of slavery. Ultimately, it was Africans who filled the labor needs of New France, particularly in Louisiana. During this period close to 4,000 Africans were forcefully brought to the colony (Hall 1992). As this history demonstrates, Africans did not become slaves because they were Black; many other cultural groups were also forced into slavery (Pitts 2012).

France produced a set of laws governing slaves and Blacks that were qualitatively different from the laws of Spain. France's Colonial Ordinance of 1685, also known as the **Black Code** (Code Noir), legislated the life, death, purchase, marriage, and religion of slaves, as well as the treatment of slaves by their masters. It formally required all slaves to be baptized and educated in the Catholic faith and prohibited masters from forcing slaves to work on Sundays and religious holidays. It required masters to provide slaves with food, shelter, and clothing, and with care when sick. It held that slaves could not own property or have any legal recourse. It further established when they could marry, where they could be buried, what punishments could be meted out to them, and under what conditions they could be freed (Buchanan 2011). These laws were an attempt to curtail the sexual and moral problems generated by frontier society, which tended to blur the lines between groups with differing status. The Black Code prohibited Whites, as well as free Blacks, from having sexual relationships with slaves. Any children who might have been born of such unions were to become wards of the state and held in perpetual slavery. In other words, a slave's status could not be altered based on marriage, and the child of a slave would become a slave. In legalizing the status of the slave, the code created a firm border between slaves and free persons. The only loophole applied to any existing sexual relationships between free Black men and Black women who were slaves. Any children born of these unions would be rendered legitimate and free.

Concealed Stories: Left-Handed Marriages and Plaçage

Within these frontier situations, "social relations were more fluid and social hierarchies less established than they would become with the entrenchment of plantation agriculture" (Spear 2003, 90). Under these circumstances, a strange norm developed whereby men often formed alliances with Creole women in what were termed **left-handed marriages**. These "marriages," temporary in nature, often resulted in children who served as interpreters and mediators (Shippen 2004, 358). While such relationships were equivalent to common-law marriages, the women were not legally recognized as wives; among free people of color, these social arrangements were referred to as **plaçage**.

Plaçage flourished throughout both French and Spanish colonies. Such relationships were celebrated as part of high society in New Orleans during what became known as the city's

Under the plaçage system, White men would take light-skinned free women of color as their common-law wives and establish them in households, often with servants.

Credit: Paul Fearn/Alamy Stock Photo

"quadroon balls." Quadroon literally means one-quarter Black by descent. These balls provided a carnival atmosphere where elite White males could make their selections from a collection of light-skinned free women of color. A woman selected was accorded a household, typically with servants, where her status was slightly less than that of a wife and greater than that of a concubine. *Plaçage* therefore constituted a socially sanctioned form of miscegenation, or the mixing of different racial groups, often lasting even after the man was legally married to a White woman. While technically free, the women involved in *plaçage* were both economically and socially dependent on their sexual objectification, availability, attractiveness, and ability to satisfy the fantasies of elite White men (Li 2007, 86). Eventually, the large number of free people of color and their relationships to others of mixed heritage caused the Louisiana Supreme Court to declare all such mixed-race people to be free (Hall 1992). This group had greater access to education and wealth and used both to become advocates for racial reform and freedom.

British Colonialism (1587)

After some failed attempts, the Plymouth Company's *Mayflower* finally reached the New World in 1620, where the ship's passengers established the next set of English colonies in a place they declared to be Plymouth in Massachusetts. These settlers shared the European rationalization for imperial expansion by declaring the indigenous peoples barbaric—and saving these pagans via Christian civilization was the goal.

Building a Tradition of Slavery

The first group of non–Native Americans to wear chains in New England were poor Whites, primarily from Ireland. These slaves began arriving in New England in the early 1600s. English slave masters looked upon the Irish as backward, lazy, unscrupulous, and fit to be enslaved (Beckles 1990, 510–11). Upwards of 50,000 Irish people, mostly women and children, were forcibly deported to the Americas. Harsh treatment, hostility, and degradation led Irish and Black slaves to engage frequently in collaborative rebellions (Bernhard 1999, 89–91).

In all likelihood, the first Blacks entered Jamestown, in the colony of Virginia, in 1619 as indentured servants, but by 1661 they were legislated servants for life. In the next year, a revised statute linked slavery to maternity by declaring that all children would be free or slave according to the status of their mothers. This Virginia law was a significant departure from previous British laws, which traced the status of children to their fathers. The lucrative commerce in Native American slaves commenced among the English with the founding of Carolina in 1670 and lasted through 1717. What emerged was a distinct racial hierarchy in which male European landowners dominated both Native American and African slaves (Gallay 2002). Thus, on the backs of African slaves, a racial hierarchy was constructed.

Like the Spanish and French, the English manipulated the ethnic conflicts among the various Native American groups. The English encouraged the Native Americans to avoid slavery by enslaving their adversaries and selling them to the English for trifles of cloth and beads, and, of course, guns (Gallay 2002, 6).

This new racial system finally gave birth to racial classification and defined race relations throughout the nation until the dawn of the Civil War. These new laws and new hierarchies were also motivated by attempts to divide those who otherwise might be inclined to join together in revolt.

Resistance Stories: Slave Rebellions

Slave rebellions represented a persistent source of both strain and stress for the White planter class. The response was the continual evolution of racial hierarchies buttressed by laws, sanctions, and privileges that pervaded the entire colonial social structure. Throughout this text, we will show how these resistance stories have become an integral part of Americans' national identity.

The first significant slave rebellion against the English occurred in Gloucester County, Virginia, in 1663. This conspiracy, which included both White indentured servants and Black slaves, aimed to overthrow the White masters. The plot was exposed by an informant, which led to the execution of several of the plotters and the passage of a series of laws that began to emphasize the ineradicable distinctions between slave masters and slaves.

Bacon's Rebellion of 1676 was the most significant challenge to the class structure (Breen 1973). The elite response to Bacon's Rebellion was to create new identities of color and race to usurp divisions of class and status. But in order to understand this threat, we must understand the labor situation in 17th-century Virginia. In this revolt, Black, Irish, Scottish, and English bond servants were pitted against a small and nervous group of planter elites. The increasing use of Africans as bonded labor had forced a large number of White laborers out of their positions. Nathaniel Bacon was one of those displaced laborers, and he found himself and his group literally between a rock and a hard place. The irony of this is that while the members of the planter class were gaining land grants with each new allotment of workers, no such provisions were being made for those displaced by the increasing numbers of cheaper laborers.

Crop failures in 1676 provided the fuel for the violence that followed. The revolt quickly became a mass rebellion of bond servants who aimed to level the government and the entire class structure. More than 6,000 European Americans and 2,000 African Americans took up arms and fought against a tiny Anglo-American slave-owning planter class. They marched to West Point, where they took over the garrisons and military arsenal. They forced the military governor to flee and shut down all tobacco production for the next 14 months.

The rebellion threatened the very heart of the British colonial system by challenging the power of the Anglo-American slave-owning planter elite. The members of the planter class responded by solidifying slavery into a racial caste system. In the process, Whiteness was created.

Borderlands and Frontiers

At the time of European colonization, most of the land in the Americas was formally under the control of various Native American federations. Europeans purposefully defined these lands as frontiers or borderlands. This designation, often preserved and presented as historical fact, fails to appreciate the reality of these contested spaces (Haan 1973). Under the guise of protecting the interests of weaker states, the Europeans placed the Native Americans and their lands into "protectorate" relationships, in which the stronger European nations took on the responsibility of protectors (Haan 1973, 146). Concurrently, these same "protected" spaces became universally

Bacon's Rebellion, in Virginia in 1676, remade class and status distinctions and hardened slavery into a racial caste system.

Credit: MPI/Archive Photos/Getty Images

known as frontiers or borderlands. This designation also provided convenient camouflage for the more aggressive actions of the various European colonial systems.

These contested spaces between the Spanish, French, and English colonies provided the colonial powers with three important benefits:

- They created the illusion of Native American national sovereignty.

- They were an outlet or safety valve for excess and displaced colonial labor and capital accumulation.

- They served as spaces where the European powers could wage imperialistic wars against each other. These wars, in which the Europeans typically encouraged or manipulated Native American tribal differences, can be viewed as proxy wars.

In this section we explore how frontiers and borderlands came to fulfill these functions.

The Turner Thesis—Our First Stock Story

Perhaps no single idea has so captured the American imagination, summarized and serialized the nation's official story, and misrepresented U.S. imperialistic ambitions as what is euphemistically called the Turner thesis. Historian Frederick J. Turner's argument is so important to our narrative because it became the dominant narrative of the United States. It represents our first stock story. Turner's basic thesis, developed in 1893, was that the American identity, which included democratic governance, rugged individualism, innovative thinking, and egalitarian viewpoints, was forged in the American frontier experience. According to Turner, the American frontier provided not only the encouragement but also the spaces to unleash the progressive spirit of freedom envisioned by various European revolutionary systems (i.e., specifically the French and English Revolutions). As significant as the Turner thesis was to the "official" narrative, it took more than 70 years for the nondominant counternarratives to be heard again. These voices told a different story, one that rejected the idea of a frontier and all of its presumptions. Rather than a blank slate of free land that was just waiting to be settled, developed, and occupied, the "frontier" was made up of sovereign lands controlled by other nations and protected by treaties. In this counternarrative, we learn of deceit and corruption, broken treaties and forgotten promises. This is the story of the frontier.

Concealed Stories: Understanding Contested Spaces

The rhetorical and political designation of the spaces between European colonies as frontiers or borderlands is central to an understanding of what and how these areas and their peoples were viewed. The crossing of frontiers and the loss of their people are typically viewed as cosmic inevitability or evolutionary truth. Such a truth positions the Native Americans as victims who passively accepted their fate. Their fate, viewed as irreversible, was that the exotic, yet inferior, native cultures would lose against the more powerful forces of civilization. While appropriately and passively sorrowful, we are left believing that these events were necessary and the natural consequences of nature, evolution, and/or civilization (Jennings 1975, 15–16). The idea of borderlands helps clarify how the three European colonial powers constructed race and space as conflicting rivalries. These conflicting rivalries not only shaped our nation but also started us on our troubled path toward a racial state (Adelman and Aron 1999, 815–16).

It is strange that our myths regarding these spaces often bring to mind such people as Daniel Boone, Davy Crockett, and James Bowie. As defenders of all that we hold dear, these men are the only forces of civilization holding back the frontier. Reality rarely lives up to such hyperbole. The Boones, Crocketts, and Bowies—as we have seen—were often displaced Whites forced into the "frontier." In this scenario, the Native Americans, defined as weak savages, are characterized as expendable and secondary to the interests of frontier survival. This feat is accomplished through the extension of the racial categories developed over time within the colonies and, by virtue of this extension, the necessity to continually extend the boundaries of civilization.

As we have seen, the patterns, practices, and realities created through the shaping of our nation were a set of choices that established the racial templates for the matrix of race. These racial templates, varying across the different colonial systems, account for the different racial trajectories that came into being. We observed that the French and Spanish colonial decisions to establish settler colonies precluded the initial immigration of European women. Within these colonial situations there was an increased likelihood that marriage unions would form with women from various indigenous tribal groups and imported Africans. These choices meant that the racial structures created were more likely to be more diverse and fluid. Creolization, reflecting multiracial family structures, were the obvious outcomes. The racial hierarchies that

Popular images of the frontier—the essence of Turner's thesis. White "frontier men" are depicted as ruggedly individualistic, noble, honest, and fiercely independent. And just as typically, they are juxtaposed against a prideful, ignoble band of savages hell-bent on destruction.

Credit: Science History Images/Alamy Stock Photo

developed tended to reflect these decisions, as gradations of skin tone favoring lighter-skinned individuals and groups were accorded higher status. Alternatively, within the English colonies, where the decision was to colonize, English women were encouraged to immigrate. Within these structures, more rigid racial rules were established that discouraged interracial unions. These rules were particularly aimed at preserving the rights and inheritance of children born of European unions, while delegitimizing the children of interracial ones. Racial hierarchies based on the presumption of White purity resulted. As a consequence, we see the creation of intersectional identities. These identities, favoring either light skin tone or presumed White purity, by definition asserted the primacy of White males and the secondary status of females, regardless of color. Within the more rigid cluster of English colonies, White women were deemed more attractive and desirable than lower-status women of color. Alternatively, within either the French or Spanish colonies, biracial and multiracial females with lighter skin tones were perceived as more attractive and higher status.

Critical Thinking

1. How might the racial matrix developed by the Spanish colonies have affected the racial matrices of the French and English colonial powers? What does this suggest about the social construction of race in the Americas?

2. Many institutions were created along with the American colonial systems. List some that were born during this early period.

3. What does the idea of borders as contested spaces in which race and conflict were orchestrated by European colonial elites suggest about the nature of these spaces and racial dynamics? What current events might reflect some of those same racial dynamics in the interaction of race and geography?

4. Neither Native Americans nor African slaves were passive during the colonial era, and they often worked together to challenge the racial matrix even as it was being constructed. What does this agency suggest about the racial matrix, identity, and the likelihood of change?

CHAPTER SUMMARY

2.1 Explain how recent events have affected how we experience race.

The United States is a nation that has historically been defined by racial and ethnic diversity. As the U.S. population increases to an estimated 458 million by 2065, we expect immigrant births and diversity to increasingly define who we are. As much of the world, including the United States, has repeatedly been traumatized by racial and ethnic violence, our continued struggle toward equality remains a dream for some. This is especially true when we examine the issue through an intersectional lens, as women, especially those of color, grapple continuously with inequalities and wage disparities. Social media has provided opportunities for challenging but also reinforcing racist, sexist, homophobic, and other forms of bigotry.

2.2 Describe the Americas before Columbus.

Before Columbus sailed the seas, the continents now known as the Americas were home to millions of indigenous peoples whose cultures spanned 12,000 to 20,000 years. The first immigrants to the Americas possibly arrived on foot from Siberia and Alaska or on boats following the currents from the Pacific Islands. More than half of U.S. state names (including Michigan, Minnesota, and Missouri) reflect these rich histories, cultures, and peoples. Contrary to both myth and Hollywood, these original Americans were skilled, knowledgeable, and sophisticated, with highly advanced agricultural and animal husbandry skills, metallurgy knowledge, and a rich tradition of pottery, weaving, and textiles. Their art decorates caves and can be found in museums all over the world.

2.3 Identify the patterns of Spanish, French, and British colonialism in the Americas.

European colonization of the Americas was most intense after the Spanish explorations of Christopher Columbus that began in 1492. Each of the major European colonial systems produced unique racial structures that ultimately blended to shape the racial fabric of the United States. Each colonial power was concerned with re-creating an image of the home country within the colonies, and each failed in its attempts. The colonizing Europeans encountered significantly different peoples with different cultural, political, and gendered systems. Their responses to these account for the variability in racial structures and the racial conflicts that came to define borders and frontiers. Slave rebellions occurred in all of the colonial lands. Bacon's Rebellion of 1676 linked White and Black bond servants and almost spelled the doom of the English colonies. The racial structures that came into being in reaction to this were intended to preclude labor organizing and revolt across racial lines. In fact, Whiteness was created as a result of this rebellion. Other racial strife was associated with frontiers, or the areas that bordered the various European colonies. Three separate European colonial powers used these borderlands to extend and expand their land and power bases. The conflicting rivalries not only shaped our nation but also started us down the troubled path toward a racial state.

KEY TERMS

Bacon's Rebellion of 1676	left-handed marriages	quadroon
Black code	miscegenation	racial caste system
colonialism	plaçage	refugees
frontiers	pull factors	settler colonies
genocide	push factors	Turner thesis

REFERENCES

Adelman, Jeremy, and Stephen Aron. 1999. "From Borderlands to Borders: Empires, Nation-States, and the Peoples in between in North American History." *American Historical Review* 104, no. 3 (June): 814–41.

Arnaiz-Villena, A. C. Parga-Lorazano, E. Moreno, C. Areces, D. Rey, and P. Gomez-Prieto. 2010. "The Origin of Amerindians and the Peopling of the Americas According to HLA Genes: Admixture with Asian and Pacific People." *Current Genomics* 11 no. 2 (April): 103–14.

Barrera, Mario. 1976. "Colonial Labor and Theories of Inequality: The Case of International Harvester." *Review of Radical Political Economics* 8, no. 2: 1–18.

Beal, Timothy K. 2008. *Religion in America: A Short History.* London: Oxford University Press.

Beckles, Hilary McD. 1990. "A 'Riotous and Unruly Lot': Irish Indentured Servants and Freemen in the English West Indies, 1644–1713." *William and Mary Quarterly* 47, no. 4 (October): 503–22.

Bernhard, Virginia. 1999. *Slaves and Slaveholders in Bermuda,* Columbia: University of Missouri Press.1616-1782.

Bonilla-Silva, Eduardo. 2008. "'Look, a Negro': Reflections on the Human Rights Approach to Racial Inequality." In *Globalization and America: Race, Human Rights, and Inequality,* edited by Angela J. Hattery , David G. Embrick, and Earl Smith, 9–22. Lanham, MD: Rowman & Littlefield.

Breen, T. H. 1973. "A Changing Labor Force and Race Relations in Virginia 1660–1710." *Journal of Social History* 7, no. 1 (Autumn): 3–25.

Brenner, Tom. 2018. "Facebook Moves to Limit Toxic Content as Scandal Swirls". *Wired.* Accessed at URL: https://www.wired.com/story/facebook-limits-hate-speech-toxic-content/

Buchanan, Kelly. 2011. "Slavery in the French Colonies: Le Code Noir (the Black Code) of 1685." In Custodia Legis (blog), Law Library of Congress, January 13. Accessed May 5, 2016. https://blogs. loc.gov/law/2011/01/slavery-in-the-french-colonies.

Cassen, Flora. 2020. "Jews Control Chinese Labs that created Coronavirus: White Supremacists' Dangerous New Conspiracy Theory."Accessed on line at url: https://www.haaretz.com/jewish/. premium-the-jews-control-the-chinese-labs-that-created-coronavirus-1.8809635

Chishti, Muzaffar, and Jessica Bolter. 2020. "Vulnerable to COVID-19 and in Frontline Jobs, Immigrants Are mostly Shut Out of U.S. Relief." Accessed online at URL: https://www.migrationpolicy. org/article/covid19-immigrants-shut-out-federal-relief

Christine. Ro, 2019. "How Underrepresentation Affects Racial Narratives and American Kids" Book Riot. Accessed online at URL: https://bookriot.com/2019/06/26/how-underrepresentation-affects-racial-narratives-and-american-kids

Cilluffo, Anthony, and D'Verra Cohn. 2019. 6 Demographic Trends Shaping the U.S. and the World in 2019." Pew Research Center. Accessed online at url: https://www.pewresearch.org/fact-tank/2019/04/11/6-demographic-trends-shaping-the-u-s-and-the-world-in-2019/

Deagan, Kathleen. 2004. "Reconsidering Taíno Social Dynamics after Spanish Conquest: Gender and Class in Culture Contact Studies." *American Antiquity* 69: 597–626.

Deagan, Kathleen, and José María Cruxent. 2002. *Columbus's Outpost among the Taínos: Spain and America at La Isabela, 1493-1498*. New Haven, CT: Yale University Press.

Deetharaman, Deepa, and Jeff Horwitz. 2020. "Facebook Creates Teams to Study Racial Bias, After Previously Limiting Such Efforts." *The Wall Street Journal*. Accessed online at URL: https://www. wsj.com/articles/facebook-creates-teams-to-study-racial-bias-on-its-platforms-11595362939? mod=djemalertNEWS.

Dettling, Lisa J., Hsu, W., Joanne Jacobs Lindsay et al. "Recent Trends in Wealth-Holding by Race and Ethnicity: Evidence from the Survey of Consumer Finances." Federal Reserve. Accessed at URL: https://www.federalreserve.gov/econres/notes/feds-notes/recent-trends-in-wealth-holding-by-race-and-ethnicity-evidence-from-the-survey-of-consumer-finances-20170927.htm

Diamond, Jared. 1999. *Guns, Germs, and Steel: The Fates of Human Societies*. New York: W. W. Norton.

Editorial Board. 2018."Trump is sending LGBTQ migrants 'back to hell.'" Accessed on line at URL: https://www.washingtonpost.com/opinions/trump-is-sending-lgbtq-migrants-back-to-hell/2018/07/24/eb305d72-8ec3-11e8-8322-b5482bf5e0f5_story.html

Fry, Richard. 2011. "Hispanic College Enrollment Spikes, Narrowing Gaps with Other Groups." Pew Research Center, August 25. Accessed June 13, 2017. http://www.pewhispanic.org/2011/08/25/hispanic-college-enrollment-spikes-narrowing-gaps-with-other-groups.

Gallay, Alan. 2002. *The Indian Slave Trade: The Rise of the English Empire in the American South, 1670–1717*. New Haven, CT: Yale University Press.

Greer, Allan. 1997. *The People of New France*. Toronto: University of Toronto Press.

Gutiérrez, Gustavo. 1974. *A Theology of Liberation*. Maryknoll, NY: Orbis Books.

Haan, Richard L. 1973. "Another Example of Stereotypes on the Early American Frontier: The Imperialistic Historians and the American Indian." *Ethnohistory* 20, no. 2 (Spring): 143–52.

Hall, Gwendolyn Midlo. 1992. *Africans in Colonial Louisiana*. Baton Rouge: Louisiana State University Press.

Hegewisch, A., & Hartmann, H. (2019). *The Gender Wage Gap: 2018 Earnings Differences by Race and Ethnicity.*Institute for Women's Policy Research. https://iwpr.org/wp-content/uploads/2020/08/C478_Gender-Wage-Gap-in-2018.pdf.

History.com editors. 2020. "Columbus Lands in South America." A &E Television Networks. Accessed online at URL: https://www.history.com/this-day-in-history/columbus-lands-in-south-america

Jackson, Robert. 2006. "República de Indios." In *Iberia and the Americas: Culture, Politics, and History—A Multidisciplinary Encyclopedia,* edited by J. Michael Francis, 901903. Santa Barbara, CA: ABC-CLIO.

Jennings, Francis. 1975. *The Invasion of America: Indians, Colonialism, and the Cant of Conquest.* New York: W. W. Norton.

Kassum, Eric. 2016. "Columbus Day? True Legacy: Cruelty and Slavery. Huffpost. Accessed online at URL: https://www.huffpost.com/entry/columbus-day-a-bad-idea_b_742708.

Krogstad, Jens Manuel. 2015. "Reflecting a Racial Shift, 78 Counties Turned Majority-Minority since 2000." Fact Tank, Pew Research Center, April 8. Accessed May 8, 2017. http://www.pewresearch.org/fact-tank/2015/04/08/reflecting-a-racial-shift-78-counties-turned-majority-minority-since-2000.

Krogstad, Jens Manuel. 2019. Key Facts About Refugees to the U.S. Accessed online at URL: https://www.pewresearch.org/fact-tank/2019/10/07/key-facts-about-refugees-to-the-u-s/

Landers, Jane L. 1997. "Africans in Spanish Colonies." *Historical Archaeology* 31, no. 1: 84–103.

Li, Stephanie. 2007. "Resistance, Silence, and Placées: Charles Bon's Octoroon Mistress and Louisa Picquet."*American Literature*79, no. 1 (March): 85–112.

Lopez, Gustavo. 2016. "About four-in-ten of the world's migrants live in the U.S. or Europe. Pew Research Center. Accessed at URL: https://www.pewresearch.org/fact-tank/2016/06/22/about-four-in-ten-of-the-worlds-migrants-live-in-the-u-s-or-europe/

Lord, Lewis, and Sarah Burke. 1991. "America Before Columbus." *U.S. News & World Report,* July 822–27. Accessed June 1, 2017. http://web.archive.org/web/20020827104452/; http://www.millersville.edu/~columbus/data/art/LORD-01.ART.

Mann, Charles. 2005. *1491: New Revelations of the Americas before Columbus.* New York: Borzoi Books.

Martinez, Maria Elena. 2004. "Limpieza de Sangre, Racial Violence, and Gendered Power in Early Colonial Mexico." *William and Mary Quarterly,* 3rd ser.,61, no. 3 (July): 479–520.

Martinez, Maria Elena. 2008. *Limpieza de Sangre, Religion, and Gender in Colonial Mexico.* Stanford, CA: Stanford University Press.

Mendoza, Ruben. 1997. "Metallurgy in Meso and Native America." In *Encyclopaedia of the History of Science, Technology, and Medicine in Non-Western Cultures,* edited by H. Selin, 702–6. Dordrecht: Kluwer Academic.

Meyere, Peter J., and Taft-Morales, Maureen. 2019. "Central American Migration: Rout Causes and U.S. Policy." Congressional Research Service.Accessed at URL: https://fas.org/sgp/crs/row/IF11151.pdf

Moje, Elizabeth Birr, Josephine Peyton Young, John E. Readence, and David W. Moore. 2000. "Reinventing Adolescent Literacy for New Times: Perennial and Millennial Issues." *Journal of Adolescent & Adult Literacy* 43, no. 5: 400–410.

Palmer, Vernon V. 1995. "The Origins and Authors of the Code Noir." *Louisiana Law Review* 56, no. 363: 363–408.

Parise, Agustin. 2008. "Slave Laws and Labor Activities During the Spanish Colonial Period: A Study of the South American Region of Río de la Plata." *Rutgers Law Record* 32, no. 1: 1–39.

Phillips, William D. 1985. *Slavery from Roman Times to the Early Transatlantic Trade.* Minneapolis: University of Minnesota Press.

Pitts, Leonard. 2012. "A Whiter Shade of Privilege." *Columbia Daily Tribune,* Accessed April 22, 2013. http://m.columbiatribune.com/news/2012/mar/28/a-whiter-shade-of-privilege/?commentary.

Poole, Robert M. 2011. "What Became of the Taíno?" Smithsonian Magazine. Accessed online at URL: https://www.smithsonianmag.com/travel/what-became-of-the-taino-73824867/.

Radford, Jynnah. 2019. "Key Findings about U.S. immigrants." Pew Research Center. Accessed online at URL: https://www.pewresearch.org/fact-tank/2020/08/20/key-findings-about-u-s-immigrants/

Shin, Hyon B., and Robert A. Kominski. 2010. *Language Use in the United States: 2007.* Washington, DC: U.S. Census Bureau.

Shippen, Peggy. 2004. "sex ratios." In *Women in Early America: Struggle, Survival, and Freedom,* edited by Dorothy A. Mays, 356–58. Santa Barbara, CA: ABC-CLIO.

Smialek, Jeanna. 2019. "Minority Women are Winning the Jobs Race in a Record Economic Expansion." New York Times. Accessed at URL: https://www.nytimes.com/2019/07/01/business/economy/minority-women-hispanics-jobs.html.

Smith, Aaron, and ,Monica Anderson. 2018. "Social Media Use in 2018". Pew. Accessed online at URL: https://www.pewresearch.org/internet/2018/03/01/social-media-use-in-2018/

Spear, Jennifer M. 2003. "Colonial Intimacies: Legislating Sex in French Louisiana." *William and Mary Quarterly,* 3rd ser., 60, no. 1 (January): 75–98.

Stasiulis, Daiva K., and Nira Yuval-Davis. 1995. "Beyond Dichotomies: Gender, Race, Ethnicity and Class in Settler Societies." In *Unsettling Settler Societies: Articulations of Gender, Race, Ethnicity and Class* edited by Daiva K. Stasiulis and Nira Yuval-Davis London: Sage.

Stone, Edward T. 1975. "Columbus and Genocide". American Heritage, Vol. 26, Issue 6. Accessed online at URL: https://www.americanheritage.com/columbus-and-genocide

Strommen, Linda Teran, and Barbara Fowles Mates. 2004. "Learning to Love Reading: Interviews with Older Children and Teens." *Journal of Adolescent & Adult Literacy* 48, no. 3: 188–2000.

Telles, Edward, and the Project on Ethnicity and Race in Latin America. 2014. *Pigmentocracies: Ethnicity, Race, and Color in Latin America.* Chapel Hill: University of North Carolina Press.

Turner, Frederick J. 1920. *The Frontier in American History.* New York: Holt.

UNHCR2020."What is a Refugee?" United Nations.Accessed online at URL: https://www.unrefugees.org/refugee-facts/what-is-a-refugee/

U.S. Census Bureau. 2017. "the Nation's Older Population is Still Growing, Census Bureau Reports". Census. Accessed at URL: https://www.census.gov/newsroom/press-releases/2017/cb17-100.html

Wilson, Jill H. 2019. "Recent Migration to the United States from Central America: Frequently Asked Questions". Congressional Research Service. accessed from https://fas.org/sgp/crs/row/R45489.pdf.

Wilson, Natalie. 2011. *Seduced by "Twilight": The Allure and Contradictory Messages of the Popular Saga.* Jefferson, NC: McFarland.

THE MATRIX PERSPECTIVE ON SOCIAL INSTITUTIONS

3

THE SOCIAL CONSTRUCTION AND REGULATION OF FAMILIES

This photo was taken on March 21, 2019, at the border between the U.S. and Mexico, in El Paso, Texas. Detained migrants were forced to wait behind bars before being transported to a more permanent detention center by the U.S. Border Patrol. On the campaign trail, President Trump blamed immigrants for many of the social problems faced by the nation, and relied on a centuries-old narrative of foreign invaders taking jobs away from American-born workers. He promised to force Mexico to build a wall between the two nations, to cut off immigration from Central America. While this did not happen, Trump held record-high numbers of children in custody.

Credit: Justin Sullivan/Getty Images

LEARNING OBJECTIVES

3.1 Describe the historical forces that have influenced the intersection of race and family in the United States.

3.2 Examine the current stock theories that explain family inequalities across racial and ethnic lines.

3.3 Apply the matrix lens to an understanding of family inequality.

3.4 Identify alternatives to the current matrix of inequality among families.

In August 2019, Miguel cried and waved at his mother as Immigration and Customs Enforcement (ICE) officials took her away, her hands tied together. Miguel's family is from Guatemala, and his mother worked in a poultry processing plant in Mississippi. When ICE employees invaded the plant, which is surrounded by barbed wire, every worker was required to show paperwork and undergo a search of their belongings. Similar raids were carried out in numerous plants in other small Mississippi towns. In all, the 600 ICE employees put 680 people, mostly Latinx, on busses to a National Guard hangar for processing. This was one of the largest raids to date carried out by the Trump administration. The raids had a devastating impact not only on the families directly affected, including Latinx U.S. citizens, but also on the towns themselves, and their local economies. These very public raids have increased fear among Latinx families and children across the nation (Fowler, 2019; Solis & Amy, 2019).

In 2019, over a million people were detained at a point of entry into the U.S., with the majority entering at the border with Mexico. Adults as well as children are held in a variety of locations, including jails and contract detention facilities owned and operated by private prison corporations. Thousands of children are detained on their own, either separated from family members at the border, or those who cross the border alone. When Donald Trump became President, the U.S. held 2,700 children in custody. In 2019 the number had increased to 13,000; their average length of stay was 55 days. Children are held in dismal conditions. These children do not have adequate healthcare (including mental health), and an average of 1,000 incidents of sexual abuse are discovered each year (American Immigration Council 2020).

Under President Trump, an Asylum Transit Ban prevented many people seeking humanitarian asylum in the U.S. from crossing the U.S./Mexican border. This race- and nation-based ban targeted immigrants from Central and South America, treating these immigrants differently from those entering at other ports, most likely from Europe and Asia (American Immigration Council 2019). In September 2020, reports were released charging that a detention center in Georgia had sterilized many women without their knowledge or consent (Amnesty International 2020).

The conditions facing families today are far different than they were just a decade ago, and they continue to be shaped by race, and the intersection of race with gender, class, immigration status, nationality, and more.

In this chapter we explore the historical development of the institution of the family, popular and sociological stock stories about family, concealed stories and stories of resistance which reveal the ways in which family narratives are used as an instrument of power and social control, and apply the matrix theory.

THE FAMILY AS AN INSTITUTION

When you hear the word *family,* what image comes to mind? In American society's idealized family, the father is the head of household and breadwinner, and the mother is comfortably enshrined in the domestic sphere, where she nurtures the couple's biological children and socializes them for middle-class adulthood. This stock story depicts the family as a private haven, separate from the public sphere. We tend to think of this family form as having a long history and being somehow natural. However, the specific family form of a married couple and their children did not rise to prominence until the mid-1800s (Coontz 2010a).

The narrative of the ideal traditional family as "natural" conceals narratives of the family as an institution constructed through domination, and by law and policy defining "appropriate" families and devaluing others (Collins 1998). But sociologists have offered alternative conceptions. **Family** has been defined as "a social arrangement that contributes to economic stability and support and advocacy systems for children and adults and is a central institution in shaping gender socialization and establishing parameters of control" (Hunt et al. quoted in Zambrana 2011: 48). We will examine a variety of family formations in the following sections.

Early Families

In 1500, an estimated 10 to 20 million indigenous people lived on the land we now call the United States, and even greater numbers ranged across the rest of the Americas (Vizenor 1995; Feagin 2000). Historians have documented great variation both in family forms and in the division of labor and power within the family (Amott and Matthaei 1996, 33).

Native American Families

Constructions of gender were essential to competing notions of the family. Many tribes were fairly egalitarian. In some tribes, women were recognized as warriors, and in others, they played the role of peacemaker. The Iroquois Confederacy's 1390 constitution gave all members of participating nations (Mohawk, Onondaga, Seneca, Cayuga, and Oneida), including women, the right to vote (Amott and Matthaei 1996, 33).

Degrees of power and status among men and women varied across different tribal nations. Many agricultural tribes were matrilineal and/or matrilocal. Some tribes had more flexible gender roles, allowing women or men to take on the traditional roles of the other gender, to move between roles, or to occupy additional genders, and to even marry someone of the same sex (Herdt 1996; Roscoe 1998; Towle and Morgan 2002).

Among many North American indigenous tribes, kinship was a central locus of community organization. Most economic production and distribution, political structures, disputes, conflicts, and battles were handled by extended kin groups. Land was not seen as private property but was often controlled by the kin group.

When European settlers began colonizing the Americas, the colonists interpreted the cultures they encountered through their own **ethnocentric** lens, seeing their own ways of life as superior, natural, and commanded by God. Many settlers were startled seeing Native women engaged in difficult physical work, which conflicted sharply with their own gender roles and ideas about appropriate work for women among the upper classes. For example, among upper-class Europeans, activities like hunting and fishing were considered leisure activities; for indigenous tribes, men hunted and fished to provide sustenance for the tribe. The Europeans did not recognize this as work, and stereotyped native men as lazy and effeminate. Native women were seen as "beasts of burden" forced to engage in agricultural labor, which settlers assumed to be men's responsibility.

Early European Colonist Families

For the European colonists, marriage was an economic relationship, and wives and children were essential family workers. On average, a White woman in colonial America gave birth to five to eight children, and it was not uncommon for women to have eleven or twelve children (Hill 2005; Hymowitz and Weissman 1978; MacLean 2014). A colonial woman's risk of dying in childbirth could be as high as one in eight, and most families experienced the death of one to two children (MacLean 2014). The colonists' definition of family at this time was not based on blood ties, but included all those living in the same household under a male household leader.

Mothers performed essential labor, meeting families' basic needs. Husbands and wives often worked side by side, and both engaged in child-rearing and training their children in gender-appropriate skills (Amott and Matthaei 1996, 98–99). Some women worked outside the home in various trades, and many lived very public lives. Nevertheless, a gendered division of labor prevailed (Hymowitz and Weissman 1978).

English common law upheld the patriarchal family. Upon marriage wives lost all legal status and all rights to their belongings, property, and income. They could not sign contracts or file lawsuits. If widowed, they could not be legal guardians to their own minor children. The notion that women literally disappeared as individuals is perhaps best demonstrated by the law's failure to recognize marital rape (Zaher 2002).

The Effects of Settler Colonialism

Settler colonialism describes an outside group that permanently settles in a new land and dominates the indigenous peoples through relocation and genocidal practices, establishes its own model of society, and becomes the dominant political and economic force (Veracini 2010). By the late 1800s, Native Americans had largely been forced to reside on reservations located in barren lands the Europeans saw as the least valuable. The settlers continued to colonize new land, drawing and redrawing the boundaries of the new nation they were building for themselves.

Surviving Native Americans were expected to assimilate—to adopt European lifestyles and modes of organization in their communities and families. Missionaries also played a key role in destroying indigenous culture and family formations. In the 1870s, the reservations were divided among 13 Christian denominations, and a federal boarding school system was created to fully assimilate the next generation of Native Americans. Children were taken from their families and cultures, forced to abandon their native languages and religious beliefs, and given new names (Vizenor 1995). Luther Standing Bear wrote: "One day when we came to school there was a lot of writing on the blackboards.… Our interpreter came into the room and said, 'Do you see all these marks on the blackboard? Well, each word is a White man. They are going to give each one of you one of these names by which you will hereafter be known'" (quoted in Vizenor 1995: 9). This policy of forced assimilation destroyed many families and future generations' family relationships. Many Native Americans resisted attempts to force them to assimilate into European cultural roles, while others saw their boarding school experiences as a path to becoming successful in the settler society.

In 1887, Congress passed the **Dawes Act**, requiring Native American nations to divide their communal reservations into individual plots of 160 acres, with each assigned to a family head.

In 1879, The Carlisle Indian Industrial School, in Carlisle, PA, was the first government-run boarding school, established in abandoned Army barracks. Hundreds more would follow. As this photo reveals, students were banned from wearing traditional tribal clothing as one step in the process of forced assimilation. Hundreds of children died at the school due to the harsh conditions, disease, and inadequate care. 186 children remain buried at the site.

Credit: Everett Collection Historical/Alamy Stock Photo

The remaining land was given to White homesteaders and various corporations, such as railroads and ranching companies. European notions of the family were reproduced and written into policy. In response to strong Native American resistance, one compromise was made: The allotments would be made to each person, rather than only to male family heads, in acknowledgment of the fact that Native cultures recognized the rights of Native women to own property (Amott and Matthaei 1996).

Colonial practices and Eurocentric notions of family had negative impacts on every minority racial and ethnic group. The culture and practice of slavery tore apart African families, beginning with the separation of individuals from their families in Africa and the common experiences of loss on slave ships. Pregnant women and infants born on the transatlantic voyage were often thrown overboard so as not to be a burden to the captain. Further, every African was insured as property, so that a dead African could be more profitable than an unhealthy living one. For slave owners, each slave was a commodity, and husbands and wives were often separated when sold; children were taken away from parents to be sold for the slave owner's profit. Slave owners often raped women slaves to produce children to be sold. The institution of slavery made it nearly impossible for Africans to maintain family relationships, yet many tried as best they could. Slaves resisted their torment in many ways. Slavery was so inhumane and horrific that some mothers would go so far as to kill their infants before they could be taken away, to protect the children from life as slaves. Patterns of intermixing produced lighter-skinned Africans, which created new status dynamics that continue into the present. The impact of the slave trade, slavery itself, and then hundreds of years of continued oppression have had far-reaching, even unimaginable effects on the formation of Black families in the United States.

Domesticity: The Emergence of the Ideology of Separate Spheres

In the early 1800s, the number of jobs outside the home was growing, and White men increasingly moved out of the domestic sphere. White women's lives became sharply defined by an **ideology of domesticity** and the creation of a public/private dichotomy. While the notion of a new version of "ideal" family took hold, diverse family formations were simultaneously evolving (Coontz 2010a). In working-class families, children and mothers had no choice but to work to help support their families. In the emerging middle class, the woman's role was seen as that of housewife and mother, responsible for the home and children, while work and politics became defined as men's sphere. Privileged White women were exalted by this "cult of domesticity," and consumer culture, such as magazines and catalogs, espoused that women's natural place was in the home and economically dependent on their husbands.

With the growth of the middle class, many families had access to domestic workers, often young European immigrant women. Working-class White families could not afford servants, and wives often had to seek paid work. European immigrant families often had to send their children to work to help the family survive. Thus, this ideology rationalized White middle-class and upper-class privilege as a result of their ability to achieve and maintain this new ideal family formation that reified inequitable gender relations.

This model, however, was actually the result of specific changes in the economy and the organization of work, and it was short-lived. It rose to prominence between 1860 and 1920, after which White women began to enter the paid workforce in greater numbers. Family sociologist Kingsley Davis (1984, 404) concludes, "Clearly, the division of labor that arose historically from the separation of the workplace and the home is not the 'normal' or 'traditional' pattern." Why, then, has this particular family formation remained the ideal?

The Legacy of Immigration

While we often refer to the United States as a nation of immigrants, neither African American nor indigenous communities are immigrant populations. Native Americans were here long before Europeans arrived, and, excluding later populations of Blacks who chose to emigrate from Africa and the Caribbean, the African American community is the historical product of slavery. Both populations, and many Mexicans, were forced to largely abandon their own cultures and family traditions. However, they were not the only racial and ethnic groups to face government regulation and intervention in their formation of families.

The Irish constituted the first significant influx of non–Western European immigrants in the 1840s, followed by Eastern and Southern Europeans and Jews. These new arrivals prompted a crisis in how Whiteness was defined. Through the end of the 19th century, being legally defined as White was critical to gaining the rights of citizenship and property ownership, so the racial classification of new immigrant groups was key to their future success in the United States. The Irish were referred to as the "Blacks of Europe" and encountered blatant discrimination by employers (Tehranian 2009, 22). Italians were also linked to Blacks by means of the common nickname "guinea," which had its origins in the European term for the western coast of Africa.

The Expanding Category of Whiteness

Different paths to assimilation were embraced to join the established dominant Northern European ideal. For Jewish immigrants, marriage was a step in the direction of Americanization but also a form of resistance. In the United States, marriages could be freely chosen and based on love, a practice that was a rejection of traditional Jewish authority regarding the arrangement of marriages. In adopting American values of freedom, love, and pleasure, Jews modeled modern American families. At the same time, they resisted Americanization through marriage by overwhelmingly marrying other Jews (Prell 1999).

Diverse immigrants turned to the law to define themselves as White, and thus as eligible for naturalization, the legal process to gain citizenship. Between 1878 and 1952 there were 52 "naturalization" trials. As Ian Haney Lopez concludes in *White by Law,* the legal apparatus played a central role in the social construction of race. It was immigrants' ability to perform Whiteness that was under scrutiny in these cases, and "the potential for immigrants to assimilate within mainstream Anglo-American culture was put on trial" (Haney Lopez 1996, 40, Tehranian 2009).

Eventually, European American ethnic immigrant groups were seen as assimilated enough to be defined as White, and the boundaries of Whiteness expanded (we look at some of the economic reasons for this shift in Chapter 4). Marriage and family formation were signs of Americanization (Prell 1999). At the same time the children of immigrants were being encouraged to assimilate through intermarriage, interracial intermarriage was illegal. The boundary between Blacks and the expanding group of Whites was being more firmly drawn.

Immigration Policy and Family Formation

In contrast with European immigrants, Asian American immigrants were excluded from the expanding category of Whiteness. The first wave of Asian immigrants came from China in the mid-1800s, primarily men who came to work in the California gold rush, in agriculture, or in railroad construction. Labor recruiters sought married men willing to leave their families in China, because they could be paid less (Yang 2011) and would eventually return home. Initially many single Chinese women immigrated, working as sex workers to support themselves, until the U.S. government enacted the 1875 Page Law, a landmark attempt to limit the immigration of "undesirables" (Luibhéid 2002, 277). The predominant view was that Chinese sex workers spread disease and debauchery among both Chinese and White men, threatening the integrity of the White family.

The scarcity of Chinese women did not mean that male Chinese laborers had no families in the United States, however. Many created family formations by establishing clans, associations based on kinship and lineage and open to people with the same last name. Following the anti-immigration Chinese Exclusion Act of 1882, Chinese continued to arrive but at a slower rate. Many petitioned to bring "paper sons," young men from China posing as their U.S.-born sons, a relationship that could not be disproven after all birth records were destroyed in the San Francisco earthquake and fire of 1906. It was not until 1943 that Chinese people could again immigrate to the United States (although only 105 Chinese were allowed to enter per year) and finally apply to become U.S. citizens.

After the supply of Chinese labor was cut off in the late 1800s, the first large groups of Japanese laborers were recruited to work in agriculture, lumber, and mining on the West Coast and in Hawaii. As the numbers of Japanese increased on the mainland, so did racism against them. Japanese were barred from joining workers' unions, and various stereotypes arose as they were scapegoated by White labor. Eventually, in 1907–8, the so-called Gentlemen's Agreement was reached, whereby Japan agreed to stop allowing Japanese men to emigrate and

The gender balance in Chinese immigration shifted after World War II, when the War Brides Act permitted Chinese wives and children of U.S. soldiers into the United States, followed by other laws that allowed American soldiers' fiancées to enter. Eventually the McCarran-Walter Act (1952) permitted Chinese wives of Chinese men in the United States to join them here, bringing the "bachelors' society" to an end and allowing Chinese people to play a greater role in shaping their own families in the United States.

Credit: Leonard McCombe/The LIFE Images Collection/Getty Images

the United States agreed to admit the family members of those men who had already immigrated. Approximately 100,000 Japanese joined their husbands, fathers, and sons in the United States, as did about 20,000 "picture brides" of arranged marriages, who often had nothing but photos or letters from the unknown husbands they were about to meet. Julie Otsuka's novel *The Buddha in the Attic* (2011, 18) brings together the voices of these women, drawing from collected historical documents and interviews:

> On the boat we could not have known that when we first saw our husbands we would have no idea who they were. That the crowd of men in knit caps and shabby black coats waiting for us down below on the dock would bear no resemblance to the handsome young men in the photographs. That the photographs we had been sent were twenty years old. That the letters we had been written had been written to us by people other than our husbands, professional people with beautiful handwriting whose job it was to tell lies and win hearts. That when we first heard our names being called out across the water one of us would cover her eyes and turn away—I want to go home—but the rest of us would lower our heads and smooth down the skirts of our kimonos and walk down the gangplank and step out into the still warm day. This is America, we would say to ourselves, there is no need to worry. And we would be wrong.

Japanese families became moderately successful in agriculture and family farming and worked hard to keep their cultural traditions alive, turning to schools, religious organizations, and Japanese-language newspapers. Between 1913 and 1920, however, despite resistance, a series of "alien land laws" were passed, banning noncitizens from purchasing land. When Japan bombed Pearl Harbor in 1941, all Japanese Americans were immediately suspect. While not one charge of espionage was ever reported, more than 110,000 first- and second-generation Japanese Americans were forced to abandon their homes, property, possessions, and businesses and were relocated to 10 internment camps in various western states. There, surrounded by barbed wire and armed guards, they faced harsh weather, low-wage labor, and lack of privacy. Family life changed dramatically. Some scholars note that internment led to some increased liberty for women, who were freed from much housework and cooking, and many young women were allowed to leave the camps for college. Nevertheless, internment was devastating for the community, and by the time they were freed in 1945, many Japanese Americans had nothing left to return to.

Both Chinese and Japanese immigrants faced a paradox when it came to the subject of assimilation. Mary Tsukamoto, in conveying her life story to an anthropologist, succinctly identifies this dilemma:

> You see, we were accused of not being assimilated into our American life, but we were always kept in limbo because every time we turned around there was some group trying to agitate to send us back to Japan or send us away from California, so we never knew for sure whether we should sink our roots deeply. And we never knew for sure if we should spend our profits building a new home and living in nice homes like we wanted. So we endured living in shacks that weren't painted because any day we might be driven out. (quoted in Buss 1985, 91–92)

RESISTANCE STORIES: ART AS RESISTANCE

Mr. Wong's Theatre Company, by Roger Shimomura

Credit: Used with the permission of Roger Shimomura

Americanese: 180 Degrees, by Margaret Kasahara

Credit: Used with the permission of Margaret Kasahara

Literature and the arts have frequently been embraced as tools for challenging and resisting oppression. These two works are examples.

The 2001Shimomura painting connects many of the most virulently racist stereotypes of racial and ethnic minorities in the United States. The biography on the artist's website states: "Roger Shimomura's paintings, prints, and theatre pieces address sociopolitical issues of ethnicity. He was born in Seattle, Washington, and spent two early years of his childhood in Minidoka (Idaho), one of 10 concentration camps for Japanese Americans during WWII" (http://www.rshim.com).

On her website, artist Margaret Kasahara says: "As an Asian American of Japanese descent, that identity crosses two disparate cultures. I don't view it as a negative or a positive reality, it simply is. . . . I often appropriate cultural symbols and the traditional iconography of Japan and America, and place them in a personal and contemporary context. . . . One person's 'exotic' was my 'everyday,' and I was left with the feeling of not quite being allowed to belong" (http://margaretkasahara.com).

Changing Families, Changing Attitudes

The **nuclear family** is often envisioned as a mother, a father, and children (biological or adopted), living together. Today, the majority of families do not fit this definition (U.S. Census 2020). The census definition of a family household, while broader, is limited to people related by birth, adoption or marriage, excluding long-time cohabiting heterosexual and gay and lesbian couples. Family formations today are very diverse:

- 64% of families with children under the age of 15 have two employed parents (Bureau of Labor Statistics 2020).

- Only two fifths of families have children (Bureau of Labor Statistics 2020).

- The number of children living with cohabiting (not legally married) parents has increased (United States Census Bureau 2018).

- The median age of marriage has increased to 30 for men and 28 for women (U.S. Census 2020b).

- More young adults (58% of all 18–24 year-olds) are living at home with their parents (U.S. Census 2020b).

- The numbers of single parents (divorced, widowed, and never married), blended families (families with children from the adult partners' previous relationships), multigenerational families (families with three or more generations residing together), and interracial and same-sex marriages have all increased.

- Postponing parenthood, never marrying, and having fewer children are increasingly common (DePaulo 2017).

- 28% of all households are one-person households, more than double the number in 1960 (U.S. Census 2020b).

- Abortion rates are declining, in part because of increased reliance on a variety of birth control methods (Jones and Jerman 2017).

- Families today are more likely than their counterparts in the past to be caring for elderly relatives at home, while we also see increasing numbers of single grandparents living with grandchildren as their primary caretakers (U.S. Census 2020b).

- About half of the number of single parents have been previously married, and they tend to have higher levels of education than cohabiting parents (Livingston 2018).

Table 3.1 provides greater insight into the kinds of families children now live in, as shaped by race and income.

While family forms are quickly changing, the gendered expectation for mothers and fathers is not. Research finds that wives still do considerably more housework and childcare than husbands, even when both are employed full-time outside of the home (Bunning 2019). Research finds that greater social supports and policy changes, such as extending opportunities for increasing men's use of parental leave, can help fathers take a more active role in the home (Bunning 2019, Tamm 2019).

Critical Thinking

1. Have you witnessed attitudes about families changing during your lifetime? Provide examples. How do you think the prevailing attitudes about families in the city where you grew up may have differed from those in other cities? Explain.

2. Can you trace your family history back to its roots in what is now the United States? How do you think those earlier generations were shaped by the practices, policies, and formation of the United States?

3. How do you think your family life was shaped by race, class, and other social identities?

4. What kind of family structure did you grow up in? Did your family or your parents' families face any stigma based on those structures?

THEORIES OF FAMILY INEQUITY

Existing sociological theories approach the family as an institution implicated in the system of race relations. Next we look at the common stock stories as well as counternarratives and critiques based on concealed and resistance stories.

Stock Stories and Assimilation

Recall that stock stories are the predominant, seemingly commonsense narratives circulating in society that naturalize inequality. The functionalist perspective sees society as an ordered system that the family helps to reproduce through the processes of assimilation and socialization.

TABLE 3.1 ■ Race and Income Can Affect Living Arrangements for Children Under Age 18

| | Total | Living with both parents | | Living with mother only | | | | | Living with father only | | | | | Living with neither parent |
		Married to each other	Not married to each other	Married spouse absent	Widowed	Divorced	Separated	Never married	Married spouse absent	Widowed	Divorced	Separated	Never married	No parent present
RACE														
White alone	53,291	37,593	2,157	564	452	3,389	1,451	3,398	78	122	1,098	307	744	1,939
Black alone	11,044	3,969	418	196	160	778	436	3,744	37	38	118	36	327	787
Asian alone	4,004	3,392	83	72	33	107	45	84	4	–	46	9	31	98
All remaining single races and all race combinations	5,401	2,992	349	113	33	328	192	820	5	5	76	33	136	317
RACE														
Hispanic[2]	18,665	11,409	1,092	336	102	1052	788	2,369	34	18	197	89	402	778
White alone, Non-Hispanic	37,244	27,514	1,236	265	354	2,520	754	1,595	45	104	931	218	444	1,263
All remaining single races and all race combinations, non-Hispanic	17,832	9,023	679	344	223	1,030	582	4,082	44	44	210	78	392	1,100

(Continued)

TABLE 3.1 ■ Race and Income Can Affect Living Arrangements for Children Under Age 18 (*Continued*)

| FAMILY INCOME | Total | Living with both parents | | Living with mother only | | | | | Living with father only | | | | | Living with neither parent |
		Married to each other	Not married to each other	Married spouse absent	Widowed	Divorced	Separated	Never married	Married spouse absent	Widowed	Divorced	Separated	Never married	No parent present
Under $2,500	2,898	348	386	73	41	171	135	766	-	2	48	28	48	851
$2,500 to $4,999	665	154	71	19	5	62	46	256	-	-	2	-	26	24
$5,000 to $7,499	829	169	65	27	10	88	99	319	-	6	6	1	10	30
$7,500 to $9,999	911	156	59	31	2	142	53	346	1	-	9	4	23	84
$10,000 to $12,499	1,347	300	119	55	30	214	128	391	1	3	7	13	22	64
$12,500 to $14,999	908	185	68	56	13	98	97	283	1	11	2	3	24	66
$15,000 to $19,999	2,404	637	199	65	62	317	179	670	1	2	54	13	77	128
$20,000 to $24,999	2,918	1,081	233	81	50	224	200	700	6	4	48	24	129	137

	Total	Living with both parents			Living with mother only					Living with father only				Living with neither parent
		Married to each other	Not married to each other	Married spouse absent	Widowed	Divorced	Separated	Never married	Married spouse absent	Widowed	Divorced	Separated	Never married	No parent present
$25,000 to $29,999	2,923	1,202	316	71	36	243	166	615	9	9	76	26	44	110
$30,000 to $39,999	6,276	2,830	341	110	81	696	311	1,211	5	3	162	75	165	285
$40,000 to $49,999	5,434	3,110	301	59	80	533	166	601	26	17	110	41	168	221
$50,000 to $74,999	11,543	7,912	418	120	132	729	286	890	39	39	268	49	225	437
$75,000 to $99,999	9,500	7,350	203	76	49	538	119	484	15	23	227	34	104	279
$100,00 and over	25,185	22,513	229	102	87	548	139	512	18	46	320	72	172	426

Source: United States Census Bureau (2018), Current Population Survey, 2018 Annual Social and Economic Supplemen: Internet Release Date: November 2018.

Many functionalist scholars have pointed to **assimilation** to argue that new racial and ethnic groups entering the United States follow specific paths of integration, gradually accepting and adapting to the cultural patterns of the dominant group. To explain the patterns of new European immigrants that we discussed earlier, sociologist Milton Gordon (1964) identified seven stages of assimilation, beginning with adoption of the dominant language and cultural patterns and advancing to increased interaction with and relationships among minority and majority group members, reduced levels of prejudice and discrimination, intermarriage, and eventually full integration and acceptance.

Assimilation theory has been criticized for a number of reasons:

1. It assumes that non-European racialized groups should and can follow the same path as European immigrants.

2. It assumes that non-Whites want to abandon their own cultures and become fully "Americanized."

3. It assumes that the dominant White culture is ideal and superior to all other cultures (Myers 2005, 10).

Conflict theorists highlight these unspoken assumptions and bring issues of power into the picture, emphasizing that the dominant group seeks to protect its economic and political interests by controlling minority groups' labor and resources. Research from a conflict perspective emphasizes the concealed story that minority groups have not all been equally welcome to assimilate and asks us to consider who benefits from the smooth functioning of an unequal society. In reviewing the research on families and race relations, scholars often draw from both functionalist and conflict perspectives, asking questions about the history of initial contact and exposing the ways in which minority groups have been both included in and excluded from the dominant group (Myers 2005).

The symbolic interactionist perspective shifts our focus to a micro level of analysis, examining how individuals and families give meaning to cultural phenomena, family relationships, and interactions, and how families struggle to pass on their own cultural values and traditions in the face of demands for socialization and assimilation. We saw clear examples of this struggle in our brief discussion of indigenous families facing cultural genocide. Families may do this by eating traditional foods, listening to music, carrying out religious and spiritual practices, or dressing in ways that reflect the traditions of their culture. Conflict between maintaining cultural practices and assumptions about assimilation are ongoing and easy to identify once we look for them—for example, consider debates in the United States over English-only rules, and in many European countries regarding the banning of burkas.

The dominant society's continued embrace of the Ideal Traditional Family are rooted in the concept of **separate spheres**, a feature of the ideology of domesticity. They are informed by a functionalist perspective that assumes this is the best family model for a well-functioning society—an essential unit that fulfills a particular function in a particular way. From this perspective, any families not fitting the ideal are defined as dysfunctional.

This logic also underlies research and public discourse about Black and Latinx families that blames them for their own presumed failure to assimilate. Here, we see how family and nation are intertwined—the ideal nuclear family is emblematic of the national family. To belong is to accept and emulate the dominant middle- and upper-class, Christian, heterosexual White cultural ideals of family.

From a conflict perspective, this family model operates explicitly to benefit some more than others. It not only reproduces inequality among racial and class groups but also reproduces gender and sexual inequality, valuing hierarchical gender roles, patriarchy, and heterosexuality. For example, consider the phrase "the African American family." What images come to mind? For many, it is a picture of a single mother raising numerous children on welfare. While African American families in reality are quite diverse, this image of the dysfunctional Black family has been especially predominant since the 1950s, when the "culture of poverty" thesis was advanced, and many politicians still rely on it to explain the high rates of African American poverty.

This narrative derived from the functionalist stock story argues that Black families are "pathological" because they do not replicate the traditional nuclear family model, and it blames poverty and other social problems on Black families themselves (Hattery and Smith 2007; Hill 2005). Single mothers are depicted as overbearing, and fathers as weak or absent. The stock story claims that these "dysfunctional" family forms are a part of U.S. Black culture, passed down over generations and firmly entrenched. Black families are often compared to other racial

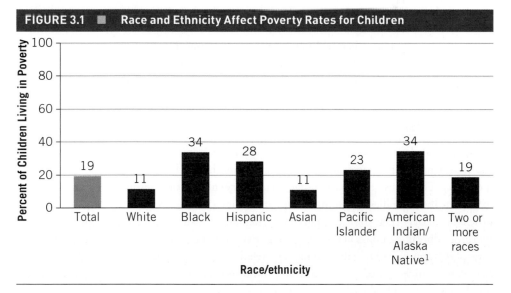

FIGURE 3.1 ■ Race and Ethnicity Affect Poverty Rates for Children

Note: Data shown are based only on related children in a family; that is, all children in the household who are related to the householder by birth, marriage, or adoption (except a child who is the spouse of the householder). The householder is the person (or one of the people) who owns or rents (maintains) the housing unit. This figure includes only children related to the householder. It excludes unrelated children and householders who are themselves under the age of 18. Race categories exclude persons of Hispanic ethnicity. Although rounded numbers are displayed, the figures are based on unrounded estimates.

Source: U.S. Department of Commerce, Census Bureau, American Community Survey (ACS), 2016. *See United States Census Bureau, American Community Survey (2017) Digest of Education Statistics 2017*, table 102.60.

and ethnic groups and are faulted for not "pulling themselves up by their bootstraps" as other immigrant groups are believed to have done.

Poverty is one of the most significant problems facing America's children (see Figure 3.1). Single-female-headed families have significantly higher poverty rates than other family types, and the percentage of single-female-headed families is much higher in the African American community than it is among Whites and other racial groups (U.S. Census Bureau 2015, 2016). Further, every racial/ethnic minority group has higher rates of childhood poverty than Whites. While marriage is frequently offered as the solution for Black poverty, Black males face such high unemployment, underemployment, and imprisonment rates that marriage to Black men is not likely to raise Black women and their children out of poverty.

Concealed Stories: The Legacy of Slavery

At least two sociological counternarratives, the legacy of slavery thesis and the revisionist thesis, have emerged to critique the assumption that African Americans are inherently inferior and incapable of sustaining proper families. These theories have roots in conflict theory, and each focuses on different historical facts—or different concealed stories—to support its arguments. Concealed stories here consist of missing or ignored history, experiences, and data, as well as alternative theoretical perspectives. Contemporary scholars have leveled critiques at both theories, pointing out that they generally accept the assumption that the traditional nuclear family is indeed ideal and focus on explaining why Black families have had a difficult time replicating that ideal. One scholar argues that even social scientists attempting to refute racist assumptions about Black families have themselves taken for granted many of the Eurocentric and race-based assumptions embedded in U.S. culture about what a family is (Dodson 2007). These theories have implications that extend far beyond the level of abstract theorizing; they inform public policy and have real impacts on people's lives.

The Legacy of Slavery Thesis

The **legacy of slavery thesis** attempts to shift the focus from Black culture as pathological to the argument that pathological family structures are the result of a long history of structural inequality. The thesis begins with the fact that slavery entailed the capture of Africans who were torn from their families and communities and thrown into a foreign culture where they had little control over their lives. E. Franklin Frazier, an African American sociologist, published two groundbreaking books in the 1930s about Black families. He was one of the strongest advocates of this approach. He embraced the "race relations cycle" proposed by W. Lloyd Warner and Ezra Parks, which posited that all racial and ethnic minority groups would eventually assimilate into U.S. society and values.

Frazier argued that the legacy of slavery had previously made assimilation impossible for Blacks, but that it would eventually become a reality (Hattery and Smith 2007; Hill 2005). According to this perspective, Black single-female-headed families have their roots in the history of slavery, which forced Black women to become strong and independent, without husbands to rely on. Black men were denied the privileges of paternity and the role of head of household that dominant narratives construct as the natural position of men in the family. This violation of the gender roles at the heart of the traditional nuclear family ideal became the basis for defining Black families as a problem.

With the end of slavery, opportunities for African Americans to form stable families did not improve. In the South, Black men were largely forced to become sharecroppers and faced lynching and imprisonment. Many children were taken from their families and forced into labor or placed in orphanages if their parents were not married or working. During the 20th century's **Great Migration**, as millions of Blacks moved to cities in the North from the rural South, many women found jobs as live-in domestics, which prevented them from forming or maintaining their own family relations. They remained vulnerable to sexual assaults by White men and they cultivated skills of resistance and resilience. Black men did not find the opportunities they sought in the North either, taking low-wage jobs instead and facing disproportionately rising rates of imprisonment for insignificant crimes. Black women often had no economic incentive to marry, because marriage could not provide a path out of poverty.

In sum, the legislation, ongoing discrimination, and high unemployment all continued to undermine Black families (Hill 2005). With the rise of the "cult of domesticity," they became increasingly defined as pathological for failing to fit the ideal.

During the Great Migration, many Black women found work as live-in domestic servants for White families, which made forming their own families difficult.

Credit: Bettmann/Getty Images

The legacy of slavery theory was repackaged in 1965 in a controversial report on the state of the Black family by sociologist and Assistant Secretary of Labor (and later U.S. senator) Daniel Patrick Moynihan. Single-women-headed families were increasingly in the public eye as a result of the high concentration of African Americans in impoverished urban centers and the increased access of Black women to public safety-net programs from which they had previously been excluded. Moynihan argued that single-women-headed families were keeping the Black community trapped in poverty and attributed a host of other problems to "dysfunctional" Black families, including crime, delinquency, and dependence on the government for financial support (Hattery and Smith 2007; Hill 2005).

The Revisionist Thesis

Scholars applying the **revisionist thesis**, including John Blassingame, Eugene Genovese, Robert Hill, and Andrew Billingsley, have responded directly to the legacy of slavery theorists by arguing for the strength and resilience of Black families (Hattery and Smith 2007; Hill 2005). These theorists have provided evidence to counter the dire stereotypes of a Black community racked by poverty, with few intact nuclear families. For example, Billingsley has pointed out that in metropolitan neighborhoods, two out of three Black families include both a husband and a wife, half of the families are middle-class, and nine out of ten are self-sufficient and have no need for welfare (cited in Dodson 2007, 57).

Revisionist scholars have drawn on concealed stories to argue that slave families were "functional adaptations" to the conditions of slavery. Families and extended kin were viable sources of strength and support, and essential to survival. Revisionist research also has demonstrated the extent to which Black fathers during slavery tried to protect their wives and children and keep their families together at any cost. Renowned historian John Hope Franklin (1947) documented the many efforts of runaway slaves to return to their families and argued that the institution of the family was central to slaves, who were denied access to other social institutions for support (see also Hill 2005). Revisionist research has drawn on basic precepts of both functionalism and conflict theory, redefining Black families as functional and as a refuge, given the context of oppression and White supremacy. Other scholars, like Carol Stack, have sought to explore the value in multiple family forms by highlighting the ways that low-income Black single mothers often join with extended kin and other households, creating functional family formations to better meet their needs. Joining to share resources, these families demonstrate that isolated nuclear families are not always the best option (Marks 2000, 610).

Revisionist scholars reveal concealed and resistance stories of African American agency, seeing their family structures not merely as the unfortunate results of slavery and inequality but as viable alternatives they formed to improve their quality of life and enable them to maintain kin connections that serve them. As revisionist theories demonstrate, it is possible to construct various stories about the past depending on which facts we highlight and which we ignore.

The Pathology Narrative and Latinx Families

The stock story of pathology for failure to assimilate was also applied to Latinx people, currently the largest minority population in the United States. According to Calderon (2005), the basic assumptions of assimilation are problematic because they imply that Chicano/as have faced a history similar to that experienced by European immigrants and can therefore follow the same path to success. Chicano/as, however, had much of their lands stolen and were forced into wage labor that was dangerous and low-paying. Their failure to achieve the levels of success reached by European Americans has led some to blame the Chicano community itself (Calderon 2005, 107). Calderon (2005, 110) argues that American schools teach children that the United States purchased the Southwest from Mexico, and that they do not learn "about the many that resisted lynching, murders, theft of land, and resources."

There are also significant numbers of Americans with roots in Cuba and various South and Central American nations. Recognizing this diversity makes it problematic to talk about Latinx families in general. The diversity among these groups is not only a product of their cultures of origin, but of the specific time period in which they immigrated, the immigration laws and restrictions in place at the time, the work opportunities available, and the communities they settled in. Before 1970, the majority of Latinx in the U.S. were from Cuba or Puerto Rico. After 1990, we see large numbers of Mexicans, and smaller numbers of immigrants from numerous other countries including El Salvador, the Dominican Republic, Guatemala, Colombia, Honduras, and elsewhere. The experiences of these families vary greatly depending on where they settled. Research demonstrates that family formations are impacted by all of these factors (Zambrana 2011). For example, foreign-born Mexican families are more likely to have larger households with extended kin, whereas Cuban households are most likely to have higher incomes and only two people.

Nevertheless, the typical Latinx family has been stereotyped as highly patriarchal, devoutly Catholic, committed to rigid gender roles for children, and valuing family over education. Some of these characteristics are more common among low-income Mexican Americans, the primary population that has been studied over the past 40 years, than among other Latinx groups. However, findings from the research are often generalized to all Latinx families, portraying them as static and unchanging and reinforcing the notion that they are all the same.

Many policy-makers, service providers, and educators have accepted these stereotypes and the assimilationist ideal (Zambrana 2011). The resulting expectations are problematic because they lead to demands that Latinx abandon the cultures, traditions, and language that for many are sources of pride and identity. The concealed story here is that the most significant obstacles to advancement are economic inequity, the criminalization of Latino men in many regions, racial profiling to identify undocumented immigrants, ongoing discrimination and racism, and barriers to opportunities in education, healthcare, and other institutions.

Critical Thinking

1. Historically, why has assimilation been emphasized so strongly in the application of stock sociological theories to immigrant families? What do you see as the costs and benefits of assimilation?

2. What might the policy results have looked like if the theories applied to various racial and ethnic groups had instead highlighted the value of maintaining diversity among families?

3. What role has racial ideology played in shaping the structures of families historically?

4. How are views about individual families depicted in the stock and concealed stories?

FAMILY INEQUALITY THROUGH THE MATRIX LENS

Our application of the matrix perspective to stock, concealed, and resistance stories reveals that ideologies about the family, as well as policies affecting real families' daily lives reproduce race, gender, class, and sexual inequality while also constructing a definition of the nation that privileges Whites (Collins 1998, 65). The family becomes a metaphor for both race and nation, with borders that require policing to prevent the invasion of "outsiders." In addition to allowing us to examine the construction of race as it intersects with other social identities, the matrix framework asks that we consider narratives, institutions, and structures as they interact with and shape each other. Finally, we also must examine resistance and agency, and all within specific social, historical, economic, and geographical contexts.

Through the matrix lens, a different narrative of family formation emerges, drawing on a wide range of research and theorizing. Our review of history was from a matrix theoretical perspective, and raised essential insights:

- Families are social constructs, and there is no single, "natural" family form.

- A diversity of family forms has always existed.

- Families are not static. They change over time, across generations, and across geographical spaces and local contexts, and they are constantly being rearticulated in new ways.

- What is considered the "ideal" family form varies historically and cross-culturally.

- Stock stories promoting hegemonic family ideals reproduce racial and other forms of inequality, privileging some families over others, and some family members over others. Examining these inequities intersectionally is necessary.

- Research presents a narrative about families that is often influenced by the culture and values of the researcher and the broader dominant culture, reproducing relationships of power, privilege, and oppression.

- Family formations are shaped by many structural factors, including material and economic, historical, and public policy and legal factors (such as immigration law and welfare policy) and other social institutions (such as criminal justice, education, and health).

- The traditional ideal family of our stock stories will not solve structural problems such as unemployment and poverty (and our focus on it as the answer prevents us from discussing real solutions).

- Gender is central to an understanding of different family formations across history and cultures, and gendered power relations influence our definitions of acceptable and dysfunctional families.

- Racism and other systems of inequality shape family formations, the experiences of individual families.

- The family, as an institution, is central to the construction of definitions of both nation and race, and their shifting boundaries over time.

- Families socialize the next generation into hierarchical systems of nation, race, gender, sexuality, and age, among others. They also can, and often do, resist such hierarchies.

- Whose stories are heard, and who tells them, shape the factors considered.

The matrix approach directs us to look at recent research that challenges the simplistic stock stories about families head-on and highlights new concealed and resistance stories that add greatly to our understanding of families.

Women's Concealed Stories

As more women have become sociologists and their research has been accepted as legitimate, we have learned more about the importance of gender and other identities in examining Black families. Sociologist Shirley Hill's work on Black families dismisses the functionalist assimilation approach we examined earlier in this chapter. Hill (2005, 10–11) argues that "race and class oppression has left most [African American families] at odds with dominant societal ideals about the appropriate roles of men and women and the proper formation of families." At the same time, the results of this oppression have been blamed on African Americans themselves, rather than on the true underlying causes.

The legacy of slavery and revisionist scholars also debated the extent to which African culture was decimated or maintained by slaves. However, family formations and culture are dynamic and are constantly re-created within specific contexts. Accumulating research provides insight into the diverse contexts that shaped the transmission of African culture over time, for instance. Josephine Beoku-Betts studied the African American Gullah community (descended from slaves) on the Georgia and South Carolina Sea Islands. The Gullah were isolated and they did not face the conditions of African Americans on the mainland. Thus, they were able to maintain cohesive communities that preserved important features of African culture. For example, they spoke their own language and passed on to successive generations traditional crafts, African birthing and naming traditions, folktales, religious beliefs, cooking techniques, and more (Beoku-Betts 2000; Joyner 2000). Beoku-Betts (2000, 415) argues that because most of these tasks have been seen as part of women's natural role in the family, they were not studied in the past. Her research uncovers a previously concealed story about what are only now being recognized as practices significant to the "maintenance of tradition."

Many women scholars have continued to make women's experiences visible, revealing further concealed stories and examples of resistance. Donna Franklin (2010) examined the Victorian era, when married Black women were largely working outside the home, often in professional careers. Many White women, in contrast, were relegated to the domestic sphere and believed they could not be successful and advance in professional careers if they were married. As Franklin observes, "Black women seemed to have an easier time juggling the role of activist with the role of mother and wife…. Historian Linda Gordon found that 85 percent of black women activists were married, compared to only 34 percent of white women activists" (64).

Black women who were both activists and working professionals were often married to professional men. Work was not stigmatized for Black women as it was for White women; rather, it was seen as contributing to the common cause of advancing the Black community. Further, because slavery had "rendered black men and women equally powerless," it had "leveled the gender 'playing field'" (Franklin 2010, 65). Among married adults today, Black women are more likely than White women to have higher salaries than their husbands, and Black husbands contribute slightly more to household chores than do White husbands (Franklin 2010).

The Concealed Story of Invisible Fathers

There is a common myth, a stock story, that the absence of Black fathers is responsible for the poverty of Black families. We see all around us stereotypes of the irresponsible Black father. We know that Black fathers are less likely to be married due to high rates of incarceration, unemployment, and changes to the welfare system (Lemmons and Johnson 2019). However, while Black fathers are less likely to marry the mothers of their children than are other fathers, this fact alone does not support the common assumption that they are not good fathers (Coles 2009). The rates of unmarried fathers and mothers living together with their children has been increasing, as more couples choose to cohabitate rather than marry. The stereotype of the absent Black father that looms so large in our culture has concealed the story of Black fathers who are strong presences in their children's lives. Research has found that people actually underestimate the numbers of interactions children have with Black fathers, for example, in daycare settings (). In fact, many Black fathers are more highly involved in their children's lives than are White or Hispanic fathers. (Blow 2015; Edin et al. 2009). Other research has found that unmarried African American fathers are more likely than their White or Hispanic counterparts to contribute to costs during pregnancy and to offer in-kind support and care for their children (Coles 2009).

- These findings are especially meaningful given the unique challenges these fathers face. They are more likely than White fathers to reside in poor communities with fewer resources available to support parents.

- They experience lower rates of education and employment.

- They are more likely to be employed in part-time and low-paying jobs that offer fewer benefits, for a variety of reasons discussed on in our chapter on work (Abdil 2018, Lemmons and Johnson 2019).

Coles (2009) conducted one of the first major studies of Black single fathers with custody of their children and found that in addition to these challenges, many experienced obstacles dealing with legal and social services, including suspicion and assumptions that they could not be good fathers, as well as institutional and policy barriers. For example, the inability to pay child support impacts the amount of time fathers are able to spend with their children. However, even without economic means, fathers can still make a positive difference in their children's lives (Harris 2018). Coles and other scholars conclude that these men are generally highly motivated, and can be and often are successful fathers even when they are not married to their children's mothers (Abdill 2018, Harris 2018). Coles implores us to see that "these are caring fathers: as good, loving, and motivated as any other father. Their existence and their experiences deserve public articulation. . . . Their stories provide a counterweight to the predominant image of black fathers" (14).

Within the larger Black Lives Matter movement, we see an emphasis on the intersectional reality of Black lives, highlighting the experiences of violence aimed at disabled, trans, and queer Black people.

Credit: David Grossman/Alamy Stock Photo

Oppression and Privilege: Support for White Families

The state's part in shaping family and reproduction practices is clearly a racialized and gendered process. It is almost always women's bodies that are targeted for control by courts and legislatures, despite the fact that men play a role in reproduction as well (Flavin 2009). Race, class, and age all influence how the state treats women's reproductive capacity, with effects on family formation.

By the 1950s, every U.S. state had passed laws preventing pregnant women from working, while at the same time withholding unemployment benefits from them (Solinger 2007). Prior to increased women's activism and the sexual liberation movement in the late 1960s, few options were available to single women who became pregnant. There was a strong culture of punishment at the time, which saw women's sexual behavior as unacceptable and unfeminine, and as breaking the hallowed bounds of the ideal nuclear family. A woman facing an unwanted pregnancy could petition the medical community for a "therapeutic" abortion based on psychiatric grounds; however, approval was hard to obtain, and if it was granted, the woman was usually also sterilized at the same time. Other alternatives varied by race. To avoid the shame of out-of-wedlock pregnancy and preserve their daughters' marriageability, White families that could afford it would hide their single pregnant daughters, sending them elsewhere to live, or confining them in maternity homes and putting their babies up for adoption. Single Black women who became pregnant were barred from Whites-only maternity homes and were more often embraced and accepted by their families and extended kin. Nevertheless, they were stigmatized and inserted into the dominant narrative as examples of broken Black families and communities (Solinger 2013).

While the public in general viewed both White and Black unmarried mothers negatively, the White women were nonetheless seen as producing a valuable commodity for which there was high demand among White married couples unable to have children. In the 1960s, welfare programs began linking the receipt of benefits to compulsory sterilization for many women, especially women of color. African American and Puerto Rican community activists fought these abuses, which were not brought to the public's attention until the mid-1970s (Flavin 2009). In 1968, more than one-third of women in Puerto Rico between the ages of 15 and 45 had been surgically sterilized, often without their knowledge, as a means of controlling the population (Lopez 1987).

In the 1950s and 1960s, numerous U.S. states passed "man in the house" laws, which gave welfare agencies the ability to cut off payments to single women who were suspected of engaging in sexual relations. The assumption was that if a woman was involved with a man, he should be "man of the house" and support her and her children, even if they were not his. In essence this law allowed the state to control women's sexual activity in a punitive fashion. This and other welfare and social programs were unevenly applied based on race, and racism often shaped the forms these policies took (Kohler-Hausmann 2007; Lefkovitz 2011). Such uneven enforcement fostered the image of the promiscuous "welfare queen" living on the public dole while indulging her own pleasures (Kohler-Hausmann 2007). This stereotype became increasingly useful in the backlash against welfare among many politicians.

The Social Security Act of 1935 established the Aid to Dependent Children (ADC) program, which became known as "welfare." ADC was not written to benefit all families equitably, however. Entire categories of workers (domestic workers, agricultural workers), those with high representations of people of color, were excluded from the benefits of the program. As a result, Whites were the primary beneficiaries of welfare. White women were often encouraged to stay at home and focus on raising their children, while women of color were strongly urged to work in the fields or as domestics (Solinger 2010).

Beginning with the President George W. Bush administration, so-called **marriage promotion programs**—programs that aim to encourage marriage by teaching relationship and communication skills—were offered as a solution to poverty for single mothers. These programs are funded by federal and state taxes on the continuing assumption that single parenting is a primary cause of poverty and marriage is the solution (Carter 2018; Heath, Randles, and Avishai 2016).

As part of the Deficit Reduction Act of 2005, under the auspices of the Department of Health and Human Services, "The Healthy Marriage and Responsible Fatherhood (HMRF) initiative" is a $150 million grant program to support organizations promoting marriage as the means to reduce family inequality. It was first authorized in 2005, reauthorized in 2010, and then again under the Trump administration. The government offers a publicly funded website that provides tips and activities for dads, including communication tips, "Dad Jokes," and suggestions for weekly activities such as celebrating "Winnie the Pooh Day," and "dad and son" dance-offs (https://www.fatherhood.gov/home).

Marriage and fatherhood promotion programs are not based on any research evidence and they reproduce the myth of the ideal family, which is dependent on a strong father. They ignore structural causes of inequality and social, historical, and economic context, instead reinforcing the belief that poverty is simply the result of individuals' poor choices. However, research finds that "the most important predictors of marriage and divorce are not whether an individual has mastered good communication skills but whether he or she has a stable job and a college education" (Avishai, Heath, and Randles 2012, 37; Carter 2018).

The Socialization of Children

A large study of mothers and their children found that when mothers had experienced racism (including verbal insults and discrimination), children struggled in school and faced more social and emotional problems (MSN News 2012). Families are a key site of future generations' socialization into the hierarchies of oppression and privilege. As groundbreaking sociologist Patricia Hill Collins (1998, 64) observes, "Individuals typically learn their assigned place in hierarchies of race, gender, ethnicity, sexuality, nation and social class in their families of origin." In communities of color, parents are forced to prepare their children to enter a world that is often hostile toward them and thus dangerous, or at best simply biased against them (Blake and Epstein 2019; Meadows-Fernandez 2020). As James Baldwin explained in his 1963 book *The Fire Next Time*:

> [The child] must be "good" not only in order to please his parents and not only to avoid being punished by them; behind their authority stands another, nameless and impersonal, infinitely harder to please, and bottomlessly cruel. And this filters into the child's consciousness through his parents' tone of voice as he is being exhorted, punished, or loved; in the sudden, uncontrollable note of fear heard in his mother's or his father's voice when he has strayed beyond some particular boundary. (40–41)

Contemporary writers continue to express this. One researcher found that the Chicana mothers she interviewed engaged in "psychological protection" of their children while also teaching their daughters "how to resist their subordination" (Hurtado 2003, 78–79).

White parents need not confront the challenging topic of race with their children, and often do not even consider it. Numerous studies have found that White parents report rarely talking about race with their children (Perry, Skinner, and Abaied, 2019; Vittrup 2016). Many embrace a color-blind perspective, assuming that if they do not talk about race, their children will grow up to see everyone as equal and the same. Results find this is not the case, however, and that bias aware-ness is more successful (Perry, Skinner, and Abaied 2019). Children as young as 6 months old recognize differences in skin color, and by the age of 7 they have already formed conclusions about race, with White children identifying Black children as more likely to be "mean." Further, living in a diverse community or attending a diverse school does not reduce these effects. The only thing that does is White parents' talking to their children about race: "This period of our children's lives, when we imagine it's most important to not talk about race, is the very developmental period when children's minds are forming their first conclusions about race" (Bronson and Merryman 2009).

There are currently many books and other resources available to help all parents in address-ing race with their children at any age. Even more important than talking to children about race is the choices privileged parents make that, often unintentionally, shape their children's experi-ences and knowledge of race. White, class-privileged parents are likely to choose "good neigh-borhoods" with "good schools." However, these are the least likely to be diverse. As a result, White children with class privilege often have very little interaction with children of color, and racial segregation persists across all socioeconomic strata (Hagerman 2018).

Critical Thinking

1. Have any of the historical factors that we have examined in this section surprised you? Which points do you think are most important for people to know?

2. How have social institutions (e.g., the criminal justice system, economies, government policies) created obstacles for some families while providing a hand up for others? Do you believe investing public funding into marriage promotion programs is worthwhile? Why or why not?

3. Do you believe that the mythical "ideal" family formation should remain the ideal for all families? Explain.

4. What did you learn about race as a child? Did your family talk about race often? If so, what kinds of issues and messages do you remember?

TRANSFORMING THE NARRATIVE OF THE IDEAL FAMILY

The myth of the ideal family obscures the reality of the diverse families we live in. Rather than asking why certain families do not conform to the ideal nuclear family model, many researchers are reframing the question, asking whether the nuclear family is necessarily the best model for all families at all times (Coontz 2010a; Hill 2005; Risman 2010).

The Rise of Multigenerational Households

While the number of multigenerational households decreased from 1900, when the number was one out of every four homes, until 1980, when they hit a low of 12%, they have been increas-ing since and currently comprise about one out of every five homes. About 20% of those 65 and older live with one or more members of the next generation (the vast majority with younger family members) (Cohn and Passel 2018). Both increasing economic inequality and increasing racial diversity have contributed to this gain.

Hispanic/Latinx and Asian immigrants are the vast majority of immigrants in the U.S. today, and they are more likely to live in multigenerational households (Wu, Sah, and Tidwell 2018); 25% of Asian, 23% of Black, 22% of Hispanic, and 13% of White households are multigenerational.

For many years, families resided in multigenerational homes so younger members could provide care for the older members of the family. One factor in the recent rise is that now grandparents are increasingly providing care for the grandchildren and contributing economically to the household, as it has become more difficult for young adults to establish financially stable homes (Miller and Nebeker-Adams 2017). In homes with children, parents, and grandparents living together, more resources are spent on children's education, and less on childcare (Amorim 2019). Additionally, many grandparents are raising their grandchildren on their own. There are approximately 1.3 million grandparents that live with, and work in the labor force to support, at least one grandchild (Census 2020). At the same time, many of our nation's aging population have no one able to provide necessary care, and subsidized and accessible housing for the elderly has declined, leaving more elderly people homeless than in the past (Joint Center for Housing Studies of Harvard University, 2019).

When the Ideal Family Is Not Ideal

Examining family violence also challenges the myth of the ideal family. Research has found that a third of women have experienced physical violence, and a quarter have survived severe physical violence (beatings, burnings, sexual violence, and other forms of violence, often leading to mental health disorders, including post-traumatic stress). Men are not immune, as one in nine men have experienced domestic abuse. Close to one-third of women who are murdered are killed by their partners (National Coalition Against Domestic Violence 2015).

While one in ten women experience rape perpetrated by their intimate partner, until the 1980s marital rape was not even a crime in many states (Hattery and Smith 2016). Domestic violence is a leading cause of the health problems and complications faced by pregnant women (Pan American Health Organization, n.d.). Native American/American Indian women are most likely to experience domestic violence, rape, and sexual assault. More than fifty percent experience sexual assault and/or intimate partner violence. Compounding the problem is the lack of culturally competent healthcare, and a lack of healthcare and domestic violence shelters or places to seek safety on reservations (National Coalition on Domestic Violence 2020).

Domestic violence has been called "the second pandemic" accompanying COVID-19. Abusers frequently isolate their targets from support systems, including family and friends, and the pandemic has provided this scenario. Couples and families are forced to spend 24 hours a day together, and as stress and anger increase as a result of isolation and economic uncertainty, the opportunities for domestic violence become more prevalent, and there are fewer options for escape. This public health problem was identified early, but measures were not put into place to deal with the predicted crisis. Calls to domestic violence and sexual assault hotlines have increased, and rates of abuse have increased and have become more severe (Fang 2020; Sharma and Bikash Borah 2020). The impact is worldwide, according to the United Nations secretary-general, who declared, "For many women and girls, the threat looms largest where they should be safest: in their own homes.… We have seen a horrifying global surge in domestic violence" (Fang 2020). Increased parental burnout, job loss, and amount of time spent at home with children has contributed to a disturbing increase in psychological and physical child abuse (Griffith 2020; Lawson, Piel, and Simon 2020).

According to Hattery and Smith () between 4.5 and 5 children die every day as a result of child abuse, most often at the hands of family members (). This is up from 3.6 in 2000. Children with disabilities are at greater risk, and all children suffer higher risks when living in foster care. African American, Hispanic, Asian American, and Native American children are more likely than White children to be removed from their homes and placed in foster care, putting them at greater risk. The most common form of child abuse is neglect, and some of this is a result of a single parent having to work full-time who cannot afford childcare. Daycare would consume the entire amount of income earned by minimum wage workers (Hatter and Smith 2020). For parents living in poverty, the very limited government support available makes it impossible to provide adequate housing and food for their children. This kind of abuse, severe illness, and death are all easily preventable if we, as a society, value the lives of the very poor.

Girls and women are more likely than their male counterparts to experience child sexual abuse and elder abuse, and African American girls and elderly women face much higher rates of abuse than do their White counterparts (). Boys who witness domestic violence while growing up are three times more like to become abusive towards their own partners. The ideology of the family as a private sphere has kept violence within families hidden from public view. Intimate partner violence often remains unreported and undetected. Hattery and Smith's (2007) research has shown that forcing poor women to find mates to escape poverty locks many into a cycle of abusive relationships. Abused women often feel they cannot leave their abusers, and those who do leave still face challenges. Many end up homeless or in other abusive relationships.

In the midst of stay-at-home orders, parents working full-time who are also providing childcare themselves are at greater risk of burnout than ever before. Parental burnout puts children's health and well-being at greater risk. Research finds that parents facing higher levels of burnout report higher levels of conflict with partners (if present), and engage in higher levels of child abuse and neglect. Research also finds that burnout is correlated with domestic violence (Griffith 2020).

Transmigration

We began the chapter with an examination of the detention of transmigrants and immigrants taken into detention centers, and often deported without their families being alerted. Some historical background and insight into the lives of undocumented Latinx peoples is important as context. The ancestors of many Chicano/as lived in regions that were once part of Mexico but today fall within the United States. National borders in these areas have been fluid over time, and for many Chicano/as, they remain so today. Many Latinx are **transmigrants**, people who "live their lives across borders, participating simultaneously in social relations that embed

Many Latinx residents of the area around the U.S.-Mexico border are transmigrants, living their lives in both countries. Many cross into the U.S. to work, often in agriculture.

Credit: inga spence/Alamy Stock Photo

them in more than one nation-state" (Glick-Schiller 2003, 105–6). Soehl and Waldinger (2010, 1496) found that the majority of Latinx transmigrants maintain activities of connectivity with their home countries, making phone calls, visiting, and sending remittances back home. Those with children or assets in their home countries engage in these activities more frequently (1505).

Undocumented immigrant parents must make difficult decisions based on their desire to do what is best for their families given their circumstances. Across the United States, close to 6 million children live with one or more undocumented family members, and more than four million live with an undocumented parent. These children live with the fear that parents or other family members could be removed from the home and deported at any time. Research is increasingly documenting the traumatic impact this is having on children, who are experiencing higher rates of "toxic stress," anxiety, depression, and behavioral and physical changes (American Immigration Council 2019; American Psychological Association, n.d.). Some scholars are also looking at the strategies that lead to family resilience in the face of such vulnerability and risk.

Reproductive Technologies

Technologies have changed the reproductive possibilities available to families, and innovations in this area will continue into the future. These technologies further destabilize our stock story that the ideal traditional family is rooted in nature.

Gestational surrogacy is deeply entwined with race and class. Hiring a surrogate in India can cost less than half what it does in the United States.

Credit: Mint/Hindustan Times/Getty Images

The United States is one of only a small number of countries in the world that allow **gestational surrogacy**, in which a woman carries an implanted embryo to term for another couple or parent but has no genetic tie to the child herself. There are currently 20 states that allow gestational surrogacy, but the regulations and legal conditions vary by state. In only some of these states is it legal to compensate the surrogate. The demand for gestational surrogates has been increasing for many reasons, including the availability of abortion and birth control, which has limited the number of White babies available for adoption. At the same time, women are marrying later and delaying attempts to get pregnant.

France Winddance Twine (2011) examines gestational surrogacy as a form of labor deeply imbued with hierarchies of race, class, and gender. She finds that it is predominantly White middle- and upper-class women and couples who are able to afford to hire surrogates, while surrogates are most often poor White women and women of color in the United States and poor women in developing nations. As Twine points out, while "contemporary gestational surrogates 'voluntarily' enter into these commercial contracts and willingly sell their 'reproductive' labor, their agency occurs within a context of a stratified system of reproduction" (15).

It is very difficult to obtain up-to-date and accurate data on surrogacy because the only source is reports obtained from medical clinics.

The number of in vitro fertilizations that involved a gestational carrier between 1999 and 2013 increased from 1 to 2.5% (Perkins, Boulet, Jamieson, Dmitry, and Kissin, 2016).

Interracial Marriage

The stock story tells us that we reside in a color-blind nation today, but intermarriage rates reveal that this is not the case; more than eight out of ten people marrying today still choose to marry someone of the same race, and gendered bias against interracial marriage persists (Skinner and Hudac 2017). Laws against interracial marriage were not declared unconstitutional in the United States until 1967. Since then, rates of interracial marriage have been climbing, most quickly in recent years. In 1970, only 1% of all U.S. marriages were interracial. By 2015 the number of new marriages that were interracial grew to 17% (Bialik 2017; Livingston and Brown 2017).

Figure 3.2 provides us with insight regarding who is more likely to marry whom, which reflects, in part, people's attitudes toward other racial groups. Whites are the least likely to intermarry, at 11%, and are significantly more likely to marry Hispanics and Asians than Black people. This mirrors historical constructions of different racial groups, the dynamics of colorism, and the power of continuing stereotypes of African Americans (Bialik 2017).

American Indians, Asian Americans, and Hispanics are most likely to marry outside their racial groups. There are generational differences as well, especially among immigrant compared to U.S.-born populations. Among U.S.-born Asians and Hispanics, 46% and 39% respectively are marrying outside their race.

Intermarriage rates also provide insight into the intersections of race and gender. For example, African American men are twice as likely to marry a White woman, than vice versa. We find the reverse dynamic with Asian Americans, where Asian American women marry White men twice as often as Asian American men marry White women (Qian and Lichter 2018). Clearly, gender stereotypes pervade our narratives and attitudes about marriageable partners. While Black women have been defined in largely negative terms as unfeminine, angry, and independent, Asian women have been depicted as exotic, erotic, and submissive (Choi and Tienda 2017; Wang, 2015; Zhenchao and Lichter 2018).

Geography is an important factor. Honolulu has the greatest number of intermarriages by far, with over 40% of recent marriages between people who identify differently by race. Of the ten cities with the least amount of outmarrying, eight are in the south (Livingston and Brown 2017). Hispanics

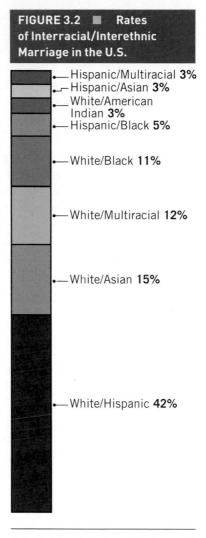

FIGURE 3.2 ■ Rates of Interracial/Interethnic Marriage in the U.S.

Hispanic/Multiracial **3%**
Hispanic/Asian **3%**
White/American Indian **3%**
Hispanic/Black **5%**
White/Black **11%**
White/Multiracial **12%**
White/Asian **15%**
White/Hispanic **42%**

Note: Racial and ethnic combinations with values of less than 2% are not shown. Whites, Blacks, Asians, and American Indians include only non-Hispanics. Hispanics are of any race. Asians include Pacific Islanders.

Source: Pew Research Center analysis of 2014-2015 American Community Survey (IPUMS).

residing in traditional Hispanic enclaves, where there is a greater concentration of Hispanics, are less likely to marry out. Whether members of racial/ethnic groups cross racial boundaries through marriage is dependent on a wide range of factors, and cannot be characterized as simply a measure of assimilation and integration (Qian, Lichter, and Tumin 2018).

As one might expect, the numbers of multiracial children are also increasing, and at last count, in 2015, were 14% of all births. More than one-fourth of these births are to couples with one Hispanic and one White parent (Bialik 2017). Parents' identity, however, may not determine how their children self-identify. There are a wide range of terms that have been embraced, including multiracial, biracial, and frequently children take on the racial/ethnic identity of the group that most closely approximates their physical features, or the identity of the group they most identify with. These are very personal choices. It is not uncommon for siblings to choose different racial classifications to describe themselves. These choices are always constrained by social factors, of course. How one classifies themselves may be at odds with how other people classify them based on assumptions, stereotypes, interacting characteristics of gender and class, as well as geographical location. Multiracial people who do not look White usually encounter discrimination and oppression, independent of whether they identify as White. As a group, multiracial people frequently experience this incongruence and mislabeling (Glover and McDonald 2019).

LGBTQ+ Families

Perhaps one of the most visible ways in which the family is changing is in the growth in numbers of openly gay and lesbian families. All the stock stories about the family that we have examined are predicated on the assumption of heterosexuality. We actively construct heterosexuality as normative, just as we construct patriarchy and Whiteness as normative (Ingraham 2013). The notion of the ideal traditional nuclear family is one of the most important sites of this construction. Same-sex desire and sexual behavior that fall outside our definition of heterosexuality have always existed. These concealed stories have often been ignored or written out of history, as heterosexuality became defined as the only "natural" and legitimate form of relationship on which to base a family. As a result, heterosexuality has been reinforced as the invisible, privileged norm.

Since the U.S. Supreme Court's decision in *Obergefell v. Hodges* (2015), the fundamental right of same-sex couples to marry has been protected in the United States, and valid same-sex marriages sealed in other jurisdictions are recognized. A Gallup poll in June 2016 found that about 123,000 same-sex couples had married since the Court's decision, bringing the national total to about 491,000. About one in ten LGBT adults is now married to a same-sex partner, up from 7.9% prior to the Supreme Court ruling (Jones 2016). Across the U.S., 39% of married, heterosexual couples are raising children. The rate among married lesbians is 30%, and 13% among gay married couples (Goldberg and Conron 2018). Marriage comes with many rights, including the right to make medical decisions for one's spouse, to inherit from one's spouse, to qualify for spousal Social Security, veteran's and other benefits, and to jointly adopt or foster children. However, many states have passed laws denying married same-sex couples some of these benefits, and allowing religious and state officials to refuse to officiate at weddings for same-sex couples. Battles over many of these issues are currently taking place in the courts (Movement Advancement Project 2017). The majority of LGBT-identifying people are White (58%), followed by Latinx (21%) and then Black (12%). On the other hand, White people are least likely to report that they identify as LGBT, and men are less likely to do so than women (Goldberg and Conron 2018;). White and class privilege may make the transition to marriage and parenthood a little bit easier. While they still face homophobia, discrimination, and structural barriers, White gays and lesbians have had the privilege of not having their loyalty to their racial community challenged (Moore 2011).

RESISTANCE STORY: NANCY MEZEY

I grew up in an upper-middle-class White suburb of New York City. My family had progressive and openly gay friends, providing me with White, economically successful role models who crossed sexual boundaries. So when I came out as a lesbian in the mid-1990s, my family and friends were neither surprised nor disappointed. Years later, I met my partner, also a White middle-class professional, who shared my desire to have children. Our White middle-class status helped us find other lesbians who were birthing and adopting children, a privilege to which Black working-class lesbians in the area did not have access.

Indeed, networking through a lesbian mothers' group, we found a fertility specialist who helped us have two children. Until that point, my partner and I had felt largely unscathed by homophobia and heterosexism. Our first real experience with individual discrimination occurred when we tried to find childcare for our oldest child. I called daycare centers in our midwestern town and explained that my son had two mothers (careful not to use the word lesbian), only to have the providers explain that "other parents would be uncomfortable" and they could not accept our child.

Later, we experienced institutional discrimination in our [pre-2015] effort to both become legal parents to our children. That process required going through a second-parent adoption in which we paid thousands of dollars for a home study, even though I was our children's biological mother and my partner and I had raised the children together in our home from birth. This was followed by my giving up my legal rights to our children in court, only to adopt them back with my partner.

When we moved to New Jersey, we found a much more welcoming environment. Our privileged status allowed us to move into a largely White middle-class town with a strong public school system. In two obvious instances, our children lost friends after their parents realized our children had two mothers. But for the most part, my partner and I buffered our children by having proactive meetings with teachers and screening parents at social events. I often wondered if the few homophobic parents we met knew that we were protecting our children from them as much as they thought they were protecting their children from us. In my personal life, transformation comes through the interactions my family and I have with others on a daily basis that create a new normal of wider acceptance.

Because of the importance of social context in family formation, the experiences of gay and lesbian families themselves differ across race and class lines. On the one hand, "Black cultures, ideologies, and the historical experiences of Black women structure lesbian identities"

(Moore 2011, 3). At the same time, Black lesbians exert influence over their own family for-mations and family lives. For example, Moore (2011) found that "respectability" was a strong theme for the Black lesbian women she studied. Consistently defined by the dominant cul-ture as lazy, poor, hypersexual, and immoral, Black women have employed numerous strate-gies to present themselves as "respectable" while at the same time asserting their own sexual autonomy.

Attitudes about gay and lesbian marriage have changed dramatically from 2004 to 2019. In 2004, 60% of Americans opposed, while 31% were in favor; this completely flipped by 2019, when 61% were in favor and 31% opposed (Masci, Brown, and Kiley 2019). These views also vary by race, gender, location, political party affiliation, age, and religion. Figure 3.3 provides a snapshot of the intersections of religion and race.

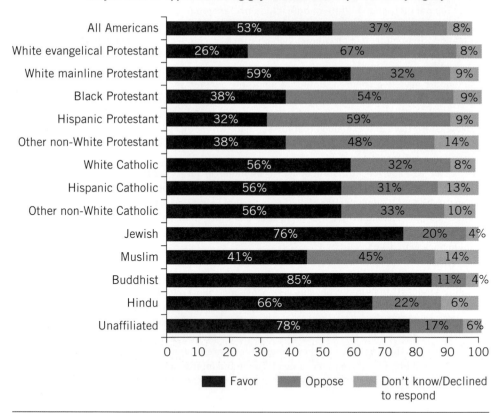

FIGURE 3.3   ■   Views on Same-Sex Marriage Vary by Race and Religion

Do you favor or oppose allowing gay and lesbian couples to marry legally?

	Favor	Oppose	Don't know/Declined to respond
All Americans	53%	37%	8%
White evangelical Protestant	26%	67%	8%
White mainline Protestant	59%	32%	9%
Black Protestant	38%	54%	9%
Hispanic Protestant	32%	59%	9%
Other non-White Protestant	38%	48%	14%
White Catholic	56%	32%	8%
Hispanic Catholic	56%	31%	13%
Other non-White Catholic	56%	33%	10%
Jewish	76%	20%	4%
Muslim	41%	45%	14%
Buddhist	85%	11%	4%
Hindu	66%	22%	6%
Unaffiliated	78%	17%	6%

Note: Totals for each category may add up to more or less than 100 due to margin of error.

Source: PRRI 2015 American Values Atlas.

The Power of Social Movements

LGBTQ+ social movements have fought not only for the right to marry, but for equal rights in every arena. They have fought to make discrimination in the workplace, housing, and businesses illegal. Most of these battles have been fought at the state level, and protections vary by state. In the past decade, LGBTQ+ movements have increasingly engaged in coalitional politics to achieve successful outcomes. For example, Adam (2017) has analyzed the collaboration between LGBTQ+ movements and immigrant rights movement in both Washington and Arizona. These two movements united to support or defeat a variety of policy proposals. These included campaigns to secure financial aid for undocumented immigrant students; a referendum to provide many of the benefits that accompany marriage to domestic partners in Washington; fighting a bill in Arizona that would have broadened the scope of the state's Religious Freedom Restoration Act, which would permit businesses to refuse to serve members of the LGBTQ+ community; and campaigns to gain marriage equality in both states. These huge victories, battles which had been lost in the past, have been attributed, in part, to these coalitions.

These movements found common ground as the foundation around which to unite. Of greatest significance was their embrace of a shared civil rights model based on previous social movements, as well as the identification of their common foes. They discovered that the movements fighting against immigrant rights were usually the same forces working against LGBTQ+ rights (Adam 2017). This example represents the power of intersectional social movement organizing, confirming the early argument of intersectional scholars who argued that intersectional movements are more successful than those which focus on a single axis of oppression (Cho, Crenshaw, and McCall 2013; Ishkanian, Armine, and eña Saavedra 2019).

Challenging the Narrative of Family

As we broaden our understanding of what counts as a family, we must reassess historical narratives that have excluded certain family formations. Researchers are not exempt from the prejudices and assumptions of the broader culture. As family researcher Stephen Marks (2000, 611) reflects: "Most family scholars continue to be White, heterosexual, married persons such as myself. The research published ... reflects the interests of those who do the studies." However, as more and more research is conducted by scholars previously excluded—men and women of color, White women, LGBTQ+ people, and working-class people, for example—the kinds of subjects that are being studied, the questions that are being asked, and the concealed stories and voices of resistance that are being brought in are changing the field. As Marks goes on, "These scholars have challenged their exclusion ... and some of us from the dominant groups who earlier saw families in a White, male, middle-class image have been listening and learning" (611).

Thus, we see broadening recognition and research on a wide array of family formations and experiences. At the same time, we need to cultivate more curious citizens who will ask the unasked questions and challenge narratives that distort the realities we see all around us.

Critical Thinking

1. How have technological changes opened up new family formations? What changes do you foresee in the future owing to technology, especially in regard to social identities including race, gender, and dis/ability?

2. How have very recently enacted government policies and laws affected families, including those formations discussed in this last section of this chapter?

3. How does the history of slavery, genocide, immigration, and inequitable access to resources help explain contemporary interracial marriage rates? How do you think future race relations will be affected by rising rates of intermarriage?

4. What other significant changes do you see taking place among families today or in the future?

CHAPTER SUMMARY

3.1 Describe the historical forces that have influenced the intersection of race and family in the United States.

Family formations were inextricably shaped by culture and race in the American colonial era. Native Americans had diverse family structures that were greatly affected by colonization, and African family structures were disrupted when Africans were ripped from their families, transported overseas, and subjected to a system of slavery that consistently broke up families, as each individual was viewed as a commodity. Various immigrating European ethnic groups and Asians were restricted in their family formation by shifting immigration laws that often dictated who could enter the United States. Today family formations continue to shift and remain diverse.

3.2 Examine the current stock theories that explain family inequalities across racial and ethnic lines.

A variety of social theories have emerged to explain inequality among families. Stock stories include the functionalist, conflict, and symbolic interactionist perspectives. The primary stock story has revolved around theories of assimilation. In order to explain the less prevalent assimilation of Africans and African Americans, other theories have revealed concealed stories examining the impact of slavery. Some of these same theories and debates have been applied to Chicanos/Latinx.

3.3 Apply the matrix lens to an understanding of family inequality.

More recent theorizing has taken an approach that explicitly addresses issues raised by the matrix perspective. Assimilation theories have been reinterpreted as maintaining inequality. Theories that have posited low rates of marriage among African Americans as the leading cause of Black poverty have been directly challenged by examinations of women's lives in particular, as well as by research into the realities facing Black men and their roles as fathers. Government funds that could contribute to decreasing family poverty have instead been directed to programs encouraging marriage, which primarily benefit White families. Some scholars have challenged the notion that the mythical ideal family is ideal at all. Inequality inevitably shapes relationships within families.

3.4 Identify alternatives to the current matrix of inequality among families.

Contemporary trends are changing the face of families. Rates of interracial marriage are increasing, and the legalization of same-sex marriage has expanded the rights of people to marry whom they choose. The phenomenon of transmigration and the explosive rise of new reproductive technologies are complicating the lives of families and will continue to do so. Our very definitions of family are shifting, as they always have.

KEY TERMS

assimilation

Dawes Act

family

gestational surrogacy

Great Migration

ideology of domesticity

legacy of slavery thesis

marriage promotion

programs

naturalization

nuclear family

revisionist thesis

settler colonialism

separate spheres

transmigrants

REFERENCES

Abdill, Aasha 2018. *Fathering from the Margins: An Intimate Examination of Black Fatherhood.* New York: Columbia University Press.

Adam, Erin. 2017. "Intersectional Coalitions: The Paradoxes of Rights-Based Movement Building in LGBTQ and Immigrant Communities." *Law & Society Review* 51(1): 132–167.

American Immigration Council. 2019. *Policies Affecting Asylum Seekers at the Border.* Accessed April 09, 2021 (https://www.americanimmigrationcouncil.org/sites/default/files/research/policies_affecting_asylum_seekers_at_the_border.pdf).

American Immigration Council. 2019. *U.S. Citizen Children Impacted by Immigration Enforcement.* Accessed April 09, 2021 (https://www.americanimmigrationcouncil.org/sites/default/files/research/us_citizen_children_impacted_by_immigration_enforcement.pdf).

American Immigration Council. 2020. *Immigration Detention in the United States by Agency.* Accessed April 09, 2021 (https://www.americanimmigrationcouncil.org/sites/default/files/research/immigration_detention_in_the_united_states_by_agency.pdf).

American Psychological Association. n.d. "Undocumented Americans." Accessed December 23, 2016. http://www.apa.org/topics/immigration/undocumented-video.aspx.

Amnesty International. 2020. "Reports of Forced Sterilization of Women in ICE Detention Deeply Alarming." Accessed April 09, 2021 (https://www.amnestyusa.org/press-releases/reports-of-forced-sterilization-of-women-in-ice-detention-deeply-alarming/).

Amorim, Mariana. 2019. "Are grandparents a blessing or a burden? Multigenerational coresidence and child-related spending." *Social Science Research* 80: 132–144.

Amott, Teresa, and Julie Matthaei. 1996. *Race, Gender, and Work: A Multicultural Economic History of Women in the United States.* Boston: South End Press.

Avishai, Orit, Melanie Heath, and Jennifer Randles. 2012. "Marriage Goes to School." *Contexts* 11, no. 3: 34–38

Baldwin, James. 1963. *The Fire Next Time.* New York: Vintage.

Beoku-Betts, Josephine A. 2000. "We Got Our Way of Cooking Things: Women, Food, and Preservation of Cultural Identity among the Gullah." In *How Sweet the Sound: The Spirit of African American Family*, edited by Nancy-Elizabeth Fitch, 414–32. Orlando, FL: Harcourt Brace.

Bialik, Kristen. June 12, 2017. Key facts about race and marriage, 50 years after Loving v. Virginia. Pew Research Center. Accessed January 10, 2021. https://www.pewresearch.org/fact-tank/2017/06/12/key-facts-about-race-and-marriage-50-years-after-loving-v-virginia/

Blake, Jamila, and Rebecca Epstein. 2019. "Listening to Black Women and Girls: Lived Experiences of Adultification Bias." The Georgetown Law Center on Poverty and Inequality. Accessed April 9, 2021 (https://www.law.georgetown.edu/poverty-inequality-center/wp-content/uploads/sites/14/2019/05/Listening-to-Black-Women-and-Girls.pdf).

Blassingame, John W. 1976. *The Slave Community: Plantation Life in the Antebellum South.* New York: Oxford University Press.

Blow, Charles. 2015. "Black Dads Are Doing Best of All." *The New York Times*, June 8 (https://www.nytimes.com/2015/06/08/opinion/charles-blow-black-dads-are-doing-the-best-of-all.html).

Bronson, Po, and Ashley Merryman. 2009. "Even Babies Discriminate." *Newsweek*, September 4. Accessed September 12, 2013. http://www.newsweek.com/even-babies-discriminate-nurtureshock-excerpt-79233.

Bunning, Mareike. 2019. "Paternal Part-Time Employment and Fathers' Long-Term Involvement in Child Care and Housework." *Journal of Marriage and Family* 81 (1): 1–2.

Buss, Fran Leeper. 1985. *Dignity: Lower-Income Women Tell of Their Lives and Struggles.* Ann Arbor: University of Michigan Press.

Calderon, Jose Zapata. 2005. "Inclusion or Exclusion: One Immigrant's Experience of Cultural and Structural Barriers to Power Sharing and Unity." In *Minority Voices: Linking Personal Ethnic History and the Sociological Imagination*, edited by John P. Myers, 106–20. Boston: Pearson.

Carter, Clarence H. 2018. Healthy Marriage and Relationship Education: Strengthening Family Bonds and Increasing Economic Independence. August 23. Accessed January 10, 2021. https://www.hhs.gov/blog/2018/08/23/healthy-marriage-and-relationship-education.html

Cho, Sumi, Kimberlé Williams Crenshaw, and Leslie McCall. "Toward a field of intersectionality studies: Theory, applications, and praxis." *Signs: Journal of Women in Culture and Society* 38, no. 4 (2013): 785–810.

Choi, K., and Marta Tienda. 2017. "Marriage-Market Constraints and Mate-Selection Behavior: Racial, Ethnic, and Gender Differences in Intermarriage." *Journal of Marriage and Family* 79(2): 301–317.

Cohn, D'vera, and Jeffrey S. Passel. April 5, 2018. A record 64 million Americans live in multigenerational households. Pew Research Center. Accessed January 11, 2021. https://www.pewresearch.org/fact-tank/2018/04/05/a-record-64-million-americans-live-in-multigenerational-households/

Coles, Roberta L. 2009. *The Best Kept Secret: Single Black Fathers*. Lanham, MD: Rowman & Littlefield.

Collins, Patricia Hill. 1998. "It's All in the Family: Intersections of Gender, Race, and Nation." *Hypatia* 13, no. 3: 62–82.

Coontz, Stephanie. 2010a. "The Evolution of American Families." In *Families as They Really Are*, edited by Barbara J. Risman, 30–47. New York: W. W. Norton.

Coontz, Stephanie. 2010b. "Not Much in Those Census Stories." In *Families as They Really Are*, edited by Barbara J. Risman. New York: W. W. Norton.

Coontz, Stephanie, and Nancy Folbre. 2010. "Briefing Paper: Marriage, Poverty, and Public Policy." edited by Barbara J.Risman, In *Families as They Really Are*, 185–93. New York: W. W. Norton.

Davis, Kingsley. 1984. "Wives and Work: The Sex Role Revolution and Its Consequences." *Population and Development Review* 10, no. 3: 397–417.

DePaulo, Bella. 2017. "More People Than Ever Before Are Single – and That's a Good Thing." *The Conversation*. Accessed April 09, 2021 (https://theconversation.com/more-people-than-ever-before-are-single-and-thats-a-good-thing-74658).

Dodson, Jualynne Elizabeth. 2007. "Conceptualizations and Research of African American Family Life in the United States· Some Thoughts." In *Black Families*, 4th ed., edited by Harriette PipesMcAdoo, 51–68. Thousand Oaks, CA: Sage.

Edin, Kathryn, Laura Tach, and Ronald Mincy. 2009. "Claiming Fatherhood: Race and the Dynamics of Paternal Involvement among Unmarried Men." *Annals of the American Academy of Political and Social Science* 621: 149–77.

Fang, Marina. 2020. "UN Chief Condemns 'Horrifying Global Surge' In Domestic Violence Amid Pandemic." April 6. Accessed January 10, 2021. https://www.huffpost.com/entry/coronavirus-covid-19-domestic-violence-surge_n_5e8b137fc5b6e7d76c672a4c

Feagin, Joe R. 2000. *Racist America: Roots, Current Realities, and Future Reparations*. New York: Routledge.

Flavin, Jeanne. 2009. *Our Bodies, Our Crimes: The Policing of Women's Reproduction in America*. New York: New York University Press.

Fowler, Sarah. 2019. "Where are Mom and Dad? School on Standby to Help Children in Aftermath of ICE Raids." *Clarion Ledger*, August 7. https://www.clarionledger.com/story/news/2019/08/07/what-happens-children-people-detained-ms-ice-raids-immigration/1947642001/).

Franklin, Donna. 2010. "African Americans and the Birth of Modern Marriage." In *Families as They Really Are*, edited by Barbara J. Risman, 63–74. New York: W. W. Norton.

Franklin, John Hope. 1947. *From Slavery to Freedom: A History of American Negroes*. New York: Alfred A. Knopf.

Frazier, E. Franklin. 1948. *The Negro Family in the United States*. New York: Citadel Press.

Gallup. In U.S., estimate of LGBT population rises to 4.5%. Accessed January 10, 2021. https://news.gallup.com/poll/234863/estimate-lgbt-population-rises.aspx

Genovese, Eugene D. 1974. *Roll, Jordan, Roll: The World the Slaves Made*. New York: Random House.

Glick-Schiller, Nina. 2003. "The Centrality of Ethnography in the Study of Transnational Migration: Seeing the Wetlands instead of the Swamp." In *American Arrivals*, edited by Nancy Foner, 99–128. Santa Fe, NM: School of American Research Press.

Glover, Victoria, and Peeper McDonald. (2019)."'But what are you, really?' Examining Multiracial Identity and Psychological Well-Being." *National Cross-Cultural Counseling and Education Conference for Research, Action, and Change*.https://digitalcommons.georgiasouthern.edu/ccec/2019/2019/20

Goldberg, Shoshana, and Kerith Conron. July, 2018. "How Many Same Sex Couples in the U.S. are raising Children?" UCLA School of Law Williams Institute. Accessed January 10, 2021. https://williamsinstitute.law.ucla.edu/publications/same-sex-parents-us/

Gordon, Milton. 1964. *Assimilation in American Life: The Role of Race, Religion and Natural Origins*. Oxford, England: Oxford University Press.

Griffith, Annette K. 2020. "Parental Burnout and Child Maltreatment During the COVID-19 Pandemic." *Journal of FamilyViolence* (2020): 1–7.

Hagerman, Margaret. 2018. *White Kids: Growing Up with Privilege in a Racially Divided America*. New York, NY: New York University Press.

Harris, Kirk. 2018. "Low-Income Black Fathers Want to be Good Dads. The System Won't Let Them." *The Guardian*, June 17 (https://www.theguardian.com/commentisfree/2018/jun/17/black-fathers-parenting-child-support-policy-flaws).

Hattery, Angela, and Earl Smith. 2016. *The Social Dynamics of Family Violence*. Boulder, CO: Westview Press.

Hattery, Angela J., and Earl Smith. 2007. *African American Families*. Thousand Oaks, CA: Sage.

Heath, Melanie, Jennifer Randles, and Orit Avishai. 2016. "Marriage Movement." In *The Wiley Blackwell Encyclopedia of Family Studies*, edited by Constance L. Shehan. Malden, MA: John Wiley.

Herdt, Gilbert H., 1996. *Third Sex, Third Gender: Beyond Sexual Dimorphism in Culture and History*. New York: Zone.

Hill, Shirley A. 2005. *Black Intimacies: A Gender Perspective on Families and Relationships*. Walnut Creek, CA: AltaMira Press.

Hurtado, Aida. 2003. *Voicing Chicana Feminisms: Young Women Speak Out on Sexuality and Identity*. New York: New York University Press.

Hymowitz, Carole, and Michaele Weissman. 1978. *A History of Women in America*. New York: Bantam Books.

Ingraham, Chrys. 2013. "Heterosexuality: It's Just Not Natural." In *Sex, Gender, and Sexuality: The New Basics*, edited by Abby L. Ferber, Kimberly Holcomb, and Tre Wentling, 99–106. New York: Oxford University Press.

Ishkanian, Armine, and Anita Peña Saavedra. 2019. "The politics and practices of intersectional prefiguration in social movements: The case of Sisters Uncut." *The Sociological Review* 67, no. 5 (2019): 985–1001.

Joint Center for Housing Studies of Harvard University. 2019. Housing America's Older Adults 2019. Accessed January 10, 2021. https://www.jchs.harvard.edu/sites/default/files/Harvard_JCHS_Housing_Americas_Older_Adults_2019.pdf

Jones, Jeffrey M. 2016. "Same-Sex Marriages Up One Year after Supreme Court Verdict." Gallup, Social Issues, June 22. Accessed December 27, 2016. http://www.gallup.com/poll/193055/sex-marriages-one-year-supreme-court-verdict.aspx?g_source=Social%20Issues&g_medium=newsfeed&g_campaign=tiles

Jones, Rachel K., and Jenna Jerman. 2017. "Abortion Incidence and Service Availability in the United States, 2011." *Perspectives on Sexual and Reproductive Health* 46, no. 1: 3–14.

Joyner, Charles. 2000. "Gullah: A Creole Language." In *How Sweet the Sound: The Spirit of African American Family*, edited by Nancy-Elizabeth Fitch, 461–86. Orlando, FL: Harcourt Brace.

Kim, Yeonwoo, Sharon Lee, Hyejin Jung, Jose Jaime, and Catherine Cubbin. "Is neighborhood poverty harmful to every child? Neighborhood poverty, family poverty, and behavioral problems among young children." *Journal of community psychology* 47, no. 3 (2019): 594–610.

Kohler-Hausmann, Julilly. 2007. "The Crime of Survival: Fraud Prosecutions, Community Surveillance, and the Original Welfare Queen." *Journal of Social History* 41, no. 2: 329–54.

Lawson, Monica, Megan H. Piel, and Michaela Simon. "Child maltreatment during the COVID-19 pandemic: consequences of parental job loss on psychological and physical abuse towards children." *Child abuse & neglect* (2020): 104709.

Lefkovitz, Alison. 2011. "Men in the House: Race, Welfare, and the Regulation of Men's Sexuality in the United States, 1961–1972." *Journal of the History of Sexuality* 20, no. 3: 594–614.

Lemmons, Brianna P., and Waldo E. Johnson. 2019. "Game Changers: A Critical Race Theory Analysis of the Economic, Social, and Political Factors Impacting Black Fatherhood and Family Formation." *Social Work in Public Health*.

Livingston, Gretchen. 2018. "The Changing Profile of Unmarried Parents." Washington, DC: Pew Research Center. Accessed April 09, 2021 (https://www.pewresearch.org/social-trends/wp-content/uploads/sites/3/2018/04/Unmarried-Parents-Full-Report-PDF.pdf).

Livingston, Gretchen, and Anna Brown. 2017. "Intermarriage in the U.S. 50 Years After *Loving v. Virginia*." Washington, DC: Pew Research Center. Accessed April 09, 2021 (https://www.pewresearch.org/social-trends/2017/05/18/intermarriage-in-the-u-s-50-years-after-loving-v-virginia/).

Lopez, Iris. 1987. "Sterilization among Puerto Rican Women in New York City: Public Policy and Social Constraints." In *Cities of the United States: Studies in Urban Anthropology*, edited by Leith Mullings, 269–91. New York: Columbia University Press.

Luibhéid, Eithne. 2002. *Entry Denied: Controlling Sexuality at the Border*. Minneapolis: University of Minnesota Press.

MacLean, Maggie. 2014. "19th Century Midwives." History of American Women (blog). Accessed December 27, 2016. http://www.womenhistoryblog.com/2014/06/19th-century-midwives.html.

Marks, Stephen R. 2000. "Teasing Out the Lessons of the 1960s: Family Diversity and Family Privilege." *Journal of Marriage and the Family* 62, no. 3 (August): 609–22.

Masci, David, Anna Brown, and Jocelyn Kiley June 24, 2019. 5 facts About Same Sex Marriage. Pew research center. Accessed January 10, 2021. https://www.pewresearch.org/fact-tank/2019/06/24/same-sex-marriage/

McAdoo, Harriette Pipes, 2007. *Black Families*. 4th ed. Thousand Oaks, CA: Sage.

Meadows-Fernandez, A. Rochaun. 2020. "Why Won't Society Let Black Girls Be Children?". *The New York Times*, April 17 (https://www.nytimes.com/2020/04/17/parenting/adultification-black-girls.html).

Miller, Richard B., and Cara A. Nebeker-Adams. 2017. "Multigenerational Households." *Encyclopedia of Couple and Family Therapy*. Lebow et al. (eds.), Springer International Publishing AG 2017J.L.

Moore, Mignon R. 2011. *Invisible Families: Gay Identities, Relationships, and Motherhood among Black Women*. Berkeley: University of California Press.

Movement Advancement Project. 2017. "Marriage and Relationship Recognition Laws." Accessed April 16, 2017. http://www.lgbtmap.org/equality-maps/marriage_relationship_laws.

MSN News. 2012. "Racism 'Harms Children's Learning.'" March 9. Accessed October 21, 2013. http://news.uk.msn.com/racism-harms-childrens-learning.

National Coalition Against Domestic Violence. 2015."Domestic Violence National Statistics." Accessed June 2, 2017. http://ncadv.org/files/National%20Statistics%20Domestic%20Violence%20NCADV.pdf.

National Coalition Against Domestic Violence. 2020. Accessed October 10, 2020. https://www.ncadv.org/

Otsuka, Julie. 2011. *The Buddha in the Attic*. New York: Vintage.

Pan American Health Organization. n.d. "Domestic Violence during Pregnancy." Fact sheet, Women, Health & Development Program. Accessed October 29, 2012. http://www.paho.org/english/ad/ge/vawpregnancy.pdf.

Perkins, Kiran M., Sheree L. Boulet, Denise J. Jamieson, Dmitry M. Kissin, and National Assisted Reproductive Technology Surveillance System. 2016. "Trends and outcomes of gestational surrogacy in the United States." *Fertility and Sterility* 106, no. 2 (2016): 435-442.

Perry, Sylvia P., Allison L. Skinner, and Jamie L. Abai. 2019. "Bias awareness predicts color conscious racial socialization methods among White parents." *Journal of Social Issues* 75, no. 4 (2019): 1035-1056.

Prell, Riv-Ellen. 1999. *Fighting to Become Americans: Jews, Gender, and the Anxiety of Assimilation*. Boston: Beacon Press.

PRRI. 2015. "American Values Atlas." Accessed April 09, 2021 (http://ava.prri.org/).

Qian, Zhenchao, and Daniel T. Lichter. "Marriage markets and intermarriage: Exchange in first marriages and remarriages." *Demography* 55, no. 3 (2018): 849–875.

Risman, Barbara J., 2010. *Families as They Really Are*. New York: W. W. Norton.

Roos, Leslie L., Elizabeth Wall-Wieler, and Janelle Boram Lee. 2019. "Poverty and early childhood outcomes." *Pediatrics* 143, no. 6 (2019).

Roscoe, Will. 1998. *Changing Ones: Third and Fourth Genders in Native North America*. New York: St. Martin's Press.

Sharma, Amalesh, and Sourav Bikash Borah. "Covid-19 and domestic violence: an indirect path to social and economic crisis." *Journal of family violence* (2020): 1–7.

Skinner, Allison L., and Caitlin M. Hudac. 2017. "Yuck, You Disgust Me!': Affective Bias against Interracial Couples." *Journal of Experimental Social Psychology* 68 (January): 68–77.

Soehl, Thomas, and Roger Waldinger. 2010. "Making the Connections: Latino Immigrants and Their Cross-Border Ties." *Ethnic and Racial Studies* 33, no. 9: 1489–1510.

Solinger, Rickie. 2007. *Pregnancy and Power: A Short History of Reproductive Politics in America*. New York: New York University Press.

Solinger, Rickie. 2010. "The First Welfare Case: Money, Sex, Marriage, and White Supremacy in Selma, 1966—A Reproductive Justice Analysis." *Journal of Women's History* 22, no. 3: 13–38.

Solinger, Rickie. 2013. *Wake Up Little Susie: Single Pregnancy and Race before Roe v. Wade*. New York: Routledge.

Solis, Rogelio, and Jeff Amy. 2019. "Largest US Immigration Raids in a Decade Net 680 Arrests." *AP News*, August 7 (https://apnews.com/article/bbcef8ddae4e4303983c91880559cf23).

Tamm, Marcus. 2019. "Fathers' parental leave-taking, childcare involvement and labor market participation." *Labour Economics* 59 (2019): 184–197.

Tehranian, John. 2009. *White Washed: America's Invisible Middle Eastern Minority.* New York: New York University Press.

Towle, Evan B., and Lynn Marie Morgan. 2002. "Romancing the Transgender Native: Rethinking the Use of the 'Third Gender' Concept." *GLQ: A Journal of Lesbian and Gay Studies* 8, no. 4: 469–97.

Twine, France Winddance. 2011. *Outsourcing the Womb: Race, Class, and Gestational Surrogacy in a Global Market.* New York: Routledge.

United States Census Bureau. 2018. *Current Population Survey: 2018 Annual Social and Economic Supplement.* Accessed April 09, 2021 (https://www2.census.gov/programs-surveys/cps/techdocs/cpsmar18.pdf).

United States Census Bureau. 2018. *Current Population Survey: All Parent/Child Situations, by Type, Race, and Hispanic Origin of Householder or Reference Person: 1970 to Present.* Accessed April 09, 2021 (https://www.census.gov/data/tables/time-series/demo/families/families.html).

United States Census Bureau, American Community Survey. 2017. "Selected Characteristics of People at Specified Levels of Poverty in the Past 12 Months." Accessed April 09, 2021 (https://data.census.gov/cedsci/table?q=S17&d=ACS%201-Year%20Estimates%20Subject%20Tables&tid=ACSST1Y2017.S1703&hidePreview=false).

U.S. Bureau of Labor Statistics. 2020. "Employment Characteristics of Families Summary." Accessed January 9, 2021. https://www.bls.gov/news.release/famee.nr0.htm

U.S. Census Bureau. 2015. "Families and Living Arrangements: Current Population Survey." Accessed January 23, 2017. https://www.census.gov/hhes/families/data/cps2015C .html.

U.S. Census Bureau. 2016."Families and Living Arrangements: Historical Time Series."Accessed January 19, 2017. https://www.census.gov/hhes/families/data/historical.html.

U.S. Census Bureau. 2020. "Families and Households Visualizations." Accessed January 9, 2021 https://www.census.gov/library/visualizations/2020/comm/grandparents-work-support-grand-children.html

U.S. Census Bureau. 2020b "Census Bureau releases new estimates on America's families and Living Arrangements." Accessed January 9, 2021 https://www.census.gov/newsroom/press-releases/2020/estimates-families-living-arrangements.html

Vittrup, Brigitte. 2016. "Color Blind or Color Conscious? White American Mothers Approaches to Racial Socialization." *Journal of Family Issues* 39(3).

Vizenor, Gerald. 1995. *Native American Literature.* New York: HarperCollins.

Wang, Wendy. 2015. "Interracial Marriage: Who Is 'Marrying Out'?" Fact Tank, Pew Research Center, June 12. Accessed December 23, 2016. http://www.pewresearch.org/fact-tank/2015/06/12/interracial-marriage-who-is-marrying-out.

Wong, Nellie. 1983. "When I Was Growing Up." In *This Bridge Called My Back: Writing by Radical Women of Color,* edited by Cherrie Moraga and Gloria Anzaldúa. Latham, NY: Kitchen Table/Women of Color Press.

Wu, Judy Tzu-Chun. 2001. "Was Mom Chung a 'Sister Lesbian'? Asian American Gender Experimentation and Interracial Homoeroticism." *Journal of Women's History* 13, no. 1 (Spring): 58–82. doi:10.1353/jowh.2001.0028.

Wu, Yi, Vivek Sah, and Alan Tidwell. 2018. "Housing preferences of Asian and Hispanic/Latino immigrants in the United States: a melting pot or salad bowl." *Real Estate Economics* 46, no. 4: 783–835.

Yang, Philip Q. 2011. *Asian Immigration to the United States.* Cambridge: Polity Press.

Zaher, Claudia. 2002. "When a Woman's Marital Status Determined Her Legal Status: A Research Guide on the Common Law Doctrine of Coverture." *Law Library Journal* 94, no. 3.

Zambrana, Ruth Enid. 2011. *Latinos in American Society: Families and Communities in Transition*. Ithaca, NY: Cornell University Press.

4 WORK AND WEALTH INEQUITY

With high expenses for healthcare and housing, many families have little money saved. A job loss, even with unemployment benefits, can be economically devastating. Eligible Californians, like those seen here, can apply for cash aid on a short-term basis.

Credit: Bob Chamberlain/Los Angeles Times/Getty Images

LEARNING OBJECTIVES

4.1 Describe the current patterns of income and wealth inequality in the United States.

4.2 Compare various stock stories about economic inequality.

4.3 Apply the matrix perspective to the historical foundations of economic inequality.

4.4 Analyze potential solutions to the problem of economic inequality.

Marvin's African American family believed a college degree was the path to success. His father taught him that the two things no one could take away from him were his integrity and his education. Marvin was lucky; according to *Consumer Reports*, only one out of ten Black high school students attending public school in his state of Ohio go on to graduate from college (2019). Marvin was a star athlete in high school and received an athletic scholarship to attend Kent State University. Nevertheless, he had to take out over $5,000 in loans his first year to pay for medical treatments for sports injuries he sustained while in high school, as well as to cover his basic needs like food and clothing. He suffered his second back injury during his sophomore year. After that he lost his athletic scholarship but was committed to completing his degree. To do this he maxed out his student loans to pay for his remaining schooling and to support himself. After graduating with $52,000 in student debt, he then pursued a graduate degree, which cost another $40,000 in student loans. He was simultaneously working full-time at a nonprofit where he earned $25,000 per year helping kids like himself to pursue their dreams of college. Earning his bachelor's and master's degrees left him with over $90,000 in debt (Consumer Reports 2019).

Marvin's story is not unusual. Americans owe nearly $1.6 trillion in student loan debt (Singeltary 2019). African Americans owe more in debt that any other racialized group. Women owe more than two thirds of all student loan debt, and at the intersection of race and gender, Black women, as a group, owe more than anyone else (AAUW 2021). This is largely due to the unequal amounts of wealth held by families in the U.S., which gives some people an advantage from the start. On the other end, income inequity after graduation makes it more challenging for some to repay this debt (AAUW 2021).

Scholars who have analyzed social identities such as class, race, gender, sexual orientation, ability/disability, and age have identified economic inequity and the organization of work as key locations where inequality originates and is reproduced in our society. In this chapter we will examine economic inequality across racial groups and how other social identities, like gender and class, intersect with race, which in turn leads to different life outcomes for people within the same racial categories. Income and wealth inequality and the various factors that contribute to it, including economic shifts and social policy, are also key to understanding how and why economic inequality exists. We will also examine the stories we tell about work, wealth, and inequality that obstruct or support social change to reduce these gaps.

TRENDS IN WORK AND WEALTH

The U.S. economy is described as **capitalist**—that is, it is an economy in which the means of production are held and controlled by private owners, not the government, and in which prices are set by the forces of supply and demand with minimal government interference. In practice, U.S. capitalism is modified by government regulation, and some resources are under public ownership (although this is on the decline). Despite its status as one of the wealthiest nations in the world, the United States is also one of the most unequal (Alston 2017). Starting around the 1920s and 1930s, economic inequality began declining in the United States and in many European nations, but from the 1970s on, we have experienced sharp increases. The World

Economic Forum has declared it a "major threat to social stability" (Oxfam 2017). Global wealth inequality is dramatically unbalanced, with only twenty-six individuals owning more than 50% of the world's wealth (Lemon 2019).

Increasing Inequality

Recently, the 2020 pandemic of the virus COVID-19 has laid bare these vast economic inequities. While everyone is feeling its effects, widespread job lay-offs are impacting those without race, class, and gender privilege the most. With less savings, lower rates of home ownership, and far fewer assets, they do not have the wealth to help mitigate the impact of job losses, lower wages, healthcare costs, and more. All of these consequences are disproportionately devastating Black and brown communities (Sandoui 2020).

Even before the pandemic, data has consistently shown that people of color and poor Whites actually pay higher prices for essential goods and services, including cars, car insurance, car loans, rent, gasoline, groceries, and even toilet paper (Badger 2016; Brown 2009; Desmond and Wilmers 2019; Orhun and Palazzolo 2019; Silber 2017). Because many live paycheck to paycheck, they aren't often able to stock up on paper goods and food when items are on sale and prices are lowest. This has long been the case and is compounded for poor communities living in food deserts where diverse, healthy food options are not available. When it comes to loans, middle- and upper-class Whites have greater access to mainstream financial institutions, so they do not have to rely on "payday lenders" or check-cashing services that charge exorbitantly high interest rates (Oliver and Shapiro 2006).

Income

Social scientists use two factors to measure economic inequality: income and wealth. **Income** consists of the flow of all incoming funds: earnings from work, profit from items sold, and returns on investments. Between 2000 and 2018, the wages earned by the lowest 10% of earners increased by less than $1.00 per hour (from $8.93 to $9.97), while the top 5% saw wages grow by almost $13.00 per hour, from $50.46 to $63.10. White workers' wage growth was strongest during the last year, reflecting the continued growth of income inequality. The differences are starker when we examine race. Figure 4.1 reveals the differences in hourly wages between 2000 and 2018, comparing Hispanics, Blacks, and Whites. The degree of inequity has increased over this period of time, even when controlling for other factors such as education, location, age, and gender.

Figure 4.1 shows us the intersections of race and class. For example, the richest Latinx population receives significantly lower wages than the richest White people ($44.23 vs. $72.05).

While education has been assumed to be an equalizer for racial income gaps, that has not been the case. Figure 4.2 examines hourly wage inequality in 2000 and 2018, broken down by both race and educational attainment. There is very little wage growth at all educational levels, and the racial wage gap has expanded.

Consequently, since 2000, White privilege has facilitated a $70,642 rise in median income, $51,450 for Hispanics, and a decrease of $41,361 for Blacks (Washington Post 6-4-20).

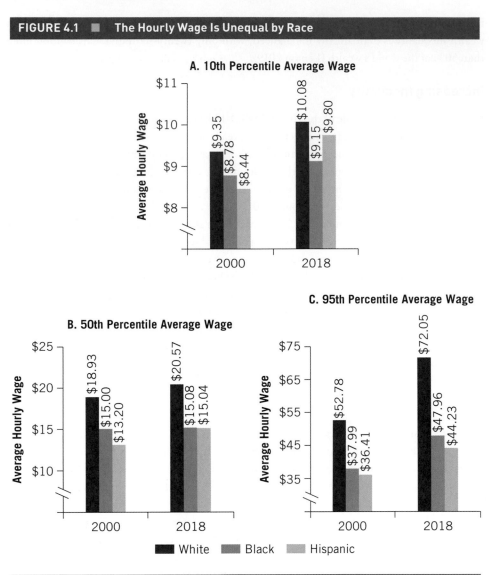

FIGURE 4.1 ■ The Hourly Wage Is Unequal by Race

A. 10th Percentile Average Wage

B. 50th Percentile Average Wage

C. 95th Percentile Average Wage

■ White   ■ Black   ■ Hispanic

Note: Sample based on all workers ages 16 and older. The xth-percentile wage is the wage at which x% of wage earners earn less and (100-x)% earn more. Race/ethnicity categories are mutually exclusive (i.e., White non-Hispanic, Black non-Hispanic, and Hispanic any race).

Source: Data from EPI analysis of Current Population Survey Outgoing Rotation Group microdata from the U.S. Census Bureau.

Wealth

In contrast to income, **wealth** (or capital) consists of the market value of all assets owned, such as a home, a car, artwork, jewelry, a business, and savings and retirement accounts, minus any debts owed, such as credit card debt, mortgages, and student loans (Saez and Zucman 2016).

FIGURE 4.2   ■   Average Hourly Wages by Race/Ethnicity and Education

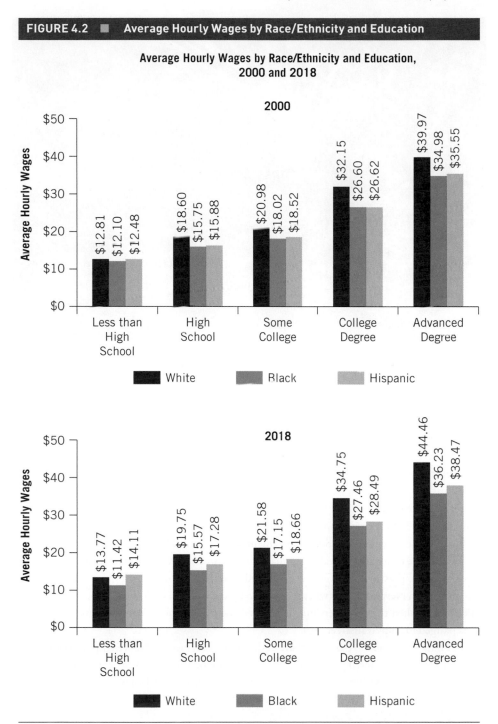

Average Hourly Wages by Race/Ethnicity and Education,
2000 and 2018

Source: Data from EPI analysis of Current Population Survey Outgoing Rotation Group microdata from the U.S. Census Bureau.

The Occupy movement began in 2011 to protest rising inequality, particularly targeting Wall Street financial firms. The group's slogan is "We are the 99%" to highlight the vast disparities in wealth and income in the U.S.

Credit: Carolyn Cole/Los Angeles Times/Getty Images

Looking closely at the wealthiest members of society, .01% own the same amount of wealth as the bottom 90%. In fact, the top .00025% (about 400 individuals) have quadrupled their wealth in the past decade (Holodny 2017; Piketty and Saez 2014; Zucman 2019). Half of all Americans saw their wealth decrease from 4% to 1% (Pedro Nicolaci de Casta 2019). 100% of the wealth increase immediately following the Great Recession (between 2009 and 2011), went to the richest 7%, while everyone else continued to lose wealth. These inequities have been the key focus of the Occupy Wall Street movement. Begun in 2011, this social movement focuses attention on the tremendous wealth gap that exists between 99% of the country and the top 1%. This leaderless, grassroots movement organized hundreds of protests in cities across the U.S. The first was in New York City where people occupied Zuccotti Park for 59 days before a major police raid pushed the protesters out or arrested them. The movement continues, but tactics have changed (occupywallstreet.org).

The data in Figure 4.3 paint a picture of dramatic class inequality. We employ a broad definition of **class** here, referring to "enduring and systematic differences in access to and control over resources for provisioning and survival" (Acker 2006, 444). When we bring in race, we see another dimension of income and wealth inequality.

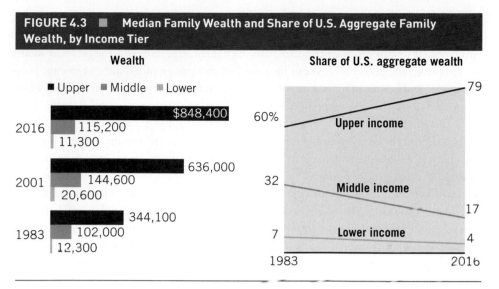

FIGURE 4.3 ■ Median Family Wealth and Share of U.S. Aggregate Family Wealth, by Income Tier

Note: Families are assigned to income tiers based on their size-adjusted income.

Source: Pew Research Center Analysis of the Survey of Consumer Finances.

While COVID-19 has economically devastated millions of Americans, some have actually benefitted:

- Between March and June 2020, the wealth of all US billionaires combined increased over $637 billion dollars.

- The top five billionaires in the nation increased their wealth by $101.7 billion.

This is an increase of 26% of their total wealth. During those same three months, approximately 44 million people were laid off and had to apply for unemployment. Latinx and African American people have been hit hardest by the layoffs, and the median wealth of Black families is only 8.7% of that of White families, a larger gap than existed in the late 1960s, and despite decades of growing Black wealth (Hansen 2020).

Economists have come to the grim conclusion that the racial wealth gap is larger than it was 100 years ago (Hansen 2020). There is a racial wealth gap at every income level, and education does not eliminate this gap. Comparing the median wealth gap for adults with a college degree, Whites have 7.2 times the amount of wealth held by Blacks, and almost four times that of Latinx (Oliver and Shapiro 2019; Pfeffer and Killewald 2019). Further, recent research finds that higher education widens the racial wealth gap (not just the income gap) due to the burden of student loan debt. If a student's tuition can be partially or fully paid by their family, they do not need to rely on loans. White students taking out loans generally pay off over 90% within

20 years, while Black students still owe over 90% after that same amount of time (Sullivan, Meschede, Shapiro, and Escobar 2019).

The racial wealth gap is much wider than the income gap, reflecting the fact that wealth is transmitted over generations. It can be passed down through inheritance of money, property, stocks, and bonds, or in the form of access to education and paid tuition. Passing a family business on to the next generation is another form of wealth transmittal (Conley 2009; Lareau 2011).

In addition, the racial wealth gap grows much larger over the average person's life span. Those with more to begin with have the resources (education, financial support) to accumulate more wealth during their lifetimes. Wealth has a far greater overall impact than income on an individual's life, because wealth also provides the opportunities that make a higher income possible. Wealth can pay for a better education, a home that may appreciate in value, and better and more accessible healthcare; it gives families opportunities to invest so that their money is making more money for them, and allows them to accumulate savings that can help them make it through rough times, job changes, and retirement. Wealth allows parents to give their children a significant head start. Recent research argues, "Wealth is where the past shows up in the present. From slavery to Jim Crow, to redlining, to mass incarceration, the division of assets on the basis of race has been explicit public policy for centuries" (Collins, Asante-Muhammed, Hoxie, and Terry 2019).

For example, valuable and resource-rich Native American lands have been stolen over hundreds of years, and Native populations have been generally forced to live on difficult-to-farm reservations with few natural resources. This has denied them opportunities to accumulate assets, not to mention support themselves as they once did. Most Indian country has been declared to have no value, and it has been extremely difficult to secure bank loans to build homes and maintain existing property. Reservation Indians have long been the poorest racial minority group in the U.S. (Carpenter and Riley 2019; Leonard, Parker, and Anderson 2018).

For African Americans freed after slavery, Reconstruction briefly helped them to make some economic and political gains. Black men were given the vote, and families were promised 40 acres to begin new, financially stable lives. Following the death of President Lincoln, it did not take long for President Andrew Johnson to reverse this promise in 1866. He proclaimed: "This is a country for white men, and by God, as long as I am President, it shall be a government for white men." The gains made under Reconstruction were destroyed as entire Black towns were decimated, and hundreds murdered by rioting Whites claiming the land for themselves. Rioters were aided and protected by local White law enforcement and faced no consequences. According to economist William Darity, "You have limited opportunity to accumulate wealth, and then you have a process where that wealth is destroyed or taken away… And all of that is prior to the effects of restrictive covenants—redlining, the discriminatory application of the G.I. Bill and other federal programs" (Lee 2019).

Poverty

The poverty levels in the United States are further evidence of the nation's inequitable distribution of income and wealth. Compared with nations around the globe, the U.S. is 33rd when it comes to the percentage of people living in poverty (Alston 2017; OECD 2020).

The U.S. Department of Health and Human Services set the federal poverty guidelines for 2020 at $26,200 per year for a family of four and at $12,760 for just one adult (Department of Health and Human Services 2020). According to the U.S. Census, the official poverty rate is 11.8% (Semega, Kollar, Creamer, and Mohanty 2019). Figure 4.4 offers a picture of poverty by race in 2019. About one fourth of all American Indian and Alaskan Natives live in poverty, followed closely by Hispanics. One-third of all African American and Native American children grow up in poverty (Hamilton, 2019).

1.5 million households with children survive (barely) on just $2.00 per person per day, significantly below the government's definition of "deep poverty." **Deep poverty** refers to those living at least 50% beneath the poverty threshold (Center for Inequality and Poverty Research 2019). Households in deep poverty have more than doubled since the mid-1990s (Edin and Shaefer 2015).

The impact of COVID-19 has been dramatic for the majority of households in the U.S., but it is hitting African American, Latinx, Native American, and immigrant communities

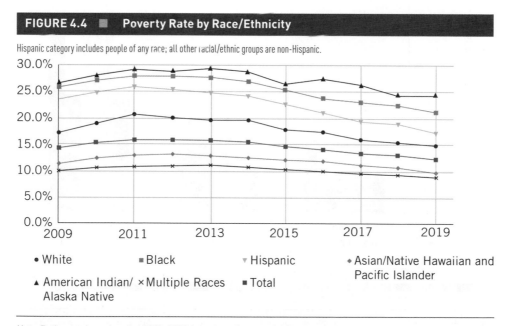

FIGURE 4.4 ■ Poverty Rate by Race/Ethnicity

Hispanic category includes people of any race; all other racial/ethnic groups are non-Hispanic.

Legend:
- White
- Black
- Hispanic
- Asian/Native Hawaiian and Pacific Islander
- American Indian/ Alaska Native
- Multiple Races
- Total

Note: Estimates based on the 2008-2019 American Community Survey.

Source: Kaiser Family Foundation's State Health Facts

the hardest. Evictions, homelessness, and hunger rates are all spiking. More than one in four children are going hungry and living in households behind in their rent or mortgage payments (Center on Budget and Policy Priorities 2020). Figures 4.5 and 4.6 reveal the rates of those struggling financially in various ways, as broken down by racial/ethnic categories and gender.

Figure 4.6 displays changes in unemployment during 2020. The Bureau of Labor Statistics does not have up-to-date numbers for Alaskan Natives and American Indians; however, in 2018 they had the highest unemployment rates of any racialized group at 6.6%, compared to the national average of 3.9%. Indigenous people of every age have higher rates of disability, have lower levels of educational attainment, and are more likely to hold jobs in the service sector than any other marginalized group (Bureau of Labor Statistics 2019).

FIGURE 4.5 ■ Everyone Facing Great Economic Hardships During COVID-19, But Impact Varies Based on Race/Ethnicity

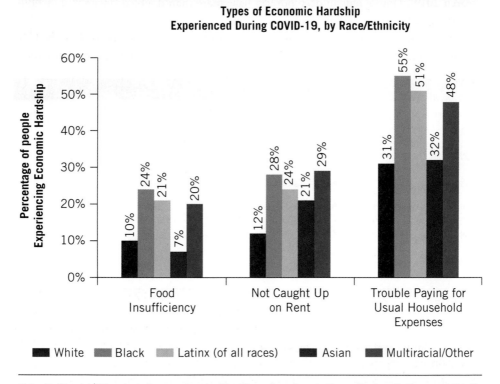

Types of Economic Hardship Experienced During COVID-19, by Race/Ethnicity

Note: Multiracial/Other includes people who identify as American Indians, Alaskan Natives, and Pacific Islanders in addition to multiracial. Those who did not respond are not included in the data. Latino includes people of any race, while the racial categories exclude those who identified their ethnicity as Latino.

Source: Data from Figures 2, 3, and 5 of CBPP's COVID Hardship Watch.

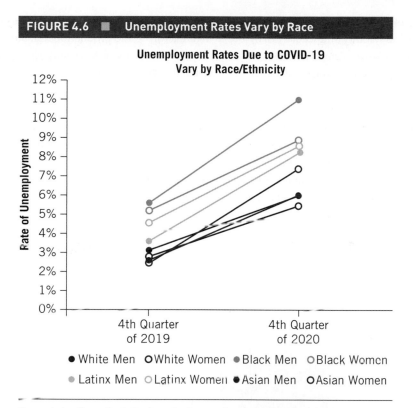

FIGURE 4.6 ■ Unemployment Rates Vary by Race

Unemployment Rates Due to COVID-19
Vary by Race/Ethnicity

● White Men   ○ White Women   ● Black Men   ○ Black Women
● Latinx Men   ○ Latinx Women   ● Asian Men   ○ Asian Women

Source: Labor Force Statistics from the Current Population Survey, U.S. Bureau of Labor Statistics, Accessed January 11, 2021.

Economic Restructuring and Changing Occupations

Today's global capitalist economy is different from the agrarian, rural economy of the past, and as it continues to change, it is altering the ways we work and live.

Economic Change

Both globalization and advances in communications and other technologies have contributed to the shift in the United States from a manufacturing economy that produced physical goods to a service economy that provides services such as banking, healthcare, retail sales, and entertainment. Cheap labor overseas, especially in developing countries, has motivated many U.S. manufacturing companies to move their production activities abroad, closing tens of thousands of U.S. factories and eliminating millions of jobs (Alderson 2015; Dunn 2012; Forbes 2004). Between 2000 and 2018 alone, the U.S. lost one-third of all manufacturing jobs, and those that remain pay relatively less than they did in the past (Bartik 2018; Levinson 2019). The result is that most U.S. job growth in recent years has been in the service sector, where work is lower paying, often part-time and temporary, and much less likely to provide benefits. These jobs also provide less stability and security than jobs in manufacturing and production did. Sociologists refer to this broad historical shift as **economic restructuring**, and it has been accompanied by growing wealth and income inequality (Andersen 2001; Dunn 2012).

Occupational Change

While the service sector also includes higher-paying, skilled jobs in fields such as information technology, growth has been far greater in more labor-intensive service-sector jobs (Collins and Mayer 2010, 7). The three largest occupational categories today—healthcare and social assistance, retail trade, and accommodation and food services—all pay significantly less than manufacturing jobs, and many require significant degrees of emotional labor, often not recognized as labor at all. These sectors employ large numbers of White women and people of color (U.S. Bureau of Labor Statistics 2015, 2016).

With the rise in joblessness starting with the financial crisis and the recession of 2007–2009, many more people are now forced to work part-time or temporary jobs, frequently

Payday loan and check-cashing businesses charge high fees and interest rates but are often the only option for people living paycheck to paycheck.

Credit: Bloomberg/Getty Images

multiple part-time jobs at once. The largest occupational categories have a few things in common:

- They employ large numbers of part-time workers (which means no benefits or retirement contributions).

- They are very low paying and have been experiencing stagnant wages.

- They offer very few opportunities for growth within the field and provide little job security.

New jobs in the service sector, such as ride-sharing (think Lyft and Uber) are similar (Condon 2019; Taylor and Omer 2019). Between June 2019 and June 2020, the service-providing industry experienced the most drastic job loss compared to all other industries, and these losses have continued to plummet as the pandemic has persisted (Bureau of Labor Statistics 2020). Small businesses and hourly employees, some of those most impacted by COVID-19, are disproportionally women and people of color.

Outsourcing

Outsourcing is another trend. For example, the Tennessee Valley Authority, which supplies electricity for numerous states, plans to build three new massive generators in Poland, and use temporary work visas to hire foreign workers to fill 20% of their technology jobs. Workers have already taken significant pay and benefits cuts they were told were required to compete with other nations. Meanwhile, the CEO has been earning approximately eight million dollars (and this is in the bottom one fourth of CEOs in large tech companies) (Miller 2020).

White-collar jobs are increasingly being outsourced in fields such as accounting and technical consulting. The foreign workers who are employed by these companies are paid 35% less than tech firm employees in the United States doing comparable work. Outsourcing this labor also exacerbates the tech industry's "diversity problem." The proportion of Blacks and Latinx working directly for tech firms is only 10%, whereas Blacks and Latinx make up 26% of white-collar contract workers and 58% of blue-collar contract workers, whose average annual pay is just $19,000 (Benner and Neering 2016; Silicon Valley Rising 2016).

We often hear about innovative tech workplaces where white-collar employees get free gourmet meals and access to on-site fitness centers, but these high-paying positions are held by a fraction of the firms' employees. The growth in the numbers of outsourced, low-paid workers has been significant. High-tech companies avoid paying worker's compensation insurance, health insurance, parental leave, childcare subsidies, and other benefits offered only to employees working directly for the company (Konkel 2020).

The Wage Gap and Occupational Segregation

Census data for 2018 reveal that for every $1.00 earned by a White man:

- Asian women earn $0.90,

- White women $0.79,

- Black women $0.62,

- American Indian and Alaska Native women $0.57, and

- Latinx women $0.54. (Bleiweis 2020)

Industry and occupation account for about 20% of the gender wage gap (Council of Economic Advisers 2015). Women in every racial category are more likely than men of the same race to be employed in service jobs, while African Americans and Hispanics have the highest rates of service employment. There are also race and gender income gaps *within* occupational categories.

The "glass ceiling" describes the forces that keep women from advancing to the highest levels of management. Recently Michael Hobbes suggested that we flip the metaphor and look at the "glass floor" that keeps the privileged from losing undeserved privilege in the workplace. For example, there are many cases of individuals born into extremely wealthy families who fail to succeed in multiple careers, but nevertheless end up with top-level jobs at major corporations. Most Americans born since 1984 have only a 50% chance of earning more than their parents, compared to 90% in 1940. This is not a concern for the very privileged, as the opportunities to bestow their own status on their offspring has only increased. Researcher Richard Reeves concludes, "There's a lot of talent being wasted because it's not able to rise, but there's also a lot of relatively untalented people who aren't falling and end up occupying positions they shouldn't" (Hobbes 2019).

In every occupation, women earn less than men in the same positions. Further, women often face a glass ceiling keeping them from advancing to the highest levels. Some have argued that women of color encounter a "sticky floor" that keeps them at the bottom rungs and in the lowest-paying jobs.

Credit: Viacheslav Iakobchuk/Alamy Stock Photo

Considering the ways in which women's experiences differ by race, women of color are said to encounter a nearly impenetrable "concrete ceiling," barring them not only from the upper echelons of power but from middle management as well. In addition to discrimination, women of color encounter a lack of mentoring and access to role models and influential people (Moore and Jones 2001; West 1999). Another factor that has a negative impact on women is wage discrimination related to parenthood; women with children often earn less than childless women, whereas income tends to increase for men who have children. Further, the lack of paid parental leave has a negative impact on women's long-term salaries and careers (Council of Economic Advisers 2015).

The U.S. ranks last among nations in terms of workers' benefits. The United States guarantees workers no paid holidays or other days off from work, and no paid sick leave or parental leave. While on the face of it this social policy is bad news for all American workers, an often-concealed story is the differential impact it has on various social groups. For example, low-income families and single parents (overwhelmingly women) whose employers choose not to offer these benefits lose proportionally more income than other workers when they must either pay extra childcare costs or take unpaid days off on national holidays, when schools are closed, or when family emergencies or illnesses require extended absences from work.

A Disappearing Social Safety Net

Soon after the inauguration of President Ronald Reagan in 1981, social benefit programs and social safety net policies that had supported workers and families through hard times saw their funding slashed. These included food stamps, education aid, and job training programs, as well as funding for mental health institutions, which led to increases in the numbers of homeless people (Eitzen and Baca Zinn 2000; Thomas 1998). At the same time, economic recessions, the shift of jobs away from manufacturing, stagnation of wages (including the minimum wage), and other structural factors led to a predicted increase in poverty. Under the Reagan presidency, from 1981 to 1989, as stable, well-paying manufacturing jobs disappeared, urban areas declined and plunged into poverty. Federal funds for public housing and rent assistance were cut in half, and 60% of federal financial support for cities was lost. Public services like hospitals, schools, libraries, and parks have continued to face funding cuts (Cohen 2014).

Taxes are another tool of government that redistributes wealth. Progressive tax rates have been slashed in recent decades, decreasing the taxes paid by the very wealthiest people and corporations. President Trump further cut taxes for those at the very top, widening the race and class wealth gap even further (Collins, Asante-Muhammed, Hoxie, and Terry 2019).

Federal and state funds have been diverted to mitigate the economic losses of businesses and individuals due to COVID-19. Without sufficient federal funds, many states are slashing budgets for preschools and childcare facilities, independent living care and programs for people with cognitive disabilities, and more (Alonzo 2020; News12 2020). The lasting economic effects of the devastating worldwide pandemic cannot be fully known yet.

The Evolution of Welfare

Welfare is a general term used to refer to policies and programs designed to support people in great financial need, providing the very basic necessities for survival. Food stamps, Social Security and Medicare benefits, and Medicaid are most frequently thought of as welfare. Today, the safety-net social policies established in the 20th century remain under attack, and many more programs are being slowly dismantled.

President Clinton replaced what was at the time called the Aid to Families with Dependent Children (AFDC) program with Temporary Assistance for Needy Families (TANF). AFDC benefits only succeeded in raising 10% of children out of poverty in the 1990s prior to the program's elimination. One of the greatest problems with AFDC was that mothers lost all benefits if they started working, even if their work income could not cover the costs of childcare and basic life necessities. A result was that welfare recipients were portrayed as people who could not take personal responsibility for their own well-being. The stereotype of the African American "welfare queen" having children in order to collect benefits became entrenched in the popular consciousness (Neubeck and Cazenave 2001; Foster 2008). This stereotype reduced resistance to the program's overhaul despite the fact that the majority of those on welfare are White (Sit 2018).

Under TANF, welfare recipients now receive less aid for a shorter period of time, and they are required to work 30 to 40 hours a week outside the home. Pursuing further education in

Corporations like Walmart now benefit from government aid to their employees, which supplements the workers' meager salaries and allows companies to keep wages low.

Credit: Gilles Mingasson/Getty Images News/Getty Images

order to get a better job is no longer an option for women receiving TANF, making it very difficult for them to improve their future opportunities. States now determine who is eligible for benefits, how much they can receive, and what work requirements are imposed, and states may limit the number of months families receive benefits. Today many people receiving TANF benefits are already working when they apply. However, their jobs pay such low wages that they cannot make ends meet. When accounting for inflation, TANF benefits today are below the levels they were in 1996 when the program began, and were no higher than 60% of the poverty line in 2020 (Safawi and Floyd 2020).

Collins and Mayer's (2010) research has found that even as the funding for government programs for the needy has been cut, such programs have also increasingly been expected to subsidize the income of the working poor and provide other safety nets once provided by employers, such as parental leave and unemployment and disability insurance (Badger 2015; Picchi 2015). For example, while Walmart pays employees so little and avoids offering employee benefits, taxpayers financially support these employees with public assistance in the form of food stamps, subsidized housing, Medicaid, and more, totaling $2.6 billion dollars (O'Connor 2014). Local governments have required other aid recipients to work as strikebreakers, taking jobs formerly held by unionized workers (Piven 2002, 26). These people are defined as "welfare recipients" rather than as workers, and in this way they are denied the rights other workers have while their efforts subsidize the labor costs of private business, and simultaneously are used to protect private corporations from workers organizing on behalf of their rights. This welfare benefits private business more than the direct welfare recipients.

When we look at the concealed story of who receives public assistance, we find that the majority of people in the United States benefit from some form of welfare, whether in the form of tax benefits, Social Security or other retirement plans receiving federal funds, Medicare, Medicaid, TANF, unemployment insurance, or food stamps. Many of these benefits are not considered "welfare" by those who receive them, especially tax benefits such as the home mortgage interest deduction, government-funded financial aid, tax-deferred savings and subsidies, business subsidies, college loans, veterans benefits, and more (Sinfield 2020).

Critical Thinking

1. Consider the ways wealth is transmitted over generations. How does this process contribute to the growing racial wealth gap? What can be done to decrease persistent racial wealth inequality?

2. What factors do you think contribute to ongoing occupational segregation based on race and gender? Which of these factors do you think are the most important contributors to the pay gap within occupations?

3. Why does wealth play a more important role than income in the perpetuation of racial inequality?

4. Have you, your family, or your friends been negatively impacted by COVID-19? How? What will have to change for you and others to recover financially?

STOCK STORIES OF ECONOMIC INEQUALITY

The myth of the American Dream is perhaps nowhere more deeply entrenched than in the institution of work. For hundreds of years, immigrants have come to the United States seeking economic opportunity and a chance at prosperity. "Work hard and you will be rewarded," we are told. As for those who do not succeed, well, they must be doing something wrong. How true is this stock story? Is success equally available to everyone in our society?

Neoliberal Theory

Relying on the stock stories we are told about economic success, we tend to blame individuals, or their cultures, for their lack of achievement. This stock story of the American Dream has become "common sense" for many of us—it pervades the media and, often, school curricula. However, it fails to consider the broader social context.

This stock story is based on **neoliberal theory** (sometimes referred to as market fundamentalism), which is a foundational perspective that shapes global economic policy today. Neoliberal theory embraces individualism, free markets, free trade, and limited government intervention or regulation (Dekker 2020; Weller and Hersh 2002; World Health Organization 2005). This approach assumes the following:

- Corporations and businesses (including banking) should be free from national and global governmental intervention and policy in order to pursue maximum growth and profit.

- Free trade benefits everyone, including all nations and their peoples.

- Privatization of many government institutions can save money and increase efficiency.

- Individual behavior is the cause of economic inequality, and redistributionist policies and taxes are unfair.

Neoliberal thinking has pervaded U.S. politics, affecting both Republicans and Democrats to varying degrees. The pervasive narratives that result from neoliberal theory include the following assumptions:

- The United States is a meritocracy, and wealth is the product of an individual's hard work and savings; consequently, those who are poor are lazy, don't want to work, or make poor choices. For example, a neoliberal theorist might argue that women make choices that lead to their lower pay, such as choosing not to pursue higher education, taking lower-paying jobs, and seeking time off to raise children.

- Discrimination on the basis of race or sex is now illegal, so poverty and inequitable employment outcomes are blamed on individual or cultural characteristics (Tilbury and Colic-Peisker 2006).

- The fact that some racial and ethnic minority groups have achieved success and assimilated into the dominant U.S. culture demonstrates that certain cultures value education and hard work while others do not (Chua and Rubenfeld 2014).

- There may be lingering individual prejudices and discrimination, but these will decrease with time.

Neoliberal theory is an oppression-blind approach in that it sees the world in terms of individual choice and a level playing field, and it assumes that the market is objective. It assumes that the economy and work institutions do not operate to the benefit or detriment of any specific groups, and that upturns and downturns affect everyone equally, independent of social identities such as race, gender, age, and sexual or gender identity (Ferber 2014). We know from our review of recent trends that this is not the case. Yet as long as people believe that inequality is a result more of individual behavior than of entrenched social structures, they are unlikely to support the implementation of policy solutions.

Marxist Theories

The other major stock story about economic inequality is rooted in **Marxist theories**, which emphasize class inequality. Karl Marx (1818–83) examined the impact of economic change, such as the shift from land-based feudalism to manufacturing-based industrialization, on class relations and social conditions. He famously declared, "The history of all hitherto existing society is the history of class struggles" (Marx [1848] 2001, 91). Industrialization introduced factory and machinery work, and the rise of the working class, a social group whose members became ever-cheaper commodities themselves. Workers became interchangeable and devalued. The products of the worker's labor were no longer her or his own, but were sold by factory owners in the marketplace for their own profit.

A plethora of Marxist approaches have been developed over the years, offering explanations of class inequality—the growing gap between the wealthy and the poor, and the decreasing wealth and power of the middle class. Some scholars have used Marxist, class-based approaches to explain racial economic inequality. However, in these explanations class relations are usually seen as primary and foundational. For example, later scholars influenced by Marx have argued that economic institutions and competition produce racial and ethnic conflict and inequity. Bonacich (1972) asserts that prejudice and discrimination are not responsible for economic inequity; rather, such inequity is a result of the priority of paying less and less for labor. This leads to a **split labor market**, where racial and ethnic minority workers compete for jobs while higher-paid earners, largely White, protect their jobs and wages by numerous mechanisms. In their analyses, Marxist approaches prioritize class relations and inequality as central to understanding all forms of inequality (including racial and gender inequality). This has been critiqued as a limited way to view race and gender relations. However, Marxist theorists importantly emphasize the role of economic production and restructuring in producing inequality, explaining some of the data we have examined above.

While many sociological theories of inequality exist, these two popular analytical approaches—neoliberal and Marxist—provide examples of two stock stories that differ in significant ways. One focuses on individual behaviors and cultural values. The other instead emphasizes the role of the economic structures and class conflict to explain economic inequality. Based on the tenets of the matrix framework, we would argue that both stock stories, to differing degrees, are insufficient for explaining the recent trend of growing racial inequality. We turn now to an application of the matrix approach and examine this theory's contributions.

Critical Thinking

1. Based on the recent trends examined earlier in this chapter, critique both of the stock stories we have reviewed. What limitations do you see in each theoretical approach?

2. Provide at least four examples of where and how neoliberal theory is reinforced in American society. Be specific.

3. Which of the two stock stories, that of neoliberal theory or that of Marxist theory, do you think provides more insight into the phenomenon of economic racial inequality? Why?

4. Do you believe the United States is a meritocracy? Defend your answer.

APPLYING THE MATRIX TO ECONOMIC INEQUALITY IN THE UNITED STATES

We can understand economic inequality by applying the matrix approach. Remember, this approach assumes the following:

1. *Race is inherently social.* Every time a policy is applied inequitably or employers or lenders invoke stereotypes and biases and discriminate against people of color, these acts are actively giving meaning to racial classifications.

2. *Race is institutional and structural.* We have seen how changes in the economy and occupations contribute to racial inequality, whether intentional or not. As we move on to examine history, we will see the foundational structures that have shaped racial inequality over time.

3. *Race is a narrative.* In opposition to dominant stock stories, concealed and resistance stories have informed the creation of emerging, transformative understandings of race throughout history.

4. *Racial identity is relational and intersectional.* We can examine many examples of the ways in which race intersects with and complicates other social identity positions, such as gender and age.

5. *We are active agents in the matrix.* As we enter the workforce we play a role, whether we want to or not, in reproducing or challenging assumptions about constructed racial differences that reproduce inequality.

From a matrix perspective, historical context is essential to any understanding of how we got to where we are today. Historical trends inform recent trends. An intersectional examination of history provides a more nuanced and complex picture of the experiences of racialized groups. Not every member of a racialized group has experienced economic inequality in the same ways, especially when other significant social identities are taken into account.

Historical Shifts in Work and Wealth

Time and place form the outer ring of the matrix image. It is essential to understand history, and the changes to institutions over time, to understand where we are today and how we can work for change.

Slavery and the Colonial Economy

In the 17th-century American colonies, wealthy land-holding Whites built plantations on which non-wealthy people began to work for others rather than for themselves, sometimes for limited periods, and sometimes for life:

- Indentured servants, brought from Europe, were legally bound to work for their masters for a set number of years.

- Slaves, brought forcefully from Africa, soon became legally defined as property, or chattel, owned by their masters for life, as were any children they had.

Children of slaves were legally defined as slaves, belonging to their mother's masters and not to their parents. Masters commonly raped women slaves and the resulting children were almost always defined as slaves (Amott and Matthaei 1996). These lighter-skinned slaves were often given preferential treatment, for example, working in their owner's home rather than the fields. In fact, the impact of this favoring of light-skinned people of color has never ended. Employers demonstrate a preference for lighter-skinned applicants, who also get better jobs and receive higher wages (Derous and Ryan 2019; Goldsmith, Hamilton, and Darity 2006). Remember that *colorism* is a form of discrimination that can also occur within racial groups, when those who most approximate Whiteness gain advantages and those with dark skin are subject to prejudice, stereotypes, and discrimination (Derous and Ryan 2019).

Both slaveowners and entire towns and cities profited from the use of slave labor on Southern sugar, tobacco, rice, and cotton plantations. Slavery was also closely linked to economic development in the Northern states, even when the practice itself was banned. Northern banking, finance, insurance, and other industries helped fund and insure the importation and sale of slaves and the products of slave labor. Northern shipbuilders made ships to carry slaves and the

African American artist Aaron Douglas's 1934 painting alludes to Emancipation via the central figure who grabs the attention of the cotton pickers, while threatening Klansmen approach from left. Throughout history, many oppressed peoples have turned to art as a means of revealing concealed stories and actively resisting the dominant stock stories.

Credit: Everett Collection Historical / Alamy Stock Photo

commodities they produced. There were about 40,000 slaves in the United States in the 1770s; by 1865, that number had increased to 4 million. Between 1770 and 1850, slaves were as large a source of capital as agricultural land in the United States (Piketty 2014).

Slave labor, and the wealth it generated, also fueled the Industrial Revolution in Europe and the Americas. The textile industry, for example, depended on the low-cost cotton grown on slave plantations (Feagin 2000). The wealth of the nation, and of its White citizens, grew as a result of slavery and was passed from one generation to the next. African Americans were denied the opportunity to earn any income or wealth from their own labor for hundreds of years. This provides one clue to the origins of the current dramatic White/Black racial wealth gap.

Following the Civil War, poor Whites in the South feared job competition from newly freed Blacks, and landowners balked at paying wages to former slaves. These concerns led to the development of Jim Crow segregation and legalized discrimination, which allowed Blacks to be barred from many jobs and to be paid much less than Whites for the jobs they were able to get. Former slaves took on contract labor as sharecroppers or domestic workers (Conrad 1982). In the South, poor Whites also had few options but to become sharecroppers.

Western Expansion

The western lands taken from Mexico and Native American tribes were offered in parcels to White homesteaders, but over time these lands became concentrated in the hands of elite Whites, and small family farmers were pushed into working for large landowners (Conrad 1982).

CONCEALED STORIES: THE HOMESTEAD ACT AND THE DAWES ACT

Native Americans have faced the devastating loss of opportunities to build wealth through property ownership as a result of a different set of policies and relationships. In 1862, Lincoln passed the Homestead Act to advance his goal of "elevate[ing] the condition of men, to lift artificial burdens from all shoulders and to give everyone an unfettered start and a fair chance in the race of life" in America (National Park Service). "Everyone" did not include Native Americans. The lands given at no cost to both men and women, including Whites, Blacks and immigrants, were lands stolen from Native American communities and families. Over one and a half million requests for the land were fulfilled; approximately 3,500 came from African Americans (National Park Service, 2021). Ten percent of what is now the U.S. was claimed and settled this way. This advanced Western settlement and the forceful removal of Native Americans to reservations.

In 1887, efforts to assimilate Native Americans and wrest additional land from reservations lead to the passage of the Dawes Act. The government took land out of tribal hands, and instituted an allotment policy, giving individual plots of land to individual families (around 160 acres). Reservation land above that amount was seized and given away to additional homesteaders. These policies transferred Native American assets overwhelmingly to White people, giving them land to build their lives on. This is an example of structural racism targeting Native Americans.

U.S. policy further curtailed the ability of Native Americans on reservations to support themselves by holding some land in trusts, to protect Native American land from being sold to non-Native Americans. However, by not fully privatizing the land in the hands of Native Americans, and keeping it under government control, the property was limited in increasing value for its owners. They did not fully own and control their own property. Research finds that for Native Americans, land held in government trusts and partially privatized also resulted in lower incomes. On the other hand, land owned and controlled by tribes themselves has had success in both keeping land in indigenous ownership, while also promoting higher earnings (Leonard, Parker, and Anderson 2018).

The U.S. philosophy of Manifest Destiny, the belief that the United States was justified to expand throughout the American continents, also shaped our nation's desire to move Westward, and capture lands that were part of Mexico, beginning with Texas. Attempted negotiations with Mexico resulted in areas of "disputed" property. In 1845, U.S. troops entered this area, Mexico fought back, and soon the two countries were at war. Between 1846 and 1848 the U.S. continued to wage war, and confiscated the areas that became California, Texas, Nevada, Utah, New Mexico, Arizona, Wyoming, Oklahoma, and Kansas. The borders of the U.S. shifted drastically. The U.S. paid Mexico $15 million dollars and gained nearly a million square miles of land. Mexicans dispossessed of their lands were reduced to sharecropping, tenant farming, and migrant farming. They were given U.S. citizenship rights, but without moving a foot, they were moved from Mexico to the U.S. Many lost their land and homes, including wealthy Mexicans.

This tremendous expansion of the U.S. led to a need for agricultural workers to farm the land, and the desire for a railroad that could transport people between the east and the west. Chinese men were recruited to construct the first transcontinental railroad in the 1850s. It was completed in 1869, and one year later Congress passed the Naturalization Act, banning citizenship to Chinese people in the U.S., and also barring the immigration of Chinese women. The goal of these laws was to force the Chinese workers to return to China. Anti-Chinese riots and attacks became frequent. In 1882, the Chinese Exclusion Act was enacted.

Before coming to the mainland, Chinese men already had a history of employment on the sugar plantations of Hawaii, which was not yet a state. As a result of the passage of the Chinese Exclusion Act, there were efforts to encourage poor men in Japan to come work on Hawaiian sugar plantations. The first 900 contract workers arrived in 1885, followed by the first handful of Filipinos in 1906. Recruitment efforts were organized by the Hawaii Sugar Planters' Association (Discover Nikkei).

In both Hawaii and then on the mainland, Asian workers faced brutality, dangerous working conditions, dismal housing, and long hours of physically demanding work. They began organizing laborers to demand better pay and working conditions. Japanese and Filipino workers went on strike. The next generation continued these battles and formed successful unions. They also followed in the footsteps of the Chinese as they began migrating to California. They continued working on the land, and by the 1920s, they owned a great deal of farm land, and were responsible for producing 10% of California's crops.

Both the Chinese and the Japanese, at the height of their constrained success, were depicted as taking away jobs form "real Americans." They faced stereotypes that depicted them as an imminent threat to White womanhood, and laws were passed barring marriage between Asians and Whites. Then, in 1913, the California congress passed a law declaring that no Asians could own land, including those who had owned their own property for decades. This one act stole the assets they had toiled to accumulate, and once again was part of a greater effort to remove Asians from the U.S. (Suzuki 2004). In 1924 the U.S. Border Patrol was created, and the Asian Exclusion Act put an end to the immigration of Chinese and Japanese workers for the next 20 years. Americans sought to eliminate any competition for the jobs they had privileged access to.

In 1935, immigration from the Philippines and other U.S. territories was limited to 50 people per year, however, the HSPA put so much pressure on Congress that they were exempt from the law, and allowed to continue recruiting Filipino labor. Asian immigration to the U.S. has always been tightly controlled by immigration laws and other government acts, in service to business needs for cheap labor. When this labor is no longer needed or desired, the immigrant workers are attacked and banned, their lands stolen, and their rights revoked.

In different ways throughout U.S. history, Native American, African American, Mexican American/Latinx, and Asian American labor has been exploited, while White people, corporations, and the nation as a whole have reaped the benefits, accruing assets and wealth denied to these oppressed groups. It is also significant that women were used as a weapon in these efforts, as they were barred from immigrating during much of this history. Asian women were not seen as a source of labor, and they were used strategically to keep men from settling in the U.S.

The Industrial Revolution

Throughout the 1800s, in Europe and the United States, the Industrial Revolution gained momentum, advancing the transition to a wage-based economy and capitalism. Jobs slowly shifted out of agriculture and into the rapidly growing and better-paying manufacturing sector in the cities. The majority of men and women of color, however, remained in agriculture and domestic labor, the lowest-paying and least secure jobs (Amott and Matthaei 1996). In 1890, half of all African American women and one-third of African American men worked in domestic labor and personal service (Amott and Matthaei 1996).

People worked largely in segregated workplaces, among others whose race, gender, and class status were similar to their own. Better-paying jobs in textile mills, as opposed to garment work done at home, were monopolized by White women and men, most often recent immigrants. In the 1800s and early 1900s, the earliest urban factories employed the daughters of poor White families and European immigrants fleeing poverty and political persecution. While these were opportunities often denied to African Americans and other people of color already in the United States, that does not mean the work was easy. Indeed, it was unregulated and extremely dangerous; long hours, health and safety risks, and very low wages were the norm.

Mining conditions were just as dismal. The families of mine workers lived in shanties in "company towns" and were allowed to shop only at the company store, which they became indebted to. Many miners were killed in accidents, and the injured were often fired. Workers fought for the right to organize into labor unions, but mine owners had huge amounts of wealth to invest in anti-union activity and to influence policy makers, lawmakers, and law enforcement. In 1931, one of the bloodiest battles between miners and mine owners ever seen in the United States took place in Harlan County, Kentucky; these events have come to be memorialized as the "Harlan County War." In addition to poor Whites, there were large numbers of Chinese immigrant miners (who were charged a special "foreigner tax").

Many Blacks moved from agriculture into mining as well during the Great Migration of 1910 to 1970 (Fishback 1984), when approximately 6 million African Americans left the South for jobs and other opportunities in the Northeast, the Midwest, and the West (Wilkerson 2010). Factory jobs also began to open up to African Americans during World War I. White workers in the North thus increasingly faced competition not only from European immigrants but also from African Americans leaving the rural South in search of jobs. Many feared their privileged access to work would be undercut by cheaper labor. In the late 1910s and the 1920s, White mobs started race riots in many cities, trying to push African Americans out of town (Amott and Matthaei 1996).

The Rise of Labor Unions and Discrimination in the Labor Movement

Between 1860 and 1910 the population of industrial workers tripled. Working conditions were deplorable. Child labor was common, as were long work hours under unsafe conditions. Laborers were at times locked in to the production floor and could not leave until they were released at the end of the day. Workers received no benefits, and were treated as easily disposable by employers. Many workers were recent immigrants, could not speak the language well, and

During the Great Migration, millions of Blacks moved out of the South in pursuit of better jobs and opportunities, like those offered in the auto factories in Detroit.

Credit: Bettmann/Getty Images

were desperate for employment. Workers began organizing to demand better working conditions. This Workers' Movement (also referred to as the Labor Movement or Union Movement) fought for unionization to increase the power of workers as a collective voice.

Some early labor unions welcomed both White and Black workers, including the Congress of Industrial Organizations (CIO), but many embraced discriminatory practices. Whites-only unions strove to exclude all people of color to protect their White members' privileged access to jobs and to expand the unions' ranks and power (Hill 1985; Kolchin 2002). Arriving immigrants worked to differentiate themselves from African Americans in order to gain acceptance as Whites, and the labor movement played a central role in this process (Brodkin 1998; Ignatiev 2008). W. E. B. Du Bois (1918) fought the American Federation of Labor's (AFL) practice of excluding Black workers, arguing that the union was reinforcing employer practices that pitted White and Black workers against one another.

History is replete with stories of resistance among workers. Excluded from the AFL, many Blacks built their own labor organizations. One of the best known and most successful was the Brotherhood of Sleeping Car Porters, founded in 1925 under the leadership of A. Philip Randolph. The porters worked as attendants on overnight trains, attending to the personal needs of White passengers, for as many as 100 hours a week, until the Brotherhood eventually won shorter hours and higher pay.

While the location and organization of work have shifted from farms to cities and from mercantilism to capitalism through the course of U.S. history, race, class, and gender inequality have remained constant. To combat the extent of inequality, especially based on class, various government policies have attempted to intervene in these dynamics. We now turn to an examination of some of these policies and their racialized results.

The Legacy of Social Policy

Largely thanks to union organizing in the 20th century, the United States, along with most other Western nations, instituted child labor laws, health and safety standards, a minimum wage, welfare programs, income protection in case of work-related injuries and disabilities, unemployment benefits, and other safety nets (Collins and Mayer 2010). Race and racial discrimination had become so ingrained in our nation, however, that many of the new policy solutions did not benefit all workers equally.

The New Deal

In response to the Great Depression (1929–39), union organizing pressure, and rising consumerism, the U.S. Congress, at the urging of President Franklin Roosevelt, passed a series of laws in the mid-1930s to provide economic relief and institute banking reform (Jacobs 2005). This **New Deal** established a federal minimum wage, AFDC, The Federal Emergency Relief Administration, and more. In 1940, older people first began receiving Social Security, and this later led to Supplemental Security Income (SSI) for the disabled.

In the late 1940s and early 1950s, President Harry Truman's **Fair Deal** expanded the safety net and sought to protect workers from unfair employment practices, raised the minimum wage, provided housing assistance, and more. Benefits from both the New Deal and the Fair Deal, however, were commonly distributed in a discriminatory manner (Katznelson 2005, 17). For example, in identifying categories of workers to be protected by New Deal legislation, legislators excluded farmworkers and domestic laborers, two groups that together accounted for more than 60% of working African Americans. Further, the administration of AFDC was put into the hands of local officers, who could choose who was "worthy" of aid and who was capable of working. Thus White women were more likely than women of color to receive aid (Amott and Matthaei 1996). At the same time, work relief programs were open to African Americans, and in the North, they provided great opportunities. Looking at all of the benefits of the New Deal, many benefitted the African American community, but many also continued the legacy of discrimination.

Asians and Mexicans were frequently denied access to most work programs and other relief because U.S. citizenship was required to participate. During the Great Depression, Mexicans were rounded up, primarily in Texas and California, and deported to Mexico to decrease job competition. Ironically, they were residing on land that not long before was part of Mexico, and many had been living there for generations. By the time New Deal programs aiding farmers were instituted, most farming jobs were being filled by Whites. Deportations decreased, and many Mexicans gained jobs and other forms of relief from new legislation. New Deal programs extended to Puerto Rico, a U.S. territory, where Puerto Ricans were hired by new works programs, and paid to build infrastructure such as roads, sewers, schools, and more.

While Asians were denied most of the benefits, there are examples, nevertheless, of life improving for some. For example, in the Chinatown area of San Francisco there was a concentration of Chinese with citizenship, and they were able to work on projects that benefitted their community. During this period of growing aid and opportunities for the majority of the nation, Roosevelt signed an executive order forcing all Japanese in the Western U.S. to be interned in concentration camps. In 1942, over 120,000 people, including Japanese American citizens, were forced to abandon their homes, property, and all belongings and were assigned to internment camps, often far from where they had lived. In addition to the dismal living conditions and lack of freedom, they lost their jobs, businesses, and any assets and wealth they had accumulated.

For Native Americans residing on reservations, there was the "Indian New Deal," which included the passage of the Indian Reorganization Act (IRA). Under the IRA, tribes were told to create their own governments with constitutions, mirroring the U.S. government. Many refused. The Commissioner of Indian Affairs, John Collier, was not concerned with providing Indians with the benefits of the New Deal, but instead emphasized the difference and separation of reservations from the larger society. He pushed for tribes to operate according to their pre-conquest ways of governing and living. He believed the Indian Allotment Act was to blame for Indian poverty, not the Depression. Collier focused only on those tribes living according to a model of Indianness from the past, excluding many tribes and urban Indians. He established a separate CCC for Indians, the Civilian Conservation Corps Indian Division (CCCID). This was kept entirely separate from the CCC and had various rules about enrollment. The CCCID produced a newspaper, "Indians at Work," and employed about 85,000 Native Americans; nevertheless, they are excluded from most histories of the New Deal. The projects they worked on transformed many more Indians from farmers to wage earners. This increased the number of Indians moving into cities in the 1940s (Morgan 2015).

The GI Bill of Rights

Congress passed The Servicemen's Readjustment Act, commonly known as the **GI Bill of Rights** or simply the GI Bill, in 1944 to aid the returning veterans of World War II. It was perhaps the most far-reaching social welfare program in U.S. history. This legislation included provisions for low-cost guaranteed loans for college degrees, new homes, and businesses; job training; and unemployment benefits. It had an enormous impact on education and economic mobility and was to a great extent responsible for the development of a large American middle class. On the eve of World War II, the United States was producing approximately 160,000 college graduates per year. By 1955, some 2.25 million veterans had received higher education under the GI Bill (Katznelson 2005, 116).

While it was touted as an egalitarian plan and did help to create a new Black middle class, the GI Bill also failed to challenge discrimination and in fact increased the wealth gap. Battles over the racial distribution of benefits were waged in the drafting of the legislation, and those arguing for federal administration of the plan, which would ensure equal distribution, lost to those who wanted to place the distribution of federal funds in the hands of state and local governments. Benefits had to be approved by the mostly White-staffed local Veterans Administration centers. In the context of Jim Crow segregation and discrimination, Southern Black veterans did not receive the same benefits as White veterans (Katznelson 2005, 128).

Numerous other obstacles to equity existed as well. Within a segregated school system, there were not enough Black colleges to serve all the Black veterans seeking a higher education. Job training programs required that applicants have employers willing to provide them with jobs after the training, but legal job discrimination made this almost impossible for the majority of Blacks. And housing loans for veterans were administered by banks, the majority of which refused to make loans to African Americans. So while in theory the benefits of the GI Bill were available to all veterans, in practice many were largely accessible only by Whites. It is frequently the case that well-intentioned programs designed to benefit everyone can end up reproducing racial or gender Inequality, especially when those who design the programs ignore widespread, ongoing discrimination.

The Civil Rights Act

It was not until the passage of the Civil Rights Act of 1964, which also established the Equal Employment Opportunity Commission (EEOC), that discrimination in employment became illegal if based on race, color, national origin, sex, or religion. As part of a compromise to get the Civil Rights Act passed, the EEOC was given no power to enforce antidiscrimination laws. For example, one-third of the complaints filed with the EEOC in the agency's first year involved sex discrimination; the EEOC's lack of action on these complaints inspired the formation of the National Organization for Women (NOW) (Freeman 1991). This act also challenged the notion of the man as the family's sole breadwinner. Prior to this time, employers assumed that their male employees were married, with families to support, and a middle-class White man was generally paid enough to support a family. Labor unions pushed strongly for this approach. However, with the Civil Rights Act's elimination of many barriers, there was a shift away from the notion that the father alone was responsible for supporting the family and toward a model of the "solitary wage." This meant a drop in wages, the increasing necessity for more than one worker in the family, and more challenges for single parents.

In 1964, President Lyndon Johnson launched the **War on Poverty**, prompting the creation of the Office of Economic Opportunity, the initiation of Medicare and Medicaid, the expansion of food aid with the Food Stamp Act, and more. This period made clear that the government does have the ability to improve the welfare of its citizens, and to decrease the tremendous wealth gap (Cohen 2014). Many of these policies were later eliminated during Reagan's presidency, ensuring that poverty remained the reality for millions in the United States, especially children.

An Intersectional Analysis of Civil Rights

While the Civil Rights Act of 1964 banned some forms of discrimination, it did not protect everyone. In 1990, the passage of the Americans with Disabilities Act (ADA) for the first time extended that protection to those with disabilities, making it possible for them to have access to

New Orleans, Louisiana
SALARY SCHEDULE -- SEPTEMBER 1942
(NOTE: Salaries of white and colored will be equal September, 1943)

WHITE TEACHERS

Years	Without Degree	With B.A.	With M.A.
1	$ 980.00	$1,100.00	$1,100.00
2	1,047.00	1,182.50	1,232.00
3	1,114.00	1,292.50	1,384.00
4	1,181.00	1,402.50	1,496.00
5	1,248.00	1,512.50	1,628.00
6	1,350.00	1,650.00	1,782.00
7	1,490.00	1,804.00	1,936.00
8	1,630.00	1,958.00	2,090.00
9	1,770.00	2,112.00	2,244.00
10	1,910.00	2,266.00	2,398.00
11	2,050.00	2,420.00	2,552.00

Substitutes -- $3.50 per day

COLORED TEACHERS

Years	Without Degree	With B.A.	With M.A.
1	$ 900.00	$1,004.50	$1,007.50
2	1,008.50	1,116.25	1,146.00
3	1,062.00	1,196.25	1,257.00
4	1,120.50	1,276.25	1,326.50
5	1,179.00	1,356.25	1,419.00
6	1,250.00	1,448.00	1,516.00
7	1,345.00	1,542.00	1,628.00
8	1,415.00	1,619.00	1,715.00
9	1,485.00	1,696.00	1,837.00
10	1,600.00	1,823.00	1,938.00
11	1,675.00	1,830.00	2,058.00

Substitutes -- $3.00 per day

WHITE PRINCIPALS -- FORMULA

$2495+M+20Y+H+5P$ = Salary in Dollars

Where 2495 is a constant which represents $75 more than the maximum salary for the teacher with a B.A. Degree;

M = $120 additional amount for possession of Master's Degree
Y = Years of service as principal (Maximum 10)
H = $120 additional amount for principal of a high school
P = Average number of pupils belonging (1200 maximum)

COLORED PRINCIPALS

Calculate on same formula as for white principals, but for session 1942-1943 last year's salary + ½ difference between formula and last year's salary will be paid.

SECRETARIES -- WHITE

Years	Elementary, Asst. High and Study Hall	High
1	$ 880.00	$ 990.00
2	946.00	1,056.00
3	1,012.00	1,120.00
4	1,078.00	1,188.00
5	1,144.00	1,254.00
6	1,210.00	1,320.00
7	1,276.00	1,386.00
8	1,342.00	1,452.00
9	1,408.00	1,518.00
10	1,474.00	1,584.00
11	1,540.00	1,650.00

SECRETARIES -- COLORED

Years	Elementary	High
1	$ 740.00	$ 795.00
2	803.00	858.00
3	866.00	920.00
4	929.00	984.00
5	992.00	1,047.00
6	1,055.00	1,110.00
7	1,118.00	1,173.00
8	1,181.00	1,236.00
9	1,244.00	1,299.00
10	1,307.00	1,362.00
11	1,370.00	1,425.00

New Orleans, Louisiana. -- September 11, 1942.

This pay chart used by a New Orleans school district in 1942 documents the widespread overt and legal pay discrimination practiced before the Civil Rights Act of 1964.

Credit: Amistad Research Center, Tulane University. Used with permission.

jobs and to participate more fully in public life. The ADA "prohibits discrimination and ensures equal opportunity for persons with disabilities in employment, State and local government services, public accommodations, commercial facilities, and transportation" (U.S. Department of Justice 2010). President Trump's 2020 budget, however, included cuts to programs serving people with disabilities, such as Medicaid, which provides healthcare and essential services for people with disabilities, independent living programs, state councils on developmental disabilities, and much more (Diament 2019). States are further cutting funding for services to people with disabilities to redirect funds as a result of Covid-19 pandemic expenses. Meanwhile, lesbian, gay, bisexual, and transgender people of every race are also still fighting for full protection. On June 15, 2020, the U.S. Supreme Court declared that LGBT people were protected from discrimination based on sex, under the Title VII protections. There are still states with laws that allow discrimination so it will likely take years before these protections are extended across the country.

Many people are perplexed when it comes to the causes of inequality and resort to blaming the victims. The more we learn about our nation's racial history, however, the better we can understand the origins of inequities and how they have been reproduced and even widened over time. It is essential that we have this full picture before we can come up with solutions.

Critical Thinking

1. How does the brief overview of history above inform your views of neoliberal, Marxist, and matrix theories? Be specific.

2. How do you think the racial inequities examined in this chapter have contributed to building the wealth and development of our nation?

3. How have social policies, meant to lift the nation out of crisis, reinforced White privilege?

4. In our application of the matrix perspective to the history of economic inequality, can you find insights that apply to your own family history? (You may need to talk with older family members to learn more about your family history.)

TRANSFORMING THE STORY OF RACE AND ECONOMIC INEQUALITY

Emergent and transformative stories grow out of a deeper examination of the versions of reality depicted in stock stories. None of the stock stories discuss the role of discrimination in reproducing economic inequality. While neoliberalism refers to individual discrimination, in the sense that there are still a few "bad apples" to be dealt with, the concealed story is much larger. Marxist theories also do not explain ongoing racial discrimination, unless it is in the service of addressing class inequality. The matrix approach, however, brings this piece of the picture into focus.

Our discussion of discrimination here will treat racial discrimination as an institutional problem actively reproduced on an ongoing basis, and an issue that should be approached intersectionally. The following research reveals that discrimination is not a thing of the past; it remains a very significant factor in the continuation of structural racism.

The Consequences of Discrimination

The Civil Rights Act of 1964 made discrimination based on race, color, religion, sex, or national origin illegal, and also banned formal, public segregation. Nevertheless, racial discrimination in housing and employment remain widespread social problems.

Housing Discrimination

Many studies have documented continuing discrimination in the housing market (Flippen and Parrado 2015; Freiberg and Squires 2015; Oliveri 2009; Pager and Shepherd 2008). Homeownership has traditionally led to the accumulation of wealth and was long denied to many groups of people of color, especially African Americans. Further, the increase in housing costs since the 1960s has hit the lower class, and people of color, disproportionally. When the housing bubble burst in the 2000s, millions of families lost their homes, with families of color facing the greatest losses.

We know that homeownership is important to the wealth gap, yet inequitable rates of homeownership and home equity are long entrenched and were exacerbated during the great recession. African Americans are 40% less likely to own homes than White people (Hansen 2020). Equalizing homeownership rates would significantly decrease the wealth gap for both Latinx and African Americans (Foster and Kleit 2015; Sullivan, Meschede, Dietrich, Shapiro, Traub, Ruetschlin, and Draut n.d.). Overt discrimination in lending and housing segregation still remain widespread. Summarizing the results of 25 different studies of rental housing discrimination, Flage (2018) found that gender discrimination is greatest among those with ethnic minority–sounding names. Overall, applications with White, female sounding names were most advantaged (Flage 2018).

One partial remedy has been implemented in numerous states and locales where they have amended the Fair Housing Act to ban landlords from asking potential renters where they receive their income from. Research has found that this decreases discrimination against people receiving government assistance to pay their rent, such as section 8 funds, and advances the FHA's goals to decrease racial segregation and provide greater opportunities for choice in housing (Schwemm 2020). In the last part of 2020 experts are expecting a devastatingly high number of evictions for people living in rentals. The U.S. already had a low-income housing crisis prior to the pandemic, and without an extension of the moratorium on rent, or housing assistance funds, the number of homeless people is expected to increase as high as 28 million by the end of 2020.

Job Discrimination

Not all discrimination is conscious or blatant; much of it is subtle, covert, and institutionalized. What happens when someone enters the job market? Most jobs are not advertised; in fact, 50% are filled without being advertised, as employers rely on their own social networks and those of people they know for their candidate pools (Dickler 2009; Kaufman 2011; Pedulla and Pager 2019). Thus, employers in occupations where people of color are already underrepresented effectively (even if inadvertently) limit the number of people of color who apply, making it particularly difficult for them to move into these fields. Other employers practice selective recruitment, placing job announcements or ads on particular websites, using social media to target a specific, narrow public that tends to be White. The most recent research finds that while White and Black job seekers receive a similar number of informal job leads from people within their social networks, White people receive greater returns. For example, White people are more likely to know someone who works at a business where they are applying for a job, and they more often have people in their networks contact the employer directly on their behalf (Pedulla and Pager 2019).

What happens when job applicants are screened? Research finds especially strong anti-Black and anti-Hispanic attitudes among employers (Bertrand and Mullainathan 2003; Doob 2005; Pager 2007, 2008; Pager et al. 2009; Pager and Western 2012; Quillian et al. 2020). Employers often focus their recruitment efforts on White neighborhoods (Neckerman and Kirschenman, 1991). Kirschenman and Neckerman (1991) and Pager (2008) found that employers have many biased attitudes about young "inner-city" Black males, assuming they will be difficult and unstable workers. Many employers engage in statistical discrimination, relying on stereotypes about race, ethnicity, and class in judging applicants' likely productivity (Wilson 1991–92; Pager and Western 2012). In recent years, access to internet and other information about job candidates online has also led to discrimination in the hiring process, including discrimination based on colorism (Derous and Ryan 2019).

Many experimental studies, or audits, have been conducted using testers, where people of various races are recruited to pose as applicants for jobs and are given nearly identical résumés to present to prospective employers (Pager and Western 2012). Similar studies have been conducted to document discrimination in other practices, such as mortgage lending. These studies consistently reveal discriminatory practices.

In a classic controlled experimental study, researchers sent out fictitious résumés that were identical except for the names on top. The invented applicants with White-sounding names (Emily and Greg) needed to send about 10 résumés for each callback they received, while those with African American–sounding names (Lakisha and Jamal) needed to send 15. The authors found that a White-sounding name yields as many additional callbacks as does an additional 8 years of experience, and they found the same statistically significant level of differences across all occupational categories and industries. They also found that race shapes the returns on other qualifications. For example, a higher-quality résumé, additional years of education, and an address in a wealthier neighborhood led to higher percentages of callbacks for those with White names than it did for those with stereotypically African American–sounding names (Bertrand and Mullainathan 2003).

Since these seminal studies, scholars have examined this kind of discrimination in more depth, finding evidence across a wide range of occupations as well as contexts beyond just the workplace, such as housing and access to public services (Flage 2018; Gaddis 2017; Giulietti, Tonin, and Vlassopoulus 2019). Gaddis (2017) found this discrimination based on gender as well. Other research has found that, like having an ethnic name, having a Latinx accent reduces an applicant's chances on the job market (Hosoda, Nguyen, and Stone-Romero 2012, Cocchiara, Bell and Casper 2016). Muslim women who wear the hijab are much less likely to be hired than all other women (Weichselbaumer 2019). Experimental regional studies found that résumés that suggested the candidate was Muslim received 26% fewer responses in the South, and one-third fewer in New England (Wallace, Wright and Hyde 2014).

While some people may assume that these forms of discrimination will disappear over time, this is not supported by research. A meta-analysis undertaken to examine results of every study using testers to identify discrimination in the job market examined whether discrimination has decreased over time. Between 1989 and 2015, a twenty-six-year period, they found no change in the degree of discrimination against African Americans, and only a small improvement for Latinx people. White privilege provided 36% more callbacks when compared to African Americans and 24% when compared to Latinx applicants. The authors conclude that "Accounting for applicant education, applicant gender, study method, occupational groups, and local labor market conditions does little to alter this result. Contrary to claims of declining discrimination in American society, our estimates suggest that levels of discrimination remain largely unchanged, at least at the point of hire" (Quillian et al. 2017). A recent study of millennials found the same kinds of discrimination based on race, as well as discrimination based on immigration status, in response to "roommate wanted" ads (Gaddis and Ghoshal 2019).

Imagine that someone has finally made it past all barriers and landed a job. For people of color, mistakes at work are more likely to be attributed to individual deficiency and taken as confirmation of stereotypes, whereas for Whites, mistakes are more often attributed to the situational context ("He was having a bad day"). People of color may be seen as tokens and assumed to be the beneficiaries of affirmative action policies established to meet government funding requirements (U.S. Department of Labor 2001). Those seen as tokens are more likely to experience sexual and racial harassment, a hostile or unwelcoming climate, and increased levels of stress on the job. They have fewer opportunities to develop the social networks that help people advance through the ranks, often face different expectations, and have fewer opportunities to be mentored (Ortiz and Roscigno 2009; Roscigno et al. 2012; Wingfield 2012). Research by the Pew Foundation provides insights into the experiences of people of color in middle-class jobs. An African American scientist stated that "people have preconceived ideas of what I am capable of doing" while an Asian American woman surgeon reported that "people look at the color of my skin and automatically begin doubting my ability and my knowledge of my job" (Funk and Parker 2018). While Asians as a group appear to have achieved high levels of success, they report being subjected to racial slurs and jokes at significantly higher rates than all other racial and ethnic groups. 29% believe they were not treated fairly when it came to hiring, promotions, and salaries (Horowitz, Brown, and Cox 2019).

Nor have demographics at the top levels of corporations changed very much. Even among middle- and upper-class people of color, barriers persist. While the Black middle class has grown, its members are more likely than their White counterparts to encounter job ceilings, slowed job mobility, and discrimination in the workplace (Funk and Parker 2018; Jones 2018; Roscigno et al. 2012; Wingfield 2012).

Finally, firing is the most frequently reported form of racial discrimination in the workplace (Roscigno et al. 2012; Couch and Fairlie 2010). Seemingly neutral policies such as "last hired, first fired" are more likely to affect White women and both women and men of color because they have only recently made inroads into many occupations. When we examine intra-racial diversity, research has found that colorism results in job discrimination and lower wages among darker people of color. Skin tone has also been found to have an impact on customers' evaluation of service providers: "With few exceptions, lighter skin tone is viewed as more aesthetically, normatively, and culturally pleasing than darker skin tone" (Cowart and Lehnert 2018, 357).

The Myth of the Model Minority

In many of the charts and figures we have examined in this chapter, Asian Americans seem to be doing as well as, if not better than, Whites. Why? According to the stock story, Asian Americans are a "model minority"; they work hard, value education, and have been able to "pull themselves up by their bootstraps." This stock story is often pointed to as evidence that minority group success is based on culture and work ethic, and that the greatest problems African Americans and Latinx face stem from their cultures. However, the picture is more complicated than the stock story suggests.

McDonald's was recently sued for racial discrimination by two senior executives who have highlighted the firing of a large and disproportionate number of African American executives, reducing the number from 42 to just seven, while also eliminating one third of Black-owned franchises, while under new leadership between 2015–2019 (Burke 2020).

Credit: Helen Sessions/Alamy Stock Photo

First, Asian American households are more often multigenerational, including more workers than the average White household does (26% versus 19%). Further, many Asians own family businesses where teens and other relatives work, thus contributing the labor of additional workers to the total household income and wealth. Even more important, we must keep in mind that the category of "Asian American" is a social construct, encompassing a very diverse group of cultures with origins in many different nations. The overarching category conceals tremendous diversity within, including inequality in employment, income, and wealth. In fact, Asians in the U.S. have the greatest gap between the wealthiest and poorest subcategories (Figure 4.7). Comparing various groups, about one third of all Burmese and Bhutanese live in poverty, while less than 8% of Indians and Filipinos do (Lopez, Neil, and Patten 2017). Most Asian ethnic groups have lower homeownership rates than the rest of the country (Lopez, Neil and Patten 2017). If we compare lower-income Asians with other racial groups, between 1970 and 2016 they made fewer gains than lower-income Blacks (67%), Whites (45%), and Hispanics (37%) (Lopez, Neil, and Patten 2017).

In addition to an income gap, there is also an education gap. 72% of Indian Americans have a college degree, a much higher proportion than is found in any other Asian American ethnic group. Only 9% of Bhutanese have graduated from college (Lopez, Neil and Patten 2017).

The concealed story reveals that various contextual factors can help explain these differences, especially year of immigration and level of education and assets accumulated before

FIGURE 4.7 ■ U.S. Asians Have a Wide Range of Income Levels

- $110K
- Indian —● $100K
- $90K
- Filipino —● $80K
- Japanese ●
- **All Asians** ●
- Chinese —● $70K
- Pakistani —●
- Korean —● $60K
- Indonesian ●
- Bangladeshi —● $50K
- Nepalese ●
- $40K
- Burmese —●
- $30K

Source: Pew Research Center Analysis of 2013–2015 American Community Survey (IPUMS).

immigration. After the Immigration Act of 1965 opened the doors to immigrants from more varied countries, the United States put in place occupational preferences, making it easier for immigrants with high levels of education and skills in desired fields to become U.S. citizens. These immigrants, coming from specific countries like India, are able to move into relatively high-paying jobs on arrival, and they have also brought more education and resources with them (Pew Research Center 2012; Zong and Batalova 2015). The Immigration Act of 1990 furthered these preferences. On the other hand, large numbers of Asian refugees have arrived in recent years, making up the majority of the poorest Asians. They are also the least likely to speak English. It is largely social and structural factors, not cultural ones, that explain economic success (Zong and Batalova 2015).

The Economic Impact of Immigration

While immigrants themselves often face discrimination and criticism, we are much less likely to hear criticism of corporate employment practices, such as hiring undocumented laborers to avoid paying minimum wage and benefits, and limiting the numbers of hours employees can work to avoid complying with labor laws. Undocumented immigrants come to the United States because there are plentiful jobs awaiting them.

Immigration to the United States has always been limited by various factors, including skill level and country of origin. Currently, having an immediate family member who is a U.S. citizen is one category under which a prospective immigrant may apply for a visa; another category is that of refugee. Temporary work visas may also be granted to some immigrants in specific categories, such as seasonal agricultural workers, and temporary work visas for highly skilled workers.

For the first 100 years of U.S. history, the nation set no limits on immigration; anyone could enter the United States. Today, the number of visas granted for permanent employment-based residency (not citizenship, which is further limited) is set at 140,000 per year, and these are divided into five preferences based on skill, profession, and money to invest in the United States (Kandel 2018). The large majority of these people are already working in the U.S. on temporary visas. Further, there are caps on the numbers of immigrants accepted from individual countries. These requirements make it extremely difficult for uneducated or poor people to immigrate to the United States, as our coauthor Abby's own great-grandparents did, and likely many of yours as well.

A recent report finds that President Trump's immigration policies have slowed and further restricted legal immigration, including refugees and asylum seekers (Caldwell 2019; Wadhia 2019).

Two-thirds of undocumented immigrants are people who came to the U.S. on legal visas and have not left the country after they expired. They are often applying for permanent residency and continuing to work. Stereotyped as lawbreakers who simply ignored legal opportunities to immigrate, Latinx immigrants are often mistakenly blamed for stealing jobs from U.S. citizens, especially other minority Americans. One often-cited explanation for minority joblessness is employers' willingness to hire undocumented immigrants at lower wages. While it might sound like a simple, commonsense assumption, this stock story is unsupported by the research. Rather, minority joblessness is the result of the economic restructuring and ongoing discrimination we have already examined. Generally speaking, undocumented workers are not competing for the same jobs as other low-wage workers. There is no correlation between the presence of undocumented workers and unemployment rates.

In an analysis of the impact of immigration on urban centers, Strauss (2013) reveals an interesting concealed story: In cities with high levels of Latinx immigration, African Americans experience lower levels of unemployment and poverty and higher wages than elsewhere. A longitudinal study in Denmark has documented the same phenomenon, finding that the presence of immigrant workers "pushes" low-wage non-immigrant workers into jobs with less manual labor and higher wages (Foged and Peri 2016). A study by the National Academies of Sciences, Engineering, and Medicine (2016) found that the presence of immigrant workers had only small impacts on job loss among existing workers, and these were largely at the expense of other immigrant workers who had arrived earlier. The researchers also found numerous benefits; however, they were not immediate. For example, after about 10 years, there was an overall positive economic impact on communities as a result of an influx of immigrants. And while communities bear the immediate costs of educating immigrant children, those children grow up to be "among the strongest economic and fiscal contributors in the U.S. population, contributing more in taxes than either their parents or the rest of the native-born population." The researchers conclude that immigrants have an overall positive impact on the long-term economic growth of the nation and that there is little evidence that immigrant workers have a negative impact on the employment of American-born workers. Additionally, while paying taxes, undocumented immigrants do not have access to food stamps, TANF, and other federal public benefits (National Immigration Forum 2018).

The presence of immigrants, both legal and undocumented, can reenergize an aging community by providing an influx of young workers and consumers, which in turn can lead to new jobs and economic growth. Facts are too often ignored in political debates. Many sociologists argue that, instead of deporting undocumented workers, we would be much better off providing mechanisms for those working and living in the United States to become permanent residents.

Many undocumented and migrant workers are clustered in agricultural labor, where conditions and wages have changed little since the days of slavery and sharecropping. We don't need to look far to find stories of their resistance.

RESISTANCE STORY: THE COALITION OF IMMOKALEE WORKERS

The Coalition of Immokalee Workers (CIW) is a farmworkers' community-based organization of low-wage-earning Latinx, Mayan Indian, and Haitian immigrants in Florida organizing for, among other things, "a fair wage for the work we do, more respect on the part of our bosses and the industries where we work, better and cheaper housing, stronger laws and stronger enforcement against those who would violate workers' rights, the right to organize on our jobs without fear of retaliation, and an end to forced labor in the fields" (Coalition of Immokalee Workers).

The CIW has recently drawn attention to the outbreaks of COVID-19 among at-risk migrant farmworkers who are living and working in unsanitary and overcrowded spaces, in deep poverty. In the Immokalee's home state of Florida, the number of deaths from COVID-19 per day steadily increased in 2020, while the number of tests made available steadily declined.

The coalition's existing tools, including their community radio station and a 24-hour hotline, are providing crucial news and support during the pandemic. They are also urging the the county and state to provide farmworkers with masks and other personal protective gear, as well as places where those who test positive for COVID can self-isolate. Many workers live in dormitories or plywood shacks, crammed closely together, where the virus can be easily spread. This housing, as well as food and transportation to the fields, is usually provided at exorbitant prices by contractors who recruit undocumented migrants for agricultural corporations. The use of contractors allows the companies to avoid any liability for these unsafe conditions, and violations of basic human rights. These are modern forms of slavery and trafficking. Sexual harassment and abuse are widespread. Many are forced to work for little to no wages and live in fear (Coalition of Immokalee Workers, Estabrook 2018;Mills 2013). The CIW's Fair Food Program has established standards, and an independent council that monitors conditions of safety, sexual harassment and assault, human rights abuses, and fair labor practices, and certifies growers adopting fair food standards. They have been credited with transforming "the tomato industry from one in which wage theft and violence were rampant to an industry with some of the highest labor standards in American agriculture" (Scheiber 2019). This worker-led organization was awarded the Presidential Medal of Honor, and is now a model for change within the international human rights movement (Fair Food Program).

Many Stories Lead to Many Solutions

Looking through the lens of the matrix at concealed and resistance stories, we can conclude that the United States has been built on and nourished by a foundation of wealth inequity. Countless suggestions have been offered to address the problem, and many can have modest impacts in specific areas. These include adopting family-friendly policies; building the pipeline of people of color to increase their numbers in higher-paying positions; and increasing EEOC enforcement of the laws concerning employer discrimination (Council of Economic Advisers

2015; Kantor, Fuller, and Scheiber 2016). In the following sections we discuss some large-scale attempts and proposals to significantly decrease racial and economic inequality.

Affirmative Action

One of the more contentious policies ever implemented to eliminate job discrimination in the United States is **affirmative action**. Put in place more than 50 years ago, it was intended to curb discrimination and create a more level playing field. Affirmative action originated in the creation of the Committee on Equal Employment Opportunity (CEEO) by President John F. Kennedy in 1961, through Executive Order 10925. That order created the CEEO in part to "recommend additional *affirmative steps* which should be taken by executive departments and agencies to realize more fully the national policy of nondiscrimination." It also ordered government contractors to "take *affirmative action* to ensure that applicants are employed, and that employees are treated during employment, without regard to their race, creed, color, or national origin" (Kennedy 1961). Under President Richard Nixon, what we today call "affirmative action" was developed further. Current affirmative action programs often establish goals, plans, and timetables in workplaces and schools where discrimination has been historically documented, and where women and people of color continue to be excluded in numbers disproportional to their representation in the population (Barnes, Chemerinsky, and Onwuachi-Willig 2015). Specific action included placing job ads in newspapers and websites that reach the general public to combat selective hiring practices. The CEEO was the predecessor of the Equal Employment Opportunity Commission, which is charged with enforcing antidiscrimination laws. Over the past 40 years, funding and staffing cuts in conjunction with the rising number of complaints has resulted in half the number of staff having to deal with twice the number of cases. Backlogs have been an ongoing problem and more and more cases are being closed without any investigation (Jameel 2019).

There are many myths about affirmative action.

- People assume that the policy translates into racial quotas, but quotas are illegal and have been since the 1972 U.S. Supreme Court case *Regents of the University of California v. Bakke.*

- Another myth is that every workplace is required to implement affirmative action policies. Most private workplaces are not affected by affirmative action guidelines; only those that receive government contracts of $50,000 or more and that employ more than 50 workers must comply.

Arguments against affirmative action are generally justified with the stock story that discrimination is a thing of the past and that poor individual choices and negative cultural characteristics are the reasons people of color and women have not had more success in the workplace. However, as we have seen throughout this chapter, discrimination continues unabated. More than 300 years of legal, government-sanctioned race and gender discrimination cannot be remedied so easily.

Reparations

A clear understanding of the extent to which African American lives, labor, and wealth have been plundered over the course of hundreds of years of slavery and discrimination should lead to a serious national dialogue about reparations (Coates 2014). While the sufficiency of the amounts can be debated, there is precedent supporting a case for reparations. In 1988, Congress allocated $20,000 for each Japanese American survivor of the internment camps established during World War II. History is full of examples of both Native American and Black individuals and groups demanding reparations (sometimes using different terminology), and they have been supported by a United Nations working group (R. Coates 2004; T. Coates 2014; McCarthy 2004; Zack 2003).

More recently, the Movement for Black Lives has made reparations a central concern, supporting its demands with a long list of reasons linking historical inequality to ongoing inequity and wealth disparity today (see Movement for Black Lives, n.d.). At local levels and through nonprofits and foundations, some White people have decided not to wait for the government to act. Coming to the Table, a nonprofit organization, established a Reparations Working Group which developed resources to guide people in advocating for public policies and also making individual monetary contributions for a range of options such as debt forgiveness, Federal income tax credits, and funds to provide mortgage down payments, home loans, business loans, education funds, and other GI Bill–like benefits. In Denver, a community group is establishing a reparations fund that can be contributed to and can offer grants. These are all about creating accountability for the history of White privilege (Coming to the Table, 2021).

William Darity Jr. has been a leading policy analyst and advocate for closing the racial wealth gap. In *From Here to Equality* (2020), he and co-author A. Kirsten Mullen present a comprehensive historical and economic analysis supporting the case for reparations and a concrete proposal for structuring a system of reparations.

Battles for reparations for Native Americans also continue. While movements to gain sovereignty and reclaim tribal culture have been an ongoing source of resistance and strength, and boosted some efforts to build security through assets, many argue that the U.S. has a moral obligation to provide reparations for the wealth it has stolen and the deep poverty the majority of Native Americans have been kept in (Carpenter and Riley 2019). Many Indigenous people choose not to use the language of "reparations," however, seeing it as a term grounded in a Western culture that values money above all else. Daniel Wildcat explains that their stolen lands are

> a source of traditions and identities, ones that have emerged from centuries and millenia of relationships with landscapes and seascapes. Reparations are ill-suited to address the harm and damage experienced by people who understand themselves, in a very practical and moral sense, as members of communities that include nonhuman life. For many Native Americans, our land (including the air, water, and biological life on which we depend) is a natural relative, not a natural resource. And our justice traditions require the restoration of our land relationship, not monetary reparations. (Wildcat 2014)

Student Loan Debt Forgiveness

Over 44 million people are saddled with student loan debt. Incomes have been stagnant, and new jobs are less stable and secure than the jobs of the past, while also offering fewer or no benefits, which now have to come out of workers' pockets. These structural economic changes, made even worse by the pandemic, make it more difficult than ever for individuals to repay these loans. About one-fourth of all borrowers, one-half of Black borrowers, and one-third of Latinx borrowers default on their student loans within 20 years (Sullivan et al. 2019).

Eliminating all or a portion of that debt would aid in decreasing the race and class inequities in wealth. It would contribute to the financial stability and success of those who otherwise could not afford to attend college (Collins, Asante-Muhammed, Hoxie, and Terry 2020). About one in five people with student loan debt would have their entire debt forgiven if the government forgave $5,000 per person, while $10,000 would eliminate the debt of one in three people. The remaining two-thirds would benefit from a decrease in their debt, lightening the burden (Demos 2019).

Revising the Tax Code

Many economists and sociologists strongly recommend revisions to the tax code (Garfinkel et al. 2016; Piketty 2014; Piketty and Saez 2014). Asset-building subsidies such as tax credits for homeowners are one example of the methods that benefit wealthy Whites much more than people of color and those in lower class brackets. Loopholes allow the wealthy to hide their assets in offshore accounts to evade taxes. Increasing the estate tax would help level the playing field for those just starting out in the world. The Federal estate tax requires that the transfer of assets from a deceased person to their heir(s) be taxed. Today, it is paid only by the extremely wealthy.

The IRS increased the amount of cash and assets that an estate can have before it is taxed to 11.4 million dollars in 2019 (and double that for a married couple). This means that when someone dies, they can pass on up to 11.4 million dollars to their heirs, tax-free. Looking back, we see a tremendous rise in the exempted amount:

- From 1987 to 1997 it remained unchanged at $600,000.

- In 2000 it had gone up to $670,000.

- In 2007, right before the recession, it was $2 million.

- In 2016 it was $5.45 million.

- In 2017 it was $5.49 million.

- Then in 2018 it jumped up to a staggering $11,180 million.

While the untaxed amount has skyrocketed, the rate at which the property above that threshold is taxed has decreased. This all amounts to a system that protects the ultra-rich from the taxes they once had to pay and allows their heirs to inherit far more than ever before, while paying far less taxes than ever before. Economists identify a number of policies that would interrupt this tax system that benefits the super wealthy at the expense of everyone else and damages an already strained economy (Asante-Muhammed, Collins and Ocampo 2020).

What do you think is a fair amount for the most highly privileged to inherit tax-free, given the other head starts they already receive? Do you believe there should be a limit on how much money an heir can inherit? (Ebeling 2018, Jacobson, Raub, and Johnson 2007). Most Americans never inherit enough to have to pay estate taxes. Inheritance is one significant way that wealth and privilege are passed on over generations. Each increase contributes further to the inequity that begins at birth, and a decrease in the revenues collected that could otherwise be used to initiate and fund programs desperately needed to support the rest of the population that has been further hurt economically as a result of COVID-19. The "deadly pandemic and deep recession have pummeled the U.S. economy. Yet even as tens of millions of Americans lost their jobs, U.S. billionaires saw their collective wealth increase by leaps and bounds" (Asante-Muhammed, Collins, and Ocampo 2020). Has COVID-19 made wealth inequality bad enough that our nation is willing to institute real change?

Asset-Based Policies

Long before the pandemic, scholars have argued for policies that focus on building wealth to decrease the huge wealth gap, which would simultaneously disproportionately benefit people of color (Garfinkel et al. 2016). Scholars have targeted the wealth gap in particular, because it has a much greater impact on opportunity and quality of life than income. Revising the tax code is one way that proven programs like matched saving and children's development accounts could be funded.

- By matching deposits to savings accounts of low-income adults and children, the government could incentivize asset building. Historically, society has helped members of the White middle class and the upper class to build wealth but excluded those in poverty (Harris and Rubenstein 2011; Oliver and Shapiro 2006).

- Children's Development Accounts, or baby bonds, provide each child with a cash allowance stored in trusts, and accessible once children reach adulthood (Hamilton and Darity 2010; Oliver and Shapiro 2019). These programs would provide greater amounts to the poor (in every racial group) with the amounts decreasing for those with more wealth. Funds would accrue interest and could be used for the down payment on a home, college education, and more. These funds would significantly decrease poverty rates for all Americans, helping to decrease financial inequity, and would at the same time have a greater impact on people of color who disproportionately are poor. Researchers determined that "if Congress had instituted a robust universal CSA program in 1979, the White-Latino wealth gap would be fully closed by now and the White-Black wealth gap would have shrunk by 82 percent for young adult households" (Collins, Asante-Muhammed, Hoxie, and Terry, 2019, p. 17).

Programs of this type have been widely tested and shown to be successful in other Western developed nations, including the United Kingdom (Sherraden 2009, Hamilton and Darity 2010; Hamilton and Darity 2012; Harris and Rubenstein 2011; Garfinkel, Harris, Waldfogel, and Wimer 2016; Madrick 2016). According to Madrick (2016), "If America makes cutting childhood poverty a priority, it can afford to do so."

Providing healthcare for everyone and decoupling it from employment would protect families from losing their savings and reduce the number of people who file for bankruptcy due to significant medical expenses. Protecting social security is essential for the millions who survive on it, disproportionately people of color. Initiating a federal job guarantee with a living wage, as we did during the Great Depression, would have an immediate, life-saving impact on people of all races, and is more urgent now than ever before (Asante-Muhammed, Collins, and Ocampo 2020; Collins, Asante-Muhammed, Hoxie, and Terry 2019; Paul, Darity, Hamilton, and Zaw 2018).

Transforming a History of Wealth Inequality

It is important that policy makers consider potential solutions that are tested and supported by research and evidence, rather than relying on ideological opinions. It is only after consideration of a wide range of stories that we can begin to develop stories that will have the power to transform the 400-year history of U.S. wealth inequality.

The workplace and the economy, like other institutions, are structured by, and actively reproduce, racial inequality. Historical inequality, occupational segregation, discrimination, inequitable application of social policy, immigration policy, and economic restructuring are some of the significant factors contributing to racial inequality in the workplace and the economy. While the impact of income inequality on families today should not be underestimated, it is essential that we also understand the concept of wealth inequality. Wealth inequality reveals the lasting impact of our history of state-sponsored racism. These factors are concealed by stock stories that blame individuals or cultures for their own lack of economic success. Finding solutions that will work is not the primary problem we face, however; rather, the problem is changing attitudes. Our stock stories must be challenged.

Until we acknowledge the full extent to which people of color have experienced unearned disadvantage and Whites, especially those with wealth, have benefited from unearned advantage, we will not have the courage to implement solutions. We continue to tell stories that serve the richest Americans. A transformational story can arise only out of an understanding of the dangers of our stock stories and a more complex knowledge of the many concealed stories and histories of resistance. A transformational story recognizes historical and ongoing patterns that reproduce inequality and is committed to taking the necessary structural steps to redress the damage done by that history of privilege and oppression. As Piketty and Saez (2014, 4) sum it up: "In democracies, policies reflect society's view. Therefore, the ultimate driver of inequality and policy might well be social norms regarding fairness of the distribution of income and wealth." Do we have the courage to challenge those norms?

Critical Thinking

1. Can you imagine living on $2.00 a day? For some readers, that has been their reality. Now, imagine living with over $20 million. Should both be allowed to exist in the same society? How much wealth do you believe a parent should be able to pass on to a child, after death, tax-free?

2. Compare and contrast current immigration policies, tied to our labor needs, with those of the past. Do you see any ways we can avoid repeating history?

3. What roles do race privilege and class privilege play in perpetuating economic inequity?

4. Of all the proposed solutions to wealth inequality, which would you be most likely to support? Why?

CHAPTER SUMMARY

4.1   Describe the current patterns of income and wealth inequality in the United States.

Since the 1960s the income gaps between Whites and Blacks and between Whites and Latinx have increased. Even more significant, however, is that the wealth gap separating Whites from Blacks and Latinx has also increased. Data on economic restructuring and changes in occupations provide more insight into the extent of this gap and the forms it takes. Wealth inequality is also affected by the disappearance of social safety-net programs and by economic cycles such as upturns and downturns. Further, significant wage gaps exist between men and women and between and within racial and ethnic groups.

4.2   Compare various stock stories about economic inequality.

Neoliberalism and Marxism are two of the most impactful social theories, or stock stories, that attempt to explain economic inequality. The neoliberal narrative sees the United States as a meritocracy and blames individuals, or their cultures, for their lack of success. Marxist theories, in contrast, focus on groups based on social class. Rather than addressing individuals, they examine the dynamics of the owning class's goal of constantly increasing profit at the expense of labor.

4.3   Apply the matrix perspective to the historical foundations of economic inequality.

Today's racial wealth gap has been significantly shaped by historical patterns of racial inequality. The expansion of the category of Whiteness was shaped by competition for jobs. The ability of minority groups to accumulate wealth has been limited by the theft of land and resources from these groups, slavery, sharecropping, Jim Crow laws, immigration policies, occupational segregation, and the inequitable application of social policies. Policy has the potential to move us in the direction of equity, but too often it has upheld and reinforced economic racial inequality.

4.4   Analyze potential solutions to the problem of economic inequality.

The United States has the ability to end the great income and wealth inequalities that have been increasing with time. Various solutions have been proffered, and many have been proven effective in other nations. However, key to real change is that we embrace a transformational story that arises out of an understanding of the dangers of our stock stories and a more complex knowledge of the many concealed stories and histories of resistance. Without this knowledge, it is unlikely that our nation will embrace change to increase equity.

KEY TERMS

affirmative action

capitalism

chattel slavery

class

economic restructuring

Fair Deal

GI Bill of Rights

income

indentured servants

Marxist theories

neoliberal theory

New Deal

split labor market

wealth

welfare

REFERENCES

Acker, Joan. 2006. "Inequality Regimes: Gender, Class, and Race in Organizations." *Gender & Society* 20: 441–64.

Alderson, Arthur S. 2015. "Globalization and Deindustrialization: Direct Investment and the Decline of Manufacturing Employment in 17 OECD Nations." Journal of World-Systems Research 3, no. 1: 1–34.

Alonzo, Amy. Aug. 4, 2020. "Lyon County faces preschool shortage as school district nixes program during pandemic." Reno Gazette Journal. https://www.rgj.com/story/news/local/mason-valley/2020/08/04/lyon-county-faces-preschool-shortage-school-district-cuts-program-during-pandemic/3292657001/

Alston, Philip. 2017. "Statement on Visit to the USA, by Professor Philip Alston, United Nations Special Rapporteur on extreme poverty and human rights*" United Nations Human Rights Office of the High Commissioner. Accessed January 10, 2021. https://www.ohchr.org/EN/NewsEvents/Pages/DisplayNews.aspx?NewsID=22533&LangID=E

Alston, Phillip. December 15, 2017 "Extreme Poverty in America: Read the UN Special Monitor's Report." The Guardian. Accessed March 12, 2021. https://www.theguardian.com/world/2017/dec/15/extreme-poverty-america-un-special-monitor-report

American Association of University Women. 2021. Women and Student debt. Accessed January 10, 2021. https://www.aauw.org/issues/education/student-debt/

Amott, Teresa, and Julie Matthaei. 1996. *Race, Gender, and Work: A Multicultural Economic History of Women in the United States*. Boston: South End Press.

Andersen, Margaret L. 2001. "Restructuring for Whom? Race, Class, Gender, and the Ideology of Invisibility." *Sociological Forum* 16 no. 2 (June): 181–201.

Asante-Muhammed, Collins and Ocampo 2020. White Supremacy is the preexisting Condition. Institute for Policy Studies. Accessed January 11, 2021. https://ips-dc.org/white-supremacy-preexisting-condition-eight-solutions-economic-recovery-racial-wealth-divide/

Badger, 2016. Why the Poor pay More for Toilet Paper and Just About Everything Else. The Washington Post. Accessed January 10, 2021. https://www.washingtonpost.com/news/wonk/wp/2016/03/08/why-the-poor-pay-more-for-toilet-paper-and-just-about-everything-else/

Badger, Emily. 2015. "When Work Isn't Enough to Keep You off Welfare and Food Stamps." Wonkblog (blog), *Washington Post*, April 14. Accessed April 7, 2016. https://www.washingtonpost.com/news/wonk/wp/2015/04/14/when-work-isnt-enough-to-keep-you-off-welfare-and-food-stamps.

Barnes, Mario L., Erwin Chemerinsky, and Angela Onwuachi-Willig. 2015. "Judging Opportunity Lost: Assessing the Viability of Race-Based Affirmative Action after *Fisher v. University of Texas.*" *UCLA Law Review* 62: 272–305.

Bartik, Timothy J. 2018. "Helping Manufacturing-Intensive Communities: What Works?" Prepared for Center on Budget and Policy Priorities (CBPP). Accessed January 10, 2021. https://research.upjohn.org/cgi/viewcontent.cgi?referer=&httpsredir=1&article=1235&context=reports

Benner, Chris, and Kyle Neering. 2016. "Silicon Valley Technology Industries: Contract Workforce Assessment." Everett Program, University of California, Santa Cruz, March 29. Accessed April 8, 2016. http://www.everettprogram.org/main/wp-content/uploads/Contract-Workforce-Assessment.pdf.

Bertrand, Marianne, and Sendhil Mullainathan . 2003. "Are Emily and Greg More Employable than Lakisha and Jamal? A Field Experiment on Labor Market Discrimination."Working Paper 9873, National Bureau of Economic Research. http://www.nber.org/papers/w9873.pdf.

Bleiweis, Robin. March 24, 2020. Quick Facts About the Gender Wage Gap. Center for American Progress. Accessed online January 10, 2021. https://www.americanprogress.org/issues/women/reports/2020/03/24/482141/quick-facts-gender-wage-gap/

Bonacich, Edna. 1972. "A Theory of Ethnic Antagonism: The Split Labor Market." *American Sociological Review* 37, no. 5: 547–59.

Brown, DeNeen L. May 18, 2009 *The High Cost of Poverty: Why the Poor Pay More.* The Washington Post. Accessed January 10, 2021. https://www.washingtonpost.com/wpdyn/content/article/2009/05/17/AR2009051702053.html?tid=lk_inline_manual_8&itid=lk_inline_manual_8

Brodkin, Karen. 1998. *How Jews Became White Folks and What That Says about Race in America.* New Brunswick, NJ: Rutgers University Press.

Burke, Minyvonne. January 9, 2020. "Black execs sue McDonald's, claim systematic racial discrimination against workers, customers." U.S. News. Accessed March 11, 2021. https://www.nbcnews.com/news/us-news/black-execs-sue-mcdonald-s-claim-systematic-racial-discrimination-against-n1112931

Caldwell, Beth. "Immigration in the Trump Era." *Sw. L. Rev.* 48 (2019): 457.

Carpenter, K. A., & Riley, A. R. (2019). Privatizing the Reservation. *Stan. L. Rev.*, *71*, 791.

Center for Inequality and Poverty Research. 2019 University of California Davis. Accessed March 11, 2021. https://poverty.ucdavis.edu/faq/what-deep-poverty

Chua, Amy, and Jed Rubenfeld. 2014. *The Triple Package: How Three Unlikely Traits Explain the Rise and Fall of Cultural Groups in America.* New York: Penguin.

Coalition of Immokalee Workers."About the CIW"Accessed March 13, 2021. http://www.ciw-online.org/Resources/tools/general/12CIWwho.pdf

Coates, Rodney D. 2004. "If a Tree Falls in the Wilderness: Reparations, Academic Silences, and Social Justice." *Social Forces* 83, no. 2: 841–64.

Coates, Ta-Nehisi. 2014. "The Case for Reparations." *Atlantic,* June. Accessed February 27, 2015. http://www.theatlantic.com/features/archive/2014/05/the-case-for-reparations/361631.

Cocchiara, F.K.,Bell, M.P.andCasper, W.J., 2016. Sounding "different": The role of sociolinguistic cues in evaluating job candidates. *Human Resource Management*, 55(3), pp. 463–477.

Cohen, Phillip. 2014. "Was the War on Poverty a Failure? Or Are Anti-poverty Efforts Simply Swimming against a Stronger Tide?" Council on Contemporary Families, January 6. Accessed February 20, 2014. http://www.contemporaryfamilies.org/was-war-on-poverty-a-failure-report.

Coleman, Rhonda Janney. 2001. "Coal Miners and Their Communities in Southern Appalachia, 1925–1941." *West Virginia Historical Society Quarterly* 15, no. 2 (April). Accessed February 20, 2014. http://www.wvculture.org/history/wvhs1502.html.

Collins, Chuck, Dedrick Asante-Muhammed, Josh Hoxie and Sabrina Terry, 2019. Dreams Deferred: How Enriching the 1% Widens the Racial Wealth Divide. Institute for Policy Studies. Accessed January 10, 2021. https://ips-dc.org/wp-content/uploads/2019/01/IPS_RWD-Report_FINAL-1.15.19.pdf

Condon P.M. (2019) Rule Five: Adapt to Shifts in Jobs, Retail, and Wages. In: Five Rules for Tomorrow's Cities. Island Press, Washington, DC.

Collins, Jane L., and Victoria Mayer. 2010. *Both Hands Tied: Welfare Reform and the Race to the Bottom of the Low-Wage Labor Market.* Chicago: University of Chicago Press.

Coming to the Table. 2021. https://comingtothetable.org/

Conley, Dalton. 2009. *Being Black, Living in the Red: Race, Wealth, and Social Policy in America.* Berkeley: University of California Press.

Conrad, David E. 1982. "Tenant Farming and Sharecropping." Oklahoma Historical Society, Encyclopedia of Oklahoma History and Culture. Accessed April 2, 2013. http://digital.library.okstate.edu/encyclopedia/entries/T/TE009.html.

Consumer Reports. America's Student Debt Crisis: Marvin's Story. Accessed January 10, 2021. https://www.consumerreports.org/video/view/money/education-debt/4983567515001/americas-student-debt-crisis-marvins-story/

Couch, Kenneth A., and Robert Fairlie. 2010. "Last Hired, First Fired? Black-White Unemployment and the Business Cycle." *Demography* 47, no. 1: 227–47.

Council of Economic Advisers. 2015. "Gender Pay Gap: Recent Trends and Explanations." Issue Brief, April. Accessed April 8, 2016.

Cowart, Kelly O., and Kevin D. Lehnert. "Empirical evidence of the effect of colorism on customer evaluations." *Psychology & Marketing* 35, no. 5 (2018): 357–367.

Darity Jr, William A., and A. Kirsten Mullen. *From Here to equality: reparations for Black Americans in the twenty-first century.* UNC Press Books, 2020.

Dekker, Sidney WA. "Safety after neoliberalism." *Safety science* 125 (2020): 104630.

Derous, Eva, and Ann Marie Ryan. "When your resume is (not) turning you down: Modelling ethnic bias in resume screening." *Human Resource Management Journal* 29, no. 2 (2019): 113–130.

Desmond, Matthew, and Nathan Wilmers. "Do the poor pay more for housing? Exploitation, profit, and risk in rental markets." *American Journal of Sociology* 124, no. 4 (2019): 1090–1124.

Diament, Michelle. 2019. Trump Proposes Cuts to Medicaid, Other Disability programs. The Disability Scoop. Accessed January 10, 2021. https://www.disabilityscoop.com/2019/03/12/trump-cuts-medicaid-programs/26159/

Dickler, 2009. "The Hidden Job Market." CNN Money, June 10. Accessed June 24, 2014. http://money.cnn.com/2009/06/09/news/economy/hidden_jobs.news/economy/hidden_jobs.

Discover Nikkei.Accessed March 13, 2021.http://www.discovernikkei.org/en/nikkeialbum/albums/392/slide/?page=2

Doob, Christopher Bates. 2005. *Race, Ethnicity, and the American Urban Mainstream.* Boston: Pearson.

Du Bois, W. E. B. 1918. "The Black Man and the Unions." TeachingAmericanHistory.org, Ashbrook Center, Ashland University. Accessed February 22, 2013. http://teachingamericanhistory.org/library/document/the-black-man-and-the-unions.

Dunn, John H., Jr. 2012. "The Decline of Manufacturing in the United States and Its Impact on Income Inequality." *Journal of Applied Business Research* 28, no. 5: 995–1000.

Ebeling, Ashlea. Nov. 15, 2018. IRS Announces Higher 2019 Estate And Gift Tax Limits. Forbes. Accessed January 10, 2021. https://www.forbes.com/sites/ashleaebeling/2018/11/15/irs-announces-higher-2019-estate-and-gift-tax-limits/?sh=5d605df14295

Edin, Kathryn, andShaefer. H. Luke 2015. $2.00 a day: Living on almost nothing in America. Houghton Mifflin Harcourt.

Eitzen, D. Stanley, and Maxine Baca Zinn. 2000. "The Missing Safety Net and Families: A Progressive Critique of the New Welfare Legislation." *Journal of Sociology & Social Welfare* 27, no. 1: 53–72.

Estabrook, Barry. 2018. Tomatoland: How Modern Industrial Agriculture Destroyed Our Most Alluring Fruit, 3rd edn.Kansas City, KS: Andrews McMeel Publishing.

Feagin, Joe R. 2000. *Racist America: Roots, Current Realities, and Future Reparations.* New York: Routledge.

Ferber, Abby L. 2014. "We Aren't Just Color-Blind, We Are Oppression-Blind!" In *Privilege: A Reader,* 3rd ed., edited by Michael S. Kimmel and Abby L. Ferber, 226–39. Boulder, CO: Westview Press.

Fishback, Price. 1984. "Segregation in Job Hierarchies: West Virginia Coal Mining, 1906–1932." *Journal of Economic History* 44, no. 3 (September): 755–74.

Flage, Alexandre. "Ethnic and gender discrimination in the rental housing market: Evidence from a meta-analysis of correspondence tests, 2006–2017." *Journal of Housing Economics* 41 (2018): 251–273.

Flippen, Chenoa A., and Emilio A. Parrado. 2015."Perceived Discrimination among Latino Immigrants in New Destinations: The Case of Durham, North Carolina."*Sociological Perspectives* 58, no. 4: 666–85.

Foged, Mette, and Giovanni Peri. 2016. "Immigrants' Effect on Native Workers: New Analysis on Longitudinal Data."*American Economic Journal: Applied Economics* 8, no. 2: 1–34.

Forbes, Kristin. 2004."U.S. Manufacturing: Challenges and Recommendations."*Business Economics* 39, no. 3: 30–37.

Foster, Carly Hayden. 2008. "The Welfare Queen: Race, Gender, Class, and Public Opinion." *Race, Gender, Class* 15, US. 3–4:162–79.

Foster, Thomas B., and Rachel Garshick Kleit. 2015. "The Changing Relationship between Housing and Inequality, 1980–2010."*Housing Policy Debate* 25, no. 1: 16–40.

Freeman, Jo. 1991. "How 'Sex' Got into Title VII: Persistent Opportunism as a Maker of Public Policy." *Law and Inequality* 9, no. 2: 163–84.

Freiberg, Fred, and Gregory D. Squires. 2015. "Changing Contexts and New Directions for the Use of Testing."*Cityscape* 17, no. 3

Fry, Richard, and Paul Taylor. 2013. "A Rise in Wealth for the Wealthy; Declines for Lower 93%." Pew Research Center, April 23. Accessed February 22, 2013. http://www.pewsocialtrends.org/2013/04/23/a-rise-in-wealth-for-the-wealthydeclines-for-the-lower-93/2/#chapter-1-the-uneven-wealth-recovery-among-the-nations-households.

Funk, Cary and Kim Parker. 2018. Women and men in STEM Often at Odds over Workplace equity. Pew Research center. Accessed January 10, 2021. https://www.pewsocialtrends.org/2018/01/09/blacks-in-stem-jobs-are-especially-concerned-about-diversity-and-discrimination-in-the-workplace/

Gaddis, S. Michael. 2017. "How Black Are Lakisha and Jamal? Racial Perceptions from Names Used in Correspondence Audit Studies."Sociological Science 4: 469–489.

Gaddis, S. Michael, and Raj Ghoshal. "Dynamic Racial Triangulation: Examining the Racial Order Using an Experiment on Discrimination by White Millennials." *Available at SSRN 3022208* (2020).

Garfinkel, Irwin, David Harris, Jane Waldfogel, and Christopher Wimer. 2016. "Doing More for Our Children: Modeling a Universal Child Allowance or More Generous Child Tax Credit." Century Foundation, March 16. Accessed April 7, 2016. https://tcf.org/content/report/doing-more-for-our-children.

Giulietti, Corrado, Mirco Tonin, and Michael Vlassopoulos. "Racial discrimination in local public services: A field experiment in the United States." *Journal of the European Economic Association* 17, no. 1 (2019): 165–204.

Goldsmith, Arthur H., Darrick Hamilton, and William Darity Jr. "Shades of discrimination: Skin tone and wages." *American Economic Review* 96, no. 2 (2006): 242–245.

Hamilton, Darrick and William A. Darity, Jr. 2010. "Can 'Baby Bonds' Eliminate the Racial Wealth Gap in Putative Post-Racial America?" *Review of Black Political Economy* 37(3–4).

Hamilton, Darrick, and William A. Darity Jr. "Crowded Out? The Racial Composition ofAmerican Occupations." *Researching Black Communities: A Methodological Guide* (2012): 60.

Hamilton, Lisa. 2019. Kids Count Data Book. The Annie E. Casey Foundation. Accessed January 10, 2021. https://www.aecf.org/m/resourcedoc/aecf-2019kidscountdatabook-2019.pdf

Hansen, Sarah, April 7, 2020. "As The Coronavirus Pandemic Spreads, The Wealth Gap Widens In America" Forbes. Accessed March 11, 2021. https://www.forbes.com/sites/sarahhansen/2020/04/07/as-the-coronavirus-pandemic-spreads-the-wealth-gap-widens-in-america/?sh=9f8ab55a8536

Harris, Karen K., and Kathleen Rubenstein. "Eliminating the Racial Wealth Gap the Asset Perspective." *Clearinghouse Rev.* 45 (2011): 74.

Hill, Herbert. 1985. *Black Labor and the American Legal System: Race, Work, and the Law.* Madison: University of Wisconsin Press.

Hobbes, Michael. October 13, 2019. "The 'Glass Floor' Is Keeping America's Richest Idiots At The Top." Huffington Post. Accessed March 11, 2021. https://www.huffpost.com/entry/the-glass-floor-is-keeping-americas-richest-idiots-at-the-top_n_5d9fb1c9e4b06ddfc516e076?

Holodny, Elena. Oct. 23, 2017. The top 0.1% of American households hold the same amount of wealth as the bottom 90%. Business Insider. Accessed January 10, 2021. https://www.businessinsider.com/americas-top-01-households-hold-same-amount-of-wealth-as-bottom-90-2017-10

Horowitz, Juliana Menasce, Anna Brown and Kiana Cox. 2019. The Role of Race and Ethnicity In Americans' Personal Lives. Accessed January 10, 2021. https://www.pewsocialtrends.org/2019/04/09/the-role-of-race-and-ethnicity-in-americans-personal-lives/

Hosoda, Megumi, Lam T. Nguyen, and Eugene Stone-Romero. 2012. "The Effects of Hispanic Accents on Employment Decisions." *Journal of Managerial Psychology* 27, no. 4: 347–64.

Ignatiev, Noel. 2008. *How the Irish Became White.* New York: Routledge.

Jacobs, Meg. 2005. Pocketbook Politics: Economic Citizenship in Twentieth-Century America. Princeton: Princeton University Press.

Jacobson, Darien B.,Brian G. Raub, and Barry W. Johnson. (2007) "The estate tax: Ninety years and counting." *SOI Bulletin* 27, no. 1 118–128.

Jameel, Maryam. Jun 14, 2019, More and more workplace discrimination cases are being closed before they're even investigated. VOX. Accessed on January 11, 2021. https://www.vox.com/identities/2019/6/14/18663296/congress-eeoc-workplace-discrimination

Jones, Brian. June 6, 2018. Growing Up Black in America: Here's my Story of Everyday Racism. The Guardian. Accessed on January 10, 2021. https://www.theguardian.com/us-news/2018/jun/06/growing-up-black-in-america-racism-education

Kandel, William A. "Permanent Employment-Based Immigration and the Per-country Ceiling." Congressional research Service. (2018).

Kantor, Jodi, Thomas Fuller, and Noam Scheiber. 2016. "Why Parental Leave Policies Are Changing." *New York Times,* April 6. Accessed April 8, 2016. http://www.nytimes.com/2016/04/07/us/why-parental-leave-policies-are-changing.html?emc=eta1&_r=0.

Katznelson, Ira. 2005. *When Affirmative Action Was White: An Untold History of Racial Inequality in Twentieth-Century America.* New York: W. W. Norton.

Kaufman, Wendy. 2011. "A Successful Job Search: It's All about Networking." *All Things Considered,* NPR, February 3. Accessed June 25, 2014. http://www.npr.org/2011/02/08/133474431/a-successful-job-search-its-all-about-networking.

Kennedy, John F. 1961. Executive order 10925. March 6. Accessed March 5, 2017. https://www.eeoc.gov/eeoc/history/35th/thelaw/eo-10925.html.

KFF. Poverty Rate by Race/Ethnicity. Accessed January 11, 2021. https://www.kff.org/other/state-indicator/poverty-rate-by-raceethnicity/?activeTab=graph&currentTimeframe=0&startTimeframe=10&selectedDistributions=white--black--hispanic--asiannative-hawaiian-and-pacific-islander--american-indianalaska-native--multiple-races--total&selectedRows=%7B%22wrapups%22:%7B%22united-states%22:%7B%7D%7D%7D&sortModel=%7B%22colId%22:%22Location%22,%22sort%22:%22asc%22%7D

Kirschenman, Joleen, and Kathryn M. Neckerman. 1991. "'We'd Love to Hire Them but. . .':The Meaning of Race for Employers." In *The Urban Underclass,* edited by Christopher Jencks and Paul E. Peterson. Washington, DC: Brookings Institution Press.

Kochhar, Rakesh, and Anthony Cilluffo. July 12, 2018. Income Inequality in the U.S. Is Rising Most Rapidly Among Asians. Pew research center. Accessed January 10, 2021. https://www.pewsocial-trends.org/2018/07/12/income-inequality-in-the-u-s-is-rising-most-rapidly-among-asians/

Kolchin, Peter. 2002. "Whiteness Studies: The New History of Race in America."*Journal of American History* 89, no. 1 (June): 154–73.

Konkel, Ann Elizabeth. July 30, 2020. Tech Sector Feeling COVID-19's Economic Pain. Accessed January 10, 2021. https://www.hiringlab.org/2020/07/30/tech-sector-covid19-impact/

Lareau, Annette. 2011. *Unequal Childhoods: Class, Race, and Family Life.* 2nd ed. Berkeley: University of California Press.

Laura Sullivan, Tatjana Meschede, Thomas Shapiro, and Fernanda 2019. Stalling Dreams: How Student debt is Disrupting life Chances and Widening the Racial Wealth gap. Institute on Assets and Social Policy (IASP), Heller School for Social Policy and Management, Brandeis University Accessed January 10, 2021.https://heller.brandeis.edu/iasp/pdfs/racial-wealth-equity/racial-wealth-gap/stallingdreams-how-student-debt-is-disrupting-lifechances.pdf

Lee, Trymaine. Aug. 14, 2019. Accessed January 10, 2021. Vast wealth gap, driven by segregation, redlining, evictions and exclusion, separates black and white America. https://www.nytimes.com/interactive/2019/08/14/magazine/racial-wealth-gap.html

Lemon, Jason. January 21, 2019. "The World's 26 Richest People Have As Much Wealth as the Poorest 50 Percent of Humanity, Report Says. Newsweek." Accessed March 11, 2021. https://www.newsweek.com/26-rich-wealth-poorest-50-percent-report-1299345

Leonard, B., Parker, D., & Anderson, T. (2018). *Poverty from incomplete property rights: Evidence from american indian reservations*. working paper, ASU.

Levinson, Marc. July 19, 2019. Job Creation in the Manufacturing Revival. Congressional research Service. Accessed January 10, 2021. https://fas.org/sgp/crs/misc/R41898.pdf

Lopez, Gustavo, Neil G. Ruiz and Eileen Patten, September 8, 2017. "Key facts about Asian Americans, a diverse and growing population." Pew Research Center. Accessed March 11, 2021. https://www.pewresearch.org/fact-tank/2017/09/08/key-facts-about-asian-americans/

Marx, Karl. (1848) 2001. "Classes in Capitalism and Precapitalism." In *Social Stratification in Sociological Perspective,* 2nd ed., edited by David Grusky, 91–101.

McCarthy, Thomas. 2004. "Coming to Terms with Our Past, Part II: On the Morality and Politics of Reparations for Slavery." *Political Theory* 32, no. 6: 750–72.

Miller, Zeke. August 3, 2020. Trump fires TVA chair, cites hiring of foreign workers. AP. Accessed January 10, 2021. https://apnews.com/0336437987fec77627c17ca9a4c781bc

Mills, Lauren. December 30, 2013"Poor housing, wage cheats still plague Midwest migrant farm workers" Investigate Midwest: The Midwest Center for Investigative Reporting. Accessed March 13, 2021. https://investigatemidwest.org/2013/12/30/poor-housing-wage-cheats-still-plague-midwest-migrant-farm-workers/

Moore, Marjorie, and Jo Jones. 2001. "Cracking the Concrete Ceiling: Inquiry into the Aspirations, Values, Motives, and Actions of African American Female 1890 Cooperative Extension Administrators."*Journal of Extension*39, no. 6 (December)

Morgan, Mindy J. 2015. " Working from the Margins: Documenting American Indian Participation in the New Deal Era." In Why You Can't Teach United States History without American Indians. Chapel Hill: University of North Caroline Press.

Movement for Black Lives.n.d. "Reparations." Accessed June 13, 2017. https://policy.m4bl.org/reparations.

National Academies of Sciences, Engineering, and Medicine. 2016. *The Economic and Fiscal Consequences of Immigration.* Washington, DC: National Academies Press. Accessed March 5, 2017. http://sites.nationalacademies.org/dbasse/cnstat/economic-and-fiscal-consequences-of-immigration.

National Immigration Forum 2018. Fact Sheet: Immigrants and Public Benefits. Accessed January 10, 2021. https://immigrationforum.org/article/fact-sheet-immigrants-and-public-benefits/

National Park Service. African American Homesteaders in the Great Plains.Accessed January 10, 2021. https://www.nps.gov/articles/african-american-homesteaders-in-the-great-plains.htm

National Park Service."Homestead: National Historic Park, Nebraska." Accessed March 11, 2021. https://www.nps.gov/home/learn/historyculture/index.htm

Neckerman, K.M.andKirschenman, J.,Hiring strategies, racial bias, and inner-city workers. *Social problems*, 1991.38(4), pp.433–447.

Neubeck, Kenneth J., and Noel A. Cazenave. 2001. Welfare *Racism: Playing the Race Card against America's Poor.* New York: Routledge.

News12 July 29, 2020. Pandemic funding cuts leave lasting effect on programs for those with intellectual, developmental disabilities. Accessed January 10, 2021. https://longisland.news12.com/pandemic-funding-cuts-leave-lasting-effect-on-programs-for-those-with-intellectual-developmental-disabilities-42428877

O'Connor, Clare. 2014. "Walmart Workers Cost Taxpayers $6.2 Billion in Public Assistance." *Forbes,* April 15. Accessed April 2, 2016. http://www.forbes.com/sites/clareoconnor/2014/04/15/report-walmart-workers-cost-taxpayers-6-2-billion-in-public-assistance/#55aa04657cd8.

Oliver, Melvin L., andThomas M. Shapiro. 2019 "Disrupting the racial wealth gap." Contexts 18, no. 1: 16–21.

Oliver, Melvin L., and Thomas M. Shapiro. 2006. *Black Wealth/ White Wealth.* 2nd ed. New York: Routledge.

Oliveri, Rigel Christine. 2009. "Between a Rock and a Hard Place: Landlords, Latinos, Anti-illegal Immigrant Ordinances, and Housing Discrimination." *Vanderbilt Law Review* 62, no. 1: 55–124.

Organisation for Economic Co-operation and development. 2020. Accessed January 10, 2021. https://data.oecd.org/inequality/income-inequality.htm#indicator-chart

Orhun, A. Yeşim, and Mike Palazzolo. "Frugality Is Hard to Afford." *Journal of Marketing Research* 56, no. 1 (2019): 1–17.

Ortiz, Susan Y., and Vincent J. Roscigno. 2009. "Discrimination, Women, and Work: Processes and Variations by Race and Class." *Sociological Quarterly* 50, no. 2: 336–59.

Oxfam. 2017. An Economy for the 99%. Oxfam briefing paper. Accessed January 10, 2021. https://oi-files-d8-prod.s3.eu-west-2.amazonaws.com/s3fs-public/file_attachments/bp-economy-for-99-percent-160117-summ-en.pdf

Pager, Devah. 2007. "The Use of Field Experiments for Studies of Employment Discrimination: Contributions, Critiques, and Directions for the Future." *Annals of the American Academy of Political and Social Science* 609: 104–33.

Pager, Devah, and Shepherd. Hana. 2008. "The Sociology of Discrimination: Racial Discrimination in Employment, Housing, Credit, and Consumer Markets." *Annual Review of Sociology* 4: 181–209.

Pager,Devah. 2008. *Marked: Race, Crime, and Finding Work in an Era of Mass Incarceration.* Chicago: University of Chicago Press.

Pager, Devah, Bruce Western, and Bart. Bonikowski. 2009."Discrimination in a Low-Wage Labor Market: A Field Experiment." *American Sociological Review* 74, no. 5: 777–99.

Pager, Devah, and Bruce Western, 2012. "Identifying Discrimination at Work: The Use of Field Experiments." *Journal of Social Issues* 68, no. 2: 221–37.

Paul, Mark, William Darity, Darrick Hamilton, and Khaing Zaw. "A path to ending poverty by way of ending unemployment: A federal job guarantee." *RSF: The Russell Sage Foundation Journal of the Social Sciences* 4, no. 3 (2018): 44–63.

Pedro Nicolaci de Casta"America's Humongous Wealth Gap Is Widening Further."May 29, 2019,Forbes.Accessed March 11. 2021. https://www.forbes.com/sites/pedrodacosta/2019/05/29/americas-humungous-wealth-gap-is-widening-further/?sh=7cf20f842ee1

Pedulla, David S., and Devah Pager. "Race and networks in the job search process." *American Sociological Review* 84, no. 6 (2019): 983–1012.

Pew Research Center. 2012. "The Rise of Asian Americans." June 19. Accessed February 21, 2013. http://www.pewsocialtrends.org/2012/06/19/the-rise-of-asian-americans.

Picchi, Aimee. 2015. "How Low-Wage Employers Cost Taxpayers $153B a Year." CBS Moneywatch, April 13. Accessed June 4, 2017. http://www.cbsnews.com/news/how-low-wage-employers-cost-taxpayers-153-billion-a-year.

Piketty, Thomas. 2014. *Capital in the Twenty-First Century.* Translated by Arthur Goldhammer. Cambridge, MA: Harvard University Press.

Piketty, Thomas, and Emmanuel Saez. 2014. "Inequality in the Long Run." *Science* 344, no. 6186: 838–43, and supplementary text online, 1–8. Accessed April 7, 2016. http://eml.berkeley.edu/~saez/piketty-saezScience14.pdf.

Piven, Frances Fox. 2002. "Welfare Policy and American Politics." In *Work, Welfare and Politics: Confronting Poverty in the Wake of Welfare Reform,* edited by Frances Fox Piven, Joan Acker, Margaret Hallock, and Sandra Morgen. Eugene: University of Oregon Press.

Quillian, L., Pager, D., Hexel, O. and Midtbøen, A.H., 2017. Meta-analysis of field experiments shows no change in racial discrimination in hiring over time. *Proceedings of the National Academy of Sciences*, *114*(41), pp. 10870–10875.

Quillian, L.,Lee, JJ and Honoré, B., 2020. Racial discrimination in the US housing and mortgage lending markets: a quantitative review of trends, 1976–2016. Race and Social Problems, 12(1), pp. 13–28.

Roscigno, Vincent J., Williams, and Lisa M. Byron. Reginald A. 2012. "Workplace Racial Discrimination and Middle-Class Vulnerability." *American Behavioral Scientist* 56, no. 5: 696–710.

Saez, Emmanuel, and Gabriel Zucman. 2016. "Wealth Inequality in the United States since 1913: Evidence from Capitalized Income Tax Data." *Quarterly Journal of Economics,* published online February 16. doi:10.1093/qje/qjw004.

Safawi, Ali and Ife Floyd. 2020. TANF Benefits Still Too Low to Help Families, Especially Black Families, Avoid Increased Hardship. Center on Budget and Policy Priorities. Accessed January 10, 2021. https://www.cbpp.org/research/family-income-support/tanf-benefits-remain-low-despite-recent-increases-in-some-states

Sandoui, Anna. June 5, 2020. Racial Inequalities in COVID-19—The Impact on Black Communities. Radcliff Institute for Advanced Study.Accessed January 11, 2021. https://www.radcliffe.harvard.edu/news/in-news/racial-inequalities-in-covid-19-impact-black-communities

Scheiber, Noam. March 7, 2019. "Why Wendy's Is Facing Campus Protests (It's About the Tomatoes)." Accessed March 13, 2021. https://www.nytimes.com/2019/03/07/business/economy/wendys-farm-workers-tomatoes.html

Schwemm, R.G., 2020. Source-of-Income Discrimination and the Fair Housing Act. *Case Western Reserve Law Review*, *70*(3), p. 573.

Semega,Jessica, Kollar, Melisssa Creamer and John Mohanty. Abinash September 10, 2019. "Income and Poverty in the United States: 2018." United States Census Bureau. REPORT NUMBER P60-266 Accessed March 11, 2021. https://www.census.gov/library/publications/2019/demo/p60-266.html

Silber, Norman I. "Discovering that the poor pay more: Race riots, poverty, and the rise of consumer law." *Fordham Urb. LJ* 44 (2017): 1319.

Silicon Valley Rising. 2016. "Tech's Invisible Workforce." Accessed April 7, 2016. http://www.siliconvalleyrising.org/TechsInvisibleWorkforce.pdf.

Sinfield, Adrian. 2020. "Building Social Policies in Fiscal Welfare." *Social Policy and Society* 19(3): 487–499.

Singletary, Michelle. September 12. 2019. There seems to be No End to the Rise in Student Loan Debt. The Washington Post. Accessed January 10, 2021. https://www.washingtonpost.com/business/2019/09/12/whos-blame-massive-amount-student-loan-debt-america/

Sit, Ryan. Jan. 12, 2018. Trump Thinks Only Black People Are on Welfare, But Really, White Americans Receive Most Benefits. Newsweek. Accessed January 10, 2021

Strauss, Jack. 2013. "Allies, Not Enemies: How Latino Immigration Boosts African American Employment and Wages." American Immigration Council, June 12. Accessed June 2, 2017. https://www.americanimmigration   council.org/research/allies-not-enemies-how-latino-immigration-boosts-african-american-employment-and-wages.

Sullivan, Laura,Tatjana Meschede,Lars Dietrich,Thomas Shapiro,Amy Traub,Catherine Ruetschlin, andTamara Draut. n.d. "The Racial Wealth Gap: Why Policy Matters." Demos. Accessed March 11, 2021: http://racialwealthaudit.org/why-policy-matters.html

Suzuki, Masao. 2004 "Important or Impotent? Taking Another Look at the 1920 California Alien Land Law." The Journal of Economic History 64, no. 1: 125–43. Accessed March 12, 2021. http://www.jstor.org/stable/3874944.

Taylor, Lance, and Özlem Ömer. "Race to the bottom: Low productivity, market power, and lagging wages." *International Journal of Political Economy* 48, no. 1 (2019): 1–20.

Thomas, Alexandar R. 1998. "Ronald Reagan and the Commitment of the Mentally Ill: Capital, Interest Groups, and the Eclipse of Social Policy." *Electronic Journal of Sociology* 3, no. 4. Accessed April 2, 2016. https://www.sociology.org/content/vol003.004/thomas.html.

Tilbury, Farida, and Val Colic-Peisker. 2006. "Deflecting Responsibility in Employer Talk about Race Discrimination." *Discourse and Society* 17: 651–76.

U.S. Bureau of Labor Statistics. 2015. "Data Tables for the Overview of May 2015 Occupational Employment and Wages." Accessed June 2, 2017.http://www.bls.gov/oes/2015/may/featured_data.htm#largest2.

U.S. Bureau of Labor Statistics. 2016. "Labor Force Statistics from the Current Population Survey." Accessed June 2, 2017. http://www.bls.gov/cps/cpsaat11.htm.

U.S. Bureau of Labor Statistics. November 2019. "American Indians and Alaska Natives in the U.S. labor force." Accessed March 11, 2021. https://www.bls.gov/opub/mlr/2019/article/american-indians-and-alaska-natives-in-the-u-s-labor-force.htm

U.S. Bureau of Labor Statistics. Current Employment Statistics. Accessed January 10, 2021. https://www.bls.gov/ces/

U.S. Department of Health and Human Services 2020. Accessed January 10, 2021. https://aspe.hhs.gov/poverty-guidelines

U.S. Department of Justice, Civil Rights Division.2010."Information and Technical Assistance on the Americans with Disabilities Act." Accessed February 22, 2013. http://www.ada.gov/2010_regs.htm.

U.S. Department of Labor. 2001. "Facts on Executive Order 11246—Affirmative Action." Accessed March 12, 2013. http://www.dol.gov/ofccp/regs/compliance/aa.htm.

Wadhia, Shoba Sivaprasad. *Banned: Immigration enforcement in the time of Trump.* NYU Press, 2019.

Wallace, Michael, Bradley RE Wright, and Allen Hyde. "Religious affiliation and hiring discrimination in the American South: A field experiment." *Social Currents* 1, no. 2 (2014): 189–207.

Weichselbaumer, Doris. "Multiple discrimination against female immigrants wearing headscarves." *ILR Review* (2019): 0019793919875707.

Weller, Christian E., and Adam Hersh. "FREE MARKETS AND POVERTY How unregulated global commerce is widening income gaps." *American Prospect* 13 (2002): 13–15.

West, Cassandra. 1999. "A 'Concrete Ceiling' Lingers over Women of Color." *Chicago Tribune,* August 4. Accessed April 10, 2016. http://articles.chicagotribune.com/1999-08-04/features/9908040296_1_glass-ceiling-minority-women-sheila-wellington.

Wildcat, Daniel R. July 10, 2014. Why native Americans Don't Want reparations. The Washington Post. Accessed January 10, 2021. https://www.washingtonpost.com/posteverything/wp/2014/06/10/why-native-americans-dont-want-reparations/

Wilkerson, Isabel. 2010. *The Warmth of Other Suns: The Epic Story of America's Great Migration.* New York: Random House.

Wilson, William Julius. 1991–92. "Another Look at The Truly Disadvantaged."*Political Science Quarterly* 106, no. 4: 639–56.

Wingfield, Adia Harvey. 2012. *No More Invisible Man: Race and Gender in Men's Work.* Philadelphia: Temple University Press

World health organization. 2005. ACTION ON THE SOCIAL DETERMINANTS OF HEALTH: LEARNING FROM PREVIOUS EXPERIENCES. Accessed January 10, 2021. https://www.who.int/social_determinants/resources/action_sd.pdf

Wright, Bradley RE, Michael Wallace, John Bailey, and Allen Hyde. "Religious affiliation and hiring discrimination in New England: A field experiment." *Research in Social Stratification and Mobility* 34 (2013): 111–126.

Zack, Naomi. 2003. "Reparations and the Rectification of Race." *Journal of Ethics* 7, no. 1: 139–51.

Zong, Jie, and Jeanne Batalova. 2015. "Indian Immigrants in the United States." Migration Policy Institute, May 6. Accessed March 5, 2017. http://www.migrationpolicy.org/article/indian-immigrants-united-states.

Zucman, Gabriel. "Global wealth inequality." *Annual Review of Economics* 11 (2019): 109–138.

5

HEALTH, MEDICINE, AND HEALTHCARE

The Affordable Care Act helped many Americans get health insurance, including 8.9 million White, 4 million Hispanic, and 3 million Black adults.

Jim West/Alamy Stock Photo

LEARNING OBJECTIVES

5.1 Describe contemporary inequity in health and healthcare.

5.2 Examine various stock narratives of inequality in health and medicine.

5.3 Apply the matrix lens to the link between race and healthcare.

5.4 Explore alternatives to the current matrix of inequality in health and medicine.

As we write this, we are in the midst of the novel coronavirus pandemic and on lockdown in our homes. Most readers will have memories from this time that they will never forget. But those memories and experiences will vary, because epidemics and pandemics, while dangerous for everyone, do not impact everyone in the same way. In fact, those populations that are already most vulnerable are disproportionally affected. For example, there has been a dramatic spike in discrimination, hate speech, and hate crime against Asian Americans. And while we are all encouraged to stay safely at home to protect ourselves and others, home is not a safe space for thousands of people who experience domestic violence (including verbal abuse), sexual assault, incest, and other forms of violence.

Many people who live paycheck to paycheck are no longer employed, and the vast majority will not receive pay and other essential benefits. Even our nation's top employers are not paying non-working employees. The elderly, one of the most isolated demographics to begin with, cannot receive visitors or interact with friends and family in face-to-face settings. For members of the Navajo Nation, it is impossible to stay home, since about 40% of Navajos living on the reservation must drive miles, some more than fifty, just to get water (Chappell 2020).

In this chapter, we will rely on the matrix framework to explore the role that health and healthcare narratives play in the construction of "normal" bodies and examine how the definition of normal has been used as an instrument of power and social control. We will briefly examine some key moments in the history of medicine in the United States as it pertains to race, analyze the stock stories about health and medicine and their consequences, and then shift our attention to a matrix-informed sociological approach that highlights concealed and resistance stories.

PATTERNS OF INEQUALITY IN HEALTH AND HEALTHCARE

Researchers have documented disparities across racial and ethnic groups in access to healthcare, quality of healthcare received, healthcare safety, sickness and death rates, and communication and care coordination (Feagin and McKinney 2003). *The National Healthcare Qualities and Disparities Report,* an annual report mandated by Congress, compares populations on 250 separate measures of health and healthcare. The 2018 report shows that African Americans, Hispanics, American Indians, Alaska and Hawaii Natives, and Pacific Islanders all received significantly worse healthcare on 35–40% of the measures than Whites. Asian Americans received worse care on 27% and better care on 28% of the measures. Figure 5.1 reveals the racial disparities among those with COVID-19. There is tremendous variation within each of these categories. For example, rates of the virus were higher in the Navajo nation than in any U.S. state (Burki 2021). It is very difficult to get accurate data on COVID-19 rates. Not all states provide data to the CDC, and among those that do, the data is incomplete. Covidtracking.com is maintained by a group of researchers trying to collect more data to provide a more complete picture, especially of the differences based on race. African Americans and native Americans have the highest death rates from the virus, followed by Latinx, then Native Hawaiian and Pacific Islanders. What accounts for these differences? By the end of this chapter you should be able to make a well-educated guess.

FIGURE 5.1 ■	Race and Ethnicity Affect COVID-19 Hospitalization and Death Rate			
Rate ratios compared to White, Non-Hispanic Persons	American Indian or Alaska Native, Non-Hispanic persons	Asian, Non-Hispanic persons	Black or African American, Non-Hispanic persons	Hispanic or Latino persons
Cases	2.8x higher	1.1x higher	2.6x higher	2.8x higher
Hospitalization	5.3x higher	1.3x higher	4.7x higher	4.6x higher
Death	1.4x higher	No Increase	2.1x higher	1.1x higher

Source: COVID-19 Hospitalization and Death by Race/Ethnicity, CDC, Updated Nov. 30, 2020. This data is based on 14 states participating in the CDC's COVID NET program, representing ten percent of the population in the U.S. It is updated weekly. Compare this chart with the data posted today.

This data is not surprising. African Americans, Hispanics, and American Indians and Alaska Natives all have higher rates than Whites of many of the deadliest diseases, such as stroke and type 2 diabetes (Centers for Disease Control and Prevention 2017; Spanakis and Golden 2013). Understanding health inequities and inequalities requires a nuanced examination of the range of factors involved. For example, while disease rates may be the same across racial groups, **mortality rates**—death rates—may differ. Research has found that while Black and White women are equally likely to be diagnosed with breast cancer, Black women are 41% more likely to die from the disease, and this gap has actually increased over the past four decades. While rates of screening have increased and treatments have improved, not all women have benefited from these advancements (Parker-Pope 2013; Wheeler et al. 2019).

Recent research finds that the reasons are less biological and more sociocultural. Black women are less likely to follow through with some forms of medical protocol, for various reasons, including socioeconomic barriers, increased likelihood of having private health insurance, and lack of trust in medical care (Parker-Pope 2013). They are also less likely to receive the most appropriate treatment options despite the fact that they benefit as much as White women from these treatments (Wheeler et al. 2019).

Traditional Healing

Traditional medicine consists of indigenous knowledge, skills, and practices that have been passed down over generations. Many forms of traditional medicine were practiced throughout the Americas prior to colonization. One example is *curanderismo,* popular among indigenous cultures throughout Latin America and parts of the United States, and still practiced today. **Curandero/as**—traditional healers—tend to specialize in specific forms of medicine, such as midwifery, bone and muscle treatment, and herbalism. Many practitioners of traditional medicine recognize a relationship between people and nature, and focus on healing the person rather than just the illness.

Latinx author and poet Pat Mora explores the work of curanderas and the importance of social and cultural context: "Listen to voices from the past and present, who evolve from their culture . . . Definitions of illness are culture bound. We might consider it essential to stay in our comfortable homes or apartments if the soles of our feet were covered with blisters. The migrant worker, however, might sigh, apply a salve, and trudge from field to field. Illness is both a biological and social reality, and our reactions are learned" (Mora 1984, 126).

Nina Raingold/Getty Images News /Getty Images

Traditional healing methods were not valued by modern medicine in the past, as medical practice became defined as the province of physicians who had graduated from medical schools (which limited admission to White men). Nevertheless, many people continued to rely on traditional methods, and they have played an important role in U.S. Latinx Indigenous cultures.

Much of our current knowledge about the medicinal qualities of specific plants and herbs comes from traditional medicine. Researchers are finding that traditional practices continue to offer insights for modern medicine and pharmacology, yet much of this knowledge is being lost as plant species become extinct, modern practices displace traditional healing, and traditional cultures around the world disappear. In the past few decades, a wide range of health professionals have shifted their focus to capturing the insights of traditional medicine. Even the World Health Organization recognizes that traditional healers are an important part of the provision of healthcare services in many countries, given the high respect they are usually accorded in their communities, local cultural beliefs that value them, and the very limited access many populations have to physicians and other health professionals. Traditional medicinal practices remain an option around the world today, especially in rural areas and developing nations.

A History of Discrimination

Before the 19th century, medicine did not exist in the United States as an organized and institutionalized discipline. Around that time, a small group of established physicians began to organize conventions designed to "defend their profession against the 'unprofessional'" (Charatz-Litt 1992, 718). Facing competition from traditional healers, midwives, and self-proclaimed healers, they created the **American Medical Association** (AMA), a formal organization through which they would define themselves as the only authentic and legitimate practitioners of medicine.

The Rise of Modern Medicine

The rise of modern medical practice in the United States was both shaped and reinforced by the broader culture of racism. Modern medicine was developed during the era of slavery, and the prevailing view which treated slaves as inhuman commodities left them vulnerable to medical experimentation (Charatz-Litt 1992; Savitt 1982; Washington 2008). Today some medical scholars argue that the role of Black people in the development of many procedures should be more widely recognized. For example, J. Marion Simms is considered the "father" of American gynecology and obstetrical medicine. He practiced his techniques and performed repeated operations on enslaved women. One woman was forced to endure thirty surgical procedures. Simms did not use anesthesia, which caused suffering, pain, and in some cases death (Vernon 2019).

Concealed Story: The National Medical Association

After the end of the Civil War, White doctors refused to treat Black patients, and segregation became the law. In fact, the institution of medicine played a prominent role in justifying Jim Crow laws. According to Southern physicians, "Blacks were pathologically different from whites, unfit for freedom, and uneducable in the ways of better hygiene" (Charatz-Litt 1992, 719).

The response from the African American community is a commonly concealed story. Denied access to White medical institutions, members of the African American community mobilized to establish their own, with assistance from White philanthropists and limited government funds. By 1900, 11 medical schools had been founded to train Black doctors. Since Black physicians were excluded from the AMA, in 1895 they created their own professional organization, the National Medical Association (NMA) (see National Medical Association, n.d.). After a 1910 report, the AMA decided that only two could remain open. This decision, made by a medical organization trying to exclude African Americans from the profession, was successful; a maximum of 20 Black physicians graduated from medical schools each year, until after the second world war (Charatz-Litt 1992; Olakanmi, n.d.; Sullivan and Mittman 2010).

Few hospitals allowed Black doctors to practice and admit patients. African Americans in the South were dramatically more likely to die due to lack of medical care than were Whites; hospitals in the South were segregated, and disproportionately fewer beds were reserved for Black patients. Black physicians and patients in the North encountered similar problems. Black patients could be admitted to only 19 of 29 hospitals in New York City, and only 3 of those allowed Black doctors to treat their patients on the premises (National Medical Association, n.d.). In 1910, life expectancy for White women was 54 years, and for White men it was 50. In

Excluded from the American Medical Association, Black doctors formed the National Medical Association and held annual conventions, like this one in Boston in 1909. The group, which still exists, is dedicated to promoting the interests of patients and doctors of African descent.

Courtesy of the National Library of Medicine

stark contrast, African American women, on average, lived to age 38, and African American men to only 34 (Pollitt 1996, 401–2). The NMA was literally fighting for the lives of African Americans across the country.

The story of the NMA is also a story of resistance. From the NMA came the National Hospital Association, a lobbying arm that pushed for the right of African American doctors to treat their patients in Southern hospitals. The NMA founded the *Journal of the National Medical Association,* which published not only medical research but political updates as well. They remain an active organization, addressing inequality in the medical professions and the provision of healthcare, and the journal is still in publication. This very recent history still affects communities today.

The Legacy in Medical Schools Continues

The Association of American Medical Colleges reports little if any significant increase in the numbers of people of color applying to medical schools or becoming doctors, and the number of Native American and Alaskan Natives entering medical schools has decreased since 2006 (Association of American Medical Colleges 2020).

While headlines have proclaimed that Whites, and men, are no longer the majority of medical school entrants, these announcements are misleading for what they conceal. In 2019–2020, Asians, Hispanics/Latinx, and Blacks each increased by less than 1%. American Indian, Alaskan and Hawaiian Native, and Pacific Islanders actually decreased from a total of 67 to 44 people, out of a total of 21,869 matriculants. The decrease in White matriculants is directly correlated with the increase of applicants self-identifying as Other, or Unknown.

Women are now the majority of entrants, but their gains are slight. There are:

- 1% more Asian women than Asian men;

- 1.8% more Black women than Black men;

- and .7% more White women than White men.

Zooming in closer, we find that among White people, the number of men *applying* to medical school dropped from 14,049 in 2016–2017, to 11,861 applicants, while the number of women grew by 105 (2019–2020). 41% of all women that applied to medical school actually attended, and the same is true for men. There is no big leap in the number of women applying and being accepted. The real change is that fewer White men are choosing to apply to medical school, and should lead us to ponder why (Association of American Medical Colleges 2020).

The Social Construction of "Fit" and "Unfit" Bodies

The emerging discipline of "science" focused on questions of human difference and hierarchy in the late 1700s, responding to the growing need for new justifications of slavery. Scientists did not agree on how many races there were, nor their characteristics, each constructing race in slightly different ways. In addition to physical features, which extended far beyond skin color to include characteristics such as the angle of the head, the size of the cranial cavity, hair, and the ability to blush, differences in personality, character, behavior, and cognitive abilities were also constructed as inborn racial characteristics. What did not vary was the placement of those seen as Whites at the top and Blacks at the bottom of the hierarchy.

Social Darwinism

Debates about how races originated and their relationship to God flourished for years, and they were not generally resolved until the publication of naturalist Charles Darwin's text on the theory of evolution in 1859. Darwin asserted that all races evolved from the same organisms and thus were part of the same species (Ferber 1998; Smedley 2018). He also described a process of natural selection, in which those species best suited to their environments were more likely to survive and reproduce, furthering their species. This new perspective focused on the inheritance of so-called genetic traits. Everything from physical characteristics to moral behavior would now be argued to have a genetic basis tied to race.

Darwin's theories, and the discoveries about genetics and inheritance published by scientist and Augustinian friar Gregor Mendel in 1866, sparked a new way of thinking about race, class, and the value of life. This new perspective focused on the inheritance of so-called genetic traits, which were believed to include everything from physical characteristics to moral behavior.

The school of thought known as **Social Darwinism** took the basic insights of the theory of evolution and applied them to social life, making the assumption that a society could distinguish between the "fit" and "unfit." Sociologist Herbert Spencer, who coined the phrase "survival of the fittest" in 1864, argued that the imagined laws of natural selection were justification for not intervening to help the poor.

These popular versions of evolutionary theory distorted the actual science of evolution in two important ways:

1. Evolution actually works extremely slowly, over millions of years, not over the course of a few generations as assumed by proponents of social Darwinism.

2. There is no way of knowing who is or is not "fit." According to the theory of evolution, "fitness" is determined by specific historical, environmental, and climatic contexts. The more diverse a species, the more likely segments of the population will survive and adapt to a changing environment. The fittest species are the most diverse.

The Eugenics Movement

The **eugenics** movement, which arose in the late 19th century, took the social Darwinist philosophy further, arguing that natural selection should be hastened through the implementation of policies that would encourage the "fit" Northern Europeans and upper classes to reproduce; in addition, the numbers of those defined as "unfit" should be reduced, most commonly by sterilizing women. Francis Galton, a cousin of Charles Darwin, coined the term *eugenics*. The idea was relatively simple: If evolution works by preserving the fittest, why not aid that process by eliminating some of the unfit? At the very least, social Darwinists argued, society should not be helping the unfit to survive by providing them with forms of charity and welfare. Eugenicists'

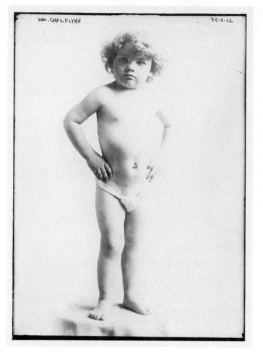

William Charles Flynn, a winner of perfect "eugenic baby" contests, circa 1910.

Courtesy of the Library of Congress Prints & Photographs Division

arguments appealed to those of all political stripes who sought answers to the "economic crisis" caused by the need to care for those in society who either could not care for themselves or were considered unfit to participate in society (Ekland-Olson and Beicken 2012; Lombardo 2008). In addition to eliminating the unfit, measures were suggested to encourage the "fittest" to marry one another and reproduce in order to increase the "fit" population. This all occurred within the broader context of a system of White supremacy, so that the White race was assumed to be the "fittest" race that could continue to be perfected.

In tracing the history of the concept of disability, Lennard Davis demonstrates that in the two decades prior to the rise of Darwinism, the concept of the "norm" came into being. Shifting from the sole focus on ideals that was then being used to judge races and bodies, the idea of a norm suggested that most people should fall within it. The concept of the norm contributed to the groundwork necessary for the rise of eugenics, when deviations from the norm were targeted for elimination (Davis 2010).

Social Darwinism and eugenics gained a broad base of support among a number of groups, including progressive organizations fighting for women's suffrage, women's right to birth control, child welfare, temperance, and prison reform. If the poor and uneducated were not competent to make educated decisions if given the vote, then it followed that those groups were most in need of limiting the numbers of births in their families and most susceptible to disease, alcoholism, violence, and crime.

Eugenics was legitimated and given the stamp of scientific truth when the AMA included among its published goals the application of a "scientific process of selection" to control the growth of the "unfortunate classes." Methods included restrictions on immigration, restrictions on who could marry, and compulsory sterilization. (Lombardo 2008, 11).

Eliminating the "Unfit"

Many people believed that by removing from society those they saw as incapable of living up to their definitions of high moral and physical standards, they could protect the purity and fitness of the White race. These efforts went so far as to attempt to protect the sensibilities of the fit by keeping "defectives" literally out of sight. The 1911 Chicago Ugly Law declared: "Any person who is diseased, maimed, mutilated or in any way deformed so as to be an unsightly or

In the early 20th century, racialized categories were created and popularized as a result of the popularity of eugenics. Laws and policies were put into place to bar "undesirable" immigrants entry and to sterilize those seen as unfit. Nazi Germany is most notable for its use of eugenics to support hte murder of millions of Jewish Europeans, such as those seen here during the raid on the Warsaw Ghetto.

Everett Collection Inc/Alamy Stock Photo

disgusting object, or an improper person to be allowed in or on the streets, highways, thoroughfares or public places in this city shall not therein or thereon expose himself or herself to public view" (quoted in Coco 2010, 23).

Eugenic ideology permeated immigration policy as well. Beginning with the Immigration Law of 1891, the federal government classified as "public charge" those immigrants thought likely to depend on government assistance. Many immigrants believed to suffer from a "loathsome or dangerous contagious disease" (which included pregnancy, poverty, and a lack of morals) were deported (Bateman-House and Fairchild 2008). Women were automatically assumed to be public charge if they were unmarried or widowed.

A plethora of new methods were devised to determine who was and was not "fit." In 1913, Henry Goddard introduced the newly created IQ test for just this purpose. A psychologist and author, Goddard argued that intelligence was inherited and largely immune to environmental factors or education, and that intelligence itself impacted behavior and morals. The IQ test was used at the immigration hub at New York's Ellis Island, where scores of women, believed to be more intuitive, were trained in methods of spotting the feebleminded and other misfits for IQ testing. Those immigrants categorized as "morons," "idiots," or "imbeciles," based on their IQ test, were deported. Goddard claimed that the IQ testing proved that about 80% of Jewish, Hungarian, Italian, and Russian immigrants were feebleminded. Deportations for the reason of feeblemindedness increased 350% that year and 570% the next, a situation that played a role in the setting of immigration quotas to limit the "inferior stock" of the not-yet-White Europeans immigrating in large numbers. Non-White immigrants had already been barred completely.

Charles Davenport, another prominent eugenicist, focused on the elimination of what he saw as undesirable inherited traits. He meticulously sought to identify every genetic trait, publishing his documentation in his 1912 *Trait Book*. The genetic traits he identified included hysteria, backwardness, prostitution, adultery, counterfeiting, and eccentricity. Public education about eugenics thus increased, and public health advocates sought methods for "race improvement through better marriage" (Lombardo 2008, 45). Eugenic sentiment fueled fears of miscegenation. "Inter-breeding" involving White people was seen as racial degeneration. (Whites cared little about interracial relationships involving only minority groups.)

In 1914 eugenicist Henry Laughlin introduced the first sterilization law. He included almost anyone that was likely to be supported by the government, such as the homeless, orphans, and the very poor. During this period, 33 U.S. states adopted laws allowing eugenic sterilizations (Ekland-Olson and Beicken 2012). People with the undesirable traits were united in the public mind as defectives deviating from the norm of the healthy racial body required for a healthy White nation.

The U.S. Supreme Court gave further legitimacy to eugenic practices in *Buck v. Bell*. The Court upheld Virginia's law requiring sterilization of those deemed "socially inadequate" and living on government support. The law went into effect the same day as another law, The Racial Integrity Act, where Virginia banned interracial marriage. Eugenicists argued that Carrie Buck, a resident at the Virginia Colony for Epileptics and Feebleminded who had given birth after being raped at age 16, could only produce socially inadequate offspring (Lombardo 2008). Writing for the majority, Justice Oliver Wendell Holmes Jr. declared: "It is better for all the world, if instead of waiting to execute degenerate offspring for crime, or to let them starve for their imbecility, society can prevent those who are manifestly unfit from continuing their kind. . . . Three generations of imbeciles are enough" (quoted in Lombardo 2008, 287).

By the mid-1930s, most states had adopted laws similar to Virginia's, and more than 60,000 U.S. citizens were forcibly sterilized (Lombardo 2008). The United States was not alone in its efforts to "improve" its population; numerous other nations followed the example set by the United States and Britain, most notably Germany. Eugenic research, much of it conducted by U.S. scientists, was the foundation of Adolf Hitler's "final solution"—the elimination of anyone identified as threatening the Aryan race, including Jews, homosexuals, Romani (then called "Gypsies"), the disabled, Jehovah's Witnesses, political prisoners, habitual criminals, the asocial, trade unionists, and more (United States Holocaust Memorial Museum, n.d.). Approximately 17 million people were killed in all. The Nazis carried out over 400,000 sterilizations of Germans under the 1933 "For the Prevention of Hereditarily Diseased Offspring" act (Barnes 2010). Going one step further, rather than waiting for the disabled to die out and having to pay the costs of their care, the Nazi regime proceeded to murder 250,000 people identified as mentally ill or disabled, and eventually killed approximately 14 million targeted people (Ridley 2017; United States Holocaust Memorial Museum n.d). The six million Jews killed was the largest single group, and only one-third of all European Jews survived the Nazi Holocaust.

German doctors played a significant role throughout, initially performing sterilizations, carrying out the murders of the disabled, and experimenting on people imprisoned in concentration camps.

Despite widespread condemnation of Nazi practices of eugenics, the United States continued to carry out forced sterilizations. California led the way, sterilizing 20,000 people by 1963 (Cohen and Bonifield 2012). California's law required that anyone deemed a "ward of the state" could not be released from state custody without undergoing sterilization. Some of the victimized included teenagers who had been removed from their families because they had been neglected or abused. Between 1929 and 1974, North Carolina sterilized more than 7,600 people, including young rape and incest victims (like Carrie Buck) who were blamed for being "promiscuous" (Snyderman 2012). Sterilization laws remained in place until 1979. By that time 60,000 people had been sterilized (Carlton 2018).

Eugenics was inherently about the construction of Whiteness, and it provides us with a clear example of the need to understand race intersectionally. Those White people who were seen as unhealthy and impure—the poor, the disabled, the homosexual, the not-quite-White Jew—were targeted for segregation or elimination. It was women's bodies, not men's, that were most often targeted for sterilization. The hierarchies of class, sexuality, ability, religion, and so on, privileged the White race as the superior race.

From the Invention of Race to the Invention of the Homosexual

The eugenic search for hereditary "defects" or abnormalities led to efforts to locate homosexuality as something inherent in certain bodies. The invention of the homosexual—the idea that there is a homosexual body and a homosexual person (as opposed to simply sexual acts and desires)—arose in late 19th-century medical discourse. Havelock Ellis's *Studies in the Psychology of Sex* was published in 1897 and became one of the founding texts of sexology. Sexologists employed many of the same methods that race scientists used to measure or locate the bodily sources of such "defects" (Blumenfeld 2012; Somerville 2000). This resulted in members of the medical professions committing lesbians, gay males, bisexuals, and those who transgressed so-called normative gender identities and expressions to hospitals, mental institutions, jails, and penitentiaries (often against their will or under tremendous pressure). Many were subjected to prefrontal lobotomies, electroshock, castration, and sterilization (Blumenfeld 2012).

The pathologizing of LGBT people of every race has continued since that time, with dire public health consequences. When the HIV/AIDS epidemic began in the early 1980s, gay men were among the first cases, and AIDS was framed as a "gay men's disease." The false assumption that the disease was a result of individual lifestyle choices led heterosexuals to believe they were safe, and doctors to limit their study of the disease to men's symptoms only. It was more than a decade before symptoms unique to women, like cervical cancer, were recognized. By then, untold numbers of women had been misdiagnosed and denied appropriate treatment (Weber 2006, 28).

So-called **conversion therapy**, treatment programs meant to change the sexual orientation of gays and lesbians, remains largely legal. Although such programs are not medically oriented and are not run by doctors, in addition to being widely discredited and often harmful, they have proliferated in some states. The basis for conversion therapy is the idea that homosexuality is a mental disorder that can be cured. Eighteen states now ban conversion therapy for minors.

Currently, there is widespread discrimination against LGBT people of all races throughout the healthcare system. There are ten states with Medicaid policy banning healthcare coverage for transgender people; 45% of the LGBT population live in states that do not have insurance protections for gender identity and sexual orientation (Movement Advancement Project 2020).

Critical Thinking

1. As you read this today, examine the impact of the coronavirus from an intersectional perspective, considering both privileged and oppressed identities. How are people being impacted in very different ways?

2. Can you think of specific innovations in contemporary medical technology that have the potential to bring the ideas of eugenics into public debate again? What safeguards might protect people from the misguided policies of the past?

3. Can you identify any characteristics you or any of your close friends or family members possess that were targeted for elimination by eugenicists?

4. Have you or anyone you know utilized traditional medicine or "alternative" medical practices? Why do you think some of these practices are more in vogue and acceptable today, after many years of being delegitimated in the United States?

STOCK STORIES OF HEALTH AND MEDICINE

Historically, medical institutions not only contributed to the system of White supremacy and supported legal and educational boundaries separating Blacks from Whites, but they also played a central role in racializing humans, and defining where they fell within the racial hierarchy. The stock story of race as a biological reality is one of the most significant narratives justifying health disparities by locating physical differences within the racialized body. This stock story, biomedicine, has prevailed ever since, among the general public as well as medical establishments and practitioners.

Biomedicine

Medicine did not become a coherent discipline until the formation of the sciences as an experimental and empirical discipline. Prior to that, wide-ranging practitioners identified and studied specific diseases and physical conditions without a common foundation of knowledge. Most practitioners saw illness and many social problems as fully rooted in bodies.

In contrast, the proponents of the natural sciences argued that they alone could provide objective scientific knowledge to control and cure bodies and the natural world, and worked to marginalize sociologists and other disciplinary perspectives. Sociologist Max Weber fought this agenda, critiquing the attempts to frame the new "natural sciences" as superior to social and cultural sciences, and argued that taking historical and social context out of the picture resulted in flawed practice. In the early part of the twentieth century, the biomedical view prevailed, claiming the social, moral, and political/power domains as irrelevant to health, disease, and mortality. Thus the stock story that shaped views of race and racialized bodies since at least slavery became the prevailing view of the institution of medicine. This is the basis of the stock story now known as **biomedicine.** As biomedicine became the normative approach to understanding health and illness, a new generation of sociologists began to accept this predominant view. These are some of the commonly accepted narratives of the biomedical theory:

1. Race is a biological reality that can (help) explain disparities in health.

2. Health is a matter of individual and genetic factors.

3. The field of medicine and healthcare employs objective science and operates independent of the social organization of society.

4. Thanks to medical advances and the elimination or minimization of many infectious diseases, people today live longer than their predecessors in previous generations.

Social Theory

The early founders of sociology were active players in the historical debates about the source of disease. In contrast to the eugenicists, they saw the connections between poverty and poor health as a matter of social forces, namely capitalism, rather than genetics. They defined things like suicide, homelessness, disability, and alcoholism as social problems, not individual problems. Sociologists advocated for social and state interventions to decrease pollution, improve sanitation and healthcare, and financial programs to assist the sick and the poor. This approach, **social theory**, is another prevailing stock story of health and medicine.

Émile Durkheim engaged issues of health and disease as social fact. For example, in his research on suicide he argued for the role of social factors, as opposed to the narrow reductionist view that sought answers innate to the individual. Karl Marx linked ill health to industrialization and the power of the owning class. German sociologist Friedrich Engels compared the life spans of the wealthy with the significantly shorter life spans of the working class, blaming social factors such as dangerous work environments and poor living conditions. Broadening the discussion to include racial inequality, *The Philadelphia Negro,* first published in 1899 by W. E. B. Du Bois, examined African Americans' higher rates of disease and mortality compared with Whites. He also argued that social factors played a significant role in these disparities, blaming nonhygienic and poor living conditions and lack of protection from the elements (see Williams 2012, 283). But Du Bois also identified racism itself as a variable:

> The most difficult social problem in the matter of Negro health . . . is the peculiar attitude of the nation toward the well-being of the race. There have . . . been few other cases

in the history of civilized peoples where human suffering has been viewed with such peculiar indifference. (Du Bois 1899, 163, cited in Williams 2012, 287)

As an African American sociologist and prolific author, Du Bois expanded sociological work beyond class.

The broader approach to health as 'well-being' is increasingly replaced in sociology by the adoption of a narrow, and reductionist, understanding. Largely ignoring earlier sociological critiques … new generations of sociologists uncritically incorporated the notion of 'disease' as an established biological, physiological 'fact.' And increasingly, ill-health disappeared as a legitimate concern of sociology. Sociologists came to regard both the management and theorization of disease as the responsibility of the medical expert. (Collyer 2010, 98).

In sociology's discipline-building process, it sought to delineate its boundaries in order to clarify the unique province of sociology, and secure its legitimacy for the future. As a part of this process, subjects seen as biological or psychological were expunged from the boundaries of the sociological. Talcott Parsons significantly contributed to this shift in his view of disease as a biological fact that could be separated from the social. In *The Sick Role*, he examined the social patterns of being sick, and the roles of the individual in society. As a functionalist theorist, he argued that the sick were temporarily deviant, because they were no longer contributing to society, and thus were required to seek medical attention to get well and become functioning members of society again. Research on ill health subsided, moving away from the kinds of work produced by the early founders. Sociologists generally limited their focus to social patterns of health, but not health or disease itself (Collyer 2010).

Today, both the biomedical and social views prevail. The subfield of Sociology of Health has reinvigorated the study of health, disease, and illness as social issues, and **medical sociology** emerged to examine the institution of medicine itself, including its organization, practices, definitions, and social effects. The Sociology of Health and Medical Sociology are courses offered by many sociology departments. While various specialized medical fields are also researching social factors, the biomedical perspective is predominant in the field of medicine, and among the general population.

In our brief historical overview, we have already examined competing biomedical and social approaches that shaped health, healthcare, and the development of the field of medicine. We have witnessed the origins of the biomedical perspective in the history of the construction of race and the eugenics movement, both of which rooted race and disease in the physical body alone. Additionally we discovered that the burgeoning field of experimental science and medicine saw itself as operating objectively without the influence of the social environment. The early theorists of race believed they were discovering the causes of racial differences and race hierarchy.

At the same time, viewing this history through a social lens revealed concealed knowledge about the inequities and foundational White supremacist views. We discovered the relations of power shaping all of these developments. The exclusion of African Americans from the medical profession, the inequitable access to healthcare and the medical experiments on slaves, were all shaped by the desire to exclude Others from access to resources, and to justify society's definition of who was valued and defined as human. These same social values and relations of power constructed "race," and constructed it in a manner that attributed a wide range of social characteristics to the body itself, rooting all differences in the racialized body. These social values produced the field of eugenics, which lead to mass sterilizations, and the death of millions of people at the hands of the Nazis, in order to consolidate power in the hands of the White elite. We saw a powerful story of resistance in the rise and continuing significance of the National Medical Association.

Critical Thinking

1. Other than those we have discussed, what additional social, economic, and institutional factors influence health and illness?

2. Identify additional examples that demonstrate the benefits of using an intersectional perspective to understand specific health inequities.

3. Which of the two stock stories do you believe is most useful for understanding racial health disparities today? Why?

4. Referring back to the key characteristics of the matrix framework, provide examples of each feature based on what we have examined so far. For example: *Race is inherently social.* We have explored this with many historical examples, ranging from the social construction of racial categories themselves, as well as the social nature of illness and disease, and the formation of medicine as a social institution that reinforces inequities and protects elite White privilege.

APPLYING THE MATRIX TO HEALTH INEQUITY AND INEQUALITY

Just like every other social institution, medicine and healthcare are imbued with hierarchies of race, gender, class, and other axes of inequality. When you were a child and had to stay home from school because you were ill, who stayed home with you? For most children in the United States, the answer to that question would be the child's mother or another female family member (Lam 2014). Health and medicine are also intertwined with the world of work. If you have an aging relative who needs more care than the family can provide, that care is most likely provided by women of color. The low-paying jobs of nursing assistant, home healthcare worker, and hospice aide are among those in which women of color are overrepresented (Glenn 2010; Himmelstein and Venkataramani 2019).

The matrix perspective draws on the insights of many social approaches, while raising new questions and subjects for investigation. This chapter has already employed a matrix theoretical approach, and will more narrowly apply it to understanding contemporary health patterns in the remainder of the chapter.

Health as a Social Issue

Today, growing fields such as public health and epidemiology are bringing social factors into medical research, practice, and policy (Conrad and Leiter 2012, 24). **Epidemiologists** focus on populations, rather than individuals, to explain why some groups may be more or less likely to develop specific diseases and health problems; they look at factors such as the characteristics of the social groups themselves, the areas in which they live, and the environmental elements to which they are exposed (Fletcher 2019).

There is also growing interest in an ecological perspective in health research which is frequently used to understand health inequities (Agbedia 2019; McLaren and Hawe 2005). *Ecological* is defined broadly here to include the entire context and range of factors that can interact to produce inequality. Researcher Clara Agbedia describes four levels examined in epidemiological research:

- The first level looks at health determinants at the individual level, such as social identities and health-related behaviors.

- The second level moves to the interrelationships between individuals, and people's status and position in the community and in the social hierarchy.

- A third level brings in health inequity as it is rooted in institutional settings such as workplaces, schools, and families. Here, there are a range of issues such as levels of violence, unemployment, geographical location and density, and more.

- The final level brings in wide-ranging social factors, such as cultural prejudices and stereotypes, and political context, as well as policy.

This approach mirrors the matrix model that similarly moves from the individual outward, acknowledging the importance of social structures and organizations, cultures and narratives of inequality, and history and place, which all must be examined intersectionally to make sense of our stark racial health gaps. Ecological methods have been used to develop more appropriate therapies for working with transgender and nonbinary people; to explore the changing global demographics of liver cancer; and to identify factors that increase the spread of infection in hospitals and practices to curb this (Drohan 2019). These four levels of that capture the full social context of health are necessary to understand the vast differences in the rates and impact of COVID-19 across racialized groups.

Seeing our own health as a social issue may be difficult today, given the number of advertisements for weight loss products, diet programs, exercise equipment, gyms and fitness clubs, and foods that promise good health. The 30-billion-dollar fitness sector is only one part of a booming industry that frames good health as the result of willpower and healthy choices (Midgley 2018). Profit motives are one driver in the definition of disease, with pharmaceutical companies investing their research and development dollars in finding medications that will sell to large numbers of people, such as drugs for erectile dysfunction, rather than prioritizing their efforts based on public health needs, or on treating life-threatening conditions that cannot be as widely marketed. Pharmaceutical companies' net profits are some of the largest among Fortune 500 companies, and they spend about 60% more on marketing than on research and development (Belk and Belk 2019; Light and Lexchin 2012). Economic interests also affect who is most likely to become ill, and the kind of healthcare they are likely to receive. Many researchers have argued that it is no coincidence that toxic waste dumps and other environmental hazards are most frequently located in or near poor communities, as we will examine later in this chapter. And because the U.S. healthcare system is driven by profits, the wealthy have better access to high-quality healthcare. Seen from this perspective, our medical system reinforces class inequality and serves as a form of social control (Daniels and Schulz 2006). If answers cannot be located in the body alone, then the narrative which blames individuals' "poor choices" is invoked. This is the biomedical view.

Yet poor choices are not the leading causes of unequal rates of illness and disease based on class, race, and gender. The matrix approach redirects our attention to find the actual causes of health inequality. In the remaining subsections we examine a sampling of the many interconnected social factors and social identities, including ethnicity, age, gender, and immigration status, that influence group health patterns in the context of historical and structural inequities.

The Gender Gap in Care

The provision of healthcare is an area in which we find many cases of both oppression and resistance that require an intersectional perspective. Age, disability, gender, race, and class are all connected in the national problem of providing care for an increasingly aging population, many members of which live with severe health impairments or chronic illness. About 44 million people in the United States provide unpaid elder care, and just as child care has historically been defined as women's responsibility, more than 75% of home healthcare has also fallen on the shoulders of women (Family Caregiver Alliance 2020). One out of every five workers, overwhelmingly women, and more often women of color, are simultaneously providing unpaid care to an elderly family member or friend (Peng et al. 2020). 70% say that it is is impacting their jobs (Clancy et al. 2020). One-third of caregivers experience poor health themselves. The stress and exhaustion they experience can lead to depression, alcohol or substance abuse, and physical health problems, including chronic illness and immune deficiency, contributing to their higher mortality rates overall. They also suffer grave financial losses, including lost wages, social security benefits, and retirement funds; informal caregivers lose about $66,000 over their lifetime. Women lose more than men (Family Caregiver Alliance 2020; Peng et al. 2020).

While there is great disparity between the amount and kind of care provided by White women caregivers compared to White male caregivers, this is not the case among Blacks and Hispanics. The amount and kind of care provided by Black women and men caregivers is very similar. This was also found to be the case comparing Hispanic women and men caregivers. Keep in mind, this is a comparison of women and men already serving as primary caregivers. Across race, women are the great majority found in the caregiving role (Cohen et al. 2019). Research also finds that differences can be found if we compare patterns among Hispanic subgroups, and among Asian subgroups. For example, specific religious beliefs and cultural patterns vary across Asian nationality groups that produce different values and expectations of families to care for their elders (Peng et al. 2020).

Paid caregiving is provided by home healthcare workers. In 2020, the average wage for home healthcare workers was $11.28 per hour. Half of home healthcare workers must rely on some form of public assistance to get by, and one in four live below the poverty level (Payscale 2020). Here again, women predominate. 89% of home healthcare workers are women, over half are women of color, and one-quarter are immigrants. Thirteen percent are not U.S. citizens. Home healthcare workers have historically been excluded from the protections and benefits guaranteed to other kinds of employees through legislation, such as a minimum wage and overtime pay, going back to the New Deal (Katznelson 2005). This is due, in part, to the fact that generally, the elderly and the disabled are undervalued and dehumanized in our culture (Rembis, Kudlick, and Nielsen 2018; Whittle 2017; Nielsen 2012). These many factors are significant in explaining the disproportionately high rates of COVID-19 in nursing homes, and among home health care workers. Providing quality care to marginalized populations is not a policy priority.

Class and Financial Impacts

For the majority of the population, old age and disability become economic crises, often plunging individuals and families into poverty or debt (Rembis, Kudlick, and Nielsen 2018; Whittle 2017). Forty percent of Americans with private insurance have high-deductible plans which reduce insurance costs, but increase out-of-pocket expenses for healthcare (Kullgren et al. 2019). In 2019, over 11.9% of severely mentally ill adults had no health insurance (National Alliance on Mental Illness). Economic and health problems can be intertwined in many ways. Living in debt and dealing with aggressive creditors can result in feelings of hopelessness and guilt, as well as clinical depression and anxiety. On the other hand, poor mental health can lead to debt when individuals forget to pay bills, lose their jobs, or rack up debt due to mental healthcare costs including prescription drugs, which frequently are not sufficiently covered by health insurance. Overwhelming debt can lead to homelessness. Many studies have found that at least one in five homeless people is seriously mentally ill (National Alliance on Mental Illness, National Association of Students in Mental Health Research 2020). Even financially successful individuals may end up living on disability benefits, unable to pay their mortgage or rent (Royal College of Psychologists 2020; Sullivan, Warren, and Westbrook 2020).

Growing up poor has lasting consequences. Despite an adult's current class status, growing up in poverty and facing the consequences of economic adversity early in life has negative impacts on health over the life span. For example, poor nutrition in childhood affects aspects of physical development, such as height, as well as cognitive development; and poverty in childhood has been associated with mental health disorders such as depression and anxiety, and decreased ability to control anger (Capistrano, Bianco, and Kim 2016; Repka 2013; Strauss and Thomas 2007).

Specific health problems are highly correlated with class and income (Syme and Berkman 2009). Class-related variables such as education, occupation, income, and wealth have all been found to influence health. Members of the lower class not only experience higher **morbidity rates**, or incidence of illness, but die younger as well. These trends apply not just to identifiable illnesses; they are witnessed across the spectrum of health and wellness, including in rates of mental illness. Scholars have concluded that "those in the lower classes invariably have lower life expectancy and higher death rates from all causes of death, and that this higher rate has been observed since the 12th century when data on this question were first organized" (Syme and Berkman 2009, 24).

The Affordable Care Act (ACA) was intended to improve healthcare access and cut costs while providing every U.S. citizen with healthcare coverage. Under the law, those with incomes below a certain level can receive subsidies to help pay their insurance premiums, and federal funding for Medicaid has been expanded to include the very poorest in the nation. The U.S. Supreme Court has ruled, however, that states can determine for themselves whether or not to expand Medicaid, and 26 states, many of them in the South, have declined to do so. These states are home to about half the country's population, and also include just under 70 percent of poor Blacks without insurance and single mothers. These states are also home to 60 percent of the country's working poor, who also happen to be uninsured (Tavernise and Gebeloff 2013). Improving access to healthcare does not fully eliminate health disparities (Syme and Berkman 2009).

President Trump's attempts to repeal and replace the ACA were unsuccessful; however, Congress did eliminate some of its mandates (Amadeo 2017; Luthra 2019). The future of the ACA has been at risk since Republican attorney general and governors challenged the constitutionality of the law in 2018 (Musumeci 2020).

The Impact of Race

Because of the intersectional nature of social identities and relationships, when we find class inequality, we are sure to find racial inequality as well. The racial health gap increased in the 1980s as a consequence of the increasing racial income and wealth gaps. While there is an overwhelming body of research documenting the impact of class on health and the interaction of class with race, the evidence also reveals that race itself is a significant factor, and sometimes a more significant factor, independent of class.

Overall, we find the greatest health inequities between Whites and Asians, compared to African Americans and Native Americans (Center for Disease Control 2018). Researchers describe the greater life expectancy for Latinx and Asian Americans as an "epidemiological paradox." These two racialized groups are heterogeneous, encompassing numerous diverse immigrant groups from different nations, with different resources, who immigrated at different points in history. All minority-group immigrants experience significantly *better* health than their racial compatriots who are U.S.-born, including healthier birth weights, longer life expectancies, and lower rates of deadly diseases, including cancer and stroke (Ruiz, Hamann, Mehl, and O'Connor 2016; Waldstein 2010). Research has found, for example, that Mexican immigrants have much better health than U.S.-born Mexican Americans. One reason is that they experience stronger health in Mexico prior to coming to the United States. The longer they are in the United States, however, the more their health declines. Research comparing Caribbean Blacks with African Americans, and Asian immigrants with Asian Americans, has had similar findings, which also help us to understand why the health gap between Whites and others is smaller for racial groups with significant immigrant populations (Latinx and Asians). These findings force us to consider the role that simply living in the United States plays in undermining the health of people of color (Betancourt-Garcia et al. 2019; Kandula et al. 2019; Tutu and Busingye 2020). These frequently concealed stories reveal that racism itself is a significant factor (Zambrana and Dill 2006).

Access to Healthcare

Less access to and lower quality of healthcare can help explain a significant degree of health inequities (Chan et al. 2019). Barriers to healthcare access are a factor in the relatively poor health of Native Americans, a group that has rarely been the focus of research on health disparities. A study examining rates of cancer among Native Americans found that, compared with Whites, Native Americans receive fewer health screenings, are diagnosed at later stages of a disease's progression, and have significantly higher cancer mortality rates. Native Americans also report higher rates of dissatisfaction with the healthcare system (Guadagnolo et al. 2009).

African Americans face multiple barriers as well. Compared with Whites, they are less likely to have a regular location to seek healthcare, less likely to receive necessary medications, and more likely to experience delays in treatment. Looking at the intersections of race and gender, Allen et al. (2019) examine the discrimination and institutional racism faced by Black men. Widespread stereotypes that they are dangerous, hypersexual and aggressive, criminal, and more, directly impact their levels of stress and poor health, resulting in higher rates of chronic health problems, that are also disproportionately severe, leading to higher rates of morbidity and shorter life spans. Allen et al. blame social stressors including harmful stereotypes, as well as institutional factors, including disproportionately high rates of incarceration, institutional discrimination, high rates of poverty and unemployment, segregated housing, and more. They concur with other medical researchers that experiences of cumulative stress directly impact physiological health and cortisol levels, which produce a wide range of health problems, both physical and mental. They also find that in cases where White men experience the same cortisol imbalances, they have less of an impact on their health (Allen 2019).

Diabetes: A Case Study in Inequality

Allen et al. (2019) emphasize that race itself does not produce health inequities. They concur with previous research arguing that White people "benefit from privileges associated with affiliation with the dominant racial group that possesses disproportionate political, economic, and social power. As such, racial categories serve as proxies for shared experiences of discrimination or privilege" (p. 2). Racial inequalities are largely a result of social, environmental, and geographic differences. Detailed and nuanced research is necessary to understand the specific contributors that shape the experiences of health among different racialized groups, as well as differences within racialized categories.

Let's consider one specific serious health problem that has been on the rise for all Americans: type 2 diabetes.

- Among White people, 7.5% have been diagnosed with diabetes.

- Prevalence is highest among American Indians and Alaska Natives who are twice as likely as Whites to be diagnosed with diabetes (14.7%).

- 12.5% of Hispanics are diagnosed with diabetes.

- 11.7% of Black people have a diabetes diagnosis.

- 9.2% of Asians have a diabetes diagnosis (U.S. Department of Health and Human Services 2020).

African American and American Indian/Native Alaskans have significantly higher mortality rates due to type 2 diabetes than all other racial groups, whose numbers are fairly similar. Mortality rates are 10% higher for Blacks, and 30% higher for American Indians and Native Americans (Clements et al. 2020).

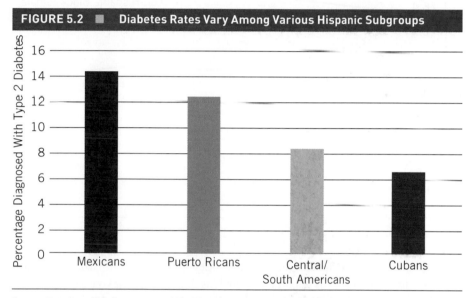

FIGURE 5.2 ■ Diabetes Rates Vary Among Various Hispanic Subgroups

Source: Data from U.S. Department of Health and Human Services, 2020.

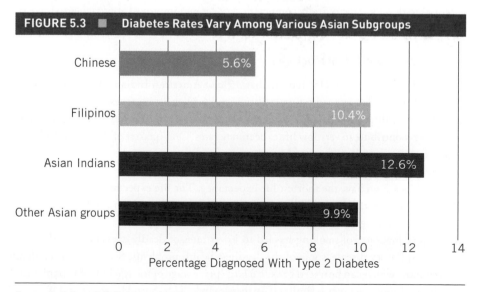

FIGURE 5.3 ■ Diabetes Rates Vary Among Various Asian Subgroups

Source: Data from U.S. Department of Health and Human Services, 2020.

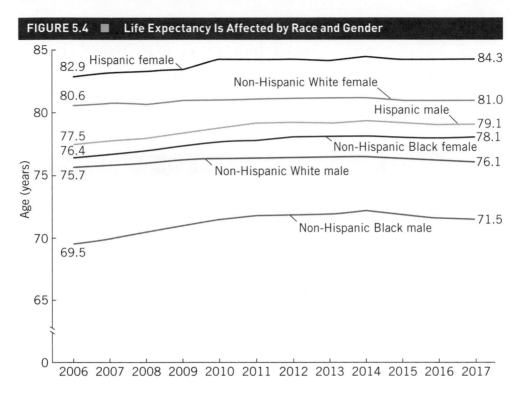

FIGURE 5.4 ■ Life Expectancy Is Affected by Race and Gender

When we examine variability within the categories of Hispanic and Asian, we see further disparities, which highlights the importance of looking deeper into these constructed categories (Figure 5.2 and Figure 5.3). Knowing the different rates of prevalence within racial groups can be essential to developing culturally competent services and improved approaches to increasing care (Cheng et al. 2019).

Life Expectancy and Infant Mortality

The Indian Health Service (IHS) reports that 36% of American Indian and Alaskan Natives' homes do not have adequate sanitation facilities, and 6.5% have no access to safe water and/or waste disposal facilities, compared to less than 1% of homes in the nation overall. These shocking inequities contribute to very low life expectancy rates. One-quarter of American Indian and Alaskan Native people die before reaching the age of 45.

Figure 5.4 shows that for infants born in 2015, Hispanic females can expect to live the longest, while Black men have the shortest life expectancy. The life expectancy for Black males is about five years lower than that of White males, and almost 13 years less than Hispanic women! The Hispanic advantage has been attributed to two factors.

First, very low rates of smoking has led to lower rates of deadly cancers, as well as heart, lung, and respiratory disease, some of the deadliest health problems. Second is the epidemiological paradox, which can be traced back to a large percentage of foreign born-Hispanics in the United States. Life expectancy is similar if we just compare U.S.-born Hispanics and Whites. As

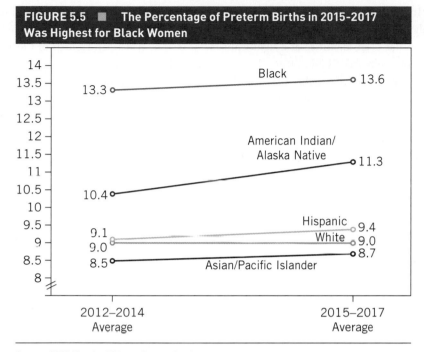

FIGURE 5.5 ■ The Percentage of Preterm Births in 2015-2017 Was Highest for Black Women

Source: 2019 March of Dimes Report Card.

we should also expect, there are differences among foreign-born Hispanics, with Cubans having longer life expectancy rates than Mexicans. For Puerto Ricans who immigrate to the mainland U.S. it is lower (Crimmins and Zhang 2019; Kochanek et al. 2019; Ruiz et al. 2016).

These health inequities begin even prior to birth. Prenatal care increases the chances of giving birth to a healthy infant, yet racialized groups of women receive vastly different care. These differences have been traced to numerous social factors including lack of easy access, mistrust of healthcare providers, lack of culturally competent care, and more (Fryer, Munoz, Rahangdale, and Stuebe 2019; Valerio et al. 2019).

Infants that are born before the completion of 37 weeks are considered preterm, and they are more likely to die. Those that survive experience a range of health problems. The number of preterm births was steadily declining until 2014, when it began increasing. But even during the earlier decline, the gap between the rate at which Black and White women delivered preterm infants was increasing (Manuck 2017). Figure 5.5 provides us with data on the preterm birth rates for the five major racial/ethnic groups.

When compared to all other racial groups, African Americans have a 49% higher rate of preterm births. Some identified factors include higher rates of hypertension, level of prenatal care, maternal education, and even source of payment for delivery. Exposure to environmental factors, such as lead, air pollution, and other toxins also increases risk for preterm births, and African American women experience the highest rates of exposure to these environmental factors (Burris, Collins, and Wright 2011; Thoma et al. 2019). State, county, and degree of racial isolation also influence preterm birth rates (Mehra et al. 2019; Thoma et al. 2019).

In line with this data, Black and Native American women are about three times more likely than White women to die due to pregnancy-related causes. Racial bias in the healthcare system has been identified as a significant factor by The American College of Obstetricians and Gynecologists (Rabin 2019). Wynn (2019) finds that racism and microaggressions are key determinants of whether Black mothers live or die. Other contributing factors that have been identified are lack of access to care, lack of culturally competent communication and support, lack of trust, financial instability, and lack of housing and transportation. One third of women report that costs keep them from seeking necessary healthcare (Gunja et al. 2018; Petersen et al. 2019; Rabin 2019). About one-third of all pregnancy-related deaths are preventable. Nevertheless, the U.S. ranks eleventh among high-income nations in deaths due to pregnancy or childbirth (Gunja et al. 2018). Maternal and infant health has not been made a national priority.

Stress and Microaggressions

Émile Durkheim was the first sociologist to recognize the impact of stress on health (White 2009). Scholars now know that experiencing overt forms of discrimination has negative effects on both the mental and physical health of most minority group members (Sue 2010). Many studies have linked institutional racism and individual experiences of racism to poor health outcomes (Williams 2012; Sue 2010). Various studies of children and adolescents have found that youths of color report experiencing significant levels of racism, whether at school, online, or elsewhere, that can be directly tied to negative mental health outcomes. Racism and stress are key factors in explaining why some health inequities increase further with age, producing a "cumulative disadvantage."

One form of stress frequently experienced by people of color, and other marginalized people, are microaggressions, which are a form of psychological stressor tied specifically to an individual's identity as a member of an oppressed group. The impact of microaggressions comes from their cumulative nature, and the way in which they evoke and serve as a reminder of a history of oppression. Imagine getting a paper cut. It stings for a moment and then you forget about it and move on. Now imagine getting a second paper cut, and then a third, and then a fourth—day after day, the paper cuts keep occurring. It is not

Constant exposure to microaggressions, for instance while working as a health aide in a nursing home, causes harm and creates health risks in every non-White group.

Phanie/Alamy Stock Photo

long before you feel as if your whole body is cut and bleeding. That is how psychologists have described the experience of being exposed to repeated microaggressions. Those who experience a paper cut only occasionally may wonder why people of color make such a big deal of such little things, instead of brushing off a comedian's racist joke as "just kidding around," or dismissing someone's inadvertent racist comment by saying, "Hey, he made a mistake, what's the big deal?" As Sue (2010, 95) describes it: "Microaggressions are linked to a wider sociopolitical context of oppression and injustice (historical trauma) . . . [for] those who understand their own histories of discrimination and prejudice. Each small race-related slight, hurt, invalidation, insult, and indignity rubs salt into the wounds of marginalized groups in our society."

Research finds that every non-White racial group experiences harm and health risks as a result of microaggressions. As with the body's reaction to more overt stressors, the ongoing experience of microaggressions can lead to physiological responses that weaken the immune system, leaving people more vulnerable to illness and disease, including diabetes, high blood pressure, heart disease, and chronic respiratory problems (Green and Darity 2010; Sue 2010; Williams 2012). The body's reaction to stress also facilitates the progression of such diseases. In a 2013 study, David H. Chae found that racial discrimination and anti-Black bias may accelerate the aging process in African American males (see Blake 2014). In addition to these physical consequences, exposure to microaggressions can threaten mental health functioning (Torino 2017). The cumulative toll may help explain why Blacks suffer from greater severity of symptoms and quicker progression of disease than Whites do, even with diseases such as breast cancer and depression, which overall Blacks are less likely to suffer from (Williams 2012).

Those who are most affected by the stress of racism, sexism, and poverty are also least likely to have access to useful coping skills, education, well-paying jobs, and access to healthcare and social services (White 2009, 72).

Researchers using complex statistical analyses have estimated the numbers of deaths each year due to specific social factors. They conclude that "245,000 deaths in the United States were attributable to low education, 176,000 to racial segregation, 162,000 to low social support, 133,000 to individual-level poverty, 119,000 to income inequality, and 39,000 to area-level poverty" (Galea, Tracy, Hoggatt, DiMaggio, and Karpati 2011, 1462). Thinking about the visual image of how each individual is situated within the matrix, we have seen that within the institution of healthcare, a wide range of social identities and social factors, all of which are context specific (shaped by history and place), play important roles. But despite widespread understanding that social factors are some of the most significant influences on health, some scholars continue to seek answers only in our biology.

A Legacy of Mistrust

Lack of trust is one reason contributing to lower rates of vaccination against COVID-19 among the African American community. A history of White supremacy has produced a climate in which people of color have decreased trust in medicine. We have examined how social factors determine the questions for study, framing them as scientific "problems" to be solved and guiding the possible answers, thus limiting what is even imaginable. This process has consequences. People defined as suffering from specific maladies can become subject to various medical, political, and legal forms of social control. Consider the case of **drapetomania**, a "mental ill-ness" invented to explain why enslaved people tried to escape slavery.

Described by Samuel Cartwright in his book *Diseases and Peculiarities of the Negro Race* (1851), this diagnosis could exist only in the context of a White supremacist society that sees slavery as the natural role for human beings defined as inferior. Slavery's stock story posited that enslaved people were happy to be enslaved and were in their natural place according to God's plan. However, if they were happy and content and slavery was God's will, what could explain the many cases of runaways? Drapetomania was the answer, and it also provided a cure—the amputation of the big toes. This remedy was successful because it physically prevented the enslaved person from running away again. The case of drapetomania "was both a product of that society and helped to reinforce the power relations of that society" (White 2009, 43).

Mistrust of medicine is frequently a barrier for people of color. As one man put it, "I think that most of the people who are in control of research don't look like me, and I don't have confidence in how they perceive my value and my worth. I would be very reluctant to give anybody a blank check with respect to experimenting with my body and my life, my health" (quoted in Freimuth et al. 2001, 806). Given the history of medical experimentation, such mistrust is certainly understandable.

Perhaps the best-known medical experiment on a U.S. minority group is the "Tuskegee Syphilis Study of Untreated Syphilis in the Negro Male, 1932–1972." This is the longest-running

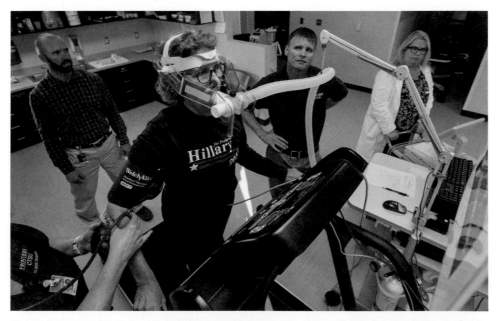

People of color are notably absent from clinical trials, in part because of this population's general mistrust of medical institutions. Other barriers to their participation in medical research include the language used in informational materials, which can be patronizing and incomplete, and the relative lack of researchers who are themselves people of color.

AP Photo/Tammy Ljungblad

nontherapeutic medical study in U.S. history. Conducted by the U.S. Public Health Service in Macon County, Alabama, 399 African American men were recruited as subjects and 201 comprised the control group. The study followed the natural progression of syphilis and denied the men treatment options, such as penicillin, which became the standard of care during the study period. The participants in the study were never informed that they had the disease, and it is estimated that between 28 and 100 men in the study died as a result of their untreated syphilis. The Tuskegee Syphilis Study "provides validation for common suspicions about the ethical even-handedness in the medical research establishment and in the federal government, in particular, when it comes to Black people" (Thomas and Quinn 1991,1499).

The story of this study (which was finally ended after a whistleblower went to the press) helps explain why many Black people harbor fears and mistrust when it comes to the medical research establishment (Alsan and Wanamaker 2016, Bienick, Romano, Kegler, and Eaton 2017; Wesson, Lucey, and Cooper 2019). Researchers argue that this history, combined with the cultural meanings of disease, has created a climate in which fears undermine public health efforts, such as those targeting AIDS in the African American community and many others (Thomas and Quinn 1991). Alsan and Wanamaker (2016) found that public news of the Tuskegee study in 1972 was directly correlated with a decline in Black men's trust of the medical establishment and a decrease in visits to physicians, and with an increase in morbidity rates. Most significant, the researchers found a 1.4-year decrease in life expectancy among Black men over 45 years old.

Most recently, a nurse working at a Georgia Immigration and Customs Enforcement (ICE) detention center has come forward as a whistleblower and claims that mass hysterectomies were performed on women who speak little English, and without their knowledge or consent. In addition, there are complaints of lack of COVID-19 protection measures, insufficient testing of detainees with symptoms, and inadequate medical care, facilitating the spread of the virus. An investigation is now under way (Alvarez 2020; Treisman 2020). This recalls many previous periods of widespread sterilizations of women of color.

The Role of Place and Environmental Racism

Where we live affects our health, and segregated housing is a significant factor in health inequality. In 1899, W. E. B. Du Bois observed that poor people of color and poor Whites faced different living conditions that produced different impacts on their health. This highlights the importance of examining racial differences among people in similar economic strata. High levels of residential racial segregation persist in the United States, and people of color are more likely than Whites to be segregated in neighborhoods that are isolated from key social services and have poor living conditions, including environmental threats to health (Schulz et al. 2016). Poor Whites are more likely than poor people of color to live in economically diverse neighborhoods, with greater access to resources. It is important to examine the neighborhoods, as specific, defined spaces, where people access healthcare. Even in highly diverse neighborhoods, people of color and immigrants often have to seek healthcare outside of their neighborhoods (Pemberton et al. 2019).

Race and class are both linked to exposure to environmental health risks. Hazardous waste dumps, landfills, incinerators, and other toxic sites are much more likely to be

Minority and poor neighborhoods are more likely to be near sources of exposure to toxins and environmental pollutants. Minority children are more likely to suffer from asthma and lead exposure as a result.

Chip Chipman/Bloomberg/Getty Images

located in poor and minority neighborhoods than in wealthier, Whiter ones. People residing in neighborhoods that are primarily minority and lower-class are also exposed to higher levels of pollution, asbestos, and lead, and playgrounds in these neighborhoods are usually older and unsafe. Exposure to high levels of lead, primarily in old houses, impacts behavioral problems and cognitive functioning and can decrease IQ levels and even lead to organ failure (Agency for Toxic Substances and Disease Registry 2000; Sorenson et al. 2019). A large body of research documents these realities and their impacts (Massey 2004; Whitehead and Buchanan 2019).

For example, people of color and low-income Whites are significantly more likely to suffer from asthma, a difference that begins early in childhood. Additionally, socioeconomics, chronic stress, and discrimination are also considered environmental factors which can also have an actual impact on biology and genes, leading to increased levels of asthma among minority groups. African Americans and Hispanics have the highest rates of asthma in the U.S. and African Americans have the highest morbidity and mortality rates among those suffering from asthma plus exposure to environmental pollutants (Barnthouse and Jones 2019). Asthma also leads to missed school days and decreased academic performance among children (Serebrisky and Wiznia 2019). Research on air quality in schools has found that greater levels of pollution contribute to lower academic performance, and children of color face the worst levels of exposure to pollution in school (Barnthouse and Jones 2019).

The Human Genome Project

Today, research on race and genetics is progressing at a faster rate than ever before. In 1990, the internationally funded **Human Genome Project** (HGP) set out to map and sequence the entire spectrum of human genes. Recalling Davenport's attempt to create a comprehensive catalog of every human trait, sociologist Troy Duster (2003) refers to these contemporary efforts as a "backdoor to eugenics."

The HGP, which was completed in 2003, sparked renewed debate over the use of race in medicine and science. While geneticists acknowledge that race has no genetic basis, there is disagreement about the usefulness of race as a system of categories for sorting human differences. Some geneticists and biomedical researchers argue that our taken-for-granted racial classifications can be used as a means of dividing people into groups based on shared ancestry (Yaylacı, ŞuleRoth, and Jaffe 2019). However, scientists have discovered that all humans are 99% genetically similar, and approximately 85% of human genetic variation occurs within so-called races—far more than can be found between any racialized groups. People categorized as belonging to the same race may have very little in common genetically or biologically (Ossorio and Duster 2005; Yaylacı, ŞuleRoth, and Jaffe 2019).

This view of genetic variation would seem to make racial categorizations useless. However, there are other interests at stake. One purpose of the HGP was to identify genetic markers for susceptibility to specific genetic disorders, so that gene therapies could be developed to prevent, treat, or cure them. According to the U.S. Government's Human Genome Project website, "An important feature of the HGP project was the federal government's long-standing dedication to the transfer of technology to the private sector. By licensing technologies to private companies and awarding grants for innovative research, the project catalyzed the multibillion-dollar U.S. biotechnology industry and fostered the development of new medical applications." The website boasts that as a result of the HGP, many wide-ranging industries are booming, and "new entrepreneurs" are popping up to "offer an abundance of genomic services and applications" (Human Genome Project Information Archive 2013).

We have seen the growth of companies offering to provide us with information about our ancestors; the launch of the first racially targeted medicine, BiDil, a heart disease drug marketed to African Americans; and new methods of screening for birth "defects" and genetic diseases. While some of these advances may be welcome, they also carry unexamined assumptions from our eugenic past. For example, disability activists warn that screening for birth "defects" once again defines disabled bodies as "unfit" and as potential targets for elimination (Saxton 2010).

These developments also target individual consumers. The individualization of health and medicine directs our attention away from the larger issue of racial inequities in health and the factors that produce those inequities, supporting the stock story that locates inferiority in the bodies of people of color (Daniels and Schulz 2006; Hubbard and Wald 1999). Scholar Emily Martin (2006, 86) addresses the ethical dilemma raised by this approach in her critique of drugs tailored to specific racial groups. She asks, "Will making more and better medicines available to African Americans who suffer more stress due to poverty and racism provide something we want to call a solution, let alone a cure?"

Sociologists Ossorio and Duster (2005, 116) offer a way out of the trap of seeing race as either useful or not. They suggest an alternative perspective, informed by a sociological lens:

> Race and racial categories can best be understood as a set of social processes that can create biological consequences; race is a set of social processes with biological feedbacks that require empirical investigation. Researchers ought to be discussing when and how best to use race as a variable rather than arguing about the categorical exclusion or inclusion of race in science. Researchers ought to interrogate the meaning of observed racial differences. In doing so, they must recognize that race may be a consequence of differential treatment and experiences rather than an independent cause of differential outcomes.

One of the foundational arguments of a sociological perspective on health and medicine is that scientific knowledge is an inherently social enterprise (White 2009, 14). The scientific-medical eugenics discourse was the product of a specific social and historical context, and reflected the values of the dominant members of society. While some scholars refer to eugenics as pseudoscience, we have chosen not to do so, but to instead emphasize the fact that *all* scientific and medical knowledge is social. Eugenics is not a unique example of how medicine can be penetrated by social prejudices. Instead, medicine is always a social practice. It is carried out by social beings in specific social and cultural contexts.

Critical Thinking

1. How has the tendency to focus on genetics changed over time? What do you see as possible positive and negative outcomes of the Human Genome Project and today's renewed interest in genetics as they shape both health and identity?

2. How do social factors pervading the institution of healthcare and medicine contribute to the greater toll of the coronavirus pandemic on communities of color?

3. What motivations may underlie drug companies' efforts to develop race-specific medications?

4. How might your own intersecting identities shape your physical and mental health?

RESISTING AND TRANSFORMING INEQUALITY IN HEALTH AND HEALTHCARE

The title of Sandra Morgen's 2002 book about the women's health movement, *Into Our Own Hands,* is an apt description of the steps taken by every community of color in the United States. In response to a long history of systemic racist violence, abuse, and neglect, we find remarkable numbers of individuals and communities facing these challenges head-on and working to meet their own health needs while simultaneously battling racist institutions and organizations.

We have already seen one example in the history of the National Medical Association. Now we examine a few more.

Urban American Indian Health Care

Overall, people of color are more likely than their White counterparts to receive low-quality healthcare. American Indians and Alaska Natives, however, face unique circumstances. Healthcare services provided by the Indian Health Service (IHS), a division of the U.S. Department of Health and Human Services on reservations, are reserved for members of the 567 federally recognized tribes. Indian Health Services also administers urban Indian health programs operating in the largest urban areas, but these are inaccessible to the majority of non-reservation Indians. This means that some tribes do not benefit at all, while some benefit more than others (Indian Health Services 2020; Marley 2019). Out of an estimated 2.7 million Native Americans, only 1.9 million are registered members of a government-identified tribe (Roygardner, Schneider, and Steiger 2019). Where available, however, IHS-provided healthcare is free and more likely to be culturally responsive and respectful of indigenous traditions, although due to lack of funding they are limited in the services they are able to offer. IHS funding is not secure and is determined each year by the President and Congress. IHS is only able to provide less than one-half of the amount of money per person as Medicaid provides. As a result, health inequities between Native Americans and Whites remain wide (Marley 2019).

About one-fifth of American Indians and Alaska Natives remain or live close to a reservation. The rest have moved, most often to urban areas, where obtaining healthcare is more difficult and expensive, and the care available is less culturally sensitive (Roygardner, Schneider, and Steiger 2019). Less than 15% of Native American children have any sort of insurance at all, and a little over half are covered by Medicaid (Rudowitz, Musumeci, and Hall 2019). Native Americans face disproportionate levels of depression and other mental health issues, suicide, alcohol and substance addiction, as well as higher rates of infants born with fetal alcohol syndrome. Native American children, when compared to every other racial/ethnic group, are more likely to grow up living below the poverty line, experiencing violent crime, and dying as a result of some kind of accident (Rudowitz, Musumeci, and Hall 2019).

In addition to the factors noted earlier, urban American Indians have few informal and formal community support networks to turn to, and they are unlikely to find traditional or even American Indian healthcare providers (Burrage, Gone, and Momper 2016; Filippi et al. 2016; Marley 2019). Dr. Joseph P. Gone, of Harvard University's Global Health and Social Medicine program, is developing an Urban American Indian Traditional Spirituality Program after research discovered a need and great desire among urban indigenous people to connect to traditional healing practices (Gone, Tuomi, and Fox 2020).

In response to these circumstances, Native Americans have founded many urban health organizations to provide prevention and treatment services in culturally appropriate and respectful ways. These organizations have also been making efforts to improve data collection and research on this community, although limited funding has curtailed this work. The Urban Indian Health Institute is improving data collection, especially around specific issues they face.

One of their projects focuses on violence against indigenous women, educating the public about the true extent of this horror. The third leading cause of death for indigenous women is murder. And they are two and a half times more likely to be sexually assaulted or raped. The Urban Indian Health Institute has published data and reports specifically examining the cases of murdered and missing Alaska Native women. The organization offers webinars and toolkits to engage the wider public to become active in addressing this urgent problem. They have recently focused on another form of genocide, "a data genocide."

Many state reports do not include the category of NAAI in their race-based data and under-report confirmed cases to the CDC. Their COVID-19 Data Report Card examines each state, showing wide variation. The nation as a whole receives a D+ (Urban Indian Health Institute, 2021).

While these organizations can produce some measure of improvement at the individual and local levels, they argue that the Native American community faces issues that cannot be remedied without broader structural changes that address federal policy, including but not limited to the provision of health services, as well as socioeconomic factors. The history of extermination, segregation, broken promises, and recent patterns of government neglect will not be remedied by individual-level responses.

Race, Reproduction, and the Women's Health Movement

The first wave of the women's movement, besides fighting for suffrage in the early 20th century, also focused on access to birth control. At the time, any public discussion of contraception was against the law, which limited information access to well-off women who could consult with private doctors. Margaret Sanger, one of the leaders of the birth control movement, was arrested for promoting contraception through the U.S. mail. Again arrested and jailed for opening the first birth control clinic in 1916, she founded the American Birth Control League, which later became Planned Parenthood. Immigrant and poor women would beg Sanger, who worked as a nurse, for information on how to prevent pregnancy, and she witnessed firsthand the poor health and needless deaths of many married women due to too many pregnancies. Keenly aware of the barriers faced by immigrant women, Sanger used the racism and eugenics ideology of the time to appeal to those in power, arguing that birth control would benefit White society by limiting the numbers of children born to immigrant families from Southern and Eastern Europe (DuBois and Dumenil 2012).

Because of the racist inflection of the debate over birth control, and its connections with the eugenics movement, Black women educated themselves about birth control and reproductive health, beginning with the women's clubs affiliated with the National Association of Colored Women. For Black women, as for many other marginalized women, the issue of reproductive rights included not only the right to use contraception but also the right to choose to have children and to be free of nonconsensual sterilization.

Women's educational and occupational opportunities are limited if they have no control over their reproduction. Growing directly out of the second wave of the women's rights movement, the women's health movement in the late 1960s and early 1970s particularly focused on increasing women's control over their reproductive and sexual health. Early on, women of color like Byllye Avery became "acutely aware of how little information existed about Black women's health and of how the movement [they were] part of defined issues, strategies, and services with little attention or awareness of the specific needs and perspectives of women of color" (Morgen 2002, 41). The mainstream women's movement's narrow focus on abortion and choice needed to be expanded to encompass the fuller range of women's reproductive needs and rights.

Avery, a board member of the National Women's Health Network, worked with others to form self-help groups for Black women, and initiated the NWHN's National Black Women's Health Project (NBWHP), which became its own organization in 1984. The NBWHP situated Black women's health within the larger context of not only sexism but also racism and class inequity, and broadened its focus from the "pro-choice" platform to one of **reproductive justice**, defined as "the right to have children, not have children, and to parent the children we have in safe and healthy environments. Reproductive justice addresses the social reality of inequality, specifically, the inequality of opportunities that we have to control our reproductive destiny" (SisterSong 2013).

Another significant focus of the White dominated women's health movement included a strong critique of the professionalization of women's health issues as medicalized matters, best left to doctors. For example, after centuries caring for women and delivering babies, midwives had been delegitimated. The movement engaged in efforts to return that control to women themselves. However, "for many women of color access to basic healthcare had been historically, and for many remained, limited. Instead of demanding that doctors, public health officials, and other healthcare professionals cede their power to ordinary women, women of color health activists were often fighting to expand professional health services into their communities" (Morgen 2002: 54).

RESISTANCE STORY: LORETTA ROSS—NOT JUST CHOICE BUT REPRODUCTIVE JUSTICE

I was born in 1953 in Temple, Texas, the sixth of eight children in a churchgoing family. I was raped by a soldier at the age of 11 and then again by my mother's adult cousin. At age 16, I had an abortion. My mother would not consent to my obtaining birth control, although I was already a teen mother and attending my first year of college thousands of miles away from home. I was lucky—abortion had been legalized in Washington, D.C., in 1970, the year I desperately needed one, so I avoided the back alley. I had a safe and legal abortion, although my older sister had to forge my mother's signature on the consent form. I do not, in any way, regret my decision. What happened to me—rape, incest, parental blocking—should not happen to any other girl, and I'm proud to be a feminist fighting for all women's human rights. African American women have made consistent and critical activist contributions to the evolution of the reproductive rights movement in the United States, expanding the movement to highlight other aspects of our struggle to achieve reproductive freedom based on our experiences of pregnancy, infant mortality, sterilization abuse, welfare abuse, and sexuality in general.

I began my work as a reproductive justice activist in the early 1970s, focusing on sterilization abuse. I have witnessed the development of a strong reproductive freedom movement among Black women during this period. In doing research to support my activism, I discovered a long tradition of reproductive rights advocacy by Black women that was either undocumented or not widely understood. I became determined to reconnect the work of Black activists at the beginning of the 20th century to the work and ideology of those at the century's end.

I have spent 38 years launching and managing nonprofit feminist organizations, including SisterSong Women of Color Reproductive Justice Collective. The Collective was formed in 1997 to fulfill a need for a national movement by women of color to organize our voices to represent ourselves and our communities. SisterSong comprises 80 local, regional, and national grassroots organizations. SisterSong educates women of color on reproductive and sexual health and rights, and works toward improving access to health services, information, and resources that are culturally and linguistically appropriate through the integration of the disciplines of community organizing, self-help, and human rights education. The mission of SisterSong is to amplify and strengthen the collective voices of indigenous women and women of color to ensure reproductive justice through securing human rights.

Joining the women's movement not only transformed my life but also saved it. On my journey, I've learned about women's human rights, reproductive justice, White supremacy, and women of color organizing.

The conferences, workshops, and other activities of the NBWHP nurtured other new grassroots organizations in the 1980s, including the National Latina Health Organization, the Native American Women's Health Education Resource Center, and the National Asian Women's Health Organization. Each of these organizations maintains an emphasis on the diversity of women's needs within these communities, while at the same time addressing some of the specific challenges each constituent group faces.

Today, a vibrant movement is fighting for reproductive justice. Women with disabilities critically advanced the reproductive justice framework based on their own history of sterilization, the treatment of people with disabilities as non-sexual beings, the risks posed by genetic testing that attempts to eliminate the disabled, and more. A reproductive justice approach moves disability rights activism from a focus on individual rights to a framework that examines access to services and support that can allow society to acknowledge the inherent value and worth of human beings with disabilities (Jesudason and Epstein 2011). While *Roe v. Wade* (1972) declared women's right to control their reproductive systems, restrictions limiting this right have proliferated. Most states have adopted laws restricting access to abortion, and continue to do so, making it increasingly difficult for women to have an abortion at all (Guttmacher Institute, 2020).

The efforts of international nongovernmental organizations supporting women's health have also increased over the past few decades, while U.S. aid declined due to our nation's "gag rule." While reproductive health inequities reflect existing social and economic inequities, they also reinforce them. International family planning programs are one key component of improving women's lives around the world (Sedgh, Hussain, Bankole, and Singh 2007, 5). According to the Global Fund for Women (2020), there are about 214 million women who want, but lack access to, contraception. This is the case when focusing on abortion access as well. For LGBTQ people of all races and ethnic groups, same-sex relationships are outlawed in 76 nations.

Researchers have found that more than one in seven married women needs or wants contraception, but is not using any. The same is true for one in thirteen women ages 15 to 29 who have never married. The most common reason these women are not using contraception is a lack of access to "supplies and services," including counseling and education about contraceptive options (Sedgh et al. 2007, 5). Around the world, women are working together locally to improve women's health. In order to improve health and healthcare access among oppressed populations, those directly affected must be a part of the process of finding solutions.

A Path to the Future

One of the most important lessons we can learn from what we have examined in this chapter is that strategies that narrowly target individual behavior are not enough. Health inequities are a social problem that requires much broader social change.

Evidence suggests that policies targeting inequity at a broader level can reduce the health gap. For example, in the United States, states with higher levels of social spending have higher overall levels of health (Gallet and Doucouliagos 2017; Verma, Clark, Leider, and Bishai 2016). As this chapter has shown, health disparities reflect social inequeties in our society and are interconnected with other institutional structures, such as economy, education, the law, and a culture that reproduces racial inequality (Weber 2006). Simplistic individual-level responses, like telling someone to lose weight, will not solve the deep-rooted problems of health inequities. Beyond the historic and cross-cultural social movements we have examined throughout the chapter, another example of positive social change is the growing recognition within medicine of the importance of social factors. In 2015, the Association of American Medical Colleges began requiring students taking the MCAT entrance exam to have background knowledge in the social sciences. In 2012 the association announced

> A new section, "Psychological, Social, and Biological Foundations of Behavior," will test the ways in which these areas influence a variety of factors, including people's perceptions and reactions to the world; behavior and behavior change; what people think about themselves and others; cultural and social differences that influence well-being; and the relationships among socio-economic factors, access to resources, and well-being.

A truly interdisciplinary and intersectional approach is essential to a real commitment to decreasing health inequities. Additionally, change can take place at different levels, within organizations, in law, among individual doctors' awareness of microaggressions, and among large numbers of people in various communities sparking social movements.

Critical Thinking

1. What examples of resistance and transformative narratives can you find in response to the inequity and inequality as a result of the pandemic?

2. Access to reproductive healthcare and options are constantly in flux, depending on federal and state legislation, and local and regional availability of care. What are the obstacles limiting equitable reproductive justice for women in your locale today?

3. Select a specific racial/ethnic subgroup, such as Hmong, Vietnamese, Puerto Ricans, immigrants from Ethiopia, etc., and discuss an example of a community response to specific health needs they have identified.

CHAPTER SUMMARY

5.1 Describe contemporary inequality in health and healthcare.

Today's disparities among racial and ethnic groups in health and mortality are evidence of the historical and ongoing effects of structural racism. Racial disparities exist in healthcare access, disease prevention, identification of disease, treatment, care coordination, outcomes, patient satisfaction, and more. Today's health disparities have been significantly shaped by historical patterns of White privilege and White supremacy. Modern medicine displaced traditional methods of healing in many cultures, and played a central role in the construction of racial classifications and corresponding notions of difference. History is replete with examples of resistance to health inequities. African Americans developed their own healthcare systems in response to their exclusion from segregated institutions.

5.2 Examine various stock narratives of inequality in health and medicine.

Our stock stories lead us to assume that medical advances are responsible for today's longer life spans; that the field of medicine and healthcare employs objective science; that race is a biological reality that can help explain disparities in health; and that health is strictly a matter of individual and genetic factors. Research, however, reveals the important roles of social factors such as hygiene and nutrition, as well as race and class.

5.3 Apply the matrix lens to the link between race and healthcare.

The matrix perspective highlights various social factors contributing to racial health inequity and inequality, including stress, social relationships, socioeconomic factors, residential segregation, environmental factors, and mistrust, as well as the interactions of race, class, gender, age, and more. The field of social epidemiology highlights the relationships among race, class, and health, and explains the "epidemiological paradox" of better *overall* health among Asians and Latinx, racial groups with significant numbers of immigrants.

5.4 Explore alternatives to the current matrix of inequality in health and medicine.

Disenfranchised groups have created many organizations to address and act as advocates for their health needs. The Urban Indian Health Institute and a wide array of health organizations founded by women of color place these groups' health needs within the broader context of social and institutional factors shaped by a history of racism. These organizations argue that health disparities cannot be remedied without broader structural changes. Organizations started and run by women of color and disabled women have fought for a more inclusive understanding of women's reproductive health needs.

KEY TERMS

American Medical
    Association

biomedicine

conversion therapy

curandero/as

drapetomania

epidemiology

eugenics

Human Genome Project

internalized racism

medical sociology

microaggressions

morbidity rates

mortality rates

reproductive justice

Social Darwinism

traditional medicine

REFERENCES

Agbedia, C. O. 2019. "Exploring Inequity in Health; an Ecological Approach." *International Journal of Forensic Medical Investigation* 4, no. 2: 35-39.

Agency for Toxic Substances and Disease Registry. 2000. *Lead Toxicity.* Publication No. ATSDR-HF-CS-2001-0001. Washington, DC: U.S. Department of Health and Human Services.

Allen, Julie Ober, Daphne C. Watkins, Linda Chatters, Arline T. Geronimus, and Vicki Johnson-Lawrence. "Cortisol and racial health disparities affecting Black men in later life: evidence from MIDUS II." *American journal of men's health* 13, no. 4 (2019): 1557988319870969.

Alsan, Marcella, and Marianne Wanamaker. "Tuskegee and the Health of Black Men." Working Paper 22323, National Bureau of Economic Research Accessed June 27, 2017. http://www.nber.org/papers/w22323.pdf.

Alvarez, Priscilla. Sept. 16, 2020. Whistleblower alleges high rate of hysterectomies and medical neglect at ICE facility. CNN. Accessed January 11, 2021. https://www.cnn.com/2020/09/15/politics/immigration-customs-enforcement-medical-care-detainees/index.html

Amadeo, Kimberly. 2017. "Donald Trump on Health Care." The Balance, June 26. Accessed June 27, 2017. https://www.thebalance.com/how-could-trump-change-health-care-in-america-4111422.

Association of American Medical Colleges. 2012. "New Medical College Admission Test Approved: Changes Add Emphasis on Behavioral and Social Sciences." Press release, February 16. Accessed March 31, 2015. https://www.aamc.org/newsroom/newsreleases/273712/120216.html.

Association of American Medical Colleges. 2018. Reshaping the Journey: American Indians and Alaskan Natives in medicine.Accessed January 11, 2021. https://store.aamc.org/downloadable/download/sample/sample_id/243/

Association of American Medical Colleges. 2020. Table A-12: Applicants, First-Time Applicants, Acceptees, and Matriculants to U.S.Medical Schools by Race/Ethnicity, 2017-2018 through 2020-2021. Accessed January 2021. https://www.aamc.org/system/files/2020-10/2020_FACTS_Table_A-12.pdf

Barnes, Colin. 2010. "A Brief History of Discrimination and Disabled People." In *The Disability Studies Reader,* 3rd ed., edited by Lennard J. Davis, New York: Routledge.

Barnthouse, Maggie, and Bridgette L. Jones. "The impact of environmental chronic and toxic stress on asthma." *Clinical reviews in allergy & immunology* 57, no. 3 (2019): 427-438.

Bateman-House, A. and Fairchild, A., 2008. Medical examination of immigrants at Ellis island. *AMA Journal of Ethics*, *10*(4), pp. 235-241. https://www.journalofethics.ama-assn.org/article/medical-examination-immigrants-ellis-island/2008-04

Belk, David, and P. Belk. "The Pharmaceutical Industry." *True Cost of Healthcare* (2019). Accessed March 30, 2020 at: http://www.truecostofhealthcare.org/wp-content/uploads/2019/03/The PharmaIndust.pdf

Betancourt-Garcia, Monica M., Kristina Vatcheva, Prateek K. Gupta, Ricardo D. Martinez, Joseph B. McCormick, Susan P. Fisher-Hoch, and R. Armour Forse. "The effect of Hispanic ethnicity on surgical outcomes: An analysis of the NSQIP database." *The American Journal of Surgery* 217, no. 4 (2019): 618-633.

Blake, Kelly. 2014. "Racism May Accelerate Aging in African American Men." UMD Right Now, January 7. Accessed June 2, 2017. http://www.umdrightnow.umd.edu/news/racism-may-accelerate-aging-african-american-men.

Blumenfeld, Warren J. 2012. "One Year Sick and Then Not: On the Social Construction of Homosexuality as Disease." Warren Blumenfeld's Blog, December 27. Accessed December 12, 2013. http://www.warrenblumenfeld.com/?s=homo sexuality+disease.

Bourree. Lam, 2014. "Who Stays Home When the Kids Are Sick?" *Atlantic,* October. Accessed May 14, 2017. https://www.theatlantic.com/business/archive/2014/10/who-stays-home-when-the-kids-are-sick/382011.

Brenick, Alaina, Kelly Romano, Christopher Kegler, and Lisa A. Eaton. 2017. "Understanding the Influence of Stigma and Medical Mistrust on Engagement in Routine Healthcare among Black Women Who Have Sex with Women." *LGBT Health* 4, no. 1: 4–10.

Burrage, Rachel L., Joseph P. Gone, and Sandra L. Momper. 2016. *American Journal of Community Psychology* 136–49."Urban American Indian Community Perspectives on Resources and Challenges for Youth Suicide Prevention." 58 nos. 1–2:

Burris, Heather H., James W. Collins Jr, and Robert O. Wright. "Racial/ethnic disparities in preterm birth: clues from environmental exposures." *Current opinion in pediatrics* 23, no. 2 (2011): 227.

Capistrano, Christian G., Hannah Bianco, and Pilyoung Kim. 2016. *Frontiers in Psychology* doi:10.3389/fpsyg.2016.01242."Poverty and Internalizing Symptoms: The Indirect Effect of Middle Childhood Poverty on Internalizing Symptoms via an Emotional Response Inhibition Pathway." 7.

Carlton, Genivieve. 2018. Virginia Ran A Secret Eugenics Program That Didn't End Until 1979. Medium. Accessed January 11, 2021. https://www.medium.com/@editors_91459/virginia-ran-a-secret-eugenics-program-that-didnt-end-until-1979-e9fcbfd23c64

Castillo, Michelle. 2013. "U.S. Life Expectancy Lowest among Wealthy Nations Due to Disease, Violence." CBS News. Accessed April 2, 2015. http://www.cbsnews.com/news/report-us-life-expectancy-lowest-among-wealthy-nations-due-to-disease-violence.

Centers for Disease Control. 2018. *Summary Health Statistics: National Health Interview Survey, 2018.* Accessed April 14, 2021 (https://www.ftp.cdc.gov/pub/Health_Statistics/NCHS/NHIS/SHS/2018_SHS_Table_P-1.pdf).

Centers for Disease Control and Prevention. 2017. "Stroke Facts." Accessed June 19, 2017. https://www.cdc.gov/stroke/facts.htm.

Chan, Kitty S., Darrell J. Gaskin, Rachael R. McCleary, and Roland J. Thorpe Jr. "Availability of health care provider offices and facilities in minority and integrated communities in the US." *Journal of health care for the poor and underserved* 30, no. 3 (2019): 986-1000.

Chappell, Bill. March 26, 2020. Coronavirus Cases Spike In Navajo Nation, Where Water Service Is Often Scarce. NPR. Accessed January 11, 2021. https://www.npr.org/sections/coronavirus-live-updates/2020/03/26/822037719/coronavirus-cases-spike-in-navajo-nation-where-water-service-is-often-scarce

Charatz-Litt, C. 1992. "A Chronicle of Racism: The Effects of the White Medical Community on Black Health." *Journal of the National Medical Association* 84, no. 8 (August): 717–25.

Cheng, Yiling J., Alka M. Kanaya, Maria Rosario G. Araneta, Sharon H. Saydah, Henry S. Kahn, Edward W. Gregg, Wilfred Y. Fujimoto, and Giuseppina Imperatore. "Prevalence of diabetes by race and ethnicity in the United States, 2011-2016."Jama 322, no. 24 (2019): 2389-2398.

Clancy, Rebecca L., Gwenith G. Fisher, Kelsie L. Daigle, Christine A. Henle, Jean McCarthy, and Christine A. Fruhauf. "Eldercare and work among informal caregivers: A multidisciplinary review and recommendations for future research." *Journal of Business and Psychology* 35, no. 1 (2020): 9-27.

Clements, John M., Brady T. West, Zachary Yaker, Breanna Lauinger, Deven McCullers, James Haubert, Mohammad Ali Tahboub, and Gregory J. Everett. "Disparities in diabetes-related multiple chronic conditions and mortality: The influence of race." *Diabetes Research and Clinical Practice* 159 (2020): 107984.

Coco, Adrienne Phelps. 2010. "Diseased, Maimed, Mutilated: Categorizations of Disability and an Ugly Law in Late Nineteenth-Century Chicago." *Journal of Social History* 44, no. 1: 23–37.

Cohen, Elizabeth, and John Bonifield. 2012. "California's Dark Legacy of Forced Sterilizations." CNN, March 15. Accessed December 11, 2012. http://www.cnn.com/2012/03/15/health/california-forced-sterilizations.

Cohen, Steven A., Natalie J. Sabik, Sarah K. Cook, Ariana B. Azzoli, and Carolyn A. Mendez-Luck. "Differences within differences: Gender inequalities in caregiving intensity vary by race and ethnicity in informal caregivers." *Journal of cross-cultural gerontology* 34, no. 3 (2019): 245-263.

Collyer, Fran. "Origins and canons: medicine and the history of sociology." *History of the Human Sciences* 23, no. 2 (2010): 86-108.

Conrad, Peter, and Valerie Leiter, 2012. *The Sociology of Health and Illness: Critical Perspectives.* 9th ed. New York: Worth.

Crimmins, Eileen M., and Yuan S. Zhang. "Aging populations, mortality, and life expectancy." *Annual Review of Sociology* 45 (2019): 69-89.

Daniels, Jessie, and Amy J. Schulz. 2006. "Constructing Whiteness in Health Disparities Research." In *Gender, Race, Class, and Health: Intersectional Approaches,* edited by Amy J. and Schulz LeithMullings, 89–127. San Francisco: Jossey-Bass.

Davis, Lennard J. 2010. "Constructing Normalcy." In *The Disability Studies Reader,* 3rd ed., edited by Lennard J. Davis, 3–19. New York: Routledge.

De la Rosa, Iván A. 2002. "Perinatal Outcomes among Mexican Americans: A Review of an Epidemiological Paradox." *Ethnicity & Disease* 12 (Autumn): 480–87.

Despotovic, Aleksa, Branko Milosevic, Ivana Milosevic, Nikola Mitrovic, Andja Cirkovic, Snezana Jovanovic, and Goran Stevanovic. "Hospital-acquired infections in the adult intensive care unit—Epidemiology, antimicrobial resistance patterns, and risk factors for acquisition and mortality." *American Journal of Infection Control* (2020).

Drohan, Sarah E., Simon A. Levin, Bryan T. Grenfell, and Ramanan Laxminarayan. "Incentivizing hospital infection control." *Proceedings of the National Academy of Sciences* 116, no. 13 (2019): 6221-6225.

Du Bois, W. E. B. 1899. *The Philadelphia Negro: A Social Study.* Philadelphia: University of Pennsylvania Press.

Dubois, Ellen Carol, and Lynn Dumenil. 2012. *Through Women's Eyes: An American History with Documents.* New York, NY: Bedford / St. Martin's.

Duster, Troy. 2003. *Backdoor to Eugenics.* 2nd ed. New York: Routledge.

Ekland-Olson, Sheldon, and Julie Beicken. 2012. *How Ethical Systems Change: Eugenics, the Final Solution, Bioethics.* New York: Routledge.

El-Serag, Hashem B. "Epidemiology of hepatocellular carcinoma." *The Liver: Biology and Pathobiology* (2020): 758–772.

Family caregiver alliance. Accessed 3-30-20. https://www.caregiver.org/caregiving

Feagin, Joe R., and Karyn D. McKinney. 2003. *The Many Costs of Racism.* Lanham, MD: Rowman & Littlefield.

Ferber, Abby L. 1998. *White Man Falling: Race, Gender, and White Supremacy.* Lanham, MD: Rowman & Littlefield.

Filippi, Melissa K., David G. Perdue, Christina Hester, Angelia Cully, Lance Cully, K. Allen Greiner, and Christine M. Daley. 2016. "Colorectal Cancer Screening Practices among Three American Indian Communities in Minnesota." *Journal of Cultural Diversity* 23, no. 1: 21–27.

Fletcher, Grant S. *Clinical epidemiology: the essentials.* Lippincott Williams & Wilkins, 2019.

Freimuth, Vicki S., Sandra Crouse Quinn, Stephen B. Thomas, Galen Cole, Eric Zook, and Ted Duncan. 2001. "African Americans' Views on Research and the Tuskegee Syphilis Study." *Social Science & Medicine* 52: 797–808.

Fryer, Kimberly E., Chris Munoz, Lisa Rahangdale, and Alison M. Stuebe. (2019): "Barriers to Prenatal Care by Race/Ethnicity in Multiparous Women [27F]." *Obstetrics & Gynecology* 133 69S.

Galea, Sandro, Melissa Tracy, Katherine J. Hoggatt, Charles DiMaggio, and Adam Karpati. 2011. "Estimated Deaths Attributable to Social Factors in the United States." *American Journal of Public Health* 101, no. 8: 1456–65.

Gallet, Craig A., and Chris Doucouliagos. 2017. "The Impact of Healthcare Spending on Health Outcomes: A Meta-regression Analysis." *Social Science & Medicine* 179(C): 9–17.

Glenn, Evelyn Nakano. 2010. *Forced to Care: Coercion and Caregiving in America.* Cambridge, MA: Harvard University Press.

Global Fund for Women. 2020. https://www.globalfundforwomen.org/sexual-reproductive-health-rights/

Gone, Joseph P., Ashley Tuomi, and Nickole Fox. 2020. "The Urban American Indian Traditional Spirituality Program: Promoting Indigenous Spiritual Practices for Health Equity." *American Journal of Community Psychology* 66(3-4): 279-289.

Green, Tiffany L., and William A. Darity Jr. 2010. "Under the Skin: Using Theories from Biology and the Social Sciences to Explore the Mechanisms behind the Black—White Health Gap." *American Journal of Public Health* 100 (suppl. 1): 36–38.

Guadagnolo, B. Ashleigh, Kristen Cina, Petra Helbig, Kevin Molloy, Mary Reiner, E. Francis Cook, and Daniel Petereit. 2009. "Medical Mistrust and Less Satisfaction with Health Care among Native Americans Presenting for Cancer Treatment." *Journal of Health Care for the Poor and Underserved* 20, no. 1 (February): 210–26.

Gunja, Munira Z., R. Tikkanen, S. Seervai, and S. R. Collins. "What is the status of women's health and health care in the US compared to ten other countries." *Commonwealth Fund, Dec* (2018). Accessed 1/6/20. https://www.commonwealthfund.org/publications/issue-briefs/2018/dec/womens-health-us-compared-ten-other-countries

Guttmacher Institute. An overview of Abortion Laws. Accessed online January 11, 2021. https://www.guttmacher.org/state-policy/explore/overview-abortion-laws

Himmelstein, Kathryn EW, and Atheendar S. Venkataramani. "Economic Vulnerability Among US Female Health Care Workers: Potential Impact of a $15-per-Hour Minimum Wage." *American journal of public health* 109, no. 2 (2019): 198-205.

Hubbard, Ruth, and Elijah Wald. 1999. *Exploding the Gene Myth*. Boston: Beacon Press.

Human Genome Project Information Archive. 2013. "About the Human Genome Project." Accessed December 30, 2013. http://www.web.ornl.gov/sci/techresources/Human_Genome/project/index.shtml.

Indian Health Services. 2020. "Locations." Accessed April 14, 2021. (https://www.ihs.gov/locations/).

Jesudason, Sujatha, and Julia Epstein. 2011. "The Paradox of Disability in Abortion Debates: Bringing the Pro-choice and Disability Rights Communities Together." *Contraception* 84, no. 6: 541–43.

Kandula, Namratha, Munerah Ahmed, Sunita Dodani, Leena Gupta, Paromita Hore, Alka Kanaya, Aijaz Khowaja et al. "Cardiovascular disease & cancer risk among South Asians: impact of socio-cultural influences on lifestyle and behavior." *Journal of immigrant and minority health* 21, no. 1 (2019): 15-25.

Katznelson, Ira. *When affirmative action was white: An untold history of racial inequality in twentieth-century America*. WW Norton & Company, 2005.

Khodneva, Yulia, Joshua Richman, Stefan Kertesz, and Monika M. Safford. "Gender differences in association of prescription opioid use and mortality: A propensity-matched analysis from the REasons for Geographic And Racial Differences in Stroke (REGARDS) prospective cohort." *Substance abuse* (2019): 1-10.

Kochanek, Kenneth D., Sherry L. Murphy, Jiaquan Xu, and Elizabeth Arias. 2019. National Vital Statistics Reports Volume 68, Number 9 June 24, 2019 U.S. DEPARTMENT OF HEALTH AND HUMAN SERVICES Centers for Disease Control and Prevention National Center for Health Statistics National Vital Statistics System Deaths: Final Data for 2017. Accessed January 21, 2021. https://www.cdc.gov/nchs/data/nvsr/nvsr68/nvsr68_09-508.pdf

Kullgren, Jeffrey T., Betsy Q. Cliff, Chris D. Krenz, Helen Levy, Brady West, A. Mark Fendrick, Jonathan So, and Angela Fagerlin. "A survey of Americans with high-deductible health plans identifies opportunities to enhance consumer behaviors." *Health Affairs* 38, no. 3 (2019): 416-424.

Light, Donald W., and Joel R. Lexchin. "Pharmaceutical research and development: what do we get for all that money?." *Bmj* 345 (2012): e4348.

Lombardo, Paul A. 2008. *Three Generations and No Imbeciles: Eugenics, the Supreme Court, and* Buck v. Bell. Baltimore: Johns Hopkins University Press.

Luthra, Shefali. 2019. 2020 Affordable Care Act Health Plans: What's New. Accessed January 11, 2021. https://www.npr.org/sections/health-shots/2019/11/21/781224043/2020-affordable-care-act-health-plans-whats-new

Manuck, Tracy A. "Racial and ethnic differences in preterm birth: a complex, multifactorial problem." In *Seminars in perinatology*, vol. 41, no. 8, pp. 511-518. WB Saunders, 2017.

Marley, Tennille L. "Ambiguous jurisdiction: governmental relationships that affect American Indian health care access." *Journal of health care for the poor and underserved* 30, no. 2 (2019): 431-441.

Martin, Emily. 2006. "Moods and Representations of Social Inequality." In *Gender, Race, Class, and Health: Intersectional Approaches,* edited by Amy J.Schulz andLeithMullings, 60–88. San Francisco: Jossey-Bass.

Martin, Joyce A., Brady E. Hamilton, Michelle J.K. Osterman, and Anne K. Driscoll, 2019. National Vital Statistics Reports Volume 68, Number 13 November 27. Births: Final Data for 2018. Accessed January 11, 2021. https://www.cdc.gov/nchs/data/nvsr/nvsr68/nvsr68_13-508.pdf

Massey, Rachel. 2004. "Environmental Justice: Income, Race, and Health." Global Development and Environment Institute, Tufts University. Accessed June 2, 2017. http://www.ase.tufts.edu/gdae/education_materials/modules/Environmental_Justice.pdf.

McLaren, Lindsay, and Penelope Hawe. 2005. "Ecological Perspectives in Health Research." *Journal of Epidemiology & Community Health* 59, no. 1: 6–14.

Mehra, Renee, Danya E. Keene, Trace S. Kershaw, Jeannette R. Ickovics, and Joshua L. Warren. (2019): "Racial and ethnic disparities in adverse birth outcomes: Differences by racial residential segregation." *SSM-population health* 8 100417.

Midgley, Ben. 2018."The Six Reasons the Fitness Industry is Booming." *Forbes*. September 26. Accessed April 14, 2021 (https://www.forbes.com/sites/benmidgley/2018/09/26/the-six-reasons-the-fitness-industry-is-booming/?sh=33f6856d506d).

Mora, Pat. 1984. *Chants*. Houston, TX: Arte Publico Press.

Morgen, Sandra. 2002. Into Our Own Hands: The Women's Health Movement in the United States, 1969–1990. New Brunswick, NJ: Rutgers University Press.

Movement Advancement Project, Healthcare Laws and Policy. Accessed January 11, 2021. https://www.lgbtmap.org/equality-maps/healthcare_laws_and_policies

Musumeci, MaryBeth. Sept. 1, 2020. Explaining California v. Texas: A Guide to the Case Challenging the ACA Accessed January 11, 2021. https://www.kff.org/health-reform/issue-brief/explaining-california-v-texas-a-guide-to-the-case-challenging-the-aca/

National Alliance on Mental Illness. Mental health by the Numbers. accessed 3-31-2020. https://www.nami.org/Learn-More/Mental-Health-By-the-Numbers

The National Healthcare Qualities and Disparities Report, 2018. Accessed January 11, 2021. https://www.ahrq.gov/research/findings/nhqrdr/nhqdr18/index.html

National Medical Association. n.d. "History." Accessed June 2, 2017. http://www.nmanet.org/page/History.

Nielsen, Kim E. 2012. *A Disability History of the United States*. Boston, MA: Beacon Press.

Obregón, Misael. "Extending the Latina Paradox: Comparative Findings of Sexually Transmitted Infections among Mexican Origin, Black, and White Birth-Giving Women." *Population Review* 58, no. 1 (2019).

Olakanmi, Ololade. n.d. "The AMA, NMA, and the Flexner Report of 1910." Paper prepared for the Writing Group on the History of African Americans and the Medical Profession, American Medical Association. Accessed June 2, 2017. http://www.ama-assn.org/resources/doc/ethics/flexner.pdf.

Ossorio, Pilar, and Troy Duster. 2005. "Race and Genetics: Controversies in Biomedical, Behavioral, and Forensic Sciences." *American Psychologist*, 60, no. 1 (January): 115–28.

Parker-Pope, Tara. 2013. "Tackling a Racial Gap in Breast Cancer Survival." *New York Times*, December 20. Accessed June 2, 2017. http://www.nytimes.com/2013/12/20/health/tackling-a-racial-gap-in-breast-cancer-survival.html?_r=0.

Payscale. 2020. "Average Home Health Care Worker Hourly Pay." Accessed April 14, 2021 (https://www.payscale.com/research/US/Job=Home_Health_Care_Worker/Hourly_Rate).

Pemberton, Simon, Jenny Phillimore, Hannah Bradby, Beatriz Padilla, Jessica Lopes, Silja Samerski, and Rachel Humphris. "Access to healthcare in superdiverse neighbourhoods." *Health & place* 55 (2019): 128-135.

Peng, Yisheng, Steve Jex, Wenqin Zhang, Jie Ma, and Russell A. Matthews. "Eldercare demands and time theft: Integrating family-to-work conflict and spillover–crossover perspectives." *Journal of Business and Psychology* 35, no. 1 (2020): 45-58.

Petersen Emily E, Nicole L Davis, David Goodman, Shanna Cox, Nikki Mayes, Emily Johnston, Carla Syverson, Kristi Seed, , Carrie K. Mendoza, William M. Callaghan, and Wanda Barfield. May 10, 2019. Vital Signs: Pregnancy-Related Deaths, United States, 2011–2015, and Strategies for Prevention, 13 States, 2013–2017. MMWR Morb Mortal Wkly Rep 2019;68: 423–429. Accessed January 11, 2021. https://www.cdc.gov/mmwr/volumes/68/wr/mm6818e1.htm?s_cid=mm6818e1_w

PHI. U.S. Home Care Workers: Key Facts. accessed 1/8/20 PHINational.org. https://www.phinational.org/wp-content/uploads/legacy/phi-home-care-workers-key-facts.pdf

Pollitt, Phoebe Ann 1996. "From National Negro Health Week to National Public Health Week." *Journal of Community Health* 21, no. 6: 401–7.

Pro, George, Jeff Utter, Jessica Cram, and Julie Baldwin. "Racial/Ethnic and Gender Differences in Associations of Medication Assisted Therapy and Reduced Opioid Use between Outpatient Treatment Admission and Discharge." *Journal of Psychoactive Drugs* (2020): 1-9.

Puckett, Jae A. 2019. "An Ecological Approach to Therapy With Gender Minorities." *Cognitive and Behavioral Practice* 26, no. 4 647-655.

Rabin, Ronni Caryn. Huge Racial Disparities Found in Deaths Linked to Pregnancy. The New York Times. May 7, 2019. Accessed 1/6/20 https://www.nytimes.com/2019/05/07/health/pregnancy-deaths-.html

Rembis, Michael A., Catherine Jean Kudlick, and Kim E. Nielsen, *The Oxford handbook of disability history*. Oxford University Press, 2018.

Repka, Matt. 2013. "Enduring Damage: The Effects of Childhood Poverty on Adult Health." *Chicago Policy Review*, November 27.

Ridley, L. (2017). The Holocaust's forgotten victims. *The Huffington Post*. https://www.huffpost.com/entry/holocaust-non-jewish-victims_n_6555604

Royal College of Psychologists. 2020. "Debt and Mental Health." Accessed April 14, 2021 (https://www.rcpsych.ac.uk/mental-health/problems-disorders/debt-and-mental-health).

Roygardner, Lauren, Andy Schneider, and Doug Steiger. "Promoting Health Coverage of American Indian and Alaska Native Children." (2019).

Rudowitz, Robin, MaryBeth Musumeci, and Cornelia Hall. "Year end review: December state data for Medicaid work requirements in Arkansas." *Kaiser Family Foundation* 17 (2019).

Ruiz, John M., Heidi A. Hamann, Matthias R. Mehl, and Mary-Frances O'Connor. 2016. "The Hispanic Health Paradox: From Epidemiological Phenomenon to Contribution Opportunities for Psychological Science." *Group Processes & Intergroup Relations* 19, no. 4: 462–76.

Savitt, Todd L. 1982. "The Use of Blacks for Medical Experimentation and Demonstration in the Old South." *Journal of Southern History* 48, no. 3 (August): 331–48.

Saxton, Marsha. 2010. "Disability Rights and Selective Abortion." In *The Disability Studies Reader*, 3rd ed., edited by Lennard J. Davis, 120–32. New York: Routledge.

Schulz, Amy J., Graciela B. Mentz, Natalie Sampson, Melanie Ward, Rhonda Anderson, Ricardo de Majo, Barbara A. Israel, Toby C. Lewis, and Donele Wilkins. 2016. "Race and the Distribution of Social and Physical Environmental Risk." *Du Bois Review* 13, no. 2: 285–304.

Sedgh, Gilda, Rubina Hussain, Akinrinola Bankole, and Susheela Singh. 2007. "Women with an Unmet Need for Contraception in Developing Countries and Their Reasons for Not Using a Method." Occasional Report 37, Guttmacher Institute, June. Accessed February 13, 2015. http://www.guttmacher.org/pubs/2007/07/09/or37.pdf.

Serebrisky, Denise, and Andrew Wiznia. "Pediatric asthma: a global epidemic." *Annals of global Health* 85, no. 1 (2019).

Sistersong. 2013. "What Is Reproductive Justice?" Accessed February 13, 2015. http://www.sistersong.net/index.php?option=com_content&view=article&id=141.

Smedley, Audrey. *Race in North America: Origin and evolution of a worldview*. Routledge, 2018.

Smedley, Brian, Michael Jeffries, Larry Adelman, and Jean Cheng. 2008. "Race, Racial Inequality and Health Inequities: Separating Myth from Fact." Briefing Paper, Opportunity Agenda and California Newsreel. Accessed June 2, 2017. http://www.unnaturalcauses.org/assets/uploads/file/Race_Racial_Inequality_Health.pdf.

Snyderman, Nancy. 2012. "North Carolina Budget Drops Payment to Forced Sterilization Victims." NBC News, June 20. Accessed December 30, 2013. http://www.usnews.nbcnews.com/_news/2012/06/20/12321330-north-carolina-budget-drops-payment-to-forced-sterilization-victims?lite.

Somerville, Siobhan B. 2000. *Queering the Color Line: Race and the Invention of Homosexuality in American Culture*. Durham, NC: Duke University Press.

Spanakis, Elias K., and Sherita Hill Golden. 2013. "Race/ Ethnic Difference in Diabetes and Diabetic Complications." *Current Diabetes Reports* 13, no. 6: 814–23.

Sorenson, Matthew, Lauretta Quinn, andDiane Klein.2019. *Pathophysiology: Concepts of Human Disease*. London, ENG: Pearson.

Strauss, John, and Duncan Thomas. 2007. "Health over the Life Course." California Center for Population Research, November. Accessed May 8, 2017. http://www.papers.ccpr.ucla.edu/papers/PWP-CCPR-2007-011/PWP-CCPR-2007-011.pdf.

Sue, Derald Wing. 2010. Microaggressions in Everyday Life: Race, Gender, and Sexual Orientation. Hoboken, NJ: John Wiley.

Sullivan IV, Teresa A., Elizabeth Warren, and Jay Lawrence Westbrook. *The fragile middle class: Americans in debt*. Yale University Press, 2020.

Sullivan, Louis W., and Ilana Suez Mittman. 2010. "The State of Diversity in the Health Professions a Century after Flexner." *Academic Medicine* 85, no. 2: 246–53.

Syme, S. Leonard, and Lisa F. Berkman. 2009. "Sociology, Susceptibility, and Sickness." In *The Sociology of Health and Illness: Critical Perspectives*, 8th ed., edited by Peter Conrad, 24–30. New York: Worth.

Tavernise, Sabrina, and Robert Gebeloff. 2013. "Millions of Poor Are Left Uncovered by Health Law." *New York Times,* Accessed June 1, 2017. http://www.nytimes.com/2013/10/03/health/millions-of-poor-are-left-uncovered-by-health-law.html?pagewanted=all&mcubz=1.

Thoma, Marie E., Laura B. Drew, Ashley H. Hirai, Theresa Y. Kim, Andrew Fenelon, and Edmond D. Shenassa. (2019): "Black–White Disparities in Preterm Birth: Geographic, Social, and Health Determinants." *American Journal of Preventive Medicine* 57, no. 5 675-686.

Thomas, Stephen B., and Sandra Crouse Quinn. 1991. "Public Health Then and Now: The Tuskegee Syphilis Study, 1932 to 1972: Implications for HIV Education and AIDS Risk Education Programs in the Black Community." *American Journal of Public Health* 81, no. 11: 1498–505.

Torino, Gina. Nov. 10, 2017. How racism and microaggressions lead to worse health. The Center for Health Journalism. Accessed January 11, 2021. https://www.centerforhealthjournalism.org/2017/11/08/how-racism-and-microaggressions-lead-worse-health

Treisman, Rachel.   Sept. 16, 2020. Whistleblower Alleges 'Medical Neglect,' Questionable Hysterectomies Of ICE Detainees. NPR. Accessed January 11, 2021. https://www.npr.org/2020/09/16/913398383/whistleblower-alleges-medical-neglect-questionable-hysterectomies-of-ice-detaine

Tutu, Raymond Asare, and Janice Desire Busingye. 2020."Migration, Social Capital, and Health." In *Migration, Social Capital, and Health*, pp. 23-28. Cham, Springer,

United States Holocaust Memorial Museum.n.d."The Murder of the Handicapped." The Holocaust: A Learning Site for Students. Accessed December 28, 2013. http://www.ushmm.org/outreach/en/article.php?ModuleId=10007683.

United States Holocaust Memorial Museum (n.d). Documenting the Holocaust. https://www.encyclopedia.ushmm.org/content/en/article/documenting-numbers-of-victims-of-the-holocaust-and-nazi-persecution

Urban Indian Health Institute. Our Bodies, Our Stories. Accessed January 11, 2021. https://www.uihi.org/projects/our-bodies-our-stories/

Valerio, Melissa, Nagla Elerian, Paul McGaha, Janani Krishnaswami, Lesley French, and Divya A. Patel. (2019): "Understanding Barriers and Facilitators to Prenatal Care in African American and Hispanic Women [12P]." *Obstetrics & Gynecology* 133 173.

Verma, Reetu, Samantha Clark, Jonathon Leider, and David Bishai. 2016. "Impact of State Public Health Spending on Disease Incidence in the United States from 1980 to 2009." *Health Services Research* 52(1): 176-190.

Verma, Reetu, Samantha Clark, Jonathon P. Leider, and David Bishai. "Impact of State Public Health Spending on Disease Incidence in the United States from 1980 to 2009." *Health Services Research* 52, no. 1. doi:10.1111/1475–6773.12480.

Vernon, Leonard F. "J. Marion Sims, MD: Why He and His Accomplishments Need to Continue to be Recognized a Commentary and Historical Review." *Journal of the National Medical Association* (2019).

Waldstein, Anna. 2010. "Popular Medicine and Self-Care in a Mexican Migrant Community: Toward an Explanation of an Epidemiological Paradox." *Medical Anthropology* 29, no. 1: 71–107.

Washington, Harriett A. 2008. *Medical Apartheid: The Dark History of Medical Experimentation on Black Americans from Colonial Times to the Present. New York: Anchor Books.*

Weber, Lynn. 2006. "Reconstructing the Landscape of Health Disparities Research: Promoting Dialogue and Collaboration between Feminist Intersectional and Biomedical Paradigms." In *Gender, Race, Class, and Health: Intersectional Approaches*, edited by Amy J.Schulz and LeithMullings, 21–59. San Francisco: Jossey-Bass.

Wesson, Donald E., Catherine R. Lucey, and Lisa A. Cooper. "Building trust in health systems to eliminate health disparities." *Jama* 322, no. 2 (2019): 111-112.

Wheeler, Stephanie B., Jennifer Spencer, Laura C. Pinheiro, Caitlin C. Murphy, Jo Anne Earp, Lisa Carey, Andrew Olshan et al. "Endocrine therapy nonadherence and discontinuation in black and white women." *JNCI: Journal of the National Cancer Institute* 111, no. 5 (2019): 498-508.

White, Kevin. 2009. An *Introduction to the Sociology of Health and Illness*. Thousand Oaks, CA: Sage.

Whitehead, LaToria S., and Sharunda D. Buchanan. "Childhood lead poisoning: a perpetual environmental justice issue?." *Journal of Public Health Management and Practice* 25 (2019): S115-S120.

Whittle, Henry J., Kartika Palar, Nikhil A. Ranadive, Janet M. Turan, Margot Kushel, and Sheri D. Weiser. ""The land of the sick and the land of the healthy": Disability, bureaucracy, and stigma among people living with poverty and chronic illness in the United States." *Social Science & Medicine* 190 (2017): 181-189.

Williams, David R. 2012. "Miles to Go before We Sleep: Racial Inequities in Health." *Journal of Health and Social Behavior* 53, no. 3: 279–95.

World Health Organization. 1996."Traditional Medicine." Accessed December 25, 2013. http://www.who.int/inf-fs/en/fact134.html.

Wynn, Gabrielle T. (2019): "The Impact of Racism on Maternal Health Outcomes for Black Women." *U. Miami Race & Soc. Just. L. Rev.* 10 85.

Yaylacı, Şule, Wendy D. Roth, and Kaitlyn Jaffe. "Measuring racial essentialism in the genomic era: The genetic essentialism scale for race (GESR)." *Current Psychology* (2019): 1-15.

Zambrana, Ruth E., and Bonnie Thornton Dill. 2006. "Disparities in Latina Health: An Intersectional Analysis." In *Gender, Race, Class, and Health: Intersectional Approaches,* edited by Amy J.Schulz and LeithMullings, San Francisco: Jossey-Bass.

6 EDUCATION

Despite the myth of education as the great equalizer, educational opportunities are not the same for all children across the United States.

Jahi Chikwendiu/The Washington Post via Getty Images

LEARNING OBJECTIVES

6.1 Describe the current state of education in the United States and the key historical factors that have shaped it.

6.2 Compare the major stock sociological theories of education.

6.3 Analyze several matrix perspectives on education.

6.4 Identify alternatives to the educational system that recognize intersectional realities.

The nation's only Catholic Black college, Xavier University in New Orleans, charges $20,110 a year for tuition and sends more Black students on to medical schools than any other educational institution in the United States. When Pierre Johnson arrived at Xavier several years ago to work toward fulfilling his lifelong ambition of becoming a doctor, he realized how inadequately he had been prepared at the all-Black Chicago high school he attended. Although he had been an outstanding student, his school had not even offered basic science courses like physics. As Johnson later told a *New York Times* reporter, "I wanted to be a doctor, but I did not even know what the periodic table was." With the intensive help and support of the faculty and his fellow Xavier students, Johnson earned admission to medical school at the University of Illinois, where he was the only Black student in his class. He is now a successful gynecologist in Illinois. Without Xavier, he says, "I wouldn't have made it" (quoted in Hannah-Jones 2015).

Johnson's shock at finding himself unprepared for college contradicts the primary stock story of the institution of education in the United States—that education is the great equalizer, that schooling can level the playing field for life opportunities and life chances, regardless of race, gender, or social and economic status. As Xavier's former president, Norman Francis, has stated, "Research shows if you are black and born poor, you are going to live in a poor neighborhood, going to go to a poor school, and by and large, you are going to stay that way. To come out of that system, you would have to rise much higher than other youngsters who had every resource" (quoted in Hannah-Jones 2015).

This story is part of a larger story—that educational opportunities are not the same for all. In this chapter, we examine how educational segregation is woven into the fabric of the United States, how different educations are creating different identities, and the important role of the matrix of race in this reality. The bottom line is this: Johnson was not "supposed" to be a doctor. Consider that in 1933, historian Carter G. Woodson argued that Black Americans were being indoctrinated and "taught their place" through the curricula in U.S. schools (Woodson [1933] 2016). In 1955, novelist and anthropologist Zora Neale Hurston criticized the Supreme Court's *Brown v. Board of Education* decision to desegregate schools, saying there were already adequate and important Black schools that more effectively served Black communities than any White school ever could (Hurston 1955).

These sorts of claims—that schools and institutions can liberate or oppress—are still debated today, as the matrix of race still matters in the institution of education and vice versa. The institution of education in the United States has been shaped by decisions, definitions, and declarations about differences. In this chapter we will explore the history of U.S. education and its expressed and concealed functions, and we will reflect on who gets an education and why. We begin with a look at who is getting an education today, and what "being educated" means.

THE SHAPING OF THE MATRIX OF U.S. EDUCATION

What does it mean to be educated? If you accept the arguments of C. Wright Mills (1956), you might conclude that education functions to maintain the social hierarchy by creating workers, who then sustain the wealth of the elite. A successful professional might tell you that education is a socialization process that is fundamentally about skills acquisition. The framers of U.S. democracy, such as Thomas Paine and Benjamin Franklin, believed that the purpose of education was to foster the critical thinking necessary for citizens in a free society. And middle-class parents paying a child's way through college might say that education is a way to move up the socio-economic ladder. Nathan Hare, who started the first Black Studies program at San Francisco State University in 1969, sees the purpose of education as bringing about change, noting, "[If] education is not revolutionary in the current day [then it] is both irrelevant and useless" (quoted in Karenga 2002, 16–17). What does this mean? Who decides what is useful and relevant to learn? And for whom?

The institution of education is both vital and complex. While some see education as a solution for inequalities of all sorts, others see the education system as rife with inequalities—especially for those who are not White or affluent. The most recently available data (from the 2015–16 school year) show that nationally, 84% of all 9th-grade public school students graduated high school after 4 years, with Asian American (91%) and White (88%) students graduating at higher rates, and Latinx (79%), Black (76%), and Native American (72%) students graduating at much lower rates (National Center for Education Statistics [NCES], 2019a). These adjusted cohort graduation rates also vary widely from state to state with the highest in Iowa (91%) and lowest in D.C. (69%) (National Center for Education Statistics [NCES], 2019a). Clearly, education does not work equally for all.

Education Today

A study by researchers at Georgetown University found that while a college degree still provides a material boost to lifetime earnings, 10 years after graduation the alumni of elite institutions are out-earning their peers from other colleges and universities, often by a significant amount, and male college graduates still earn much more per year than female graduates almost across the board (Carnevale, Rose, and Cheah 2011). Rising tuition costs and a weak job market have contributed to these inequalities, but as we will discuss in more detail below, they did not create them. Via the Executive Order on Improving Free Inquiry, Transparency, and Accountability at Colleges and Universities, the government plans to continue monitoring 10-year earnings data as well as document student loan debt loads by college/university on its new College Scorecard website, collegescorecard.ed.gov (Carey 2015).

Who Goes to School?

Many children in the United States begin their structured experience of education soon after birth, in institutionalized and organized childcare settings. In the most recent nationwide data available, in 2010, there were about 20 million children under the age of 5 in the United States.

- Of these 20 million, 43.2% attended organized daycare or preschool facilities, and the remainder were under the care of parents, grandparents, siblings, or other relatives.

- Black and Latinx children were a little less than half as likely as White and Asian children to attend preschool.

- Mothers with only high school educations were five times less likely to enroll their children in preschool than were mothers with college degrees. (U.S. Census Bureau 2011)

From 2015 through 2016, there were more than 105,000 elementary schools in the United States (some of which were combined elementary and secondary schools). Almost three-fourths (69.9%) of these were public schools, while the rest were private (including religious schools) (30.1%). Public elementary schools enroll slightly more than 35 million students, taught by some 2.2 million teachers. That makes the average student–teacher ratio 16.1 to 1 (NCES 2018). Secondary schools (hosting different combinations of grades 7 through 12) number more than 43,000 in the United States. The vast majority of these are also public schools (71.0%). In public secondary schooling, 15 million students are taught by more than 1.2 million teachers— an average student–teacher ratio of 16.2 to 1 (NCES 2018). From 2008 to 2015, public school enrollment increased by about 2.4%, while enrollment in private and religious schools declined over the same period. However, the public school enrollment of certain groups increased much more (Latinx, 18%; Asian Americans, 6%), while that of others decreased over this period (7% decrease for both Whites and Blacks; 11% decrease for Native Americans). By 2024, projections indicate a continued increase mirroring what was seen in the 2008–15 period, largely due to immigration from Asia (first) and from Central and Latin America (second) (NCES 2016a) (see Figure 6.1).

In the same school year (2015–16), 19.8 million students, ages 18 to 24, were enrolled in 7,021 Title IV institutions of postsecondary education (i.e., colleges and universities) (NCES 2017). The majority of these students (56.9%) were White, while Blacks (13.7%), Latinx

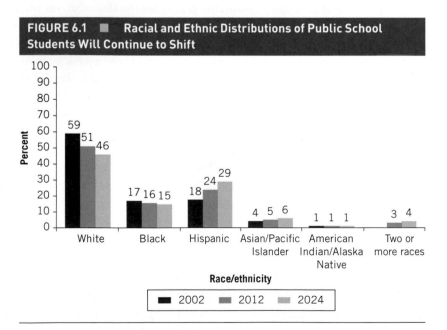

FIGURE 6.1 ■ Racial and Ethnic Distributions of Public School Students Will Continue to Shift

Source: National Center for Education Statistics (2016).

(18.2%), Asian Americans (6.9%), and Native Americans (0.8%) made up the rest. Compare this to a decade earlier, when Whites made up 69.1%, Blacks 12.7%, Latinx 10.5%, Asian Americans 6.6%, and Native Americans 1.1%. Hussar and Bailey (2016) have projected college enrollments to 2024, and they estimate that the proportion of Whites will decrease to 56%, that of Blacks will increase to 16.7%, and that of Latinx will increase to 17.5%, while the proportions of Asian Americans and Native Americans will remain largely the same; in many ways their projections have already arrived, with Latinx students already surpassing those projections (in line with an earlier Pew study by Roach in 2013), with Blacks lagging somewhat behind.

While the vast majority of preK-12 students attend public schools in the United States, about 10% attend private schools (NCES 2017) and, of those who do, Whites are significantly overrepresented while non-Whites are underrepresented given their proportions of the school-aged population. Attending a private school often provides a significant boost to a child's opportunities within the educational and, therefore, socioeconomic structure. In places like New York City, scholars are finding that local, state, and national policies often help Whites continue to hoard these rare educational opportunities. For instance, Quealy and Shapiro (2019) found that a federal designation, dubbed 504s, which are supposed to give New York City students with mental and physical disabilities more time when taking the elite private high school entrance exams, are systematically given more often to White students. These White students tend to get admitted to private schools more often, and further rig the private school game (Quealy and Shapiro 2019).

We see that who enrolls and attends school has changed over time, and Figure 6.2 shows an even more interesting and disturbing pattern that requires explanation: The gains that Blacks, Latinx, and Native Americans have made in graduating from high school, as well as their immense gains in enrolling in and attending college, have not resulted in proportionate *attainment* of the bachelor's degree or the pursuit of higher graduate or professional education. These gains are not only racialized, but gendered as well. Figure 6.2 shows very clearly the different educational pipelines for American students. For instance, For every 100 Latinx girls and boys, 63 of the girls will get their high school diploma compared to 60 of the boys; only 13 of the girls and 11 of the boys will get a bachelor's degree; and only 4 Latinas and 3 Latinos will get a graduate/professional degree, with a doctorate almost out of reach. The system clearly works very differently depending on one's position.

The challenges faced by graduate students of color as they attempt to gain doctoral and professional degrees are even more pronounced (Brunsma, Embrick, and Shin 2017). Students of color face a pattern of poor access to the higher education pipeline, or the pathway to higher education, and the explanations for this pattern reside in the ways that the institution of education is woven by and within the matrix of race.

Education Yesterday

Regardless of type or level of schooling, the institution of education in the United States has almost always been the site of conflict, debate, and confrontation over access, meanings of education, and what is taught, why, and to whom (as well as whose knowledge counts as knowledge worth having). This conflict is often between dominant (White, male, upper-class,

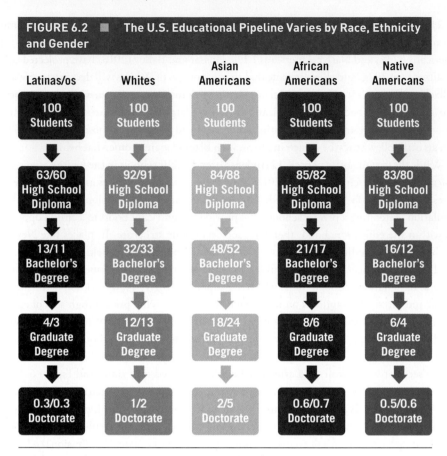

FIGURE 6.2 ■ The U.S. Educational Pipeline Varies by Race, Ethnicity and Gender

Latinas/os	Whites	Asian Americans	African Americans	Native Americans
100 Students	100 Students	100 Students	100 Students	100 Students
63/60 High School Diploma	92/91 High School Diploma	84/88 High School Diploma	85/82 High School Diploma	83/80 High School Diploma
13/11 Bachelor's Degree	32/33 Bachelor's Degree	48/52 Bachelor's Degree	21/17 Bachelor's Degree	16/12 Bachelor's Degree
4/3 Graduate Degree	12/13 Graduate Degree	18/24 Graduate Degree	8/6 Graduate Degree	6/4 Graduate Degree
0.3/0.3 Doctorate	1/2 Doctorate	2/5 Doctorate	0.6/0.7 Doctorate	0.5/0.6 Doctorate

Source: Chart: "The U.S. Educational Pipeline, by Race/Ethnicity and Gender, 2012." From *Still Falling Through the Cracks: Revisiting the Latina/o Educational Pipeline* by Perez Huber et al. UCLA Chicano Studies Research Center, November 2015.

Note: The first number represents females, the second, males.

heterosexual) groups and Blacks, Latinos, women, poor and working-class families, sexual minorities, and those with physical and mental disabilities. To understand current educational realities, we must first understand the formative moments in the shaping of the matrix of education.

The first public schools in the United States were established shortly after the American Revolution, and public education expanded rapidly in the 19th century, thanks to the efforts of such advocates as reformer Horace Mann and Tuskegee University founder Booker T. Washington. By 1910, nearly 72% of all children in the United States attended at least elementary school, and by 1930 most children received some form of compulsory education.

Native American Boarding Schools

Harvard University, founded by the Massachusetts legislature as Harvard College in 1636, was the first university built and chartered in the United States. The Harvard Indian College was established in 1655 to educate "the English & Indian Youth of this Country in knowledge and godliness" (the school was closed in 1698) (McGrory 2011). Beginning in the early 1870s, the federal government set up boarding schools to educate Native American students in English, "civilization," Christianity, and the agricultural vocational trades. As one historian has observed, many Native Americans were, in this way, "stripped of their hair, their clothes, their beliefs, their language, and their culture, including, when possible, their prayers" (Owings 2011, xiv).

Until 1903, more than 460 boarding and day schools were built close to reservations; they were run by religious organizatios using federal funds. Ultimately, more than 100,000 indigenous children were "educated" out of their cultures, languages, and ways of life. The effects linger, as recounted by Lakota woman Karen Artichoker:

> You see the impact of removing children from their homes, forcibly, putting them in a concentration camp type of setting, a POW type of setting, the boarding schools, and telling them anything Indian is not good, then sending them out into their community to do their work and to raise children they don't have a clue how to raise. We see our bonding with the oppressor still when we don't see each [other] competent as Indians. We don't see each other as being honest. We don't see ourselves as having a work ethic. If we didn't have that mainstream type of thinking about what's honorable and ethical, we're still sort of "savages." (quoted in Owings 2011, 155)

One of the key functions of Native American boarding schools run by Christian organizations and the federal government was to eradicate students' culture. The effects of this "soul wound" are still felt today, more than half a century after the program ended.

© CORBIS/Corbis via Getty Images

Consider the profound impacts that such cultural, spiritual, and psychological damage and erasure can have on a people—loss of language, community norms, parenting skills, tribal relationships, knowledge of one's own history, understanding of indigenous worldviews and identities, ability to develop skills useful to the life of the tribe, and more. The effects of such a collective experience linger, despite the fact that the last generation that went through the system was born in the 1950s; the long-term effects of the boarding school system have been described as a "soul wound" by some scholars (King 2008; Smith 2007). In a collective effort to move toward healing that wound, Native American activism arose in the 1960s and, along with several pieces of legislation concerning the Bureau of Indian Affairs, led to the closure of the vast majority of these schools and to the establishment of community schools and colleges run by the tribes themselves. Scholarship has identified the role of "resiliency," rooted in Native family, community, and supportive campus systems, in helping Native American women to succeed even with the lingering effects of cultural trauma (Waterman and Lindley 2013).

Early African American Education: "Separate but Equal"

After the emancipation of enslaved African Americans in 1863 and the end of the Civil War in 1865, the period known as Reconstruction began. The nation faced four challenges in "reconstructing" the South after slavery and the Civil War:

1. To rebuild the crucial Southern economy on free labor instead of slave labor

2. To change the South so that it could more effectively rejoin the United States

The first sorority for Native American women, Alpha Pi Omega, was founded at the University of North Carolina at Chapel Hill in 1994, and currently supports 800 indigenous sisters nationwide and has been recognized for academic excellence and community service (ASU 2019).

©Norma Jean Gargasz/Alamy

3. To integrate the freed African Americans into U.S. society

4. To protect the freed African Americans from harm

In the face of industrialization and capitalist development occurring in the Northern United States, however, only the first challenge was achieved. The "education of the Negro" began in earnest as well, in schools that were separate from but supposedly equal to schools for Whites. The goal was to keep Blacks domesticated and subservient, with very limited skills exchangeable in the urban labor markets of the North and South. Not surprisingly, by 1870 the institutionalization of comprehensive and separate public school systems for Whites and Blacks was well under way.

Soon, however, educator and orator Booker T. Washington grew concerned about the increasing violence targeting the Black community and Black schools. In a now-famous speech given at the Atlanta Cotton States and International Exposition on September 18, 1895, Washington articulated the so-called **Atlanta Compromise**. Under this compromise, Southern Blacks would agree to work, forgo their own political ambitions, and submit to White political rule. In exchange, Southern Whites would guarantee basic education for Blacks, reduce intimidation toward them, and allow for due process in all legal matters involving Blacks. One year later, the U.S. Supreme Court, in the landmark *Plessy v. Ferguson* case, declared that racial segregation in public facilities was constitutional and fell under the doctrine of separate but equal. This decision heralded the Jim Crow era of legal segregation.

School Desegregation

In 1900, W. E. B. Du Bois and the Black civil rights group he founded, the Niagara Movement, called for free education for all, *real* education, they cried, for "either the United States will destroy ignorance, or ignorance will destroy the United States" (Du Bois 1900). From Du Bois's criticism, the Harlem Renaissance was born, a period when Black scholars, scientists, and artists aimed to reject the negative characterizations of Blackness and assert the existence of the "New Negro." Thirty years later, Carter G. Woodson, as mentioned earlier, would lambast the educational system and decry the poverty it produced among Blacks. These critiques and the social unrest they produced laid the foundation for what has been termed the modern civil rights movement. Several seminal court cases paved the way for this movement and significantly transformed the United States and its discourses regarding race, class, and gender. The launching event was the 1954 Supreme Court case of *Brown v. Board of Education of Topeka*.

Brown v. Board of Education effectively set aside the *Plessy v. Ferguson* decision and held that "separate" was by definition "unequal." Thurgood Marshall, who argued the case for the plaintiffs (and would later become the first Black American to sit on the U.S. Supreme Court), asserted that "separate but equal" was unfair and unconstitutional. He argued that the Southern educational establishment should be forced to make all schools—both Black and White—equal. The South was trapped. For decades, Black schools had been significantly underfunded compared to White schools. According to testimony offered to the Court, the costs of equalizing the Black and White schools would essentially bankrupt the South. Evidence offered by child psychologist Kenneth Clark further demonstrated the damaging stigmas that were borne by Black children as a result of segregation. The psychological traumas inflicted by segregation

W. E. B. Du Bois and the Niagara Movement he founded inspired Blacks to reject the negative associations with their Blackness and laid the foundation for the modern civil rights movement.

Universal History Archive/Getty Images

further aggravated the already hostile situation faced by Blacks living in the South. Observing the paradox that produced "wholly unequal" educational systems for Black students, the Court was forced to recognize that equality could not be provided under the current system, and that the only remedy was to set aside *Plessy. Brown v. Board of Education* followed a lesser-known but precedent-setting 1946 case, *Mendez et al. v. Westminster School District of Orange County*, in which the Court declared unconstitutional the segregation of Mexican and Mexican American students into separate schools (Martinez-Cola 2019).

Even with the desegregation orders from the highest court in the land, there was significant White backlash. Indeed, the recent controversies of prominent politicians' yearbook photos showing them in blackface (e.g., Virginia Governor Ralph Northram) shows a post-*Brown* reality where blatant and overt racism and racist imagery was completely normal in many schools across the country. As discussion of these issues continues, we are uncovering a history of the normalization (and even celebration) of racism in American schools, as well as uncovering the fact of segregation academies, 2000 of which were opened after *Brown* across 11 Southern states (Onion 2019).

While we have focused here on the early histories of racialized minorities and socioeconomic classes' engagement with the institution of education, these were fully wrapped up,

Before the Supreme Court decision in *Brown v. Topeka Board of Education*, segregated schools for Blacks, like this one in rural Georgia, were legally considered "equal" to those available to Whites.

Bettmann/Getty Images

in the matrix, with religion, region, and certainly with gendered experience and the experience of disability. Girls and women faced significant marginalization throughout American history, often with separate curricula, expectations, and even separate schools focusing on keeping women in caretaking domestic and professional roles. Title IX of the 1972 Education Amendments Act radically changed this reality and the institutions began to open up, mostly for White women initially. Those who suffered disabilities of a wide variety of kinds (physical, learning, sight, hearing, developmental, etc.) were treated largely as outcasts throughout American history. The period of eugenics was particularly brutal for those with disabilities; they would wait until 1975's Education for All Handicapped Children Act as well as 1990's Americans with Disabilities Act for the institution of education to begin treating their educations with dignity. The history of education has affected our present and foreshadows our future.

The institution of education in the United States has fundamentally involved decisions, definitions, and declarations about differences, including who is considered fully human, who is valued, whose histories are valued, who deserves what kind of education, and what kinds of futures can be envisioned for different classifications of peoples. All of these issues and more are related to interactions, opportunities, and outcomes within the institution of education. We will continue to examine the way the matrix operates in the institutionalized education system

Prior to the *Brown v. Board of Education* ruling, separate facilities for Black people, such as this movie theater in Waco, Texas, were pervasive in the South.

IanDagnall Computing / Alamy Stock Photo

in the United States, mostly through the ways students from racialized groups experience and navigate them. Some groups, even since "desegregation," have worked to establish their own schools in order to help their people navigate the racist American education system, like the Latino College Preparatory Academy, a chartered, Spanish-speaking high school in San Jose, California, which opened its doors in 2001 for some 500 students (Koven 2009).

Critical Thinking

1. What does it mean to be educated? What does it mean to "get" an education? What does it mean to "give" an education? These are core questions that any society must wrestle with. Be sure to start from the matrix of experience to begin discussing and answering these questions.

2. The institution of education was forged within the American crucible of race, class, and gender. How did these differential experiences in early American society aid in the formation of the institution of education? What do you see as some of the consequences and aftereffects of this early shaping of the matrix of education?

3. Is it important who controls the decisions that affect the institution of education? Give some historical and contemporary examples of the importance of such control. What happens when those who have been oppressed by the system control their own schools, curricula, and educations?

4. Can you describe any evidence of educational inequality in your schooling experiences up to this point?

THEORIES OF EDUCATION: STOCK STORIES

How do we grapple with and begin to understand how education has functioned within the matrix of race in the United States? Sociology offers many potential theoretical perspectives, and these theories can help us understand the origins of our stock stories about education as an institution. In this section we discuss two of the primary theories of education—social-functional theory and human capital theory—and show how stock stories reflect each of these theories in the real world.

Education as a Socialization Process

One of the primary theoretical stock stories of education is the narrative of education as socialization. This rests on the idea that schools socialize students. **Socialization** is the process whereby members of a society are taught that society's dominant roles, norms, and values. Families once served the socialization function, but in postindustrial societies, other organizations have grown in socializing influence, including the media (see Chapter 11). The socialization function of education and school is to teach students to be competent members of society.

For French sociologist Émile Durkheim (1956, 1962, 1977), education's purpose was to instill a sense of "morality" and "cohesion" within individuals. By "morality," Durkheim meant that through education, children are subconsciously infused with the norms, rules, and values of their society (such as patriotism and the value of individual effort). This infusion of morality takes place through the structure of the classroom, the relationship between teacher and student, the structure of rules enforced throughout the school day, and other social and cultural structures in the school, among others. The resulting conformity helps maintain the bonds between us that make us follow norms, thus producing **social cohesion**.

However, a theory that predicts social cohesion also implies that there are processes that might lead to breakdowns of that cohesion, inequalities within the system, and so on. The question, of course, is whose norms and values are being instilled? Whose cohesion is valued, and who has been excluded, marginalized, or devalued? If education socializes individuals to be competent members of society, then who benefits from such "competencies," and who benefits from this process? These and other questions have motivated social scientists interested in critical studies of education for a very long time. The history laid out earlier in this chapter gives some indication of the answers.

Education as Skills Acquisition

Many high schools, colleges, and universities aim to give their students the "skills they need to compete in the global economy" or for membership in the workforce in general. This theory invokes what we might call an **apprenticeship model of education**. In precapitalist societies, a master craftsman (usually a man) would take on one or more apprentices to train—whether in blacksmithing, baking, cobbling, or some other craft—passing on the skills the apprentices would need to eventually fill the master's role. In "dame schools" of the 17th, 18th, and 19th centuries, female teachers taught girls sewing, knitting, and embroidery (Forman-Brunell and Paris 2011), while during this same period boys from affluent families went to grammar schools to learn arithmetic, writing, Latin, and Greek (Zhboray 1993).

The skills acquisition function of education is echoed throughout many communities today in the common belief that education provides the skills we need to engage productively in society. In New York City, for instance, Mayor Bill de Blasio wants the city's public schools to offer computer science classes to all students by 2025, in a plan projected to cost $81 million and requiring the training of 5,000 teachers. With tech jobs increasing in the city, the director of the Office of Strategic Partnerships has stated, "I think there is acknowledgment that we need our students better prepared for these jobs and to address equity and diversity within the sector as well" (quoted in Taylor and Miller 2015, A22). By the end of 2019, there was a 72% increase of NYC public school students taking computer science classes (NYC Department of Education 2019).

This provision of skills that are exchangeable within a social structure, or market, for other forms of capital has been described by economists, sociologists, and educational researchers alike as the development of **human capital** (Schultz 1961; Becker 1964; see also Coleman 1988). As Coleman (1988, S100) describes the concept: "Just as physical capital is created by changes in materials to form tools that facilitate production, human capital is created by changes in persons that bring about skills and capabilities that make them act in new ways."

Yet the knowledge we gain from the educational system often has little relevance to the specific skills we need in the workforce or on the job (Moore and Morton 2017). In contemporary society, as in the apprentice model, most of the skills that people need to perform their jobs are learned *on* the job, through doing (practice), and not through knowing (theory). Despite this fact, the notion that education allows us to acquire job skills and/or makes us more desirable to potential employers remains one of the key legitimating narratives of education. The assumption that education leads to skills and skills lead to jobs has serious consequences for non-White and lower-class members of society, because it posits (a) that the playing field is level, (b) that education delivers needed skills, and (c) that race, class, and gender play no moderating role in the effects of these processes. Yet, though we wish to believe these ideas, we know these things are not true in practice; the data do not bear them out.

Critical Thinking

1. How do the stock theories of education help us understand the formative experiences that shaped the matrix of education, especially those of Native Americans and African Americans? Are these theories helpful for understanding these experiences?

2. Education, its socialization functions, and its human capital functions do not exist in a vacuum within our society. Education is linked to other institutions—work, family, and the mass media, for instance—in fundamental ways. How are any two of these institutions linked? How are the linkages the same or different for individuals from different locations within the matrix of race?

3. The institution of education is, according to the theories, central to both socialization and skills acquisition. It is also clearly important in the formation of identities. What lessons do these theories and/or the histories discussed above hold for our understanding of the relationship between education and identity for racial and ethnic minorities?

4. How were you socialized in high school? What norms and values were forged within your secondary education? Does attending the same high school as others mean that you experienced the same high school they did?

APPLYING THE MATRIX TO THE CONCEALED STORY OF RACE AND EDUCATION

The story of U.S. education is actually several parallel stories, as we can see if we use the matrix to view education as a social institution. What these parallel stories have in common is the recognition that we have created many different educational structures that serve different groups and purposes.

Education is a dominant institution that appears to carve several pathways for individuals from different locations in the matrix, while promising equality of educational opportunity for all. Given all these different structures, some of which are based on race, gender, or ethnicity, it is not surprising that concealed stories are critical of the dominant educational narratives of the United States—that schools serve primarily as socializers and skill developers. These concealed stories speak to the stock stories we have examined in this chapter; sociologists themselves have told many of them. We will examine four concealed stories: education as a conversion tool, education as a site of class construction, education as a means of creating workers, and education as a citizen machine.

Education as a Conversion Tool

As societies spread across geographic and cultural space over time, whether through migration, conquest, colonialism, or imperialism, their members encounter others who are different from them in many ways. Often the institution of education becomes a tool that migrating settlers, conquering armies, or globalizing corporations use in the attempt to change the cognitions, the social arrangements, and even the meaning systems of their host societies. Like missionary work, education can be seen as an effort at a "conversion" of sorts. The story of education as a conversion tool is a critical take on the stock theory of education as socialization, and it goes something like this: "Your socialization is wrong; use ours. We will educate yours out of you, in order that you might become like us."

We can clearly see the role of education as conversion by looking at those who wrestled with their role as colonial subjects (or internal colonial subjects within the United States—some scholars consider Native Americans, African Americans, and Latinx, for instance, to constitute domestic, or internal, colonies *within* the United States, providing an exploitable workforce from which labor power can be extracted), and who continue to try to reclaim aspects of their social and cultural structures and identities. Frantz Fanon, in his classic books *Black Skin, White Masks* (1952) and *The Wretched of the Earth* (1961), writes caustically of the symbolic, cognitive, and cultural violence done to Algerians throughout French colonialism and the dominance of White supremacy. Introducing the concept of **colonization of the mind**, Fanon discusses the indelible mark of inferiority left on the psyches of colonized individuals and communities long after the colonizers have left. A deep and profound **resocialization** experience takes place in those who have been stripped of their dignity and self-determination.

In the United States, many education-as-conversion stories have been uncovered in the disciplines of Black studies, Chicano studies, women's studies, gender and sexuality studies, and indigenous studies. Many of these disciplines began as student movements aimed at changing dominant U.S. institutions—education, law, health, government—and they grew in earnest as a result of the civil rights movement. In the late 1960s, for example, the civil rights, freedom of speech, antiwar, and Black Power movements converged on U.S. campuses, and Black students began demanding programs relevant to their lives and aspirations.

The first 4-year Black studies program was organized by Nathan Hare and Jimmy Garrett at San Francisco State University in 1968. Between 1969 and 1973, approximately 300 to 600 programs sprang up across the United States at predominantly White colleges and universities; today more than 200 schools maintain African American studies units, with 10 offering master's degrees (Patillo, cited in West 2012). While the discipline of Black studies provides a story of resistance, the fact that it is needed in the first place is evidence of the strength of the education-as-conversion reframing of the socialization stock story.

Consider too the rise of Black, Latinx, Asian, indigenous, and multicultural fraternities and sororities, especially since the 1980s, that have largely emerged to provide "safe spaces for college students of color as well as students who value diversity and acceptance more generally" than those traditional White Greek spaces that have been consistently exclusionary (Zeilinger 2015). These too are evidence of the socialization story.

Education as a Site of Class Construction

Education has consistently perpetuated class inequality, going back as far as the earliest social structures of literacy. The notion that education provides a society and its members with the academic and cultural knowledge necessary to function is encouraged by the dominant classes in most contemporary societies. One interpretation of this belief is that if you do not receive an education, you are not a full-fledged member of society.

Scholars have been interested in this narrative primarily because of its obvious ties with class, control, and domination in virtually every known society (Apple 2013). Education has played a role not only in creating social classes but also in reproducing them generation after generation. One of the ways schools do this is by implicitly, structurally, and culturally embedding

These women are members of Delta Sigma Theta Sorority, one of many Greek organizations for students of color.

Wim Wiskerke / Alamy Stock Photo

processes of distinction and the social construction of difference within their walls. Consider dress codes and even school uniforms. Dress codes are lists that schools create to specify what items of clothing *may not be worn* at school (e.g., bandanas, baggy pants), while uniform policies mandate what *must be worn* (e.g., specific khaki pants, specific colors)—many dress code and uniform policies have race, class, and gender overtones (Brunsma 2004).

Cultural capital consists of the cultural resources—the meanings, codes, understandings, and practices—that individuals can accumulate and utilize to exchange for other goods in a social or economic market (Bourdieu and Passeron 1977; Bourdieu 1984; Lareau 1989, 2011). Cultural capital exists in three forms, according to Pierre Bourdieu (1986), an important 20th-century French sociologist:

- Embodied personal characteristics (such as the ability to see, feel, and think about the world in ways acceptable to the dominant class)

- Physical objects (like books, music, movies, and clothing recognized by the dominant class as worthy of attention)

- Institutionalized recognition (a college degree, for instance, which is an accepted credential that determines the graduate's worth in the job market)

Cultural capital is like a road map that helps us navigate social life because we have learned the "rules of the game."

At this point you might be saying, "Well, that sounds good, actually, because we want to be sure that schools imprint the rules of the game on their students so they can be competent members of society." However, the question is, *whose* rules and *whose* game? Lee, Park, and Wong (2016) studied second-generation Asian American students in the public education system and found that their identities were being shaped and also policed by the Whiteness of the structure of education. What's more, whose institution is education itself? For if Bourdieu is correct (and there is substantial evidence that he is), the dominant institutions of any given society serve the interests of the dominant classes. From this perspective, we can see a concealed story: that education reproduces the class structure by creating schools in society's image that expect students to know the rules of the game but do not actually teach them the rules. This has led to charges that schools are organized along male, White, middle-class, and heteronormative principles. Indeed, sociologist Lauren Rivera (2016), in her award-winning book *Pedigree: How Elite Students Get Elite Jobs,* finds clear evidence of this in the process of matching college students who attend elite universities with investment banking, management consulting firms, and legal firms, through cultural indicators of "fit," "poise," and narratives of "merit," all benefitting White students with White socialization experiences. Institutionalized cultural capital keeps this structure invisible to those who do not already have cultural capital—especially girls, non-Whites, and students from lower-class and disadvantaged families and communities. Thus, those without cultural capital have an increased probability of being unsuccessful from the institution's perspective.

Education as a Means of Creating Workers

While we generally assume, based on our stock stories about education, that we need an education in order to get a job, an alternative narrative focuses on the idea that schools exist to *create* (not educate) workers for the labor force. To consider this possibility further, think about the general rules we learn at school from a very early age, as listed in Table 6.1.

If we replace the school with the factory, the desk with the assembly line, the teacher with the boss, students with coworkers, and schoolwork with making products, we can see that the discipline of school literally mirrors the pulse of the factory, the rhythm of the workplace, the striving for output and profit for the corporate machine. Scholars have also argued that schools serve to create workers for the capitalist structure—not the *skills* needed, but the *identities* needed.

Karl Marx, in his analysis of capitalist development, argued that all institutions in capitalist societies are "epiphenomenal to social class." What he meant by this is that the dominant institutions in society—government, religious institutions, families, schools, and so on—all exist in the forms they do, and operate in the ways they do, with the relationship structures they encourage, because they benefit the bourgeoisie (the owning class) and their interests.

In their classic (and still strikingly relevant) 1976 book *Schooling in Capitalist America,* Bowles and Gintis echo this argument by comparing the structures of schools to the forms, relationships, and rules that operate within the world of work. Furthermore, they argue that schools (whether secondary or post-secondary) do not actually provide employers with workers who have the skills needed for particular jobs but instead provide employers with "suitably socialized workers," who come into the workforce trained not to question the system and to

TABLE 6.1 ■ Dominant School Rules and Their Corresponding Roles at Work	
School Rule	*Function for Occupational Structure*
Arrive on time.	Punctuality
Keep your desk clean.	Image
Sit in your assigned seat.	Order
Ask the teacher for permission.	Hierarchy
Be silent and focus on your own work.	Individualism
Do what the teacher tells you to do.	Authority
Line up.	Rules
Eat when it is time for lunch.	Schedules
Do your best work.	Evaluation

accept their socioeconomic fate. Scholars who follow this Marxist line of inquiry raise serious questions about the role education systems actually play in capitalist and other societies. In fact, as more people have attained higher levels of education, we would expect income inequality to be reduced, but it has actually worsened over time (Mayer 2010). There is also evidence that the system of "tracking" within schools has created separate experiential, curricular, and, ultimately, opportunity pathways for students, and that these pathways are fundamentally grounded in class and race. Sociologist Whitney Pirtle lays it out clearly, "The implication is clear: Black students are regularly excluded from schools' conceptions of what it means to be gifted, talented, or advanced" (2019)—and the effects of tracking do not only affect Black students; they tend to systematically favor White students to the detriment of racialized minorities.

Scholars who embrace the matrix perspective have also asked how the educational system fashions and constructs individuals' identities *as* women, *as* heterosexuals, *as* Blacks or Latinx, *as* (dis)abled, and *as* the myriad intersections across all these that fully inform their positions in the system. In his landmark work "The Afrocentric Idea in Education," Molefi Asante (1991) writes about the experiences of Blacks in the American context and their interactions with dominant institutions like education. He makes clear that, because education is fundamentally about socializing a child to become part of the larger social group, and because schools mirror the societies that develop them, ultimately, then, a White supremacist–dominated society will develop a White supremacist educational system which works hard to craft identities and selves that glorify and uphold the superiority of Whiteness.

This narrative points to one of the most important lessons of sociology—the distinction between individual and group realities. On the one hand, it is clear that an individual who has more education will earn more income, on average, than someone with a lower level of education. On an individual level, the relationship between educational attainment and income is a strong one, supporting the stock stories about education as a skill provider and a path to social mobility.

Scholars like Bowles and Gintis (1976) argue that school prepares children to be docile members of the workforce by teaching obedience, cooperation, and deference to authority.

Design Pics Inc/Alamy Stock Photo

However, on the group level, this has not been the case. Educational equity has *not* led to more income equality. In fact, the opposite has occurred—while more and more people have attained higher educational credentials over time, the income disparities between the rich and the poor have continued to widen. Thus, as a society, we have increased our human capital (e.g., skills, education) without increasing our socioeconomic equality. In fact, scholars recognize that the most efficient way to increase a nation's productivity is by increasing its mechanization and technological advancement (Chang 2010). Countries that do so, that actually "de-skill" their populaces through education institutions, make workers more replaceable and easier to control. The narrative that schools create workers for the bourgeoisie helps to partially account for this.

Education as a Citizen Machine

While we may like to imagine that education allows individuals to learn to question their reality, there is abundant evidence that it carefully constructs that reality for a specific purpose and with certain goals in mind. Through the curricula, social structures, and cultural meaning systems embedded in both, schools and the social institution of education socially construct age hierarchies, gender identities, student roles, consumer identities, and ways to think, create, and question—including the creation of nationalistic sentiments, patriotic affiliations, and, ultimately, citizens. From the morning's recitation of the Pledge of Allegiance through a politically constructed curriculum, students in the United States (like students elsewhere) learn prescribed knowledge, from history and English to math and science. Education is continuously creating national citizens as well as citizens of a globally dominant, imperialist power.

Social scientists have been interested in this concealed narrative for education for some time. The primary research approach, often called **critical pedagogy**, stems from the work of Brazilian educator and philosopher Paulo Freire ([1970] 2000) and British sociologist of education Basil Bernstein (1971) and their students and colleagues. In his foreword to Freire's most important work, *Pedagogy of the Oppressed,* Richard Shaull ([1970] 2000, 34) explains Freire's view of education:

> Education either functions as an instrument that is used to facilitate the integration of the younger generation into the logic of the present system and bring about conformity to it, or it becomes "the practice of freedom," the means by which men and women deal critically and creatively with reality and discover how to participate in the transformation of their world.

Students of the institution of education must therefore pay very close attention to the old sociological adage that things are not what they seem. Education is a tool for both social control and liberation. The creation of citizens, the decision about who is and is not one, and the determination of what citizens should think and do are mechanisms of social control for specific state purposes. According to a recent report by the Institute for Social Policy and Understanding (Mogahed and Chouhoud 2017), after the election of Donald Trump, the bullying of Muslim children in public schools skyrocketed to some 42% reporting such experiences (four times the level of the general public) with 25% of these incidents coming from these Muslim children's public school teachers.

Throughout its history, education in the United States has been the subject of continual efforts at reform by the federal government. In 1983, the National Commission on Excellence in Education published the report *A Nation at Risk: The Imperative for Educational Reform,* which prompted action from Ronald Reagan's administration. Since then, we have seen programs such as George H. W. Bush's Goals 2000, George W. Bush's No Child Left Behind, and Barack Obama's Race to the Top. With these national platforms, the federal government typically mandates reform but rarely funds it, and critics claim that such efforts also fundamentally fail to understand the structure and functioning of the institution of education. Nevertheless, all these reform efforts share one element: the goal of the development of the citizenry (especially imperial citizens, or citizens of the U.S. empire) and the furthering of the interests of multinational corporations.

President Donald Trump's educational platform was driven by his choice for secretary of education, Betsy DeVos: "school choice." The basic idea of school "choice" is this: While taxpayer dollars fund our public schools (and we will discuss later how this particularly American structure rigs the educational game), those who advocate school choice want taxpayer moneys to go to *all* schools (charter schools, private schools, religious schools, and so on), with parents then allowed to "choose" the schools their children attend. This idea has its foundations in the White flight that occurred after the 1954 order to desegregate public schools. Indeed, as Singer (2017) observes, "Before the federal government forced schools to desegregate, no one was all that interested in having an alternative to traditional public schools. But once whites got wind that the Supreme Court might make their kids go to school with black kids, lots of white parents started clamoring for 'choice.'" Time will tell the extent of the damage done by the Trump administration's policies. Among other unprecedented actions, DeVos encouraged public schools to call ICE on undocumented public school children (Ballinget 2018).

Education, Race, and Intersectional Realities

Each year since 1970, the U.S. Department of Education's National Center for Education Statistics has published a report titled *The Condition of Education,* a recent edition of which we have referenced and will continue to reference in this chapter (NCES 2017), along with other sources that together represent the institution's official presentation on the developments and trends in education. Data do not speak for themselves, however; all of us use lenses to interpret data, as we will see next. Education is compulsory in the United States until the age of 16, but the ages at which children begin and end their education vary by state (NCES 2017). And depending on their positions within the matrix of experience—their race, class, gender, sexuality, and abilities—the ways in which individuals experience the institution of education vary dramatically. Now that we have established a set of stories and lenses with which to understand the way education works (or does not work) for its constituents, we can map out its official structure, while recognizing that there are alternative structures, and that some children experience neither the official one nor any alternatives.

Social Class

We are born into the matrix and gendered, raced, and located in our positions in the socioeconomic structure. From Durkheim (1956) to Lareau (2011), sociologists of education have long identified social class as one of the most fundamental axes of inequality in all societies, determining who gets what and why in the educational system (for an overview of the field, see also Sadovnik 2011). Put another way, all educational processes and outcomes are grounded firmly in the student's class position and affected by the student's race, gender, and other locations.

The United States is the only nation that funds its public schools primarily on the basis of local and state, not federal, tax revenues (see Kozol 1991). That is, a given neighborhood or community can support the quality of its school system only to the extent that its local tax revenues, based on the income and wealth of its residents, can afford. This is why there are disadvantaged schools in disadvantaged neighborhoods and advantaged schools in advantaged neighborhoods. In addition, given the historical and contemporary linkages of class, race, immigration, poverty, and segregation, in the end, the school system is in a certain sense rigged.

One disastrous consequence of such economic rigging is what some scholars have called the school-to-prison pipeline, in which race plays a fundamental part. The monetary and social disinvestment in and abandonment of many predominantly Black, Latinx, and Native American schools and school districts disproportionately affect students of color, who achieve at lower rates, are not expected to achieve as much, are more likely to repeat a grade, are subject to increased surveillance and punishment, and, as we have seen, drop out at higher rates when compared to students from more affluent areas and more privileged positions within the matrix.

So, we underfund certain schools, these students' opportunities are dismal, they drop out and commit crimes, and then they are put into prison (Redfield and Nance 2016). The United States currently spends much more on keeping an individual in prison than it would have cost to shepherd that same person through the education system as a child.

Given our narratives about the role of education in skills acquisition and social mobility, we should first ask whether the payoff is worth it. As Figure 6.3 shows, the answers are yes, no, and, well, it depends. On average, those with more education earn more income. The median income for college graduates in 2017 was about $52,019 (Jeffrey 2019) which was some 74.5% (or $22,204/year) higher than high school graduates. However, there are significant gender and race differences. White men reap greater rewards at every educational level. And within every racial group there is a gender gap. White men with a high school diploma still earn significantly more money than White women with an associate of arts (AA) degree. This simple fact helps explain why more women today are seeking college degrees; men have greater income options without attending college.

Many students see a college degree as a requirement for landing a decent-paying job. However, college has grown increasingly expensive, and the past decade has shown that many graduates accumulate enormous debt in their pursuit of a degree. Overall, it is estimated that about 44.2 million U.S. adults have outstanding student debt and that the total owed is more than $1.5 trillion (Irby 2019). According to a recent study, more Black and Latinx undergraduate students take out student loans than do Whites or Asians (Scott-Clayton and Li 2016) and even

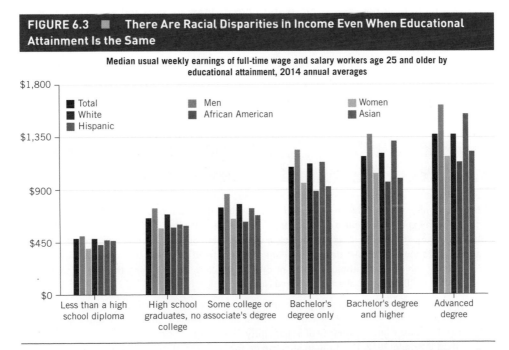

FIGURE 6.3 ■ There Are Racial Disparities in Income Even When Educational Attainment Is the Same

Median usual weekly earnings of full-time wage and salary workers age 25 and older by educational attainment, 2014 annual averages

Source: Bureau of Labor Statistics, U.S. Department of Labor, *The Economics Daily*, Median weekly earnings by educational attainment in 2014 on the Internet at https://www.bls.gov/opub/ted/2015/median-weekly-earnings-by-education-gender-race-and-ethnicity-in-2014.htm (visited January 06, 2021).

15 years after graduation, Blacks, for instance, held 186% more debt than Whites (Houle and Fenaba 2018). Additionally, Blacks and Latinx are more likely to shoulder a heavier debt burden than Whites or Asians while also having less income after graduation and coming from families with less wealth—the matrix of race allows us to see how entangled all these elements are.

Gender

Worldwide, according to UNESCO's most recent *World Atlas of Gender Equality in Education* (2012), only a handful of nations have achieved gender parity in education. They are most of the countries of the European Union, Indonesia, the Russian Federation, a few South American countries, Canada, and the United States. For the vast majority of these nations, this situation represents a significant gain since 1970. Despite advancements in school enrollment for girls around the world, however, women still make up the majority of illiterate adults—especially in South and West Asia, sub-Saharan Africa, and the Arab states. The Global Partnership for Education has been working to remedy this situation across the globe since the early 2000s. In 2002, some 57% of girls (on average) finished primary school throughout Africa, Southeast Asia, and the Middle East; that number has risen to 75%, and across the same time period the percentage of girls completing lower secondary school increased from 35 to 50% (Global Partnership for Education 2020).

In their Pulitzer Prize–winning book *Half the Sky: Turning Oppression into Opportunity for Women Worldwide,* Kristof and WuDunn (2009) observe that "education is one of the most effective ways to fight poverty. . . . [It] is also a precondition for girls and women to stand up against injustice, and for women to be integrated into the economy." In 2011, Malala Yousafzai of Pakistan, 14 years old at the time, was shot in the head and neck by a Taliban attacker because of her political blogging, organizing, and activism with girls and women in her community (and beyond) centered on the importance of education for all. Her experience reminds us that, worldwide, the education of girls and women fundamentally matters—but also that, while gains have been made, we still have far to go.

RESISTANCE STORY: MALALA YOUSAFZAI

Some children receive stronger educations because the color of their skin is forever linked to opportunity; other children are not able to succeed in school because the curriculum is centered in experiences quite different from their own; still others are denied an education because they are female. This was the case with Malala Yousafzai. When she resisted, she almost paid for it with her life, but now she speaks for all of those children marginalized because of their racial, ethnic, gender, or other identities, emphasizing the importance of education. In 2013, she spoke at the United Nations:

> I raise up my voice . . . so that those without a voice can be heard. Those who have fought for their rights: Their right to live in peace. Their right to be treated with dignity. Their right to equality of opportunity. Their right to be educated . . . . On the 9th of October, 2012, the Taliban shot me on the left side of my forehead. They shot

Malala Yousafzai
Simon Davis/DFID

ny friends too. They thought that the bullets would silence us. But they failed. And then, out of that silence, came thousands of voices . . . . In many parts of the world, especially Pakistan and Afghanistan, terrorism, wars, and conflicts stop children to go to their schools. . . . Dear sisters and brothers, now it's time to speak up. . . . We call upon the world leaders that all the peace deals must protect women and children's rights. A deal that goes against the dignity of women and their rights is unacceptable. We call upon all governments to ensure free compulsory education for every child all over the world. . . . We call upon all communities to be tolerant—to reject prejudice based on caste, creed, sect, religion, or gender. To ensure freedom and equality for women so that they can flourish. We cannot all succeed when half of us are held back. . . . Let us empower ourselves with the weapon of knowledge and let us shield ourselves with unity and togetherness. . . . Education is the only solution. Education first.

Source: Malala Yousafzai, speech to the United Nations Youth Takeover, July 12, 2013, https://secure. aworldatschool.org/page/content/the-text-of-malala-yousafzais-speech-at-the-united-nations.

The matrix structures the schooling experiences of boys and girls very differently, and these structures intersect with race, class, and many other dimensions of that experience. An older, but comprehensive review of gender inequalities in education by Buchmann, DiPrete, and McDaniel (2008) highlighted that the research showed then that girls did less well on standardized tests than boys but got better grades; that girls' behavior in school, compared with that of boys, is more in line with institutional expectations of students; and that girls show more interest in schooling than boys do.

A more recent review Yu, McLellan, and Winter (2021) shows the persistence of societal gender roles structuring classroom experiences including:

- boys are more likely to speak up in classroom discussions than girls;

- teachers interact and respond to boys and girls differently without realizing it; and they praise and criticize the genders differently.

- These come with consequences for the experience of education in the matrix.

In general, girls engage much more fully than boys in many aspects of school. One of the reasons for this is society's very limited definition of masculinity. Teenage boys do not see engaging in schoolwork and getting good grades as a path to proving their masculinity. Instead, if they do these things, they may be bullied as geeks. When gender and race intersect, school success is even more problematic for boys. Among Black youth, getting good grades is often seen as "acting White." A recent study by Stanford University's Center for Educational Policy Analysis shows that while, on average, boys and girls perform the same in mathematics, in affluent, White, suburban schools, boys consistently outperform girls. The researchers believe this has to do with local norms and more traditional socialization patterns which are stereotypically gendered, where these "high-income parents spend more time and money on their children, and invest in more stereotypical activities …enrolling their daughters in ballet and their sons in engineering" (Miller and Quealy 2018).

In the wake of the founding of the Black Lives Matter movement, sparked by the 2014 shooting death of Michael Brown in Ferguson, Missouri, the African American Policy Institute released a report titled *Black Girls Matter: Pushed Out, Overpoliced, and Underprotected* (Crenshaw 2015). The report reviews research on Black girls' lives, particularly their lives and experiences in schools, details key findings, and offers suggestions. The following are some of the research findings described in the report:

- In New York and Boston, while both Black boys and Black girls are subject to larger achievement gaps and harsher forms of discipline than their White counterparts, for girls these consequences are often more stark.

- At-risk girls describe zero-tolerance schools as chaotic environments where discipline is prioritized over educational attainment; this leads them to disengage.

- Increased levels of law enforcement and other security measures within schools sometimes make girls feel less safe and less likely to attend school.

- Girls' attachment to and sense of belonging in school can be undermined if their achievements are overlooked or undervalued.

- Punitive rather than restorative responses to conflict contribute to girls' feelings of separation from school.

- The failure of schools to intervene in sexual harassment and bullying of girls contributes to girls' insecurity at school.

- Girls sometimes resort to "acting out" when their counseling needs are overlooked or disregarded.

- School-age Black girls experience a high incidence of interpersonal violence.

- Black and Latina girls are often burdened with familial obligations that undermine their capacity to achieve their schooling goals.

- When teen pregnancy occurs, the experiences of both pregnancy and parenting make it difficult for girls to engage fully in school.

Clearly, the data show that race and gender together create the experience of schooling for Black girls. This report recommends the expansion of opportunities in schools to include Black girls, increase their feelings of safety, and ensure environments that are free of sexual harassment. So, while Malala rightly encourages us to work to ensure an education for all, especially girls, it is important to recognize that we must also keep a close eye on how education does and does not work for all girls, depending on their position within the matrix. Currently, with increasing Islamophobia in the United States and in American schools, girls like Malala are now daily undergoing a process of racialization the likes of which Muslim Americans have previously never seen—and it is deeply affecting their ability to succeed in American society (Selod 2015).

Sexual Minorities

In 1999, the Gay, Lesbian, and Straight Education Network (now known simply as GLSEN) began conducting the National School Climate Survey. This important survey, conducted every 2 years, seeks to measure students' experiences within their schools. In the most recent data collection, from the 2016–17 school year, a sample of 23,001 students across all 50 states and more than 3,000 school districts was canvassed (Kosciw, Greytak, Zongrone, Clark, and Truong 2018). The results of the survey, since 1999, have consistently revealed a previously concealed story: LGBTQ students experience hostile school climates, absenteeism, lower educational aspirations and achievements, and poor psychological well-being. Respondents have reported verbal assaults on their sexuality, gender, and gender expression (while transgender identites are not about sexual orientation or sexuality, the data reported include these students along with LGB youth) (see Figure 6.4). Physical assaults have been reported as well, and reports of intervention by fellow students have been rare. Such incidents are reported to school authorities only about 42% of the time, and to family members only about 43% of the time.

The report on the National School Climate Survey for the 2016–17 school year shows that while all LGBT students experience verbal and physical harassment in their schools, LGBT students of color experience such harassment in addition to the daily microaggressions that they receive when others make assumptions about their other statuses (such as race and class;

In part because getting good grades is not seen as incompatible with femininity, as is often the case with masculinity, girls tend to be more engaged with many aspects of school.

Katherine Frey/The Washington Post via Getty Images

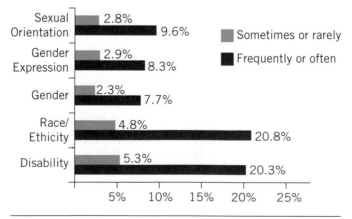

FIGURE 6.4 ■ Harassment, Bullying, and Physical Assault Experienced by LGBTQ Students

Percentage of LGBTQ students who have experienced harassment or assault in the past school year, based on...

- Sexual Orientation: 2.8% / 9.6%
- Gender Expression: 2.9% / 8.3%
- Gender: 2.3% / 7.7%
- Race/Ethnicity: 4.8% / 20.8%
- Disability: 5.3% / 20.3%

■ Sometimes or rarely
■ Frequently or often

Source: Kosciw, Greytak, Zongrone, Clark, and Truong. The 2017 National

School Climate Survey: The Experiences of Lesbian, Gay, Bisexual, Transgender, and Queer Youth in Our Nation's Schools. New York. GLSEN.

Kosciw et al., 2016). The report, and LGBTQ students themselves, offer several solutions to these problems:

- Increased opportunities for gay-straight alliances have been shown to have significant positive impacts on school cultures and climates.

- Curricula must be inclusive of the experiences of LGBTQ individuals, histories, and voices.

- Supportive teachers and administrators are essential.

- Comprehensive anti-bullying and anti-harassment policies and laws should be in place.

Critical Thinking

1. If the concealed story that education serves to create workers is correct, what other kinds of behavioral rules and normative expectations would employers in today's labor market find desirable? Do you think these differ for Blacks, Whites, Latinx, Native Americans, or Asian Americans? For men and women? How are such expectations manifested in schooling practices?

2. Now that you have been in college for a bit of time, can you explain the "rules of the game" (cultural capital) for college? Do these rules privilege certain locations in the matrix?

3. How has your education thus far encouraged you to question reality? What kinds of structures and relations have facilitated this? How has your education discouraged you from questioning reality?

4. Have you ever taken a Black studies/African American studies course? A women's studies or gender studies course? A sexualities course? If so, how did these classes function to, as Frantz Fanon would say, "decolonize your mind"? If not, how do you think such courses would help students to decolonize their minds? How would different students—Whites? Men? African Americans? Lesbians?—benefit differently from such courses?

TRANSFORMING THE FUTURE OF EDUCATION

There have always been movements rooted in educational reform, in fact we have discussed several of these throughout this chapter. But reform for whom? By whom? With whose experiences in mind? With what goal propped up as indicative of "success"? As we have seen, the institution of education does not work equally or effectively for all, and often works to reproduce inequalities that exist outside of the school, within the walls of our schools. Evidence indicates that federal-, state-, and even corporate-led "reforms" have often served the needs of those who are already advantaged within the system, and the interests of those in power; thus, it is clear that we need social movements to move toward educational justice for all of those in the matrix.

Educational Movements

Those who are on the front lines fighting for a more equitable educational system rightly question whether the education "reforms" of the past several decades add up to a "movement" to make a better system.

Drawing from the full matrix of experience, such educational movements will be more likely to focus on the issues that are determined to be significant for those within the system—students, teachers, parents—more reflective of their experiences of the institution of education within the matrix of experience. According to Mark Warren, who studies such educational justice movements in the United States, in the era of the New Jim Crow (Alexander 2020) where significant proportions of Black and Latinx students live in poor neighborhoods, attend schools that lack funding, and deal with daily burdens of policing and mass incarceration, we require a "renewed educational justice movement that is connected to a broader movement to address poverty and racial inequities across schools and communities" (2018). Some organizations, like Allies for Educational Equity, work to collectivize and amplify the realities of educators and education reforms across the country, with a mission "to unite the political voices of education reforms so that zip codes don't determine destinies" (2020).

The 21st century is vibrant with such movements for educational justice in this sense. Perhaps you are involved in one or more right now! Those involved in them come from all intersections of the matrix as advocates and activists for education—working to erase the inequalities that have been present since America's founding and reproduce themselves through dominant institutions like education (El-Mekki 2018).

Educational justice moves in a wide variety of arenas including, but not limited to:

- the school-to-prison pipeline,

- the intersectional gap in achievement driven by experience in the matrix,

- the fundamental inequities in school funding,

- the number of Black, Latinx, and male teachers (recognizing that experience in the matrix matters for educating about the matrix),

- issues of food insecurity,

- college preparation and student debt,

- zero-tolerance policies, and so on.

These movements represent the unceasing voices, protests, letter-writing campaigns, speaking at boards of education, and so much more that work to bend the functioning of our educational system toward the needs of children and their communities rather than the needs of the majority, the capitalist workplace, or party politics.

Some have even been calling for the creation of a student-to-activism pipeline (El-Mekki 2018) to produce those who, having undergone the experience of indignity, punishment, and silencing within America's schools, will become the next wave of organizers who will fight for educational justice. Those marginalized by the system often are the ones who are on the front lines of movements to change the system of education and to propose alternatives. Indeed, the front lines are disproportionately Black, Latinx, and Native students and parents from low-income families and communities that have been disinvested in by the system; their children and communities have the most to gain.

There are many Whites who also work for educational justice, although their privilege often distances them from the realities on the ground and they are often the ones who can take the benefits that the system, built for them, offers, instead of continuing to fight for those who need a new system.

Consider the recent movements to fight against the Trump administration's ending of the DACA (Deferred Action for Childhood Arrivals) program. This dismantling of protection (and even acknowledgment of these children) has put almost 1 million children and young adults at risk in many institutions, including education. The fight to ensure that these students can become citizens and even have the hope of receiving educations in the U.S. is a critical one right now. One organization at the forefront of this consolidated movement to protect Dreamers, United We Dream, has effectively staged coordinated protests in Washington, DC, and walk-outs across the nation. These movements, often through a combination of research, protesting, personal stories of experience in the educational system, and connecting to broader moral imperatives, have indeed connected with other movements for social justice (across other institutions), and have broadened the constituencies invested in educational justice and are winning some policy successes across the country.

Education as a Human Right

Much of this movement work was inspired, in the late 1960s and early 1970s, by the work of Paulo Freire, an educator from Brazil, whom we met earlier, who sought to reveal the oppressive foundations of capitalist educational systems, particularly in colonized countries, while simultaneously calling for the construction of a **pedagogy of liberation** whereby education can free people, not confine them. Freire was born into a middle-class family in Brazil but suffered from hunger in childhood as a result of the collapse of the Brazilian economy. He was inspired by this and by his later experiences in political exile to fight a colonial system that was built on, and essentially maintained by, the dehumanization and exploitation of the colonized such as himself. Believing that the capitalist system of education was instrumental in silencing the oppressed, he argued for a form of education through which the oppressed, in dialogue with one another and by drawing from personal experience, would come to critically question the oppressive system. As Freire ([1970] 2000, 68) explains, "The struggle begins with men's recognition that they have been destroyed." The oppressed are then able to actively participate in their own liberation, and therefore in the transformation of society as a whole.

This is all to change existing structures, yes, but also to return dignity to the institution of education and those whose lives it touches. Many of these movements for educational justice emerged from and continue to acknowledge education as a human right. Dignity is fundamental to human rights. Indeed, much of this stems from the Universal Declaration of Human Rights (1948), which states, in Article 26, that "everyone has the right to education," that it should be

These demonstrators gathered in support of DACA in front of the United States Supreme Court in November 2019.

Jahi Chikwendiu/The Washington Post via Getty Images

free, that it should be grounded in the "full development of the human personality" and "promote understanding, tolerance and friendship among all nations, racial or religious groups," and that education should work toward universal peace. We are far from this reality in the United States, and around the world, but these movements for educational justice continue to fight.

Perhaps we need alternative models to civics, to political science, to social science, to history as taught in our schools and universities. Currently the structure trains and prepares citizens, not humans. Perhaps we need human rights principles not only to be taught in our classrooms but also to be structured into the social relationships that exist in our schools—and indeed wherever learning to be human takes place, which is everywhere. Perhaps we need to move toward a liberation curriculum, one that recognizes that the world is socially constructed and shaped by human action and inaction, and that each person has a voice, experience, and knowledge, and therefore ideas and practices that we can use to alter the structure of the world for the betterment of all.

Critical Thinking

1. Have you ever studied abroad? Have you ever experienced education in another country? Have you had discussions with anyone else who has had these experiences? How would living in, studying in, or even studying/hearing about alternative

The Brazilian educator Paolo Freire believed that traditional education, as in this classroom near Rio de Janeiro, reinforces systems of oppression and inequality.

Three Lions/Getty Images

educational experiences help us envision new educational realities that are more effective for all in the matrix?

2. Taking into account the ideas discussed above about imagining new educations and education as a human right, engage your peers in dialogue about ways in which we might forge new educational systems.

3. How might the institution of education and the process of schooling in the United States be different if African Americans had been centrally involved in the creation of the education system? If Latinx had been? If Asian Americans had been? If women had been? If the poor had been?

4. After reading this chapter, what actions can you take to improve the educational experience and outcomes for all students?

CHAPTER SUMMARY

6.1 Describe the current state of education in the United States and the key historical factors that have shaped it.

Key factors that helped shape the contemporary educational system in the United States include the treatment of Native Americans, the development of the university system, the establishment of separate schools for Blacks and Whites, and the creation of training opportunities that differ by race, gender, ethnicity, and class. Experiences of schooling are fundamentally woven together with the threads of gender, class, and sexuality. These experiences are themselves critically about race. In order to understand the current realities and distributions of opportunities and outcomes for students, one needs to examine their locations in the matrix of race.

6.2 Compare the major sociological theories of education.

Social-functional theory and human capital theory are two dominant explanations of education within the discipline of sociology. The former focuses on socialization, while the latter focuses on skills acquisition. These are similar stock theories, but they have different implications for our understanding of how education works in the matrix of race.

6.3 Analyze several matrix perspectives on education.

From a critical matrix perspective, education can be seen as a site of conversion (to White American culture), a site of class construction (as a space for the dominant culture's ideas and interests), a site of creating workers (for the capitalist labor market), and a site where citizens are crafted (as Americans).

6.4 Identify alternatives to the educational system that recognize intersectional realities.

Imagining new educations requires seeing our reality for what it is and allowing our vision to extend beyond that reality at the same time. Students will think about contemporary movements for educational justice. Paulo Freire provides us with some inspiration in this regard, as does conceptualizing education as a human right.

KEY TERMS

apprenticeship model of education
Atlanta Compromise
Brown v. Board of Education of Topeka
colonization of the mind
critical pedagogy
cultural capital
human capital

Mendez et al. v. Westminster School District of Orange County
pedagogy of liberation
Plessy v. Ferguson
resocialization
social cohesion
socialization

REFERENCES

Alexander, M., 2020. *The new Jim Crow: Mass incarceration in the age of colorblindness.* The New Press.

Allies for Educational Equity. 2020. "What We Do" Accessed on April 28, 2020 online at https://www.alliesforedequity.org/what-we-do

Apple, Michael. 2013. *Knowledge, Power, and Education: The Selected Works of Michael Apple.* London: Routledge.

Asante, Molefi Kete. 1991. "The Afroectric Idea in Education." *Journal of Negro Education* 60, no. 2: 170–80.

ASU. 2019. "Alpha Pi Omega, the first sorority for native women." Arizona State University website. Accessed November 21, 2019. https://studentlife.asu.edu/content/alpha-pi-omega-first-sorority-native-women

Ballinget, Moriah. 2018. "Civil rights groups criticise US education secretary for saying schools can report undocumented students" May 13. Accessed Janaury 20, 2020 at https://www.independent.co.uk/news/world/americas/report-students-schools-us-civil-rights-betsy-devos-immigration-education-a8365596.html

Becker, Gary. 1964. *Human Capital.* New York: National Bureau of Economic Research.

Bernstein, Basil. 1971. *Class, Codes and Control, Vol. 1, Theoretical Studies towards a Sociology of Language.* Oxford: Routledge.

Bourdieu, Pierre. 1984. *Distinction: A Social Critique of the Judgment of Taste.* Cambridge, MA: Harvard University Press.

Bourdieu, Pierre. 1986. "The Forms of Capital." In *Handbook of Theory and Research for the Sociology of Education,* Westport, CT: Greenwood Press.241–58.

Bourdieu, Pierre, and Jean-Claude Passeron. 1977. *Reproduction in Education and Society.* London: Sage.

Bowles, Samuel, and Herbert Gintis. 1976. *Schooling in Capitalist America.* New York: Basic Books.

Brunsma, David. L. 2004. *The school uniform movement and what it tells us about American education: A symbolic crusade.* R&L Education.

Brunsma, David L., David G. Embrick, and Jean H. Shin. 2017. "Graduate Students of Color: Race, Racism, and Mentoring in the White Waters of Academia." *Sociology of Race and Ethnicity* 31. doi:10.1177/2332649216681565.

Buchmann, Claudia, Thomas A. DiPrete, and Anne McDaniel. 2008. "Gender Inequalities in Education." *Annual Review of Sociology* 34: 319–37.

Carey, Kevin. 2015. "How One's Choice of College Affects Future Earnings." *New York Times,* September 15, A3.

Carnevale, Anthony P., Stephen J. Rose, and Ban Cheah. 2011. "The College Payoff: Education, Occupations, Lifetime Earnings." Center on Education and the Workforce, Georgetown University. Accessed March 11, 2017. https://www2.ed.gov/policy/highered/reg/hearulemaking/2011/collegepayoff.pdf.

Chang, Ha-Joon. 2010. *23 Things They Don't Tell You About Capitalism.* New York: Bloomsbury.

Coleman, James S. 1988. "Social Capital in the Creation of Human Capital." *American Journal of Sociology* 94 (suppl. 1): S95–S120.

Crenshaw, Kimberlé Williams. 2015. *Black Girls Matter: Pushed Out, Overpoliced, and Underprotected*. New York: African American Policy Forum. Accessed June 2, 2017. http://www.aapf.org/recent/2014/12/coming-soon-blackgirlsmatter-pushed-out-overpoliced-and-underprotected.

Du Bois, W. E. B. 1900. "Address to the Nation." Accessed December 3, 2012. http://users.wfu.edu/zulick/341/niagara.html.

Durkheim, Émile. 1956. *Education and Sociology*. New York: Free Press.

Durkheim, Émile. 1962. *Moral Education*. New York: Free Press.

Durkheim, Émile. 1977. *The Evolution of Educational Thought*. London: Routledge & Kegan Paul.

Educational Psychology. "Gender differences in the classroom," accessed on April 28, 2020 online at https://courses.lumenlearning.com/suny-educationalpsychology/chapter/gender-differences-in-the-classroom/

El-Mekki, Sharif. 2018. "educational Justice: Which Are You – an Advocate, Ally, or Activist?" September 24 *The Education Trust* Accessed online on April 28, 2020 at https://edtrust.org/the-equity-line/educational-justice-which-are-you-an-advocate-ally-or-activist/

Fanon, Frantz. 1952. *Black Skin, White Masks*. New York: Grove Press.

Fanon, Frantz. 1961. *The Wretched of the Earth*. New York: Grove Press.

Forman-Brunell, M. and Paris, L. eds.,2011. *The girls' history and culture reader: the nineteenth century*. University of Illinois Press.

Freire, Paulo. (1970) 2000. *Pedagogy of the Oppressed*. 30th anniversary ed. New York: Bloomsbury.

Global Partnership for Education. 2020. https://www.globalpartnership.org/what-we-do/gender-equality

Hannah-Jones, Nikole. 2015. "A Prescription for More Black Doctors." *New York Times Magazine*, September 9. Accessed June 5, 2017. https://www.nytimes.com/2015/09/13/magazine/a-prescription-for-more-black-doctors.html?mcubz=1&_r=0.

Houle, Jason N. and Fenaba R. Addo. 2018. "Racial Disparaities in Student debt and the Reproduction of the Fragile Black Middle Class," *Sociology of Race and Ethnicity*, 5(4): 562-577.

Huber, L. P., Malagón, M. C., Ramirez, B. R., Gonzalez, L. C., Jimenez, A., and Vélez, V. N. (2015, November). *Still Falling Through the Cracks: Revisiting the Latina/o Education Pipeline*. CSRC Research Report, Number 19. UCLA Chicano Studies Research Center.

Hurston, Zora Neale. 1955. "Court Order Can't Make the Races Mix." *Orlando Sentinel*, August. Accessed March 11, 2017. https://www.lewrockwell.com/1970/01/zora-neale-hurston/court-order-cant-make-the-racesmix.

Hussar, William J., and Tabitha M. Bailey. 2016. *Projections of Education Statistics to 2024. NCES 2013–008*. Washington, DC: U.S. Department of Education, National Center for Education Statistics.

Irby, Latoya. 2019. "Breakdown of Student Loan Debt in the U.S." *The Balance*, May 14. Accessed on April 30, 2020 online at https://www.thebalance.com/student-loan-debt-statistics-4173224

Jeffrey, Terence P. 2019. "Median Earnings of U.S. College Grads 74.5% Greater Than High School Grads." *CNSNews*, March 21. Accessed November 14, 2019. https://www.cnsnews.com/news/article/terence-p-jeffrey/median-earnings-college-grads-745-greater-high-school-grads

Jeffrey, Terrence. 2019. "Median Earnings of U.S. College Grads 74.5% Greater Than High School Grads" *CNS News.com*. March 21. Accessed on January 9, 2021 at https://www.cnsnews.com/news/article/terence-p-jeffrey/median-earnings-college-grads-745-greater-high-school-grads

Karenga, Maulana. 2002. *Introduction to Black Studies*. 3rd ed. Los Angeles: University of Sankore Press.

King, Marsha. 2008. "Tribes Confront Painful Legacy of Indian Boarding Schools." *Seattle Times*, February 3. Accessed March 11, 2017. http://www.seattletimes.com/seattle-news/tribes-confront-painful-legacy-of-indian-boarding-schools.

Kosciw, J. G., Greytak, E. A., Zongrone, A. D., Clark, C. M., & Truong, N. L. (2018). *The 2017 National School Climate Survey: The experiences of lesbian, gay, bisexual, transgender, and queer youth in our Nation's schools*. New York: GLSEN.

Kosciw, Joseph G., Emily A. Greytak, Noreen M. Giga, Christian Villenas, and David J. Danischewski. 2016. *The 2015 National School Climate Survey: The Experiences of Lesbian, Gay, Bisexual, Transgender, and Queer Youth in Our Nation's Schools*. Washington, DC: Gay, Lesbian and Straight Education Network. Accessed June 5, 2017. https://www.glsen.org/sites/default/files/2015%20National%20GLSEN%202015%20National%20School%20Climate%20Survey%20%28NSCS%29%20-%20Full%20Report_0.pdf.

Koven, K.A., 2009. *Establishing college preparatory conditions and a college-going culture in California charter high schools*. University of California, Los Angeles.

Kozol, Jonathan. 1991. *Savage Inequalities: Children in America's Schools*. New York: Crown.

Kristof, Nicholas D., and Sheryl WuDunn. 2009. *Half the Sky: Turning Oppression into Opportunity for Women Worldwide*. New York: Alfred A. Knopf.

Lareau, Annette. 1989. *Home Advantage: Social Class and Parental Involvement in Elementary Education*. Lanham, MD: Rowman & Littlefield.

Lareau, Annette. 2011. *Unequal Childhoods: Class, Race, and Family Life*. 2nd ed. Berkeley: University of California Press.

Lee, Stacey, Eujin, Park, and Jia-Hui Stefanie Wong. 2016. "Racialization, Schooling, and Becoming American: Asian American Experiences." *Educational Studies*, published online December 14. doi:10.1080/00131946.2016.1258360.

Martinez-Cola, Marisela. 2019. "Visibly Invisible: TribalCrit and Native American Segregated Schooling." *Sociology of Race and Ethnicity*. https://doi.org/10.1177/2332649219884087

Mayer, Susan. 2010. "The Relationship between Income Inequality and Inequality in Schooling." *Theory and Research in Education* 8, no. 1: 5–20.

McGrory, Brian. 2011. "Centuries of Interruption and a History Rejoined: Wampanoag Grad to Be Harvard's First since 1665." *Boston Globe*, May 11. Accessed June 5, 2017. http://www.boston.com/news/local/massachusetts/articles/2011/05/11/wampanoag_grad_to_be_harvards_first_since_1665/?page=2.

Miller, Claire Cain and Kevin Quealy. 2018. "Where Boys Outperform Girls in Math: Rich, White and Suburban Districts." *The New York Times*. June 13. Accessed on November 26, 2019. https://www.nytimes.com/interactive/2018/06/13/upshot/boys-girls-math-reading-tests.html

Mills, C. Wright. 1956. *The Power Elite*. New York: Oxford University Press.

Mogahed, Dalia and Youssef Chouhoud. 2017. *American Muslim Poll 2017: Muslims at the Crossroads*. Institute for Social Policy and Understanding. Washington, DC. Accessed November 26, 2019. [link]

Moore, T. and Morton, J., 2017. The myth of job readiness? Written communication, employability, and the 'skills gap' in higher education. *Studies in Higher Education*, 42(3), pp. 591–609.

National Center for Education Statistics. 2017. *The Condition of Education: 2016*. Washington, DC: National Center for Education Statistics. Accessed March 11, 2017. https://nces.ed.gov/pubs2016/2016144.pdf.

National Center for Education Statistics. 2018. *Digest of Education Statistics: 2017*. Washington, DC: National Center for Education Statistics. Accessed November 11, 2019. https://nces.ed.gov/programs/digest/d17/

National Center for Education Statistics. 2019a. "Trends in High School Dropout and Completion Rates in the United States." Accessed November 11, 2019. https://nces.ed.gov/programs/dropout/ind_05.asp

NCES. 2016a. *Projections of Educational Statistics to 2024*. Washington DC: National Center for Education Statistics. Accessed online at https://nces.ed.gov/pubs2016/2016013.pdf

NYC Department of Education. 2019. "Chancellor Carranza Announces 72 Percent Increase in Students Taking Computer Science Sicne Launch of Computer Science For All" December 11. Accessed January 20, 2020 at https://www.schools.nyc.gov/about-us/news/announcements/contentdetails/2019/12/11/chancellor-carranza-announces-72-percent-in-students-taking-computer-since-launch-of-computer-science-for-all

Onion, Rebecca. 2019. "The Stories of 'Segregation Academies,' as Told by the White Students Who Attended Them." *Slate.com*, November 7. Accessed November 24, 2019 https://slate.com/news-and-politics/2019/11/segregation-academies-history-southern-schools-white-students.html

Owings, Allison. 2011. *Indian Voices: Listening to Native Americans*. New Brunswick, NJ: Rutgers University Press.

Pirtle, Whitney. 2019. "The Other Segregation." *The Atlantic*. April 23. https://www.theatlantic.com/education/archive/2019/04/gifted-and-talented-programs-separate-students-race/587614/

Quealy, Kevin and Eliza Shapiro. 2019. "Some Students Get Extra Time for New York's Elite High School Entrance Exam. 42% Are White." *The New York Times*. June 17. Accessed November 21, 2019. https://www.nytimes.com/interactive/2019/06/17/upshot/nyc-schools-shsat-504.html

Redfield, Sarah E., and Jason P. Nance. 2016. *School to Prison Pipeline: Preliminary Report*. Washington, DC: American Bar Association. Accessed June 27, 2017. https://www.americanbar.org/content/dam/aba/administrative/diversity_pipeline/stp_preliminary_report_final.authcheckdam.pdf.

Rivera, L.A., 2016. *Pedigree: How elite students get elite jobs*. Princeton University Press.

Sadovnik, Alan R., 2011. *Sociology of Education: A Critical Reader*. 2nd ed. New York: Routledge.

Schultz, Theodore. 1961. "Investment in Human Capital." *American Economic Review* 51: 1–17.

Scott-Clayton, Judith, and Jing Li. 2016. "Black—White Disparity in Student Loan Debt More than Triples after Graduation." *Evidence Speaks Reports* 2, no. 3 (October 20), Brookings Institution. Accessed March 14, 2017. https://www.brookings.edu/research/black-white-disparity-in-student-loan-debt-more-than-triples-after-graduation.

Selod, Saher. 2015. "Citizenship Denied: Racialization of Muslim American Men and Women Post 9/11." *Critical Sociology* 41: 77–95.

Shaull, Richard. (1970) 2000. *Foreword to Pedagogy of the Oppressed, by Paulo Freire*. 30th anniversary ed. New York: Bloomsbury.

Singer, Steven M. 2017. "The Racist Roots and Racist Indoctrination of School Choice." Gadfly on the Wall (blog), January 15. Accessed March 11, 2017. https://gadflyonthewallblog.wordpress.com/2017/01/15/the-racists-roots-and-racist-indoctrination-of-school-choice.

Smith, Andrea. 2007. "Soul Wound: The Legacy of Native American Schools." *Amnesty International Magazine*, March 26. Accessed March 11, 2017. http://www.amnestyusa.org/node/87342.

Taylor, Kate, and Claire Cain Miller. 2015. "Mayor to Put Schools' Focus on the Science of Computers." *New York Times*, September 16, A25.

UNESCO. 2012. *World Atlas of Gender Equality in Education*. Paris: UNESCO. Accessed March 28, 2013. http://www.unesco.org/new/en/education/themes/leading-the-international-agenda/gender-and-education/resources/the-world-atlas-of-gender%20equality-in-education.

U.S. Census Bureau. 2011. "Who's Minding the Kids? Child Care Arrangements: Spring 2010, Detailed Tables." Accessed July 12, 2013. http://www.census.gov/hhes/childcare/data/sipp/2010/tables.html.

Warren, Mark. 2018. "The Power of Educational Justice Movement," *Learning Policy INtitutte*, November 1, accessed on April 28, 2020 online at https://learningpolicyinstitute.org/blog/power-educational-justice-movements

Waterman, Stephanie J. and Lindley, Lorinda S. 2013. "Cultural Strengths to Persever: Native American Women in Higher Education." *NASPA Journal About Women in Higher Education* 6(2): 139-165.

West, Cassandra. 2012. "Black Studies Programs Now Flourishing despite Early Struggles." *Diverse Issues in Higher Education* 29, no. 11. Accessed June 26, 2017. https://www.questia.com/magazine/1G1-296952044/black-studies-programs-now-flourishing-despite-early.

Woodson, Carter Godwin. (1933) 2016. *The Miseducation of the Negro*. Baltimore: Black Classic Press.

Yu, J., McLellan, R. & Winter, L. (2021). Which Boys and Which Girls Are Falling Behind? Linking Adolescents' Gender Role Profiles to Motivation, Engagement, and Achievement. *Journal of Youth and Adolescence* 50, 336–352. https://doi.org/10.1007/s10964-020-01293-z

Zeilinger, Julie. 2015. "Multicultural Fratnernities and Sororities Flip the Script on What We Think About Greeks." Mic.com. October 5. Accessed November 24, 2019. https://www.mic.com/articles/125195/multicultural-fraternities-and-sororities-flip-the-script-on-what-we-think-about-greeks

Zhboray, Ronald. (1993). *A fictive people: antebellum economic development and the American reading public*. New York: Oxford University Press.

7 CRIME AND DEVIANCE

Black people are more than twice as likely than Whites to be victims of police violence, a fact that has prompted numerous protests and confrontations between citizens and police.

Nicholas Kamm/AFP/Getty Images

LEARNING OBJECTIVES

7.1 Examine the history of race, crime, and deviance.

7.2 Analyze stock theories of race, crime, and deviance.

7.3 Apply the matrix lens to the relationships among race, crime, and deviance.

7.4 Formulate transformative narratives of crime and deviance.

On September 6, 2018, Amber Guyger, a White Dallas Police Officer, entered what she thought was her apartment and saw an "intruder," a Black male, who she shot and killed. As the shots were fired, Officer Guyger realized that the unarmed Back man, Botham Shem Jean, was her neighbor. She was the intruder; her apartment was actually one floor down. She was arrested and charged with first-degree manslaughter. Days of protest followed the incident, as people across the nation protested another Black life cut short at the hands of police. Guyger testified that she had been working 10-hour shifts, four days a week, that she was on "autopilot" when she entered the residence, and that she feared for her life when she fired the shot that killed Jean. Prosecutors argued that the five-year police department veteran missed several clues that she was in the wrong apartment "including a red doormat, a neighbor's planter, a missing table and clutter on the kitchen counter."

In 2017, of the 1,147 people killed by police, Blacks comprised 25%, despite making up only 13% of the population. Black victims are also more likely (21%) than either Whites (14%) or Hispanics (17%) to be unarmed (Sinyangwe 2018). While much attention has been given to excessive force used against Blacks, there is less conversation about the hidden stories of other racial and ethnic groups. For instance, Native Americans are almost 5 times more likely than Whites, a third more likely than Blacks, and three times more likely than Hispanic/Latinx to be killed by police in the United States (Guardian 2016).

Gender, age, and sexuality also have an impact. Over a lifetime, men and boys are more than 15 times more likely than women and girls to be killed by police (Edwards, Lee, and Esposito 2018). A national survey of LGBTQ+ people and those living with HIV reported that over 70 percent of respondents had had direct contact with police in the past five years. Of these, 21% reported that this encounter was hostile, with 14% reporting verbal assaults by police, 3% reporting sexual harassment, and 2% reporting physical assault by law enforcement officers (Mallory, Hasenbush, and Sears 2015).

Our stock stories teach us that laws protect us; they are created to preserve peace, promote tranquility, and allow us to pursue our collective best interests. These stories tell us that the deviants who violate laws are committing crimes and must be punished accordingly. In the pursuit of justice, democracy is preserved and enhanced, and freedoms are procured and embraced. Our stock stories assume that the law is color-blind—enforced the same way everywhere, for everyone, and without concern for race, class, or other differences. Using the matrix approach, we can reveal the concealed stories of crime and deviance in the United States, stories that have always been complicated by race, ethnicity, gender, and class. Historically, crime and punishment have been associated with attempts to preserve the racial order. In this chapter we will examine this and other narratives and observe how the matrix has influenced both our perceptions and the realities of crime and deviance.

A HISTORY OF RACE, CRIME, AND DEVIANCE

What happens when being different defines criminal behavior and deviance? The historical record demonstrates that in the early days of the United States, high-status White males (e.g., ministers, merchants, landowners) were rarely the subjects of criminal proceedings. Punishments were most frequently meted out to Native Americans, enslaved African Americans, single women (particularly servants), poor White males, and unruly children (Patrick 2010). **Deviance** encompasses all actions or behaviors that defy social norms, from crimes to social expectations. Deviance can be as mild as wearing the wrong colors to a high school football game or as extreme as not wearing anything at all. When deviance takes forms that violate moral and ethical standards, like murder or theft, it may be covered under law and become a **crime**. Deviance in many ways defines a significant portion of our national identity. We will discover that, as the social construction of "Whiteness" came into being, it also became the normative, or standard, structure by which our laws are constructed and deviance is defined.

Building a Foundation of Whiteness

English colonists arrived in America with decidedly racist stereotypes about Africans, Native Americans, and others, assuming that members of these groups were savage, indolent, and sexually promiscuous (Jordan 1968). In fact, the Europeans who settled the Americas believed it was their destiny to extend Christian civilization and White supremacy around the globe.

Legislating White Privilege

Elite European males institutionalized, or established, Whiteness in an effort to control Blacks, Native Americans, women, and others. Women, across all socioeconomic statuses and racial groups, typically received harsher punishments than their male counterparts for violating sexual or marriage taboos. Gender-specific laws affecting all racial, ethnic, and class groups helped to sustain White privilege and White normative structures. White privilege, as we discussed briefly in Chapter 1, results from laws, practices, and behaviors that preserve and (re-)create societal benefits for those people identified as White. White normative structures are those norms and institutions that obscure the racial intent of such laws, practices, and behaviors, creating the illusion that White privilege is natural and normal.

One of the first recorded instances within the English colonies in which judicial processes decreed differential judgments along both racial and gender lines occurred in 1630 in Jamestown, when colonist Hugh Davis was ordered to be "soundly whipt" for dishonoring God and shaming Christianity by sleeping with a Black woman (Bernasconi 2012, 215). Ten years later, also in Jamestown, another White man was ordered to do penance for impregnating an African female, while the African female was sentenced to whipping. So, even though the interracial relationship was condemned, the more extreme punishment was shifted to the Black female (Bernasconi 2012, 216).

Over the next few decades of the 17th century, the pattern of race, gender, and status inequities was replicated repeatedly. While all women experienced unique discrimination and bias, racial hierarchies were also gendered. White women, given authority over women of other races through their connection to White males, were also given authority over Blacks regardless of gender. White women could lose their status if they married or had intercourse with African,

Native American, or Asian men. Colonial laws did not protect either Black or Native American women from rape. Laws also precluded them from defending themselves, either directly against their attackers or through the courts. Females of color were often cast as seducers (Browne-Marshall 2002).

Racial consciousness and fear have shaped our views of law and deviance since colonial times. **Racial consciousness** is the awareness of race shared by members of a racial group and the wider society. This consciousness perpetuates, legitimates, and normalizes racial hierarchies by making the notions of Whiteness, White privilege, and White supremacy real at the expense of people of color. The linking of White racial consciousness with notions of normalcy was first engraved into our national laws as early as 1790, with the passage of the U.S. Naturalization Law. This law limited citizenship to those immigrants who were "free white persons of good character." And when we look further into this law, we note that, of children born abroad, only those whose fathers were U.S. residents were granted citizenship. The exclusion of children whose mothers might have been residents points to the gender bias of these early laws as well. This process justified and perpetuated White male privilege.

White privilege in the United States has its foundations in sets of rules created and preserved through a series of laws, mores, and beliefs that guaranteed White personal privilege over Blacks, Native Americans, Asians, Hispanics, and others. Privilege encouraged all Whites, including those of lower status, to identify with the ruling White elite, often at the expense of Black slaves. Whiteness and its privilege provided the illusion of elite status and control of the economic, political, and judicial systems, the ultimate arbiters of White privilege. More punishment could be meted out to Blacks than to Whites; Whites, not Blacks, could own and bear arms; Whites, not Blacks, had the right to self-defense. The lowliest of White servants could chastise, correct, and testify against Blacks (either free or enslaved). And the ultimate forms of degradation were reserved for Blacks, often at the hands of Whites. Only Blacks could be whipped naked; Black slave women could be raped, and any offspring that resulted would be slaves. Further, any White woman or free woman of color who, forgetful of her status, elected to have sex with or marry a Black male slave could be forced into slavery herself.

These laws were codified into what came to be called **slave codes** throughout the Southern colonies. Beginning in 1757, under these laws White males were further empowered when they joined **slave patrols** (Durr 2015)—organized groups of White men with police powers who systematically enforced the slave codes. A patrol, usually consisting of no more than seven men, would ride throughout the night, challenging any slaves they encountered and demanding proof that they were not engaging in unlawful activities (Cooper 2015). Slave patrols were active throughout the South until slavery's abolishment at the end of the Civil War.

With the end of the Civil War came a great many new laws aimed at controlling the now freed Blacks. These laws were known as **Jim Crow laws** (also known as **Black Codes**), and they held sway across the United States from the 1880s onward, with some surviving into the 1960s.

Reservations and treaties served the same function for Native Americans. For many other racial and ethnic minority Americans, Whiteness and the laws were also effectively used for social control and the construction of deviance.

Defining Whiteness in the West

During the latter half of the 19th century, Whiteness was also being defined on the western frontier, this time at the expense of Native Americans. Formal U.S. policies and laws were formulated to aid White settlers and railroad corporations in the forcible expulsion of Native Americans from their tribal lands. The U.S. Army supplied the force whereby thousands of acres of land were acquired. No new treaties were ratified, as "raid" replaced "trade" in White–Indian treaties (DiLorenzo 2010).

As the result of battles with the army, hundreds of Native Americans were held as prisoners and subjected to military "trials." Most of the adult male prisoners were quickly found guilty and sentenced to death. In the largest mass execution in U.S. history, 38 members of the Dakota tribe were hanged in 1862 in Mankato, Minnesota, on orders of the president of the United States, Abraham Lincoln. They were accused of killing 490 White settlers, including women and children, during the Santee Sioux uprising earlier in the year. The story that rarely gets told is that these Sioux were angered by repeated broken treaties and the failure of the United States to live up to its promises of food, supplies, and reparations. Enraged and starving, the Native Americans attempted to take back their lands by force. After the execution, the remaining Native Americans were resettled on "reservations" under a presidential executive order. From this period through the next few decades, Native Americans were consistently vilified

Slave rebellions demonstrate that deviance can be both deliberate and political. In the pre–Civil War United States, several rebellions and insurrections fanned the flames of White anxiety and fears, while legitimating the humanity of those considered slaves. During the 1831 rebellion led by Nat Turner, slaves went from plantation to plantation, freeing other slaves and killing Whites. A total of 55 to 65 Whites died. In retaliation, White militias and mobs killed more than 200 Blacks.

Stock Montage/Getty Images

as criminals, deviants, and savages, and their lands were systematically taken as Whites and Whiteness marched westward. Even a bloody civil war did not stop the U.S. attack on Native Americans. In 1867, General William Sherman, who was tasked with securing western lands and dealing with the Native Americans, wrote to Ulysses S. Grant, then commanding general of the U.S. Army, "We are not going to let a few thieving, ragged Indians check and stop our progress" (quoted in Goldfield 2011, 450). The consolidation of Native American lands, along with the end of the Civil War, marshaled a new period of Whiteness and social control.

The Effects of Immigration

How we as a nation have dealt with immigrants has consistently demonstrated the problems and the possibilities of intersectional differences. Immigration specifically presents problems that our laws, our customs, and our institutions have had to frequently grapple with. Who is welcomed? Why are some treated with favor and others with disfavor? What do our responses demonstrate about the character of our nation? Through the experiences of the "less desirable," we are able to see the irony of a nation where freedom is presumed, but some are greeted with both fear and resentment.

Fear and Resentment

One of the first groups deemed unfit for immigration to the U.S. were Asians, particularly those from China. During the California gold rush of 1848–52, Chinese immigrants began arriving in the United States to work as laborers on large construction projects. Following the 1862 Anti-Coolie Act enacted in California, Chinese were stereotyped as criminals and prostitutes and thus were excluded from entry into the country. Other ethnic groups also deemed "undesirable" included Middle Easterners, Hindus, East Indians, and Japanese, and some Europeans.

While Asians were being targeted in the Western U.S., immigrants from Southern and Eastern Europe were being targeted in the Eastern and Midwestern parts of the country. Previous European immigrants (those from the British Isles, Germany, Scandinavia, Switzerland, and Holland) resented new immigrants from Austria-Hungary, Italy, Russia, Greece, Romania, and Turkey. These resentments fostered prejudices, similar to those regarding Asians, that the new Southern and Eastern Europeans were too different to properly assimilate. The greatest hostilities were leveled at non-western Europeans, particularly Jews. Economic downturns fueled both fear and resentment of these new European immigrants. They were also being singled out for their supposed criminality, cultural differences, and experienced threats to their personal welfare. Ultimately, these fears led to the changes in the Immigration Act of 1875 (Fuchs and Forbes 2003).

Immigration laws and policies explicitly targeting Chinese and other ethnic/racial groups, in various forms, held sway until 1943, when Chinese immigrants were finally made eligible for U.S. citizenship. Then in 1952, race was formally removed as grounds for exclusion, allowing a limited number of Chinese and other Asians to be admitted. In 1965 a sweeping Immigration and Naturalization Act was created that favored family reunification and skilled immigrations

Chinese immigration to the U.S. began in earnest around 1850, when "coolies" came to the country to work on major construction projects. Legislation aimed at preventing Chinese immigration, driven by fears of innate criminality, could not entirely stem the flow, and by the 1920s Chinese laborers had branched out into other industries, like salmon canning in Oregon.

Keystone-France/Gamma-Keystone/Getty Images

and eliminated specific country quotas. For the first time, immigrants from the Western Hemisphere were limited, while favoring people born in Asia and Latin America (Cohn 2015). These policies have had a direct impact on who we are as a people.

Asserting Heteronormativity

In one of the strangest court rulings ever, in 2019 a set of twins, Aiden and Ethan Dvash-Banks, were deemed unequal. In the ruling, and in the eyes of the U.S. government, Aiden is a citizen while his brother Ethan is undocumented. The boys' parents are a married gay couple who legally share parenthood. One is a U.S. citizen, while the other is a citizen of Israel. Both fathers are listed on the birth certificates, but because Ethan has DNA from his Israeli father, and Aiden has DNA from his U.S. father, the government denied Ethan citizenship. Thus, the

Andrew Dvash-Banks, 37, and his husband Elad Dvash-Banks, 32, feed their twins.

Lucy Nicholson/Reuters/Newscom

government's decision to treat these twins differently, simply based on the parental DNA sends a clear message to LGBT couples: "You are not equal" (Levin 2019).

Such unequal treatment is not new; in fact, it has long been used to restrict access to immigration and citizen rights based on sexuality, or sexual orientation.

"Moral turpitude" was also utilized to exclude and target a group of citizens and potential immigrants based on their sexuality. *Moral turpitude* is an extremely vague legal term that attempts to define acts or behaviors that gravely violate the sentiment or acceptable standards within a community. In this regard, moral turpitude asserted heteronormativity, or a belief that heterosexuality predicated on the gender binary was not only the norm but also the legal default of sexual orientation. These laws presumed that biological sex, sexuality, gender identity, and gender roles were aligned with biological sex (Minter 1993).

It was not until 1974, when the American Psychiatric Association removed homosexuality from the list of recognized illnesses, that there was any significant movement to change immigration policy around sexuality. Despite this, the INS (Immigration and Naturalization Service) as late as 1980 deemed homosexuality a reason to deny full citizenship. These laws were invalidated with the 1983 Supreme Court ruling of *Hill v. Immigration and Naturalization Service*. And in 1990, the INS statutes mandating excluding persons committing sexual deviant acts or exhibiting psychopathic personalities were repealed. The issue was not completely settled until 1994, when the Board of Immigration Appeals ruled a gay Cuban man eligible for asylum. Attorney General Janet Reno followed up with a directive to immigration officials that considered lesbians and gays as a "social group," thus giving them greater access to existing regulations having to do with asylum (Ridinger 2019).

A Legacy of Racial Profiling

Crime, laws, and perceptions of deviance create, (re)produce, and reinforce status hierarchies based on race and ethnicity. At the intersections of these racial hierarchies are both gender and class. Consequently, as we look at how deviance is both constructed and enforced, we find that people of color, and males of color in particular, are most likely to be racially profiled by police and to receive the stiffest sentences from the courts, are incarcerated at higher levels than Whites, and are more likely to face the death penalty.

Racial profiling is the targeting of particular racial and ethnic groups by law enforcement and private security agencies, resulting in their subjection to ridicule, detention, interrogation, and search and seizure, often with no evidence of criminal activity. Racial profiling is based on the perception that certain racial, ethnic, religious, and national-origin groups are guilty until proven innocent. And while racial profiling violates the U.S. Constitution's guarantees of equal protection under the laws, and freedom from unreasonable searches and seizures, it continues to be utilized.

Slightly more than half of all adults in the United States believe that racial profiling is widespread. Some 53% believe that racial profiling plays a role in which motorists police pull over, and many believe that security personnel use racial profiling at airport security checkpoints (42%) and when deciding which shoppers to watch at stores and malls (49%). The majority of Blacks (67%) and Hispanics (63%), compared to only 50% of non-Hispanic Whites, feel that racial profiling is widespread (Bergner 2014).

Finally, LGBTQ+ people of color are twice as likely to experience hate crimes then either Blacks or Jews (Park and Mykhyalyshyn 2016). This was clearly reflected in the 2016 mass shooting at the Pulse nightclub in Orlando, Florida, that killed 49 people. Many believe that this was "undeniably a homophobic hate crime targeting the clubs' mostly LGBTQ+ clientele" (Coaston 2018; Fitzsimons 2018). While transgender people of color face higher levels of victimization, crimes against them are less likely to be reported or investigated than crimes against other minority groups (Caspani 2015).

Critical Thinking

1. How do immigration status, sexuality, and race impact perceptions of deviance, acceptability, and crime? How do police and the wider community respond to these groups differently based on these differences?

2. Racial profiling by police has consistently been demonstrated to lead to the increased surveillance and criminalization of both Blacks and Hispanics. How might similar types of racial profiling affect not only these groups but others within major institutions such as education, the military, and the economy? While we have

concentrated on the negative aspects of racial profiling, could such profiling have positive effects for Whites or females? Speculate on how these may manifest, not only in crime but also in other institutions.

3. Are there some individuals that we assume to be more violent, criminal, or deviant, simply because of the groups to which they belong? What does this say about the social construction of deviance?

4. Consider your hometown or university. Does it include certain groups that are more likely to be associated with crime and deviance? Does this behavior surface in specific ways, at particular times, or in specific situations? Has this behavior been evidenced across several different periods?

SOCIOLOGICAL STOCK THEORIES OF CRIME AND DEVIANCE

The disciplines of sociology and criminology have always been concerned with crime and deviance. These concerns have mirrored society's attempts to justify racial, gender, and class hierarchies. Accordingly, the standard theories within sociology and criminology may be considered as stock stories. The theoretical orientations of these stock stories may be separated into two broad categories: biosocial theories of deviance and ecological perspectives on crime.

These standard stories have a common thread—they place the source of deviance at the micro, or personal, level. Therefore, either the individual or the individual's community, culture, or environment is at odds with societal norms. And, by implication, if the individual or the community, culture, or environment could just be reformed, fixed, adjusted, or rehabilitated, then the deviance would be reduced or would cease to exist. Finally, as we shall see, these stock stories all fail to account adequately for the macro, or structural, factors that at best intervene in and at worst are the primary contributors to the social construction of deviance. As we will see later in the chapter, after a troubled start, sociologists armed with an intersectional or matrix perspective have been more adept at unraveling the discourse regarding race, class, gender, and crime and deviance. Let us now turn to these theories.

Biosocial Theories of Deviance

The earliest and most systematic attempts to understand deviance linked it to biology. In the 19th century, Cesare Lombroso, viewed as the founder of modern criminology, ascribed crime and deviance to both ethnicity and race. He held that Africans, Asians, and American Indians were especially prone to crime and deviance (Greene and Gabbidon 2012, 96). According to Lombroso, all non-Europeans were more likely to be criminals because they were lower on the evolutionary scale. He argued that crime and deviance were biologically determined. This theory, based in **biological determinism**, holds that an individual's behavior is innately related to components of physiology, such as body type and brain size. Lombroso's theory was later criticized for being too simplistic and highly ethnocentric. The samples he relied on for his studies were unrepresentative of the population as a whole, because he focused primarily on Italian criminals who were convicted of crimes, comparing them with Italian soldiers. A whole range of structural, economic, and cultural factors were ignored or subsumed under these differences.

By the time Lombroso's research became known in the United States at the beginning of the 20th century, biological determinism was the dominant explanation for crime and deviance. Within the United States, the overrepresentation of African Americans and some immigrants in crime statistics caused many to link race and ethnicity to crime and deviance (Gould 1981). With time, the leading arguments regarding deviance and crime were linked to IQ and race.

While some recent scholars have revived the discourse linking crime and biology, they have stressed that a person's behavior is influenced by both biology and environment. Critiques of this approach have quickly pointed out the implicit race, gender, and class biases inherent in it, and that it fails to take into consideration social environment, a failure that can lead to the biological and social determinism of previous periods (Gould 1981).

If crime is related to environment, what does that say about the environment in which you live? If we were, for example, to do a measure of crime on many college campuses, we might conclude that offenders are likely to be White, male, and educated. This is primarily because most college campuses are predominantly White and presumably more educated than the general population. And it recognizes that males are most likely to be risk takers, hence more likely than females to be associated with deviance. Alternatively, Black male offenders receive on average 19.1 percent longer sentences than White male offenders for the same kinds of crime (United States Sentencing Commission 2019). Clearly, something more is happening.

Ecological Perspectives on Crime

From its inception, sociology in the United States was concerned with solving the myriad problems associated with industrialization, urbanization, slums, poverty, and crime that were rapidly transforming the nation at the beginning of the 20th century (Orcutt 1983). Sociologists attempted to explain the apparent links between crime and social location (including ethnicity, race, class, and gender). Some believed that members of minority communities received much more scrutiny from criminal justice professionals and thus were more likely to be prosecuted by the legal system (Tonry 1995). Others argued that Blacks and other minorities were simply more likely than Whites to commit serious crimes (Hindelang 1978).

For almost half of the 20th century, the ecological approach dominated the discourse on deviance within American sociology. This approach situates human behavior (norms, social control, deviance, and nondeviance) within the social structures external to the individual. The causes of crime, these theorists argued, are found in the community structures in which people live and interact. Community members interact to socially (re-)create the conditions that account for criminal and noncriminal behavior. Several theoretical strands have been derived from the ecological approach to crime and deviance. The three most important of these are social disorganization, the culture of poverty, and broken windows theory.

Social Disorganization

Social disorganization, one of the first derivatives of the ecological approach, links crime to neighborhood ecological patterns. Place matters, and the apparent ecological differences in levels of crime are explained by the structural and cultural factors that shape, distort, or encourage social order within communities. For example, high levels of immigration and migration often produce rapid community changes. These rapid changes may then lead to either the disruption or the breakdown of the structure of social relations and values, resulting in the loss of social controls over individual and group behavior. During the period of stress, social disorganization prevails, and crime, which is thus situational and not group specific, develops and persists.

Culture of Poverty

Rather than the community, some theorists began to think of culture as connected to deviance. It was argued that different levels of crime among various groups arose from differences in morality (Wirth 1931). Theorist Louis Wirth (1931, 485) wrote, "Where culture is homogeneous and class differences are negligible, societies without crime are possible." **Differential association theory** elaborates on this perspective, proposing that differences in criminal involvement among groups result from their different definitions of criminality. Those groups that normalize crime essentially develop a "culture of poverty," accounting not only for their lack of success but also for their continued leaning toward criminal lifestyles (Moynihan 1965; Lewis 1961, 1966a, 1966b). The **culture of poverty** approach views poverty as a set of choices made by unwed mothers that perpetuate crime, deviance, and other pathologies across generations. The process produces children who are both morally deficient and more apt to commit crime; in addition, they produce more unwed mothers with unwanted children. This self-perpetuating cycle of dependencies, it has been argued, is associated with poor families, and specifically with poor families of color. This perspective has been criticized as essentially blaming the victim— that is, holding the injured party entirely or partially responsible for the harm suffered. Such a perspective ignores the structural inequities that underlie poverty, and it reveals an intersection between racism and sexism.

Crenshaw (1991, 2005) argues that the intersection of racism and patriarchy accounts for the increasing levels of violence faced by women of color. These intersecting patterns of racism and sexism reflect the dynamics of structure rather than culture. When we understand that many women of color are also more likely to be burdened with children, underemployed or unemployed, and consequently poor, the problems associated with racial discrimination are further compounded. Intersectionality shapes the experiences of these women of color, and impacts where they live, how they live, and the context in which they experience violence throughout our country and history. Their experiences demonstrate that it's not just race, or class, or gender, but *how* these structures intersect. The same types of intersectional structures have also been shown to account for the increased likelihood of transgender women of color to be victimized by acquaintances, partners, and strangers. And while some of these cases are clearly due to anti-transgender bias, for most victims it is their intersectional identities that put them at greater risk. These risks also include unemployment, poverty, homelessness, and/or survival sex work (Human Rights Council 2018).

Broken Windows Theory

Beginning in the early 1980s, criminologists began to speculate on the relationship between urban disorder and vandalism. Could cities fix their crime problems by simply fixing up the neighborhoods, picking up the litter, and, yes, fixing broken windows? **Broken windows theory** (Wilson and Kelling 1982) argues that stopping vandalism can lead to a significant decrease in serious crime. Police surveillance may be a means of controlling crime, but it does not eliminate or even curtail it. The presence of abandoned properties, vandalism, litter, and filth not only demoralizes community residents but also produces a form of nihilism (i.e., an extreme form of fatalism) that leaves people feeling overwhelmed, hopeless, and apt to give up. But while fixing broken windows and sprucing up neighborhoods may lead to increasing pride in a community, these actions do not sufficiently explain lower levels of crime and deviance. Combatting fear, making citizens feel empowered, and establishing partnership relations between community members and police are among the factors that lead to decreased crime levels (Xu, Fiedler, and Flaming 2015). Similar arguments have linked crime with the prevalence of lead in the environment.

The broken windows theory holds that addressing minor crimes like vandalism and jaywalking reinforces social norms around lawfulness and thus reduces crime.

pjhpix/Alamy Stock Photo

Critical Thinking

1. What does the acceptance of stock stories suggest regarding the natural, cultural, biological, or community basis of crime?

2. How might stock stories influence the way that crime is both perceived and prosecuted? How might such beliefs affect jury members in cases involving suspects who are members of racial minorities? How might these differences impact different intersectional groups differentially?

3. How do stock stories mirror our assumptions about racial and ethnic differences?

4. Have you experienced being categorized according to others' conceptualizations of how you should or should not act based on the group(s) with which you identify? If so, in what ways did this experience affect your choices? How did you ultimately deal with the characterizations of others? What does this suggest about your individual agency and stereotypical assumptions about you?

APPLYING THE MATRIX TO CRIME AND DEVIANCE

The matrix approach argues that powerful elites construct and enforce laws that protect their interests. Du Bois (1904) was the first to theorize and document the intersectional or matrix approach to crime and deviance. He began by dismissing the biological basis of crime and pointing out how social structures influence crime and deviance. Du Bois argued that crime and racial status are definitely linked, with the linkage most obvious among African Americans. He pointed out that in the United States, race, class, and gender are manipulated to maximize profits.

The matrix perspective helps us interrogate our assumptions about what is deviant and what is normal, or what is considered criminal and what is noncriminal.

Assigning Deviance

Some types of crimes, victims, and criminals have become closely associated with particular races, classes, and genders. Dominant racial and ethnic groups, because they are better positioned than others, are more able to avoid criminal sanctions and being labeled deviant. The systematic linking of deviance with difference has much to do with both who is doing the linking and where the observations are being conducted. In most cases the assignment of deviance serves to legitimate both the status and the privileges of those in power. Deviance typically has been associated with young males who are members of racial and/or ethnic minorities. The fact that these youth also tend to be concentrated within urban areas, on reservations, or in rural enclaves has given rise to a long history of linking deviance to specific kinds of communities and groups. Crimes targeting women in all of these situations have tended to be either ignored or marginalized.

Differential labeling occurs when some individuals and groups are systematically singled out and declared deviant by virtue of their being in those particular groups. This labeling derives from the social construction of crime, law, and deviance by those who have power. Differential labeling underlies a persistently held belief within the United States that Blacks, Hispanics, and other disadvantaged groups are more prone to crime, violence, and disorder; more likely to receive support from welfare programs; and more likely to live in undesirable communities. Such stereotypes may also lead members of the stigmatized groups to respond in ways that confirm the beliefs. Women of all groups have also experienced differential labeling. Women of color in particular bear the historic scars of being labeled promiscuous and money-seeking (Farrell and Swigert 1988, 3).

Differential labeling makes us more likely to associate racial minorities with crime. Deviance is in the eye of the observer. If we expect to see crime, then we will see it (Thomas and Thomas 1928, 571–72).

Differential labeling highlights the significance of the perceptions and social construction of deviance and crime. All too often, it can have devastating consequences. Over the past 7 years, the U.S. Department of Justice has been increasingly asked to evaluate incidents of the use of lethal force by local police. While it has identified 14 municipal law enforcement agencies suspected of engaging in a "pattern or practice" of violating civil rights through the use of excessive force, these findings have resulted in few lasting reforms (Weichselbaum 2015). Some have gone so far as to suggest that law enforcement has developed a warrior mindset rather than a guardian mindset (Stoughton 2015).

The Spaces and Places of Crime and Deviance

Even casual observation reveals that a given behavior might be rewarded in one context and penalized in another. Space often determines the appropriateness of specific acts. Consider war and contact sports: In both settings the use of certain forms of violence is considered legitimate, but that same behavior at a party or in a college classroom would not be appropriate. The matrix approach also reveals that certain persons occupying certain social spaces or identities, such as racial, class, and gender identities, may similarly find their actions differentially circumscribed and labeled deviant. When various physical spaces interact with social identities, different types and definitions of deviance can be identified.

Have you ever wondered when and where crime is most prevalent? The matrix approach focuses our attention on how individual behavior interacts with larger social structures. Issues of race and racism produce stress. One important theory helps us understand how this stress influences deviance.

General Strain Theory

One of the seminal sociological approaches demonstrates the causal link between levels of stress and deviance. **General strain theory** (Agnew 1992) proposes that racism produces stressful events and environments, which in turn lead to "negative emotions such as anger, fear, depression, and rage, and these emotional reactions lead to crime either directly or indirectly depending upon other contingencies such as coping mechanisms, peer and familial support, and self-esteem" (Piquero and Sealock 2010, 171). Thus, it is suggested that people of color may view the United States from a particularly racialized perspective, where "race matters" because it significantly alters their chances for survival and success (Unnever and Gabbidon 2011). Systemic racism—that is, a system of inequality based on race, often within institutional settings, such as law enforcement and the criminal justice system—is often associated with differential outcomes in crime and deviance. Because of systemic racism, people of color are more likely than Whites to be victims of police abuse, racial profiling, and differential criminal sanctioning under get-tough policies associated with the war on crime and drugs. Systemic racism is at the root of the current mass incarceration of Blacks, who then experience a lifetime of legal and employment discrimination, housing segregation, and diminished opportunities (Alexander 2010).

Some criminologists argue that until we understand how race and racism create a hegemonic structure that has historically criminalized people of color, we will not be able to account for the apparent permanence of racial disparities in deviance and incarceration rates.

Intersectional Differences: Gender, Race, and Class

Gender and race consistently are demonstrated to be associated with criminal behavior. In fact, they are the strongest predictors of deviant behavior according to most research. Men commit more violent and conventional crime than females (Beirne and Messerchmidt 2006). Alternatively, while Whites are more frequently victims of violent crime, less than half of the perpetrators were White, and close to a quarter were Black (23%). Fourteen percent of the perpetrators were Hispanic (Morgan 2017).

But if we consider gender, we see stark differences. For example, Native American women have the highest rate of homicide among women, followed by Hispanic or Latinx women, but this is just the opposite for their male counterparts. In fact, as demonstrated in Figure 7.1, while violent crimes such as homicide have decreased from 1980 to 2015, the racial disparities in male murder continue to persist with slight variations. Black males consistently are more likely to be victims of murder than all other men across either racial or ethnic groups (Widra 2018).

But if we control for class, particularly economic disadvantages, we observe that extremely disadvantaged White neighborhoods have similar rates of murder and victimization as extremely disadvantaged Black neighborhoods (Lee 2000). When we talk about crime, White victims seem to get most of the press, while the victimization of persons of color is grossly underreported. In the next section we will discuss incarceration rates by race to see how national policies may account for some of these differences.

Types of Crime

As we have seen, crime, laws, and perceptions of deviance create, (re)produce, and reinforce status hierarchies based on race and ethnicity. We have seen how being different defines criminal

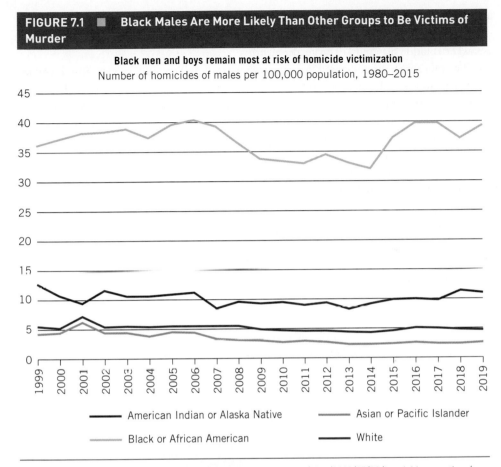

FIGURE 7.1 ■ **Black Males Are More Likely Than Other Groups to Be Victims of Murder**

Black men and boys remain most at risk of homicide victimization
Number of homicides of males per 100,000 population, 1980–2015

— American Indian or Alaska Native   — Asian or Pacific Islander

— Black or African American   — White

Source: Prison Policy Initiative, 2018, https://www.prisonpolicy.org/blog/2018/05/03/homicide_overtime/.

behavior and deviance. We have also seen how historically this difference is associated with the intersection of various racial categories and other social, gender, and class designations. In this section we will examine how various types of crime are reflected interjectionally.

Hate Crimes

Crimes targeting individuals because of their group membership fall under the classification of **hate crimes**. The perpetrators of such crimes use violence and intimidation to further stigmatize and marginalize disenfranchised individuals and groups. These offenses are intended to protect and preserve hegemonic hierarchies associated with race, gender, sexuality, and class (Perry and Alvi 2011). The first federal legislation in the United States concerning hate crimes was the 1990 Hate Crime Statistics Act (Perry 2001, 2–3).

In 2017, just over half of hate crimes were racially motivated crimes. Others targeted sexual orientation, religion, ethnicity, gender identity, disability, and gender (Figure 7.2). The FBI reported that although overall hate crimes had increased by over 17%, hate crimes motivated by gender identity bias in 2017 decreased. Of the 7,175 hate crime incidents, 1,130 were based on sexual orientation bias and 119 on gender identity.

Bias-motivated crimes based on race, religion, disability, and gender also increased. According to the FBI report, anti-Black hate crimes increased by 16% (from 1,739 incidents in 2016 to 2,013 incidents in 2017). While hate crimes targeting Black people constituted 28% of all reported hate crimes in 2017. All other racial and ethnic groups also saw increased hate crimes in 2017 (HRC Staff 2018).

Violence, Gender, and Sexuality

Violence against women has historically been a problem within the United States. In 1994, President Bill Clinton signed the Violence against Women Act. Prior to this act, domestic abusers could avoid prosecution for beating, raping, or other acts of violence against their spouses by simply crossing state lines. Overall the rate of intimate-partner violence dropped 64% from 1993 to 2010 (Law 2019).

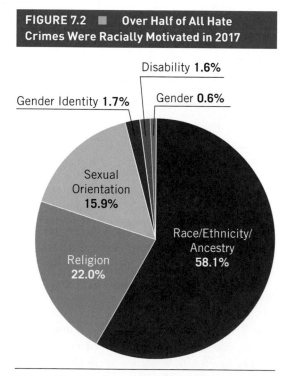

FIGURE 7.2 ■ **Over Half of All Hate Crimes Were Racially Motivated in 2017**

Disability **1.6%**

Gender **0.6%**

Gender Identity **1.7%**

Sexual Orientation **15.9%**

Religion **22.0%**

Race/Ethnicity/ Ancestry **58.1%**

Source: 2019 Hate Crime Statistics, US Department of Justice, https://www.justice.gov/hatecrimes/2017-hate-crime-statistics.

But some males, particularly lower-income Black males in urban settings, are most likely to be victims of violence. Race, class, and gender have consistently been elements in the selection of particular groups for victimization. The rate of victimization for people of color is higher than that for Whites. These rates, consistent over the past four decades, have demonstrated that Blacks and Hispanics were more at risk for serious violence, at a rate of 1.2 to 2 times greater than Whites. Non-Hispanic American Indians report even higher rates of serious violence—approximately 2.4 times greater than those of non-Hispanic Whites. Those with multiple race backgrounds also have higher rates than Whites (about 4.1 times greater). Adding income, gender, and geography completes our intersectional matrix. When doing so, we observe that Black males under the age of 35 residing in urban households with annual incomes under $25,000 are at the highest risk of violent victimization (Warnken and Lauritsen 2019).

Among women of color, sexual abuse has been used as a means of social control and to buttress a system that upholds both racial and masculine supremacy. There were more than 320,000 sexual assaults in 2016; that amounts to about 1.2 per thousand people aged 12 and older. Based on victim survey responses, 84% of women reported to being raped or assaulted in the past year. Of these, 66% were non-Hispanic White women, 15% Hispanic, and 13% non-Hispanic Black respondents. Approximately 44% of the victims were in low-income households earning less than $25,000 per year. People with household incomes of less than $75,000 were almost 12 times more likely (about 4.8 incidents per 1,000 age 12 or older) to be victims of sexual assault than those with household incomes greater than $75,000 (.4 per 1,000) (Fessler 2018).

Across the United States, 1 in 5 women and 1 in 71 men will be raped at some point in their lives. Bisexual women report the highest rates of rape (74.9%), followed by lesbians (46.4%) and then heterosexual women (43%). Among high school youths, female students of color are more likely to report sexual violence:

- 12.5 percent of American Indian/Alaska Native students,

- 10.5 percent of Native Hawaiian/Pacific Islander students,

- 8.6 percent of Black students,

- 8.2 percent of Hispanic students,

- 7.4 percent of White students, and

- 13.5 percent of multiple race students reported being sexually assaulted. (Planty, Langton, Krebs, et al., 2013)

The most common violent crime on U.S. college campuses is rape (Sampson 2002). By the time they graduate, at least a quarter of female college students have experienced sexual assault. Only 4% of these incidents are reported to law enforcement and 7% to any school official. A significant proportion of sexual assaults on college campuses involve LGBT students (9%) (National Sexual Violence Research Center 2015).

Drug-Related Crime

Between 1999 and 2017, more than 700,000 people died from drug overdoses (CDC 2020). Opioids fall into two different categories: illegal (including heroin and fentanyl) and legal (pain relievers such as oxycodone, codeine, and morphine). Since the 1980s, this country has engaged in a so called "war on drugs" which has focused our attention on the illegal categories.

The response to this "crack epidemic" was increased law enforcement and expanded prison capacity to deal with the increasing number of identified addicts. According to the **disease model of addiction**, people addicted to drugs were morally flawed and lacked willpower. This model, holding sway since the 1930s, helped shape our society's response to what many felt was a moral failing rather than a health problem. Addicts were therefore punished rather than treated (NIDA 2018). The war on drugs specifically singled out African Americans and Latinx, particularly males, who had higher arrest and incarceration rates. The mass criminalization of these groups and individuals had little to do with actual drug possession law violations or high levels of drug sales. As a consequence, nearly 80% of those serving in federal prison and close to 60% of those in state prison for drug offenses are either African Americans or Latinx. Blacks and Latinx are also more likely to receive mandatory minimum sentences (Drug Policy Alliance 2018).

In 1996 Purdue Pharma introduced OxyContin, which was marketed as being virtually risk-free of addiction. Through an extremely aggressively marketing campaign, its sales grew from $48 million to almost $1.1 billion in 2000. Between 2009 and 2018, sales increased more than 28%, more than $35 billion (Armstrong and Ernsthausen 2019). Opioid deaths, disproportionately high among Whites (80% of opioid overdose deaths in 2017) have been declared our new epidemic (Kaiser Family Foundation 2020). Ironically, as the opioid use continues to increase in the White communities, these addicts have been classified as victims in need of treatment. Thus, this form of addiction has been medicalized. Put simply, White people who are addicted to opioids are victims in need of treatment; Black and Latinx people addicted to drugs are perceived as criminals and sent to jail (Murch 2019).

Crime and Punishment

Over the past few decades serious crime has been steadily decreasing, yet incarceration rates for select populations has been skyrocketing. What accounts for this apparent contradiction? And what does this contradiction say about how crime and incarceration relate to intersectionality?

Donald Trump, along with several other governors, legislators, and pundits, declared that fighting crime would be a major focus of his administration. Consequently, several measures, both legal and judicial, were put into place to get tough on crime. But while we were getting tough on crime, crime, at least violent crime in the U.S., has been sharply falling over the past two decades. According to the FBI, serious reported violent crime, which includes rape, robbery, and assault in more than 18,500 jurisdictions across our country, fell 51% between 1993 and 2018. Property crime in the same period also fell by about 54% (Morgan and Oudekerk 2019). But while these statistics are real, the average American perceives that crime is on the increase. Therefore, during the period when crime has been decreasing, at least 60% of Americans believe

Abuse of prescription drugs, like oxycodone, is now outpacing that of street drugs like crack cocaine.

Science History Images/Alamy Stock Photo

that there were more crimes being committed (Gramlich 2019). These perceptions have fueled not only our political discourse, but also intersectional outcomes.

Most people, including scholars, policymakers, and citizens, often misunderstand the relationship between crime and punishment. It seems logical that crime and punishment should be correlated. But what we have witnessed over the past decade is that while crime has gone down, our prison populations have skyrocketed. Consequently, for the past two decades there has been no clear relationship between crime and incarceration rates (Gramlich 2019). Incarceration rates reflect the public's belief that crime is a serious problem that needs to be addressed. Their views are what drives both policymakers and social scientists to push for more incarceration and stiffer punishments (Enns 2016). Understanding why there would be an increase in incarceration rates does not explain who tends to be targeted; for this we must understand the structure and context of crime and deviance.

CONCEALED STORY: KERI

Hello, my name is Keri Blakinger. I was a senior at Cornell University when I was arrested for heroin possession. As an addict—a condition that began during a deep depression—I was muddling my way through classes and doing many things I would come to regret, including selling drugs to pay for my own habit. I even began dating a man with big-time drug connections that put me around large amounts of heroin. When police arrested me in 2010, I was carrying six ounces, an amount they valued at $50,000—enough to put me in prison for up to 10 years. Cornell suspended me indefinitely and banned me from campus. I had descended from a Dean's List student to a felon.

But instead of a decade behind bars and a life grasping for the puny opportunities America affords some ex-convicts, I got a second chance. In a plea deal, I received a sentence of 2 and a half years. After leaving prison, I soon got a job as a reporter at a local newspaper. Then Cornell allowed me to start taking classes again, and I graduated in 2014. What made my quick rebound possible?

I am white, female, and middle-class.

Source: Keri's story is used by permission of the author and the *Washington Post*, http://www.washingtonpost.com/posteverything/wp/2015/01/21/heroin-addiction-sent-me-to-prison-white-privilege-got-me-out-and-to-the-ivy-league.

Incarceration Rates, Race, and Ethnicity

Blacks have historically been more likely to be incarcerated then either Whites or Hispanics, but over the past few years there has been a steady decline in the incarceration racial gap. Between 2007 and 2017 there has been a 25% decrease in the number of Blacks incarcerated. This reflects a significant decrease in Black inmates compared to Whites. Although the gap between Hispanic and White incarceration also narrowed during this same period, it reflects an increase in the number of White prisoners. As Figure 7.3 shows, across all three racial groups, there has been a significant decline from 2007 (Gramlich 2019).

State incarceration levels by race show similar patterns. In some states (Iowa, Minnesota, New Jersey, Vermont, and Wisconsin) Blacks are more than 10 times more likely to be incarcerated than their White counterparts. In Alabama, Delaware, Georgia, Illinois, Louisiana, Maryland, Michigan, Mississippi, New Jersey, North Carolina, and Virginia, Blacks constitute more than half of the prison population. And in Maryland, which leads the nation, Blacks comprise 72% of the total prison population. Hispanics, at a rate of 1.4 times that of Whites, are particularly likely to be incarcerated in Massachusetts, Connecticut, Pennsylvania, and New York (Nellis 2016). While most attention is focused on the disparities between Blacks and Hispanics compared to White offenders, the incarceration rates of Native Americans tend to be concealed. Native Americans are incarcerated at 38% higher than the national rate (Bell 2017).

Even though incarceration rates have been declining primarily due to reforms in the last decade, the United States continues to incarcerate a larger percentage of its population than any other country in the industrialized world. As of 2015, Black men were the most represented among those incarcerated, at more than 5.7 percent of young Black males. As many as

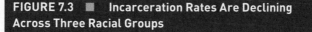

FIGURE 7.3 ■ Incarceration Rates Are Declining Across Three Racial Groups

Racial and ethnic gaps shrink in U.S. prison population

Sentenced federal and state prisoners by race and Hispanic origin, 2007–2017

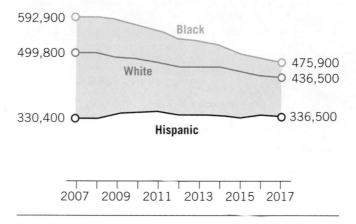

Source: Pew Research Center, Data from Bureau of Justice Statistics.

10 percent of Black children had at least one parent incarcerated in 2015, compared to 3.5% among Hispanic children or 1.7% percent of White children. Incarceration is disproportionately associated with those with limited formal schooling and tends to be intergenerational. For example, in 2010 at the peak of U.S. incarceration rates, nearly one-third of young Black males incarcerated had dropped out of high school, and by the end of 2015 this portion had increased substantially (Pettit and Sykes 2017).

Juvenile justice systems reflect the same racial disparities as we've seen with their adult counterparts across the United States. Again, the most likely sources of these disparities is associated with differential sentencing, criminalization, and deviance labeling associated with nonviolent, low-level offenders. Black youths under the age of 18, who comprise less than 14% of all youth, make up 43% of the male population in juvenile detention facilities, while Black girls comprise 34% of girls incarcerated. Native Americans, representing less than 1% of the U.S. population, comprise 3% of all girls and 1.45% of all boys in detention. Throughout the juvenile justice system, youth of color are disproportionately overpoliced in their communities, criminalized in their schools, and are more likely to be treated as adults and serve time in adult facilities (Sawyer 2018).

According to a 2017 poll, close to half of Americans believe that immigrants contribute to crime (Gallup 2017). Recent research however demonstrates that no such relationship has been demonstrated (Flagg 2018). Similarly, increasing numbers of undocumented populations do not lead to increased criminal sanctions (Flagg 2018). In fact, legal immigrants are 75% less likely to be incarcerated, and undocumented immigrants are 49% less likely to be incarcerated, than people born in the U.S. (Landgrave and Nowrasteh 2019).

Teens of color more likely to serve time in adult detention facilities.

Spencer Grant/agefotostock/Newscom

Incarceration Rates, Gender, and Sexuality

While racial disparities are frequently discussed, the disparities regarding women of color often are ignored. Research documents the reality that women of color are disproportionately more likely to be prosecuted and convicted for felonies compared to their White counterparts (Schiffer 2015).

Persons that identify as LGBTQ are more likely to be more vulnerable when entering the criminal justice system. For example, one in five of the youth in U.S. juvenile justice facilities identify as LGBTQ+, and 85% of these are youth of color. These youth are also more likely to spend a longer time in custody. For older populations, LGBTQ+ people of color are also less likely to have access to legal counsel, less likely to obtain pre-trail release, and less likely to get a fair sentence. While detained, they are more likely to face discrimination and more vulnerable to harassment and inhumane treatment (MAP and Center for American Progress 2015).

Capital Punishment

The NAACP Legal Defense Fund has a long history of resisting and attempting to prevent travesties of justice, particularly concerning persons of color. This was especially true in the brief it filed in the case of *Flowers v. Mississippi*. In this trial, Mississippi death-row prisoner Curtis Giovanni Flowers appealed his conviction of a quadruple murder in Winona, Mississippi. It took lead Prosecutor Doug Evans, the District Attorney in Mississippi's Fifth

Circuit Court District, six separate trials to get this conviction. Three of the first trials and convictions were reversed due to prosecutorial misconduct, and the next two trials ended with hung juries. A conviction was finally obtained in the sixth trial and Mr. Flowers was sentenced to death. A defense appeal to the Mississippi Supreme Court, arguing a pattern of continued and repeated racially discriminatory behavior and unconstitutional removal of all Blacks from the jury pool, was rejected. The case then proceeded to the United States Supreme Court. In a classic *story of resistance*, through the efforts of the NAACP Legal Defense Fund and others, on June 21, 2019, the High Court vacated the conviction in a 7-2 decision (Higgins and Mangan 2019).

The NAACP Legal Defense and Educational Fund also condemns the death penalty as unconstitutional. Over 50 years ago, the NAACP argued that persistent racial discrimination was rampant in the administration of capital punishment. These arguments were consistently rejected by the Supreme Court as it refused to use race as the lens for evaluating the efficacy of the death penalty. Consequently, the NAACP decided to expand its efforts and argue for reforms and the abolition of capital punishment. A partial victory was obtained in 1972 when the Supreme Court voided the capital punishment in the case *Furman v. Georgia*. In striking down this case, the court argued that, in the absence of a consistent policy for determining who was eligible for capital punishment, the death penalty was cruel and unusual punishment. It would be four years before the death penalty was resumed. In the interim, 35 states passed new laws clarifying the death penalty. And although the high court, in 1976, struck down new state laws that made the death penalty mandatory for anyone convicted of a capital crime, it left standing those laws that gave discretion to juries and judges to impose the death sentence.

Today, the United States is virtually alone in using capital punishment, as over 149 other nations have abolished the death penalty. In 2020, the United States ranked third, behind China and India, in the number of prisoners it executed (World Population Review 2020). Within the United States, many states have consistently imposed the death penalty in ways that show clear patterns of discrimination by race, gender, and geography (Caplan 2016). Further, Blacks are more likely to be on death row across the United States, and those convicted of killing White people are more likely to face the death penalty than those convicted of killing Black people. In 2019, 59% of the death row inmates were Black (Ndulue 2020), yet Black people make up less than 14% of the U.S. population.

Several states, recognizing that these disparities are imposed arbitrarily and reflect racial biases, have instituted a moratorium on death penalties. Since 2007, New Jersey, New York, New Mexico, Illinois, Connecticut, Delaware, Maryland, Nebraska, and Washington have abolished capital punishment. Today, a total of 21 states (and DC) have made the death penalty illegal, while 29 states still impose the death penalty (ProCon 2019).

Critical Thinking

1. We all have at one time or another been involved with both crime and deviance. Thinking about one specific occurrence in your life, in what ways did this event demonstrate the interaction of race, class, and gender? How might such events affect

your perceptions of those within particular groups and the causes of deviance? Which groups are most likely to be exonerated? What does this suggest regarding the costs to the individual? Society?

2. In what ways do space and place impact perceptions and incidents of deviance? How is this impacted by race, class and gender? What does the matrix suggest regarding the types and forms of deviance associated with these differences? (Explain at least three ways based on the readings, research, and class discussions.)

3. What are hate crimes? Explain how hate crimes are related to social/political and or economic conditions. (Cite at least three examples of this.) What types of hate crimes are most prevalent? What accounts for their prevalence? In what ways does the matrix help us understand the complexity of hate crimes?

4. Which theories best explain differential incarceration rates of Blacks, Hispanics, Whites, and others? What does this suggest with reference to the interaction of race, class, and gender with different types of crime and deviance?

TRANSFORMING THE NARRATIVE

The matrix lens alerts us to the reality that groups and individuals throughout the American narrative have been quite effective at both resisting and surviving oppressive systems. Resistance consists of the conscious and unconscious attempts by individuals and groups to challenge the dominant values of society. Resistance counters oppression by providing sites and spaces where stereotypes can be challenged and social and cultural hegemonies can be transformed. Where the normative structures define deviance as moral irregularity, resistance redefines it as resilience and moral alternative (Scott 1985, 1992). Black, Latinx, Native American, and other cultures developed in resistance to and negation of the dominant culture that not only racializes them but also defines them as deviant. These oppositional cultures reject the often demonized and ostracized racial identities inherent in racialized structures (Gardner 2004). When laws and structures are perceived as arbitrary and unjust, people feel anger, lack of self-control, and less committed to the community and each other. In such a situation deviance is likely (Colvin, Cullen, and Vander Ven 2002)—but deviance can also lead to forms of resistance.

Transformative stories are happening all around us. They are hidden within criminal proceedings and on the back pages of our newspapers, while the stock story is reported in the headlines. During a trial the victim is asked, "Do you see the person who attacked you?" And, typically, the victim confidently points a finger at the handcuffed and nervous defendant. Nothing is more gripping; nothing is more definitive for jurors than that moment. But what happens when there is a case of mistaken identity, when the wrong person is accused, then convicted, then sentenced for a crime he or she did not commit?

Scientific Advances

The 2019 Netflix miniseries, *When They See Us,* documents the transformative story of five Black and Latinx teenagers from Harlem who were wrongly convicted of raping a White woman who was jogging in New York City's Central Park in 1989. After serving between 6 and 13 years, the boys were released after serial rapist Matias Reyes admitted to the crime. In 2002, the convictions were reversed and, in 2014, the city of New York settled with the five men for $40 million dollars (Evans 2019). Unfortunately, the story of these exonerated five is not unique, nor are the stories of hundreds of others who have been exonerated.

The Innocence Project demonstrates, through its advocacy for those who have been wrongly convicted and imprisoned, just how transformative stories happen. Since it was founded in 1992, the Innocence Project has been tracking possible cases of wrongful conviction (Figure 7.4). By 2019, through its efforts, a total of 2,522 convictions had been overturned by both DNA (485) and non-DNA (1,926) evidence. Among these cases, Blacks, who comprise just 12% of the population, were close to half of those who had been exonerated. Most of these exonerations were of Blacks convicted of homicide. If we were to compute the total years served by these wrongly convicted

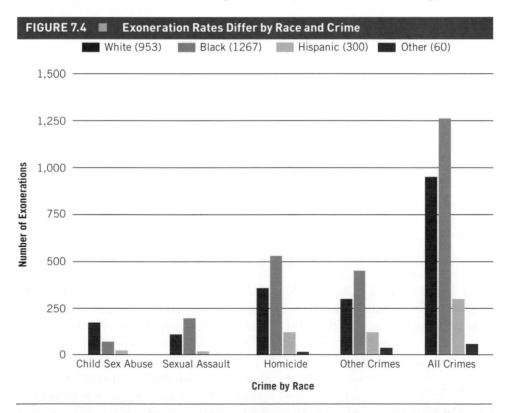

FIGURE 7.4 ■ Exoneration Rates Differ by Race and Crime

White (953)   Black (1267)   Hispanic (300)   Other (60)

Number of Exonerations (y-axis: 0 to 1,500)

Crime by Race (x-axis: Child Sex Abuse, Sexual Assault, Homicide, Other Crimes, All Crimes)

Source: Exonerations by Race/Ethnicity and Crime, The National Registry of Exonerations, https://www.law.umich.edu/special/exoneration/Pages/ExonerationsRaceByCrime.aspx.

men, we would arrive at a staggering 4,730 years. At the time of their wrongful convictions, the average age of those eventually exonerated was 26.5. And consider how much this has cost the U.S. taxpayers—a total of 4.12 billion dollars has been spent since 1989 to incarcerate innocent men and women. And a quarter of this has been spent to incarcerate innocent Blacks ($944 million) and Hispanics ($256 million) (National Registry of Exonerations 2019).

Collective Action

Laws and norms must be perceived as being just if they are to be effective at controlling deviant and criminal behavior. When there is a perception among targeted groups that these laws and norms are in fact being enforced differently across groups, then people are more likely to not only systematically disobey or ignore such norms and laws, but to do so in collective social movements that range from uprisings to civil disobedience. These collective social movements demonstrate that targeted groups are active agents that frequently transform institutions and the laws and norms that perpetuate racial and other hierarchies. These groups and others not only survived, but actively engaged in social movements to reclaim their identities and recast the narratives. Although history offers an abundance of examples, we will limit ourselves to just a few to demonstrate the dynamic and creative ways in which groups have utilized intersectional identities and the matrix to inventively bring about change.

Native American Resistance Stories and Social Movements

Resistance stories, often in the context of what we frequently call social movements, have long been a part of the reality of Native Americans. In Chapter 2 we discussed the over one hundred years of protests where Native Americans took up arms to resist European encroachment of their lands, genocide, and colonial imperialism. In this section we focus on some of the more recent social movements Native Americans have engendered to combat laws, criminalization, and policies that targeted them.

In July 1968 in Minneapolis, Minnesota, the American Indian Movement (AIM) was born. This grassroots movement was initially formed in urban areas to protest the systematic issues associated with poverty and police brutality targeting Native Americans. The founders of this movement, Clyde Bellecourt, Dennis Banks, and George Mitchell, were graduates of the "Indian finishing school"—the Minnesota State Penitentiary. The first action taken by AIM was to form patrols that would monitor the police and justice systems that frequently targeted American Indians. With time AIM became the face of Native American activism (Maxey 2018). It also inspired Native American social movements across the country, including the Native American Lives Matter movement.

Unfortunately, the deaths of Native Americans at the hands of police rarely gets wide attention. Native American males rank second to Black males as being most likely to be killed by police (Vicens 2015).

Allen Locke, a 30-year-old Lakota man, was shot and killed by an officer of the Rapid City Police Department in South Dakota in December 2014. According to police reports, Officer Anthony Meirose fired his weapon after Locke charged him with a knife. After an internal

The Native American protest of the Dakota Access Pipeline was unprecedented in the scope of participation. Yet it was part of a centuries old tradition of protest and activism

Justin Sullivan/Getty Images

investigation, the police department found no grounds to pursue criminal charges against the officer. Lakota leaders maintain that this case follows a long history of Rapid City Police Department's unwillingness to indict or prosecute officers interacting violently with the local Native community (Lakota Peoples Law Project 2015).

After several wrongful death lawsuits and assault charges were dismissed, Native Americans responded by starting the Native American Lives Matter movement, modeled after Black Lives Matter, in 2014. The group has more than 160,000 members, and uses such hashtags such as #NativeLivesMatter and #NativeAmericanLivesMatter. They have been successful at raising funds and protesting injustice; the most prominent recent action was the 500+ Native American activists that showed up to protest the Dakota Access Pipeline (Hensen 2017).

In 2018 a social movement called Not Invisible was created to ensure that the deaths and disappearances of Native American women and girls would not remain under the radar (Golden 2019). Native women living on tribal lands are 10 times more likely to be murdered than others in our nation (Golden 2019). 84% of indigenous women experience physical, sexual, or psychological violence in their lifetime (Rosay 2016). One in three Native American women have been raped or experienced an attempted rape. According to the Justice Department this is more than twice the national average (Williams 2012).

The movements have been successful, as evidenced by new federal legislation with bipartisan support that has introduced a bill called the Not Invisible Act of 2019. The bill includes creating an advisory committee that will make recommendations to combat the problem.

Asian American Resistance Stories and Social Movements

The Chinese Exclusion act was the first federal law that placed limits on access to immigration specifically based on a potential immigrant's nationality. While the language of this law was not explicitly racial, it effectively drew a racial line in the sand that extended the privileges of Whiteness to Europeans while permitting a series of anti-Asian laws to come into existence at not only the federal, but also the state and municipal levels.

Organized Asian American sociopolitical movements surfaced and peaked in the late 1960s to mid-1970s. This period also saw the development of a pan-Asian social movement, and the associated coining of the term Asian American (as opposed to "Orientals"). The primary focus of the Asian American movement was to protest American imperialism and the constant U.S.-backed wars that targeted various Asian countries (Maeda 2016).

In the aftermath of 9/11, the U.S. government, laws, police, and criminal justice system increasingly targeted South Asians and Muslims. In 2002 and 2003, male non-citizens above the age of 16 from 25 countries were required to register with the Department of Homeland

Chol Soo Lee, a Korean American man wrongfully convicted of murder in 1973, spent 10 years in jail and sparked a social movement. For the first time in U.S. history, thousands of Asian Americans from all backgrounds mobilized to seek justice for what they believed was a wrongful conviction. They raised tens of thousands of dollars for legal defense from car washes and church fundraisers. In 1982 a San Francisco jury overturned his murder conviction. Lee was not freed immediately due to a second conviction of murder and death sentence in 1977 for the stabbing death of a fellow inmate. Lee pleaded self-defense against a neo-Nazi. It was not until 1983 that this conviction was nullified and reduced to second-degree murder. He was then released for time served.
Reuters/Alamy Stock Photo

Security. Islam is the principal religion of these 25 countries. Out of the 80,000 who registered, 13,100 were put into deportation proceedings (Kampf and Sen 2015).

Across the country, Muslim Americans were targeted with a wave of violence, racial profiling, and harassment (Peek 2010). According to a 2017 Pew Survey, 48 percent of U.S. Muslims reported experiencing at least one kind of discrimination in the previous 12 months. These discriminatory actions seem to be correlated with U.S. electoral cycles, as politicians increasingly have relied on anti-Muslim rhetoric to mobilize their bases. Fighting the negative stigma and stereotypes targeting Muslims, several advocacy organizations have surfaced. These organizations, such as the Council of American-Islamic Relations, the Muslim Public Affairs Council, and the U.S. Council of Muslim Organizations, aim to reframe the narrative, demonstrating that U.S. Muslims are not only integral to the fabric of our nation, but that they uphold the central ideals of democracy, liberty, equality, and justice (Cury 2017).

African American Women's Resistance Stories and Social Movements

Black women, even before the end of slavery, were creating organizations to sustain the Black community (Scott 1990). Black women organized themselves for self-help, survival, and revival in what is known as the Club Movement.

The first of these clubs, The Female Benevolent Society of St. Thomas, was created as early as 1793 in Philadelphia. Another group, launched in Salem, Massachusetts, in 1818, known as the Colored Female Religious and Moral Society, aimed to combat the negative stereotypes that often portrayed Black women as sexually aggressive, amoral, and deviant. By the 1890s, more deliberate social and political reform was taking place (Mjagkij 2001). In 1896, under the leadership of Mary Church Terrell, Black women's clubs banded together to form the National Association of Colored Women's Clubs. Soon, mutual benefit societies, settlement houses, and schools created safe havens, communities, and training for young Black women fleeing the South (Scott 1990).

The emergence of the Black Lives Matter Movement (#BlackLivesMatter), a response to the brutal, systematic violence and racism against Black people by police, attests to the reality that we continue to deal with these problems. Today, with over 40 chapters, the group organizes and builds local movements to intervene in police-instigated violence inflicted on the Black community.

LGBTQ+ Resistance Stories and Social Movements

The central event that many argue triggered the national gay liberation movement was the New York Stonewall Riots of June 1969. They were precipitated by a New York City police raid on a gay club located in Greenwich Village in New York called the Stonewall Inn. In 1969, homosexual sex was illegal in every state except Illinois. There were no laws at the federal, state, or local levels that protected gay men or women from discrimination, harassment, or acts of bigotry (Carter 2014). The movement took form during the 1970s as gay and lesbian activists created small and local organizations celebrating gay pride and promoting empowerment of sexual

(left to right) Opal Tometi, Patrisse Cullors, and Alicia Garza receive a Glamour Women of the Year 2016 award for their founding of the #BlackLivesMatter movement.

Kevork Djansezian/Getty Images for Glamour

minorities. These tended to separate into lesbians and gay men, resulting in the organizations being segregated along gender lines.

When we look at how sexuality intersects with race and gender, we can identify more nuanced resistance movements (Armstrong 2002). The mid-1970s saw the emergence of the first antiracist and queer people of color organizations. Several such groups worked to end police violence, including:

- Gay Asian Pacific Alliance,

- Gay American Indians,

- Salsa Soul Sisters (the first Black lesbian group),

- National Coalition of Black Lesbians and Gays,

- Black and White Men Together (BWMT), and

- Dykes against Racism Everywhere (DARE).

After the September 29th, 1982, police raid of the Blues Bar, a predominantly Black gay bar on 43rd Street in Midtown Manhattan, DARE, Salsa Soul Sisters, BWMT, and other New York local activists joined forces to mobilize a response (Gossett, Gossett, and Lewis 2012).

Most recently, LGBTQ+ social movements advocate for the inclusion of gender identity and sexual orientation in state and federal hate crime statutes. Unfortunately, Blacks who identify as transgender, as well as Black girls in general, are stereotyped as more knowledgeable about sex, therefore less in need of protection (Epstein, Blake, and Gonzalez 2017). Consequently their victimization often is either ignored, dismissed, or downplayed.

- Since 2013, of a total of 157 violent attacks on transgender people, 111 were against Black trans women.

- Of the 22 trans people killed in 2019, all but two were Black trans women. (Human Rights Campaign 2019)

Groups like Southerners on New Ground, the Safe Outside the System Collective at the Audre Lorde Project, Critical Resistance, and Women of Color Against Violence continue the struggle (Gossett, Gossett, and Lewis 2012). As a consequence, as long as these problems persist, social movements will continue to be part of our landscape.

Transforming the Relationship Between Police and Communities of Color

I (Rodney) was born in a police family; both my father and younger brother are law enforcement professionals. Most police are doing their best in a difficult job. But if members of specific groups perceive that the laws and their enforcement are being used to marginalize, criminalize, and punish them essentially for being different, then police, courts, and laws will be held in disdain. And if these biased structures are prevalent across multiple institutional structures, then social control (the ability of a community to regulate their own behavior) will devolve into chaos, and crime will run rampant. The institutional framework taken in the matrix theory helps us to understand that institutions function collaboratively to produce specific societal goals. What this means is that until and unless race, racial ideologies, processes, and practices are viewed systemically, then we will continually see the racialized results of bigotry, discrimination, prejudice, and hate. Given these realities, how can we transform our legal system, our criminal processes, and our ideas regarding deviance as it relates to communities of color?

Currently, many criminal justice professionals are advocating an evidence-based approach as a way of dealing with increasing levels of social unrest, mass criminalization, and decades of economic, social, and political marginalization (Greenwood 2008; Howel and Lipsey 2012). Unfortunately, such approaches continue to focus on short-term programs aimed at transforming individuals rather than structural, long-term system-wide interventions. Again, we find ourselves "blaming the victims" and ignoring the socio-structural sources of risk factors that continually marginalize and criminalize specific individuals from specific social groups (Goddard and Myers 2017). Rather than focusing on the individual, we could focus on the risk. If, for example, we were to identify geographic areas where individuals are most at risk for being criminalized for low-level offenses, such as those associated with drug use, mental illness, and homelessness, we may be able to identify more cost-effective solutions outside of the criminal justice system. Services for drug treatment, psychological counseling, and shelter are not only cheaper but are more beneficial than incarceration (United States Sentencing Commission 2017). Then we could work to change the systems and structures that govern police, increase community control, and enhance individual responsibility.

One of the leading causes of racial disparities among police are implicit biases, which as we learned in Chapter 1, are subjective attitudes or stereotypes that affect how we view others based on their race, class, and/or gender. Experiments with police demonstrate complex patterns that show differential treatment of persons of color. For example, in "shoot-don't-shoot" training, evidence demonstrates bias in officers' reaction times that align with racial stereotypes. Further, police that frequently interact with minority gang members are more likely to exhibit racial bias in their decision to shoot (Sim, Correll, and Sadler 2013).

Since 2015, as more attention is given to implicit bias, more of our nation's police academies are instituting implicit bias training for police recruits in an attempt to help individuals understand their biases and overcome them. Implicit bias training gets mixed reviews and has not yet been shown to fix the myriad of problems associated with police misconduct, harassment, and targeting of individuals and communities of color.

The risk of becoming entangled in the criminal justice system needs to be understood in structural terms that identifies the links between external and internal community variables with the risk of criminal sanctions and risks and the needs of the individual in such systems (Hannah-Moffat 2015). While implicit bias training may reduce racially disparate policing, it can't be the only answer. Implicit bias is part of the whole fabric of not only our criminal justice systems but also our society (Smith 2015). We must recognize that our criminal justice systems are not isolated from the rest of our society, but in fact respond and react to social, political, and economic constraints.

TRANSFORMATION STORY: ADDRESSING THE DNA RAPE KIT BACKLOG

One transformative story details the efforts of Eli Travis, who was raped at knifepoint in 2008. The man who she identified as the rapist was exonerated through DNA evidence almost ten years later, when the rape kit from the crime was finally analyzed. As one of the more than 11,000 victims whose rape kits were abandoned, Ms. Travis questioned why it took 7 years for the kit to be analyzed, and decided to do something about it. She, along with other Black women, started the movement "Voices from the Backlog" which aims to force the Detroit Police Department to resolve the rape kit backlog (Kozlowski 2019).

Prosecutors have finally begun to test the 11,000 untested rape kits. As a result, over 3,000 cases have been closed with 197 convictions. Another 588 cases are currently being investigated or are awaiting investigation (Cwiek 2019). The voices of these activists are being heard and over 100,000 backlogs are being challenged in states across the country (Svokos 2019).

Emphasizing Choice

Any remedy must take into consideration individual agency. People make choices, including the choice to commit crimes, although, as we have learned throughout this chapter, some choices are more constrained than others. Some people's criminal actions seem to be reactions to their being left out of the American Dream. When agency is denied or circumscribed by race, class, and gender, there is an increased likelihood that deviance will result. This deviance does not reflect a culture of crime or a culture of poverty; rather, it reflects a poverty of opportunities.

Neither crime nor deviance is caused by race, ethnicity, gender, or class. People make choices, some good and some bad. These choices are circumscribed by environments, histories, and structural inequities. The prevalence of one specific type of crime or deviance is determined by the kinds of resources available within a particular community, institution, or situation, and the kinds of choices people make.

The overwhelming majority of people in all racial and ethnic groups do not commit crimes—they make other choices. While society cannot force individuals to make different choices, it can both hold them accountable and provide effective alternatives to deviance. Even for those currently caught up in deviance, alternatives to detention have been demonstrated to deter further criminality. These alternatives include suspended sentences, probation, fines, restitution, community service, and deferred adjudication/pretrial diversion.

Finally, we must shift away from an individualistic approach that defines specific individuals and communities as in need of "fixing." Using the matrix lens instead of the dominant cultural lens of White middle-class male privilege, we must understand that some differences in life outcomes are rooted in structural inequities. One size does not fit all, and racism, sexism, poverty, and homophobia influence identity, group formation, and community.

The matrix lens does not present people, communities, and groups as victims, though they might have been victimized. Rather, it presents them as agents, who see not only what is available but also what obstacles they must overcome to obtain it. By changing the lens, we therefore ask a different set of questions: How do we empower, how do we incorporate, and how do we embrace the power of difference?

Critical Thinking

1. In what ways do the transformation stories of people of color reflect similar strategies? What is unique about them? How might space, historical context, and cultural specifics of each group account for these differences and similarities?

2. What might be the outcome if rape kits were analyzed? Based on the exoneration data, which intersectional groups might be the most likely beneficiaries? What might this mean for both victims and accused?

3. What role does intersectionality play in crime and deviance? Identify and explain at least three ways in which this occurs. What does this suggest regarding the social construction of crime and deviance?

4. In what ways does your identity and social status affect the likelihood that you will be charged with a crime or with being deviant? Are there types of crime or deviance that are strictly related to your being a student? Are there some behaviors that are considered deviant on a college campus that would be considered normal elsewhere?

CHAPTER SUMMARY

7.1   Examine the history of race, crime, and deviance.

Race, gender, and class disparities are represented in who gets defined as either criminal or deviant. Historically these differentials can be traced to the slave codes, immigration policy, and the development of reservations for Native Americans. Taken together, these practices, policies, and laws account for the racially differentiated criminal justice system. Whiteness was created as a means of assuring that the racial state would be preserved. Laws were created to fortify this structure at the expense of people of color. Contemporary trends in scholarship on crime and deviance highlight the racial, gendered, and class differentials in how justice is administered across the United States. These disparities are observed throughout the justice system, in differential policing, racial profiling, and differential sentencing and incarceration rates.

7.2   Analyze stock theories of race, crime, and deviance.

Our stock stories teach us that laws protect us; they are created to preserve peace, promote tranquility, and allow us to pursue our collective best interests. Our stock stories assume that the law is color-blind—enforced the same way everywhere, for everyone, and without concern for race, class, or other differences. Classical sociological theories of crime and deviance represent a portion of our stock stories. As such, they reflect the dominant view that not only is our system just, but also those who violate the laws are appropriately sanctioned. Most of the theoretical orientations of these stock stories fall into four broad categories: biosocial theories of deviance, ecological perspectives, culture of poverty explanations, and broken windows theory. All of these have a common theme—they place the source of deviance at the micro level. Therefore, the individual or his or her community, culture, or environment is at odds with societal norms. And by implication, if the individual or his or her community, culture, or environment could just be reformed, fixed, adjusted, or rehabilitated, then the deviance would be reduced or nonexistent.

7.3   Apply the matrix lens to the relationships among race, crime, and deviance.

Using the matrix approach, we revealed the concealed stories of crime and deviance in the United States, stories that have always been complicated by race, ethnicity, gender, and class. Historically, crime and punishment have been associated with attempts to preserve the racial order. In this chapter we will examine this and other narratives and observe how the matrix has influenced both our perceptions and the realities of crime and deviance.

The matrix informs us that certain socially defined people and groups (reflecting the interactions of race, class, and gender) situated in particular spaces and places are more apt to be labeled deviant than others. It also informs us that the nexus of various spaces interacts with social identities to produce different types and definitions of deviance. As we consider the various dimensions of the matrix lens, space and place help us to understand that crime and deviance are situationally and contextually specific. Therefore, urban areas produce different types of deviance possibilities than corporate spaces. Hate crimes, which constitute a particular type of deviance, are utilized as means of social control. Among the outcomes of the linking of national and corporate policies around crime and deviance have been the militarization of the police and the creation of the prison-industrial complex. These policies have called for increased surveillance, criminalization, and incarceration of the members of designated racial and ethnic groups. Ultimately, this process also accounts for the fact that Blacks, Hispanics, and the poor are more likely to receive the death penalty.

7.4 **Formulate transformative narratives of crime and deviance.**

Most police are doing their best in a difficult job. But if members of specific groups perceive that the laws and their enforcement are being used to marginalize, criminalize, and punish them essentially for being different, then police, courts, and laws will be held in disdain. And if these biased structures are prevalent across multiple institutional structures, then social control (the ability of a community to regulate their own behavior) will devolve into chaos, and crime will run rampant. The institutional framework taken in the matrix helps us to understand that institutions function collaboratively to produce specific societal goals. What this means is that until and unless race, racial ideologies, processes, and practices are viewed systemically, then we will continually see the racialized results of bigotry, discrimination, prejudice, and hate. Rather than focusing on the individual, we could focus on the risk. If, for example, we were to identify geographic areas where individuals are most at risk for being criminalized for low-level offenses, such as those associated with drug use, mental illness, and homelessness, we may be able to identify more cost-effective solutions outside of the criminal justice system. Services for drug treatment, psychological counseling, and shelter are not only cheaper but are more beneficial then incarceration. Then we could work to change the systems and structures that govern police, increase community control, and enhance individual responsibility.

Over the past few years, many people have begun to question the racial, gender, and class disparities that dominate every phase of the American criminal justice system. Scientific developments have added additional resources for both the victims and accused. Social justice movements, such as organizations calling for quicker analysis of rape kits, might speed up both trials and exonerations. Alternatives to detention and incarceration, particularly for nonviolent criminal acts, are showing promise in several states. And while we must continue to hold individuals responsible for their actions, we also need to recognize that some crimes and forms of deviance are the result of racism, sexism, poverty, and homophobia. The most effective way to reduce crime and deviance would be to decrease all forms of discrimination, increase opportunities, and enhance training and education.

KEY TERMS

biological determinism	differential labeling	social disorganization
Black Codes	general strain theory	structural inequities
broken windows theory	Jim Crow laws	welfare fraud
crime	organized crime	White normative structures
culture of poverty	prison—industrial complex	White privilege
deviance	racial consciousness	white-collar crime
differential association theory	racial profiling	
	slave patrols	

REFERENCES

Agnew, Robert. 1992. "Foundation for a General Strain Theory of Crime and Delinquency." Criminology 30, no. 1: 47–87.

Alexander, Michelle. 2010. The New Jim Crow: Mass Incarceration in the Age of Colorblindness. New York: New Press.

Armstrong, David and Ernsthausen. Jeff 2019. "Data Touted by OxyContin Maker to Fight Lawsuits Doesn't Tell the Whole Story." ProPublica. Accessed online at URL: https://www.propublica.org/article/data-touted-by-oxycontin-maker-to-fight-lawsuits-doesnt-tell-the-whole-story.

Armstrong, Elizabeth A. 2002. Forging Gay Identities: Organizing Sexuality in San Francisco, 1950–1994. Chicago: University of Chicago Press

Beirne, Piers, and James Messerschmidt. 2006. Criminology. 4th ed. Los Angeles: Oxford University Press.

Bell, Kerryn. 2017. "Prison Violence and the Intersectionality of Race/Ethnicity and Gender". Criminology, Criminal Justice, Law and Society. Vol 18(1) 106–121.

Bergner, Daniel. 2014. "Is Stop-and-Frisk Worth It?" Atlantic, April. Accessed November 17, 2016. http://www.theatlantic.com/magazine/archive/2014/04/is-stop-and-frisk-worth-it/358644.

Bernasconi, Robert. 2012. "Crossed Lines in the Racialization Process: Race as a Border Concept." Research in Phenomenology 42, no. 2: 206–28.

Blau, Judith R., and Peter M. Blau. 1982. "The Cost of Inequality: Metropolitan Structure and Violent Crime." American Sociological Review 47: 114–29.

Browne-Marshall, Gloria J. 2002. "The Realities of Enslaved Female Africans in America." Excerpted from Gloria J. Brown-Marshall, "Failing Our Black Children: Statutory Rape Laws, Moral Reform and the Hypocrisy of Denial." Accessed October 17, 2011. http://academic.udayton.edu/race/05intersection/gender/rape.htm.

Caplan, Lincoln 2016. "Death Throes: Changing how Americans think about capital punishment." Accessed online at URL: https:\harvardmagazine.com\2016\11\death-throes.

Carter, David. 2014. "It's Time to Write LGBT History into the Textbooks." Time Magazine. Accessed online at URL: https://time.com/2935029/stonewall-riots-lgbt-school-curricula/.

Caspani, Maria. 2015. "Police discrimination against U.S. LGBT community pervasive: report" Reuters. Accessed online at URL: https://www.reuters.com/article/us-usa-lgbt-police-idUSKBN0M02JM20150304.

CDC (Centers for Disease Control and Prevention).2020."Understanding the Epidemic". Center for Disease Control. Accessed online at URL: https://www.cdc.gov/drugoverdose/epidemic/index.html.

Coaston, Jane. 2018. "New evidence shows the Pulse nightclub shooting wasn't about anti-LGBTQ hate". Vox. Accessed online at URL: https://www.vox.com/policy-and-politics/2018/4/5/17202026/pulse-shooting-lgbtq-trump-terror-hate.

Cohn, D'Vera. 2015. "How U.S. immigration laws and rules have changed through history." PEW Research Center. Accessed online at URL: https://www.pewresearch.org/fact-tank/2015/09/30/how-u-s-immigration-laws-and-rules-have-changed-through-history/

Colvin, Mark, Francis T. Cullen, and Thomas Vander Ven. 2002. "Coercion, Social Support, and Crime: An Emerging Theoretical Consensus." *Criminology* 40, no. 1: 1942

Cooper, Hannah L. F. 2015. "War on Drugs Policing and Police Brutality." Substance Use and Misuse 50 , nos. 8–9: 1188–94.

Crenshaw, Kimberlé. 1991."Mapping the Margins: Intersectionality, Identity Politics, and Violence against Women of Color."*Stanford Law Review* 43,no. 6: 1241–99.

Cury, Emily. 2017. "How Muslim Americans are fighting Islamophobia and securing their civil rights" The Conversation. Accessed online at URL: https://theconversation.com/how-muslim-americans-are-fighting-islamophobia-and-securing-their-civil-rights-82235

Cwiek, Sara. 2019. "After ten years Detroit rap kit backlog cleared, but still a long way to go". Michigan Radio. Accessed online at URL: https://www.michiganradio.org/post/after-ten-years-detroit-rape-kit-backlog-cleared-still-long-way-go.

DiLorenzo, Thomas J. 2010. "The Culture of Violence in the American West: Myth versus Reality." *Independent Review (Fall)*. http:// www.independent.org/ publications/tir/article .asp?a=803.

Drug Policy Alliance. 2018. "Leading the fight for lasting change: Annual Report." Accessed online at URL: https://drugpolicy.org/sites/default/files/dpa-annual-report-2018_0.pdf

Du Bois, W. E. B. 1904. *Some Notes on Negro Crime, Particularly in Georgia.* Atlanta: Atlanta University Press. Accessed November 5, 2014. http://scua.library.umass.edu/digital/dubois/dubois9.pdf.

Durr, Marlese. 2015. "What Is the Difference between Slave Patrols and Modern- Day Policing? Institutional Violence in a Community of Color." *Critical Sociology* 41, no. 6: 873–79.

Edwards, Frank, Hedwig Lee and Michael Esposito. 2019. "Risk of being killed by police use of force in the United States by age, race-ethnicity, and sex." Proceedings of the National Academy of Sciences. Accessed online at URLRisk of being killed by police use of force in the United States by age, race–ethnicity, and sex | PNAS

Enns, Peter K. 2016. Incarceration Nation: How the Unites States Became the Most Punitive Democracy in the World. UK: Cambridge University Press.

Epstein, Rebecca,Jamilia J. Blake, and Thalia Gonzalez. 2017. Girlhood Interrupted: The Erasure of Black Girls' Childhood". Center for Poverty and Inequality. Accessed online at URL: https://www.law.georgetown.edu/poverty-inequality-center/wp-content/uploads/sites/14/2017/08/girlhood-interrupted.pdf

Evens, Rhonda. 2019. "When They See US: Researching the Story of the Exonerated 5 and Beyond at the New York Public Library." New York Public Library. Accessed online at URL: https://www.nypl.org/blog/2019/06/25/when-they-see-us-researching-story-exonerated-five-and-beyond-new-york-public

Farrell, Ronald A., and Victoria Lynn Swigert. 1988. "General Introduction." In Social Deviance, 3rd ed., Belmont, CA: Wadsworth.

Federal Bureau of Investigation. 2014. "Sixteen Juveniles Recovered in Joint Super Bowl Operation Targeting Underage Prostitution." Press release, February 4. Accessed February 14, 2014. http://www.fbi.gov/news/pressrel/press-releases/sixteen-juveniles-recovered-in-joint-super-bowl-operation-targeting-underage-prostitution.

Fessler, Leah 2018. "The poorest Americans are 12 times as likely to be sexually assaulted as the wealthiest". Quartz. Accessed online at URL: https://qz.com/1170426/the-poorest-americans-are-12-times-as-likely-to-be-sexually-assaulted/.

Fitzsimons, Tim. 2018. "What really happened that night at Pulse". NBCNEWS. Accessed online a t URL: https://www.nbcnews.com/feature/nbc-out/what-really-happened-night-pulse-n882571.

Flagg, Anna. 2018. "The Myth of the Criminal Immigrant". The Marshall Project. Accessed at: https:\www.themarshallproject.org\2018\03\30\the-myth-of-the-criminal-immigrant

Fuchs, Lawrence, and Forbes, Susan Martin. 2003. "Immigration and U.S. History – The Evolution of the Open Society." InImmigration and Citizenship: Process and Policy. St. Paul, MN: Thomson West.

Gallup, 2017. "Immigration", Accessed online at URL: https://news.gallup.com/poll/1660/immigration.aspx

Gardner, Trevor. 2004. "The Political Delinquent: Crime, Deviance, and Resistance in Black America." Harvard Black Letter Law Journal 20: 137–61.

Goddard, T., & Myers, R. R. (2017). Against evidence-based oppression: Marginalized youth and the politics of risk-based assessment and intervention. Theoretical Criminology, 21(2), 151–167. https:\doi.org\10.1177\1362480616645172

Golden, Hallie. 2019. "Sister, where did you go? The Native American women disappearing from US cities." The Guardian. Accessed online at URL: https://www.theguardian.com/us-news/2019/apr/30/missing-native-american-women-alyssa-mclemore

Goldfield, David. 2011. America Aflame: How the Civil War Created a Nation. New York: Bloomsbury.

Gossett, Che, Gossett, Reina, Lewis, AJ. Fall 2011/Spring 2012. "Reclaiming Our Lineage: Organized Queer, Gender-Nonconforming, and Transgender Resistance to Police Violence." Scholar & Feminist Online no. 10.1-10.2. http://sfonline.barnard.edu/a-new-queer-agenda/reclaiming-our-lineage-organizedqueer-gender-nonconforming-and-transgender-resistance-to-police-violence/0/

Gould, Stephen Jay. 1981. *The Mismeasure of Man*. New York: W. W. Norton.

Gramlich, John. 2019. "Five facts about crime in the U.S." Pew Research. accessed at URL: https:\\www.pewresearch.org\fact-tank\2019\10\17\facts-about-crime-in-the-u-s\

Gramlich, John. 2019. "The gap between the number of blacks and whites in prison is shrinking". Pew Research Center. Accessed at: https:\www.pewresearch.org\fact-tank\2019\04\30\shrinking-gap-between-number-of-blacks-and-whites-in-prison\

Greene, Helen Taylor, and Shaun L. Gabbidon. 2012. "Theoretical Perspectives on Race and Crime." In Race and Crime: A Text/Reader, 95168. Thousand Oaks, CA: Sage.

Greenwood, P. W. 2008. Prevention and intervention programs for juvenile offenders. Juvenile Justice 18(2): 185–210.

Guardian. 2016. "The Counted: People Killed by Police in the U.S." Accessed September 27. https://www.theguardian.com/us-news/ng-interactive/2015/jun/01/the-counted-police-killings-us-database.

Hannah-Moffat, K. (2015). Needle in a haystack: Logical parameters of treatment based on actuarial risk–needs assessments. Criminology & Public Policy 14(1): 113–120.

Hansen, Elise. 2017. "The forgotten minority in police shootings". CNN. Accessed online at URL: https://www.cnn.com/2017/11/10/us/native-lives-matter/index.html

Hensen, Elise. 2017. "The forgotten minority in police shootings."*CNN*. Accessed online at URL: https://www.cnn.com/2017/11/10/us/native-lives-matter/index.html.

Higgins, Tucker and Mangan Dan. 2019. "Supreme Court rules for Curtis Flowers, black man tried six times for Mississippi murders. CNBC. Accessed online at URL: https:\www cnbc.com\2019\06 \21\supreme-court-rules-for-curtis-flowers-black-man-tried six-times-for-murder.html www. cnbc.com\

Hindelang, Michael J. 1978. "Race and Involvement in Common Law Personal Crimes," American Sociological Review 43 no. 1 (February): 93–109.

HRC Staff. 2018. "New FBI Statistics Show Alarming Increase in Number of Reported Hate Crimes." Accessed online at URL: https://www.hrc.org/blog/new-fbi-statistics-show-alarming-increase-in-number-of-reported-hate-crimes.

Human Rights Campaign. 2019. "A National Epidemic: Fatal Anti-Transgender Violence in the United States in 2019."https://www.hrc.org/resources/a-national-epidemic-fatal-anti-trans-violence-in-the-united-states-in-2019

Innocence Project.2016. "DNA Exonerations in the United States." Accessed November 12, 2016. http://www.innocenceproject.org/dna-exonerations-in-the-united-states.

Kaiser Family Foundation, 2020. "Opioid Overdose Death by Race/Ethnicity". Accessed online at URL: https://www.kff.org/other/state-indicator/opioid-overdose-deaths-by-raceethnicity/?currentTimeframe=0&sortModel=%7B%22colId%22:%22Location%22,%22sort%22:%22asc%22%7D.

Kampf, Lena, and Sen, Indra. 2015. "History Does Not Repeat Itself, But Ignorance Does: Post-9/11 Treatment of Muslims and the Liberty-Security Dilemma." Humanity in Action. Accessed online at URL: https://www.humanityinaction.org/knowledge_detail/history-does-not-repeat-itself-but-ignorance-does-post-9-11-treatment-of-muslims-and-the-liberty-security-dilemma/

Kelling, George L., andJames Q. Wilson. 1982. "Broken Windows: The Police and Neighborhood Safety." Atlantic Monthly, March. Accessed February 1, 2014. http://www.manhattan-institute.org/pdf/_atlantic_monthly-broken_windows.pdf.

Kozlowski, Kim. 2019. "Elle Travis: A voice from the Detroit rape kit backlog". The Detroit News. Accessed online at URL: https://www.detroitnews.com/story/news/local/wayne-county/2019/08/13/elle-travis-detroit-rape-kit-backlog/1983913001/

Lakota Peoples Law Project. 2015. "Native Lives Matter". Accessed online at URL: https://s3-us-west-1.amazonaws.com/lakota-peoples-law/uploads/Native-Lives-Matter-PDF.pdf

Landgrave, Michelangelo and Alex Nowrasteh 2019. "Criminal Immigrants in 2017: their Numbers, Demographics, and countries of Origen". Accessed at: https:\www.cato.org\publications\immigration-research-policy-brief\criminal-immigrants-2017-their-numbers-demographics

Law, Tara. 2019. "The Violence Against Women Act Was Signed 25 Years Ago. Here's How the Law Changed American Culture." Time. "The Violence Against Women Act Was Signed 25 Years Ago. Here's How the Law Changed American Culture." Accessed online at URL: https://time.com/56750 29/violence-against-women-act-history-biden/.

Lee, Mathew R. 2000. "Concentrated Poverty, Race, and Homicide." The Sociological Quarterly." Vol. 41. No. 2 (Spring): 189–206.

Levin, Sam. 2018. "One Ruled a US citizen, the other not: gay couple's twins face unusual battle." The Guardian. Accessed online at URL: https://www.theguardian.com/world/2018/jan/23/gay-cou ple-twin-sons-citizenship-ruling-lgbt-discrimination.

Lewis, Oscar. 1961. *The Children of Sanchez: Autobiography of a Mexican Family.* New York: Random House.

Lewis, Oscar 1966a. "The Culture of Poverty." *Scientific American*, October, 1925.

Lewis, Oscar 1966b. *Vida: A Puerto Rican Family in the Culture of Poverty—San Juan and New York.* New York: Random House.

Lipsey, Mark W., and James C. Howell. 2012. "A Broader View of Evidence-Based Programs Reveals More Options for State Juvenile Justice Systems." Criminology and Public Policy. Vol 11 (3).

Maeda, Daryl Joji. 2016. The Asian American Movement". Oxford University Press. Accessed online at URL: https://oxfordre.com/americanhistory/view/10.1093/acrefore/9780199329175.001.0001/ac refore-9780199329175-e-21

Mallory, Christy, Amira Hasenbush, and Brad Sears. 2015. "Discrimination and Harassment by Law Enforcement Officers in the LGBT Community." UCLA Williams Institute. Accessed online at U RL: http://williamsinstitute.law.ucla.edu/wp-content/uploads/LGBT-Discrimination-and-Harass ment-in-Law-Enforcement-March-2015.pdf

Map and Center for American Progress"Unjust: How the Broken Criminal Justice System Fails LGBT People of Color". Accessed online at URL: http://www.lgbtmap.org/policy-and-issue-analysi s/criminal-justice-poc.

Maxey, Mark. 2018. "American Indian Movement founded 50 years ago." People's World. Ac cessed online at URL: https://www.peoplesworld.org/article/american-indian-movement-founded-50-years-ago/

McLaughlin, Eliott C. and Darran Simon. 2019. Murder trial focuses on whether Dallas police-woman did enough to save man she shot in his own apartment. CNN. Accessed online at URL: https: /www.cnn.com/2019/09/24/us/botham-jean-amber-guyger-murder-trial/index.html

Minter, Shannon. 1993. "Sodomy and Public Morality Offenses under U.S. Immigration Law: Penalizing Lesbian and Gay Identity," *Cornell International Law Journal:* Vol. 26: No. 3, Article 11. Avai lable at: https://scholarship.law.cornell.edu/cilj/vol26/iss3/11.

Mjagkij, Nona 2001. *Organizing Black America.* London: Routledge.

Morgan, Rachel. E. 2017. "Race and Hispanic Origin of Victims and Offenders, 2012-15. U.S. Department of Justice. Accessed on line at URL: https://www.bjs.gov/content/pub/pdf/rhovo1215. pdf.

Morgan, Rachel E. and Barbara A. Oudekerk. 2019. "Criminal Victimization, 2018. U.S. Department of Justice. Accessed online at URL: https:\www.bjs.gov\content\pub\pdf\cv18.pdf .

Moynihan, Daniel P. 1965. *The Negro Family: The Case for National Action.* Washington, DC: U.S. Department of Labor, Office of Policy Planning and Research.

Murch, Donna. 2019. "How Race Made the Opioid Crisis." Boston Review. Accessed online at URL: ht tp://bostonreview.net/forum/donna-murch-how-race-made-opioid-crisis

National Registry of Exonerations, 2019. Newkirk Center for Science and Society at University of California Irving, the University of Michigan Law School and Michigan State University College of Law. Accessed at URL: https:\www.law.umich.edu\special\exoneration\Pages\about.aspx

National Sexual Violence Research Center. 2015. "SAAM 2015: An Overview on Campus Sexual Violence Prevention." Accessed June 21, 2017. http://www.nsvrc.org/publications/nsvrc-publicati ons-sexual-assault-awareness-month/saam-2015-overview-campus-sexual.

Ndulue, Ngozi. 2020. "Enduring Injustice: The Persistence of racial Discrimination in the U.S. Death Penalty." The Death Penalty Information Center. Accessed online at URL: https:\files.deathpenaltyi nfo.org\documents\reports\r\Enduring-Injustice-Race-and-the-Death-Penalty-2020.pdf

Nellis, Ashley (2016). The Color of Justice: Racial and Ethnic Disparity in State Prisons. Accessed on line at URL: https://www.sentencingproject.or/ublication/olor-of-justice-racial-and-ethnic-dispar ity-in-state-prisons/>.

NIDA.2018, July 20. Drugs, Brains, and Behavior: The Science of Addiction. National Institute on Drug Abuse. Accessed online at URL: https://www.drugabuse.gov/publications/drugs-brains-beh avior-science-addiction/preface.

Orcutt, James D. 1983. *Analyzing Deviance*. Homewood, IL: Dorsey Press.

Pager, Devah. 2003. "The Mark of a Criminal Record." American Journal of Sociology 108, no. 5: 937–75.

Park, Haeyoun and Iaryna Mykhyalyshyn. 2016. "L.G.B.T. People Are More Likely to BE Targets of Hate Crimes Than Any Other Minority Group." The New York times. Accessed online at URL: https:// www.nytimes.com/interactive/2016/06/16/us/hate-crimes-against-lgbt.html.

Patrick, Leslie. 2010. "Crime and Punishment in Colonial America." In Encyclopedia of American History, Vol. 2, Colonization and Settlement, 1608–1760, rev. ed., edited by Billy G. Smith and Gary B. Nash. New York: Facts on File.

Peek, Lori 2010. *Behind the Backlash: Muslim Americans After 9/11*. Philadelphia, PA: Temple University Press.

Perry, Barbara. 2001. *In the Name of Hate: Understanding Hate Crimes*. New York: Routledge.

Perry, Barbara, and Shahid Alvi. 2012. "We Are All Vulnerable': The In Terrorem Effects of Hate Crimes." International Review of Victimology 18, no. 1: 57–71.

Pettit, Becky and Bryan Sykes 2017. "State of the Union: Incarceration. The Stanford Center on Poverty and Inequality. accessed online at: https:\www.themarshallproject.org\documents\43165 17-Pettit-Sykes-2017-incarceration-report

Piquero, Nicole Leeper, and Sealock. Miriam D. 2010. "Race, Crime, and General Strain Theory." Youth Violence and Juvenile Justice 8, no. 3: 170–86.

Planty, M., Langton, L., Krebs, C., Berzofsky, M., and Smiley-McDonald, H. 2013. "Female victims of sexual violence, 1994-2010." https://www.bjs.gov/content/pub/pdf/fvsv9410.pdf

ProCon 2019. States with the Death Penalty and States with Death Penalty Bans. accessed at: https: \deathpenalty.procon.org\view.resource.php?resourceID=001172

Ridinger, Robert B. 2019. "Gay and Lesbian Immigrants -Immigration to the United States."{ Immigrationtounitedstates.org. Accessed online at URL: https://immigrationtounitedstates.org/5 15-gay-and-lesbian-immigrants.html.

Rosay, Andre B. 2016. Violence Against American Indian and Alaska Native Women and Men." National Institute of Justice Journal. Accessed online at URL: https://nij.ojp.gov/topics/articles/violence-against-american-indian-and-alaska-native-women-and-men

Sampson, Rana. 2002. "Acquaintance Rape of College Students." Problem-Oriented Guides for Police Series, No. 17. Washington, DC: U.S. Department of Justice, Office of Community Oriented Policing Services

Sawyer, Wendy 2018. "Youth Confinement: The Whole Pie." Prison Policy Initiative. Accessed online at URL: https:\www.prisonpolicy.org\reports\youth2018.html

Schiffer, Molly A. 2015. "Women of Color and Crime: A Critical Race Theory Perspective To Address Disparate Prosecution"> Arizona Law Review. Accessed online at URL: http://arizonalawreview.org/pdf/56-4/56arizlrev1203.pdf

Scott, James C. 1985. *Weapons of the Weak: Everyday Forms of Resistance*. New Haven, CT: Yale University Press.

Scott, James C. 1992. Domination and the Arts of Resistance: Hidden Transcripts. New Haven, CT: Yale University Press.

Scott, Anne Firor 1990. "Most Invisible of All: Black Women's Voluntary Associations". The Journal of Southern History. 56 (1): 3–22. doi:10.2307\2210662. JSTOR 2210662

Sim, J.J., Correll, J., Sadler, M.S. 2013. "Understanding police and expert performance: when traning attenuates (vs. exacerbates" stereotypic bias in the decision to shoot." Pers Soc Psychol Bull. 2013 Mar; 393): 291–304. doi: 10.1177\0146167212473157.

Sinyangwe, Samuel. 2018. "Mapping Police Violence." Mapping Police Violence. Accessed at URL: https:\mappingpoliceviolence.org\

Smith, Robert J. Reducing Racially Disparate Policing Outcomes: Is Implicit Bias Training the Answer?, 37 HAWAII L. REV. 295 (2015).

Stoughton, Seth. 2015. "Law Enforcement's 'Warrior' Problem." Harvard Law Review 128: 225–34.

Svokos, Alexandra. 2019. "Massive backlog of untested rape kits is 'a public safety issue' that may be letting offenders slip away, experts warn." *ABC News*. https://abcnews.go.com/US/massive-backlog-untested-rape-kits-public-safety-issue/story?id=60540635.

Thomas, William I., and Dorothy Swaine Thomas. 1928. *The Child in America: Behavior Problems and Programs*. New York: Alfred A. Knopf.

Timothy. Williams, 2012. "For Native American Women, Scourge of Rape, Rare Justice." *New York Times*, May 22. Accessed February 1, 2014Accessed February 1, 2014 http://www.nytimes.com/2012/05/23/us/native-americans-struggle-with-high-rate-of-rape.html?pagewanted=all.

Tonry, Michael. H. 1995. *Malign Neglect: Race, Crime, and Punishment in America*. New York: Oxford University Press.

United States Sentencing Commission.2017."Federal Alternative-to-Incarceration Court Programs" . United States Sentencing Commission. Accessed online at URL: https://www.ussc.gov/sites/default/files/pdf/research-and-publications/research-publications/2017/20170928_alternatives.pdf

Unites States Sentencing Commission 2019. Opioid Epidemic Blacks United States Sentencing Commission. Accessed online at URL: https:\www.nytimes.com\2019\11\25\upshot\opioid-epidemic-blacks.html.

Unnever, James D., and Shaun L. Gabbidon. 2011. *A Theory of African American Offending: Race, Racism, and Crime*. New York: Routledge.

Vicens, A.C. 2015. "Native Americans Get Shot By Cops at an Astonishing Rate." Mother Jones. Accessed online at URL: https:\www.motherjones.com\politics\2015\07\native-americans-getting-shot-police\

Warnken, Heather and Janet L. Luaritsen. 2019. "Who experiences Violent Victimization and Who Accesses Services" Center for Victim Research. Accessed online at URL: https:\ncvc.dspacedirect .org\bitstream\item\1270\CVR Article_Who Experiences Violent Victimization and Who Accesses S ervices.pdf?sequence=1.

Weichselbaum, Simone. 2015. "The Problems with Policing the Police." Marshall Project, April 23. Accessed October 24, 2016. https://www.themarshallproject.org/2015/04/23/policing-the-police# .w3g6ycqRd.

Wildra, Emily. 2018. "Stark racial disparities in murder victimization persists, even as overall murder rates decline." Prison Policy Initiative. Accessed online at URL: https://www.prisonpolicy.org/b log/2018/05/03/homicide_overtime/.

Winthrop D. Jordan, 1968. *White over Black: American Attitudes toward the Negro, 1550–1812.* Chapel Hill: University of North Carolina Press, for the Institute of Early American History and Culture

Wirth, Louis. 1931. "Culture Conflict and Delinquency, I: Culture Conflict and Misconduct." Social Forces 9: 484–92.

World Population Review, 2020. Countries With Death Penalty 2020. Accessed online at URL: https: \worldpopulationreview.com\country-rankings\countries-with-death-penalty

Xu, Yiuli, Fiedler, and Mora L. Flaming. Karl H. 2015. "Discovering the Impact of Community Policing: The Broken Windows Thesis, Collective Efficacy, and Citizens' Judgment." Journal of Research in Crime and Delinquency 42, no. 2: 147–86.

8 POWER, POLITICS, AND IDENTITIES

2020 Presidential Debate at Belmont University.

Kevin Dietsch/UPI/Bloomberg via Getty Images

LEARNING OBJECTIVES

8.1 Explain contemporary political identities.

8.2 Evaluate stock sociological theories regarding power, politics, and identity.

8.3 Apply the matrix approach to U.S. political history.

8.4 Formulate alternatives to the matrix of race and politics.

The 2020 Presidential race, between incumbent Donald J. Trump and former vice president Joe Biden provided competing visions for transforming the United States. Trump's slogan, reframing his successful 2016 bid for the presidency, challenged the electorate to stay the course and "Make America Great Again; Promises Made, Promises Kept." Contesting this vision, Biden declared that the campaign was a "Battle for the Soul of the Nation; Our Best Days Still Lie Ahead." The road to his eventual victory was overshadowed by events like a global pandemic, which had already claimed over 220,000 lives, and the rise of multiple social movements from both the left and the right. At the core of these social movements is the increasingly fragmented electorate. But this period is not unique within our nation, nor is it cause for undue concern. In fact, the very purpose of a democracy is to allow for the free assembly and expression of its citizenship. The continual vibrancy of our political system and increasing engagement of our various intersectional constituencies is a testament to the efficacy of our democratic system.

Every four years, the people of the United States elect a president, and candidates from each of the major political parties attempt to obtain the largest share of the votes. Success often is dependent on how well a candidate navigates the various political identities that define U.S. politics. What exactly are these political identities, and how do they define U.S. politics? In this chapter we will explore those questions, examine how various forms of political behavior have traditionally been accounted for, analyze political history and its lessons through the matrix, and discuss how new forms of political and social movements have affected political processes and power in the United States.

CONTEMPORARY POLITICAL IDENTITIES

Politics encompasses all of the processes, activities, and institutions having to do with governance. Like all other institutions, politics provides unique spaces and places in which various identities come into play. Political identities are the political positions, based on the interests and perspectives of social groups, with which people associate themselves. Across the United States, these political identities—representing race, gender, sexuality, language, region, and class—frequently intersect, interact, and intervene in multiple forms of political expression. Political identities have historically been a means by which nondominant groups can resist and transform political systems.

Understanding the Electorate

Traditionally, political analysis within the United States has stressed single group comparisons. The problem with comparing groups on a single indicator is that this method fails to capture the complex reality of political behavior. **Intersectional politics** refers to the political identity groups (i.e., the patterning of intersectional identities of race/ethnicity, class, and gender) that forge alliances, develop strategies, and attempt to control political discourses, issues, processes, elections, and events. In this way, intersectional identities produce intersectional politics that reflect the complicated terrain that defines American political structures.

Intersectional Political Identities

Voters can't be classified by just one identity. Race, class, gender, and other identities matter when it comes to how and if people vote. Since 2014, voter turnout for women in general, and younger women across Black, White, and Hispanic groups specifically, was higher than for their male counterparts. This gap was highest among non-Hispanic Black women, where there was an 8% gender gap in voting (Misra 2019). Since 2016, women with some level of higher education are increasingly identifying as Democrats, while White voters without college degrees increasingly report identifying with the Republican Party (Pew 2018).

Racially, while the Democratic Party is becoming more diverse, the Republican Party is becoming less so. Blacks remain solidly Democratic, but there have been minor declines. In the 2016 Presidential election, 8% of Black voters identified with the Republican Party. The political leanings of Hispanics, who are more than twice as likely to lean Democratic, have changed little over the past decade; about 63% vote for Democratic candidates. Among Asian voters, about 65% identify as Democrats (Figure 8.1).

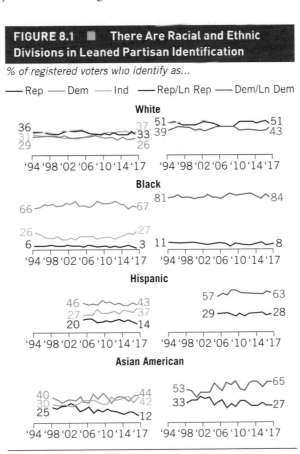

FIGURE 8.1 ■ There Are Racial and Ethnic Divisions in Leaned Partisan Identification

% of registered voters who identify as...

— Rep — Dem — Ind — Rep/Ln Rep — Dem/Ln Dem

Source: Annual totals of Pew Research Center survey data (U.S. adults).

Regardless of which party they identify with, U.S. voters have grown more diverse in recent years. More than 122 million people voted in the 2018 elections, the highest midterm election year turnout since 1978. And while voter turnout rates for Whites (57%) and Blacks (51.4%) increased, they increased by only 11.7 and 10.8 percentage points respectively, over the 2014 elections.

Voter turnout rate increased sharply across racial and ethnic groups during 2018 midterm elections (Figure 8.2).

Hispanics and Asians witnessed the highest turnout rates (about 40%). It would be incorrect to assume that Hispanics and Asians are monolithic groups. The reality is that many differences exist depending on whether they were native-born or are naturalized citizens. The largest increase in voter turnout between the 2014 and 2018 elections among Latinx and Asians was among naturalized citizens. Among Latinx, naturalized-citizens turnout rates were 44.2%, compared to 39% for U.S.-born Latinx. Asian naturalized citizens also turned out at higher rates, 42.7% compared to 36.7% (Krogstad, Noe-Bustamante, and Flores 2019).

The 2018 midterm elections further made history with the most diverse set of candidates to ever run for offices across the United States. For the 116th Congress, 103 women were elected to serve in the House. That represented a 22% increase from the previous Congress. Women of color now represent 42% of the women serving in the House. Political affiliation also changed, as 34% of the incoming House Democrats identified as people of color, compared to about 2% of the Republicans. And for the first time two Native American and Muslim females were

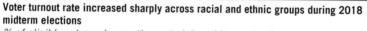

FIGURE 8.2 ■ Voter Turnout Rate Increased Sharply Across Racial and Ethnic Groups in 2018

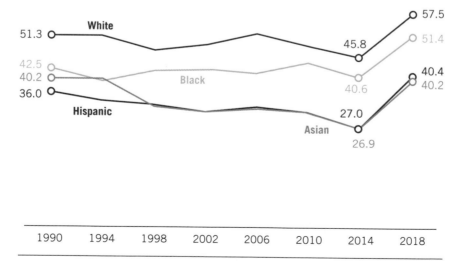

Voter turnout rate increased sharply across racial and ethnic groups during 2018 midterm elections
% of eligible voters who say they voted, by midterm election year

Source: Pew Research Center analysis of the Current Population Survey, November Supplements, 1990–2018.

Rep. Matt Gaetz, shown here with former president Trump, was quoted as saying "I am a white male, I guess I'm a little old-fashioned. I identify as a white male because I am a white male and . . . I guess it's because I was born that way" (Hall 2019). Ironically, his comment harkens to the 2011 hit song by Lady Gaga, "Born This Way," which is considered by many as an anthem for marginalized and disenfranchised minorities, including those who identify as LGBTQ, and an expression of self-empowerment.

MediaPunch Inc/Alamy Stock Photo

elected to Congress (Williams 2019). Of the newly elected people of color, most were elected from primarily White districts. Of the 10 newly elected Senators, 5 were females. Females now make up almost a quarter of the Senate (Edmondson and Lee, 2019). There were some changes around age too. More than 20% of the newly elected Congresspeople were millennials (Brown 2019).

Political Identities by Place

Political identities are more than just social groups—they intersect across multiple dimensions. Space is one dimension in which political identities vary significantly in the United States. For example, most Whites living in urban communities tended to vote Democratic (57%) in the 2018 midterm elections. On the other hand, most Whites living in small or rural towns or in suburban communities tended to vote Republican (63% and 51%, respectively). Non-Whites, regardless of community size, overwhelmingly voted for a Democratic candidate (McGill, Dougherty, and Friedman 2018).

Across all groups, those living in the South and the Northeast are most likely to view reality through the lens of race, and those living in the West are most likely to view class as central to their identities (McElwee 2016). Immediately, the questions of identity and intersectionality come into play. For example, how would living in a particular region affect different racial and class identities? More important for our purposes here, how might these differences play out politically?

Some research provides potential answers. Among predominantly White political districts, the relationship between income and political partisanship varies very little. Regional differences linking political partisanship and race are most likely to be associated with racially heterogeneous districts within states. So, as Figure 8.3 shows, in the Northeast, where large numbers

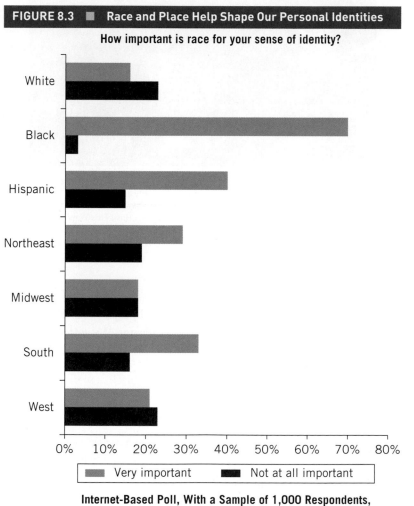

FIGURE 8.3 ■ Race and Place Help Shape Our Personal Identities

How important is race for your sense of identity?

Legend: Very important | Not at all important

Internet-Based Poll, With a Sample of 1,000 Respondents, Performed in January 2016

Source: Adapted from Sean McElwee, "Race versus Class in the Democratic Coalition," *The Nation*, March 7, 2016, https://www.thenation.com/article/race-versus-class-in-the-democratic-coalition.

of African Americans reside, there is an increased likelihood that the voters are Democrats. On the other hand, voters who live in affluent areas are only slightly more Republican than those in less affluent areas. In contrast, in specific rural areas with high concentrations of minority poverty (particularly the Black Belt, the Rio Grande Valley, and California's Central Valley), the links among White identity, income, and partisanship become more apparent. Alternatively, for racially diverse areas outside of the rural South, the link between party identification and income are very weak (Hersh and Nall 2015).

Voter Disenfranchisement

Laws regulating voter **disenfranchisement**, or revocation of the right to vote, also differ regionally. Current laws in many states revoke the voting eligibility of anyone with a criminal conviction. The rate of disenfranchisement in the United States has kept pace with the growth in incarceration. Forty years ago, almost 1.2 million people were denied the right to vote due to criminal convictions. Twenty years later, that number had risen to 3.3 million. And between 2016 and 2018, at least 17 million more voters were denied the right to vote (Morris 2019). Race continues to be associated with disenfranchisement, as Blacks are nearly six times more likely than Whites to be incarcerated. Thus 1 of every 13 Black Americans of voting age currently cannot vote (Amritt, 2017).

States vary significantly in how they apply disenfranchisement laws. Seven states have revoked the right to vote for 2–3% of their populations, amounting to tens of thousands of people losing their right to vote in each state (Rafei 2020). In Alabama, Florida, Kentucky, Mississippi, Tennessee, and Virginia, more than 7% of the adult population are disenfranchised. The disenfranchised are disproportionately likely to be Hispanics, African Americans, and the poor. Many of these potential voters were caught in our nation's "get-tough" crime policies.

Voting rights groups have launched efforts across the nation, particularly in the South, to overturn felony disenfranchisement. In 2019 the Florida Rights Restoration Coalition encouraged the Florida voters to amend the state constitution to allow people with felony convictions to vote. Consequently, once they finish serving their felony convictions, 1.4 million individuals will be allowed to vote. Kentucky passed a similar amendment, which means that more than 140,000 people will regain their voting franchise once they complete their sentences (Barber 2019).

Native Americans have also historically experienced disenfranchisement. The Navajo Nation extends across Arizona, Utah, and New Mexico, but because the tribe falls under the jurisdiction of different individual Secretaries of State overseeing federal elections, the Navajo have three different sets of rules with which they must comply in order to vote (Bogado 2018).

Native Americans in several states, including Nevada and Arizona, have mobilized to combat voter suppression and disenfranchisement. These states have heavy concentrations of Native Americans and voter identification laws that require proof of address, which can be an obstacle since many potential voters live in rural areas without formal addresses. Additionally, polling places are generally not located on reservations, which also increase the cost and burdens of voting (Hayoun 2019).

Disenfranchisement is not only a result of race. According to a 2018 study, as many as 78,000 transgender voting-eligible people face significant barriers in eight states. These barriers are often associated with strict photo ID laws. Transgender citizens were significantly less likely to have accurate identification than were people of color (48%), young adults (aged 18–24; 69%), and students (54%) (Herman and Brown 2018). Currently 34 states have laws requiring potential voters to prove their identity at the polls. Often it is left to poll workers to determine if the identification accurately matches the information on the identification card issued by the state (Moreau, 2018).

The Role of Race, Class, and Gender

Other intersectional aspects of political identities are associated with how race and income interact. For example, slightly more than three-fourths of likely voters identify as White, compared to 9% identifying as Black and 6% as Hispanic or Latinx. Hispanics are almost four times as likely (23%) as Whites to be nonvoters, while those identifying as Black are 6% more likely to be nonvoters. An inverse relationship exists between nonvoting and both income and education (Pew Research Center 2015). The highest levels of nonvoting are associated with the lowest levels of education and income. And while higher income seems to be associated with a greater likelihood of voting, the same does not hold true for higher levels of education. The likelihood of voting is mixed across various levels of education (Pew Research Center 2015).

Aimee Allison—seen here during a keynote discussion at the Netroots Nation progressive grassroots convention in Philadelphia, PA, on July 13, 2019—joins millions of Americans that are involved, both financially and personally, in political campaigns. She observes that many women of color, believing that they are not valued, tend to be apathetic. This apathy is most obvious in the realm of political donors where the most influential tend to be White and male. To address this problem, Allison founded and serves as president of She the People (Lee 2019). While difficult to document, Black, Latina, and Asian women made up a much smaller percentage of donors in the elections from 2008 through 2014, compared to men of color, White women, and White men (McElwee, Schaffner, and Rhodes 2016).

Reuters/Alamy Stock Photo

Being eligible or likely to vote and actually voting are two different things. Women across all racial groups are more likely to vote than men, and in the last two presidential election cycles, Black women have been the most likely to vote. Before that, White women had maintained this record. Women, including women of color, are increasingly being elected to political offices at all levels. The current election cycle represents a set of transformative stories. We have witnessed waves of women, including women of color taking office in 2018-2020. These elections highlight the important, and often overlooked, impact of intersectional politics that currently shape our electoral processes (Zhou 2019).

Critical Thinking

1. Intersections of race, gender, and education affected the 2018 midterm elections, but these were not the only factors. How might differences between geographical regions have influenced the election outcome?

2. An individual's education level may have an impact on how he or she votes. How might other factors, such as marital status, employment status, religion, and military service, affect a person's voting behavior?

3. Different levels of voting are associated with different gendered identities within race. In what ways might these patterns affect electoral outcomes? What does this suggest for future voting and electoral outcomes?

4. In what ways do your own political beliefs reflect your identities (race, class, and/or gender), and in what ways do your identities shape your political beliefs?

CRITIQUING SOCIOLOGICAL THEORIES OF POWER, POLITICS, AND IDENTITY

Political sociology is the study of government, political behaviors, institutions, and processes that occur between the state and its society and citizens. More simply, political sociology is the study of power, politics, and identity. Our discussion of the stock sociological theories here is not intended to be an exhaustive look at the rich theoretical landscape; rather, our goal is to illustrate how power, politics, and identity have been explained. These theories—pluralist approaches, the power elite model, and class approaches to power, politics, and identity—are central to the discipline and have long served to inform and guide political theorizing, research, and policy.

The Pluralist Approach

Pluralism posits that power within society is decentralized, widely shared, diffuse, and fragmented. Groups throughout society, reflecting business, labor, professions, religions, and cultures, compete and often hold conflicting interests. Because no single group is dominant, **democratic equilibrium** (a dynamic working balance between and among various groups) is established. This means that democratic governance is conceived of as a system that regulates conflict between and among various interest groups. These interest groups include, but are not limited to, groups concerned with the economy (markets, industries, and finance), education, religion, and the military. Individuals join groups because groups have more power than individuals when it comes to achieving goals. The larger the group, the more influence it has. Political policies develop as a result of the continuous bargaining and compromises among various groups (Dahl 1961).

The essential democratic function of political institutions is to regulate the conflict among various groups. Multiple forms of conflict can surface along distinct interest-group lines, so various political elites tend to be more or less engaged in the political process depending on which interests are prominent. For example, while Black political and civil rights elites were actively involved with the water crisis in Flint, Michigan, few mainline political elites were so heavily involved. Alternatively, consider the Asian American electorate—a group that is virtually invisible in American politics. This reflects the fact that the "Asian" label suggests a monolithic group, when in fact there is a significant degree of variation among Asian cultural groups (Wagner 2016). The democratic process is therefore dynamic, changing continually as different lines of conflict produce multiple and shifting power bases. Two types of groups are associated with the pluralist approach: **insider groups**, which hold the bulk of the power, and **outsider groups**, which are marginalized and have limited power (Dahl 1961).

Insider groups tend to be well recognized and established, holding positions of power and prestige within their communities. Their positions mean that they have considerable influence over elected officials at various levels of government. Members of these groups tend to have similar perspectives on several issues. The list of insider groups is virtually endless. It includes unions and professional organizations like the Teamsters Union and the American Medical Association; identity groups such as Protestants, Whites, and Blacks; gender groups; and corporations and marketing groups. Insider groups may use direct means such as voting, lobbying, and boycotts to influence political outcomes, political processes, and politicians.

Many of today's insider groups were outsider groups in the past. Blacks, Jews, and Catholics have become insider groups through effective political organizing, protests, and other forms of political activism. Outsider groups, which have significantly less power and prestige within their communities, tend to be marginalized in the political process and have less access to elected officials. Members of these groups may be recent immigrants (documented and undocumented, political refugees, and so on), people who belong to socially marginalized groups (including LGBTQ people), and people with special interests (such as animal rights or environmental justice).

The pluralist approach presumes that, at least among the various insider groups, power is dispersed equally. It also suggests that the system is fair, and that outsider groups get a chance at influencing the structures and one day achieving the status of insiders. The reality is that power tends to coalesce among a very few, well-placed insiders. For example, even as women and Blacks have become relative insiders over the past four decades, they do not share power equally with men and Whites. Also, their presence as insiders produces **binary constructs** (White/Black, male/female) that normalize and legitimate racial and gender hierarchies at the expense of other outsiders, such as other racial and gender minorities.

The AARP is an insider group founded to promote the interests of retired people. The organization claims membership of more than 37 million people and has an annual budget of $1.6 billion (2016 AARP Annual Report), giving it considerable clout.

Jim West/Alamy Stock Photo

The pluralist approach has limited ability to deal with changing political climates and conditions. During these times of unrest, major upheavals are presented as interest group dynamics and conflicts that disrupt political processes. Since the terrorist attacks of September 11, 2001, many political candidates and elected officials have focused on Americans' fears of Islamic extremism. Muslims, regardless of political involvement or national origin, have become more likely to be targeted by political outcomes such as racial profiling laws and new immigration quotas and standards. The democratic equilibrium that pluralism assumes might be too simplistic and unrealistic (Domhoff 2005).

The Power Elite Model

The **power elite model** suggests that power is concentrated among a discrete group of elites who control the resources of significant social institutions. The power elite consists of members from three specific realms:

1. Holders of the highest political offices, such as the president of the United States, key cabinet members, and close advisers

2. Heads of major corporations and directors of corporate boards

3. High-ranking military personnel

While inherited wealth and position can help an individual attain the status of a power elite, individuals can also gain admittance to the highest circles by working hard and adopting elite values (Mills 1956). The power and authority derived from elite positions allow these members to influence governmental, financial, educational, social, civic, and cultural institutions. A relatively small group of elites, consequently, can have a significant impact on most people across a nation. Over the past few decades, the power of the elites has been enhanced through the development of a military–industrial complex with strong governmental ties. Simultaneously, links between corporations and government elites have strengthened as the role of government has expanded into many aspects of our daily lives. In the United States, the Food and Drug Administration (FDA) must approve all foods and medicines intended for human consumption. But the FDA and Congress are frequently targeted by lobbying activity. In 2018, leading all other industry, pharmaceutical companies spent about $27.5 million to influence Congress (Scutti 2019).

The first major criticism of the power elite model is that it erroneously assumes equality among economic, political, and military elites. The link between political and military elites might be tenuous at best. For example, in 2018, 18 members of the House were veterans (Provost 2019). Alternatively, veteran status might be a road to the White House. Slightly more than half (26 of 45) of U.S. presidents have served in the armed forces.

Another criticism of the power elite model is that it presents political and corporate elites as unified, while regional and economic interests interact to produce specific types of power structures. Consider the Northern industrial and financial elites, who currently align with the Republican Party, and their common interests with Southern Democrats and agricultural elites. Coming out of the Civil War, the Democratic Party surfaced in the South to thwart Reconstruction and the rising ambitions of the freed slaves (Ager 2013). The coalition of Southern and Northern elites remained constant for much of the 20th century, with only two deviations: one in 1935, when industrial union organizing dominated politics and elections in the North (forcing a split between Northern and Southern elites), and one in 1964, with the advent of the civil rights movement in the South (when again the Northern and Southern elites split). In the sections that follow, we will return to this example, as it demonstrates how White Southern elites pursued a policy of segregation that not only harmed their long-term interests but also served to pit low-status Whites against low-status Blacks and Hispanics. The repercussions of these actions have lasted even to this day.

The Class Approach

The **class approach** to power, politics, and identity assumes that the type of economic system a society has determines the kind of political structures that evolve. Within the United States, those who control the economic production control the political processes. As implied by the saying "What is good for corporate America is good for America" (Nussbaum 2010), major corporations dominate our economy, and that translates to power across all major social institutions (Miliband 1977). We live in a society where major corporations and industries greatly influence political processes and outcomes. The social elites who control the markets control the government, and they in turn dominate other classes to perpetuate their power (Marx [1852] 1964). Two different intellectual traditions derive from this perspective:

1. **Instrumentalism** views the state as being dominated by an economic class that controls both political and economic spheres (Goldstein and Pevehouse 2009).

2. **Structuralism** posits that the state and all political institutions exist relatively independent of each other and are essentially by-products of conflict between and within class groups (Poulantzas 2008).

Critics of the class approach and its derivatives claim that they tend to reduce all aspects of power to what happens in the market. These approaches do not account for those instances when members of the dominant class do not act in their own self-interest as they pursue either racial or gendered objectives. For example, from the 1920s to the 1940s, elite corporation owners were silent partners with the White labor force as labor unions denied membership to racial minorities and women. Elite employers first instigated racial strife by recruiting Black workers to take the place of White strikers, resulting in many riots across the country. Once settlements were reached, the newly hired Blacks were replaced by White immigrants, who were more acceptable to the unions (Restifo, Roscigno, and Qian 2013).

Further, class approaches tend to minimize racial, ethnic, and immigrant bases of power, such as the Congressional Black Caucus and the Congressional Hispanic Caucus, that serve as resistance and countervailing forces in our political structure. The biggest challenge for social change has to do with the gaps that exist among the various identity groups. Critical scholars point out that if coalitions could be forged across these various social locations (of race, class, gender, and age), a massive social movement could be fostered. Such a movement would be most effective in challenging the U.S. power structure. The civil rights movement of the 1960s could serve as a model for this kind of movement (Domhoff 2005).

Critical Thinking

1. What might account for the different geographical patterns observed among states that disenfranchise voters? What does this say about intersectional identities? How effective have the resistance efforts to combat them been? How effective are stock stories in explaining the outcomes?

2. We have seen how some institutions (such as the military and the economy) might influence political outcomes, and similarly how political institutions can affect the wider society. What other major institutions might have similar effects?

3. Over different historical time periods, different types of identities might be more prevalent or more visible than others. What does this suggest regarding political outcomes? How might the matrix help us understand these outcomes? What does this suggest about the relevance of stock stories?

4. What are your political beliefs? To what extent do they reflect your family, education, gender, race, or geographical region? What intersections can you identify based on this?

APPLYING THE MATRIX TO U.S. POLITICAL HISTORY

According to our nation's stock story, the original intent of our system of government was to diminish the conflict between "the haves" and "the have-nots." That is, since various interests divide people into different classes with radically different objectives and rationales, the principal purpose of government is to regulate these conflicts and ensure that fairness, or justice, is achieved. Our form of government, which is based on representation, is an attempt to ensure that we will not be governed by either the tyranny of the majority or the tyranny of the minority. The stock story of U.S. politics teaches us that our nation is a democracy in which every citizen, regardless of identifying characteristics, has a voice in the political process. The stock narrative also suggests that inequalities associated with race, class, gender, sexual orientation, and other forms of identity are aberrant and not part of the core values of our culture. This idea is part of the American Dream that draws thousands of immigrants and refugees to the United States each year. Accordingly, democracy fosters pluralism and welcomes diversity, as both are essential to the interests of freedom.

Using our stock story to guide us, we understand that conflicts arise in situations where resources are scarce (whether the scarcity is real or only perceived). **Power**, therefore, might be defined as the ability to acquire scarce resources. And if indeed the central role of political institutions is to diminish conflict, then they also serve the function of regulating power. It stands to reason that resource scarcity and the power associated with the acquisition of resources are both keyed to specific historical situations, institutional settings, and geographical locations. Further, individuals seeking to maximize their access to resources are likely to organize into groups to increase the efficiency of their resource acquisition. These assumptions align perfectly with the expectations of the matrix.

Certain resources associated with work and the economy, housing, and access to education are always scarcer than others. A person or group must first have access to these things, so citizenship or immigration status is of equal importance. We can also expect that both geographical and historical situations can have impacts on each of these potential sources of conflict. Our task in the next sections will be to explore how these conflicts have been resolved, and to what extent they reveal the importance of the intersections of race, class, and gender.

Legislating a Nation Built on Racial and Intersectional Differences

When the so-called Founding Fathers convened to write the U.S. Constitution, they not only established the founding principles of our nation, they also declared that basic rights were associated with land ownership. Since land was owned primarily by a small elite group of White males, they thus enshrined race, class, and gender into the very fabric of our nation. Race and

The Congressional Black Caucus is composed of most of the African American members of the U.S. Congress and is an example of identity politics. The group is "committed to using the full Constitutional power, statutory authority, and financial resources of the federal government to ensure that African Americans and other marginalized communities in the United States have the opportunity to achieve the American Dream."

Tom Williams/CQ-Roll Call Group/Getty Images

intersectional differences have been part of our legislative and political processes since the inception of our nation.

The Geography of Slavery

While slavery existed in all of the colonies, political, social, and geographical conditions resulted in distinctly different attitudes toward slavery.

The Southern colonies, consisting of Maryland, Virginia, the Carolinas, and Georgia, were staunch supporters of slavery. Their political economies rested on an agricultural base and almost year-round growing seasons. Elite landowners found that by using slave labor, their plantations could more profitably produce such crops as rice, cotton, and tobacco.

Slaves in the Northern colonies (New Hampshire, Massachusetts, Rhode Island, and Connecticut) likely had more diversified skills than those in the heavily agricultural South (Melish 1998). The complex economies of the Northern colonies allowed slaves to develop a wide variety of skills, from domestic to skilled trades. The tradition of Northern slavery therefore allowed expansion from small-time farms to large agricultural production, the growth of local and regional markets, increased entrepreneurial activity, and the rise of industrialization. Some slave owners encouraged their slaves to work harder and more efficiently by offering them a share in the profits, which the slaves often used to buy their freedom. Ultimately, the Northern elites determined that free labor was more productive than slave labor (Melish 1998). As the united colonies entered the Revolutionary War, these different regional political economies and attitudes regarding slavery served to produce the nation's first set of political compromises.

The establishment of the U.S. Congress as a bicameral legislature, with the Senate and House of Representatives, was a direct result of debates over whether and how to count slaves as part of the country's population. The Southern states, with their relatively smaller populations, wanted the slaves to be counted equally to Whites to bolster their populations and thus their power in the government. The Northern states, with their considerably larger populations and virtually no slaves, were in opposition. The **Great Compromise of 1787** was the result of this disagreement. According to the compromise, the Congress would be composed of two governing bodies, one in which population would determine the number of seats each state would hold (the House of Representatives), and one in which each state would have two members (the Senate). It was further decided that each slave would be counted as three-fifths of a person in population counts determining numbers of representatives as well as presidential electors, and for purposes of taxation.

Consequently, the Southern states received a third more seats in congress and a third more votes for the Electoral College than they would have if slaves were not counted. This directly impacted the five Southern states with a majority slave population. The compromise also resulted in fewer taxes owed to the federal government. Interestingly, Native Americans, excluded from these provisions, were defined in subsequent sections of the same article.

The Framers of the Constitution settled on the Great Compromise of 1787 to resolve a dispute between Northern and Southern states about how to fairly allot representation in Congress. The Compromise created the House of Representatives, where seats are distributed based on population, and the Senate, where each state is represented equally.

Ian Dagnall/Alamy Stock Photo

Native American Sovereignty

In article 1 section 8, clause 3 of the Three Fifths Compromise, Congress was empowered to regulate commerce with foreign nations and particularly with Native Americans (called tribes in the Constitution). Three Supreme Court decisions, known as the Marshall Trilogy, between 1823 and 1832, set out the legal and political perimeters of Native American sovereignty.

- The first ruling, *Johnson v. M'Intosh* (1823), granted the federal government the rights to occupy and settle any lands. Those lands granted by the federal government to Native Americans could not be sold to either individuals or states with indigenous standing. Only the federal government could negotiate with Native Americans over land rights.

- The second case, *Cherokee Nation v. Georgia* (1831), defined Native American tribes as domestic dependent nations, not as sovereign ones. This distinction meant that Native American tribes and boundaries were not like states, nor were they foreign nations. They had limited authority within the boundaries established by the United States. This created a reciprocal relationship whereby the Native Americans ceded their lands to the federal government, which was obligated to provide the basic necessities of food, shelter, and services.

- The last decision, *Worcester v. Georgia* (1832), declared that federal and not state laws controlled activities on tribal lands. (Fletcher 2014)

Free or Slave: Legislating Away Rights

In Norwich, Connecticut, shortly before the Civil War, the assets of R. I. Stoddard were seized for failure to pay taxes. The executor, Charles Johnson, sued the town to recover the seized amount. Ironically, the Connecticut Supreme Court ruled that the funds were improperly seized because of Stoddard's race. Connecticut's General Assembly had exempted all persons of color from taxation because the Connecticut Constitution denied them the right to vote. Connecticut and Rhode Island were the only two states to exempt free Blacks' personal and real property from all taxation because they were not allowed to vote. Many states not only denied free Blacks the right to vote, but also created special taxes just for them (Bryant 2015).

Virginia was the first of the British colonies to import slaves, and its legislators enacted more than 130 slave statutes between 1643 and 1865. Among these were seven major slave codes, containing more than fifty provisions (Palmer 2006), including the following:

- A 1643 Virginia law stipulated that all Blacks over the age of 16 were obliged to pay taxes.

- 18 years later, the same Assembly decreed that a child's status (slave or free) was to be determined by the status of the mother. Therefore, if she was free, her children would be free, and if enslaved, then her children would be born slaves.

- These laws also stipulated that if a "Christian, white" male or female were to have sex with a Black person, they would be fined.

- In 1691, a set of laws stated that if an unmarried White woman had sex with a Black man, she could be fined or forced to work for the community. Any mixed-race children from these relationships were deemed illegitimate, and their mothers had to pay fines to the local government, the local church, and the person reporting the crime. These mixed-race children were forced to work as indentured servants until they reached the age of 30.

- In 1705, Virginia passed laws that allowed a master to kill a slave with impunity, if the killing occurred while the slave was undergoing "correction" or punishment.

- Further, if slaves were declared runaways, it was legal for anyone to kill them by any means necessary. Even if killing was not desirable, "dismembering" was approved.

These laws helped to make race, slavery, and Whiteness central features of American political culture and reality. By 1700 about 30,000 enslaved people lived in the British Colonies, and by 1776 a total of 450,000 were counted (Ruane 2019).

Citizenship and Immigration

The next step in nation building that cemented the intersectional basis of our political institutions involved citizenship and immigration. One of the most significant aspects of power within any political system is to whom citizenship is granted. The status of **citizenship** reflects the legal processes that a country uses to regulate national identity, membership, and rights. Citizenship also establishes the political boundaries that define who is and is not included in the democratic franchise. The Naturalization Act of 1790 granted citizenship to "free white aliens" with 2 years' residence in the United States but withheld it from slaves and women. The law further excluded all non-Whites, including Asians, enslaved Africans, and Native Americans, from citizenship. While citizenship was extended to all Whites after they had established residency, only property-owning men could exercise the right to vote or to hold political office (Tehranian 2000).

U.S. immigration policies were created expressly to preserve the racial character of the nation. Persons from Northern Europe and Western Europe, followed by Southern Europe, were favored over all other potential immigrants. The Northern free states, with their concentration of both commercial businesses and manufacturing, were the clear choice of immigrants. In the 1840s, nearly half of immigrants to the United States were from Ireland alone. Of the approximately 4.5 million Irish immigrants who arrived between 1820 and 1930, most settled close to their points of arrival in cities along the East Coast (Omi and Winant 2015).

The mid-1800s gold rush attracted a significant number of Asian immigrants to the West Coast. By the early 1850s, some 25,000 Chinese had immigrated (Omi and Winant 2015). Almost 5 million German immigrants, also coming in large numbers during the 19th century, arrived in the Midwest, where they bought farms or settled near cities such as Milwaukee, St. Louis, and Cincinnati (Omi and Winant 2015).

Anglo-Saxon Protestants, nervous about the influx of so many newcomers, began voicing anti-immigrant sentiments. The anti-immigrant, anti-Catholic American Party (also known as the Know Nothings) lobbied for significant restrictions on immigration. The first group targeted was the Chinese in 1882, and immigrants from other Asian Pacific countries were targeted in 1917 (Jacobson 2006). In 1921 the Emergency Quota Act was adopted, limiting the numbers of immigrants to the United States by imposing quotas based on countries of birth, as determined by a **national origins formula.** The formula set quotas at 3% of the total number of foreign-born persons from a country, as recorded in the 1910 U.S. Census. This meant that persons from Northern Europe had a higher likelihood of being admitted to the United States than persons from Eastern or Southern Europe and those from non-European countries. Latin American immigrants were excluded from these quotas until 1965, the same year that the discriminatory quotas based on race and national origins were limited. Actual numerical quotas limiting immigration from individual Latin American countries were imposed in 1976 (Ewing 2012). Use of the national origins formula continued until 1965, when it was replaced by rules laid out in the Immigration and Nationality Act of 1965.

The Black civil rights movement of the 1960s, which linked human rights and social justice, sheds light on American immigration policy. The 1965 Immigration and Nationality Act formally committed the United States, for the first time in its history, to accepting immigrants of all nationalities on roughly equal terms. The law eliminated quotas based on countries of origin, a system under which immigrants coming from Northern and Western Europe were given preferential treatment. The impact of this law was immediate and dramatic. For example, in 1960, seven out of every eight immigrants to the United States came from Europe; by 2010, nine out of ten came from other parts of the world. No other law passed in the 20th century has had such a significant demographic impact on our nation (Jelten 2015).

Civil War and Its Aftermath

Geography and history interact in particular ways. Over these unique spaces and places, two distinct patterns of racial political processes can be identified: **de jure political practices,** or processes that were enacted as formal laws, and **de facto political practices,** processes that, although not enshrined in law, were carried out by various entities. Collectively these political practices served to restrict or marginalize the political power, as well as the economic and social power, of specific racial and ethnic groups.

De Jure Political Practices

The Civil War, although centered on the issue of slavery, was equally about what political system should govern the country. In August 1862, in response to concerns about his resolve to free the slaves, President Abraham Lincoln wrote an open letter that appeared in the *New York*

The 1965 Immigration and Nationality Act ended the preferential treatment enjoyed by immigrants from northern and western Europe, radically changing the demographic makeup of new arrivals to the country.

Kevork Djansezian/Getty Images News/Getty Images

Times. Lincoln stated that the issue for him was not slavery but the preservation of the political union. He went further, declaring that he was prepared to abolish, uphold, or partially abolish slavery to uphold the union (Lincoln 1862). In the Emancipation Proclamation, issued one month later, Lincoln took the third choice, freeing some slaves while leaving others in slavery. Most historians agree that Lincoln's proclamation "freed" only those slaves under Confederate control, over which he had no power. The strategy worked in that it relied on either open rebellion or the fear of open rebellion among slaves. And this is what tipped the Civil War in the direction of the Union (Morris 2015).

The 14th and 15th Amendments, which finally granted African Americans the right to vote, were ratified by the states in 1869 and 1870. Unfortunately, these laws granted differential rights based on gender. The 14th Amendment, for the first time in our history, declared that only male citizens over the age of twenty-one years old could vote. And the 15th Amendment clarified that the right to vote could not be denied because of race.

In the aftermath of the Civil War, a half million Black men became voters in the South during the 1870s. Former slaves, now making up more than half of the voting population in many Southern states, easily gave the Republican Party, the party of Lincoln, the political power. And for the first time, Blacks were elected to national, state, and local positions. But even with these majorities, Whites were still the majority of those elected at both the state and local levels. When federal troops left the old Confederacy, voting significantly declined among Blacks as White employers and groups like the Ku Klux Klan sought to preserve White political supremacy at all costs (Chancellor 2011).

Over the next few decades, many new laws were created that affected all aspects of life in the South. Most public spaces were segregated by race, and significant restrictions on voting were introduced, including **poll taxes**, taxes that individuals had to pay for 2 years in advance in order to register to vote; **literacy tests**, which required persons seeking to vote to read and interpret a section of the state constitution to the (always White) county court; and **grandfather clauses**, which gave the right to vote to anyone whose grandfather was qualified to vote prior to the Civil War. All these laws benefited only White citizens. Prior to the enactment of these laws and during Reconstruction, 90% of Black males of voting age were eligible to vote. In 1892, after these laws were passed, less than 6% were eligible (Omi and Winant 2015). Blacks were not the only ones harmed by these devices. So-called old immigrants, mostly British, Irish, Germans, and Scandinavians, were strongly in favor of these restrictions. Those newly arrived from Italy, Russia, and other parts of Southern and Eastern Europe were not so fortunate, as they also found it difficult to pass the new voting tests (Omi and Winant 2015).

With Blacks effectively removed from the electorate, Whites were in control of all federal and state legislative and executive offices, and so were able to pass a whole range of Jim Crow laws that enforced racial segregation throughout the South. These laws led not only to political disfranchisement but also to economic discrimination and social ostracism. In many ways, the laws specifically targeting African Americans were intended to deal with Native Americans and Chinese Americans as well (Upchurch 2004).

De Facto Political Practices

Vagrancy laws, and other Black Codes, were de facto (in fact) ways to limit the civil and political rights of Blacks. In this regard the concealed story of Green Cottenham is instructive.

THE FREEDMEN'S BUREAU.—Drawn by A. R. Waud.—[See Page 201.]

In the aftermath of the Civil War the New Freedmen's Bureau was established, providing hope for progress and harmony that was soon dashed as Black Codes re-emerged as Jim Crow.

Granger

In 1908 a young Black man named Green Cottenham was sold to the Tennessee Coal, Iron and Railroad Company and forced to work at the Pratt coal mines, near Birmingham, Alabama. Cottenham joined 1,000 other men, all of whom could be whipped if they did not dig the minimum eight tons of coal a day. At night he slept in chains. How could he be sold? He was a vagrant (Ruane 2019). Vagrancy laws were established when White planters complained about labor shortages and utilized their political clout to control Blacks. Although Blacks did not stop working, they wanted more rights, such as a reduction of Saturday work hours, and women wanted to spend more time caring for their children (Wilson 1965). These laws required Blacks to have written evidence that they were employed each year in January. If they left prior to fulfilling their contract, they could be forced to return, forfeit earlier wages, and were subject to arrest. South Carolina further restricted Blacks from occupations other than farming or service unless they paid an annual tax ranging from $10 to $100. Farmer slave artisans, particularly in Charleston, were not only forced out of their professions but were also declared vagrants and forced to work on plantations. Vagrancy laws joined a whole slew of other laws, which politically proscribed race and rights throughout the South (Hammad 2019). Similar de facto political laws also served to limit the political and civil rights of Blacks and others.

States in both the South and the North passed residential segregation laws. But in 1917, the U.S. Supreme Court held that such ordinances were unconstitutional. As a result, real estate agents and private developers began to write their own provisions into real estate contracts. These **restrictive covenants** barred the resale of houses to purchasers of a race different from that of the original homeowner. In 1948, the Supreme Court ruled that restrictive covenants were also unconstitutional. Unfortunately, the damage had already been done, as residential segregation had become entrenched. National housing policies from 1930 to 1950, under the Federal Housing Authority (FHA), also reinforced residential segregation. FHA rules required developers to include restrictive covenants and supported local housing policies that segregated public buildings owned by municipalities. In a practice known as **redlining**, areas worthy of mortgage lending were ranked and color coded, and those with the lowest rankings (typically outlined in red), so designated because they held "inharmonious" racial groups, were systematically denied good mortgage rates (Badger 2015).

Redlining was in use by the federal government until 1968, and it was also used by private banks as the country went through one of its most massive homeownership expansions in history. Income restrictions and income differences between Blacks and Whites helped create White suburbs, Black urban ghettos, and Hispanic barrios (Tushnet 2003). In a 2015 suit against the largest bank in Wisconsin, the U.S. Department of Housing and Urban Development (HUD) argued that in the period 2008–9, Black and Hispanic borrowers in Wisconsin, Illinois, and Minnesota were wrongly excluded from getting loans. While the bank settled the dispute and denied any wrongdoing, HUD declared that it had gained a victory in "one of the largest redlining complaints" ever brought by the federal government against a lender (Badger 2015).

Redlining causes a domino effect, as lower-valued houses fall into disrepair, businesses and employment vacate the neighborhood, and only the poorest and most vulnerable are left behind. Schools decline, because their revenues are tied to local property and income taxes, and the level of education and the motivation to succeed dwindle, resulting in generations of youth that struggle to escape the cycle. The people who became involved in the 1960s civil rights movement found these circumstances ample reason to wage their war on racism.

CONCEALED STORY: CLAUDETTE COLVIN—BEFORE ROSA, THERE WAS CLAUDETTE

When she was 15, Claudette Colvin refused to give up her seat to a white passenger on a Montgomery, Alabama bus in 1955.

Dudley M. Brooks/The Washington Post/Getty Images

In 1955, Claudette Colvin, a 15-year-old Black woman, refused to give up her seat on a Montgomery, Alabama, bus to a White person. Someone knocked the books from her hands, beat her, and dragged her forcibly from the bus. When the police arrived, Colvin was arrested, charged with disorderly conduct for violating the segregation ordinance and with assault and battery. Her case immediately got the attention of local civil rights leaders, who debated whether it was worth contesting the charges. Colvin's mother was a maid and her father mowed lawns. Although they were churchgoing people, they lived in the poorest section of Montgomery. As the civil rights local leaders continued to debate whether the Colvin case could be used to challenge segregation on Montgomery buses, it became known that Colvin was pregnant by a married man. While the leaders helped raise money for her defense, Colvin was deemed unacceptable to become the face of the Montgomery bus protest. Nine months later, another woman, Rosa Parks, would ride on the same bus and follow the same script originated by Colvin. The rest is history, as Rosa Parks became the face of the Montgomery bus boycott and the mother of the modern civil rights movement (Colvin 2016).

The Rise of Coalitional Politics and Social Movements

In many ways, identity politics paved the way for the massive political protests, resistance, and transformations associated with the civil rights movement of the 1950s and 1960s. This period is also distinguished by the rise to prominence of **coalitional politics**, in which political alliances are formed among various identity groups with the shared purpose of establishing specific political agendas.

Perhaps no single movement captured this new form of politics better than the **Black civil rights movement**, which began roughly in 1955 and continued through 1968. In this movement, Southern Blacks—in partnership with their Northern Black and White allies—challenged and effectively nullified the intimidation and segregation of the Old South. The movement was politically organized to effect change, resist oppression, and redefine the racial order through the courts, on the streets, through boycotts, and at the ballot box.

The Black civil rights movement utilized a series of well-orchestrated nonviolent protests and civil disobedience actions to force dialogues between activists and political institutions. Federal, state, and local governments, as well as businesses and communities that discriminated against African Americans were targeted and highlighted. The protests included boycotts such as the Montgomery bus boycott of 1955–56; sit-ins targeting restaurants that refused to serve Blacks, such as in Greensboro, North Carolina, in 1960; and large-scale marches, such as the one from Selma to Montgomery in 1965, protesting the inability of Blacks to vote.

Several major pieces of federal legislation resulted from these activities. One of the major victories of the movement came with passage of the Civil Rights Act of 1964. This act officially banned discrimination in employment practices based on race, color, religion, sex, or national origin. It also prohibited racial segregation in schools, workplaces, and public accommodations. This was followed the next year by the Voting Rights Act of 1965, which ended voting discrimination and extended federal protections to minorities. In that same year, the Immigration and Nationality Act removed racial and national barriers to immigration, which meant that Blacks from other nations could immigrate to the United States. In 1968, the Fair Housing Act banned discrimination in the sale and rental of housing.

During this same period, significant movements were also taking place among other identity groups. On September 8, 1965, a group of mostly male Filipino American grape workers, members of the Agricultural Workers Organizing Committee, walked out of the fields and began a strike against the Delano-Area Table and Wine Grape Growers Association. The workers were protesting decades of poor pay, substandard living conditions, and lack of benefits. They asked Cesar Chavez, leader of the mostly Latinx National Farm Workers Association, to join their strike, along with his union's members. Chavez was a veteran union activist and understood how growers had historically pitted different low-skilled workers in disadvantaged racial groups (such as Blacks and Hispanics) against each other. Growers were able to keep wages low by continuously hiring the lowest bidders for services. When Chavez's union voted to join the Filipino workers by walking out on Mexican Independence Day, on September 16, 1965, a coalition was formed that bridged two different and often adversarial racialized labor groups. Soon the strike became a national boycott. As Latinx and Filipino strikers banded together, their plight captured the attention of middle-class families in the

By crossing racial lines and allying his National Farm Workers Association with Filipino groups, Cesar Chavez built a coalition that won major concessions from their employers.

Arthur Schatz/The LIFE Picture Collection/Getty Images

big cities, who ultimately sided with the poor farmworkers and their families. Millions of people stopped buying and eating grapes. By 1970, the table grape growers admitted defeat and agreed to sign the first union contracts granting workers increased benefits and wages (United Farm Workers of America 2016).

In 2016, the Standing Rock Indian Reservation in North Dakota became a household name when Native Americans defied large corporations and the government of the United States to protest the building of the Dakota Access Pipeline near the reservation. This was in the tradition of several other Native American protest movements aimed at preserving sacred sites, ensuring the protection of natural resources, and resisting corporate takeovers. The Standing Rock Sioux were not alone, as thousands of people from across the United States, from environmentalists to Black Lives Matter activists, traveled to the reservation to join hands and say no. Another Native American resistance action took place in 2015, when the Rosebud Sioux tribe in South Dakota fought to keep the Keystone XL pipeline off its lands; also involved in those protests were environmentalists and other Native American tribes (Donnella 2016). These modern forms of resistance illustrate the viability and the reality of coalitional politics as an effective form of political activism.

Critical Thinking

1. Identities and political systems have changed over both time and place. Given the types of changes that we have seen, what may be the sources of change in the future? Alternatively, are there any political patterns linking identity to specific political

parties or outcomes that may either endure into the future or be subject to change? What might account for these outcomes?

2. The labor and civil rights movements had significant impacts not only on identity but also on political coalitions. What other movements might have significantly influenced political institutions, identities, and outcomes? What does this suggest regarding the stability of political institutions?

3. Political identity is a unique part of our political processes. What kinds of events might increase or decrease the likelihood that a political identity or collection of identities will remain viable or have the ability to transform political processes?

4. Identity politics is a very effective organizational tool, but identity movements can become mired in single issues. How might concentration on single issues and single identities serve not only to marginalize but also to limit the effectiveness of a social movement?

BUILDING ALTERNATIVES TO THE MATRIX OF RACE AND POLITICS

The past four decades have been marked by historic lows when it comes to public trust in government (Figure 8.4). In fact, in 2019 American trust in government was at an all-time low. A survey revealed that only about 17% of U.S. citizens trusted their political system. Of these only 3% believed that they could trust governmental officials in Washington to do the right thing "just about always," and 14% believed that they would do the right thing "most of the time." This distrust in government is observed across all racial and ethnic groups, regardless of age or party affiliation (Pew 2019).

Political participation is often a result of political activism. Consequently, while much of our attention is drawn to political participation, other components of this terrain are just as important, including various forms of action where the primary goal is to promote, impede, or raise awareness of a particular issue or set of issues. **Political activism** normally involves various types of actions that go beyond voting. It may be as simple as posting opinions online or getting involved in a letter-writing campaign, or it may involve active participation in boycotts, protests, or demonstrations.

The Power of Political Activism

One of the major insights revealed by the intersectional approach is that while race, class, gender, sexuality, and other sites of identity interact to produce unique forms of inequality and discrimination, they can also become the basis of **agency**—that is, the ability to effect change, to act independently, and to exercise free choices. This agency, a vital component of identity politics, reflects the multiple ways and mechanisms by which individuals and groups challenge, resist, and cope with inequality and discrimination. The various forms of political activism, such as boycotts and harnessing social media, have been quite effective at

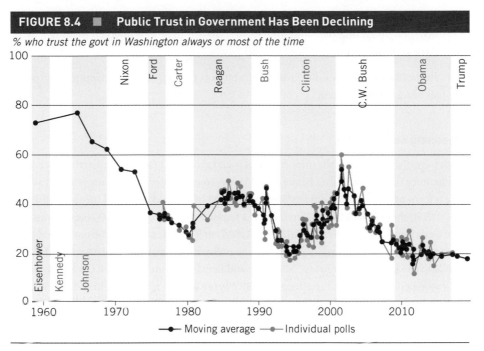

FIGURE 8.4 ■ Public Trust in Government Has Been Declining

% who trust the govt in Washington always or most of the time

Source: % who trust the government in Washington always or most of the time, Pew , 2019.

producing social change. Identity politics also highlights the coalitions that form both within racial groups (as multiple ethnic groups coalesce into a panethnic or panracial identity) and across them. The various examples below highlight how identity politics significantly alters the political landscape.

Boycotts

Boycotting is one of the most significant forms of political activism. **Boycotts** are voluntary acts of protest in which individuals or groups seek to punish or coerce corporations, nations, or persons by refusing to purchase their products, invest in them, or otherwise interact with them. Boycotts are often used to raise awareness of issues while simultaneously pressuring the entities involved to change policies, practices, or structures. The earliest boycotts in the United States occurred during the American Revolution, when colonists refused to purchase British goods. Other boycotts have served as means by which marginalized groups have challenged the political process, for example:

- In 1905, the Chinese boycotted U.S. products in reaction to the extension of the Chinese Exclusion Act.

- From 1965 to 1970, the United Farm Workers of America led nationwide boycotts of grapes and lettuce in retail grocery stores to pressure growers to improve wages and working conditions.

- From 1954 to 1968, participants in the Black civil rights movement conducted several boycotts (including the Montgomery bus boycott) to protest unequal treatment of African Americans.

- From 1973 to 1995, LGBT groups led a boycott of Coors Brewing Company to protest its antigay hiring practices.

Harnessing Social Media

Groups have also discovered the importance of social media as a tool for facilitating social activism. The story of the Black Lives Matter (BLM) movement demonstrates how political activism can be a form of resistance and transformation. BLM originated on social media in 2013 with the Twitter hashtag #BlackLivesMatter. It was a response to the acquittal of George Zimmerman for the shooting death of 17-year-old African American Trayvon Martin. The movement gained momentum and went national in 2014 after the police killings of two more African American males: Michael Brown in Ferguson, Missouri, and Eric Garner in New York City. This modern social movement is devoted to challenging police brutality and racial profiling. Since its inception, BLM has documented and protested the deaths of several African Americans who have been killed by police or died while in police custody. During the 2016 presidential campaign, representatives from BLM on several occasions entered political discourse by attending candidate forums and pointing out how systemic racism is pervasive in the United States (Griffith 2016). While BLM has become an effective voice calling for both resistance and transformation, it has also produced some unanticipated consequences, including the revelation of underlying racial tensions affecting other minority groups.

Hashtags such as #LoveWins, #JeSuisCharlie, #BlackLivesMatter, #MeToo, and others demonstrate how causes and events can emerge almost spontaneously, garner substantial support, then almost as quickly fade. For example, in January 2015, after the newspaper office shooting in France, the #JeSuisCharlie hashtag appeared on social media, and in 2 short days, the tag appeared over a million times on social media. Now, it is rarely seen. Similarly, major upsurges have been associated with #LoveWins and the #MeToo movement.

There is a link between hashtag "movements" and the intersection of race, law enforcement, and violence. But this pattern is not constant. For example, protests and fatal encounters with police, while quite common, may lead to a great deal of variation regarding tweets (Figure 8.5). When it was announced that police Officer Darren Wilson would not face trial for the shooting death of Michael Brown in Ferguson, Missouri, that news accounted for about 35% of the Black Lives Matter tweets that appeared on social media. The protests associated with the NFL and Black Lives Matter issues accounted for only 2% of the tweets (Anderson, Toor, Rainie, and Smith 2018).

The day after Donald Trump became the 45th president of the United States, women across the United States and around the globe marched in protest. According to some estimates, as many as 2.5 million people—women as well as men and others who support women's rights—took to the streets. The demonstrations dominated the news and social media and elicited several tweets from the president. The movement to stage a Women's March began on Facebook

FIGURE 8.5 ■ **Tweets Mentioning Social Movement Hashtags at Key Points in Time**

Among tweets using the #BlackLivesMatter, #BLM, #AllLivesMatter, and #BlueLivesMatter hashtags during the following time periods, the % that mention the following topics:

Time period (with corresponding major events)	Fatal police encounters	Violent acts	Police, law enforcement	National politicians/ parties	Race	Protests
Nov. 24–Dec. 4, 2014 (Ferguson, Mo., police officer not indicted in shooting death of Michael Brown)	35%	13%	9%	1%	25%	10%
July 7–17, 2016 (Alton Starling, Philando Castile, Dallas, Texas, and Baton Rouge, La., shootings)	8	18	22	8	27	11
June 17–27, 2017 (Acquittal of police officer in shooting death of Philando Castile)	22	20	23	6	26	4
Sept. 22–Oct. 2, 2017 (President Trump addresses NFL protests, Black Lives Matter rallies)	2	20	23	18	24	31
March 19–29, 2019 (Stephon Clark is shot and killed by Sacramento, Calif., police officers)	20	25	20	10	15	14
Aggregate average	11%	18%	21%	8%	25%	12%

Source: Table: "Large Share of Tweets mentioning #Black Lives Matter, #BlueLivesMatter and #AllLivesMatter at key points in time explicitly mention, race, law enforcement and/or violent acts." Pew Research Center Activism in the Social Media Age. July 11, 2018.

the day after Hillary Clinton lost the November election, and the idea for the protest quickly went viral as many feared the consequences of a Trump presidency for reproductive, civil, and human rights (Przybyla and Schouten 2017). Although touted as an all-inclusive protest, drawing participants across all racial, ethnic, gender, and class groups, many criticized it as being a movement of primarily White, middle-class women (Bates 2017).

The Role of Generational Change

The voters from younger generations are essentially products of the internet, social media, and advancing globalization, and therefore are more likely to be linked with the global universe.

While young people have historically voted in much lower numbers than other age groups across the United States, the number of college students casting ballots doubled between 2014 and 2018. These voters were often concerned with climate change and the Trump presidency. In the 2018 midterm elections these two groups, along with Generation X (those born between the mid-1960s and the early 1980s) obtained a slim majority of voters. These three groups cast 62.2 million votes compared to the 60.1 million cast by Baby Boomers and older generations. This same pattern, which first surfaced in the 2016 presidential election, suggests what the future political landscape might look like. For example, the number of eligible voters among Millennials and Gen Xers grew by 2.5 million over the past 4 years, primarily due to the fact

Muhammad Hoshur loved his iPhone so much that he decided to learn how to fix them. Hoshur, at 23 years old, owns three electronic repair shops in the Washington, D.C. area. The only problem is that, for obvious reasons, corporate America would rather you buy a new phone rather than repair your old one. Newly developing special interest groups such as The Repair Association are being formed to help Hoshur and other small businesspeople. Over the past five years, they have introduced 50 similar "fair repair" bills in 23 different states. These bills would require manufacturers of everything from phones to tractors to make all manuals, hardware, and software available to consumers and repair shops like those owned by Hoshur. These fair repair model bills are just a few of the thousands of proposed laws drafted by special interests groups (Hernandez and Rabala, 2019).

that the number of people who became naturalized citizens exceeded the rate of mortality in these age groups (Cilluffo and Fry 2019). We therefore can expect that issues of immigration will increasingly be of importance when it comes to politics in the United States.

Harnessing the Power of Immigrants

As we have seen in earlier chapters, immigrants have historically been targeted by both federal and state policies. Immigrants are currently undergoing similar sources of stress amid political rhetoric about building a wall along the U.S.–Mexico border, banning Muslim immigration, and deporting "undocumented" immigrants. Immigrants, their communities, and organizations concerned with immigrants' rights are not being idle. The DACA (Deferred Action for Childhood Arrivals) program has been highly successful. An estimated 68% of those in the program have achieved significant social mobility, attend classes in at least 19 states and Washington, D.C., and continue to progress. Unfortunately, variability of state laws, including uncertainty at the Federal level, continues to cast doubt on the continuance of the program. More permanent solutions are needed, as immigrant activists call for more protections and long term, national legislation that includes pathways to legalization and citizenship (Acevedo 2019).

Some conservative groups have complained about the millions of illegal ballots they claim were cast during the 2020 presidential election. While this has been shown to be false, a similar but concealed story is that of the hundreds of non-citizens that are being allowed to vote in local elections. In San Francisco, one out of three children attending public school has an immigrant parent. In 2017 voters in the city granted noncitizen parents and guardians the right to vote for school board elections. Several other cities have passed similar resolutions, such as Hyattsville

The DACA (Deferred Action for Childhood Arrivals program) has been highly successful and provides hope for millions.

David Grossman/Alamy Stock Photo

and Takoma Park in Maryland and Cambridge and Amherst in Massachusetts. These local efforts to expand voting rights are a counter to, and attempt to transform, efforts to restrict voting (Douglass 2017).

Immigrants are also making gains in political office. When Ilhan Omar, a Black Muslim woman from Somalia, immigrated to the United States in 1992, she joined other refugees trying to escape restrictive governments, where political freedoms of speech and assembly were denied. The Somali Civil War, which has been ongoing since the 1980s, has fueled the exodus of thousands of Somalians. In large part, they came to the United States because the freedoms denied to them at home are not only protected but celebrated here. Many became outspoken activists, community organizers, and even elected officials. Representative Omar, elected as the U.S. Representative for Minnesota's 5th congressional district in 2019, brings this point home, as she has spoken out on U.S. foreign policy, Palestinian liberation, and immigrants' rights (Gessen 2019).

TRANSFORMATION STORY: REPRESENTATION MATTERS

It is estimated that among all U.S. adults, 4.5% (or more than 11 million) may identify as LGBTQ. In 2019, some 1.4 million identified as transgender. At least 161 openly gay candidates were elected to the federal (10), state (106), and local levels (45) (LGBTQ Victory Fund 2018). And in the 2018 elections, riding on the wave, Sharice Davids from Kansas won a seat to the House of Representatives, becoming the first lesbian congresswoman from the state and one of the first two Native American women elected to Congress (Caron 2018). In a historic letter to the 116th Congress, 152 LGBTQ elected officials urged the passage and promotion of a number of issues, including the Equality Act, which mandates that sex, sexual orientation, and gender identity be included in the Civil Rights Act of 1964, increases funds for HIV/AIDS research, and supports LGBTQ rights as human rights (International LGBTQ Leaders Conference 2018).

Critical Thinking

1. In what ways might millennials effect transformative change? How might geography affect the likelihood of change?

2. How might political institutions better interact with other institutions (those dealing with the economy, family, education, or the military) to improve outcomes? What types of barriers or opportunities can you identify?

3. Our identities are shaped by and help shape the various institutions of which we are a part. In what ways might your identity become transformed given political actions that are now taking place? How might you, given your identity, be part of these changes?

4. The future belongs to all of us. Each generation, from oldest to youngest, has a stake in how well the political process operates. How might you, even at this point, become

more involved in politics? What can you do within your institution or in the wider community?

CHAPTER SUMMARY

8.1 Explain contemporary political identities.

The U.S. electorate is made up of various identity groups that reflect the matrix of race, class, gender, and region. These identities do not share equally in political outcomes, as witnessed by the significant number of Black and Hispanic felons who have been disenfranchised in recent years. Gender cannot be ignored, as we see how it interacts with race, education, and class, which helps to explain some recent political outcomes. Black women, and women in general, are more likely to vote than their male counterparts but less likely to hold political office.

8.2 Evaluate stock sociological theories regarding power, politics, and identity.

Political sociology has traditionally provided three central theories for understanding power, politics, and identity. These stock theories are pluralism, the power elite model, and the class approach. Pluralism argues that power is decentralized and widely shared among approximately equal groups. This perspective fails to provide enough insight into those systems in which power is not shared equally. The power elite model posits that power is concentrated among discrete groups of elites who control the resources of significant social institutions. Controlling these resources allows the elites also to control power and authority over governmental and political processes. Again, the model assumes both equality and consensus across the various elites. It fails to address what happens when power is in conflict across elites or how nonelite individuals and groups produce political change. The class approach argues essentially that those who control the economic system control the political processes. The class approach therefore tends to be reductionist, evaluating all politics from the vantage point of a person's position in the economic system. It fails to consider how social movements radically outside the mainstream economic institutions have served to resist and transform the political process.

8.3 Apply the matrix approach to U.S. political history.

Resource scarcity often underlies political struggles, and political systems come into being to regulate conflicts over these resources. In the process, differences associated with race, class, gender, and geography often become politicized. Our application of the matrix allows us to see how these political processes have played out over time, producing both de jure and de facto outcomes that have unique impacts. In the South, certain de jure forms of political structures came into being. These legal, more obvious forms of racialized politics had negative and differential impacts on Blacks, Chinese, and Native Americans, and influenced how citizenship, freedom, and immigration were defined. In the North, less obvious de facto procedures were used in discriminatory federal housing policies that created White, middle-class suburbs and urban ghettos through redlining. Coalitional politics are associated with the convergence of identity politics in the form of massive political protests, resistance, and transformations during the civil rights movement of the 1950s and 1960s. This movement, driven by a coalition of Southern Blacks and Northern Whites and Blacks, effectively nullified the intimidation and segregation of the Old South. Such movements have not been exclusive to Blacks; among others, Filipino and Latinx farmworkers and Native Americans have utilized similar social activism to influence political discourse.

8.4 Formulate alternatives to the matrix of race and politics.

The members of the millennial generation are less likely than their counterparts in earlier generations to vote based on political party loyalty, but they might be more motivated by specific issues. Recent elections demonstrate that compared to other age cohorts, millennials are most likely to be politically independent. Millennials may change the very course of this country as they become the largest generation and as they become more economically viable and politically active. More diverse than any preceding generation, and with a strong understanding of the effective use of social media, millennials have a huge potential for bringing about political change. The question is not if they will create change, but when, and what forms these changes will take.

KEY TERMS

agency

binary constructs

Black civil rights movement

boycotts

citizenship

class approach

coalitional politics

critical race theory

de facto political practices

de jure political practices

democratic equilibrium

disenfranchisement

grandfather clauses

Great Compromise of 1787

identity politics

insider groups

Instrumentalism

literacy tests

millennials

national origins formula

outsider groups

pluralism

political activism

political identities

political sociology

politics

poll taxes

power

power elite model

redlining

restrictive covenants

silent generation

structuralism

REFERENCES

Acevedo, N. 2019. "DACA has transformed young immigrants' lives, a new report says. Will the Supreme Court save it". *NBC NEWS*. Accessed online at URL: https:\www.nbcnews.com\news\latino\daca-has-transformed-young-immigrants-lives-new-report-says-will-n1077686.

Ager, Phillip. 2013. "The Persistence of De Facto Power: Elites and Economic Development in the U.S. South, 1840–1960." Working Paper 38, European Historical Society. Accessed February 17, 2017. http://econpapers.repec.org/RePEc:hes:wpaper:0038.

Amritt, Carl. (2017). "A Quick History Lesson on Voter Disenfranchisement". *Roosevelt Institute*. Retrieved from https://rooseveltinstitute.org/2017/05/22/a-quick-history-lesson-on-voter-disenfranchisement/

Anderson, Monica, Skye Toor, Lee Rainie, and Aaron Smith. 2018. "An Analysis of #BlackLivesMatter and other Twitter hashtags related to political or social issues." *Pew Research Center*. Accessed online at URL: https://www.pewresearch.org/internet/2018/07/11/an-analysis-of-blacklivesmatter-and-other-twitter-hashtags-related-to-political-or-social-issues/.

Badger, Emily. 2015. "Redlining: Still a Thing." *Washington Post*, May 28. Accessed February 22, 2017. https://www.washingtonpost.com/news/wonk/wp/2015/05/28/evidence-that-banks-still-deny-black-borrowers-just-as-they-did-50-years-ago/?utm_term=dbbc1c4a0709.

Barber, Benjamin 2019) "The push to overturn felony disenfranchisement in Southern States". *Facing South*. Accessed online at URL: https:\www.facingsouth.org\2019\12\push-overturn-felony-disenfranchisement-southern-states.

Bates, Karen Grigsby. 2017. "Race and Feminism: Women's March Recalls the Touchy History." *Code Switch*, NPR, January 21. Accessed June 22, 2017. http://www.npr.org/sections/codeswitch/2017/01/21/510859909/race-and-feminism-w-omens-march-recalls-the-touchy-history.

Bogado, Aura 2018. "How Native Voters are routinely Disenfranchised in Arizona". *Colorlines*. Accessed online at URL: https:\www.colorlines.com\articles\how-native-voters-are-routinely-disenfranchised-arizona

Brown, 2019. "America\'s Most Diverse Congress: Meet the Class of 2019". *Time*. Accessed online at URL: https:\time.com\longform\new-members-of-congress-2019\

Bryant, Christopher J. 2015. "Without Representation, No Taxation: Free Blacks, Taxes, and Tax Exemptions Between the Revolutionary and Civil Wars". *Michigan Journal of Race and Law*, Vol 21(1). Accessed at URL: https:\repository.law.umich.edu\cgi\viewcontent.cgi?article=1051&context=mjrl

Caron, Christina. 2018. "In \'Rainbow Wave,\' L.G.B.T. Candidates Are Elected in Record Numbers." *The New York Times*. Accessed online at URL: https:\www.nytimes.com\2018\11\07\us\politics\lgbt-election-winners-midterms.html.

Chancellor, Carl. 2011. "After Civil War, Blacks Fought for Rights for 100 Years." *USA Today*, April 11. Accessed February 21, 2017. http://usatoday30.usatoday.com/news/nation/2011-04-11-civil-war-civil-rights_N.htm.

Cilluffo, Anthony and Richard Fry. 2019. "Gen Z, Millennials and gen X outvoted older generations in 2018 midterms". *Pew Research Center*. Accessed online at URL:https:\www.pewresearch.org\fact-tank\2019\05\29\gen-z-millennials-and-gen-x-outvoted-older-generations-in-2018-midterms\ www.pewresearch.org\ www.pewresearch.org\

Colvin, Claudette. 2016. "History: Claudette Colvin." Congress of Racial Equality. Accessed February 20, 2017. http://www.core-online.org/History/colvin.htm.

Dahl, Robert A. 1961. *Who Governs? Democracy and Power in an American City*. New Haven, CT: Yale University Press.

Domhoff, G. William. 2005. "Social Movements and Strategic Nonviolence." *Who Rules America*, March. Accessed June 17, 2017. http://www2.ucsc.edu/whorulesamerica/change/science_nonvio lence.html.

Donnella, Leah. 2016. "The Standing Rock Resistance Is Unprecedented (It's Also Centuries Old)." *Code Switch*, NPR, November 22. Accessed December 12, 2016. http://www.npr.org/sections/code switch/2016/11/22/502068751/the-standing-rock-resistance-is-unprecedented-it-s-also-centuri es-old.

Douglass, Joshua A. 2017. "Noncitizens are gaining the right to vote. Good. *Washington Post*. Acce ssed online at URL: https:\www.washingtonpost.com\opinions\noncitizens-are-gaining-the-right- to-vote-good\2017\08\18\805b86e2-4d3e-11e7-9669-250d0b15f83b_story.html.

Edmondson, Catie and Jasmine C. Lee. 2019. Meet the New Freshmen in Congress" *The New York Times*. Accessed online at url: https:\www.nytimes.com\interactive\2018\11\28\us\politics\congre ss-freshman-class.html

Ewing, Walter. 2012. "Opportunity and Exclusion: A Brief History of U.S. Immigration Policy." American Immigration Council, January 13. Accessed June 22, 2017. https://www.americanimmigr ationcouncil.org/research/opportunity-and-exclusion-brief-history-us-immigration-policy.

Fletcher, Mathew L.M. 2014. "A Short History of Indian Law in the Supreme Court." *American Bar Association*. Accessed online at URL: https:\www.americanbar.org\groups\crsj\publications\hum an_rights_magazine_home\2014_vol_40\vol--40--no--1--tribal-sovereignty\short_history_of_in dian_law\.

Gessen, Masha. 2019. "The Dangerous Bullying of Ilhan Omar". *The New Yorker*. Accessed online a t URL:https:\www.newyorker.com\news\our-columnists\the-dangerous-bullying-of-ilhan-omar

Goldstein, Joshua S., and Jon C. Pevehouse. 2009. *Principles of International Relations*. New York: Pearson/Longman

Griffith, Erin. 2016. "The Black Lives Matter Founders Are among the World's Greatest Leaders." *Fortune*, March 24. March 24. Accessed June 2, 2016. http://fortune.com/2016/03/24/black-lives- matter-great-leaders.

Hammad, Neveen. 2019. "Shackled to Economic Appeal: How Prison Labor Facilitates Modern Slavery While Perpetuating Poverty in Black Communities". *Virginia Journal of Social Policy & the Law*, Vol. 26(2): 65-91. Accessed online at URL: https:\heinonline.org\HOL\Page?collection=journal s&handle=hein.journals\vajsplw26&id=100&men_tab=srchresults.

Hayoun, Massoud 2019. "Native American Rights Groups Are Targeting Six States to Fight Voter Suppression in 2020. *PS Magazine*. Accessed online at URL: https:\psmag.com\social-justice\nativ e-american-rights-groups-are-gearing-up-to-fight-voter-suppression-in-2020.

Herman, Jody L. and Taylor N.T. Brown. 2018. "The Potential Impact of Voter Identification Laws on transgender Voters in the 2018 General Election. *The Williams Institute*. Accessed online at URL: https:\williamsinstitute.law.ucla.edu\wp-content\uploads\Voter-ID-Laws-2018.pdf.

Hernandez, Kristian., & Rabala, Pratheek. (2019). Puppies, phones and porn: How model legislation affects consumers' lives. *USA Today*. Retrieved from https://www.usatoday.com/in-depth/news/in vestigations/2019/11/20/puppies-phones-porn-meat-milk-how-model-legislation-and-copycat-bi lls-affect-consumers/2525454001/

Hersh, Eitan D., and Clayton Nall. 2015. "The Primacy of Race in the Geography of Income-Based Voting: New Evidence from Public Voting Records." *American Journal of Political Science* 60, no. 2: 289–303.

International LGBTQ Leaders Conference 2018. *LGBTQ Elected Official\'s Letter to the 116 Congress*. Accessed online at URL: https:\victoryinstitute.org\116congressletter\.

Jacobson, Matthew Frye. 2006. "More 'Trans,' Less 'National.'" *Journal of American Ethnic History* 25, no. 4: 66–84.

Jelten, Tom G. 2015. "The Immigration Act That Inadvertently Changed America." *Atlantic*, October. Accessed February 20, 2017. https://www.theatlantic.com/politics/archive/2015/10/immigration-act-1965/408409.

Krogstad, J. M., Luis Noe-Bustamante and Antonio Flores. 2019. "Historic highs in 2018 voter turn-out extended across racial and ethnic groups." Pew Research center. Accessed online at URL: https://www.pewresearch.org/fact-tank/2019/05/01/historic-highs-in-2018-voter-turnout-extended-across-racial-and-ethnic-groups/.

LGBTQ Victory Fund 2018. "Results 2018". *LGBTQ Victory Fund*. Accessed online at URL: https://victo ryfund.org/results2018/.

Lincoln, Abraham. 1862. "A Letter from President Lincoln: Reply to Horace Greeley. Slavery and the Union, the Restoration of the Union the Paramount Object." *New York Times*, August 24. Accesse d February 21, 2017. http://www.nytimes.com/1862/08/24/news/letter-president-lincoln-reply-ho race-greeley-slavery-union-restoration-union.html.

Marx, Karl. (1852) 1964, *The Eighteenth Brumaire of Louis Bonaparte*. New York: International Publishers.

McElwee, Sean. 2016. "Race versus Class in the Democratic Coalition." *The Nation*, March 7. https://www.thenation.com/article/race-versus-class-in-the-democratic-coalition.

McGill, Brian, Dougherty, Danny and Dov Friedman. 2018. "How We Voted in the 2018 Midterms". *Wall Street Journal*. Accessed online at url:https:\www.wsj.com\graphics\election-2018-votecast-poll\

Melish, Joanne Pope. 1998. *Disowning Slavery: Gradual Emancipation and "Race" in New England, 1780–1960*. Ithaca, NY: Cornell University Press.

Miliband, Ralph. 1977. *Marxism and Politics*. Oxford: Oxford University Press.

Mills, Wright C. 1956. *The Power Elite*. New York: Oxford University Press.

Misra, Jordan. 2019. Voter Turnout Rates Among All Voting Age and Major Racial and Ethnic Groups Higher Than in 2014 U.S. Census. Accessed online at URL:https:\www.census.gov\library\stories\2019\04\behind-2018-united-states-midterm-election-turnout.html.

Moreau, Julie. (2018, August 17). "Strict ID laws could disenfranchise 78,000 transgender voters, report says". *NBC News*. Retrieved from https://www.nbcnews.com/feature/nbc-out/strict-id-law s-could-disenfranchise-78-000-transgender-voters-report-n901696

Morris, Aldon. 2015. *The Scholar Denied: W. E. B. Du Bois and the Birth of Modern Sociology*. Berkeley: University of California Press.

Morris, Kevin. 2019. "Voter Purge Rates Remain High, Analysis finds". Brennan Center for Justice. Accessed online at URL: https:\www.brennancenter.org\our-work\analysis-opinion\voter-purge-rates-remain-high-analysis-finds.

Morrison, Toni. 1993. "On the Backs of Blacks." *Time*, December 2. Accessed March 21, 2016. http://content.time.com/time/magazine/article/0,9171,979736,00.html.

Nussbaum, Bruce. 2010. "Is What's Good for Corporate America Still Good for America?" *Harvard Business Review*, October 26. Accessed February 17, 2017. https://hbr.org/2010/10/is-whats-good-for-corporate-am.

Omi, Michael, and Howard Winant. 2015. *Racial Formation in the United States*. 3rd ed. New York: Routledge.

Palmer, Vernon Valentine April 2006. "The Customs of Slavery: The War Without Arms". *American Journal of Legal History*. 2(48): 177

Pew 2018. Wide Gender Gap, Growing Education Divide in Voters' Party Identification." Accessed onl ine at URL: https://www.pewresearch.org/politics/2018/03/20/wide-gender-gap-growing-educati onal-divide-in-voters-party-identification/.

Pew 2019. "Public Trust in Government." *Pew Research Center*. Accessed online at URL: https:\www. people-press.org\2019\04\11\public-trust-in-government-1958-2019\.

Pew Research Center. 2015. "A Deep Dive into Party Affiliation: Sharp Differences by Race, Gender, Generation, Education." April. Accessed December 9, 2016. http://www.people-press.org/2015/04/ 07/a-deep-dive-into-party-affiliation.

Poulantzas, Nicos. 2008. *The Poulantzas Reader: Marxism, Law and the State. Edited by James Martin*. London: Verso Books.

Provost, Julie. 2019. "Military Veterans in Congress". *College Recon*. Accessed online at URL: https: \collegerecon.com\veterans-in-congress-2019\

Przybyla, Heidi M., & Schouten, Fredreka. (2017, January 22). "At 2.6 mission strong, women's marches crush expectations". *USA Today*. Retrieved from https://www.usatoday.com/story/news/ politics/2017/01/21/womens-march-aims-start-movement-trump-inauguration/96864158/

Rafei, Leila 2020. "Block the Vote: Voter Suppression in 2020." *ACLU*. Accessed online at URL: https: \www.aclu.org\news\civil-liberties\block-the-vote-voter-suppression-in-2020\

Restifo, Salvatore J., Vincent J. Roscigno, and Zhenchao Qian. 2013. "Segmented Assimilation, Split Labor Markets, and Racial/Ethnic Inequality." *American Sociological Review* 78, no. 5: 897–924.

Ruane, Michael E. 2019. "Freedom and slavery, the 'central paradox of American history'". *The Washington Post*. Accessed online at URL: https://www.washingtonpost.com/local/freedom-and-sl avery-the-central-paradox-of-american-history/2019/04/30/16063754-2e3a-11e9-813a-0ab2f17e 305b_story.html.

Scutti, Susan 2019. "Big Pharma spends millions on lobbying amid pressure to lower drug prices. *CNN*. Accessed online at URL: https:\www.cnn.com\2019\01\23\health\phrma-lobbying-costs-bn\ index.html

Tehranian, John. 2000. "Performing Whiteness: Naturalization Litigation and the Construction of Racial Identity in America." *Yale Law Journal* 109, no. 4: 817–48.

Tushnet, Mark V. 2003. "Segregation." In *Dictionary of American History*, 3rd ed., edited by Stanley I. Kutler. New York: Scribner.

United Farm Workers of America. 2016. "The 1965–1970 Delano Grape Strike and Boycott." Acces sed October 20, 2016. http://www.ufw.org/_board.php?mode=view&b_code=cc_his_research&b_ no=10482.

Upchurch, Thomas Adams. 2004. *Legislating Racism: The Billion Dollar Congress and the Birth of Jim Crow*. Lexington: University Press of Kentucky.

Villarreal, Vezmin. 2016. "Nation's Largest Latino Civil Rights Group Joins LGBTs in N.C. Boycott." *Advocate*, May 18. Accessed May 31, 2016. http://www.advocate.com/transgender/2016/5/18/nation s-largest-latino-civil-rights-group-joins-lgbts-nc-boycott.

Wagner, Alex. 2016. "Why Are Asian Americans Politically Invisible?" *Atlantic*, September. Accessed April 4, 2017. https://www.theatlantic.com/politics/archive/2016/09/why-dont-asians-count/498893.

William, Vanessa. 2019. "Women of color in Congress are challenging perceptions of political leadership." *The Washington Post*. Url: https:\www.washingtonpost.com\nation\2019\01\04\women-color-congress-are-challenging-perceptions-political-leadership\.

Wilson, Theodore Brantner 1965. *The Black Codes of the South*. University of Alabama Press.

Wines, Michael. 2016. "Virginia's Governor Restores Voting Rights for 13,000 Ex-Felons." *New York Times*, August 23. Accessed February 24, 2017. https://www.nytimes.com/2016/08/23/us/virginia-governor-mcauliffe-voting-rights-felons.html?_r=1.

Wines, Michael. 2019. "The Student Vote Is Surging. So Are Efforts to Suppress it." *The New York Times*. Accessed online at URL: https:\www.nytimes.com\2019\10\24\us\voting-college-suppression.html.

Zhou, Li 2019 A Historic new Congress will be sworn in today. *Vox*. Accessed at URL: https:\www.vox.com\2018\12\6\18119733\congress-diversity-women-election-good-news

9 SPORTS AND THE AMERICAN DREAM

There are many more opportunities for boys to participate in school sports than for girls and the increasing cost of participation can make it hard for lower income students to play.

AP Photo/Paul Sancya

LEARNING OBJECTIVES
9.1 Explain the state of sport in the United States.
9.2 Compare stock theories about U.S. sport.
9.3 Apply the matrix approach to sport.
9.4 Describe strategies for transforming the institution of sport.

In 2019 officials from The Army West Point football program rebranded their team logo after an internal investigation discovered that the phrase on its team flag originated with White supremacist biker gangs. The original logo included the slogan "GFBD," which stands for "God Forgives, Brothers Don't." Embarrassed by the discovery, Gen. Darryl Williams, West Point Commandant, admitted that the team was ignorant of the slogan's origins, and that its selection had nothing to do with any covert or internal beliefs in White supremacy or other bigoted organizations or beliefs (Murphy 2019). West Point and its athletic program join countless other professional and collegiate sports that have had to come to grips with imagery which links race to sport.

Sport is not an isolated institution, but rather an integral part of the institutional structures that comprise the United States. Sports have historically been linked to males and attitudes of dominance, and the West Point example shows how different sport contexts—race, gender, and class—intersect. Sports are highly stratified, segregated, and reflective of these intersections. This means that while some sports may appear to be more diverse than others, closer analysis of ownership, coaching, and fan bases reveals that an examination of sport, as an institution, can benefit from an intersectional approach. Let's first look at contemporary trends in sports and how they relate to the American dream.

THE STATE OF SPORT TODAY

Sport encompasses a range of activities that involve physical exertion and skill. These activities are organized around sets of rules and can be played at either the individual or the team level. Today's athletes are remarkable, and some of the best set some dazzling new records that continue to amaze us:

- In 2020, 24-year-old Patrick Mahomes became the second-youngest quarterback to ever win a Super Bowl and the youngest player in NFL history to win a regular-season MVP (Freiman 2020).

- At the 2019 World Championships, gymnast Simone Biles took home five of the six golds. With a total of 25 world gold medals, she is now considered the greatest gymnast of all time (Wamsley 2019).

- Major league club owners, such as Linda G. Alvarado (co-owner of the Colorado Rockies), demonstrate that women can be not only CEOs and innovators in corporate roles, but also transformative leaders who shape American sports culture and industry (Echegaray, Gray, and Kolur 2017).

- Tampa Bay Buccaneers quarterback Tom Brady is considered by many sports analysts to be the greatest quarterback of all time (Harrison 2019). To date he has 34 postseason wins and has participated in 10 Super Bowls (earning 7 wins), the most of any player in NFL history.

Across the country and in many of our colleges, high schools, and local communities, athletes are writing new chapters in a long tradition of competition and victory, sometimes earning fame, high salaries, and lucrative endorsement deals. But all sports are not equal, as we will see in our exploration of the business of sports.

The Business of Sports

The most watched sport in the United States has traditionally been football, and the Super Bowl leads all other single sporting events. Games run by the National Football League (NFL) generated 40 of the top 50 U.S. sports audiences in 2018, and accounted for 80% of the sports audiences in 2018 (Paulsen 2019).

We can identify some interesting demographics among the NFL viewership numbers:

- The NFL fan base is 41% more likely to be males than females.

- They are, on average, between 50 and 59 years old.

- They have an average annual income of $75–100,000.

- Politically they are more likely to be Republicans (Johnson 2017).

- Over two thirds of the fan base is White, while Blacks (16%), Hispanics (9%), and Asians (4%) make up the remaining third (Kertcsher 2017).

The statistics for Major League Baseball (MLB) fans are similar to NFL fans.

- They are slightly older (more likely to be aged 56–60).

- They are slightly wealthier (more likely to have incomes of $150–250,000).

- They are even more likely to be male (48%).

- They are about evenly split politically between Republicans and Democrats (Johnson 2017).

- MLB fans are also most likely to be White (Z2solutions 2016).

The National Basketball Association (NBA) has the most diverse fan base. During the 2016–17 regular season, 66% of NBA television fans were racial minorities. Of these, Blacks were 47%, Hispanics 11%, and Asians 8%. The least diverse fan base was associated with National Association for Stock Car Racing (NASCAR). For example, its most popular televised event in 2017 had an over 90% White audience (Piacenza 2018). Let's now consider the link between the popularity of sports and their impact upon the economy.

It is not surprising that the sports we choose to watch reveal something about our values and interests, and that certain fan bases made up of distinct social groupings can have large impacts on the business of sport. In fact, the makeup of a sport's fan base not only affects television viewership but also links directly to both the salaries athletes can earn and the endorsement contracts they are offered.

Sport constitutes a significant portion of the U.S. economy, and the popularity of sports means that billions of dollars are generated each year. In 2017, Americans spent $100 billion on sports. Over half, $56 billion, included attending sporting events, with money spent on tickets, transportation, food, and beverages. The next sport expenditure, $33 billion, was on sports equipment, followed by gym memberships ($19 billion) (Kutz 2017). In 2016 the NFL, with income of $13 billion, led all other professional sports leagues in revenue (Kutz 2016). Also, in 2016, among colleges and universities, 24 schools had revenues of at least $100 million annually for their athletic departments (Gaines 2016).

After the stunning victory of Naomi Osaka over Coco Gauff in the 2019 U.S. Open Tennis Championship, Osaka invited her 15-year-old opponent to join her in the on court interview. When asked why she was willing to share the spotlight, Ms. Osaka remarked "I think it's better [for her] than going into the shower and crying." This tremendous moment of compassion is not unique among women athletes who regularly support each other both directly and indirectly. Even as access to sports for young women and girls is increasing, women athletes receive minimal media coverage across all sports leagues. During the same U.S. Open match, a 90-second spot aired discussing the problems associated with women's professional sports. In the ad, tennis great Billie Jean King pointed out that women athletes receive only 4% of all sports coverage. She invited viewers to use the hashtag #womenworthwatching to inspire others to watch and encourage female athletes (Beato 2019).

The same issues apply to scholarships, positions, and endorsements. While female athletes make up more than half of the college student athlete population, they get only 43% of NCAA athletic scholarship opportunities. In 2018–19, women received 62,225 fewer NCAA athletic positions than their male counterparts (NCAA 2019). Men received about 56% of NCAA support for college athletes, while women received 45% (NCAA 2019). These inequities continue into professional sports.

Coco Gauff of the U.S. celebrates her win over Anastasia Potapova of Russia during their first-round match of the women's 2019 U.S. Open tennis tournament August 27, 2019, in New York.

Shi Tang/Getty Images

U.S. athletes, primarily from the NFL or the NBA, accounted for the majority (62%) of the world's highest-paid athletes in 2019. Of these, over half (42) were Black, and 18 were White. Surprisingly, 11 were immigrants. There were only 4 Hispanics and no Asians were in this elite grouping. One woman—Serena Williams made it onto the list of the world's highest-paid athletes (see Table 9.1). Her earnings, at $29.2 million, made her 63 on this list out of 100. Four African American men—Russell Wilson, LeBron James, Stephen Curry, and Kevin Durant—were among the 10 highest-paid athletes in 2019. The top-grossing world athletes in 2019 were 3 male international soccer players (Forbes 2019).

The Intersection of Race and Class

The majority of college athletes (61%) are White, and they get the bulk of the athletic scholarships. At more prestigious colleges, this figure goes as high as 65%. In 2019, a scandal dubbed "Operation Varsity Blues" revealed a criminal conspiracy in which 53 people were charged with attempting to influence undergraduate admissions at several elite American universities. Thirty-three parents of potential students were accused of paying more than $25 million between 2011 and 2018 to inflate their children's entrance examination scores and bribe college officials. The organizer of the scheme, William Rick Singer, admitted "helping" children from as many as 750 families (Winter and Burke 2019). According to allegations, Singer bribed coaches to fill slots at the universities allocated for new players with his clients' children. Applicants would pose for pictures that showed them performing a sport, or their faces were digitally manipulated onto athletes' bodies to support their athletics-based applications (Lam and Fedschum 2019).

TABLE 9.1 ■ The World's Highest Paid Athletes			
	Name	**Pay**	**Sport**
1	Lionel Messi	127M	Soccer
2	Cristiano Ronaldo	109M	Soccer
3	Neymar	105M	Soccer
4	Canelo Alvares	94M	Boxing
5	Roger Federer	93.4M	Tennis
6	Russell Wilson	89.5M	Football
7	Aaron Rodgers	89.3M	Football
8	LeBron James	89M	Basketball
9	Stephen Curry	79.M	Basketball
10	Kevin Durant	65.4M	Basketball
63	Serena Williams	29.2M	Tennis

Source: "The World's Highest-Paid Athletes," *Forbes*, 2019.

Children get involved in sports from an early age.

iStock.com/Geber86

"Operation Varsity Blues" demonstrates that rather than sports being a level playing field, students of color are systematically disadvantaged. The systematic disadvantages include reliance on ACT/SAT test scores and legacy admissions at elite institutions that continually favor White upper-class admits (Byrd 2019). Ivy League universities such as Harvard privilege athletes for admissions. Consequently, athletes with a top academic score are 83% more likely to get an acceptance letter compared to just 16% of non-athletes with the same academic score. In fact, at 30 selective colleges, athletes were given a 48% advantage in admissions, compared to the 25% boost for legacies (children whose parents attended the school in question) and 18% for racial minorities (Desai 2018).

But race and gender disparities begin long before athletes enter college. Some believe that participation in sports is a way to keep kids engaged in school and off the streets. But the total number of high school athletes that participated in 11-player tackle football declined 6.6% in the period between 2008–09 and 2017–18 (Semuels 2019). Fueling this decline are recent studies that link brain damage, particularly chronic traumatic encephalopathy (CTE), to repeated blunt impacts like those that occur with head tackles in football. At least 21% of high school players are expected to develop CTE (Chen 2017).

The precipitous decline in football participation demonstrates the perceived choices available to different families. And these choices reflect the race/class divide as kids from mostly White upper-income communities in the Northeast, Midwest, and West are opting to play lacrosse or baseball, avoiding the potential for CTE and other injuries more common in contact sports. So while Whites continue to make up the largest number of youths playing tackle football, their proportion is shrinking. In 2018, of the 50,000 eighth-, tenth-, and twelfth-grade students, 44% were Black compared to 29% that were White (Semuels 2019).

Players, Coaches, and Owners

The intersections of race, class, sexuality, and gender are reflected in the biographies of successful athletes, coaches, and owners. An examination of these intersectional background structures demonstrates the unequal pathways into professional sports (Keating 2011). As we will see, these intersectional realities help us understand many of the variabilities associated with sports in this country.

Often when we speak of diversity, we are actually referencing binary constructions of diversity—that is, we are accounting for only two major racial or ethnic groups. A more realistic measure of diversity would be one that accounts for the a greater number of racial, ethnic, and gender groups.

Most professional sports are at least somewhat segregated by race, ethnicity, and gender.

In the 2018 NBA season, players of color dominated, as about 80% of players so identify, and the percentage of White players reached an all-time low at just under 30%. Only 9% of the managers in the league offices are people of color. Major League Baseball was the least diverse organization in 2018; only 42.5% of its players were people of color. The majority of the players of color were Latinx, constituting 31.9%, while African American players made up 7.7% (Tower 2018).

Only one professional sports league can truly be called international (see Figure 9.1). In 2019, Major League Men's Soccer (MLS) had the best overall record with respect to international people of color in professional sport, with 40.9%. MLS also has the largest number of international players (55.4%).

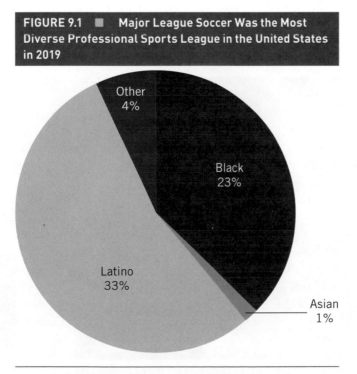

FIGURE 9.1 ■ Major League Soccer Was the Most Diverse Professional Sports League in the United States in 2019

Source: Data from "The 2019 Racial and Gender Report Card: Major League Soccer," Lapchick, Richard et al., November 13, 2019, page 6, https://43530132-36e9-4f52-811a-182c7a91933b.filesusr.com/ugd/7d86e5_de133092e061432aaf36518bf49436f8.pdf.

The Women's National Basketball Association (WNBA) has consistently been the leader with reference to racial and gender hiring practices in professional sports. In 2019, just under 50% of its professional-level staff positions were people of color. Five women and three African Americans were general managers. Just over 60% of assistant coaching positions, which often lead to head coaching positions, are held by women (Lapchick 2019).

The NBA has the most owners of color (43) and the most female owners (10) of all professional leagues. The NBA also has the highest number of coaches of color (33.3%). While there are 32 head coaches in the NFL, only four of them are people of color. This is in a league where 70 percent of the players are Black (Cornish 2020).

To address this, the National Football League mandated that the league develop a diverse pool of manager and general manager candidates. This was called the Rooney Rule, and it went into effect in 2003. The rule specifically requires teams to interview minority candidates for head coaching and senior football operation jobs. But a 2018 study documented that, for the 35 head coaching positions open in the NFL between 2013 and 2017, 29 went to White men, while only six were awarded to Black men. 22 interviews took place from 2013 to 2017, but only one Black candidate for the coach position had been interviewed. Alternatively, in cases (12 in total) where two or more Black coaches were in the pool of candidates, four (33%) were hired. During the same period, Black coaches were more likely to be fired than their White counterparts. Part of the issue is that while the Rooney Rule requires teams to interview at least one minority applicant, the approach does not address the underlying problems (Gibbs 2019).

It's important to note that the Rooney Rule does not apply to the offensive and defensive coordinators, or any other coaching positions that are logical feeders into the coaching pipeline

The NFL now has only three non-White head coaches: Anthony Lynn of the Los Angeles Chargers, shown here; Mike Tomlin of the Pittsburgh Steelers; and Ron Rivera of the Carolina Panthers.

Jayne Kamin-Oncea/Getty Images

(Gibbs 2019). For example, out of 80 positions, there were only two Black offensive coordinators in 2019. Also in the 2019 season, there were only four Black quarterback coaches across the entire league (Gibbs 2019). By 2020, there were only three coaches of color. Only by increasing the diversity of the lower rungs of the coaching ladder will there be changes in the diversity of head coaches.

In 1997, Bud Selig, then acting commissioner of baseball (he became commissioner in 1998), mandated that MLB create a diverse pool of managerial candidates in a manner similar to that which was later established in the NFL. In 2019, people of color comprised 23.2% of the senior executive-level positions. Professional staff in the MLB central office included 33.3% people of color, with 37.3% of the directors and managers being persons of color. In a league where 42% of the players are minorities, only 4 head coaches are persons of color (Lapchick 2019).

Critical Thinking

1. Why might different U.S. regions, such as the South, the North, the Southwest, and the Midwest, produce different interactions among race, gender, and sport? How might both history and economic conditions affect these differences?

2. Sport is significantly influenced by other institutions, such as educational and community organizations. How might changes in these institutions (values, structure, or resources) lead to the increased or decreased participation of various groups in sport?

3. How have the interactions among race, gender, and sport changed across the United States? What might be some future trends in sport, based on current demographic and other potential shifts? For example, how might fan bases influence trends?

4. Are you into sport? If so, is your interest as an athlete, as a fan, or a little of both? What sports are you active in (either as a fan or as a participant)? What intersectional factors, such as your race, gender, class, and family background, might account for your support of particular sports?

EXAMINING STOCK SOCIOLOGICAL THEORIES OF SPORT

The link between race and sport predates the actual sociology of sport, which has emerged as an academic field only in the past half-century. Scholarly interest in the field may be linked to the increasingly significant amount of time devoted to sports on television and other media, the development of professional sporting leagues, and the expansion of youth sports in local communities and educational institutions. There are four popular sociological theories about sport. Two pit biology and socialization against each other, with the biological viewpoint holding that certain groups are born with athletic abilities. The nurture perspective, in contrast, assumes that individuals are socialized into becoming, or not becoming, athletes. Other scholars, assuming either nature or nurture, have been more interested in the functions served by sport in society and how sport serves to perpetuate certain myths about the United States. Finally, scholars who take a critical perspective argue that sport is a by-product of the U.S. economic system, where group differences in athleticism associated with race, gender, and class are manipulated to preserve power differentials. These dominant theories, reinforced and promoted by media and popular culture, are our sport stock stories.

The Nature Perspective

We live in a time when many of our behaviors have been linked to specific sets of genes. It's not surprising, then, that in our competitive culture companies have capitalized on this by claiming they can help parents identify, through genetic testing, which sports their kids are biologically programmed to succeed in and then recommend specific workouts based on the children's "innate" skills. One company claims that it can determine which youths are more susceptible to concussions, heart attacks, and other health problems. Critics point out that the advice being offered by these companies, based on questionable genetic testing, is not only likely to be inaccurate but also may pose potential ethical issues and health threats (Stein 2011). Let's take a look at the science.

The **nature perspective** posits that biological differences between genders and among racial, cultural, and national groups account for variations in athletic ability, performance, and success. On the surface, the link between biology and sport seems logical. Of course, some might argue, certain people and groups are just more athletic than others. These common stereotypes about race, gender, and sport are supported by the larger social narrative that defines differences as rooted in biology. Biological determinism argues that human behavior, intelligence, and athleticism are determined by genetics or by some other aspects of physiology (such as brain size or body type). Accordingly, it argues that Blacks run faster, run longer, and jump higher than

Women are now emerging and finding success in traditionally male-dominated sports such as wrestling. Here, Joice da Silva of Brazil fights against Louise Marlouis of the United States in the Women's Freestyle 55kg during the 2011 Pan American Games in Guadalajara, Mexico.

Buda Mendes/LatinContent via Getty Images

Whites, but are genetically deficient in intelligence (Hall 2002, 114). No evidence, biological or otherwise, exists to support this linking of race, athleticism, and intelligence.

Research has found more than 200 genetic variants associated with physical performance, and more than 20 genetic variants associated with elite athletic status. Genetic variants may also be associated with particular injury risks and outcomes. While these associations may exist, to date no genetic variations have been identified that provide predictability in terms of either athletic success or injury risk outcomes (Guth and Roth 2013). Further research has concluded that there is no association between genotypes and elite competitive status (Coelho et al., 2016). Other sports scholars and researchers theorize that rather than nature, nurture accounts for athletic success and related outcomes.

The Nurture Perspective

The **nurture perspective** views gender, racial, cultural, and national group differences in athleticism as products of socialization and environment. A whole range of behaviors are socialized, including those associated with notions of meritocracy, teamwork, rule conformance, gender norms, and sportsmanship. For example, sport is a space where the best athletes are rewarded, and in theory these rewards are not associated with race, gender, or class.

For years, gender norms have been reinforced by gender segregation within individual sports. Women rarely compete directly with men in a given sport, a practice that reinforces gender norms. Women athletes are, however, consistently challenging these norms. Stock car racer Danica Patrick, winner of the 2008 Indy Japan 300 and third-place finisher in the 2009 Indianapolis 500, demonstrates that women can perform just as well as men in car racing. In 2003, professional golfer Annika Sörenstam decided to enter a PGA (men's) tournament. She faced a lot of backlash, but nevertheless, she competed.

The pushback that women encounter when they enter what are perceived to be male spaces in sport demonstrates how sport socialization tends to mirror the perceptions of sport within the wider community and nation. Major institutions, such as schools, media, teams, and local, state, and national government, use rewards and sanctions to reinforce this socialization (Sage and Eitzen 2015). Performing within a sport helps members learn how to obey rules, as they are rewarded when they accomplish acceptable tasks in acceptable ways and penalized when they violate these rules. Think for a moment about the following aspects of sport and how they reinforce rules:

- If a football player trips an opponent during a play, the player receives a foul for inappropriate or unfair behavior. The player has violated the rules—not only the rules of the game but also the rules of life.

- Sport teams and athletes are some of the most visible members of their schools and colleges, communities, and states.

- Team seasons, competitions, and rivalries structure our time in unique ways. There is March Madness, when college basketball teams vie for national honors, and bowl season, when college football dominates the airwaves and conversations. Baseball enthusiasts eagerly wait for spring training and the World Series. Then there are the Olympics, cheerleading competitions, fantasy bowls, and other competitions.

All of these aspects of sport provide opportunities for people to participate in a wide range of athletic activities. But participation is also to a great extent dictated by what is available within a community.

As we will examine in more depth, critical scholars have pointed out that sport socialization serves to preserve the dominant gender, racial, and class hierarchy. For example, fishing is typically cast as a male-dominated sport, and researchers have pointed out that women are rarely featured in fishing magazines. When they are depicted, usually in advertisements, they are often sexualized (their clothing and other "feminine" qualities are shown as obstacles to fishing for men) or they are presented as valued fishing companions for men (Carini and Weber 2015).

The links among race, nurture, and sport have also been demonstrated repeatedly. African American youth, compared to their White, Hispanic, and Asian counterparts, are more likely to receive encouragement to participate in sports from both family members and nonrelatives (Shakib and Veliz 2012). While there are more than 150 major league professional sports franchises in the United States, there is a significant lack of diversity among team ownership. Only six people of color serve as principle owners in the three biggest leagues in professional sports franchises. There are only two people of color among the principal owners of the NFL's 32 teams; they are Shahid Khan (Pakistani American), owner of the Jacksonville Jaguars, and Kim Pegula (Asian American), co-owner of the Buffalo Bills. Of the 30 NBA teams, three principal owners can be identified: Sacramento Kings owner Vivek Ranadivé (Native American), Marc

New West Point field logo.

Mike Lawrie/Getty Images

Lasray (Moroccan American), co-owner of the Milwaukee Bucks, and Michael Jordan (African American), owner of the Charlotte Hornets. Only one person of color is a principal owner in MLB: Arte Moreno (Mexican American), owner of the Anaheim Angels (Garcia 2018).

Critical theorists currently argue that **agency** (the capacity of individuals to make choices and to act independently given access, resources, and ability) interacts with sport in a process that links identities, nature, and nurture. This process recognizes that there are obvious biological differences among infants. These differences, related to motor skills and early childhood development, can have impacts later in life. Family and prenatal care can influence not only cognitive but also fine motor skills associated with sport. Lastly, if there is an environment, reflected in either culture or community, that values, encourages, and rewards athleticism, then we would expect outcomes to reflect those values. For example, we tend to encourage gender differences in sport and athleticism, and this produces obvious gendered differences associated with specific types of sports (Hofstede, Dignum, Prada, Student, and Vanhée 2015). In high schools, girls have 1.3 million fewer opportunities than boys have to be involved in sports. This leads to an increased likelihood that female athletes have to look outside both high school and college to be involved in sports, and such alternative options typically do not exist, or if they do, they cost more money than school sports participation (Women's Sports Foundation 2017).

Indeed, finances are the major factor accounting for youth participation in sports. At least 21% of children, those living in households with incomes below the federal poverty threshold, lack athletic opportunities. Children in families with less than $25,000 annual income, between the ages of 6 and 12, are nearly three times less likely to play some sport during the year, and half as likely to play team sports even for one day.

Some of the biggest losers might be girls. Girls who participate in athletics are significantly less likely to develop heart disease and breast cancer, have fewer unplanned pregnancies, are less likely to be obese, and have higher levels of body self-esteem. Female athletes are also markedly more likely to be successful as adults—four out of five female business executives were athletes as kids. They are more likely to go to college, and 25% more likely to go into politics (Flanagan 2017). The youth sports industry, now larger than professional baseball and close to the size of the NFL, is currently a $17 billion industry (Thompson 2018). Poverty, gender, and race need not be the total determinants of who gets to play what sports. There are some (almost) concealed stories about people who are helping to transform who gets to play.

CONCEALED STORY: SCHONE MALLIET

For over seven years, Schone Malliet, co-founder of the National Winter Sports Education Foundation (NWSEF), has helped to improve the chances of poor children of color by helping them engage and compete in winter sports. Malliet, born and raised in the projects in the Bronx, was introduced to skiing while in the Marine Corps by one of his squadron mates. He fell in love with the sport and joined the National Brotherhood of Skiers (NBS), which is comprised of African Americans. Across the country Malliet and the NWSEF build programs that allow urban youth to get the resources and coaching to engage in skiing and snowboarding. In recent years, over 1,000 kids have been able to ski for free. Of these participants, 85% come back to the program each year, demonstrating that, yes, Blacks can ski (Hall 2017).

The Functions of Sport

Functionalists believe that society is composed of a system of interrelated institutions that are structured according to the functions they perform (or the vital societal/community needs they fulfill). The **functionalist theory of sport** argues that sport fulfills a multitude of needs.

- Shared values: Sport both teaches and reinforces societal values. Parents encourage their children to play sports in the hopes that they will develop positive social values such as fair play, respect for others, and competition (Macri 2012).

- Life skills: Sport teaches and reinforces a set of core skills associated with moral development, social relationships, self-perception, motivation, and achievement. Ethics and good sportsmanship are considered vital, as they help individuals become good citizens who respect and abide by laws. Sport also teaches cooperation, respect for authority in the form of parents and coaches, and leadership (Weiss 2016).

- Socioemotional function: Sport helps individuals learn how to deal with conflict and anger management, encourages community bonding, and highlights the importance of rituals (Delaney 2015).

- Social mobility: Sport provides individuals and groups with opportunities to advance in socioeconomic status, both directly (through professional sport participation) and indirectly (through college scholarships) (Delaney 2015).

The principal critique of the functionalist theory of sport is that it tends to overemphasize the positive consequences of sport and assumes that all identity groups (race, class, and gender) benefit equally from sport. Proponents of this theory fail to grasp that sport is a social construction that preserves social hierarchies benefiting privileged individuals and groups while disadvantaging others.

Identity through Competition

Finally, the **symbolic interaction perspective on sport** posits that sports are created and maintained by shared meanings and social interaction. In other words, athletes' identities are formed as they participate in various sports and sport cultures. Sporting events are seen as ritual contests in which individuals seek to obtain heroic or iconic status. Competition provides order and control for these identities and various communities. For example, when the head coach of Auburn University's women's basketball team, Nell Fortner, walked onto the court for her first game in 2004, there were just 200 people in the stands. By 2012, when she left Auburn, her team was attracting crowds in excess of 12,000. Under Fortner, Auburn won the Southeastern Conference championship in 2009—the first time Auburn had won since 1989. Women's basketball is now the most popular team sport at Auburn. The fans come out in numbers because they want to see winners, and Auburn's success has helped to advance the profile of women's basketball nationally (Robinson 2017).

As various identity groups challenge the stereotypical assumptions that relegate them to subservient positions within sport, many have called into question the basic premises of the symbolic interaction perspective. The principal critique of the symbolic interaction perspective is that it provides limited ability to understand structural processes that create, maintain, and perpetuate inequalities among various identity groups (Giulianotti 2016). Consider the women coaches who are currently challenging gendered stereotypes by coaching men's teams:

- Kathryn Smith: In 2016 she became the first woman to hold the position of full-time assistant coach in the NFL.

- Nancy Lieberman: One of the greatest women's basketball players in history, she became the first woman to coach a professional men's team as coach of the NBA Development League team of the Texas Legends in 2009.

- Bernadette Mattox: She made NCAA history as the first female assistant coach in Division I men's basketball.

Among executives, Kim Ng is the highest-ranking female executive in Major League Baseball as general manager of the Miami Marlins. Sarah Thomas became the first woman to officiate a bowl game, and the first hired by the NFL in 2015 (Radcliffe 2018). In 2019, Thomas became the first women to referee an NFL playoff game.

We are left with the conclusion that while stock theories on sport do provide some insight, they leave much unanswered. For the rest of the picture, we turn to the matrix approach to sport.

Critical Thinking

1. Clearly sport fulfills some useful functions within society. But in what ways do these functions reflect values specific to certain geographical areas? How might historical factors help explain the potential differences between these areas? More specifically, in what ways might history within specific areas, communities, or schools have impacts on who plays and what sports they might engage in?

2. Both the nature and nurture perspectives on sport seem to offer plausible arguments. But how might institutions such as family, school and community environment, and culture affect athleticism? What impact might sport have on the likelihood that an individual will be successful, marry, and have kids? What does this suggest about how sport may influence genetic outcomes? (For example, if society placed a great value on tallness, would this lead to more tall people getting married and therefore propagating?)

3. Symbolic interactionism argues that how we interact with sport symbols and images can affect how sport is perceived or valued. How does this symbolic interaction reflect cultural values? How might identities, as reflected in cultural, gendered, class, or school

values, affect how sport is perceived? How might this account for the differences in athleticism associated with gender, race, and class?

4. In what ways do you believe your athleticism or lack thereof might be associated with nature or nurture?

APPLYING THE MATRIX TO SPORTS IN THE UNITED STATES

The matrix of race, class, and gender operates throughout the institution of sport. Geographic and social locations and identities across time influence how sport and athleticism develop, which groups and identities become involved, and the ways in which these intersections might serve to facilitate change.

The stock story of U.S. sports has been central to our national narrative. However, our concealed stories reveal the historical, political, cultural, and social processes that have shaped the development of sport in the United States. What this history reveals is that for some, sport has provided access to the American Dream. Racial, ethnic, class, and gendered groups have frequently used sport as a means of social mobility when other pathways were blocked. However, sport can be a source of both resistance and transformative change, as individuals and groups engaged in sport use their status to effect changes both within sport and in the wider society.

Analyzing Space and Place: Early American Sports Narratives

From the earliest point in U.S. history, sports blended the cultural and athletic traditions of Native Americans and European immigrants. Each new immigrant group arriving in North America brought along its own sporting traditions, which were absorbed and transformed to produce a unique American sport culture (Crawford 2013, 1–2). When Europeans settled the Americas, indigenous peoples, comprising as many as 500 separate nations, were actively engaged in a range of sport and game activities, including many that provided children with life experiences that would help them develop the competencies and experiences necessary for survival.

Sports and the Colonists

Several variations in sport and athleticism can be identified across U.S. regions and across historical times. Religious attitudes within the American colonies governed the recreational activities considered proper for men and women. In the North, elite White women were encouraged to participate in ice skating, while Southern women were expected to develop equestrian skills. Other recreational activities for women included dancing, quilting, and swimming. Women were also expected to be spectators at both horse and boat races (Borish 2014).

Puritans, believing that time was a sacred gift not to be wasted, condemned all sport (Daniels 1995). The Protestant Dutch in New York were more liberal, however, and allowed for bowling, golf, and boat and horse racing. The Quakers of Pennsylvania banned boxing but did allow those sports deemed useful and necessary for recreation, such as swimming, skating, hunting, and fishing.

The 19th-century Southern planters modeled themselves on European nobility and attempted to duplicate their leisure activities. Within this culture, horse racing became a major sport. Fox and quail hunting and bloody sports such as bare-knuckle boxing and eye-gouging fights were also frequent events. All of these sport activities were associated with heavy gambling, where generations of wealth could be won or lost in a single match (Zirin 2000). Through gambling, Southern elite gentlemen asserted their manliness while distinguishing themselves from poorer Whites and Black slaves (Carroll 2003). Sport not only helped reinforce the White gentry's values, but it also served to distinguish them from subordinate groups. Sporting venues quickly became the places where politics, economics, and culture were controlled. In many ways, sport became a proxy for power in the South (Crawford 2013).

Race, Gender, and Early American Sports

Slaves, both male and female, were often the featured attractions providing entertainment and profit to the Southern plantation elite (Gems, Borish, and Pfister 2008). And while boxing and other sports provided Black slaves with entertainment and momentary escape from the harsh realities of slavery, for some they provided a more direct route to emancipation (Harris 2000).

Black women, regardless of their status, found that sport could be a means of rebellion. Many slave women excelled at swimming, which they often did in the nude, a practice that tended to go against religious prohibitions (Gems et al., 2008, 24). For Northern White females, the bicycle became an instrument of rebellion. After the Civil War, women's colleges were a vanguard in this movement. Schools offered athletic options that included bicycle races. The bicycle became a symbol of women's liberation and resistance for suffragists such as Elizabeth Cady Stanton, Susan B. Anthony, and other feminists during the late 19th century (LaFrance 2014).

Latinx and Hispanics have also had an impact on sports within the United States. From 1519 to 1700, the Spanish imported cattle and horses and established ranches throughout the South and the Southwest. Cattle ranching became a dominant economic activity as early as the 1700s in Texas, Arizona, and New Mexico. The vaqueros (cowboys—the term is derived from *vaca,* the Spanish word for cow) on these ranches developed a range of skills using ropes made from braided rawhide, as well as skills in horsemanship, and they showed off these skills by competing with each other at rodeos, which were held to celebrate the annual cattle round-ups. Rodeos became popular throughout the West and Southwest, and "Wild West" shows featuring some of the most famous rodeo stars toured the country through much of the 1890s (Alamillo 2013).

Institutionalizing Sport: Industrialization, Immigration, and Team Sports

Theorists employing a matrix or intersectional approach have characterized sport as a mirror of capitalist society and have examined how sport has increasingly become globally commercialized. A matrix analysis of sport demonstrates that sporting events are more than media representations or cultural products. They become major institutional spaces where race, class, and

Tom Molineux (1784–1818), born into slavery, was possibly the first heavyweight bare-knuckle boxing champion in the United States. Starting on the Virginia plantation of his birth, he often would fight fellow slaves while plantation owners placed wagers on the outcomes. After a particularly successful boxing match, for which his owner took in $100,000 in prize money (equivalent to about $1 million today), Molineux was granted his freedom and given $500 (equivalent to about $11,000 today).

Schomburg Center for Research in Black Culture, Photographs and Prints Division, The New York Public Library. (3 October 1811). The battle between Crib (Cribb) and Molineaux. Retrieved from http://digitalcollections.nypl.org/items/510d47df-bb84-a3d9-e040-e00a18064a99.

gender intersections are manifested. The club movement served to preserve and magnify sport and race, class, and gender hierarchies.

The Club Movement

Industrialism encouraged increased immigration from Europe and spurred the **club movement** in the United States. The team sports that we know today developed out of this early movement, in which elite White ethnics formed exclusive clubs in urban industrial areas to promote group identity and enhance status. Typically, as these new ethnic groups entered the urban industrial centers, they were met with either acceptance or rejection. Immigrants from England, Scotland, and Wales tended to be more acceptable within the status communities of racialized White elites. These elite clubs tended to exclude Catholics, Jews, and women as part of an unwritten and often unspoken agreement among White Anglo-Saxon Protestant (WASP) men to preserve White male privilege and racial exclusion (Kendall 2008). Lower-status White ethnics, from other European countries such as Ireland, Italy, and Poland, responded by creating their own status clubs, which were closely linked to sports. Thus was born the sports club movement.

The sports club movement was a means by which lower-status White ethnics could gain elite status. The first sports clubs in the United States were formed by these groups. Cricket, racquetball, and yacht clubs welcomed young men who shared an interest in various sports, and club membership became a principal means of status enhancement. Massive immigration and the perception that the United States was being swamped by the swarthy, unwashed masses led sports clubs to emphasize their aristocratic British cultural connections and lineage; thus they began introducing golf in the 1890s (Starn 2006). Golf courses and club facilities emulated aristocratic gardens and manor houses (Ceron-Anaya 2010).

Baseball and the American Dream

Baseball, considered by many to be the quintessential American game, has been far from a "field of dreams" for people of color. In the early 1850s, like its probable forerunner, cricket, the game was essentially a source of entertainment for middle-class White males. As industrialism and urbanization brought increasing numbers of immigrants to the United States, this rural pastime became part of the urban landscape and a form of escape. Baseball allowed many urban residents to imagine a more rural existence. Played in park-like settings with green fields and plenty of fresh air, it evoked images of a safe, secure haven from the harsh world. Baseball was from its inception a male-dominated sport with definite racial overtones (Kimmel 2005, 64). The historical view of baseball as a homogenized space where middle-class White males could be legitimated and glorified held sway up until the 1960s (Butterworth 2007).

The first baseball club originated in 1845 in Manhattan, when a group of young firefighters formed the Knickerbocker Baseball Club. Blue-collar workers were the mainstay viewers of the game until increased admission prices, lack of accessibility, and elimination of Sunday games transformed the audience to middle-class workers by the 1860s. The national leagues that developed continued to draw their players primarily from new immigrants and their audience from the White middle class until the late 1940s. This changed with the advent of World War II, when, for the first time, fans saw both Blacks and women on the field. Once these groups appeared on the national scene, it was too late to put them back in the bleachers or on the sidelines.

As many as 55 professional Black baseball teams existed from 1883 to 1898. Interestingly, about half of Black players in that period were part of these all-Black teams, while the remainder played on integrated teams. From the end of the Civil War until 1890, a number of Blacks played alongside Whites in both minor and major baseball league teams (Kleinknecht 2017). When the National Association of Base Ball Players was formed in 1867, it formally banned all Black players. Despite this ban, as late as the 1870s several Black players were still active on mostly White minor league teams, and some persisted longer. In 1883, Moses "Fleetwood" Walker, from Oberlin College, signed with the Toledo, Ohio, team in the Northwestern League and became the first Black to play in a major league franchise. In the same year, another Black player, John W. "Bud" Fowler, a veteran of 10 years, signed with the Northwestern League. Even these slots were soon lost, however, when segregation became law and increased hostility toward Black, Hispanic, Asian, and other racial minority athletes became rampant. By the end of the 19th century, the ban on Black players in baseball was firmly established (Pennington 2006). Rather than admit defeat, Blacks and other athletes of color continued to play, but were often segregated into their own leagues. The first Black professional team, the Cuban Giants, was formed in 1885. Ironically, there were no Cubans or Hispanics on the team.

The story of baseball, with minor alterations, mirrors what was also happening in football, basketball, and other team sports. Therefore, as we move into the 20th century, segregated sports (by race, gender, and class) can be identified.

Identities and Resistance

Critical race theorists stress that confronting race and racism is central to any analysis of sport. This perspective argues that sport is a central social process that regularly legitimates, modifies, and re-creates racial hegemony. Critical race theory also aims to combat racial hegemony within sport, while at the same time recognizing that race is a social construction (Hylton 2010). Within sport, racism both dehumanizes and legitimates the racial "other." Thus, while the members of a given group might be the objects of racial derision, their participation in sport might also reconstruct or legitimate certain racial stereotypes.

The Legacy of Civil Rights

The civil rights movement of the mid-20th century had significant impact on sport in the United States. Through legislation, court actions, and organized efforts, the movement helped to abolish many of the formal mechanisms of racial discrimination. Almost every institutional sphere was affected, including sport.

As a registered conscientious objector, Black heavyweight boxing champion Cassius Clay repeatedly drew attention to racial injustices prevalent in the United States.

After converting to Islam, Cassius Clay changed his name to Muhammad Ali. One of his first announcements after his conversion concerned his objection to the Vietnam War: "I'm expected to go overseas to help free people in South Vietnam and at the same time my people here [African Americans] are being brutalized and mistreated, and this is really the same thing that's happening in Vietnam" (quoted in Hunt 2006, 285).

Critical scholars researching sport also became highly successful in bringing about change. Harry Edwards, political activist and scholar, was a key participant in a protest at the 1968 Olympic Games. Edwards concluded that U.S. sport needed a wake-up call to address the long-standing racism that existed. He called for Black athletes to boycott the 1968 Olympics and other sports activities to dramatize the racial inequities and obstacles confronting Blacks. But during a period of heightened racial awareness, Black athletes could not simply quit and be labeled as "failures." Instead, during the medal awards ceremony for track and field, U.S. gold and bronze medalists John Carlos and Tommie Smith raised their fists as they stood on podium.

Women and the Impact of Title IX

Taking an intersectional approach to sports reveals that while sport can be transformative, it can also uphold some of our nation's most blatant forms of discrimination. By age 14 girls withdraw from sport at twice the rate of boys. This is for a myriad of reasons, including barriers to participation that include lack of access, social stigmas, and lack of positive role models. When we add race, low socioeconomic status, disability, inadequate or inappropriate cultural coaching, non-segregated activities, lack of equipment, prejudice, and

On Dec. 3, 1943, singer/actor Paul Robeson headed a group of Blacks who met with baseball commissioner Kennesaw Mountain Landis and Major League owners at the Roosevelt Hotel in New York. After being introduced Robeson remarked: "The time has come when you must change your attitude toward Negros... Because baseball is a national game, it is up to baseball to see that discrimination does not become an American pattern. And it should do this this year" (Robeson 1978,152). Here, supporters of integrating Major League Baseball march in a May Day parade.

Science History Images/Alamy Stock Photo

non-inclusive practices, the barriers to participation for young women only become more severe (Moore 2017).

It is only in the last two generations that young women in the United States have been able to grow up actively engaged in sports. In 1972, President Richard M. Nixon signed into law the landmark U.S. Education Amendments, including **Title IX**, which declared that "No person in the United States shall, on the basis of sex, be excluded from participation in, be denied the benefits of, or be subjected to discrimination under any program or activity receiving federal financial assistance." The impact of Title IX was profound. In 1971, before it became law, fewer than 295 females participated in high school varsity athletics. This was just under 7% of all high school athletes. By 2001, a total of 2.8 million or 41.5% of all high school varsity athletes were females.

By 2012, the number of females in high school and college sports had grown to 3,373,000 (Dangerfield and Barra 2012; TitleIX.info n.d..a). Title IX did not solve gender inequities in sports, however. Today, roughly 28% of total money spent on high school and college athletes goes to women, and colleges spend 31% of recruiting dollars and 42% of athletic scholarship money on women (TitleIX.info n.d..a).

In 1972, prior to the implementation of Title IX, the overwhelming number of women's teams head coaching positions were held by women (90%). Title IX, which forced colleges and universities to provide the same amount of funding for female athletics as it did for males, led to a significant increase in the number of female college athletes. Unfortunately, this same act led to just the opposite impact for female head coaches. As more money poured into women's sports programs, universities began to pay coaches significantly higher salaries. This meant that more men began applying and being hired as coaches for women's teams. Currently, women hold less than half of the head coaching jobs for women's teams (Elsesser 2019). If we consider all eight conferences, there is an even more stark reality. While White coaches comprised just under 90% of all head coaching positions, just over 12% were coaches of color. Among these, 6.9% were African American, 2.8% were Latinx, 2.2% were Asian, and less than 1% were Hawaiian/Pacific Islanders. Only 18.2% of the women's teams were coached by coaches of color (Caple, Lapchick, and LaVoi 2017).

Increasing Diversity

In the 2018 Winter Olympics, Team USA was one of the most diverse teams in history. Forty-five percent of the team members were females. The team also consisted of ten African Americans, eleven Asian Americans and, for the first time, two openly gay athletes. Four of the five members of the U.S. women's bobsled team were women of color (Chappell and Mayes 2018). Approximately 6% of the 178 Olympians that participated in the 2018 games were immigrants. Even more significant were the 12 nations who were represented exclusively by foreign-born athletes, including Nigeria, Tonga, Bermuda, and Thailand. And during these games, Team USA athletes of diverse backgrounds made some remarkable contributions to our efforts. Mirai Nagasu, the child of Japanese immigrants and restaurateurs, became the first American woman to land a triple axel (when a skater completes 3.5 rotations before landing successfully) in the Olympics. Another descendant of recent immigrants is Chloe Kim. Known as the "Queen of Snow," Chloe won a gold medal in the women's halfpipe finals. Lastly, Maame Biney, who was born in Ghana, became the first Black woman to qualify for a U.S. Olympic speed skating team (Scott 2018).

At the college level, gay coaches and athletes often fly under the raider, but their stories show both resistance and resilience. The number of openly gay coaches reached 39 across all college levels, with 24 publicly declaring their sexuality just last year (Hall 2018).

This is a 62.5% increase over the previous year, when there were 24 publicly out LGBTQ college coaches. During the same school year, a total of 76 college athletes were publicly out as LGBTQ. These coaches and athletes demonstrate that you can be a successful coach and athlete and still be involved in activism, community, and the institutions that you serve (Hall 2018).

RESISTANCE STORY: MEGAN RAPINOE

Megan Rapinoe poses with her individual awards at the end of the 2019 Women's World Cup final soccer match between the U.S. and The Netherlands.

Alex Grimm/Getty Images

Megan Rapinoe is the two-time World Cup champion and co-captain of the United States women's national soccer team. She has a long history of combining sports and social activism. Rapinoe used her 2016 victory to kneel in support of the Black Lives Matter protest started by NFL former quarterback Colin Kaepernick. Rapinoe is also a staunch advocate for closing the gender pay gap and ensuring equal rights for members of the LGBTQ community. In 2019 Rapinoe became one of just four women ever declared the Sportsperson of the Year by *Sports Illustrated*. True to form, she used the ceremony honoring her to criticize *Sports Illustrated* for its poor record covering women athletes. She also castigated FIFA, soccer's governing body, for paying women athletes less than men, despite the winning record of American women (Kelley 2019).

In 2019 you would have had to look hard to find a single LGBTQ professional athlete in the NHL, NBA, MLB, NFL, and WWE. This does not mean that none have ever existed, but they have tended to be less open or public about their sexual identity. Some notable exceptions do exist. Major League Baseball outfielder Glenn Burke became the first openly gay player in MLB history; he played for the Los Angeles Dodgers and Oakland Athletics from 1976 to 1979. The first openly gay NFL player was Michael Sam, who came out in his senior year at the University of Missouri and was drafted by the St. Louis Rams in 2014. Jason Collins, who played 13 seasons for the NBA between 2001 and 2014, came out in 2013 publicly. Darren Young, who fought numerous bouts for the WWE between 2005 and 2010, became the first openly gay professional wrestler in 2013. Currently, free agent Ryan Russell, who has played in the past for the Tampa Bay Buccaneers, is the only openly bisexual or gay male athlete in all of U.S. professional sports (Gameday News 2019).

Critical Thinking

1. In what ways might either geography or history affect how sport is perceived and received? What does this suggest regarding our attitudes toward sport?

2. How does sport, or participating in sport, affect other institutions? How might other institutions affect sport?

3. How might sport affect an individual's identity? In what ways might this sport identity be influenced by other identities, such as race, class, and gender? How might differences in regional or community values influence these identities?

4. How has sport affected your life? What kinds of racial messages have been associated with your contacts with sport? What does this suggest about you, race, and sport?

CREATING A NEW PLAYING FIELD

Sport is an important institution within the United States. It not only provides needed exercise and opportunities but also helps stimulate change within both local communities and the wider society. How different athletes use their status in sport can enhance the visibility of often marginalized members within society.

The Role of Agency and Resistance

Much of our understanding of agency (i.e., sense of control, the ability to initiate, execute, and control one's actions, particularly to effect change) and resistance within sports is derived from personal narratives of athletes and coaches. Their stories have generated our knowledge of homophobia, sexism, racism, and ethnocentrism in sport. These narratives also help us understand how we can create more tolerance within our communities, our institutions, and, ultimately, our society. They demonstrate how individuals have been able to transform not only how they perceive themselves but also how their identities are perceived and received within the wider community. These stories show that racial identities are not fixed and one-dimensional; rather, they are fluid and multifaceted (Iannotta and Kane 2002).

Athletes and Activism

Laura Ingraham, conservative television host on Fox News, criticized the political activism of NBA star LeBron James when she challenged him to just "shut up and dribble." In fact, many believe that the sole purpose of athletes is to perform; they fail to realize the long history of activism, particularly among athletes of color (Carter 2019). Political activism among athletes, such as Colin Kaepernick's protests against police violence, often mobilizes other Black Americans to political activism (Towler, Crawford, and Bennett 2019).

In southern Colorado in 2019, athletes of the Ignacio High School girls' basketball team were photographed wearing face paint to call attention to the Missing and Murdered Indigenous Women (MMIW) movement. Most of the players are members of the Southern Ute tribe. The face paint colors have symbolic meanings. The red handprint symbolizes the only color, according to some Native American folklore, that the spirits can see. The hand over the mouth symbolizes giving voice to those who have been displaced. Of the 5,712 missing and murdered indigenous women and girls reported in 2016, only 116 were entered into the U.S. Department of Justice database (Ploen 2020). The action of these young women demonstrates a history not only of continuous resistance but also of the agency through which various intersectional groups have challenged and attempted to transform their communities and society as a whole.

Creating Opportunities for Girls

Gender continues to be ignored in much of our conversations about sports, and this is especially true of girls of color. We have learned that girls of color face diminished sports opportunities from the earliest ages through college. These diminished opportunities are associated with highly segregated schools that reflect both racial and economic inequalities. These inequalities typically result in fewer resources for both academic and extracurricular activities like athletics. Forty-two percent of our public schools are either 90% White or more, or over 90% minority. Of those minority schools, 40% have large female opportunity gaps when compared to 16% of heavily White schools. This is important because as we have learned, sports play a critical role in self-esteem, physical and mental development, and economic opportunities. Policymakers at all levels (federal, state, and local) must redouble efforts to increase the opportunities for girls of color to participate in playing sports. Enforcing Title VI and Title IX, particularly for girls of color, would enhance the availability of equitable educational resources to include athletic opportunities to all school districts (.Graves, Chaunchry et al. 2015).

Transgender Athletes

What constitutes gender? And how is this question complicated by transgender athletes? For the last half-decade Olympic gold medalist Caster Semenya has been a central figure in this conversation. A Swiss court has forbid the South African runner the opportunity to defend her 800-meter title unless she adheres to requirements passed by the sport's governing body, the International Association of Athletics Federation (IAAF). The requirement is that all intersex athletes like Semenya take testosterone-suppressing drugs. This ruling might influence the 20 states and the District of Columbia that prohibit against transgender students in athletic programs. Currently, the Department of Education's Office of Civil Rights is investigating if these policies violate Title IX by allowing transgender athletes to compete with cisgender students. And while there is no evidence that cisgender or transgender athletes have an unfair advantage, such actions pose threats to their continued access to sports (Stern 2019).

Transforming Stock Stories through Acts of Resistance

We have all heard the stock story that Native Americans are not offended when sports teams use Native American mascots or chants in general (Annenberg Public Policy Center 2004; Cox, Clement and Vargas 2016). The reality is that as many as two-thirds of Native Americans who frequently identify with and participate in tribal and cultural practices take offense to such actions and mascots (Wadley 2020).

Beginning with the 1960s Native American Civil Rights movement, a number of highly publicized and effective protests have been orchestrated by Native Americans and their

Jesse Owens, by taking four gold medals in 1936, destroyed Hitler's myth of Aryan supremacy. Tommie Smith and John Carlos, raising their fists, asserted the importance of all humans as they took the gold medals in 1968. In 1988, the world was shocked as Jamaican bobsledders became internationally famous with their entry into the Olympics. And in Rio 2016, Ibtihaj Muhammad (pictured) became the first U.S. athlete to compete in the Olympics wearing a hijab.

Ezra Shaw/Getty Images Sport/Getty Images

supporters. These protests targeted the use of mascots, the tomahawk chop, and war chants (King 2010). Although the numbers have dropped, sports teams from the professional levels down to Little League teams continue to use Native American mascots. While no exact counts exist, the most prevalent Native American team name is "Indians," ranking among the top 10 for high schools (Brown and Kraus 2019).

Hundreds of resistance stories have transformed our stock stories. Different types of protest can change not only the conversation but also the system that justifies the use of dehumanizing stereotypes. For example, in 2019, high school students in Salt Lake City successfully protested and renamed their "Redmen" mascot to "Reds." And even when a Utah legislator proposed a resolution to discourage schools from renaming mascots involving Native Americans, several dozen protestors showed up to ensure that the bill did not pass (Associated Press 2020). Change can come about, but only if we act as agents willing to change the story.

Critical Thinking

1. How does participation in sports affect racial identity? How does racial identity affect perceived competency in different sports? Some racial groups participating in sports appear to have different outcomes when it comes to college graduation. How might gender or class or even type of sport influence these outcomes?

2. Over time different racial groups appear to dominate particular sports. In what ways might this be a result of racial hierarchies operant within society, in different geographic areas, or in different historical periods? What does this suggest regarding the social construction of sport?

3. Sport provides many different types of opportunities and challenges for athletes. In what ways is racial identity reflected in these opportunities and challenges?

4. What might you do to effect changes in the institution of sport? As a student? As a consumer? As an athlete?

CHAPTER SUMMARY

9.1 Explain the state of sport in the United States.

Clear gender and racial hierarchies are reflected in what sports are played by whom, who is most rewarded (in terms of both income and endorsement deals), and who makes up the fan bases. Clearly the gendered segregation of sports has implications for both viewers and endorsement deals, accounting for the small number of women among the athletes who earn the highest salaries (just 2 of the top 100 earners are women). Also, the fact that males dominate in viewership explains to some extent their much higher levels of pay and their more lucrative endorsement contracts. Once we consider these, we are still left with the fact that only one professional sports league, Major League Soccer, is truly diverse; most national professional leagues have high concentrations of players in one or two racial groups.

9.2   Compare stock theories about U.S. sport.

Four theoretical perspectives have traditionally been supported regarding U.S. sport: the nature perspective, the nurture perspective, the functionalist perspective, and the symbolic interactionist perspective. These represent stock stories, or the standard justifications that are used to explain the prevalence of sport and athleticism. The nature argument posits that biology and talent account for athleticism and sport development within specific groups and across the nation. The nurture perspective argues that environment, culture, and socialization explain how athletes and sport develop. Research indicates that both nature and nurture are significant but not sufficient to account for athletic ability and sport development. Functionalist theory explains the development of sport in terms of the vital or important needs accomplished by sport. These functions include shared values, life skills, socioemotional functions, and social mobility. The limitations of this theory include its overemphasis on the positive consequences of sport and its failure to account for unequal results for race, class, and gendered groups, and how sport serves to preserve inequalities. Symbolic interaction investigates the shared meanings that are created and maintained within sport, communities, and athletes. These shared meanings help produce sport cultures that replicate rituals, create sport heroes, and symbolically link sport to the community. Symbolic interaction provides limited insight into the structural processes that create, preserve, and distribute inequalities among various identity groups within sport. Collectively, while providing some insight into sport and athleticism, traditional stock theories offer a limited understanding regarding sport and athleticism.

9.3   Apply the matrix approach to sport.

The matrix, with its focus on intersectional differences, helps fill the gaps in our understanding of how sport and athleticism create institutions that have differential impacts on racial, class, and gendered groups within U.S. society. The perspective anticipates that geographic and social locations, identities across time, and agency provide necessary insights into how this process operates. Institutional analysis demonstrates that sport and sporting events produce media and cultural products. Through these processes race, class, and gender interactions are manifested. Space and place concerns within the matrix approach highlight the importance of geographical and historical spaces that affect social identities within sport. Identities are constantly affected by sports as they legitimate, modify, and re-create racial hegemonies. Finally, both agency and resistance have been demonstrated by multiple individuals and groups who have utilized their status within sport to transform both sport and the nation. An examination of U.S. sport through time reveals many concealed stories. Native Americans, long before European colonization, were active creators of sport and games. Most of these were directly associated with the needs of hunting and gathering communities. Consequently, stick games, racing, hunting, and archery were frequently vital parts of youth socialization. Industrialization served to transform the U.S. sport landscape as it drew an increasingly large number of immigrants and others into the urban centers. One of the significant outcomes of this transformation was the rise in team sports. From the early 19th century, elite sport clubs catering to White ethnics were established throughout the Northeast. Baseball and other team sports were soon to follow.

9.4 Describe strategies for transforming the institution of sport.

Transformative stories are possible as athletes both individually and collectively push for change. But this change just does not happen, it must be concerted, deliberate, and continuous. In many cases concerted efforts to discourage resistance must be overcome. In the process, we are able to transform our stock stories. Different types of protest, targeting different aspects of the sport structures, can cause us to reflect on, engage with, and critically evaluate the system that justifies dehumanizing others through stereotypes. Change can come about, but only if we act as agents willing to change the story.

KEY TERMS

agency	nurture perspective
club movement	sport
functionalist theory of sport	symbolic interaction perspective on sport
nature perspective	Title IX

REFERENCES

Alamillo, José M. 2013. "Beyond the Latino Sports Hero: The Role of Sports in Creating Communities, Networks, and Identities." American Latino Theme Study, National Park Service. Accessed April 10, 2013. http://www.nps.gov/Latino/Latinothemestudy/sports.htm.

Amritt, Carl. 2017. "A Quick History Lesson on Voter Disenfranchisement." Roosevelt Institute. https://rooseveltinstitute.org/2017/05/22/a-quick-history-lesson-on-voter-disenfranchisement/

Annenberg Policy Center.2004. "Most Indians Say Name of Washington "Redskins" Is Acceptable While 9 Percent Call It Offensive." Accessed online at URL: https://www.annenbergpublicpolicycenter.org/most-indians-say-name-of-washington-redskins-is-acceptable-while-9-percent-call-it-offensive/

Associated Press 2020. "Utah American Indian mascot change resolution draws protests." *Modesto Bee.* Access online at URL: https:\www.modbee.com\news\politics-government\national-politics\article239658688.html.

Beato, Kendra Nordin 2019. "More women are playing sports. Why is no one watching?" *The Christian Science Monitor.* Accessed online at URL: https:\www.csmonitor.com\The-Culture\2019\0909\More-women-are-playing-sports.-Why-is-no-one-watching.

Borish, Linda J. 2014. "Women in American Sport History." In *A Companion to American Sport History,* edited by Steven A. Riess. Chichester: John Wiley.

Brown, Xanni and Michael Kraus 2019. "When the School Is a Native American Stereotype". *Insights.* Accessed online at URL: https:\insights.som.yale.edu\insights\when-the-school-mascot-is-native-american-stereotype.

Butterworth, Michael L. 2007. "Race in 'The Race': Mark McGwire, Sammy Sosa, and Heroic Constructions of Whiteness." *Critical Studies in Media and Communication* 24, no. 3: 228–44.

Byrd, Carson 2019. "Varsity blues and Lawsuits." Context. Accessed online at URL: https:\contexts.org\blog\varsity-blues-and-lawsuits-too\#wong

Caple, N., R., Lapchick, N. M. LaVoi, 2017. "Gender, race, and LGBT inclusion of head". *Tucker Center: Regents of the University of Minnesota.* accessed at URL: https:\www.cehd.umn.edu\tuckercenter\library\docs\research\2017_Title_IX_at_45_Report.pdf.

Carini, Robert M., and Jonetta D. Weber. 2015. "Female Anglers in a Predominantly Male Sport: Portrayals in Five Popular Fishing-Related Magazines." *International Review for the Sociology of Sport* 52, no. 1: 45–60.

Carroll, Bret E., 2003. *American Masculinities: A Historical Encyclopedia.* Thousand Oaks, CA: Sage.

Carter, Dylan Hunter 2019. "Study: Athlete activism increased African American activism". *Global Sport Matters.* Accessed at URL: https:\globalsportmatters.com\culture\2019\09\25\study-athlete-activism-increased-african-american-activism\.

Ceron-Anaya, Hugo. 2010. "An Approach to the History of Golf: Business, Symbolic Capital, and Technologies of the Self." *Journal of Sport and Social Issues* 34, no. 3: 339–58.

Chappell, Bill and Brittany Mayes 2018. "Bigger Than Ever, and More Diverse: Team USA at the 2018 Winter Olympics." *NPR.* Accessed at URL: https:\www.npr.org\sections\thetorch\2018\02\09\583565914\bigger-than-ever-and-more-diverse-team-usa-at-the-2018-winter-olympics.

Chappell, Bob. 2001. "Race, Ethnicity and Sport." In *The Sociology of Sport and Physical Education: An Introductory Reader,* edited by Anthony Laker. New York: Routledge Falmer.

Coelho, Daniel, Eduardo Pimenta, Izinara Rosse, Christiano Venerosa, Lenice K. Becker, Maria Raquel Santos Carvalho, Guilherme de Azambuja Pussieldi, and Emerson Silami Garcia. 2016. "The Alpha-Actinin-3 R577X Polymorphism and Physical Performance of Soccer Players." *Biology of Sport* 56, no. 3: 241–48.

Cornish, Audie 2020. "NFLPA's DeMaurice Smith on Pro Football Head Coaching Diversity". *NPR.* Accessed online at URL: https:\www.npr.org\2020\01\16\797098345\nflpas-demaurice-smith-on-pro-football-head-coaching-diversity. www.npr.org\

Cox, John Woodrow, Scott Clement and Thomas Vargas 2016. "New pol finds 9 in 10 Native Americans aren't offended by Redskin name". *Washington Post.* Accessed online at URL: https:\www.washingtonpost.com\local\new-poll-finds-9-in-10-native-americans-arent-offended-by-redskins-name\2016\05\18\3ea11cfa-161a-11e6-924d-838753295f9a_story.html.

Crawford, Russ. 2013. "America Plays: Sports in Colonial Times." In *American History through American Sports: From Colonial Lacrosse to Extreme Sports,* edited by Danielle Sarver Coombs and Bob Batchelor. Santa Barbara, CA: Praeger.

Dangerfield, Whitney, and Allen Barra. 2012. "Before and After Title IX: Women in Sports." *New York Times Sunday Review,* June 16. Accessed January 15, 2014. http://www.nytimes.com/interactive/2012/06/17/opinion/sunday/sundayreview-titleix-timeline.html?_r=0#/#time12_265.

Daniels, Bruce C. 1995. *Puritans at Play: Leisure and Recreation in Colonial New England.* New York: Palgrave Macmillan.

Delaney, Tim. 2015. "The Functionalist Perspective on Sport." In *Routledge Handbook of the Sociology of Sport,* edited by Richard Giulianotti, 18–28. London: Routledge.

Desai, Saahil 2018. "College Sports Are Affirmative Action for Rich White Students". *The Atlantic*. Accessed online at URL: https:\www.theatlantic.com\education\archive\2018\10\colle ge-sports-benefits-white-students\573688\

Echegaray, Luis Miguel, Andy Gray and Nihal Kolur. 2017. "The 30 Most Influential Hispanics in Sports". *Sports Illustrated*. Accessed online at URL: https:\www.si.com\extra-mustard\2017\10\13 \30-most-influential-hispanics-sports. www.si.com\

Edwards, Harry. 1970. *The Revolt of the Black Athlete*. New York: Free Press.

Elsesser, Kim. 2019. "Here's Why Women's Teams Are Coached by men". *Forbes*. Accessed at URL: https:\www.forbes.com\sites\kimelsesser\2019\03\01\heres-why-womens-teams-are-coa ched-by-men\#34dfa645b3f9.

Flanagan, Linda 2017. "What's Lost When Only Rich Kids Play Sports". *The Atlantic*. Accessed online at URL: https:\www.theatlantic.com\education\archive\2017\09\whats-lost-when-only-rich-kids-play-sports\541317\.

Forbes 2019."The World's Highest-Paid Athletes". *Forbes*. Accessed at URL: https:\www.forbes.com\athletes\list\#tab:overall. tab:overall.

Freiman, Jordan. 2020. Super Bowl 2020: Kansas City Chiefs top San Francisco 49ers, 31-20. *CBS News*. Accessed online at URL: https:\www.cbsnews.com\live-updates\super-bowl-kansas-city-chiefs-defeat-san-francisco-49ers-31-20\www.cbsnews.com\ www.cbsnews.com\

Gaines, Cork. 2016. "The 25 Schools That Make the Most Money in College Sports." Business Insider, October 13. Accessed January 20, 2017. http://www.businessinsider.com/schools-most-revenue-college-sports-2016-10.

Gameday News 2019."Professional athletes Who Have Been Open About Being Part of the LGBTQ+ Community". *Gameday News*. Accessed online at URL: http:\www.gamedaynews.com\sports\profe ssional-athletes-open-lgbtq-community\?chrome=1.

Garcia, Ahiza 2018. "These are the only two owners of color in the NFL." *CNN*. Accessed online at URL: https:\money.cnn.com\2018\05\18\news\nfl-nba-mlb-owners-diversity\index.html

Gibbs, Lindsay 2019. "Only 2 Black head coaches remain in NFL despite the Rooney Rule." *Think Progress*. Accessed online at URL: https:\thinkprogress.org\rooney-rule-nfl-4d0f17baa469\

Giulianotti, Richard. 2016. *Sport: A Critical Sociology*. 2nd ed. Malden, MA: Polity Press.

Graves, Fatima Goss, Neena Chjaunchry, Katharine Gllagher Robbins, et al. 2015. "Finishing Last: girls of color and school sports opportunities." *National Women's Law Center and The Poverty and Race Research Action Council*. Accessed online at URL: https:\prrac.org\pdf\GirlsFinishingLast_Report.pdf.

Guth, Lisa M., and Stephen M. Roth. 2013. "Genetic Influence on Athletic Performance." *Current Opinion in Pediatrics* 25, no. 6: 653–58.

Hall, Erik. 2018. Gay Illinois diving coach part of a trend of out LGBTQ college coaches." *Outsport*. Accessed online at URL: https://www.outsports.com/2018/8/23/17758032/lgbt-sports-roundup-g ay-coach-illinois.

Hall, Mia 2017. "Black People Can Ski? Bridging the Race Gap in Winter Sports". *NBC News*. Acce ssed online at URL: https:\www.nbcnews.com\news\nbcblk\black-people-can-ski-bridging-race-gap-winter-sports-n731921.

Hall, Ronald E. 2002. "The Bell Curve: Implications for the Performance of Black/White Athletes." *Social Science Journal* 39, no. 1: 113–18.

Harris, Othello. 2000. "African Americans." In *Encyclopedia of Ethnicity and Sports in the United States*, edited by George B. Kirsch, Othello Harris, and Claire E. Nolte.Westport, CT: Greenwood Press.

Harrison, Elliot 2019. "Top 25 Quarterbacks of all times: Tom Brady leads list". *NFL.com*. Accessed online at url: http:\www.nfl.com\news\story\0ap3000001035041\article\top-25-quarterbacks-of-all-time-patriots-tom-brady-leads-list www.nfl.com\

Hernandez, Kristian, and Pratheek Rabala. 2019. Puppies, phones and porn: How model legislation affects consumers' lives. USA Today. https://www.usatoday.com/in-depth/news/investigations/2019/11/20/puppies-phones-porn-meat-milk-how-model-legislation-and-copycat-bills-affect-consumers/2525454001/

Hofstede, Gert Jan, Frank Dignum, Rui Prada, Jillian Student, and Loïs Vanhée. 2015. "Gender Differences: The Role of Nature, Nurture, Social Identity and Self-Organization." In *Multi-Agent-Based Simulation XV: International Workshop, MABS 2014*, edited by Francisco Grimaldo and Emma Norling.Berlin: Springer.

Hunt, Thomas. 2006. "American Sport Policy and the Cultural Cold War: The Lyndon B. Johnson Presidential Years." *Journal of Sport History* 33, no. 3: 273–97.

Hylton, Kevin. 2010. "How a Turn to Critical Race Theory Can Contribute to Our Understanding of 'Race,' Racism, and Anti-racism in Sport." *International Review for the Sociology of Sport* 45, no. 3: 335–54.

Iannotta, Joah G., and Mary Jo Kane. 2002. "Sexual Stories as Resistance Narratives in Women's Sports: Reconceptualizing Identity Performance." *Sociology of Sport Journal* 19: 347–69.

Johnson, Jim. 2017. A Look inside Modern Sports Fan: NFL vs. NCAA vs. MLB. *Huffington Post*. Accessed online at URL: https:\www.huffpost.com\entry\a-look-inside-the-modern-sports-fan-nfl-vs-ncaa-vs_b_5a3a9ed9e4b0df0de8b061a3.

Kahn, Lawrence M., and Malav Shaw. 2005. "Race, Compensation and Contract Length in the NBA: 2001–2002." *Industrial Relations* 34, no. 3: 444–62.

Keating, Peter. 2011. "Importance of an Athlete's Background." ESPN, Accessed January 19, 2017. http://www.espn.com/espn/story/_/id/6777581/importance-athlete-background-making-nba.

Kelley, Keith. "'Sportsperson of the Year' Megan Rapinoe slams Sports Illustrated". *New York Post*. Accessed at url: https:\nypost.com\2019\12\10\sportsperson-of-the-year-megan-rapinoe-slams-sports-illustrated\.

Kendall, Diane Elizabeth. 2008. *Members Only: Elite Clubs and the Process of Exclusion*. Lanham, MD: Rowman & Littlefield.

Kerr, Ian B. 2010. "The Myth of Racial Superiority in Sports." Hilltop Review (Spring). Accessed March 24, 2013. http://scholarworks.wmich.edu/hilltopreview/vol4/iss1/4/

Kertcsher, Tom. 2017. "Amid anthem protests, checking if 'NFL family' is diverse". *Politifact: The Poynter Institute*. Accessed online at URL: https:\www.politifact.com\article\2017\sep\28\amid-anthem-protests-checking-if-nfl-family-divers\.

King, C. Richard 2010. "Introduction". In C. Richard King (ed.). *The Native American Mascot Controversy: A Handbook*. Lanham, Maryland: Scarecrow Press.

Kleinknecht, Merl F. 2017. "Blacks in 19th Century Organized Baseball." Society for American Baseball Research. Accessed January 18, 2017. http://research.sabr.org/journals/Blacks-in-19th-c-baseball.

Kutz, Steven 2017. "$100 billion –that's how much Americans spent on sports over the past 12 months". *Market Watch*. Accessed at URL: https:\www.marketwatch.com\story\heres-how-much-americans-spend-on-sports-in-one-chart-2017-09-11.

LaFrance, Adrienne. 2014. "How the Bicycle Paved the Way for Women's Rights." *Atlantic,* June. Accessed January 18, 2017. http://www.theatlantic.com/technology/archive/2014/06/ the-technology-craze-of-the-1890s-that-forever-changed-womens-rights/373535.

Lam, Katherine and Travis Fedschun. 2019. "Felicity Huffman, Lori Loughlin among several dozen snared in elite college cheating scheme, authorities say." *Fox News*. https:\www.foxnews.com\us\felicity-huffman-lori-loughlin-among-several-dozen-snared-in-elite-college-cheating-scheme-authorities-say.

Lapchick, Richard 2019. "The WNBA Racial and Gender Report Card. "*TIDE: The Institute for Diversity and Ethics in Sport*. Accessed online at URL: https:\docs.wixstatic.com\ugd\7d86e5_918fdf4e8051461d8f8f5f8f4180deb4.pdf

Lapchick, Richard 2019. The MLB Racial and Gender Report Card. *TIDE: The Institute for Diversity and Ethics in Sport*. Accessed online at URL: https:\docs.wixstatic.com\ugd\7d86e5_e943e1c08a514661a86b449dea5bcfd2.pdf

Moore, Michelle 2017. "The question of Intersectionality in Women's Sport" *Michelle in blog*. Accessed online at URL: http://michellemoore.me/the-question-of-intersectionality-in-womens-sport/.

Moreau, Julie. 2018, Aug. 17. "Strict ID laws could disenfranchise 78,000 transgender voters, report says." NBC News. https://www.nbcnews.com/feature/nbc-out/strict-id-laws-could-disenfranchise-78-000-transgender-voters-report-n901696

Murphy, Dan. 2019. "Army football program dropped motto of white supremacist origin." ESPN. Accessed at URL: https:\www.espn.com\college-football\story_\id\28232249\army-football-program-dropped-motto-white-supremacist-origin.

Paulsen 2019. "2018 Ratings Wrap NFL Laps the Field, Again". Sports Media Watch. Accessed at URL: https:\www.sportsmediawatch.com\2019\01\top-sports-audiences-2018-list\

Pennington, Bill. 2006. "Breaking a Barrier 60 Years before Robinson," *New York Times*. Accessed April 17, 2013. http://www.nytimes.com/2006/07/27/sports/27hall.html.

Piacenza, Joanna 2018. "The NFL Isn't the Only Divisive Sport in America". *Morning Consult*. Accessed online at URL: https:\morningconsult.com\2018\01\25\nfl-isnt-divisive-sport-america\

Ploen, Brendan 2020. "Sisters in red: Ignacio girls basketball brings uncomfortable conversation to gymnasium. *Durango Herald*. Accessed online at URL: https:\durangoherald.com\articles\312756.

Przybyla, Heidi M., and Fredreka Schouten. 2017, Jan. 22. "At 2.6 mission strong, women\'s marches crush expectations." USA Today. https://www.usatoday.com/story/news/politics/2017/01/21/womens-march-aims-start-movement-trump-inauguration/96864158/

Radcliffe, J. R. 2018. "As Bucks ponder Becky Hammon, a look at women who have made history coaching and officiating in pro college sports." *Milwaukee Journal Sentinel*. Accessed online at URL: https:\www.jsonline.com\story\sports\nba\bucks\2018\05\11\like-becky-hammon-list-female-coaches-mens-athletics\601577002\

Robinson, Manie. 2017. "Community, Competition Builds SEC Women's Hoops Brand." Greenville Online. Accessed March 1, 2017. http://www.greenvilleonline.com/story/sports/college/2017/02/25/sec-womens-basket-ball-tournament-dawn-staley/98307078.

Sage, George H., and D. Stanley Eitzen, 2015. *Sociology of North American Sport*. 10th ed. New York: Oxford University Press.

Scott, Cleo-Symone 2018. "Who are the real winners of Team USA? Immigrants". Study Breaks. Accessed at URL: https:\studybreaks.com\news-politics\immigrants.

Semuels, Alana 2019. "The White Flight From Football". The Atlantic. Accessed online at URL: https:\www.theatlantic.com\health\archive\2019\02\football-white-flight-racial-divide\581623\

Shakib, Sohaila, and Phillip Veliz. 2012. "Race, Sport and Social Support: A Comparison between African American and White Youths' Perceptions of Social Support for Sport Participation." *International Review for the Sociology of Sport* 48, no. 3: 295–317.

Starn, Orin. 2006. "Caddying for the Dalai Lama: Golf, Heritage Tourism, and the Pinehurst Resort." *South Atlantic Quarterly* 105, no. 2: 447–63.

Stein, Rob. 2011. "Genetic Testing for Sports Genes Courts Controversy." *Washington Post,* May 18. Accessed January 12, 2017. https://www.washingtonpost.com/national/genetic-testing-for-sports-genes-courts-controversy/2011/05/09/AFkTuV6G_story.html.

Stern, Mark Joseph 2019. "Betsy DeVos May Force High Schools to Discriminate Against Trans Athletes". *Slate*. Accessed at URL: https:\slate.com\news-and-politics\2019\08\trump-education-department-title-ix-trans-athletes-discrimination.html.

Thompson, Derek. 2014. "Which Sports Have the Whitest/Richest/Oldest Fans?" *Atlantic*. Accessed June 23, 2017. https://www.theatlantic.com/business/archive/2014/02/which-sports-have-the-whitest-richest-oldest-fans/283626.

Thompson, Derek 2018. "American Meritocracy Is Killing Youth Sports". *The Atlantic*. Accessed online at URL: https:\www.theatlantic.com\ideas\archive\2018\11\income-inequality-explains-decline-youth-sports\574975\

TitleIX.info. n.d. "Athletics under Title IX." Accessed January 15, 2014. http://www.titleix.info/10-key-areas-of-title-ix/athletics.aspx.

Tower, Nikole 2018. "In an ethnic breakdown of sports, NBA takes lead for most diverse." *Global Sport Matters*. Accessed online at URL: https:\globalsportmatters.com\culture\2018\12\12\in-an-ethnic-breakdown-of-sports-nba-takes-lead-for-most-diverse\

Towler, Christopher, Nyron N. Crawford, and Robert A. Bennett 2019. "Shut Up and Play: Black Athletes, Protest Politics, and Black Political Action". *Perspectives on Politics*. Accessed online at URL: https:\www.cambridge.org\core\journals\perspectives-on-politics\article\shut-up-and-play-black-athletes-protest-politics-and-black-political-action\F9266D6D87A357726B19EC51C6266068\core-reader#.

Wadley, Jared 2020. "Study Shows Much Opposition to Native American mascots names". *The University of Michigan Record*. Accessed online at URL: https:\record.umich.edu\articles\study-opposition-high-to-native-american-mascots-names\.

Wamsley, Laurel 2019. Simone Biles Becomes The Most Decorated Gymnast In World Championship History". *NPR*. Accessed at URL: https:\www.npr.org\2019\10\13\769896721\simone-biles-becomes-the-most-decorated-gymnast-in-world-championship-history. www.npr.org\

Weiss, Maureen R. 2016. "Old Wine in a New Bottle: Historical Reflections on Sport as a Context for Youth Development." In *Positive Youth Development through Sport,* 2nd ed., edited by Nicholas L. Holt, 7–20. London: Routledge.

Winter, Tom and Minyvonne Burke 2019. "College cheating ringleader says he helped more than 750 families with admissions scheme". *NBC News*. Accessed online at URL: https:\www.nbcnews.com\news\us-news\college-cheating-mastermind-says-he-helped-nearly-800-families-admissions-n982666.

Women's Sports Foundation. 2017. "Factors Influencing Girls' Participation in Sports." Accessed March 1, 2017. https://www.womenssportsfoundation.org/support-us/do-you-know-the-factors-influencing-girls-participation-in-sports.

z2solutions2016.Baseball demographics -viewer demographics & 2016 baseball season. *Z2SSolutions*. Accessed online at URL: http:\z2solutions.com\demographics\2016-baseball-season-demographics\.

Zirin, David. 2000. *A People's History of Sports in the United States: 250 Years of Politics, Protests, People, and Play.* New York: New Press.

10 THE MILITARY, WAR, AND TERRORISM

Tammy Duckworth is a decorated veteran, the daughter of a veteran and an immigrant, and an exemplar of the unique mix of race, class, and gender that characterizes the United States.

Saul Loeb/AFP/Getty Images

LEARNING OBJECTIVES

10.1 Examine the contemporary reality of race, class, and gender in the U.S. military.

10.2 Explore the stock sociological theories regarding the U.S. military, war, and terrorism.

10.3 Apply the matrix approach to U.S. military history, war, and terrorism.

10.4 Evaluate the possibilities for a more inclusive future.

Politician, mother, wife, double amputee, disabled combat veteran, and hero—all of these describe U.S. Senator Tammy Duckworth of Illinois. Her story, like that of thousands of veterans throughout history, is entwined with society's collective narrative. Duckworth's father was a U.S. Marine Corps veteran who could trace his family's military roots back to the American Revolutionary War (Weinstein 2012). Her mother was a native of Thailand and of Chinese ancestry. Duckworth joined the Army Reserve Officers' Training Corps as a graduate student and was soon commissioned a lieutenant in the U.S. Army Reserve. Since piloting was one of the few combat jobs open to women, she attended helicopter flight school. After graduation, she joined the Illinois National Guard. While she was earning her PhD in political science, her unit was deployed to Iraq, and on November 12, 2004, her UH-60 Black Hawk helicopter was hit by a rocket-propelled grenade. She lost both of her legs and much of her right arm. Her valor earned her the Purple Heart, the Air Medal, and the Army Commendation Medal.

After leaving the military, Duckworth served as the director of the Illinois Department of Public Affairs from 2006 to 2009, after which she became assistant secretary of public and intergovernmental affairs at the U.S. Department of Veterans Affairs. Thousands were moved by her story when she spoke at the 2008 Democratic National Convention, and in 2011 she resigned her position at the Department of Veterans Affairs and announced her candidacy for the U.S. House of Representatives. She went on to win that election and represented Illinois's Eighth Congressional District from January 2013 to January 2017. In November 2016, she was elected to the U.S. Senate, where she now serves along with 20 other women and 79 men. Senator Duckworth has been a staunch supporter of American veterans and those who have disabilities, and her story, and all those who have served throughout our history, reflects the matrix of race and how it intersects with the military, war, and terrorism.

A single act of war or violence can define the life of a person, a community, and a nation. Consider the U.S. use of atomic bombs in Japan during World War II, or the terrorist acts carried out against the United States on September 11, 2001. Nothing seems so central to our collective experience, or as controversial, as war. Similarly, nothing seems so apt to bring us together or tear us apart, and nothing seems so central to the understanding of these moments as race, class, ethnicity, and gender.

REPRESENTATION IN THE U.S. MILITARY

The five branches that make up the U.S. military—the Army, Navy, Air Force, Marine Corps, and Coast Guard—are authorized to use deadly force to support the national interests, specific entities, and citizens of the United States. The U.S. Department of Defense (DoD), an executive branch department of the federal government, is charged with coordinating all agencies and functions associated with national defense and U.S. armed forces. In 2020, the DoD was the largest employer in the world, with an estimated 1.4 million service members on active duty and another 860,000 in reserve; these numbers make it the third-largest military in the world, following China and India (Global Fire Power).

The United States spends more on its military than any other country. In fact, U.S. military expenditures, $639 billion in 2018, exceeded the combined expenditures of China, Saudi

Arabia, India, France, Russia, the United Kingdom, and Germany, which was collectively $609 billion (Stockholm International Peace Institute 2019). The defense budget for the period of October 1, 2020, through September 30, 2021, represents 16% of the entire federal budget and is devoted primarily to costs related to the DoD. This makes military spending the second-largest item in the federal budget after Social Security. The base budget for the Department of Defense is $636 billion. The second largest expenditure is the $69 billion in overseas contingent operations devoted to fighting the Islamic State group (Amadeo 2020).

The U.S. military continues to be one of the most diverse institutions within our country. As we will learn, it was the first major institution to become racially integrated, providing upward mobility for U.S.-born people of color as well as immigrants that used it as a route to citizenship. The military has also been a space for women to demonstrate that they too have "the right stuff." This section will explore how these different groups are currently being represented in the military.

Representation by Gender and Sexuality

Today's military are mostly from middle-class neighborhoods. Increasingly these recruits are both female and diverse. At the end of the draft in 1973, women only represented 2% of the enlisted and 8% of the officer corps. Now they comprise 16% and 18% respectively for enlisted forces and officer corps. The distinction is important, as those in the enlisted ranks are lower paid, lower status, and lower training. Officers on the other hand, with greater pay, specialties, and authority, are of higher status. In the corporate world, this might be the difference between the managers and the line workers.

Our diverse military serves many vital functions.

Bob Daemmrich/Alamy

Figure 10.1 shows clear gender differences by service branch. Female recruits are more diverse than their male counterparts or the civilian population. Among the enlisted corps, 56% of the women are either Hispanic or a racial minority. The Army and Navy tend to be the most racially diverse, while the Marines and Air Force are the least. Even more to the point, within the Army, Black women are almost at parity with their White female counterparts. Women are more likely to be both enlisted and in the officer corps in the Air Force and Navy (where they comprise at least one in five) and least likely to be present in the Marines (where they make up about 8% in both categories) (Reynolds and Shendruk 2018). Higher female enlistments, at least among Black women, might be a result of fewer economic opportunities in society in general and the lack of an adequate safety net. But while female veterans might not reap the same level of economic and social mobility as their male peers, the military may provide more than what is otherwise available (Melin 2016).

Many people frequently confuse gender with sexuality, but clear distinctions can be identified across all institutions. These distinctions have been a continual debate within the military. Tracking the number of military personnel that are gay, lesbian, transgender, and bisexual is

FIGURE 10.1 ■ Female Recruits Are More Diverse Than Their Male Counterparts

Race and Ethnicity of Enlisted Recruits by Service and Gender, 2018
Hispanic, considered an ethnicity and not a race, overlaps with racial categories.

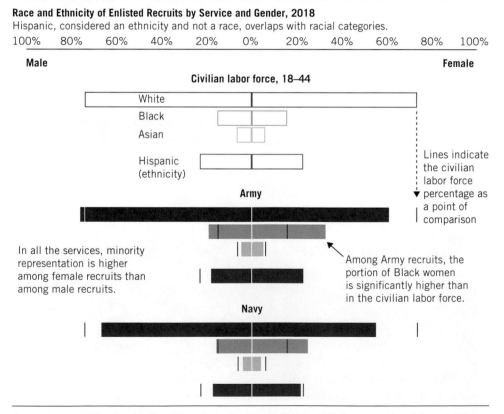

Source: Race and Ethnicity of Enlisted Recruits by Service and Gender, 2018, Demographics of the U.S. Military, Council on Foreign Relations, 2020.

consistently a problem given the various government policies. For example, President Clinton's "Don't Ask, Don't Tell" policy unofficially lifted the official ban on transgender people serving in the military.

Then in 2016, President Obama formally ended all restrictions on openly transgender service members. For the first time, thousands of transgender troops could serve openly, and not in silence. This period lasted for only 3 years, as one of President Trump's first orders in 2019 was an executive order banning transgender people from service. Even after a 2020 Supreme Court ruling that civil rights law protects gay, lesbian, and transgender people from discrimination in employment, the U.S. military ban was unaffected. Hence, the military is the only institution in the United States that can still legally discriminate based on gender identity (Limon 2020).

Representation by Class, Race, and Immigration Status

Recruiting within the Armed Forces is closely tied to the economy and job prospects. In fact, the high unemployment rate among youth during the past decade has been associated with higher rates of enlistment. The number of recruits therefore fluctuates with the economy. As economic uncertainty increases the number of unemployed, we note an increase in those who seek the military. The current active duty military, although smaller, is more racially and ethnically diverse than in previous generations of service personnel (Barroso 2019).

Every year close to 180,000 young people enlist for active duty in the Armed Forces. Over 90% of these recruits have a high school diploma, and nearly two-thirds score in the top half of the math and verbal aptitude test given at the time of induction. Urban areas are most underrepresented, with most recruits coming from suburban and rural areas. Recruits from the South accounted for 41% of the total, with the Northeast generating 14% of recruits, and the West and North Central parts of the country producing respectively 21% and 24% of all new recruits.

Casualties in war are most likely to be White (67%) followed by African Americans (17%), and Hispanics (9%). These figures roughly reflect the demographic distribution of these groups within the military:

- Whites (67%)

- African Americans (17%)

- Hispanics (11%) (Military.com 2020)

According to the latest available data from 2017, enlisted personnel (i.e., those who were not officers) were more racially diverse than the U.S. population as a whole. Non-White service members accounted for close to one-third of all active duty enlisted and almost 40% of senior enlisted personnel. The only enlisted minority groups underrepresented among active and reserve components were Asian and Hispanic service members. Just the opposite is the case among the officer corps, and particularly among the senior leadership levels, where racial and ethnic minorities are underrepresented relative to either the U.S. population or the enlisted corps (Kamarck 2017) (see Figure 10.2).

	Rank and Grade	White	Black	Asian	Other	Multi/ Unknown	Hispanic*
Active Duty	General/Flag Officer (O-7 and above)	87.6%	8.2%	2.1%	0.3%	18%	1.4%
	Officer (all)	76.99%	8.7%	4.9%	1.2%	8.3%	7.7%
	Warrant Officer	66.7%	17.8%	3.2%	1.4%	10.8%	11.3%
	Senior Enlisted	62.3%	20.1%	3.9%	2.3%	11.4%	14.0%
	Enlisted (all)	67.0%	19.1%	4.4%	2.6%	7.1%	17.0%
	Total Active Duty	**68.7%**	**17.3%**	**4.5%**	**2.3%**	**7.3%**	**15.4%**
Selected Reserve	General/Flag Officer (O-7 and above)	91.3%	4.0%	2.3%	0.8%	1.7%	3.0%
	Officer (all)	74.8%	9.8%	4.4%	1.0%	5.8%	6.4%
	Warrant Officer	8.3%	8.7%	2.4%	0.9%	2.9%	6.5%
	Senior Enlisted	76.1%	14.7%	2.4%	1.3%	5.5%	9.5%
	Enlisted (all)	72.7%	17.8%	4.2%	1.5%	3.7%	12.5%
	Total Selected Reserve	**73.9%**	**16.5%**	**4.2%**	**1.5%**	**4.0%**	**11.5%**
U.S. Resident Population (age 18-64, estimated)		**76.6%**	**13.7%**	**6.1%**	**1.5%**	**2.1%**	**17.5%**

FIGURE 10.2 ■ **Representation of Racial and Ethnic Groups Show Differences Across Military Ranks and Duties**

Notes: Race and Hispanic origin are self-identified. * The concept of race is separate from the concept of Hispanic origin. Hispanic may be more than one race (e.g., Hispanic and White or Hispanic and Black). Percentages for race should not be combined with percent Hispanic. The "Other" category includes Native Hawaiian and Other Pacific Islanders, and American Indian and Alaskan Natives.

Source: Congressional Research Service, Diversity, Inclusion, and Equal Opportunity in the Armed Services: Background and Issues for Congress, 2017.

From the inception of our country, military service, particularly during times of war, has been the principal means by which foreign-born individuals could become citizens of the United States. There has never been a U.S. war in which foreign-born persons have not participated on the side of the United States. From the Revolutionary War to the 1840s, nearly half of military recruits were foreign-born, and during the Civil War, nearly 20% of the Union army included foreign-born troops. These numbers have been constantly increasing, as over 500,000 immigrants served in the military during World War I. Close to 18% of these immigrant veterans were eventually granted citizenship. There were over 300,000 immigrants serving in World War II, which included 109,000 noncitizens. About 1,000 of these noncitizens were eventually naturalized for their service. After the Korean War ended in 1953, another 31,000 foreign-born soldiers became naturalized citizens.

Currently, close to 511,000 foreign-born people are serving in the armed forces. 1.5 million veterans have at least one parent that was an immigrant (Mason 2017). Figure 10.3 shows the trends in the number of non-citizens that have become citizens through military service. Since 2002, a total of 129,587 non-citizen military service members have been naturalized. But these trends have not been consistent over the entire period. Specifically, these trends have been generally increasing since 9/11, peaking at over 11,000 in 2011 and leveling off to slightly less than 8,000 annually until 2018. In 2018, there was a a deep cut in naturalized service members following President Trump's order discharging immigrant reservist and recruits in 2017 (Mendoza and Burke 2018).

A whole range of theories have been proposed, and a great deal of research has been conducted over the years in attempts to answer questions about the military, including who serves and under what conditions. As we have seen, various groups have radically different paths and, as we will see below, experiences within the military. Further, external factors such as their race, gender, sexuality, or citizenship status can be dramatically impacted by current policies and practices. We have looked at these differences singularly, but what might an intersectional lens produce? Theories, both stock and intersectional, help us to grapple with these complexities. Let us begin.

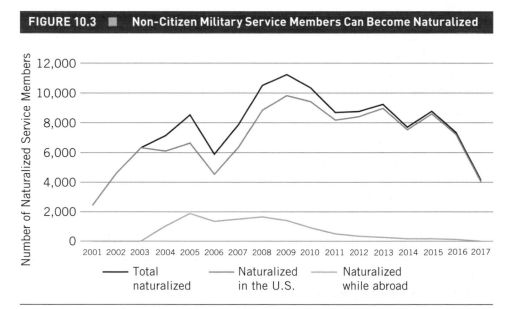

FIGURE 10.3 ■ Non-Citizen Military Service Members Can Become Naturalized

Source: Compiled by authors with data from Military Naturalization Statistics, U.S. Citizenship and Immigration Services, https://www.uscis.gov/military/military-naturalization-statistics.

Critical Thinking

1. Does the fact that the United States has one of the world's largest military budgets improve the security of the United States or of the world?

2. How might other institutions, such as education, family, and healthcare, be influenced by the current U.S. military? How might these same institutions influence the military?

3. What kinds of policies might increase diversity, including diversity in race, gender, and class, in the U.S. military?

4. In what ways are you affected by the military? Would you consider joining/serving? Why or why not?

MILITARY SOCIOLOGY STOCK THEORIES

Military sociology, the sociological analysis of armed forces and war, has been a central concern within the sociological discipline since at least World War I (Bottomore 1981). Three key sociological theories have controlled the field: functionalism, symbolic interactionism, and monopoly and materialist perspectives. Like all stock stories, these theories are both dominant within the discipline of sociology and traditionally relied upon as explanations. In many ways they also justify our use of the military, our involvement in wars, and our concerns regarding terrorism.

Functionalism

Functionalist theory assumes that institutions come into being to meet specific and basic societal needs. A **functionalist approach to the military** argues that the military, war, and terrorism serve specific and important tasks, or functions, within society. Some of these functions are socialization, integration, and reduction of conflict. **War**, defined as the use of organized force, represents a state of armed conflict between different nations, states, or groups within a nation or state. War legitimates state claims, regulates conflict between states, minimizes collateral damage among noncombatants, and extends the social, political, and economic values of the victor over the vanquished (Park 1941). **Terrorism** is the unlawful use of force, particularly against civilians, in pursuit of political, economic, or social aims. Functionalism views terrorism as **dysfunctional**, as it disrupts social structures, increases stress, and violates norms and rules of engagement. An examination of how functionalist theorists view the military, war, and terrorism provides some key insights.

The Military Preserves Social Values

The military functions to preserve social values by encouraging patriotism, compliance with normative expectations, and order, both domestically and internationally. Accordingly, the stratification that occurs within the military, such as along racial and gender lines, reflects these functions. Those tasks considered most functionally important, such as those performed by officers and in combat roles, require higher levels of training and responsibility, and are therefore rewarded to a higher degree than other tasks and roles. For example, generals in the U.S. Army are graduates of the United States Military Academy at West Point; have advanced training in military tactics, troop deployment, leadership, and logistics; and have spent several years advancing through the ranks. On the other hand, an army private typically is qualified to serve after just 8 weeks of basic training. It is presumed that the inequality that results reflects the functional differentiation associated with the valuing of different tasks. Structural functionalists also stress the integrative functions served by the military (Cardoso 2001, 164). The military provides these functions at multiple levels. At the national level, a strong military helps maintain social cohesion and relative calm, as it is perceived as a deterrent to hostile and wanton attacks. The military also serves at the individual level by socializing individuals and advancing such notions as patriotism, maturity, and solidarity.

War Is a Bonding Experience

War, viewed functionally, helps citizens develop a form of social bonding or solidarity. A nation and its citizens must come together to fight a common enemy. Recall images from the scene at the U.S. Capitol in the aftermath of the attacks on September 11, 2001, and similar scenes across the nation. Republicans and Democrats; Asians, Blacks, Whites, and Hispanics; urbanites, suburbanites, and rural dwellers; gay and straight—all appeared to join hands in a collective show of solidarity. Wars produce cultural artifacts such as art, shared collective memories, and a sense of common purpose. And with the billions of dollars associated with modern wars, war also functions to stimulate the economy by providing jobs in the production of war/military goods and services. As we will see in our examination of the history of war, war has been a significant factor in the social mobility of women, people of color, immigrants, and the poor across the United States. Finally, wars have served to stimulate advances in technology, production processes, and sciences, leading to leaps forward in many areas, from airplanes and jets to space flight, medical innovations, mass transit, and the internet (Lin 2010).

Terrorism Is Dysfunctional

Most sociologists ignored the topic of terrorism prior to the attacks on September 11, 2001. Since those pivotal events, a great deal of scholarly attention has been expended in efforts to understand the events and prevent similar attacks. Terrorists, from a functionalist perspective, are viewed as deviants who violate basic norms of both civilization and war by targeting noncombatants. Unfortunately, the label of "terrorist" is applied depending on an individual's perspective. A person might be viewed as a terrorist by one group but seen as a revolutionary or even a patriot by another.

Race/Ethnicity Is the Missing Piece

Functionalist approaches to the military, war, and terrorism ignore how these institutions serve the interests of the powerful within society and fail to provide specific analysis of race and ethnicity. The emphasis on the idea that the military and war unify society obscures the fact that

War, or violent attacks like those of September 11, 2001, can bring people together, like the more than 1,000 who gathered at this candlelight vigil in the wake of al-Qaeda's attack.

Steve Liss/The LIFE Images Collection/Getty Images/

Terrorism can be in the eye of the beholder. The United States originated from an act that may be seen as terrorism, when the Sons of Liberty boarded ships belonging to the East India Company in Boston Harbor and threw 342 chests of tea overboard to protest what they believed to be an unjust law.

Courtesy of the Library of Congress Prints and Photographs Division

they can also be forces for disunity and oppression. As we have observed earlier, terrorism, while viewed as dysfunctional, may be functional and a form of resistance for those who feel that their freedoms are being denied. Specifically, who gets to label an individual or group as terrorist in many cases reflects the very power dynamics that the acts are intended to alter. The definition is critical, and it is political, and often it also mirrors our concerns with race, class, and gender.

Symbolic Interactionism

A **symbolic interactionist approach to the military** investigates how we attach meaning to things (flags and memorials), events (wars), and other representations (heroes and patriotism) in support of war, and the military. Symbolic interactionists point out that military organizations have their own values, symbols, hierarchies, cultural rituals, and forms of socialization. The military socializes individuals to facilitate their entry into a specific community whose goal is to engage in war and conflict. In other words, the military creates symbolic meanings, representations, and recognitions that attempt to create a specific military personality that fosters group interaction, cohesion, and conformity.

Symbolic interactionism studies military life histories, the process of recruitment, and how civilians are transformed into soldiers. Establishing the legitimacy of the military and war is accomplished through the manipulation of symbols and concepts such as patriotism, heroes, enemies, and justice. The legitimacy of war, particularly, relies on the redefining of the killing of enemy soldiers, or combatants, as casualties of war. For example, using the term *collateral damage* instead of *victim* is one way this symbolism is extended to legitimate the "accidental" killing of innocents, or noncombatants (Cockerham 2003).

One of the critiques of symbolic interactionism is that it fails to account adequately for how social structures, identities, and military organizations interact (Giddens 1984). Symbolic interactionists have provided no insight, for example, into how racial, ethnic, and religious hostilities erupt into war, leading to events such as the 9/11 attacks (Cockerham 2003).

Monopoly and Materialist Perspectives

Finally, the **monopoly and materialist perspectives** posit that military organizations must maintain a legitimate monopoly on the use of force, and the use of this force is uniquely tied to the material instruments of war. In other words, the military argues that a central feature of the modern state is its monopoly over the legitimate use of coercive force (Weber 1978, 50–56). **Coercive force** is force in which intimidation is used to obtain compliance. The monopoly perspective suggests that the state and its agents have an exclusive right or privilege, granted by the citizens of the state, to use such force to gain compliance.

Contextualizing the Military

Clearly, the link between the military and its use of coercive force is important. Some scholars have argued that military institutions are a direct result of either the real or potential struggles of war and armed conflict (Kestnbaum 2009). They insist that if we are to understand the military, we must understand war. War highlights not only inequities but also the structural and organizational foundations of both conflict and coercion. National resources and their effective military mobilization determine the origins and likelihood of successful military campaigns. The basic questions that come from these lines of interest are concerned with how wars are waged and the consequences of wars for national existence (Kestnbaum 2009). Further, it is argued that the military force represents the essential quality of the modern state. By extension, both war and military violence are uniquely social events that create, maintain, and transform states as well as individuals and societies (Weber 1991).

Assuming Legitimacy

The major criticism of this approach is that it assumes that the military has a monopoly on the coercive use of force and, further, that such use is legitimate. This theory also assumes that **interstate forms of war** (conflicts involving national states, such as World Wars I and II) are somehow more legitimate than **intrastate forms of war** (conflicts that exist or occur within the boundaries of particular states). Third, this approach tends to overemphasize the material basis of war, dismissing or marginalizing other major sources of struggle, such as political, cultural, and other social dimensions and roots of both international and intranational forms of conflict (Kestnbaum 2009). Several implications follow from these criticisms. First, most of the wars fought by the United States prior to 9/11 were against nations, with clearly defined and universally recognized rules of war (as governed by the United Nations). The terrorist attacks of 9/11 signaled a shift in how wars are fought. Now, what are termed **nonstate actors** (individuals or organizations with economic, political, or social power that allows them to influence both national and international events, typically with violence) are most often the initiators of terrorist attacks, wars, and other conflicts. The reality is that most recent wars and other conflicts have involved nonstate actors. As we will see, nonstate actors such as ISIS (the so-called Islamic State), al-Qaeda, and Boko Haram are on the rise and pose a definite threat, not only to the United States but also to the world in general (Brady 2017).

Second, and more central to our concerns within the matrix, is that this approach ignores how the military, war, and terrorism tend to reflect, duplicate, and in some cases actually transform the race, class, and gender hierarchies present within society. Both state and nonstate actors utilize both organized and unorganized strategies to effect change. Wars and other conflicts are waged on multiple fronts and include actual combat as well as, and increasingly, campaigns of terror that may include lone terrorists and cells. Methods and strategies might range from simple tactics such as writing editorials and holding press conferences to hacking into secure networks and planting fictitious stories in formal news and social media outlets. As we will see when we apply the matrix theory to this institution, race, class, and gender differences in the military's allocation of human resources duplicate the hierarchies within the host society. This means that military hierarchies, such as the hierarchy of the chain of command and the hierarchy of honors and other sanctions, tend to reflect status arrangements that are present within the wider society. Finally, this approach does not address the issues involved when a state uses the military to coerce compliance by domestic and/or indigenous groups, as when the U.S. military was used to control the Native American populations during westward expansion. The very presumption of the state's legitimacy hides the racial and gendered use of this force to preserve the racial hierarchy.

CONCEALED STORIES: CRITICAL RACE THEORY AND MILITARY SOCIOLOGY

Critical race theorists began to challenge the overly conservative and apologetic approach typically taken within military sociology. The earliest work by military sociologists found military organizations to be necessary features of modern democracies. At the core of such societies is a tension between violence and reason that war and the military regulate and mediate (Foucault 1977). All our moral values and intellectual definitions of right and wrong are derived from this viewpoint. Finally, the laws that we ultimately construct are a direct consequence of violence and war. Their intent, critical theorists insist, is to preserve peace and tranquility by establishing order, minimizing conflicts, and punishing violators. This means that power, inequalities, and social existence are anchored in relationships of force that are controlled through institutions, particularly those of the military (Foucault 2008). Therefore, the race, gender, and class inequities that exist are not only manifested but also in many ways preserved in military hierarchies. Obviously, as we will see, these inequalities preceded military hierarchies.

Finally, the military serves the interests of the corporate elite in their pursuit of profits and power. An informal alliance exists between the nation's military and the major industries that produce arms and other military materials, which seek to influence public policy. This alliance, termed the military–industrial complex, is dominated by major U.S. corporations and serves to preserve race, class, and gender hierarchies. By separating ownership from management, the corporations in the military–industrial complex have effectively emancipated themselves from stockholders. By reinvesting profits, they have eliminated the influence of both financiers and the capital market. And through effective lobbying, they have come to dominate and manipulate the state and governmental control (Galbraith 1967). The U.S. military–industrial complex is structured by violence and aimed at creating, preserving, and manipulating racial boundaries. This was clearly the case during the country's period of nation building and the Indian removal process (Perret 1989).

Contemporary research also highlights a stratified internal labor market within the military consisting of two spheres: one for enlisted personnel (working class) and one for officers (middle or managerial class). The different social locations or backgrounds of the people in each sphere reflect societal norms. For example, typically enlisted ranks require a high school degree, while officer grades require some college. These status distinctions, reflecting access to and quality of educational institutions, consequently, tend to reflect the racial, gendered, and class hierarchies in the wider society. Hence, racial and ethnic minorities tend to be concentrated in the enlisted ranks, and women tend to be concentrated in the support, clerical, and medical fields (Booth and Segal 2005). Up until recently, women in the armed forces were also limited to noncombat positions, which further reduced their likelihood of promotion.

Lastly, as critical theorists have considered terrorism, again they have identified how race, class, and gender affect not only how particular acts are perceived but also who is most likely to be at risk of harm from terrorism. And, as to be expected, White, privileged males are less likely to perceive themselves at risk for various types of terrorism—typically, they view themselves as invulnerable. Women, across all groups, are more likely to be anxious about being the targets or victims of terrorist attacks (Finucane, Slovic, Mertz, Flynn, and Satterfield 2000). After 9/11, a national study found that women and racial/ethnic minorities were more likely than White males to have experienced sustained psychological distress and emotional as well as physical health problems (Chu, Seery, Ence, Holman, and Silver 2006).

Critical Thinking

1. How might the stock stories of military sociology account for the terrorist attacks on 9/11?

2. In what ways do the stock stories reflect both the historical periods in which they were developed and the official perspective of the United States? Why are such stock stories appealing? What is the difficulty in automatically assuming their reliability?

3. How might the stock stories be utilized to minimize the concerns of racial, gender, and class groups, or to marginalize such groups?

4. Almost all of us are affected in some way by the military, war, and acts of terrorism. How have these affected you or your family?

APPLYING THE MATRIX APPROACH TO U.S. MILITARY HISTORY, WAR, AND TERRORISM

The military has been historically racially segregated. In the early years of the nation, non-Whites were only considered as potential military recruits when there was a shortage of soldiers. And while Blacks did serve in limited capacities during the Civil War, it was not until the Army Reorganization Act of 1866 that Congress authorized the permanent presence of "colored" units, which then consisted of two cavalry and four infantry regiments. This same act called for the recruitment and enlistment of 1,000 Native Americans who would serve as scouts during combat or other missions. When the 1896 Supreme Court case of *Plessy v. Ferguson* established legal racial segregation, states began implementing a series of segregation-based laws that also impacted military service. Eventually, extreme shortages forced the Army to increase its non-White recruits for both World War I and World War II. In 1948, President Truman, by executive order, abolished discrimination based on race, color, religion, or national origin in the United States Armed Forces. The Korean War marked the moment that the military was integrated and began the transformations that have led to our contemporary military (Kamarck 2019).

Each war has not only shaped the racial ethnic makeup of the military, but also created new traditions and new social norms, heroes, and methods of military engagement. Exploring how various wars have also reflected our changing intersectional landscape of race, class, and gender provides insight into the operation of the matrix within military organizations. One way to organize our discussion is to focus on those wars that have defined us as a people, and that have cost us the most in terms of human life.

Revolutionary War

The Revolutionary War (1775–1783) involved 217,000 colonial soldiers. Of those, 4,435 died in combat, and another 6,188 were wounded (U.S. Department of Veterans Affairs 2017). The U.S. military has always been a complex mix of race, class, gender, and sexual identities. Native Americans, Blacks, immigrants, Whites, women, the affluent class, the middle class, the working class, and the poor have all constituted significant portions of our military. This was also true of the first group of patriots to give their lives for this nation during the Boston Massacre on March 5, 1770. Crispus Attucks, an American of African and Native descent; a sailor by the name of Patrick Carr, an Irish immigrant; and two Englishmen, Samuel Maverick, a teenage apprentice, and a rope maker named Samuel Gray—all died from shots fired by the British soldiers that day. None were armed (Brooks 2011). These first to die in our country's history remarkably reflected the diversity of our nation and those willing to pay the ultimate sacrifice.

Boston silversmith Paul Revere called the nation to arms in 1775 and was answered by thousands of militiamen. On April 19, 1775, the first battle was waged in Concord, Massachusetts, where 89 men from Massachusetts died or were wounded. Within weeks of the first call, 6,000 men were mobilized. These were soon joined by 16,000 more from the other four New England colonies (Ferling 2010).

Black Soldiers

Black service members have fought in every war since the founding of America. The British were the first to tap the support of Black slaves. Black militias were established in all the English colonies. Virginia governor John Murray issued a proclamation on November 7, 1775, that granted full freedom to all Blacks willing to serve. The only caveat was that the offer applied only to slaves owned by the rebels, not to those owned by British Loyalists. The offer was aimed at punishing and threatening the rebels. North Carolinian Joseph Hews, one of the signers of the Declaration of Independence, accused the British of planning to "let loose Indians on our Frontiers" and to "raise the Negros against us" (quoted in Ashe 1908, 473).

Black men and women worked as British spies in New York. They created networks that helped others to escape, planned sabotage in rebellious cities, and otherwise aided in the British cause. More than 300 escaped slaves immediately joined the British within the first month of the war. Over the next few months more than 30,000 slaves would escape and fight for the British. This represented the single largest emancipation to take place within the United States until the Civil War. With the former slaves, the British established three full companies of colonial marines. These regiments took part in the sacking of Washington and fought in the Battle of Baltimore and along the coast (Lender 2016, 114).

George Washington was adamantly against the use of slaves in the military, but the ravages of the winter of 1777–78 and the devastation of the Continental army by both disease and desertion forced him to reconsider. He reluctantly granted Rhode Island permission to raise a regiment of free Blacks and slaves. A total of 5,000 free Blacks and slaves served in the Continental army, and the first integrated units of the U.S. military were created. Black and White men fought alongside each other almost on an equal footing, receiving the same pay, facing the same dangers, and providing the same levels of skill and courage (Lanning 2000, 73).

White Ethnic Soldiers

All forms of immigration were halted when the Revolutionary War began, but a large percentage of White immigrants and their descendants served in the Revolutionary War. For example,

Irish and German immigrants fought on both sides of this war, but those living in the Mid-Atlantic states comprised the largest proportion of recruits in the Continental army. Roughly one out of every four Continental soldiers were of Irish descent, and both groups fought in all-Irish and all-German battalions. When the Revolutionary War broke out, many European nations provided soldiers to both sides. Of these, several German states provided mercenaries to the British army (Lutz 2008).

The Role of Women

The Revolutionary War afforded women on both sides of the conflict a variety of roles, including combat. One of the little-known achievements of women during the Revolutionary War was a successful boycott of British goods starting in the 1760s and continuing through the 1770s. Many women avoided purchasing British goods by making their own products at home, particularly clothing, and therefore effectively changed the consumption patterns of households. Acts of sabotage were also frequently carried out by women; for example, Catherine Van Rensselaer Schuyler, wife of General Philip Schuyler, burned the wheat fields around Albany, New York, thus denying the harvest to British forces (Best 2012, 23). Both the British and colonial forces utilized women in their traditional roles as homemakers and domestic servants to carry out espionage. As cooks and maids, who were routinely ignored, women were able to gain unrestricted access to military operations and move easily to gather information about troop movements, leadership changes, and equipment shortages. Some reported directly to General Washington and became highly accomplished spies. Of special note is Ann Simpson Davis, whom Washington personally selected to carry messages to his generals in Pennsylvania. Slipping through British-occupied areas unnoticed, she would often carry secret messages in sacks of grain or in her clothing. She received a letter of commendation for her services from Washington (Rhoades-Piotti 2017, 251). Women also served in more conventional roles as nurses and medics (Figley, Pitts, Chapman, and Elnitsky 2015).

Wars and Native Americans

Currently, Native Americans, who are 1.4% of the U.S. population, account for 1.7% of enlisted and officers in the military (Flanagan 2018). Native American nations, with strong warrior traditions, have been influential in shaping our U.S. military traditions. Consider the Native American tribal names the Army uses for its aircrafts, including Apache, Black Hawk, Chinook, Kiowa, Lakota, Creek, Cayuse, Huron, and Ute. Or consider the Tomahawk cruise missile, a long-range, all-weather, subsonic cruise missile used by the U.S. Navy in both ship and submarine-based land-attack operations.

Despite this, some of the most violent and cruel wars in U.S. history took place on our own soil, and against Native American populations. American military forces fought 29 major wars against Native Americans, stretching from precolonial times to well into the 20th century. These wars cost thousands of lives, and Native Americans lost thousands of acres of land, from Georgia to Ohio, from Illinois to Alabama, and from Florida to Texas. The only other war on our soil to match this dreadful toll in both destruction and lives lost was the Civil War (Stout 2009).

Native Americans and the Revolutionary War

With few exceptions, Native Americans sided with the British in the Revolutionary War. Four of the six Iroquois nations joined forces with the British, and Loyalist forces devastated Continental forces in western New York and Pennsylvania in 1778 and 1779. Despite significant Native American support, not a single Native American representative was invited to the European treaty negotiations that concluded the war in 1783. As a result, the British ceded much of the lands occupied by Native Americans between the Appalachian Mountains and the Mississippi River (Callaway 1995).

During the Revolutionary War, the Seminoles and a large contingent of Black ex-slaves also allied with the British. This alliance was not without its difficulty, as the Seminoles also held slaves. Slavery among the Native Americans was radically different from that found among the Europeans. Among the Seminoles, slaves gradually became part of the group through marriage. After the Revolutionary War, Southern slaveholders became increasingly alarmed at the armed Black and Native American communities throughout Florida. Formally under Spanish rule, the territory was a safe haven for escaped slaves. The first effort to deal with these escaped slaves was in the Treaty of New York (1790), which attempted to force Seminoles to honor new boundary lines and return African slaves to their masters. The Seminoles and other Native Americans refused to honor the treaty and return the Black fugitive slaves. From these humble beginnings the Black Seminoles came into being. Black Seminole culture, a blend of African, Native American, Spanish, and slave traditions, solidified during the 1800s (Ray 2007, 100).

War of 1812

A total of 286,730 soldiers fought in the **War of 1812** (1812–15). Of these, 2,260 died in combat, and another 4,505 were wounded (U.S. Department of Veterans Affairs 2017). Land, specifically Native American land, was the principal source of the tensions that gave rise to this conflict between the United States and Great Britain over British violations of U.S. maritime and trading rights with Europe. It quickly became a war that pitted the United States against the Native Americans, who were allied with Britain and France. All the major players wanted to consolidate or actuate their claims on Native American homelands throughout the interior of the continent. Tribal nations immediately understood the risk to their lands, and a diverse group of Native American military leaders banded together. A faction of the Seneca joined with the Americans in the Battles of Fort George and Chippewa. Most other Native Americans sided with the British against the United States, believing that a British victory would lead to a cessation of land expansions. About a dozen Native American nations participated in the war (Fixico 2008).

One of the most diverse groups of soldiers participating in this war consisted of Choctaw Indians, free Blacks, Creoles, slaves, pirates, and Filipino sailors. Operating out of a swamp, this motley crew fought the decisive **Battle of New Orleans** in January 1815. In this battle, considered the final major battle of the war, the invading British army was defeated; the British had been intent on seizing New Orleans and subsequently all the lands associated with the Louisiana Purchase. Although the British were defeated, the increasingly bitter relationship between the United States and the Seminoles continued. The War of 1812 was also the harbinger of the various Seminole Wars (Warshauer 2007).

The U.S. victory in the War of 1812 marked the acceleration of westward expansion and the destruction of much of what had been Native American lands. Andrew Jackson wasted no time in pushing for passage of the Indian Removal Act; this 1830 law banished all Native Americans to lands west of the Mississippi River. The Indian Removal Act is most directly associated with what became known as the Trail of Tears (1838–39), the name given by Native Americans to the devastating relocation process, which resulted in thousands of deaths from disease and exposure as tribes were forced to leave their lands (Warshauer 2007).

Seminole Wars

During the War of 1812, both African escaped slaves, known as maroons, and Black Seminoles waged war against the United States. Their combined strength made them targets of General Andrew Jackson. After the War of 1812 was concluded, Jackson led army forces in an attack on Fort Gadsden (also known as the Negro Fort) to disrupt Florida's maroon communities. Thus, the first of the Seminole Wars (1817–18) began. The Seminole Wars were three conflicts in Florida between the United States and the Seminoles. Often these conflicts were instigated by the British against U.S. settlers migrating south into Seminole territory. The fact that the Seminoles provided sanctuary to escaping Black slaves also precipitated these conflicts. The three Seminole Wars were never officially declared "wars" by the U.S. government. They were essentially the continuation of the U.S. policy aimed at stripping Native Americans of their lands and forcing them west of the Mississippi. Collectively, the Seminole Wars resulted in the removal of almost 4,000 Seminoles to Oklahoma. In later years, some Black Seminoles went on to become members of the famed Buffalo Soldiers (Calvin 2015).

By 1837, John Horse was an ex-slave and a formidable military leader and member of the Seminole tribe. He launched several successful campaigns throughout the Florida Everglades. At the age of 36, he was elevated from subchief to war chief. He commanded both fellow ex-slaves and Black Seminoles. Black Seminoles had been instrumental in the liberation of slaves from plantations throughout Florida and Georgia and were frequent instigators of Native American rebellions against the U.S. policy of forced removal to present-day Oklahoma. Captured by Union troops in November 1837, John Horse met and became allies with another Seminole war leader—Wild Cat. After their escape, they inspired hope and resistance among both Black and Seminole people. The ultimate battle would come on Christmas Day in 1837, as a sizable U.S. force pursued the Seminoles into the Everglades of southern Florida. With fewer than 380 defenders, the Seminoles faced Union soldiers totaling more than 1,000. Thus began the Battle of Lake Okeechobee, the bloodiest contest of the Seminole Wars. His forces decimated, John Horse and his followers fled south with the Seminoles toward the last safe zone in Florida. Fearing for the survival of his own wife and children, John Horse surrendered during the spring of 1838. By the end of the summer of 1838, he and his family had joined other Native Americans in Indian Territory in present-day Oklahoma (Bird 2008; Tucker 1992).

Mexican–American War

A total of 78,718 soldiers were engaged in the Mexican–American War (1846–1848). Among those who served, a total of 1,733 died, while 4,125 suffered nonmortal wounds (U.S.

Department of Veterans Affairs 2017). The Mexican–American War was primarily an outcome of the U.S. Government's desire to annex Texas, California, and other Mexican territories. U.S. forces launched a three-pronged offensive: from the north through Texas, from the east through the Port of Veracruz, and from the west through present-day California and New Mexico. The Mexican–American War was concluded in 1848 with the signing of the Treaty of Guadalupe Hidalgo. In this treaty, Mexico ceded all lands now considered the American Southwest. In return, all Mexicans living on that land were to be granted full U.S. citizenship. Actions taken by both the U.S. Congress and the Supreme Court denied American citizenship to both Black Mexicans and Pueblo Indians, even though both groups had previously been Mexican citizens. Black Mexicans in Texas were given the choice of staying in Texas and becoming slaves or being deported to Mexico, where slavery was outlawed. Pueblo Indians would not gain the right to vote until 1924. Finally, many other Mexican Americans lost their lands to White American settlers. The Mexican–American War highlighted not only the differences between regions but also the influence of slavery. The nation was on a collision course that could only lead to civil war.

Civil War

If the Revolutionary War defined the United States as a republic, then the Civil War defined it as a nation. The Civil War was a struggle over who would be covered under "we the people" and who would not. Consequently, this conflict also helped define the meaning of U.S. citizenship. The war affected not only U.S.-born Whites and African Americans but also foreign-born residents and Native Americans. A total of 2,213,363 soldiers served in the Union army, and 1,050,000 served in the Confederate army. A total of 140,414 Union soldiers died in battle, as

After the Mexican–American War, Mexico ceded a huge swath of land to the U.S. with the condition that all the Mexican citizens residing there be granted American citizenship. Despite these terms, the U.S. denied citizenship to many Black Mexicans and Pueblo Indians in the region.

William Edward Hook/Library of Congress

did 74,524 Confederate soldiers. Among Union soldiers, 281,881 suffered nonmortal wounds; it is unknown how many Confederate soldiers were wounded (U.S. Department of Veterans Affairs 2017).

The Union, the Confederacy, and Ethnicity

On the eve of the Civil War, the United States was truly becoming a nation of immigrants. For the first time the **old immigrants** (people who came in the earliest waves of immigration, from England, Scotland, and Wales) were being supplanted by **new immigrants** (people from Ireland, Switzerland, Poland, Germany, and Southern European countries). In 1860, about 13% of the U.S. population was foreign-born. This group overwhelmingly not only supported the Union cause but also volunteered for the army in numbers that far exceeded their proportion in the U.S. population. A quarter of the Union armed forces were foreign-born (i.e., 543,000 out of the more than 2 million Union soldiers). Collectively, immigrants and the sons of immigrants accounted for about 43% of the Union army. Many of these were segregated into ethnic regiments (Doyle 2015). In contrast, the Confederate army was 91% U.S.-born, primarily the descendants of old immigrants.

Race and Gender in the Civil War

The Union army, despite intense prejudices, actively recruited Native Americans under the condition that they would fight only in Indian Territory. Two regiments—the First and Second Indian Home Guards—were established. Initially serving under White officers, Native Americans eventually assumed leadership of these regiments.

The start of hostilities put a strain on the Union army and forced it to abandon many of its forts in Indian Territory. This provided a unique opportunity for the Confederates to open an alliance with the Creek, Cherokee, Choctaw, Chickasaw, and Seminole. Their geographic location also ensured that they were culturally tied to the Confederacy. Native American tribes siding with the Confederates were part of the Texas regiments and fought against Union troops (National Park Service 2010).

Although it is difficult to document the contributions of women during the Civil War, we do know of distinguished service by some women. At least 250 women, dressed as men, are known to have fought on both sides of the war (Blanton and Cook 2002). Harriet Tubman, who was born a slave, served as a spy, scout, and hospital nurse during the war. Because of Tubman's knowledge of escape routes from the South, Union officers recruited her to organize an intelligence service to provide troop deployment and other tactical information on Confederate military operations (Moore 1991).

Rape is one of those atrocities of war particularly visited upon women, and it remains a widespread weapon of war today. The Civil War was no exception. Even though President Lincoln—in General Order No. 100, known as the Lieber Code of 1863—established strict guidelines prohibiting wartime atrocities, particularly rape, such atrocities nevertheless occurred. What is important about the Lieber Code is that it represents the first time Black women were afforded protections against rape by White men. As many as 450 cases involving sexual crimes were tried by Union military courts (Feimster 2013), and at least 20 of these cases were prosecuted on behalf of "colored" women (Stutzman 2009).

RESISTANCE STORY: CATHAY WILLIAMS

Cathay Williams, who later altered her name to William Cathay, hid her gender as the nation's only known female Buffalo Soldier, as a private from 1866 to 1868. A bronze bust memorial was dedicated to her on July 22, 2016, at the Richard Allen Cultural Center and Museum in Leavenworth, Kansas.

Courtesy of the National Archives and Records Administration

Cathay Williams (1844–92) was the first documented woman ever to enlist and serve in the U.S. Army while posing as a man. Williams was born a slave on the Johnson plantation on the outskirts of Jefferson City, Missouri. In 1861, as Union forces occupied Jefferson City during the early period of the Civil War, the slaves were declared contraband, and many were forced into military service in support roles such as cooks, laundresses, and nurses. Williams, then 17 years old, was pressed into service in the Eighth Indiana Volunteer Infantry Regiment, under the command of Colonial William Plummer Benton. Over the next few years, as a soldier in the Eighth Indiana, Williams participated in campaigns in Arkansas, Louisiana, and Georgia. She participated in the Battle of Pea Ridge and the Red River Campaign. Later, Williams was transferred to Washington, D.C., where she served with General Phillip Sheridan's battalion. As the war ended, she worked at Jefferson Barracks. After the war, Williams enlisted for a 3-year term in the U.S. Regular Army on November 15, 1866, in St. Louis, Missouri. During this term she served with the famed Buffalo Soldiers. When she suffered a bout of smallpox, a medical examiner discovered that she was a woman. As a result, she was discharged from the army on October 14, 1868.

After the Civil War, the army disbanded all the volunteer "colored" regiments and established six segregated Black regiments under White officers. In 1869, the infantry regiments were reconstituted into the 24th and 25th Infantries. Two cavalry regiments, the 9th and 10th, remained intact. These regiments saw combat in both the Southwest and the West in the so-called Indian War, and during the Spanish–American War.

World War II

World War II (U.S. involvement 1941–45) was, among other things, a scramble for raw resources such as oil, gold, and diamonds that spanned Europe, Africa, Asia, and the Middle East. A total of 16.6 million men and women served. Of those, close to 407,000 American service personnel died, including 292,000 in battle and another 115,000 through other circumstances. Of the total deaths, 79,000 were lost in combat and never receeovered, while another 672,000 suffered non-fatal wounds. In 2017, 1,711,000 World War II veterans were still living (U.S. Department of Veterans Affairs 2017).

Unrest at Home and Abroad

From its beginning in 1939, World War II was cast as a race war, as Adolf Hitler and Nazi Germany stormed through Poland and the Soviet Union, killing Jews (some 6 million over the course of the war) and declaring Slavs (mainly ethnic Poles, Serbs, and Russians) to be subhuman (Timm 2010). The Japanese, allied with Germany in this effort, believed that they were the superior race and attempted to overpower China and other Asian countries. The Japanese held the United States in equal contempt, describing Americans as a decadent and mongrel people (Baofu 2014).

Meanwhile, here in the United States, after the bombing of Pearl Harbor by the Japanese in December 1941, 120,000 citizens of Japanese ancestry were ordered into concentration camps. As our nation castigated both Germany and Japan for their racist imperialism, Jim Crow laws ruled the South and the military. American cities were repeatedly rocked by race riots. Whites attacked Blacks in shipyards in Mobile, Alabama; Whites targeted both Blacks and immigrants in Detroit; White workers rioted in Beaumont, Texas; and White servicemen assaulted Mexican

Americans in Los Angeles during the so-called Zoot Suit Riots. In 1943 alone, 242 separate violent attacks targeting African Americans occurred in 47 U.S. cities as Southern White migrants clashed with Black residents over access to public spaces, jobs, and housing (Honey 2007).

African Americans: Upward Mobility and Continued Discrimination

During the war, some 400,000 women served in the American military, primarily in the Women's Army Corps and the Army and Navy Nurse Corps. Black women constituted the largest group of women of color within the Women's Army Corps, accounting for 10.6% of the total (Honey 2007). Black women made significant gains in the labor force during the war, although these advances were significantly curtailed by legally sanctioned racial and gendered segregation across the entire country.

While President Franklin Roosevelt's 1941 Executive Order 8802 prohibited racial discrimination in the defense industries and civil service jobs, this rule was rarely enforced. Most employers turned to non-Whites only when they had exhausted the White labor supply. Even then, non-Whites were relegated to the most menial and dangerous positions, frequently on night shifts and in janitorial slots. Unions further hindered Black women's ability to gain employment in unionized blue-collar jobs. When Black people were hired, they were forced to use separate restrooms and were often paid the lowest salaries for the most difficult work. **Hate strikes**, a series of White supremacist wildcat strikes, were triggered throughout the war, such as in 1943 when White women working at the Baltimore Western Electric plant demanded toilet facilities separate from those used by the Black women working at the plant. Ultimately, the racial restrictions in the military–industrial complex forced Black women to remain in the private sector, serving as maids (Honey 2007).

Fully qualified African American nurses often found that racial segregation and discrimination hampered their entry into military service during World War II. And even those who made it in found Jim Crow discrimination waiting for them at the door. In 1945, thanks to pressure applied by First Lady Eleanor Roosevelt, 60 Black women were sent to Lovell Hospital at Fort Devens (outside Boston) to be trained as medical technicians. The commanding officer objected to Black medical technicians placing thermometers in the mouths of White servicemen, and he ordered these women to be reclassified from medical technicians to orderlies. A group of African American servicewomen met with the commanding officer, only to be insulted and dismissed. They walked out of the meeting and refused to report to work the next morning. After being threatened with charges of mutiny, most returned to work. Six did not. When these six were threatened with execution, still four stayed away. They were eventually court-martialed for refusing to obey orders, found guilty, and sentenced to a year of hard labor. They also received dishonorable discharges. A national protest led by the NAACP, the ACLU, and Mary McLeod Bethune's National Council of Negro Women forced a reversal of the decision (Bray 2016), but resistance to African American women serving across all of the armed forces persisted throughout the war (Wynn 2010).

For many Black men, the military offered decent wages and the potential for upward mobility after the war. But the military life, they discovered, was a continuation of the discrimination and segregation prevalent in the wider society. Often both the military and government officials looked on Black soldiers as inferior. They rejected Blacks as leaders, claiming Blacks would serve best under White officers. While the U.S. Army maintained separate Black regiments, the Navy restricted Blacks to positions as cooks, janitors, and waiters. The Marine Corps refused to allow Blacks to join altogether. But possibly the worst treatment occurred among those Blacks serving in the South. Here even Nazi prisoners of war were accorded better treatment than Black soldiers. Prisoners of war could dine with Whites, often ride on the trains, and even go into town to view movies. Black soldiers and civilians were denied all of these (Wynn 2010).

In 1940 just 4,000 African Americans served in the U.S. Navy, most of them as cooks or dishwashers or in the engine rooms. Another 12,500 served in naval construction units such as the Seabees and another thousand in the Coast Guard. It was not until 1943 that African Americans were admitted into all naval branches on a proportional basis, and the first Black naval officers were appointed in February 1944. Segregation still prevailed, and the only way Blacks could crew a ship was if it were entirely Black. In 1944 the USS *Mason* and the submarine chaser USS *PC-1264,* both with all-Black crews, were commissioned to escort destroyers. That same year the first integrated crews were introduced on 25 auxiliary vessels. By the end of the war, 165 African Americans were serving in the Navy and 5,000 in the Coast Guard. The overwhelming majority of these, 95%, still served in mess halls. Only 54 Black naval officers and 700 Coast Guard officers were serving at the close of hostilities, in 1945 (Wynn 2010).

Labor Shortages and the Bracero Program

Latinx men and women also benefited from the labor needs of the military–industrial complex during World War II. In 1942, labor shortages on railroads, in mining operations, at shipyards, and in agriculture forced the U.S. government to establish the **Bracero Program**, which allowed 50,000 agricultural workers and 765 railroad workers from Mexico to enter the United States as contract guest workers (*bracero* is the Spanish word for manual laborer). These workers were critical to the nation's wartime economy. The program established basic workers' rights (sanitation, adequate shelter, and food) and a minimum wage of 30 cents an hour. Through various extensions of the program, 4.6 million contracts were signed from 1942 to 1964, with many workers coming back year after year. From its inception, however, the Bracero Program was fraught with problems, as desperate Mexican workers were often relegated to the most difficult, least desirable, and lowest-paying jobs in agriculture. In theory the workers were protected, with guaranteed sanitary housing, decent meals at reasonable prices, occupational insurance at the farm owners' expense, and free transportation back to Mexico at the ends of their contracts. These rules were often and flagrantly broken as farm wages dropped and abuses ran rampant (Gonzalez 2013).

Asian Americans in the Enlisted Ranks

One particular group that faced systematic discrimination during the war consisted of about 500 Nisei (second-generation Japanese—i.e., children of immigrants) women who served in the U.S. forces in the enlisted ranks and worked as office personnel, translators, and medical professionals. They had to contend not only with the reality that their families were being held in internment camps but also with the gender expectation that women should be subservient to men. For many of these women, their wartime experience was a turning point in their lives as they navigated racial, gender, and national identities. The military experience for Japanese American (as well as for Korean and Chinese American) women was different from that of African American women in that they did not serve in segregated units (Moore 2003).

Correcting the Record

The **Medal of Honor**, often called the Congressional Medal of Honor because it is awarded in the name of Congress, is the highest military honor that an individual can receive for combat heroism. Racial discrimination was so extreme during World War II that not a single African American received a Medal of Honor during the war or immediately after. This injustice began to be remedied somewhat only after researchers at Shaw University conducted a study in the mid-1990s and found that systematic racial discrimination had prevented Blacks from being considered (Converse, Gibran, Cash, Griffith, and Kohn 1997).

Of the 3,488 Medals of Honor awarded as of June 2016, 263 have gone to Irish Americans, 87 to African Americans, 42 to Hispanic Americans, 47 to Asian Americans, 22 to Native

The 100th Infantry Battalion, or the 42nd Regimental Combat Team, composed exclusively of Japanese Americans, was one of the most highly decorated units in the U.S. military, yet the battalion's members were denied the nation's highest combat award. Among the unit's citations were an accumulated 18,000 individual decorations, but only one wartime Medal of Honor, 53 Distinguished Service Crosses, 9,486 Purple Hearts, and 7 Presidential Unit Citations. Anti-Japanese sentiment would deny many the nation's highest honor. It would take another 57 years before 21 more would receive the Medal of Honor (Williams 2000).

Bettmann/Getty Images

Americans, 25 to Italian Americans, and at least 28 to Jewish Americans. Only one Medal of Honor has been awarded to a woman. The numbers of Medal of Honor recipients of various races and ethnicities are even more telling when we look behind the scenes. Most of the Jewish, Hispanic, Asian, and African American recipients have been recognized only after decades of anonymity and historical amnesia. Over the past three decades, each U.S. president has held special ceremonies to honor these heroes for their service and sacrifices. These delayed recipients of the nation's highest recognition of valor have been identified through a congressionally mandated review.

On January 13, 1997, President Bill Clinton awarded the Medal of Honor to seven African American World War II veterans. Only one recipient, Vernon Baker, was still alive to receive it. On June 21, 2000, after more than 50 years, the government recognized and awarded 22 Asian American soldiers for their valor during World II. In awarding these medals, President Clinton stated, "It's long past time to break the silence about their courage . . . Rarely has a nation been so well-served by a people it has so ill-treated" (quoted in Williams 2000). Most recently, President Barack Obama awarded the Medal of Honor to 24 overlooked Black, Hispanic, and Jewish heroes. In all these cases, a military tribunal declared that all were "denied Medal(s) of Honor years ago because of bias" (Straw 2014).

CONCEALED STORY: MARCARIO GARCÍA

Marcario García receiving the Medal of Honor from President Harry S. Truman.

Courtesy of the National Archives and Records Administration

Marcario García answered his nation's call to go to war. García, a native of Mexico, grew up in the Fort Bend area in Texas. In November 1942 he was drafted and was soon bound for the European theater. There, during the Normandy attack in November 1944, he was wounded. When VE Day ended the war in Europe on May 8, 1945, he returned to the United States and his hometown. VJ Day, announcing the Japanese surrender and the end of World War II, occurred on August 14, 1945. Less than two weeks later, on August 23, 1945, Harry Truman awarded García the Medal of Honor in a White House ceremony. García was a hometown hero.

A fabulous party was held to celebrate the local hero. A story in the *Houston Post* on September 7, 1945, was headlined "Sugar Land War Hero." But just a day after this public welcome, Staff Sergeant García was refused service at the Oasis Café in the nearby city of Richmond. He was then beaten with a bat, resulting in his hospitalization; he was subsequently charged with drunkenness and disorderly conduct. The charges were ultimately dropped, but this incident illustrates the racial climate in America at the time—a climate in which individuals could honorably serve, putting their lives on the line on foreign battlefields, and still come home to a place where their basic freedoms were circumscribed by race, class, and gender.

Source: Michael A. Olivas, "The 'Trial of the Century' That Never Was: Staff Sgt. Marcario García, the Congressional Medal of Honor, and the Oasis Café," *Indiana Law Journal* 83, no. 4 (2008): 1391–1403.

Although five Native Americans who served in World War II were Medal of Honor recipients, few have acknowledged the clandestine and important mission served by the group known as code talkers. Their story is both unique and important. The Japanese military had become very adept at breaking the sophisticated codes utilized by the U.S. forces. In the search for a solution, it was suggested that the language of the Navajo might be effective in thwarting the Japanese code breakers. This language, without an alphabet or symbols, was in use only in remote areas of the American Southwest. At the onset of World War II, no more than 30 non-Navajo could understand the language. Therefore, its potential as code was immediately recognized. During one of the most hard-fought battles in the Pacific theater, at Iwo Jima, a strange language was intercepted coming from American radios. The secret messages were derived from the Navajo language and transmitted by Native American soldiers. A total of 400 Navajo served in the Marines Corps as code talkers. While the value of what they contributed was significant, it was not until September 17, 1992, that they were honored in a ceremony at the Pentagon (Asturias 2008).

Vietnam War

Currently, the largest group of veterans within the U.S. served during the Vietnam era (33%). By 2045, the largest share of living veterans will be those who first served during the era encompassing the post-9/11 Gulf War (35%) (Barroso 2019). The Vietnam War (1954–75), one of the most contentious conflicts this nation has seen, continues to define U.S. politics, military wisdom, and national policy. President George H. W. Bush declared that the 1991 Persian Gulf War would "not be another Vietnam," and all succeeding presidents have found themselves arguing with the war's ghost—Bill Clinton in the Balkans, George W. Bush in Iraq, and Barack Obama in Afghanistan. The Vietnam War resulted in an estimated 1.1 million Vietnamese army and Viet Cong military deaths and another 533,000 civilian deaths. Of the 2.1 million U.S. men and women who served, 90,220 died and 153,303 were wounded. Today, an estimated 7,391,000 Vietnam veterans are living (U.S. Department of Veterans Affairs 2017). The Vietnam War coincided with various civil rights movements—the Black civil rights movement, the women's liberation movement, the Native American movement—and a whole slew of countercultural movements, and, of course, it was the entire reason for the antiwar movement. But this does not totally explain why this was the most unpopular, most debated, most contentious war in U.S. history.

More Blacks served in Vietnam than in any war before or since. During the height of the war (1965–69), Blacks accounted for 11% of the American population but made up 12.6% of the soldiers in Vietnam. They also made up 14.1% of the war dead (National Archives 2016). Military recruitment advertisements were carefully crafted to feature African American men and women but avoided overrepresenting them. The advertising agencies charged with crafting these ads took into consideration both the arguments of civil rights activists that Blacks were overrepresented among war casualties and the fears that an all-volunteer military would become disproportionately populated by lower-income minorities. The ads they developed attempted to strike a balance, featuring Blacks and Whites, and males and females, in identical environments (Bailey 2009).

Black people were overrepresented in the military during the Vietnam War and made up a yet larger proportion of casualties.

Ian Brode/Hulton Archive/Getty Images

Most of the deaths of Black soldiers in Vietnam occurred during the war's first phase. Blacks were overrepresented in the infantry at that time and consequently had significantly higher casualties. Interestingly, as the military shifted to a withdrawal phase, deaths among Black servicemen declined, while a disproportionate number of Hispanics died in combat. Some speculate that this shift reflects the effectiveness of civil rights activism, which applied pressure to decision makers to replace African Americans with members of less politically mobilized ethnic groups, such as Hispanics, during the withdrawal phase of the war (Talbot and Oplinger 2014).

Obviously absent from the binary construct of military advertisements was the possibility of recruiting either Latinx or Asian Americans. Part of this might have been deliberate avoidance, particularly of Hispanics, as Latinx antiwar leaders were extremely vocal about their opposition to any form of military service (Oropeza 2005).

Vietnam veterans constitute nearly half of all homeless veterans today. Among all veterans, people of color, constituting 18.4% of the general veteran population, were disproportionately (43.2%) likely to experience homelessness. African Americans, comprising just 12.3% of the general veteran population, were 33.1% likley to experience homelessness. And Native Americans and Alaska Natives, comprising respectively 0.7% and 2.1% of the general veteran population, were respectively 3% and 4.8% likely to be homeless. White veterans, significantly less likely to be homeless, comprising 81.6% of all veterans, constituted 56.8% of homeless veterans (National Alliance to End Homelessness 2018).

Wars on Terrorism

Terrorists function to disrupt social, political, and economic processes, with the aim of accomplishing specific ends. There are three forms of terrorism: individual, group, and state sponsored. Many observers today believe that state-sponsored terrorism is the biggest challenge to world peace.

The **war on terrorism**, also often called the global war on terrorism or the war on terror, consists of a series of military and legislative campaigns that began after the September 11, 2001, attacks on the United States. These have involved both covert and overt military operations, new legislation aimed at increasing national security, and efforts to block the flow of money going to terrorists. Those critical of such efforts argue that they stem primarily from an ideology of fear and repression that targets specific groups, and that they promote violence, thus strengthening terrorist recruitment efforts (Hafetz 2011).

The phrase "war against terrorism" first appeared in 1984 in reaction to the 1983 Beirut barracks bombings, a set of terrorist attacks that occurred during Lebanon's Civil War. In the attacks, two truck bombs were used to target separate buildings that housed peacekeeping forces, specifically U.S. and French soldiers. In the suicide attacks, 241 American and 58 French soldiers, 6 civilians, and the 2 attackers were killed. The Reagan administration used these provocations to seek enhanced powers to freeze the assets of terrorist groups and respond quickly to perceived threats with military action. The U.S. strike on Libya in April 1986 was the first strategic use of this policy. In this attack, code-named Operation El Dorado Canyon, the U.S. military conducted air strikes in retaliation for Libyan sponsorship of terrorism against Americans. During the same period, the Reagan administration was also covertly involved in trying to topple several governments. One example is the Iran-Contra affair, in which senior administration officials violated the law by facilitating the acquisition of military arms for both Iran and the Contras in Nicaragua, as part of an attempt to destabilize autonomous governments. A total of $212 million in covert U.S. military aid flowed into Central American states in 1986 alone. By 1992, when a United Nations–brokered peace was established, more than 80,000 Salvadorans had been killed, 8,000 more had disappeared, and more than a million of El Salvador's 5 million citizens had been displaced (Sandford 2003, 70). Often indigenous peasants were targeted, as was the case in Guatemala, where more than 200,000 people died (Sullivan and Jordan 2004). These covert operations included disseminating propaganda and arming and training Indian leaders willing to fight (Krauss 1986, 569).

The current war on terrorism is associated with the events that occurred on September 11, 2001. Since that time, Arab and Muslim Americans have been systematically targeted, racialized, and often ostracized for acts they did not commit, accused of things they did not do, and presumed guilty simply because they were perceived different. There were 481 hate crimes in just 2001, up from 28 just the year before. But during the period between 2002 and 2014 anti-Muslim crimes receded to between 105 and 160 annually. These numbers began to again spike in 2015, as all hate crimes increased. They now make up 4.4% of victims of all reported hate crimes while constituting only 1% of the U.S. population (Levin 2017). Most recent data reveal that the number of anti-Muslim hate crimes continues to rise, reaching 127 in 2016 (See Figure 10.4).

Pervasive levels of **Islamophobia**, or intense fear and paranoia regarding Muslims and Arabs (both those living in the United States and those abroad), have consistently and

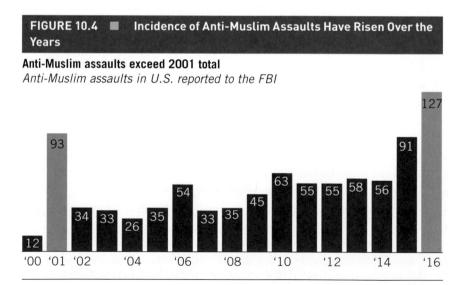

FIGURE 10.4 ■ Incidence of Anti-Muslim Assaults Have Risen Over the Years

Anti-Muslim assaults exceed 2001 total
Anti-Muslim assaults in U.S. reported to the FBI

Source: Data from the Federal Bureau of Investigation, compiled by Pew Research Center.

increasingly been identified among U.S. citizens, and hate crimes against people assumed to be Muslim have spiked dramatically (Ogan, Wilnat, Pennington, and Bashir 2013). These issues, often reflected by our leading politicians, suggest simmering resentment and condemnation of Arab and Muslim Americans. Islamophobia ultimately asserts that a fundamental incompatibility exists between Islam and "Western values," here associated with democracy, tolerance, and civility (Malik 2019).

How we ultimately view terrorism is structured by the intersectional lens that we have constructed. We rarely think of terrorists as being rich, White, or female (Cole 2011). The reality is that women, particularly affluent White women, are being effectively recruited by various terrorist organizations. These women are attracted to such organizations because they perceive that by joining, they can be empowered and add meaning to their lives. These groups use Twitter, Facebook, and other social media sites as primary arenas for recruitment of both women and men (Ferran and Kreider 2015).

Early in his administration, President Donald Trump vowed that he would protect the American people from terrorists by restricting entrance to the United States by people from predominantly Muslim countries. After several court challenges, the ban was upheld by the Supreme Court. The ban included all persons from the Muslim-majority countries of Iran, Iraq, Libya, Somalia, Syria, and Yemen, and instituted travel restrictions on citizens of Chad, North Korea, and Venezuela (Harb and Akkad 2019). None of the terrorists responsible for any attacks within the United States has come from any of the countries included in this travel ban. In fact, most individuals involved in terrorism since 9/11 were citizens, either born in the United States or naturalized. Moreover, a U.S. citizen is 253 times more likely to die from ordinary homicide than from a terrorist attack carried out by a foreigner in the United States (McCarthy 2017).

Critical Thinking

1. In what ways have the wars in which the United States has been involved changed over both time and place? What does this suggest about us as a nation? What are the implications for our future?

2. The U.S. military, as an institution, has been transformed by wars and terrorism. What changes have occurred in how the United States conducts wars?

3. What does the belated awarding of Medals of Honor suggest about the operation of the racial matrix (both historically and in contemporary times)? What may account for these shifts?

4. How have you been affected by the war on terrorism? How have your family and friends been affected? What does this suggest about race, gender, and class?

STORIES OF RESISTANCE, SOCIAL MOVEMENTS, AND TRANSFORMATION

Stock stories do not tell us how change and resilience come about within the military. Neither do they demonstrate how people of color find ways to transform the structures. For this we need to explore stories of resistance, agency, and transformative social movements.

Activism and Social Movements

Military service influences veterans in very real ways. It can serve as a platform by which they push for racial equality and justice (Parkier 2009). In this section we will examine some of these stories of resistance, agency and the social movements they sparked to transform the military and even the outcomes of the various wars that comprise our history.

African American Activism

An estimated 180,000 African Americans served in the Civil War. These Black regiments, commonly referred to as the United States Colored Troops, faced several forms of discrimination. Not only were they segregated, but they were confined to positions such as laborers, cooks, and caretakers. Despite their willingness to serve, African American soldiers in the Union army were paid significantly less than their White male counterparts. Despite, or possibly because of, their low status, Blacks increasingly used their position as veterans to challenge the system. The story of Sgt. William Walker is instructive in this regard.

Mourners visit a mural in Austin, Texas, dedicated to Army Specialist Vanessa Guillen, who was murdered by another soldier.

Sergio Flores/Getty Images

In November of 1863, Sgt. William Walker of South Carolina and other Black soldiers went on strike demanding equal pay. The Union threatened to charge the soldiers with mutiny, and many of the Black soldiers went back to work. Sgt. Walker refused, and in February 1864 he was tried, convicted, and executed by firing squad. Soon a social movement, instigated by abolitionist groups, mobilized as their cause was picked up by newspapers and politicians. Joining their struggle was Harriet Tubman, who refused to meet with Abraham Lincoln until Blacks received equal pay. This protest was successful and Black soldiers were awarded equal pay in March of 1865 (Beard 2018).

Black women also found ways to serve during this period. For example, Susie King Taylor, who was raised as a slave off the coast of Georgia, was one of the first Black nurses to serve in the military. As a laundress and nurse for the First South Carolina Volunteers, she set up a school for Black children and soldiers. Although she served for four years and three months, she did not receive any pay. Following the war, King set up a school for freed slaves (Sheldon 2019). This tradition of service and activism continued into the next century as the World Wars fostered change both locally and globally.

World War I had barely been concluded; Black veterans were just returning home when they had to go to war again. One incident that will go down as a travesty of both justice and shame happened during the Huston Riot of 1917. The Huston Riot of 1917 was a reaction of 156 soldiers of the all-Black Third Battalion of the Twenty-fourth United States Infantry Regiment to the harassment of local Black residents as well as Black soldiers. In one night, over 11 civilians, five policemen, and four soldiers were killed. The soldiers involved were court-martialed. 19 were executed, and 41 sentenced to life imprisonment. Although President Wilson commuted, or lifted, the sentences of 10 of those condemned to execution, the rest of the sentences were carried out. No White civilian was ever brought to trial. Even today, many seek justice for these men and demand that they be exonerated (Mitchell 2018). Similar actions took place in Chicago, Washington, and throughout the South (Balto 2019). In several Southern towns it was common to see Black veterans creating self-defense units and calmly carrying guns to protect their communities against White rioters (McWhirter 2011). World War II veterans continued this tradition of service and activism.

Black veterans returning from World War II were determined that the past would not be repeated in their generation. Almost from the start, their activism and agency began transforming the United States, particularly in the South. On July 2, 1946, this is what motivated twenty-one-year-old Medgar Evers, his brother, and four other World War II Black veterans to appear at the courthouse in Decatur, Mississippi, determined to vote. They were the first group of Black people since Reconstruction to try to register in this small town. Evers and his fellow veterans were met by a White mob. They went home and got their guns but decided not to vote or fight. Evers would rise to become the field secretary for the NAACP, a worker on the Emmett Till trial, and one of the most critical leaders in the Mississippi Freedom Movement. He was killed in 1964 by White supremacists (SNCC No Date). Black veterans continue in their activism as they protest police brutality and homelessness, and fight for access to healthcare and rehabilitation for both veterans and the community at large (Walker 2016).

Asian American Activism

The stories of Asian American activism, agency, and social movements are concealed stories. Although time and space preclude us investigating all of them, we can examine one that demonstrates resilience and the determination to be more than a victim. President Franklin Roosevelt forced more than 110,000 Japanese Americans to live in concentration camps during World War II. This event, more than any other, mobilized a generation of Japanese Americans to activism.

One such activist was Fred Korematsu, who was arrested when he refused to relocate to an internment camp in 1942. His case ultimately went to the Supreme Court; Korematsu fought the legality of President Franklin's Executive Order 9066 (the order that forced the relocation of Japanese citizens to internment camps). The Supreme Court ruled in favor of the government, in what current Supreme Court Justice Scalia (2000) argued was one of the worst rulings ever made. Most of the court argued that the detentions were based on suspicions of Japanese Americans' loyalties and not racially discriminatory. After being released, Korematsu contested his conviction. It was not until 1983, 40 years later, that his conviction was overturned (Nittle 2019).

TRANSFORMATION STORY: FIGHTING FOR WHAT IS RIGHT

Dan Choi, a former Army infantry officer who saw combat in the Iraq War during 2006–2007, is an LGBTQ rights activist. His story demonstrates the intersections of sexuality, ethnicity, and military service. As a spokesman for *Knights Out*, an organization of West Point alumni, staff, and faculty who support LGBTQ people, he declared his sexuality on national television and publicly challenged the "Don't Ask, Don't Tell" policy forbidding lesbian, gay, and bisexual service members from openly serving (Caron 2009). Two different federal courts ruled in 2010 that the ban on openly gay, lesbian, and bisexual service personnel was unconstitutional. As we discussed earlier, President Trump, through executive order, banned transgender individuals from serving in the military.

Hispanic American Activism

The Chicano Movement, dating back to end of the U.S.–Mexican war in 1848, aims to combat discrimination in both public and private institutions. World War II Hispanic groups, led by Mexican American veteran Dr. Hector P. Garcia, formed the American G.I. Forum (AGIF) and joined with other civil rights organizations to wage a concentrated effort to expose racism targeting Hispanics. The first major event to receive national attention was when the AGIF advocated for Felix Longoria, a Mexican American veteran denied burial services in his hometown of Three Rivers, Texas, after being killed during WWII. AGIF became a national civil rights advocacy group by the 1950s (Estrada 2015).

In 1966, the AGIF joined Black civil rights groups to force Texas to repeal the poll tax (a tax levied on every individual which served to disenfranchise many Blacks from voting in the former Confederate States). In 1967 they marched on the Texas state capitol protesting the low wages of Mexican agricultural workers. From 1969 to 1979, the AGIF led a national boycott against the Adolph Coors Company, one of the largest brewing producers in the country, to challenge its discriminatory policies affecting Chicanos (Ramos 1998).

Building a More Inclusive Future

Since the United States began its war on terrorism in late 2001, it has appropriated $6.4 trillion on counterterrorism efforts through the end of 2020. Our counterterrorism efforts and other operations now involve more than 80 countries. Veterans benefits will add an additional $1 trillion over the next several decades. To date, over 801,000 people have died as a direct consequence of war violence. Of these, 335,000 were civilians. And there were 21 million war refugees and displaced persons (War Institute 2020).

It is almost inconceivable to think of a time when we might be free of conflict. However, we can develop saner, more reasonable, and more just ways of resolving conflict that avoid the destructive and vastly inequitable structures, processes, and practices that all too frequently reflect race, class, and gender. Engaged citizens are the most significant deterrent to domestic terrorism. Engaged citizens are also the most effective safeguards when national policies are misdirected.

Strength through Diversity

Our best chance of averting wars lies in efforts to increase world security by working toward sustainable jobs and economies. Asserting the basic dignity of all, regardless of race, class, ethnicity, religion, age, or gender, is a good starting place. Measures such as random bag checks, airport strip searches, and racial profiling have done little to make us any safer, but they have increased the threats to our basic freedoms. At the core of the American judicial system is the presumption of innocence, yet we have targeted our citizens for internment, hostility, and even death, with no basis for our accusations other than our fear. Fear is a poor substitute for trust, and it erodes the very democratic principles that we cherish.

Our military institutions, the most diverse institutions in the nation, hold the key to the effective and efficient use of all our human resources. Encouraging all citizens to serve in, participate with, and provide oversight of our military institutions can be the greatest deterrent to abuses, the greatest safeguard to peace, and the most effective weapon against terrorism.

If we are going to diversify the military, the change needs to start from the top (Sicard 2016)—something on which 25 four-star generals, admirals, and other military leaders agree (Duster 2013). This means getting more women and people of color into the officer pipeline. This is indeed what is happening at West Point. In 2019 the U.S. Military Academy (West Point) welcomed its most diverse group of cadets in history. Among the 1,190 cadets, 43% were people of color (Fink 2019). These same patterns need to be replicated across all military academies if the armed forces are going to become truly diverse.

World Security through Sustainable Economies

The enemy of democracy is tyranny. And the principal allies of tyranny are poverty, hopelessness, and inequity. If we are going to stop terrorism, then we must first prevent it by supporting equal access to education; alleviating poverty, hunger, and misery; and promoting civil liberties and freedom (Martin 2015).

Wars are more likely to occur where lawlessness, hopelessness, and helplessness prevail. The most likely to suffer are those most vulnerable, regardless of whether they are in the United States or abroad. In such situations it is difficult to determine who is right or wrong, good or evil. None of these terms make any sense in the face of devastated lives, pain, and suffering. We should realize that during our own Revolutionary War, we were the extremists, the terrorists, and the discontents.

We cannot however continue to see our military budget increase unchecked, now close to $1 trillion. This is unsustainable. Also unsustainable are the more than 6,900 U.S. military personnel that have died since 9/11, and the more than 30,000 wounded in Iraq and Afghanistan alone. And of course, this does not take into consideration the hundreds of thousands of returning troops that will suffer from post-traumatic stress disorder (Hartung and Smithberger 2019). We need to find alternatives to war and militarism, particularly when responding to terrorism. As a nation among other nations, the United States needs to join with the United Nations to help sustain the rule of law around the world. All parties need to be brought to the table, and all need to be held to the same standard. The International Criminal Court offers a place where the world can hold accountable those who commit crimes against humanity, whether they are state agents or nonstate actors (Rothkopf and Lord 2013).

Within our own country, we need to encourage service by all as part of what it means to be a citizen. The idea that military service and other forms of public service should be shared equally by all, regardless of race, class, or gender, reflects the fact that we all have a stake in this democracy. The most secure democracy is one in which all citizens participate.

Critical Thinking

1. How do the societal values of diversity and inclusion become manifested in the military? How might our values effect changes in the military?

2. How could the establishment of more global institutions lead to decreasing numbers of terrorist acts? What role should the United States play in such institutions? What role should the United Nations and the International Criminal Court play?

3. How does veteran activism influence social change within the U.S. In what ways do veterans with marginalized identities affect wider civil rights and social movements?

4. What kinds of information, messages, or images prevail regarding people who are not like you, not of your same culture or nationality? Are these barriers or bridges to interactions?

CHAPTER SUMMARY

10.1   Examine the contemporary reality of race, class, and gender in the U.S. military.

The contemporary U.S. military accounts for 16% of the total U.S. budget, which represents a third of all moneys spent globally on defense. Although it is predominantly male, White, and young, the U.S. military is one of the most diverse institutions in the nation. Race, gender, and age differences occur across all the branches. Younger recruits tend to join the Marine Corps, while the Air Force attracts older recruits. Women are underrepresented in all branches, but they are most likely to enlist in the Air Force. Close to a third of all enlisted personnel are members of racial minority groups. While racial minorities constitute 23.4% of those eligible to enlist, they make up 32.9% of enlisted ranks. Middle- and upper-class individuals are least likely to be found among enlisted personnel. Clear gender differences are evident across the various services. Women of color are more likely to serve in either the Army or the Navy than in other military branches. Immigrants continue to join the military as a means of becoming naturalized citizens.

10.2   Explore the stock sociological theories regarding the U.S. military, war, and terrorism.

Three central sociological theories dominate the field of military sociology and represent stock stories. The functionalist approach holds that the military, war, and terrorism serve specific and important tasks within society. Symbolic interactionism investigates how we attach meaning to such things as war and remembrance, flags and memorials, and other representations that support wars, terrorism, and the military. Monopoly and materialist perspectives posit that military organizations maintain a legitimate monopoly on the use of coercive force that is uniquely tied to the material instruments of war. Stock theories tend to oversimplify the military, war, and terrorism while underemphasizing the impacts of race, class, and gender. Functionalism, specifically, fails to anticipate change and tends to ignore powerful interests within society. Symbolic interactionism, with its emphasis on micro-level analysis, fails to account adequately for social structure, identity, and military organizations. And monopoly and materialist perspectives, by linking all manifestations of the military, war, and terrorism to the state, fails to anticipate how nonstate entities, civil war, and ethnic/racial conflict can be the sources of war and military conflict. Critical sociologists have stressed the intersections of race, class, and gender as being central in any theories, scholarship, and research interrogating the military, war, and terrorism. Critical race theory also examines how military hierarchies represent internally stratified labor markets that reflect hierarchies in wider society. Terrorism often highlights the vulnerability of specific racial groups.

10.3   Apply the matrix approach to U.S. military history, war, and terrorism.

Concentrating on the most significant wars throughout our history provides a central set of events by which and through which the matrix lens can be utilized. The Revolutionary War highlights that the military of the United States has never been homogeneous, as Native Americans, Blacks, immigrants, women, and various class groups have always participated. Our national identity was initially forged in this war. Across our history, the U.S. military engaged in 29 major wars with Native American populations. These wars were responsible for the loss of thousands of lives as well as Native Americans' loss of tribal lands. The Civil War highlights the importance of race, class, and gender. At least 250 women, often dressed as men, fought on both sides. Rape, a particular atrocity of war, targeted women, especially Black women. World War II highlighted the nation's bifurcated stance regarding race. On the one hand, the United States was waging a war against fascism and racial imperialism, while on the other it was upholding Jim Crow laws in both the South and the military. The Vietnam War, our most contentious war, revealed the ugly scars of racism as both Blacks and Hispanics were significantly overrepresented among U.S. casualties. Agitation over these deaths and questions about the morality of the war challenged our country and its leaders to reconsider how wars should be fought. Amid these controversies an all-volunteer force was created. Wars against terrorism, involving both covert and overt military operations, security legislation, and new regulations, derive from the September 11, 2001, attacks on U.S. soil. The current war on terrorism has tended to target Muslims, principally from the Middle East. Such concerns seem to be misplaced, as the average U.S. citizen is more than 253 times more likely to die from a homicide than from a terrorist attack carried out by a foreigner in the United States.

10.4 Evaluate the possibilities for a more inclusive future.

Our military institutions, the most diverse institutions in the nation, hold the key to the effective and efficient use of all our human resources. Encouraging all citizens to serve in, participate with, and provide oversight of our military institutions can be the greatest deterrent to abuse, the greatest safeguard of peace, and the most effective weapon against terrorism. Wars are more likely to occur where lawlessness, hopelessness, and helplessness prevail. The most likely to suffer are those most vulnerable, regardless of whether they are in the United States or abroad. In such situations it is difficult to determine who is right or wrong, good or evil. None of these terms make any sense in the face of devastated lives, pain, and suffering. We should realize that during our own Revolutionary War, we were the extremists, the terrorists, and the discontents.

KEY TERMS

Battle of New Orleans

Bracero Program

coercive force

dysfunctional

functionalist approach to the military

hate strikes

interstate forms of war

intrastate forms of war

Islamophobia

Medal of Honor

Mexican–American War

military sociology

military–industrial complex

monopoly and materialist perspectives

new immigrants

nonstate actors

old immigrants

Seminole Wars

symbolic interactionist approach to the
   military

terrorism

Trail of Tears

war

War of 1812

war on terrorism

World War II

REFERENCES

Amadeo, Kimberly. 2017. "War on Terror Facts, Costs and Timeline." The Balance. Accessed June 18, 2017. https://www.thebalance.com/war-on-terror-facts-costs-timeline-3306300.

Amadeo, Kimberly. 2020. "US Military Budget, Its components, Challenges and Growth." Accessed online at URL: https://www.thebalance.com/u-s-military-budget-components-challenges-growth-3306320

Ashe, Samuel A'Courte. 1908. *History of North Carolina: From 1584 to 1783*. Greensboro, NC: Charles L. Van Noppen

Asturias, Lani. 2008. "Navajo Code Talkers." In *Encyclopedia of Bilingual Education,* edited by Josué M. González. Thousand Oaks, CA: Sage.

Bailey, Beth. 2009. *America's Army: Making the All-Volunteer Force.* Cambridge, MA: Harvard University Press.

Balto, Simon 2019. *Red Summer to Black Power.* Chicago: The University of Chicago Press.

Baofu, Peter. 2014. "Racism and Inferiority Complex in Japan's Current Foreign Policy towards China." *Foreign Policy Journal.* Accessed May 11, 2017. https://www.foreignpolicyjournal.com/2014/07/22/racism-and-inferiority-complex-in-japans-current-foreign-policy-towards-china.

Barroso, Amanda 2019. " The changing profile of the U.S. military: Smaller in size, more diverse, more women in leadership." *Pew Research Center.* Accessed online at URL: https://www.pewresearch.org/fact-tank/2019/09/10/the-changing-profile-of-the-u-s-military/www.pewresearch.org/

Beard, Rick. "Black Union Soldiers Fought a costly battle for equal pay". Military Times. accessed online at URL: https://www.militarytimes.com/military-honor/black-military-history/2018/02/12/black-union-soldiers-fought-a-costly-battle-for-equal-pay/

Best, James D. 2012. *Principled Action: Lessons from the Origins of the American Republic.* Tucson, AZ: Wheatmark.

Bird, J. B. 2008. "Rebellion: John Horse and the Black Seminoles, the First Black Rebels to Beat American Slavery." Accessed November 21, 2015. http://www.johnhorse.com/index.html.

Blanton, DeAnne, and Lauren M. Cook. 2002. *They Fought Like Demons: Women Soldiers in the Civil War.* Baton Rouge: Louisiana State University Press.

Booth, Bradford, and David R. Segal. 2005. "Bringing the Soldiers Back In: Implications of Inclusion of Military Personnel for Labor Market Research on Race, Class and Gender."*Race, Gender & Class* 12, no. 1: 34–57.

Bottomore, Tom P. 1981. "A Marxist Consideration of Durkheim." *Social Forces* 59, no. 4: 902–17.

Brady, Kyle R. 2017. "Beware the Limits of Hard Power in 2017." *Small Wars Journal,* May 6. Accessed May 10, 2017. http://smallwarsjournal.com/jrnl/art/beware-the-limits-of-hard-power-in-2017.

Bray, Chris. 2016. Court Martial: How *Military Justice Has Shaped America from the Revolution to 9/11.* New York: W. W. Norton.

Brooks, Rebecca Beatrice. 2011. "The Boston Massacre." History of Massachusetts. Accessed June 26, 2017. http://historyofmassachusetts.org/the-boston-massacre.

Callaway, Colin G. 1995. *The American Revolution in Indian Country: Crisis and Diversity in Native American Communities.* Cambridge: Cambridge University Press.

Calvin, Mathew J. 2015. *Aiming for Pensacola: Fugitive Slaves on the Atlantic and Southern Frontiers.* Cambridge, MA: Harvard University Press.

Cardoso, Fernando H. 2001. *Charting a New Course: The Politics of Globalization and Social Transformation.* Lanham, MD: Rowman & Littlefield.

Caron, Christina 2019. "Dan Choi Explains 'Why I cannot stay quiet'". ABCNEWS. Accessed online at URL: https://abcnews.go.com/US/story?id=7568742&page=1

Chu, Thai Q., Mark D. Seery, Whitney A. Ence, E. Alison Holman, and Silver. Roxane 2006. "Ethnicity and Gender in the Face of a Terrorist Attack: A National Longitudinal Study of Immediate Responses and Outcomes Two Years after September 11." *Basic and Applied Social Psychology* 28, no. 4: 291–301.

Cockerham, William. 2003. "The Military Institution." In *Handbook of Symbolic Interactionism,* edited by Larry T. Reynolds and Nancy J. Herman-Kinney, 491–510. Lanham, MD: Rowman & Littlefield.

Cole, Juan. 2011. "Islamophobia and American Foreign Policy Rhetoric: The Bush Years and After." In *Islamophobia: The Challenge of Pluralism in the 21st Century,* edited by John L. Esposito and Ibrahim Kalin, 127–42. Oxford: Oxford University Press.

Converse, Elliott V. III, Daniel K. Gibran, John A. Cash, Robert K. Griffith Jr., and Richard H. Kohn. 1997. *The Exclusion of Black Soldiers from the Medal of Honor in World War II.* Jefferson, NC: McFarland.

Doyle, Don H. 2015. "The Civil War Was Won by Immigrant Soldiers." *Time.* Accessed May 11, 2017. http://time.com/3940428/civil-war-immigrant-soldiers.

Duster, Troy. 2013. "Merit Scholars, the Military, and Affirmative Action." The Conversation (blog), *Chronicle of Higher Education,* January 23. Accessed June 26, 2017. http://www.chronicle.com/blogs /conversation/2013/01/23/merit-scholars-the-military-and-affirmative-action.

Estrada, Josue 2015. LULAC and American Gi Forum: History and Geography 1929-1988. Accessed online at URL: https://depts.washington.edu/moves/LULAC_map.shtml

Feimster, Crystal N. 2013. "Rape and Justice in the Civil War." Opinionator (blog), *New York Times,* April 25. Accessed June 26, 2017. https://opinionator.blogs.nytimes.com/2013/04/25/rape-and-justice-in-the-civil-war.

Ferling, John. 2010. "Myths of the American Revolution." *Smithsonian Magazine,* January. Accessed June 26, 2017. http://www.smithsonianmag.com/history/myths-of-the-american-revolution-10941835.

Ferran, Lee, and Randy Kreider. 2015. "Selling the 'Fantasy': Why Young Western Women Would Join ISIS."ABC News, February 20. Accessed September 9, 2015. http://abcnews.go.com/ International/young-women-join-isis/story?id=29112401.

Figley, Charles, Barbara L. Pitts, Chapman, and Paula Elnitsky.Christine 2015. "Female Combat Medics." In *Women at War,* edited by Elspeth Cameron Ritchie and Anne L. Naclerio. New York: Oxford University Press.

Fink, Jenni 2019. "West Point's Newest Class Has More Minority New cadets Than Last Year." Newsweek. Accessed online at URL: https://www.newsweek.com/west-point-class-2023-minority-cadets-1446958

Finucane, Melissa L., Paul Slovic,C. K. Mertz, Flynn, and James Theresa A. Satterfield. 2000. "Gender, Race, and Perceived Risk: The 'White Male' Effect." *Health, Risk & Society* 2, no. 2: 159–72.

Fixico, Donald. 2008. "A Native Nations Perspective on the War of 1812." *The War of 1812,* PBS. Accessed November 21, 2016. http://www.pbs.org/wned/war-of-1812/essays/native-nations-perspective.

Flanagan, Meg. 2018. "These Meaningful Military Traditions Come From Native American Culture." Under the Radar, Military.Com. Accessed at URL: https://www.military.com/undertheradar/2018/04/16/these-meaningful-military-traditions-come-native-american-culture.html

Foubert, John D., and Ryan C. Masin. 2012. "Effects of the Men's Program on U.S. Army Soldiers' Intentions to Commit and Willingness to Intervene to Prevent Rape: A Pretest-Posttest Study." *Violence and Victims* 27, no. 6: 911–21.

Foucault, Michel. 1977. *Discipline and Punish: The Birth of the Prison.* London: Routledge.

Foucault, Michel. 2008. *The Birth of Biopolitics: Lectures at the Collège de France, 1978–1979.* Translated by Graham Burchell; edited by Michel Senellart. Basingstoke: Palgrave Macmillan.

Galbraith, John Kenneth. 1967. *The New Industrial State.* Princeton, NJ: Princeton University Press.

Giddens, Anthony. 1984. *The Constitution of Society: Outline of the Theory of Structuration.* Berkeley: University of California Press.

Global Fire Power 2020. Military Strength Comparisons. Accessed online at URL: https://www.globalfirepower.com/countries-comparison.asp.

Gonzalez, Gilbert G. 2013. *Guest Workers or Colonized Labor? Mexican Labor Migration to the United States.* Boulder, CO: Paradigm.

Hafetz, Jonathan. 2011. "Targeted Killing and the 'War on Terror.'" Al Jazeera, October 19. Accessed May 11, 2017. https://www.globalpolicy.org/war-on-terrorism/50878-targeted-killing-and-the-war-on-terror.html?itemid=id#609.

Harb, Ali and Dania Akkad 2019. "'Muslim ban': Two years on, Trump's order still destroying lives." Middle East Eye. Accessed online at URL: https://www.middleeasteye.net/news/muslim-ban-two-years-trumps-order-still-destroying-lives

Hartung, William D. and Mandy Smithberger 2019. "America's Defense Budget Is Bigger Than You Think." The Nation. Accessed online at URL: https://www.thenation.com/article/archive/tom-dispatch-america-defense-budget-bigger-than-you-think/

Honey, Maureen. 2007. "African American Women in World War II." History Now. Accessed February 10, 2017. https://www.gilderlehrman.org/history-by-era/world-war-ii/essays/african-american-women-world-war-ii.

Institute 2020. Cost of War. Accessed online at URL: https://watson.brown.edu/costsofwar/papers/summary

Kamarck, Kristy 2017. "Diversity, Inclusion, and Equal Opportunity in the Armed Services: Background and Issues for Congress". *Digital Commons*. Accessed online at URL: https://digitalcommons.ilr.cornell.edu/cgi/viewcontent.cgi?article=2968&context=key_workplace.

Kamarck, Kristy 2019. "Diversity, Inclusion, and Equal Opportunity in the Armed Services: Background and Issues for Congress." *Congressional Research Service*. accessed online at URL: https://fas.org/sgp/crs/natsec/R44321.pdf.

Kestnbaum, Meyer. 2009. "The Sociology of War and the Military." *Annual Review of Sociology* 35: 235–54.

Krauss, Clifford. 1986. "Revolution in Central America?" *Foreign Affairs* 65, no. 3: 564–81.

Lanning, Michael L. 2000. *African Americans in the Revolutionary War.* New York: Kensington.

Lender, Mark Edward. 2016. *The War for American Independence: A Reference Guide.* Santa Barbara, CA: ABC-CLIO.

Levin, Brian 2017. "ISLAMOPHOBIA IN AMERICA: RISE IN HATE CRIMES AGAINST MUSLIMS SHOWS WHAT POLITICIANS SAY MATTERS," Newsweek. Accessed online at URL: https://www. newsweek.com/islamophobia-america-rise-hate-crimes-against-muslims-proves-what-politicians-640184.

Lin, Patrick. 2010. "Robots, Ethics and War." Center for Internet and Society. Accessed January 27, 2017. http://cyberlaw.stanford.edu/blog/2010/12/robots-ethics-war.

Lutz, Catherine. 2008. "Who Joins the Military? A Look at Race, Class, and Immigration Status." *Journal of Political and Military Sociology* 36, no. 2: 167–88.

Malik, Nakita 2019. "Instead of Islamophobia, We Should Focus On Defining Anti-Muslim Hatred." *Forbes.* Accessed online at URL: https://www.forbes.com/sites/nikitamalik/2019/05/20/instead-of-islamophobia-we-should-focus-on-defining-anti-muslim-hatred/#1bcd72dd69e5.

Martin, Paul Kawika. 2015. "Is There an Alternative to War with ISIS?" MSNBC, February 12. Accessed May 11, 2017. http://www.msnbc.com/msnbc/alternative-war-isis.

Mason, Jeff. 2017. Immigrants in the Military: A History of Service". *Bipartisan Policy Center.* Accessed online at URL: https://bipartisanpolicy.org/blog/immigrants-in-the-military-a-history-of-service/.

McCarthy, Niall. 2017. "Most Terrorists in the U.S. since 9/11 Have Been American Citizens or Legal Residents." *Forbes,* January 31. Accessed February 13, 2017. http://www.forbes.com/sites/niallmc carthy/2017/01/31/most-terrorists-in-the-u-s-since-911-have-been-american-citizens-or-legal-residents-infographic/#6e28894482c6.

Melin, Julia 2016. "Desperate Choices: Why Black Women Join the U.S. Military at Higher Rates than Men and All Other Racial and Ethnic Groups. *New England Journal of Public Policy*, Vol. 28, Issue 2. Accessed at URL https://scholarworks.umb.edu/cgi/viewcontent.cgi?article=1697&=&context= nejpp&=&sei-redir=1&referer=https%253A%252F%252Fwww.bing.com%252Fsearch%253Fq%25 3Dblack%252Bwomen%252Bprotest%252Bmilitary%2526qs%253Dn%2526sp%253D-1%2526pq% 253Dblack%252Bwomen%252Bprotest%252Bmilitary%2526sc%253D1-28%2526sk%253D%2526 cvid%253D70D8CD8DA1D1409CBAE486F6FB2A495E%2526first%253D13%2526FORM%253DPER E%23search=%22black%20women%20protest%20military%22.

Mendoza, Martha, and Garance Burke. 2018. "U.S. Army quietly discharging immigrant recruits." *Associated Press News.* https://apnews.com/article/immigration-us-army-united-states-military-ap-top-news-international-news-38334c4d061e493fb108bd975b5a1a5d

*Military.com.*2018."Who's Joining the Military: Myth vs. Fact". *Military.com.*Accessed online at URL: https://www.military.com/join-armed-forces/whos-joining-military-myth-vs-fact.html

Mitchell, Mitch 2018. "Buffalo Soldiers hanged after 1917 race riot should be pardoned, advocates say". Accessed online at url: https://www.star-telegram.com/news/state/texas/article221379955. html. www.star-telegram.com\

Moore, Brenda L. 1991. "African American Women in the U.S. Military." *Armed Forces & Society* 17: 363–84.

Moore, Brenda L. 2003. *Serving Our Country: Japanese American Women in the Military during World War II.* New Brunswick, NJ: Rutgers University Press.

National Alliance to End Homelessness. 2018. People of Color Make Up a Disproportionate Share of the Homeless Veteran Population." *End Homelessness.* Accessed online at URL: https://endhomelessness.org/resource/people-color-make-much-larger-share-homeless-veteran-population-general-veteran-population/

National Archives. 2016. "Statistical Information about Casualties of the Vietnam War." Accessed February 8, 2017. https://www.archives.gov/research/military/vietnam-war/casualty-statistics.html#category.

National Park Service. 2010. "Forgotten Warriors: Fort Scott National Historic Site." Accessed May 11, 2017. https://www.nps.gov/articles/forgotten-warriors.htm.

Nittle, Nadra Kareem. 2019. "History of the Asian American Civil Rights Movement". ThoughtCo. Accessed online at URL: https://www.thoughtco.com/asain-american-civil-rights-movement-history-2834596.

Ogan, Christine, Lars Wilnat, Rosemary Pennington, and Manaf Bashir. 2013. "The Rise of Anti-Muslim Prejudice: Media and Islamophobia in Europe and the United States." *International Communication Gazette* 76, no. 1: 27–46.

Olivas, Michael A. 2008. "The 'Trial of the Century' That Never Was: Staff Sgt. Marcario García, the Congressional Medal of Honor, and the Oasis Café." *Indiana Law Journal* 83, no. 4: 1391–1403.

Oropeza, Lorena. 2005. *¡Raza Si! ¡Guerra No! Chicano Protest and Patriotism during the Viet Nam War Era.* Berkeley: University of California Press.

Park, Robert E. 1941. "The Social Function of War: Observations and Notes." *American Journal of Sociology* 46, no. 4: 551–70.

Parker, Christopher 2009. "When Politics Become Protests: Black Veterans and Political activism in the Postwar South." *The Journal of Politics,* Vol. 71, No. 1, January. 113–131.

Perret, Geoffrey. 1989. A Country Made by War: From the Revolution to Vietnam—*The Story of America's Rise to Power.* New York: Random House.

Ramos, Henry 1998. The American GI Forum: In Pursuit of the Dream, 1948-1983. Houston, TX: Arte Publico Press

Ray, Celeste. 2007. *The New Encyclopedia of Southern Culture, Vol. 6, Ethnicity.* Chapel Hill: University of North Carolina Press.

Reynolds, George M. and Amanda Shendruk. 2018. "Demographics of the U.S. Military". Council on Foreign Relations. Accessed online at URL: https://www.cfr.org/article/demographics-us-military

Rhoades-Piotti, Tiffany. 2017. "Ann Simpson Davis." In *Women in American History: A Social, Political, and Cultural Encyclopedia and Document Collection,* edited by Peg A. Lamphier and Rosanne Welch. Santa Barbara, CA: ABC-CLIO.

Rothkopf, David, and Kristin Lord. 2013. "The Alternative to War." *Foreign Policy,* October 3. Accessed May 11, 2017. http://foreignpolicy.com/2013/10/03/the-alternative-to-war.

Sandford, Victoria. 2003. "Learning to Kill by Proxy: Colombian Paramilitaries and the Legacy of Central American Death Squads, Contras, and Civil Patrols." *Social Justice* 30, no. 3: 63–81.

Scalia, J. 2000. "Dissenting: Don Stenberg, Attorney General of Nebraska, et al., Petitioners V. Leroy Carhart". Accessed online at URL: https://www.law.cornell.edu/supct/html/99-830.ZD1.html

Segal, David R. 2008. "Military Sociology." In *21st Century Sociology,* edited by Clifton D. Bryant and Dennis L. Peck. Thousand Oaks, CA: Sage.

Segal, Mady Wechsler, and David R. Segal. 2007. "Latinos Claim Larger Share of U.S Military Personnel." Population Reference Bureau, October. Accessed September 3, 2015. http://www.prb.org/Publications/Articles/2007/HispanicsUSMilitary.aspx.

Sheldon, Kathryn 2019. "Brief History of Black Women in the Military". The Women's Memorial. Accessed online at URL: https://www.womensmemorial.org/history-of-black-women

Sicard, Sarah. 2016. "How Affirmative Action Works at West Point." Task & Purpose, July 19. Accessed May 12, 2017. http://taskandpurpose.com/race-factors-west-point-admissions.

SNCC No Date."Black Veterans Return From World War II". SNCC Digital Gateway, *SNCC Legacy Project and Duke University.*Accessed online at URL: https://snccdigital.org/events/black-veterans-return-from-world-war-ii/

Stockholm International Peace Research Institute, SIPRI Military Expenditure Database, April 2019. Accessed online at URL: https://www.pgpf.org/chart-archive/0053_defense-comparison.

Stout, Harry S. 2009. "Review Essay: Religion, War, and the Meaning of America." *Religion and American Culture* 19, no. 2: 275–89.

Straw, Joseph. 2014. "Obama Awards Medal of Honor—the Military's Highest Decoration for Bravery—to 24 Veterans across Three Wars Who Were Originally Overlooked Due to Their Race." *New York Daily News,* March 19. Accessed March 24, 2014. http://www.nydailynews.com/news/politics/president-obama-award-medals-honor-tuesday-article- 1.1725488.

Stutzman, Maureen. 2009. "Rape in the American Civil War: Race, Class, and Gender in the Case of Harriet McKinley and Perry Pierson." *Transcending Silence* (Spring). Accessed April 23, 2013. http://www.albany.edu/womensstudies/journal/2009/stutzman.html.

Sullivan, Kevin, and Mary Jordan. 2004. "In Central America, Reagan Remains a Polarizing Figure." *Washington Post,* June 9. Accessed May 24, 2013. http://www.washingtonpost.com/wp-dyn/articles/A29546-2004Jun9.html.

Talbot, Richard P., and Jon T. Oplinger. 2014. "Social Stratification and Ethnic Mobilization: U.S. Military Deaths in Southeast Asia." *Race, Gender & Class* 21, nos. 1–2: 195–210.

Timm, Annette F. 2010. *The Politics of Fertility in Twentieth-Century Berlin.* Cambridge: Cambridge University Press.

Tucker, Phillip. 1992. "John Horse: Forgotten African-American Leader of the Second Seminole War." *Journal of Negro History* 77, no. 2: 74–83.

U.S. Department of Veterans Affairs. 2017. "America's Wars." Accessed May 11, 2017. https://www.va.gov/opa/publications/factsheets/fs_americas_wars.pdf.

Walker, Hiannon. 2016. "An Open Letter by black military veterans in support of Colin Kaepernick". The Undefeated. Accessed online at URL: https://theundefeated.com/features/an-open-letter-from-american-military-veterans-in-support-of-colin-kaepernick/

Warshauer, Mathew. 2007. "Andrew Jackson and the Constitution." History Now. Accessed April 20, 2017. https://www.gilderlehrman.org/history-by-era/age-jackson/essays/andrew-jackson-and-constitution.

Weber, Max. 1978. *Economy and Society.* Translated and edited by Guenther Roth and Claus Wittich. Berkeley: University of California Press.

Weber, Max. 1991. "Bureaucracy." In *From Max Weber: Essays in Sociology,* translated and, edited by H. H. Gerth and C. Wright Mills, London: Routledge.

Weinstein, Adam. 2012. "Nobody Puts Tammy Duckworth in a Corner." *Mother Jones*, August. Accessed March 19, 2014. http://www.motherjones.com/politics/2012/08/tammy-duckworth-versus-joe-walsh-congress.

Williams, Rudi. 2000. "21 Asian American World War II Vets to Get Medal of Honor." Armed Forces Press Service, May 19. Accessed April 20, 2013. http://www.defense.gov/news/newsarticle.aspx?id=45192.

Wynn, Neil A. 2010. *The African American Experience during World War II*. Lanham, MD: Rowman & Littlefield.

THE MEDIA AND COMMUNICATION TECHNOLOGIES

A large "Q" sign, for QAnon, a conspiracy theory group, is held aloft while awaiting President Trump at a 2018 rally in Pennsylvania.

Rick Loomis/Getty Images

LEARNING OBJECTIVES

11.1 Examine the historical and contemporary role of media in the construction of difference.

11.2 Explain the stock stories that have helped us think through the role of mass media in our lives.

11.3 Apply the matrix theory to how we consume media.

11.4 Investigate the importance of critical media literacy.

As the internet was just taking off in the early 1990s, former Ku Kux Klan leader Don Black created the internet site Stormfront. The first website devoted to racial hatred, today Stormfront distributes digital literature, leaflets, and announcements. It includes a Whites-only dating page, multiple links to other hate sites, and boasts over 6 million annual posts, 490,000 discussion threads, and 170,000 members (ADL 2013). According to the Southern Poverty Law Center (2019), the internet in general and **social media** in particular has encouraged the rapid rise of hate groups. internet hate groups use the very simplicity of the Internet to garner new members as they intimidate others—some even recruit via videogame chat rooms, and their influence is being increasingly seen on college campuses.

Social media potentially connects us to a wide variety of people and ideas, and algorithms that control our online activity connect us potentially with those "just like us." Think about your social networks and online relationships, as well as the things that you "click," "follow," and "like." Now, ask yourself how those things compare to what you "like" in your real life.

There is evidence that our gender, race, class, and sexuality social orders offline are actively being reproduced online. At the same time, there is also research that shows that the virtual world is helping to change these "real-life" structures to a degree. Millennials, those born roughly between the years of 1981 and 1996, are the first generation who has spent most of their lives on social networking sites like Facebook, Instagram, and Twitter (Sackmann and Winkler 2013; Tapscott 1998). All of these cutting-edge forms of social media rest on a deep history of technology and media innovations, innovations that act back on us—social media are but the latest manifestation—and we need to recognize this history, in order to more fully understand the present and future.

Welcome to the mediated matrix—it is a place where things are not quite what they seem.

HISTORICAL AND CONTEMPORARY DEVELOPMENTS IN MEDIA

All of the different forms of media—literature, magazines, news, advertising, comics, film, television, radio, video games, the internet, and new forms of social media—have a role in the construction of difference in our lives. Developing critical **media literacy** skills will allow you to:

1. gain important tools to use and conceptual lenses through which to look at, interpret, understand, and discuss media, and

2. actively assess your own media consumption practices and the ways that these support or challenge the race, gender, class, and sexuality social order.

Media transmits and reproduces our values, ideas, ways of being, and histories. **Media** is a means by which various groups collect, transmit, and preserve their symbolic communications. As we examine the development of various media within the U.S., we may be surprised to see just how diverse we are as a people. Let's start at the beginning.

Early Media

The exciting thing about media is also the daunting thing about media—it is always morphing and shifting as it always morphs and shifts us. History shows us this. Every ethnic group that ventured on these shores brought with them a range of symbolic communications that told their stories, captured their identities, and projected their values.

Native American Media Forms

Throughout time people have invented a variety of systems and objects to transfer information. One of the oldest is the Native American media known as the *Quipu*. The natives of Andean South America utilized the Quipus, sometimes referred to as talking knots, to record specific historical events. The Quipu, strung with colored and plied threads or strings from llama or alpaca hair, represent complicated systems that we are still trying to decode. One Incan set was used to record information and collect data for a variety of purposes, from monitoring tax obligations to census records to military organizations (D'Altroy 2001, 18).

Sandpainting is another Native American media form, associated with the Navajo. Intended to be transitory and therefore destroyed upon completion, this media form was restricted to sacred and healing contexts. Thanks to drawings and artistic reproductions, we have some examples dating from the late 1800s and early 1900s. Some of these are captured in the work of

Rugs woven by Navajo weavers on display at a shop in Santa Fe, New Mexico.

Robert Alexander/Getty Images

Hosteen Klah, a medicine man and weaver, who reproduced these images in Navajo rugs and drawings. This visual history of life represents traditional Navajo healing designs. Today they are considered the rarest of all Navajo rug styles.

CONCEALED STORIES: HOSTEEN KLAH–BERDACHE–TWO SPIRIT

We-Wa, a Zuni berdache, weaving.

Alpha Stock/Alamy Stock Photo

Some Native American groups have descriptions of gender and sexuality that do not fall into the conventional English-language categories of homosexual, gay, lesbian, transgender, or heterosexual, but rather on a continuum of acceptable activities. Hosteen Klah was such a person. Within Native American culture, weavers were typically women and medicine men (hataa-lii) were typically men. Hosteen Klah was both. The Navajo considered Klah to be a *nádleeh* which loosely translates to "one who is changed" or "one who is transformed." It is unclear if Klah was born intersex or experienced a genital injury in a childhood accident. Klah identified at times as a man and at other times as a woman. What is clear is that, in the 1880s, Klah learned weaving from his mother and sister. And he learned Navajo medicine ways—chanting and sandpainting—from an uncle. After 24 years of study, Hosteen Klah performed his first Nightway Ceremony, which lasted nine days. As part of this ceremony he produced a sandpainting which calls on the power of the Holy People. In 1911 Klah wove a blanket representing yeibichai dancers which portrayed sacred masks. Many viewed this as a sacrilege and urged Klah to destroy the blanket. Not bowing to pressure, Klah continued to produce blankets that recorded the Navajo traditions. Over his lifetime he produced hundreds of drawings, paintings, and weavings. Many are on display at the Wheelwright Museum. Thanks to Klah and the media produced, many of the Navajo traditions have been preserved (Roscoe 1988).

The Colonial Era

Almost every group that settled in the Americas similarly brought and preserved their symbolic cultures, which also reflected race, class, ethnicity, and gender. Often we restrict our attention to the written word, and by default ignore the race, class, and gender realities represented in nonverbal media forms. Among these media forms, research into quilting, needlepoint, and scrapbooking have produced a richly textured look into our American story. With the patterns, designs, and colors, people (typically women) recorded life events and developed community. Quilts not only represented culture, but they also asserted and conveyed values, and preserved traditions.

As with all media, quilts, needlepoint, and scrapbooks also reflect the different historical events that captured the spirit of the time (Wahlman 1986). For example, during build-up to the American Civil War, quilts were made to raise funds to support abolitionist actions. On one such quilt, sold by the Boston Female Anti-Slavery Society in December 1836, features the following inscription in its center block:

Mother! When around your child

You clasp your arms in love

And when with grateful joy you raise your eyes to god above

Think of the negro-mother

When her child is torn away

Sold for a little slave—oh, then

For that poor mother, pray!

(Aptheker 1989: 72)

African American women also produced similar quilts. Some quilt patterns, reflected in strip-weaving technology, have been traced to the Mandé peoples of West Africa. These weaves were created by diverse groups associated with Maroon peoples, or by escaped slaves living in Haiti and the Suriname rainforest. These quilt patterns use strips of old clothing or other fabric such as feed, flour, tobacco, or sugar sacks. Quilting parties were important social events among slave women on the plantations. This tradition has been preserved by a group of women in Gee's Bend, Alabama. In 2006 the quilts of Gee's Bend were part of the American Treasures Series issued by the U.S. Postal Service. The work of contemporary African American artist Faith Ringgold has been celebrated as taking this media to its fullest expression.

The ground-breaking work of Faith Ringgold, shown here at a 2019 exhibit at the Serpentine Galleries, her first in a European institution for more than five decades.

Malcolm Park/Alamy Stock Photo

Triptych of the Sedano family by Gerard David, 1450-1523.

Peter Horree/Alamy Stock Photo

The Development of Mass Media

Our story now takes several divergent, yet frequently intersecting, routes that ultimately converge. These routes reflect both the technological and sociological as shown in newspapers, radio, television, and, most recently, the internet. Each of these media forms were in one way or another considered the most prominent, if not dominant, form for a given historical period. Consequently, they mirror and also re-create the race, class, and gender stereotypes, identities, and imagery of our society through time. Sociologists González and Torres (2011) concluded that media forms such as newspapers, radio, and television were central in perpetuating racist views by representing non-Whites as threats to a White society.

Mass media are the social and organizational structures of communicating information throughout a given society to its members (McChesney 2000). There are dominant, mainstream outlets of mass media that use varieties of communication technologies in any given era.

Newspapers

The development of newspapers in America tells a story of freedom, but also one of oppression and even resistance. The story of the press in America is the story of the *The Wall Street Journal* and the *The New York Times*. It is also the story of the *Griot, Telemundo, Chinese American News* and the *Native American Times*.

James Franklin, at his own expense and risk, in 1721 published the *The New-England Courant*, and may have been the first person to be jailed for seditious libel due to a set of stories he published that were critical of British rule. Thus began the English-language press in the U.S., and the birth of rebel editors and their newspapers.

Many of the colonial-era publishers were on the leading edge of revolutionary efforts. Newspapers and their editors were central political figures throughout most of our nation's history (González and Torres 2011, 4). Newspaper outlets (whether paper or digital) have always distributed information to the masses—but which masses? Papers that are owned by Whites, with primarily White audiences and/or White stockholders, will produce information that a White supremacist society deems important for its primary constituents—Whites. Thus, minority and ethnic communities have worked hard to create their own outlets to communicate the information their communities find important.

Every major ethnic group in America has produced their own new media. In fact, the Center for Community and Ethnic Media, at City University of New York, recently produced a directory of nearly 270 community and ethnic outlets producing news in 36 languages, in print, on the radio, on TV, and online (Bartlett 2013). According to a poll, nearly half of all African American, Latinx, Native American, Asian American, and Arab American adults would rather get their media fix from ethnic media over mainstream media, and one-quarter of the total U.S. population regularly tunes into ethnic media (New America Media 2013). There are over 3,000 ethnic media organizations in the United States. These media provide news and other information to over 57 million ethnic adults in the U.S. (New America Media 2013).

Ethnic presses serve a variety of functions, including:

- education and advocacy

- providing news and recording history

- preserving ethnic identity and bridging ethnic boundaries

In most major U.S. cities ethnic presses were represented by all significant language groups. Alongside the major newspapers, these ethnic newspapers became the major source of news, sports, entertainment, and issues from their home country (Rhodes 2010, 46).

The first Native American newspaper, the *Cherokee Phoenix* (or *Tsa-la-ge-Tsi-hi-sa-ni-hi*), was founded in 1828. Each issue of this weekly carefully documented Cherokee efforts to resist White settlers (González and Torres 2011, 99) and became a critically influential voice against Indian removal, even though the Post Office deliberately attempted to curtail the distribution. The newspaper was perceived as a threat to local settlers. In 1835, as the newspaper was relocating to a more secure location on Indian land in Tennessee, the Georgia Guard blocked the wagon carrying the printing equipment and destroyed it. The significant voice of the *Phoenix* was silenced.

Today, the newsroom at companies that have focused on print newspaper creation and marketing for their product have always been predominantly White, male spaces, as has the ownership of such companies. Total circulation of U.S. daily newspapers has been declining since the mid-1980s when it was around 63 million readers, to today where it hovers around 28 million (Pew Research Center 2019b). Advertising revenues took a particularly large hit at newspaper organizations since 2000, declining over 300% in 20 years. The frequency of daily newspaper readership has steadily declined among all major racial groups. This is more pronounced among younger, less educated, and lower-income readers (Edmonds, Guskin, and Rosentiel 2011).

Radio

In 1920 commercial radio was born in the United States. By 1933, two thirds of households in the U.S. had a radio (Barnouw 1968). The massive growth of listeners was directly associated with the formation of major networks such as NBC (National Broadcasting Company, 1926), CBS (Columbia Broadcasting System, 1927), and MBS (Mutual Broadcasting System, 1934). And with these networks came the emergence of a national market platform for products (Douglas 2012). Radios soon became a staple of American life.

Radio, particularly during times of crisis, was often used to create and encourage adherence to prevailing notions of Americana. During World War II, "The University of Chicago Round Table" and "America's Town Meeting of the Air" showed what was possible at the time regarding discussions of racial oppression and provided spaces for early discourses regarding civil rights (Savage 2002). At the opposite extreme, the extremely popular "The Green Hornet" served to mobilize audiences against "Oriental" troops and stereotyped anti-Axis war rhetoric (Russo 2002).

Certainly radio has been used for **propaganda**, the mass-mediated distribution of misinformation to influence public opinion and collective sentiment. Yet we also have seen widespread subversive uses of radio by gendered, ethnic, and racial groups. New media scholarship shows how the radio often played a subversive role by challenging and even ridiculing conventional social norms.

Perhaps the most significant event to occur in radio following World War II was the development of minority or ethnic radio. Several factors are associated with this rise.

- In 1952 nearly 20 million homes had TVs. This resulted in a major shift in advertising budgets as companies attempted to gain access to this new medium.

- From 1948 to 1952, the advertising budgets for radio stations dropped by 38%. Soon analysts were predicting the death of radio.

- The invention of the transistor radio allowed the production of cheap mobile radios between 1955 and 1960. The total number of AM radio stations increased by 27% during this same time. Despite this, radio broadcasting revenues still declined.

These trends caused both advertisers and radio programmers to increase their access to the growing, and economically more visible, Black communities. One of the first stations to capture this exclusively Black audience was WDIA in Memphis beginning in 1947. In 7 short years, more than six hundred stations were programming to large, primarily Black communities in thirty-nine states. But while these stations targeted Black communities and provided significant space for Black talent and music to be heard, few were actually owned by Blacks (Rothenbuhler and McCourt 2002, 373-4).

Nevertheless, these formats paved the way for the creation and re-creation of Black art forms, stereotypes, and caricatures. One of the key cultural contributions of Black radio was the creation of a market to disseminate rhythm and blues and soul music (Rothenbuhler and McCourt 2002, 375). Changes in music, led by guitar-based melding of soul and country, brought forth a new sound—rock and roll. New stars like Elvis Presley, Buddy Holly, and Bill Haley were part of a new generation of "boppers" (Peterson and Berger 1975). And of course, this media space would provide a place for the new sound being experimented with by Berry Gordy's Motown (also known as the Detroit sound) and artists such as Marvin Gay, The Temptations, and The Supremes. Ultimately, hip-hop and rap owe their existence to Black radio as well. Today, radio is facing challenges from every angle, largely from the increase of the digital realm, social media, and changing possibilities of advertising revenues. Podcasts and streaming services are both filling demand, but also providing new outlets for marginalized voices.

Television

We are what we watch, as the saying sometimes goes. But what if the majority of what is written, produced, filmed, and distributed is done so by and for a particular segment of the population? Consider the following reality. A recent report by the Federal Communications Commission (FCC 2020) showed that while women comprise some 51% of the entire U.S. population, they own only about 4.5% of all broadcast television stations. Men own the other 95.5%. The same report showed that racial minorities, when *combined,* make up 23.6% of the U.S. adult population, but own only about 1.5% of the television stations. Whites own the other 98.5%.

Television has had a profound effect on the construction of difference, and indeed, television has not been kind over its history to women (Boyle 2018), the LGBTQ+ community (Mendos 2019), the working class (Deery 2017), and racial and ethnic minorities (Jhally 2019)—instead supporting White supremacy at the expense of minorities and their expression.

Even in this new media world, television viewing—in one form or another—continues to dominate media consumption, taking up about 4 hours a day in young people's lives. According to recent industry research, Black Americans spend an average of 3.55 hours per day watching TV, Latinx an average of 2.45 hours per day, and Asian Americans about 1.75 hours, many watching programming aimed at Black, Latinx, and Asian Americans that are more likely to appear in streaming services (Watson 2019). There is also little doubt that the production of our most cherished and dominant television programming over the past 50 years was created largely by White, heterosexual men.

In an important study from 2004, researchers Jane Brown and Carol Pardun tested the idea that there is a common youth culture reflected in television programming, or whether television is further segregating its viewers. They analyzed the television watching preferences and associated behaviors of some 3,000 middle school children and found that, across 140 television shows, there was very little overlap between the television diets of Black boys, White boys, Black girls, and White girls. Thus, where television was once considered by communications scholars to be the common glue that binds the disparate elements of American experience together, it is now clearly a segregated and segmented communication technology—largely designed to sell products, but also, by extension, identities, relationships, and ideologies.

RESISTANCE STORIES: VISION MAKER MEDIA

Native Americans are virtually nonexistent on television, and their voices are missing as producers, writers, and actors. Vision Maker Media is an organization working to make those voices heard.

On their website, the organization describes their mission: "Vision Maker Media shares Native stories with the world that represent the cultures, experiences, and values of American Indians and Alaska Natives. ...Vision Maker Media exists to serve Native producers and Indian country in partnership with public television and radio. Vision Maker Media works with Native producers to develop, produce and distribute educational telecommunications programs for all media including public television and public radio. Vision Maker Media supports training to increase the number of American Indians and Alaska Natives producing quality public broadcasting programs, which includes advocacy efforts promoting increased control and use of information technologies and the policies to support this control by American Indians and Alaska Natives." http://www.nativetelecom.org/about-us

The Corporation for Public Broadcasting funds Vision Maker Media and other members of the National Minority Consortia, including Black Public media, Center for Asian American Media, Latino Public Broadcasting, and Pacific Islanders in Communications. Diversity is one of the core values of public media (http://www.cpb.org/). Without public media, would some of these voices be heard at all on television?

Television shows produce and reinforce racial, ethnic, and gender stereotypes. For example, crime dramas have frequently depicted different races and ethnic groups (particularly, Italians, Blacks, Asians, and Hispanics) as members of gangs, thugs, or organized crime families. Historically, TV audiences have seen the Black stereotypes such as the mammy (big, mean, loud mother figure), the coon (lazy, unreliable buffoon), the buck (savage, ruthless brute), and the tom (the submissive, loyal slave/Black). Latinx Americans have been often portrayed as the comic (funny, but lazy), the Latin Hottie (oversexed, promiscuous seducer), or the thug (violent criminal). Today, many TV shows actually attempt to include "positive" stereotypes, like police officers or court officials, to present a more balanced portrayal.

Shows like *South Park* utilize token stereotypes as symbols to poke fun while actually trying to make a point. For example, there is the young Black character actually named Token. Some media personalities like Flip Wilson, Moms Mabley, and Redd Fox made a career out of making comedy out of these negative stereotypes. As comedy, it allowed them not only to demystify stereotypes but also to delegitimize much of the negativity. Current comics such as Aisha Tyler, Dave Chappelle, Eddie Murphy, and Chris Rock continue in these traditions. You cannot help but laugh. But in the process, you see that beneath the humor "lies a rich layer of social commentary about race relations in the United States" (Cohen and Richards 2006).

While stereotypes are often used against different race, gender, and class groups, group members can actually use them to reflect back on the society, forcing us to confront the harsh realities of beliefs (Cohen and Richards 2006). Norman Lear took this to a new height as he introduced America to the racial bigots —both Black and White—with George Jefferson (*The Jeffersons*) and Archie Bunker (*All in the Family*); delegitimized our stereotypical conceptions of the poor, Black family by presenting its opposite in *Good Times* with Florida and James Evans; and, with Dorothy, Rose, Blanche, and Sophia (*The Golden Girls*) demonstrated the flaws with various stereotypes regarding gender, sexuality, and age. These series brought issues like racism, classism, sexism, and homophobia into our living rooms, and made us laugh at ourselves. Today we still respond to these stereotypes, and to the programs that make us think. A recent survey of high school students conducted by Lichter and Lichter (2013) reveals that a large group (40%) sees television as a learning tool that accurately reflects the real world. A quarter believes that "TV shows what life is really like" and "people on TV are like real life." A full third of students believed that the portrayal of ethnic characters actually reflect real life (Lichter and Lichter 2013). The good news is that those TV shows that are ethnically diverse in both their casts and their writers are also more likely to receive higher ratings. Racial diversity therefore does indeed impact the profitability of TV programing (Hunt 2013). The real question that remains is: Does this demonstrate life imitating art, or art imitating life?

Music

Sociologists who study music focus both on the active social construction of music as well as the distribution and impact of music within societies.

One of the most instructive stories to understand the importance of music in experience in the matrix is the trajectory of African American music in the context of the United States. Early Black music, on transportation to North America, was decidedly West African. Plantation

Jackie (Moms) Mabley was one of the most prominent entertainers on the Chitlin' Circuit, primarily for Black artists and audiences.

RBM Vintage Images/Alamy Stock Photo

experience and its subsequent dehumanization and constant surveillance led to work songs and spirituals as African American cultural expressions within the context of a culture grounded in White Anglo Saxon Protestantism. Musical expression, like the blues, served a variety of functions for African Americans—as comfort, as communication, as resistance, as critique, as liberation.

After the Civil War and "emancipation," Blacks carved their life in the United States—and so too came new musical resistances to the new structures of racial inequality. Informal and "underground" juke joints, honky-tonks, and after-hours clubs emerged away from the social gaze of Whites as well as the church—here was created an early version of the blues and, with the movements North, instrumental blues (or early jazz) was being created as well. In the North, where there were class schisms within the Black community itself, jazz and ragtime, spurred by the emerging mass-mediated form of recorded music, became popular. This popularity of jazz became so widespread that it was no longer niche marketed to Blacks, but to everyone, especially, and importantly, Whites.

Starting in the 1830s, the "minstrel show" rose in popularity. Minstrel shows were a uniquely American entertainment form consisting of comic skits, variety acts, dancing, and music, performed by Whites in blackface. These shows became extremely popular after the Civil War, with Blacks often portrayed as lazy, dim-witted buffoons. Minstrel shows were the main form of American entertainment, often performing to packed opera houses (Mahar 1998, 9).

After the war, rhythm and blues was the industry's packaging of "black music," but Black artists, with newly amplified instrumentation, began writing and performing across the spectrum of Black music through the decades, from gospel, blues, and jazz to soul, bebop, and funk.

Of course, it was White artists who, covering Black artists' songs, were able to profit from "rock n roll."

From the Black Arts Movement to Black protest music, the 1960s brought Black music and musicians to prominence, both socially and culturally, through music. The 1970s would see an attempt (e.g., disco) to create integrative music cultures. All of this would lead to the rise of Black culture, Black expression, and Black styles through R&B and, ultimately, hip-hop, one of the most influential genres of—again—Black music. This rise paralleled the industry's commodification of this culture, these expressions, these styles—with Whites its largest consumer base. Whites, as scholar Greg Tate (2003) has expressed, are able to share in "everything but the burden" of being Black in a racist America, through their purchase of clothes, music, and style.

One researcher argues that Whites employ a color-blind ideology to allow them to embrace hip-hop and feel a part of the hip-hop cultural milieu, while simultaneously seeing race as irrelevant in their own lives. Color-blind ideology allows Whites to justify their presence in the scene, but they purchase and consume everything about the hip-hop culture (e.g., clothes, music, slang, etc.) except the burden of being Black in America. This, according to Perry Hall (1997), amounts to exploitation. For when you separate the art from the people and their experience, you are commodifying their art and making Black meanings null and void.

Lil Nas X was the first openly gay artist to win a Country Music Award.

Taylor Hill/Getty Images

While music creation is, importantly, rooted in context, the product becomes **mediated,** taken out of its immediate social context and its message sometimes lost in translation to a wider audience, when it is recorded, distributed, and consumed by audiences. By the 1930s, most people in the U.S. were listening to music on the radio or on their home phonographs—no longer was the live experience necessary. Recorded music (from analog to digital) has been the primary mediated form of music production and distribution.

While the music production and distribution industry has gone through myriad changes over the 20th and into the 21st century in terms of genres, technologies, and audiences, by 2012 only four corporate conglomerates controlled the vast majority (88%) of the entire market in musical products. These four conglomerates are predominantly White-owned and only one (EMI) is not from the United States. The demography of corporate owners is largely American, White, and male, controlling a 67.6-billion-dollar industry worldwide. Such structures have consequences for the mediation of musical products across mass media and communication technologies.

The Recording Industry Association of America (RIAA) collects data on the industry every year. Figure 11.1 shows data taken from their most recent (2019) report (RIAA 2020). We can see several intriguing patterns related to engaging with recorded music in the matrix:

- Overall, men are more likely to purchase and download music across most outlets and formats than women.

- Women are slightly more likely to occasional digitally stream music.

- Those in their primary working ages (25–44), likely because they have more disposable income and available technologies, are more likely to have paid subscriptions and download music from servers.

- There are some racial/ethnic differences in music consumption, as well.

The Internet and Social Media

The Pew Research Center has been tracking Americans' internet usage since 2000 (2019a). What we know from that data collection effort is that, almost two decades ago, just over half (52%) of U.S. adults used the internet; that figure is now 90%. The largest demographic utilizing the internet were 18–29-year-olds (100%), followed very closely by 30–49-year-olds (97%), with usage rising across all age groups over time consistently. There are still fewer rural internet users (78%) than those from urban and suburban spaces (91% and 94% respectively) and significant income and education gaps; therefore, continued class inequality in internet usage. There is only a slight racial gap (with Whites at 92%, Latinx at 86%, and Blacks at 85%) and no gender difference in internet usage. Much of the decreasing inequality has to do with the increase in smartphones over the past decade—35% of Americans owned one in 2011, and 81% in 2019 (Anderson 2019). This form of communication technology has led to an increase in our primary mode of sociability in the 21st century: online social media.

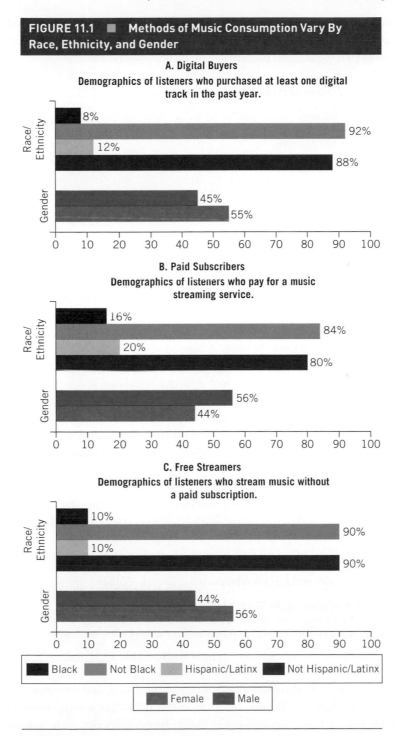

FIGURE 11.1 ■ Methods of Music Consumption Vary By Race, Ethnicity, and Gender

A. Digital Buyers

Demographics of listeners who purchased at least one digital track in the past year.

B. Paid Subscribers

Demographics of listeners who pay for a music streaming service.

C. Free Streamers

Demographics of listeners who stream music without a paid subscription.

Black   Not Black   Hispanic/Latinx   Not Hispanic/Latinx

Female   Male

Source: MusicWatch/2019 Annual Music Study.

Depending on ever-shifting data sources on social media usages and/or "market penetration," it appears that well over three-quarters (79%–83%) of us are using social networking sites. The most used social media platforms in the world, in order, are:

- Facebook (2 billion users worldwide),

- YouTube (1 billion),

- Instagram (800 million),

- Twitter (317 million),

- Snapchat (300 million),

- Pinterest (200 million), and

- LinkedIn (106 million) (Khoros 2019).

In the U.S., Snapchat and Instagram are much more popular among 18–24-year-olds, while Facebook is consistently popular with the rest of the age ranges (30–65-year-olds). Women prefer Pinterest, Instagram, and Facebook more than men, while YouTube and Reddit appear to be much more male spaces. Social class differences, perhaps not surprisingly, seem to impact LinkedIn and Pinterest the most. In terms of how the matrix of race plays out on these social media usage statistics, there is some unequal usage in Instagram, Pinterest, and LinkedIn (Figure 11.2). Yet, we know, if we were to look at intersectional data and look at usage for Black Muslim American women, or for LGBT Latinx, or for rural indigenous high school graduates, it is there we would see significant differences from these experiential positions; such data are very difficult to obtain. This means that the diversity that exists in the United States is in these online spaces. While the growth and reach of these tools have skyrocketed, their adoption has not been even. Race and other significant social identities play a role, even here, in shaping how we engage with new media technologies.

The increase of these social media platforms represents the cutting edge of media and communication technology in the 21st century, and has had several results, including:

- Reuniting old friends and making new friends (Utz and Jankowski 2016)

- Providing health-seeking behavior outlets (Lin et al., 2016)

- Starting revolutions (Juris 2012; Mansour 2012)

- Increasing surveillance and government information gathering (Trottier 2016)

- Creating new and insidious forms of bullying (Kowalski and Giumetti 2017).

Sociologists have studied community, community formation, and community experience since its earliest foundations (Tonnies 1887; Durkheim 1893). These early communities were rooted in being in the same space and place. Twenty-first-century electronic communications provide new kinds of communal forms—forms that you are currently deeply embedded in, and, like those early communal formations and the individuals within them, you are becoming less and less aware that you are so profoundly embedded in these electronic communal matrices, at the very same time they are affecting you and your life with others.

What is at stake in 2021 and beyond is the ways in which our relationships are mediated in these new virtual spaces, how they affect our daily experiences in our "real" life, who participates in these "communities," and how this participation is both similar to and different from the realities of segregation, exploitation, privilege, and power outside of these virtual spaces. As the statistics above show, we are like fish trying to study water here and it is very difficult to do so. Just ask the fish.

FIGURE 11.2 ■ Demographic Groups Use Different Online Platforms

% of U.S. adults who say they ever use the following online platforms or messaging apps

	YouTube	Facebook	Instagram	Snapchat	Twitter	Reddit
U.S. adults	73%	69%	37%	24%	22%	11%
Men	78	63	31	24	24	15
Women	68	75	43	24	21	8
White	71	70	33	22	21	12
Black	77	70	40	28	24	4
Hispanic	78	69	51	29	25	14
Ages 18-29	91	79	94	62	38	22
18-24	90	76	75	73	44	21
25-29	93	84	57	47	31	23
30-49	81	79	47	25	26	14
50-64	70	68	23	9	17	6
65+	38	46	8	3	7	1
<$30,000	68	69	35	27	20	9
$30,000-$74,999	75	72	39	26	20	10
$75,000+	83	75	42	22	31	15
High school or less	64	61	33	22	13	6
Some college	79	75	37	29	24	14
College+	80	74	43	20	32	15

Note: Respondents who did not give an answer are not shown. Whites and Blacks include only non-Hispanics. Hispanics are of any race.

Source: Pew Research Center, data from survey conducted Jan. 8-Feb. 7, 2019.

Critical Thinking

1. Feminists have documented the work of other women, representing other cultures and their lives. Can you identify any local artists and their link to culture? What does this say about both media and symbolic cultures?

2. How are your online social media networks the same as and/or different from your offline friendship networks? What do you think explains the patterns in your own (socially mediated) life?

3. In 1864 Rev. E. Warren published a book called *Happy Slaves.* It argued that slaves were content in slavery, and accepted it as their natural place. What types of stories do you think would emerge if we were to read the actual autobiographies of slaves? What does this say about media, representations, and our beliefs?

4. In your experience of these mass-mediated communication forms—news(papers), radio (or podcasts), television (whether network or streaming), and music—what have you learned about the experiences of other positioned groups in the matrix? Of Black women? Of White lesbians? Of immigrants? Of Muslim Americans? Of children? Of the elderly?

5. Does life imitate art or does art imitate life? You decide.

MASS MEDIA STOCK STORIES AND THEORIES

Scholars have been interested in the institutional and organizational structure of the various mass media throughout the past century. These scholars and cultural critics have looked at who owns the media, the technologies, and the overlapping networks across companies, and the prominent families that run media companies (Davis 2003). They have also examined:

- Organizational networks and how they are interconnected within media institutions (Castells 2011)

- The role of occupational careers, specifically, the importance of specific roles

- Technological innovation (Havens, Lotz, and Tinic 2009)

- Who are the authors/writers of content? Whose voices are heard? Whose work gets published?

- What are the various effects of all of this on the content and form, and on the potential effects on individuals, their communities, and societies? In other words, what messages are being delivered and how are they packaged? (Thompson 1995)

This has been an important and central stock story within the disciplines of communications and sociology, as well as providing significant theoretical material that we have used to make sense of mass media and its effects on our lives. We will now focus on the medium *as* the message, the media as the dominant ideas of the ruling class, and the media as filling our cultural tool kits.

The Medium Is the Message

Marshall McLuhan's prophetic body of work (1964; 1967/1999), written largely throughout the 1950s and 1960s, is considered one of the most influential bodies of scholarship and theoretical insights into the mass media. His now famous phrase "the medium is the message" captures these important insights.

To say that "the medium is the message" is to say that the personal and social consequences of any medium—that is, as McLuhan conceptualizes media, of any *extensions of ourselves*—result from the new scale that is introduced into our lives. The *form* that mass media takes, for instance, the written word in a book, brought to human societies the ability to freeze both individual and communal expressions, set them on the page, and, as such, increase an individual's and their community's expressive longevity and reach. In this approach, the content, per se, is not the most important component of the mass media because the content distracts us from the actual structure of the mediated *form* and thus blinds us to its effects on ourselves and our relations with others.

In the introduction to McLuhan's work, *Understanding Media* (1964), Lewis Lapham clarifies what his friend and colleague meant by this famous insight that "the medium is the message." Individuals in societies become that which they "behold"; we craft our technologies and our media and those, in turn, change us and our relations with each other. In other words, McLuhan, if he were with us today, would help us understand and ask us to think about how we are currently being shaped by social media and smartphones, to take two examples. Social media and smartphones, as media technologies, come with different "structures of feeling, thought, and interaction" than the email and cell phone revolutions in technologies that came before them. Regardless of content, we have already changed because of the media we utilize. Ryan and Wentworth (1999) highlight this stock story as well by arguing that "each mass medium represents a large-scale transformation of social and economic relations" (91).

Media as the Dominant Ideas of the Dominant Classes

While we have thought about the importance of media structure and ownership, now we can think through *who* owns the media and *who* benefits from its structure. These are critical questions for understanding the role of mass media and communication technologies within the matrix of experience—especially regarding race, class, gender, sexuality, and so on. This subsection investigates how the form and content, effects and ideologies, and identities and relationships of mass media are constructed by those in power in order that they remain in power.

Most scholars investigating these questions begin with the work of Karl Marx, particularly his work in *The German Ideology* (1846/1970). This is an important work for understanding the role of ideas, and, therefore, the mass-mediated spread of those ideas, especially in a capitalist society. He powerfully states, "the ideas of the ruling class are in every epoch the ruling ideas, i.e., the class which is the ruling material force of society, is at the same time its ruling intellectual force" (Marx 1846/1970, 64). Controlling the institution of the mass media, according to this perspective, means distributing ideas that support the interests of the ruling, capitalist class—ideas such as racial inferiority, gender superiority, the pathologies of the poor and working classes, and so on. Such scholars and public intellectuals have focused on the ways in which the dominant classes "engineer popular consciousness" through propaganda—driven largely by the political economy of the mass media—a barrage of dominant messages and **controlling images** designed to etch themselves into the psyche and consciousness, and effectively internally and cognitively colonize a population.

Such controlling images serve the dominant classes by hiding domination, oppression, and inequality. Instead of encouraging a society to critically assess the level of racism, economic inequality, sexism, and so on, these controlling images actually shield us from the structural and cultural, political and economic causes of inequality and, instead, place the blame squarely on those who are oppressed, by encouraging society to individualize these social problems and blame the victims of structures of inequality and domination. According to Collins (2008), for instance, the "mammy" image hides the fact that Black female labor is hyperexploited by a White society—the smiling mammy (e.g., Aunt Jemima) signals to Whites (and White society, via the White imagination) that she is okay with this situation—which, of course, she is not. The "matriarch," the "strong Black woman," the Black woman who does not "need a man," the assertive Black woman—is demeaned in multiple ways through these representations as Black women are then stereotyped as "too aggressive," "bad mothers" (who do not spend enough time with their children) and, due to these, cannot "keep a man." Then there is the "welfare mother," who is symbolized as a Black woman who does not work and spends too much time with her children. The jezebel is represented as sexually aggressive Black women—the ultimate underlying threat of all of these stereotypes—Black sexuality.

Can you find examples of these stereotypes in the mass media today? According to Gross (1991), marginalized groups, like our example of Black women here, are underrepresented and "symbolically annihilated" from the rest of society. Because we live in a segregated society, where groups live, work, and play in separate spaces, it is actually the mass media itself that makes the variation in American society "visible" to us. However, *how* groups become visible to the society, *how* they are represented, is key. Gross reminds us, "their representation will reflect the biases and interests of those elites who define the public agenda" (p. 21) and, according to other scholars, such representations typically serve to reinforce the gender, class, race, sexuality status quo, and to support the agenda of the elite. Stemming from this critical story of the mass media and communication, the **Thomas Theorem** (Thomas & Thomas 1928) states that "if men [sic] define situations as real, they are real in their consequences." In other words, the power elite (the heads of corporations, government, military, etc.; see Mills 1956) define society in their own image in order to increase profits, keep the public unquestioning, and maintain their power.

The Media as Culture, Meaning, and Symbols

If things are real if they are real in their consequences, and if the media landscape exists to maintain how things have always been, then why are some individuals and some positions within the matrix more affected by the media and others less so? For that, we turn to another stock story used to understand mass media and communication technology, one that asks *how* these mass media and communication technologies affect our thoughts and behaviors, through what processes do they do so, and how these differ according to the experience in the matrix, etc.

Scholars and social theorists as varied in their research as Goffman (1974), Bandura (2002), Swidler (1986), and Zerubavel (1993) have provided several ways for us to think about this—although, interestingly, none of these authors ever really grappled with race, class, or gender. Goffman originally helped scholars think about the importance of understanding how bodies, interactions, and the extensions of those things, like media, are *framed*. **Frames** give us the "what is going on here" *before* perception kicks in to put pieces together, a cognitive and cultural template of meaning-making that is socially constructed, but also socially utilized to make sense of the world. Goffman states, "Given their understanding of what it is that is going on, individuals fit their actions to this understanding and ordinarily find that the ongoing world supports this fitting" (247). Media helps frame things for us so that we do not have to interpret anew each time; however, such frames can become cognitive crutches, so to speak, where we come to accept the frame and cease being critical of it.

One of Goffman's students, Eviatar Zerubavel (1993), would later develop a theoretical framework to understand how our cognitions are indeed social—that we cognitively map the world in order to understand it. Similarly, Bandura's (2002) large body of work focused our attention on how individuals use a "symbolizing capability" to rework their experiences into symbolic cognitive models which then serve as guides for their behaviors and attitudes. Therefore, "people may learn behaviors through symbolic modeling of stereotypes that they observe on television," for instance (Bandura, 2002). The point of all this is to think about the media as a set of cultural materials that help us think, act, and do in society—the media as culture, the media as filling our cultural tool kit.

Swidler (1986) sees culture as a **tool kit** to understand how culture, even mediated culture, influences individual behavior. Mass media is a prominent and profoundly influential reservoir of publicly available ideas, styles, ideologies, values, symbols, and so on, that can be appropriated by individuals. This model envisions all of us as having a tool kit that we fill with all this stuff. When faced with a dilemma, a decision, an interaction, a conversation, etc., we pull from this tool kit in order to form "strategies of action" and use these strategies to act in the world. Thus, culture influences our behavior by providing certain sets of understandings, precedents, meanings, and strategies of actions. This concealed story asks us to think of the media as providing us, the audience, with scripts, frames, **cognitive maps**, strategies of action, and even identities.

The mass media and our communication technologies create symbols and signs that are not fixed, images and "virtual realities" that are floating, and, as such, they are easily manipulated and can attach to bodies, identities, relationships, social structures, and institutions.

This is not to say, however, that individuals and the groups that attach themselves to these floating symbols have no agency in such a system. Indeed this approach to understanding media is one of the looser frameworks in that it allows for more fluidity in how people and their communities use mass media and communication technologies given what is available.

Young Thai kathoey ("third gender") poses for the camera in front of good-luck souvenirs at a stall in Bangkok's Chinatown.

Matt Hahnewald Photography/Alamy Stock Photo

This has been exacerbated in the 21st century with the rise of social media and web technologies. Not only are identities crafted through the tools that media place in our tool kits, but sometimes entire subcultures can be created as they attach themselves to these sets of meanings. A classic study in this was Radaway's (1991) work on how women read and interpret romance novels. She developed a concept of **interpretive communities** in her analysis of how audiences come at these cultural products, like romance novels, from their positionality and experiences through shared worldviews, from the matrix that informs their understandings of culture in systematic ways. And, indeed, as Grazian puts it, "sometimes mass media exists to grease the wheels of interaction by providing something for us all to talk about" (Grazian 2010).

Critical Thinking

1. How can we see that "the medium is the message" in social media platforms like Instagram, Snapchat, or even TikTok? How are these algorithms potentially raced? Gendered? Classed?

2. Whites tend to own the vast majority of media outlets, including broadcast news outlets (e.g., CNN, Fox, MSNBC, etc.). Using a Marxist lens, how might this fact affect racialized minorities? Whites?

3. Do you see evidence of "controlling images" in today's popular television? Give a few examples. In what ways do people resist such images?

4. How does your mass media consumption affect your interracial interactions and relationships?

APPLYING THE MATRIX: INVESTIGATING MEDIA AND ITS MESSAGES

We will investigate how the social construction of difference is shaped by these mediated forms as well as how those who exist in different places within the matrix approach these forms in their daily lives, and to what effect. Our hope is that this will help you build **_media literacy_** and to be a more conscientious consumer of mass mediated cultural products. This includes resisting their racist, sexist, classist, and heteronormative effects, and perhaps, building new, more inclusive and respectfully representative forms of media in the future as we move deeper into the 21st century.

Media Exposure and Usage

The 2010 Kaiser Family Foundation Study surveyed over 2,000 American children at three points in time (1999, 2004, 2009), covering a wide range of media, even including measures of "multitasking" (i.e., using more than one form of media technology concurrently). Overall, 8–18-year-olds' media consumption has increased by 43% between 1999 and 2009. Total media exposure (including multitasking) from 1999 to 2009 increased by 22%. This is a significant change in 10 years.

In the past decade, 8–18-year-olds have increased their cell phone (39% to 66%) and laptop (12% to 29%) ownership to a staggering degree, allowing more opportunity for media consumption. At the same time, this dramatic shift in consumption contributes to reproducing age-based identities and reinforcing a gap between older and younger populations.

As Figure 11.3 shows, overall, TV use was highest in 2009, followed by listening to music/audio, then computer use, video game playing, and finally reading print media and watching movies/films. And, indeed, youth are multitasking across multiple media and communication technologies. We also find racial differences: Blacks and Hispanics, in almost every category

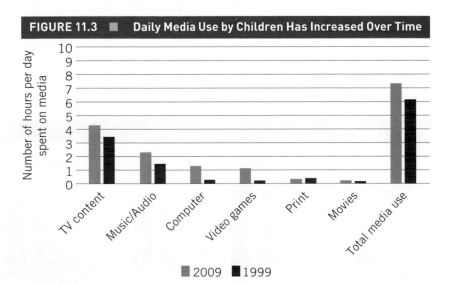

FIGURE 11.3 ■ Daily Media Use by Children Has Increased Over Time

■ 2009 ■ 1999

(TV, music, computers, video games), are *using* and *exposed to* media at higher rates, on average, than their White counterparts (Figure 11.4). Concerning total media exposure, it appears that teenagers, non-Whites, boys, and children with less educated parents are exposed to media at higher rates. As we will see, this also varies by media type.

Books and Magazines

The overall patterns are interesting to think about. In a society like the United States, where the social world is grounded in white-supremacist-capitalist-patriarchy (hooks 1981), we find cultural products are being mostly created and delivered by a White and male-owned media to an increasingly diverse audience. It is important to note that all new forms of media, whether radio, television, or the Internet, were all created to be free and open to all, yet, in all cases, they eventually were bought and concentrated in the hands of a few.

There are six dominant publishers in the world and they are *all* European. Book industry ownership is still predominantly White and male, while the book industry workforce is predominately White and female. This means that it is more difficult for minorities and women to get their work published, and therefore, to be more effectively represented within the print media (Greco et al., 2007). The works of women and people of color are often marginalized and seen as filling a "niche" market. For example, books published by women that address women's lives are often specifically marketed to women, and labeled "chick lit." Is there a genre of books called "White man lit"? Of course not. The dynamics of privilege mean that works by White men are assumed to be universal, and capable of speaking to all humans.

News

News and its related propaganda began in the 19th century through the production and distribution of daily newspapers. Regularly scheduled broadcast news programs did not begin entering the homes of Americans (those who owned TVs) until the 1940s—the era of WWII. Before this, propaganda-based newsreels were often broadcast in movie theaters before the feature film. The more familiar scripted news model began by the 1950s—when well over half of American households had at least one television.

Over 26 million people tune in nightly to get their information from the networks (Edmonds, Guskin, and Rosenstiel 2011). The Pew data from 2010 shows that 23% regularly

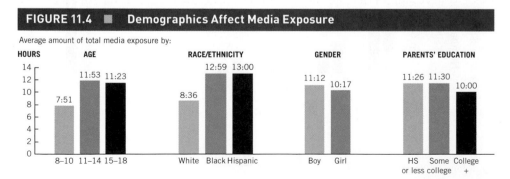

FIGURE 11.4 ■ Demographics Affect Media Exposure

Average amount of total media exposure by:

	AGE	RACE/ETHNICITY	GENDER	PARENTS' EDUCATION
	8–10: 7:51, 11–14: 11:53, 15–18: 11:23	White: 8:36, Black: 12:59, Hispanic: 13:00	Boy: 11:12, Girl: 10:17	HS or less: 11:26, Some college: 11:30, College +: 10:00

get their news from Fox News, 18% from CNN, 11% from MSNBC, 14% from ABC, 12% from NBC. The data also show that the type of news (and television programming in general) consumed varies by race, class, gender, and age.

All this is particularly interesting in terms of the concerns raised by Farai Chideya in her 1995 book *Don't Believe the Hype: Fighting Cultural Misinformation about African Americans.* In this study she shows that in the newsrooms of our journalistic outlets, dominant news staff, editorial staff, and reporters are predominantly White. Such gaps, as Chideya deftly argues, lead to misinformation, misrepresentation, and misunderstanding of reality when Whites control what is considered news, how to present news facts, and which stories to cover. Such a reality (which has really not changed in the past 40 years) leads to classic cover-ups like the one revealed by 1977 Censored News Project, which showed a cover-up of the plight of Black farmers in the United States. The news media is capable of completely ignoring entire regions (like Appalachia) and entire groups (like Black farmers).

These methods are evident in research on racial discrimination in the news. For example, one study showed clearly that while about a third of the poor in the United States are Black, periodical covers like *Time* and *Newsweek,* when covering poverty in the U.S. showed Blacks two-thirds of the time. The same was true of evening newscasts—overrepresenting the issue of poverty as one of Black poverty (Ehrlich 2009, 70).

Discrimination also manifests itself in how the news defines who is a worthy "victim" (for example, rapes of White women are more likely to get news coverage than when any woman of color is the victim); who they invite to serve as "experts" (most often White men); and even which issues are covered. Howard Ehrlich and his colleagues at The Prejudice Institute have conducted a series of five studies over time "documenting institutional discrimination in the treatment of news." Examining local evening news broadcasts in cities around the country, their findings continue to confirm that Whites were significantly overrepresented in positive news roles, whereas stories that dealt with crime were more likely to have Black men as their major characters and there were, on average, four minutes of negative stories for every minute of positive stories (Ehrlich, Weller, and Eden, n.d.).

Advertising

Advertising, like the news, is a supreme propaganda machine. However, instead of creating citizens it creates consumers for capitalism. This makes sense given the purchasing power of these groups in 2019 (Catalyst 2019):

- Whites: 13.2 trillion dollars

- Minorities: 4.7 trillion dollars, with Latinx and Asian American purchasing power expected to continue rising quickly

- Gays and lesbians: 1 trillion dollars

Advertising proliferates and creates desire, creates demand, and it does so by creating the very identities it desires.

Advertising explicitly contributes to the social construction of both race and ethnicity in contemporary United States. Advertising executives write advertising copy and create original artwork that produces "index brand identities." These stereotypical representations use both material and linguistically significant values to target specific audiences. In this way marketing becomes both a preserver but also a manufacturer of race and ethnic images (Shankar 2012).

The commodification of race, class, and gender identities provides new marketing realms. Cars, clothing, cosmetics, video games, and the whole assortment of ethnically defined products are being promoted through the use of these identities (Davila, 2001/2012). Similar strategies have also been used to target and manipulate gay and lesbian identities (Baxter 2010). A recent study shows how Facebook's advertising delivery algorithm interfaces directly with race and gender stereotypes. For instance, the scholars ran ads for job listings in North Carolina without specifying any demographic targets, and they found that, all things equal, "Facebook delivered our ads for jobs in the lumber industry to an audience that was 72% White and 90% men, supermarket cashier positions to an audience of 85% women, and jobs with taxi companies to a 75% black audience even though the target audience we specified was identical for all ads" (Biddle 2019).

Film

From *The Birth of a Nation* (1915) to *Metropolis* (1927), from *The Wizard of Oz* (1935) and *King Kong* (1933) to *Gentlemen Prefer Blondes* (1953), to today, Whiteness in the film industry has been revered. The invention of Hollywood corresponded with the "rise" of the White woman, gender portrayals that legitimiate men's societal dominance, masculinity, and racist formations. Consider the early minstrel shows and blackface appearing alongside the likes of dominant actresses like Shirley Temple and Judy Garland. All of this has resulted in the invisibility of and the misrepresentation of all others.

While the industry is a significant extension of Whiteness, patriarchy, and overrepresented upper-class lifestyles, it is particularly problematic to witness the extent of how we engage with these forms of media. Figure 11.5 shows that Latinx are overrepresented in their engagement with motion pictures—a medium that does not represent them very well at all. While they are the largest minority group in the U.S., they are depicted in very limited roles in film. Like the controlling images of Black women, Latinx tend to be limited to the images of maid; sexpot; Latin lover; thug; or immigrant (Nittle 2013). Clearly these images are gendered as well. Can you think of examples for each of these stereotypes? Can you think of many Latinx actors or actresses that have been able to break out of these roles?

Among younger people, according to the previously mentioned Pew Report, Latinx and Black Americans are overrepresented in their engagement. Attending and viewing films appears to decline as one becomes a teen, is more frequent for boys, and is more likely to be experienced by those from the lower socioeconomic classes. What does all of this mean? Perhaps it means that the experience in the matrix in real life is not reflected and represented at all in the matrix of film. There are many who rarely, if ever, see themselves positively and variably represented at the movie theater. It also may mean that the virtual representation of the matrix may serve the interests of those in power, of the status quo, as it plays more and more of a strong socialization

Detail from poster for *Metropolis*, the 1926 UFA film classic directed by Fritz Lang.

Pictorial Press Ltd/Alamy Stock Photo

King Kong, 1933.

Pictorial Press Ltd/Alamy Stock Photo

FIGURE 11.5   ■   Moviegoers Vary by Race and Ethnicity

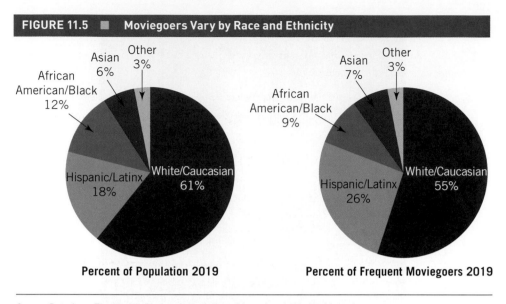

Source: Data from The Motion Picture Association of America via *Variety* Magazine.

role in the lives of individuals and their communities in the real matrix. Films have been specifically utilized to construct differences and maintain the racial status quo in the United States. From racial representation on the silver screen to the overabundance of celebrity culture, movies serve Whiteness, capitalism, patriarchy, and heteronormativity well.

This also means that film plays a fundamental role in constructing difference and mediating reality in our daily lives. The past ten years saw a significant rise in films that centered race, racism, and the voices, talents, and technological prowess of racial and ethnic minorities (e.g., *Black Panther, Get Out, Moonlight, Selma, Sorry to Bother You, Spider-Man: Into the Spiderverse,* etc.; see Ware 2019), and yet the industry's critics are mostly male and White (Mendez Berry and Yang 2019).

Research suggests that mass-mediated culture is an important place where some frames, some narratives, and some images of groups and their stories rise to the top of our collective consciousness, while others remain hidden. Here we are, entering the second decade of the 21st century, fighting for #BlackLivesMatter, while the #OscarsSoWhite continues (Schulman 2018).

Critical Thinking

1. What messages have you learned from the media about race? Stop and think about each racial group, and jot down the images that come to mind and specific examples from the media. Think about the specific media you engage with: How often do you see each racial group represented—for example, do you ever see Native Americans in television sitcoms or dramas? How are they presented? What is missing/excluded? And what are some of the consequences of this?

2. Though we did not cover video games in this chapter, they are another significant form of mass media that is consumed by the society. In fact, the gaming industry is huge! How do the processes described in this section play out similarly or differently in the virtual world of video gaming?

3. Advertising preys on our fears, hopes, desires, and insecurities in order for corporations to make a profit. How is the Whiteness of society revealed through the things that are advertised? Give some examples.

4. Can mass media also be used to create social change for racial justice? If so, how?

TRANSFORMING OUR MASS-MEDIATED COMMUNICATION TECHNOLOGIES

After all of this, we must ask the obvious question. If all these mass media and communication technologies have been so fundamental to the construction of difference in the 19th, 20th, and now 21st centuries, what will be the mediated forms of the future? As demographics change radically, will the mediated forms change accordingly? If media both reflects *and* alters our identities, our relationships, our communities, and our societies on a large scale, it represents a very important institution to critically understand *and* learn how to harness in order to create a more just world for all. For that we need more critical media literacy and social movements that can harness media for the empowerment of humanity.

Critical Media Literacy

We hope you have become much more critical of your media intake and the ways that sometimes even the sheer partaking of mass-mediated images, stories, and identities takes us further from understanding and respecting differences and experiences within the matrix. On the other hand, some newer technologies, like social media and online communities, may hold some promise for creating new racial, gender, class, and sexuality understandings and relationships. Or do they?

From freely accessible public channels to very strictly regulated broadcast entities, scholars have shown that the technologies that have positive potential for transformative change can also quickly be used for social control, but that there is always hope that such media forms can be cracked open again and used for positive human and social transformative potential (Wu 2010). The internet, that most democratic of systems, is currently facing the same dichotomy. A recent piece urges us to remember that currently "90% of all media consumed in the United States [is] owned by six companies. This includes print, television, film, music, video games and related investments. And it includes the internet. In other words, these six companies control 90% of what Americans see and hear" (Alyn 2019).

We all must work hard at developing our critical media literacies—learning to "read" the media. According to Durham (2008), in a world that is saturated with media, people need to be taught how to understand this ever-encroaching part of their environments, just like they need to understand how gravity works—it is that important. In an era of fake news and wide-sweeping, corporate-controlled mass media, we must be vigilant, especially people and communities of color, because the information spread by Whiteness and White supremacy will serve its constituents' blindness. Diversity and inclusion media consultant Jody Alyn has some advice for critically evaluating media:

- Discuss these topics openly with friends and colleagues. Share information and tools for being a responsible news consumer.

- Join organizations that work on responsible journalism, holding media accountable, and a free and open internet.

- Support alternate news sources that are transparent about their ownership, funding, mission, and motives.

- Publicly call on news organizations to uphold journalism's purpose and ethics, and to encourage independence and diversity of opinion.

- When editorials present false equivalencies or inaccuracies, call for the newsroom side of that outlet to report on falsehoods with journalistic investigation and fact.

- Register public complaints when racist or other propaganda statements by public figures are "given a pass" or reported as fact.

- Write to your elected representatives. Support net neutrality and specific regulatory practices to break up the "big six" and to restore integrity and equity to media ownership policies. (Alyn 2019)

These are fairly simple things we can all do to enhance media literacy in our families, communities, and society.

Mass Media and Social Movements

The 21st century has seen an intense pushback by groups and communities that have been devalued, stereotyped, and rendered invisible by the institution of mass media. These groups harnessed the very media that have dehumanized, invalidated, and excluded them to speak for themselves, instead of having others speak for them.

Groups like the Institute for Nonprofit News bring together hundreds of news outlets that seek truth instead of profits, corporate interests, and partisan politics. This kind of news structure holds much more potential for coverage that strengthens communities instead of creating division simply for profits.

The rise of the podcast (originally called "audioblogging" in early personal computing), with its availability to literally anyone with a computer or mobile device and ability to be easily shared, can bring disparate communities together and to create community. Podcasts such as *The Black (Un) Conscious, Hella Black Podcast, All My Relations,* and *LatinoUSA* among many others show us the power of the medium for minority-owned, minority-produced, and minority-distributed content.

Streaming services like Netflix, Hulu, Amazon Prime, and others initially held promise for more onscreen diversity and more realistic representation of non-White characters, stories, and identities, but due to their for-profit nature, they have issues similar to those that plague broadcast television and Hollywood. Although some media critics see Netflix as trying to break the mold (Boboltz and Williams 2016), only time will tell.

It has indeed taken social movements to push against the for-profit motives of the majority of mass-mediated industries to force them to alter who writes and produces content and how content is distributed to better reflect the true diversity that exists in the matrix. The more critical media literacy we develop in this society, the more social movements will be organized around the change we demand, and the more likely our society will respect the experiences of those who have been made invisible and silenced by our mediated matrix.

Critical Thinking

1. In our contemporary democracy in the United States, what should the role of the news be? The radio/podcasts? Television/streaming services?

2. The hashtag has revolutionized social movement organizing. How so? What was its predecessor?

3. How are national, state, and local elections mediated? How does race play a role in this process? Gender? Class? Sexuality? Give examples from a recent election that you followed fairly closely.

CHAPTER SUMMARY

11.1 Examine the historical and contemporary role of media in the construction of difference.

All of the different forms of media have a role in the construction of difference in our lives. Media not only transmits, but also reproduces our values, ideas, ways of being, and histories. The exciting thing about media is also the daunting thing about media—it is always morphing and shifting as it always morphs and shifts us. Every ethnic group that ventured on these shores brought with them a range of symbolic communications that told their stories, captured their identities, and projected their values. Throughout time people have invented a variety of systems and objects to transfer information, including indigenous peoples, whose creative developments in the uses of media inform our own contemporary realities. Almost every group that settled in the Americas similarly brought and preserved their symbolic cultures, which also reflected race, class, ethnicity, and gender—African American quilting is one of many colonial examples that still exists today. Mass media, the social and organizational structures of communicating information throughout a given society to its members, developed primarily through the forms of newspapers, radio, television, music, and the internet. All offer glimpses into the mediated matrix of reality.

11.2 **Explain the stock stories that have helped us think through the role of mass media in our lives.**

Scholars are interested in understanding the *whys* and *hows* of media development, as well as how mediated realities reproduce and/or challenge the racial status quo through the information and messages deployed throughout society. One approach has been to focus on the shape of the media form and the kinds of relationships it encourages; since media is an extension of ourselves and our communities, perhaps the medium, itself, is the message. In this approach, the content is not the most important component of the mass media because the content distracts us from the actual structure of the mediated form and blinds us to its effects on ourselves and our relations with others. Another way to understand the role of media in our lives in the mediated matrix is to look specifically at the role that power plays in the production, distribution, and consumption of media. Often, from a fundamentally Marxist lens, the media and its messages are expressions of the dominant class and the ruling relations of its power—in order to secure that power, dominant messages and controlling images are designed to etch themselves into the psyche and consciousness, and effectively internally and cognitively colonize a population. Finally, we can also look at the media as filling our cultural tool kits that we draw from as individuals and communities differently to make sense out of our world and our position in it. This also creates avenues for pursuing change.

11.3 **Apply the matrix theory to how we consume media.**

The media are embedded within our society and our relations in a variety of ways; yet, these ways are more or less enhanced and effective depending on our exposure to and our engagement with those forms of media. Whether books and magazines, news, advertising, or film, our position within the matrix affects how we choose (and are able) to engage with those media. The matrix not only impacts individual use and interpretation of these mediated forms, but our positions in the matrix also determines who writes, produces, distributes, and markets such messages and information to which communities, and with which desires (e.g., profit, power, empowerment, etc.).

11.4 **Investigate the importance of critical media literacy.**

Knowing the historical development of the media and various mass-mediated forms, understanding the various stock stories used by those in power as well as the powerless, and grappling with how the matrix of race differentially provides exposure to and engagement with the media and its production, distribution, and consumption is only part of the story. Such processes can alter us or we can alter those mediated processes. In order to make media an effective tool of liberation and community organization, we need to develop our media literacy and learn how to harness it in order to create a more just world for all. This is done through hard work, study, and practicing critical media literacy skills. Many minority and racialized groups who have learned how to harness the power of media are using that power to create social movements to effect change for themselves, and ultimately, for all.

KEY TERMS

cognitive maps

controlling imagesframes

interpretive communities

mass media

media

media literacy

mediated

propaganda

social media

Thomas Theorem

tool kit

REFERENCES

ADL 2013. "Don Black/Stormfront", accessed online on January 13, 2014 at URL: http://archive. adl.org/learn/ext_us/don-black/stormfront.html?LEARN_Cat=Extremism&LEARN_SubCat= Extremism_in_America&xpicked=5&item=DBlack.

Alyn, Jody. 2019. "Of Minds and Media," *Inclusionalysis*. January 10, 2019. Accessed online on Janua ry 5, 2020 at http://www.alynconsulting.com/diversity-blog/key-concepts-conversations/of-mind s-and-media/

Anderson, Monica. 2019. "Mobile Technology and Home Broadband." Pew Research Center. Acces sed January 4, 2019 at https://www.pewresearch.org/internet/2019/06/13/mobile-technology-an d-home-broadband-2019/

Aptheker, Bettina 1989. *Tapestries of Life: Women's Work, Women's Consciousness and the Meaning Life: Women's Work, Women's Consciousness, and the Meaning of Daily Experience*. Boston, Ma.: University of Massachusetts Press.

Bandura, Albert. 2002. "Social cognitive theory of mass communication." In J. Bryant & D. Zillmann (Eds.), *Media effects: Advances in theory and research* (2nd ed., pp. 121-153). Mahwah, NJ: Erlbaum.

Barnouw, Erik. 1968. *A History of broadcasting in the United States: Volume 2: The Golden Web, 1933 to 1963*. Oxford: Oxford University Press.

Bartlett, Sarah. 2013. Ethnic media is more than a niche: It's worth your attention." Neiman Journalism Lab, Harvard University. Accessed online on January 13, 2014 at URL: http://www.niem anlab.org/2013/07/ethnic-media-is-more-than-a-niche-its-worth-your-attention/.)

Baxter, Susan C., 2010. "Evidence on the Marketing Approaches Targeting Gay and Lesbian Consumers." *Global Journal of Business Research*, Vol. 4(2): 125-139.

Biddle, Sam. 2019. "Facebook's Ad Algorithm is a Race and Gender Stereotyping Maching, New Study Suggests," *The Intercept*, April 3. Accessed online on January 4, 2020 at https://theintercept. com/2019/04/03/facebook-ad-algorithm-race-gender/

Boboltz, Sara, and Brennan Williams. 2016 https://www.huffpost.com/entry/streaming-sites-dive rsity_n_56c61240e4b0b40245c96783

Boyle, K., 2018. Hiding in plain sight: gender, sexism and press coverage of the Jimmy Savile case. *Journalism Studies*, 19(11), pp. 1562-1578.

Brown, Jane D. and Carol J. Pardun. 2004. "Little in Common: Racial and Gender Differences in Adolescents' Television Diets." *Journal of Broadcasting and Electronic Media*, 48(2): 266-278.

Castells, M. 2011. *The Rise of the Network Society: Volume One: The Information Age: Economy, Society and Culture.*Second edition. Wiley Blackwell

Catalyst. 2013. *Catalyst Quick Take: Buying Power.* New York: Catalyst.

Chideya, Farai. 1995. *Don't Believe the Hype: Fighting Cultural Misinformation about African Americans.*

Cohen, Roger and Ryan Richards. 2006. "When the Truth Hurts, Tell a Joke: Why America Needs Its Comedians", *Humanity in Action*, accessed online on January 22, 20-14 at URL: http://www.humani tyinaction.org/knowledgebase/174-when-the-truth-hurts-tell-a-joke-why-america-needs-its-co medians).

Collins, P.H. 2008. *Black feminist thought: Knowledge, consciousness, and the politics of empowerment.* London: Routledge.

Davila, Arlene *Latinos, Inc: the Marketing and Making of a People.* Berkeley and Los Angeles, Ca: The University of California Press.

D'Altroy, Terence N. N. 2001. *The Incas.* Victoria, Australia: Blackwell Publishing.

Davis, Aeron. 2003. "Whither Mass Media and Power? Evidence for a Critical Elite Theory Alternative." *Media, Culture & Society*, 255): 669-690.

Deery, J., 2017. TV Screening: the entertainment value of poverty and wealth. In *Media and Class* (pp. 53-67). Routledge.

Douglas, Susan J. 2012. "Radio and Television". *History Channel.* (Accessed on January 15, 2014 at URL: http://www.history.com/topics/radio-and-television.)

Durkheim, Emile. 1893/1997. *The Division of Labour In Society.* Trans. Lewis A. Coser. New York, NY: Free Press.

Edmonds, Rick, Emily Guskin and Tom Rosenstiel. 2011. "The State of News Media: Annual Report on American Journalism." Pew Research Center. Accessed online on 1/20/2014 at URL: http:// stateofthemedia.org/2011/newspapers-essay/data-page-6/.)

Ehrlich, Howard J. 2009. *Hate Crimes and Ethnoviolence: The History, Current Affairs, and Future of Discrimination in America.* Westview.

Ehrlich, Howard J., Jason Weller & Allison Eden. n.d. "If It Bleeds It Leads, If It's White It's Right: Local TV News in 12 Cities." http://prejudiceinstitute.com/IfItBleeds.html accessed 1-11-14.

FCC. 2020. Fourth Report on Ownership of Broadcast Stations. February. https://www.fcc.gov/ media

Goffman, Erving. 1974. *Frame Analysis.* Northeastern.

González, Juan and Joseph Torres 2011. *News for All the People: The Epic Story of Race and the American Media.* Brooklyn, NY: New Left Books.

Greco, Albert N., Clara E. Rodriguez, and R. M. Wharton. 2007. *The Culture and Commerce of Publishing in the 21st Century.* Stanford, CA: Stanford University Press.

Gross, L. 1991. "Out of the mainstream: Sexual minorities and the mass media." In M. Wolf & A. Kielwasser (Eds.), *Gay people, sex and the media* (pp. 19–46). New York: Haworth.

Guskin, E. and Mitchell, A., 2011. Hispanic media: Faring better than the mainstream media. *The State of the New Media. An Annual Report on American Journalism*, 22(02), p. 2012.

Hall, P. A. 1997. The Ebonics debate: Are we speaking the same language?. *The Black Scholar*, 27(2), pp. 12-14.

Havens, Timothy, Amanda D. Lotz, and Serra Tinic. 2009. "Critical Media Industry Studies: A Research Approach" *Communication, Culture & Critique*, 2(2): 234- 253.

hooks, b. 1981. *Ain't I a woman: Black women and feminism*. Boston: South End.

Hunt, Darnell. 2013. "Hollywood Diversity Brief: Spotlight on Cable Television". *Ralph J. Bunche Center for African American Studies at UCLA*. Accessed online on January 5, 2014 at URL: http://www.bunchecenter.ucla.edu/wp-content/uploads/2013/10/Hollywood-Diversity-Brief-Spotlight-10-2013.pdf.)

Jhally, S., 2019. *Enlightened racism: The Cosby Show, audiences, and the myth of the American dream*. Routledge.

Juris, Jeffrey S. 2012. "Reflections on #Occupy Everywhere: Social Media, Public Space, and Emerging Logics of Aggregation." *American Ethnologist*, 39(2): 259-279.

Kaiser Family Foundation. 2010. Rideout, V.J., Foehr, U.G. and Roberts, D.F., 2010. Generation M 2: Media in the Lives of 8-to 18-Year-Olds. *Henry J. Kaiser Family Foundation*.

Khoros. 2019. "The 2019 Social Media Demographics Guide." https://khoros.com/resources/social-media-demographics-guide

Kohut, A., Wike, R., Horowitz, J.M., Simmons, K., Poushter, J., Barker, C., Bell, J. and Gross, E.M., 2011. *Global digital communication: Texting, social networking popular worldwide*. Washington, DC: Pew Research Centre.

Kowalski, R.M. and Giumetti, G.W. 2017. Bullying in the digital age. In *Cybercrime and its victims* (pp. 167-186). Routledge.

Lichter, Robert S. and Linda S. Lichter. 2013. "Does TV Shape Ethnic Images?" *Media Literacy*, Issue 43, Accessed online on January 12, 2014 at URL. http.//www.medialit.org/reading-room/does-tv-shape-ethnic-images.)

Lin, W.Y., Zhang, X., Song, H. and Omori, K., 2016. Health information seeking in the Web 2.0 age: Trust in social media, uncertainty reduction, and self-disclosure. *Computers in Human Behavior*, 56, pp. 289-294.

Mahar, William 1998. *Behind the Burnt Cork Mask: Early Blackface Minstrelsy and Antebellum American Popular Culture*. Champaign, Il: University of Illinois Press.

Mansour, Essam. 2012. "The Role of Social Networking Sites (SNSs) in the January 25th Revolution in Egypt." *Library Review*, 61(2): 128-159.

Marx, Karl. 1846/1970. *The German Ideology*.

McChesney, Robert. 2000. *Rich Media, Poor Democracy: Communication Politics in Dubious Times*. New York, NY: The New Press.

McLuhan, Marshall. 1964. *The Medium is the Massage*. Columbia Music.

McLuhan, Marshall. 1999 (1967). *Understanding Media: The Extensions of Man*. Cambridge, MA: The MIT Press.

Mendez Berry, Elizabeth and Chi-hui Yang. 2019. "The Dominance of the White Male Critic," *The New York Times*, July 5. Accessed online on January 4, 2020 at https://www.nytimes.com/2019/07/05/opinion/we-need-more-critics-of-color.html?auth=login-facebook&fbclid=IwAR3SScPKlVMMz_ECDAFqyHuDxCiPr66c7RVnLLpPev1U-eiqyeHCNFYQ8h0&smid=nytcore-ios-share

Mendos, L.R., 2019. *State-sponsored homophobia*. ILGA, Geneva.

Mills, C.W. (1956/1981). *The power elite*. Oxford: Oxford University Press.

New America Media. 2013. "Our History", (Accessed online on January 18, 2014 at URL: http://newamericamedia.org/about/.)

Nittle, Nadra Kareem. 2013. "Five Common Latino Stereotypes in Television and Film." http://racerelations.about.com/od/hollywood/a/Five-Common-Latino-Stereotypes-In-Television-And-Film.htm accessed 1-11-14.

Perrin, Andrew and Monica Anderson. 2019. "Share of U.S. Adults Using Social Media Including Facebook is Mostly Unchanged since 2018," Pew Research Center. Accessed on January 5, 2019 at https://www.pewresearch.org/fact-tank/2019/04/10/share-of-u-s-adults-using-social-media-including-facebook-is-mostly-unchanged-since-2018/

Peterson, Richard A., and David G. Berger. 1975. "Cycles in Symbol Production: The Case of Popular Music." *American Sociological Review*, Vol. 40 (2): 158-173.

Pew Research Center. 2019a. "Internet/Broadband Fact Sheet," Pew Research Center. Accessed on January 4, 2019 at https://www.pewresearch.org/internet/fact-sheet/internet-broadband/

Pew Research Center. 2019b. "Newspapers Fact Sheet," Pew Research Center, July 9. Accvessed online on January 4, 2019 at https://www.journalism.org/fact-sheet/newspapers/

Radaway, Janice. 1991. *Reading the Romance: Women, Patriarchy, and Popular Culture*. Chapel Hill: University of North Carolina Press.

Rhodes, Leara 2010. *The Ethnic Press: Shaping the American Dream*. New York: Peter Lang Publishers.

RIAA. 2020. Music Concsumer Profile. Accessed online at https://www.riaa.com/wp-content/uploads/2020/04/MusicWatch-Consumer-Profile-2019.pd

Roscoe, Will. 1988. "We'Wha and Klah: The American Indian Berdache As Artist and Priest". *American Indian Quarterly*, Vol. 12 (12): 127-150.

Rothenbuhler, Eric and Tom McCourt. 2002. "Radio Redefines Itself, 1947-1962". In Michele Hilmes and Jason Loviglio (eds.) *Essays in the Cultural History of Radio: Radio Reader*, New York: Routledge.

Russo, Alexander. 2002. "A Dark (ened) Figure on the Airwaves: Race, Nation, and the Green Hornet". In MicheleHilmes andJasonLoviglio (eds.) *Essays in the Cultural History of Radio: Radio Reader*, New York: Routledge.

Ryan, John W., and William M. Wentworth. 1999. *Media & Society*. New York: Pearson.

Sackmann, R. and O. Winkler. 2013. *Gerontechnology*, 11(4): 493-503. "Technology Generations Revisited: The Internet Generation."

Savage, Barbara. 2002. "Radio and the Political Discourse of Racial Equality": In MicheleHilmes andJasonLoviglio (eds.) *Essays in the Cultural History of Radio: Radio Reader*, New York: Routledge.

Schulman, Micheal. 2018. "Is the Era of #oscarssowhite Over?" *The New Yorker*, January 23. Accessed online on January 4, 2020 at https://www.newyorker.com/culture/cultural-comment/is-the-era-of-oscarssowhite-over

Shankar, Shalini 2012. "Creating model consumers: Producing ethnicity, race and class in Asian American advertising." *American Ethnologists*, Vol. 39 (3): 578-591.

Southern Poverty Law Center. 2019. "Hate Groups Reach Record High," SPLC, February 19, 2019. Accessed online on January 5, 2019 at https://www.splcenter.org/news/2019/02/19/hate-groups-reach-record-high

Swidler, A., 1986. Culture in action: Symbols and strategies. *American sociological review*, pp. 273-286.

Tapscott, D. 1998. *Growing up digital: The rise of the net generation*. New York: McGraw-Hill.

Tate, Greg. 2003. *Everything But the Burden: What White People are Taking from Black Culture*. New York, NY: Broadway Books.

Thomas, W.I., and D.S. Thomas. 1928. The methodology of behavior study. *The child in America: Behavior problems and programs*, pp. 553-576. New York: Knopf.

Thompson, John B. 1995. *The Media and Modernity: A Social Theory of Modernity*. Stanford, CA: Stanford University Press.

Tonnies, Ferdinand. 1887. *Gemeinschaft und Geselchaft*. Leipzig: Fues's Verlag.

Trottier, D., 2016. *Social media as surveillance: Rethinking visibility in a converging world*. Routledge.

Utz, S. and Jankowski, J., 2016. Making "friends" in a virtual world: The role of preferential attachment, homophily, and status. *Social Science Computer Review*, 34(5), pp. 546-566.

Wahlman, Maude Southwell. 1986. "African Symbolism in Afro-American Quilts, *African Arts*, Vol, 2(1):68-76+99.

Ware, Lawrence. 2019. "The Most Important Decade for Movies About Black Lives," *The New York Times*, December 30. Accessed online on January 4, 2020 at https://www.nytimes.com/2019/12/30/movies/movies-black-lives.html?fbclid=IwAR1lo5cPo8RP49ZJa5oZEOvoRwLsIBJ-Iu6nCTIlIV1kZvdY-JYxFw2TSB8

Watson, Amy. 2019. "Media Consumption among Ethnic Groups in the U.S. – Statistics and Facts," Statistica.com. November 28. Accessed online on January 5, 2019 at https://www.statista.com/topics/5108/ethnic-groups-in-the-us-media-consumption/

Wu, Tim. 2010. *The Master Switch: The Rise and Fall of Information Empires*. New York, NY: Alfred A. Knopf.

Zerubavel, E., 1993. *The fine line*. University of Chicago Press.

12 TRANSFORMING THE MATRIX, TRANSFORMING THE FUTURE

John Brown, 1800–1859.

Pictorial Press Ltd./Alamy

LEARNING OBJECTIVES

12.1 Explore the connections between the past and the present, the global and the local, and the individual and collective action.

12.2 Compare social movements that are organized for racial justice and those designed to maintain the racial status quo.

12.3 Identify the differences between activism and allyship and evaluate your own engagement in transforming the matrix of race.

In 1856, John Brown, who had dedicated his life to abolishing the institution of slavery in the United States, pointed a finger at the so-called abolitionist movement and spoke the rallying cry that would organize a slave rebellion: "These men are all talk. What we need is action! Action!" Three years later he would be tried, convicted, and hanged for his beliefs. Fast forward to Charlottesville, Virginia, in August of 2017. Thirty-two-year-old Heather Heyer was counter-protesting the assemblage of White nationalists, neo-Nazis, and White supremacists at the "Unite the Right" rally when she was killed by a far-right White supremacist. Her last public Facebook post before her death was "If you are not outraged, you're not paying attention."

As we have learned throughout this course, the United States was established upon fundamentally racist institutions and practices. A variety of antiracist actions and pushback against such a racist foundation have also been a part of the social fabric of the United States since its inception (Aptheker 1992). Throughout this history, antiracist activists have been mobilized around issues like abolitionism, and opposition to structural and systemic racism, individual racist speech acts, individual racist acts, institutional racism, racial ideology, implicit bias, and inequitable distribution of land, wealth, and power (Olson 2004; Feagin 2013, Kendi 2017).

While the oppressed and racialized have always been at the center of individual and organized action against the racial order, at every stage along the way, White antiracist action has taken varying shapes, been birthed from varied locations in the intersectional social structure, narrated its motivations in various ways, etched itself into individual and organization identities, taken aim at particular manifestations of racial domination, and had differential (re)productive impacts.

More recently, the racially charged rhetoric used by the Trump administration was seen as emboldening, energizing, and giving permission for White fascists, neo-Nazis, White supremacists, Ku Klux Klan members, and other White bigots, nativists, nationalists, and members of the alt-right to fight to preserve their perceived heritage, express their opinions, and publicly torment those who do not look or think like they do. As has always been the case, however, alongside these newly motivated defenders of White supremacy, there is potentially renewed hope for a new wave of antiracist activism to overcome this surge of hatred and push the United States closer to its democratic ideals of equality and justice for all.

The actions of John Brown and Heather Heyer are but two moments in centuries of antiracist activism in the United States. Both were located in privileged positions within the matrix, where Whiteness expected them to remain silent in the face of structural racism; yet, both were individuals who stood up and consistently challenged the racial order that reproduced and justified racial inequality.

Throughout this course we have examined examples of resistance and transformational stories coming from social movements, creative and innovative proposed policies, and the interventions of activist organizations working to collectively organize and shift the way we look at specific forms of inequity. In this chapter we extend that discussion further and examine various ongoing attempts to create transforming stories. We begin by examining social movements fighting both for and against racial justice. We then discuss possibilities for change within institutions. Finally, we arrive back into the center of the matrix: the individual. What can individuals possibly do to work for change when such problems operate on such a massive scale? Every individual can do something, beginning here and now. Massive change will not happen without the involvement of countless individuals. Just as certain as the matrix fundamentally shapes us and our relations, each of us individually, and in relation to each other, fundamentally can alter the matrix—indeed, it is the only thing that ever has.

CONNECTING THE PAST AND THE FUTURE

The key to creating new solutions is understanding our own particular experiences of race in two ways:

- through the intersectional lens of the matrix, and

- by grappling with our experiences as they continue to be informed by the global context to which we are all connected.

We learned in Chapter 2 that "the problem of race" originated in the global context of imperialism and colonialism. It makes sense that any problems of racism and racial inequity must be addressed within that very global context in order to create contemporary social change for racial justice. The dynamics of inequality that we witness in our institutions of work, education, families, health, the economy, and so on, are also intricately tied to the world's economy and the international matrix of race.

Emerging/Transforming Stories

Globalization, the increasing interweaving of economic, cultural, and social realities across regions, nations, and localities, has created a much more connected world. This is clearly the case as we experience the ongoing impact of COVID-19 that has exposed the deep racialized disparities in healthcare, as well as the widespread protests against racialized police brutality and anti-Blackness in the wake of the murder of George Floyd on May 25, 2020. Right now, multiple narratives are competing to become the predominant stock story to explain both public health crises and police brutality. There are also many stories being concealed as well as revealed. Resistance stories will take multiple forms and shift with time and new information, and with experience and initiative—all within the matrix.

Lee Anne Bell is an expert in intersectionality in higher education. In her influential book, *Storytelling for Social Justice*, she encourages us all to engage with emerging/transforming stories because such stories "envision alternatives to the status quo and generate strategies to realize our visions for racial equity" (Bell 2010, 75). The terms *emerging* and *transforming* highlight the deep importance of connecting the past to the future. For instance, "emerging" acknowledges that there have been previous stories whose forms have helped us realize the need to develop other ways of knowing, acting, and, ultimately, storytelling, which push against earlier forms that encouraged maintaining the status quo or "just the way things are." When a story is "transforming," it draws inspiration from other realms of experience (e.g., art, theatre, etc.) to encourage change. For Bell, when we combine the two, emerging/transforming stories allow us to envision and "act in alignment with one's dreams toward a better future" (Bell 2010).

The site where Heather Heyer was killed during a protest of the Unite the Right rally in Charlottesville, VA, in 2017.

AgnosticPreachersKid, CC BY-SA 4.0

After learning about the matrix of race and myriad examples of how the stock stories, concealed stories, and resistance stories have filled the library of human existence, and informed the collective conscience of groups, you can now connect the dots as to how the stories we *will* tell within the matrix are dependent on the stories we *have* told and *are* telling right now. While it can feel like the story has already been written, and that things are the way they are and always will be, you know better.

We are the ones we have been waiting for to write, acknowledge, share, and utilize the emerging/transforming stories to reshape the world we live in toward social justice.

NGOs, Globalization, and the Matrix

While we know that the world is deeply interconnected and that the lives we lead in our own communities are linked to those on the other side of the globe, it can be difficult sometimes to keep this front and center as we try to create change.

Over the past 30 years **nongovernmental organizations (NGOs)**—typically nonprofit groups that operate independently of any national government, and whose operations often seek solutions to pressing social problems (e.g., climate change, hunger, etc.)—have helped to paint a clearer picture of the global matrix within which we are all interconnected. NGOs are able to advance democratic processes, promote human rights, and provide essential services for some of the world's most needy. Starting at the local and national level, these organizations are now global in their impact. Global transformations have occurred within the context of United Nations agencies, regional organizations, finance and trade institutions, and transnational corporations. Some examples include Doctors Without Borders, Heifer International, and the One Acre Fund.

NGOs arrived on the scene when it became clear that the neoliberal policies of the Global North (those developed nations of Western Europe, North America, Australia, New Zealand, Singapore, South Korea, and Taiwan, led by the United States) were wreaking havoc on the communities of the Global South (mostly Latin America, Asia, Africa, and Oceania nations that are also known as the "periphery"). Although there have also been significant criticisms of the potential cooption of NGOs by imperial world powers, they have rapidly transformed the way international systems and processes operate.

As the poor get poorer, NGOs appear to gain in influence as the clients they serve expand in number and in needs. NGOs do a number of things, including, but certainly not limited to:

- Facilitating opportunities for indigenous peoples to self-organize

- Aiding citizens in promoting social values and civic goals deemed important

- Allowing local initiatives to develop for solving problems in a wide array of areas such as environment, health, poverty alleviation, culture and the arts, and education

Taken together, NGOs can reflect the complexity and diversity within each society as they establish and sustain individuals collectively working to improve their communities.

By working at the grassroots level, NGOs both advance and reflect diversity and pluralism necessary to sustain vibrant and successful social institutions. NGOs also help preserve essential spaces between nonprofit and governmental sectors. NGOs help create and sustain public goods through which diverse publics, those within the matrix of experience, women, racialized minorities, sexual minorities, the differently abled, the neurodiverse, children, the poor, and others can express agency. And finally, NGOs provide spaces for social experimentation where indigenous groups can learn to solve and engage in solutions to their most pressing problems (Heintz 2006). NGOs are potentially well positioned to author emerging/transformative stories that advance creative solutions.

The more globalized the world becomes, the more localized the solutions must be. This is because, as the forces of globalization impact more and more nations—of both the Global North and the Global South—there will be a tendency to protect and preserve national borders, identities, and interests. These identities frequently described and defined as sovereignty, culture, language, and political spheres are increasingly feeling the strain of globalization. Yet the borders, interests, and identities are often solidified at the expense of human rights, equality, and dignity. Thus, because they are not rooted in the ebbs and flows of political influence of the ruling party or at the mercy of local traditions and politics, NGOs are, for many, the logical answer to these sorts of tensions specifically because they are based locally.

We can identify several current examples of the significance of NGOs (though there are many, many more):

- In Ecuador the indigenous people's movement was able to identify international allies in their fight against land reform. In Brazil similar groups were able to identify international actors to halt proposed dam construction. In both of these cases, both top-down and bottom-up alliances helped establish global exchange of information and contributed key personal contacts.

- NGOs, aligning with local groups, have successfully targeted major corporations, the World Bank, and the IMF, and have won important concessions for their communities and livelihoods.

- NGOs and NGO alliances have been critical in articulating and facilitating the empowerment of women. The Global Network of Women's Shelters has successfully identified and illuminated many common themes of violence around the world to include dowry deaths in India, female genital mutilation in Africa, spousal abuse in North America, and the rape and torture of prisoners in Latin America (Brown, Khagram, Moore, and Frumkin 2000).

The emergent and transforming stories that have sprung forth from the spaces that are created by the local work of NGOs can be shared, validated, acknowledged, and compounded as more become available, leading to a larger story and greater possibility of change for the indigenous globally (not just in Ecuador), for land reform globally (not just in Brazil), for women and girls' opportunities globally (not just in Latin America), and so on.

NGOs demonstrate just how much can be done, if people are willing to just get involved. Indeed, NGOs have helped to encourage the development of social movements as well as to suture a variety of social movements across societies together. We do, you see, live in a very small and interconnected world, even though it may not feel that way at times.

Critical Thinking

1. After working through your textbook and learning about the matrix of race, how do you see the role of stories in maintaining/reproducing and challenging/changing our society?

2. Why are NGOs particularly well positioned to create social change? Do you see any pitfalls to the work they are engaged in?

3. In what ways can you see the matrix of race as *global?* What is the role of U.S. racial dynamics in that global racial order and its processes?

A doctor examines a boy in a small Maasai village in Southern Kenya.

hadynyah/Getty Images

THE POWER OF SOCIAL MOVEMENTS

The actions of individuals are the building blocks for the coming together of common interests. These actions can grow into social movements toward social justice—a rallying cry of knowing a better world is possible for all and collectively building identities, relationships, communities, and institutions to buttress that better world.

But on the other side are social movements against social justice—a collective backlash against an acknowledgment of the matrix of experience, resistance to social change from those whose lives and identities have been marginalized, and a vote (even if against one's own interests) for the racialized, classed, and gendered status quo. This section wil discuss both types of movements so that you can understand the ways we can work to build a more just and equitable matrix of experience, by transforming it through collective action.

The #BlackLivesMatter Movement

We have to reckon with the fact that social change that makes lives better for *all* rather than a select *few* has always come from mass social movement. We have seen countless social movements, and the results of those movements, throughout this course:

- the trans justice movement,

- the Black Power movement,

- the abolitionist movement,

- the women's suffrage movement,

- the Occupy Wall Street movement,

- the gay rights movement,

- and the civil rights movement, to name but a few.

In all cases, despite the reverence our history books tend to give certain individuals, these movements were joined, organized, and led by ordinary people.

There have been myriad *moments* across the 400+-year history of the United States—murder, discrimination, genocide, sexual violence, segregation, unequal opportunity, disenfranchisement, theft, stolen stories, stolen identities, stolen votes, stolen resources, stolen land, stolen dreams—moments from within the matrix that came to define experience within that matrix across generations, as individuals, families, and communities interacted with the dominant institutions of those in power. Over the years, these moments are shared, passed down between generations, fought against, written about, sung about, and so on, until they eventually form a common tapestry. This common experience, organized across time and space, results in a chorus that amplifies otherwise marginalized voices and echoes inside the walls of power—demanding to be seen and heard, demanding change, and demanding life, liberty, and the pursuit of happiness. These are the social movements for social justice.

BlackLivesMatter could have been another moment in the long, painful arc of Black experience in the matrix, but it now represents a movement seeking fundamental change and racial justice in the American system. We have briefly discussed this movement in previous chapters, but its importance is now central to the fight for racial justice in the United States (and beyond).

Following the acquittal of Trayvon Martin's murderer in 2013, the phrase "Black lives matter" was used in a Facebook post by Alicia Garza on July 13, 2013:

> "stop saying we are not surprised. That's a damn shame in itself. I continue to be surprised at how little Black lives matter. And I will continue that. Stop giving up on black life. Black people. I love you. I love us. Our lives matter"

Patrisse Cullors shared Garza's post using the hashtag #BlackLivesMatter through her social media feeds; Garza, Cullors, and Nigerian-American human rights activist Opal Tometi co-founded, envisioned, organized, and continues to craft strategies for the Black Lives Matter movement.

Then, in 2014, Mike Brown was murdered by a Ferguson, Missouri, police officer. Protests followed and a brutal, militarized crackdown reigned down on those in the streets demanding justice, not only in the St. Louis area, but across the country—again. The Black Lives Matters Freedom Ride occurred in September of 2014, just days after Brown's murder. It was funded via crowdsourcing (through GoFundMe), and some 600 journalists, lawyers, medics, organizers, students, videographers, and others travelled from Boston, Chicago, Columbus, Detroit, Houston, Los Angeles, Nashville, Portland, Tuscon, Washington, DC, Winston-Salem, and other cities to support Ferguson, to "help turn a local movement into a national movement" (Solomon 2014).

By 2016 there were over 30 local chapters in the U.S., spread throughout the cities around the country, where the police treat Black and Brown communities like occupied territories—indeed, most cities in the U.S. Today the movement is a full-fledged NGO itself, the Black Lives Matter Foundation, Inc., in the United States, the United Kingdom, and Canada, with a mission "to eradicate white supremacy and build local power to intervene in violence inflicted on Black communities by the state and vigilantes" (blacklivesmatter.com 2020). They continue to organize around the issues of racial injustice, criminal justice reform, Black immigration, economic injustice, LGBTQIA+ rights, environmental conditions, voting rights and suppression, healthcare, government corruption, education, commonsense gun laws, and, most centrally, police brutality.

The Black Lives Matter movement has encouraged the country, and the world, to acknowledge, honor, and #saythenames of those unarmed people of color murdered by the police. Since Trayvon Martin, sadly the list is very long, including:

- Tamir Rice

- Eric Garner

- Philando Castile

- Breonna Taylor

These names have been at the forefront of the movement, but there are others, including:

- Lavall Hall

- Salvado Ellswood

- India Kager

- Dyzhawn Perkins

- Levonia Riggins

- Alteria Woods

- Jean Pedro Pierre

- James Leatherwood

- Atatiana Jefferson

- Donnie Sanders

As we write this conclusion, the deaths of Ahmed Arbery, Tony McDade, Rayshard Brooks, and, most prominently, George Floyd, are forcing the United States and the world to finally grapple with the realities of systemic racism and police brutality that have made Black lives not matter in this society. Woven with the Black Lives Matter movement, these moments and movements in the matrix, we hope, will create space for "Black imagination and innovation, and centering Black joy" (blacklivesmatter.com 2020), and will reclaim the "mattering" of Black lives, Black experiences, Black histories, and Black voices, and begin the weaving of writing the new, emergent story of Black liberation, for until Black lives matter, all lives do not matter. A moment can spark a movement.

TRANSFORMATION STORIES: AFROFUTURISM AND OTHER FUTURISMS IN THE MATRIX

- In 1975, from the experience of being Black in "dystopian" Detroit, the band Parliament landed the *Mothership Connection* album and tour, along with the utopian funk brought by "extraterrestrial brothers."

- In 1979, novelist Octavia Butler published *Kindred,* where she imagined that her Black female protagonist, Dana, time-traveled from the 20th century to the pre–Civil War South, and revealed that our past is embedded in our ideas of the present, which will impact our imagining of the future.

- In the 1990s, Detroit electronica band Drexciya crafted a mythology imagining that the babies of the pregnant African women on transatlantic slave ships who were thrown overboard survived, and founded a Black Atlantis—a mythology further developed recently by the experimental hip-hop group Clipping (This American Life 2017).

- On his third studio album, *To Pimp a Butterfly*, Kendrick Lamar released the song "Alright," a protest chant against police brutality, the video of which shows Kendrick able to fly above the streets, escaping them and the police for a while to let his people know "we gon' be alright."

- Originally envisioned by Wesley Snipes in the early 1990s, Marvel studios released *Black Panther* in 2018, with a predominantly Black cast, showing an alternative reality where an African nation named Wakanda is the most technologically advanced nation in the world.

Whether in the 1970s or today, all of these are examples of Afrofuturism.

Afrofuturism centers on the fact that Blacks have survived all that they have endured, that they are a resilient and strong community—a technology in and of itself—and, that this history means that they will survive and thrive in the future as well. Afrofuturism takes "black histories and realities and adds a dose of magic, mysticism, superpowers, or all three to create new worlds where the protagonists are black people. These stories can be sci-fi, they can be horror, they can imagine a past that never happened or a distant future that by today's standards seems impossible" (Wellington and Hardnett 2020). It is about Blacks acting on this world, making this world, and making, therefore, the future, their future. This is as opposed to the traditional narrative, the stock story, where Blacks are only acted on, have things done to them, and have their experiences and possibilities parameterized—a bleak present that will equal a bleak future. But, this is not the case! Ariell Johnson, the first Black female comic book store owner on the east coast, said, "Black people today, black people who are alive and walking around, it's like, we are Afrofuturism. There's a quote that says, 'I am my ancestors' wildest dreams.' And I think that's true." As such, Afrofuturism is the parallel narrative to the one currently being told and, indeed, taken together it is a transformative story! This movement is having quite a significant impact on Black children, giving them new ways to imagine, invent, and interpret their futures, and, by extension, their presents and pasts.

Rapper Grafh raises his fist in the Black Lives Matter Plaza in Washington, D.C., during the 2020 George Floyd protests.

Michael Ventura/Alamy

The White Nationalist/Supremacist Movement

Advancement in economic or political equity for people of color is usually accompanied by a backlash. The organized White nationalist movement overtly fights to protect White supremacy and privilege. When it appears to be threatened, their numbers and activity increase. We have seen it happen throughout the history of the United States.

Ku Klux Klan

The Ku Klux Klan was birthed by Confederate veterans after the Civil War who were afraid of the political power of newly freed Blacks. During Reconstruction, Whites felt their privilege threatened by the enfranchisement of Black men and civil rights granted to all Blacks. Approximately 2,000 African Americans were elected to public office during this time. Small Klan groups terrorized the African American community, and White supremacy was again enshrined more deeply in law and policy by the Black Codes (Du Bois 2017;Holt 1977).

In the 1920s, a widespread White supremacist movement bloomed, no longer limited to the South (Blee 2008). This expansion was fueled by the large numbers of European immigrants that did not already have much presence in the U.S. (for example, the Irish, Italians, Jews, and Catholics). These groups were initially identified as non-Whites.

African Americans were most likely to face rioting White mobs, lynching, and banishments of entire populations from many towns across the U.S., forcing people to abandon any property they had accumulated. These are only some of the examples of what should be rightly labeled domestic terrorism. This second wave of the Klan counted approximately five million members, including many elected officials, with a minority now in the South. Even Whites who did not perpetuate violence generally legitimated it. Crowds of White families attended lynchings and officers of the law were complicit. Klan groups no longer had to operate in secrecy.

Kathleen Blee's (2008) groundbreaking work *Women of the Klan* introduced an intersectional approach to the study of White supremacist movements, and was the first to examine gender differences in the Klan. She focused specifically on the different ways in which wives supported the movement. Women played an important role in sustaining the work of the Klan through their reproductive and domestic labor.

Developing a White Supremacist Narrative

The third wave of increased movement activity occurred in the 1950s–1970s. During the Civil Rights and Black Power Movements, the KKK and other organized White supremacist groups like the neo-Nazis became more visible again to defend against threats to institutionalized White supremacy. The growth in other movements, including the women's movement, further fanned their flames, and writing and publications of White supremacist groups became more hostile toward women, depicting them either as ideal White mothers reproducing White children for the movement, or race traitors involved in interracial relationships with non-Whites.

The controlling image of White women being raped or "stolen away" by oversexualized Black men was a constant theme. The threat many men felt was posed by the women's movement was part of the White supremacist appeal to White men to "reclaim their women" and "reclaim their nation" (Ferber 1998).

During this time, the White supremacist narrative remained largely unchanged at its core, but reflected the country's shift in expanding the category of Whites to embrace the immigrants of the previous wave of immigration. The White supremacist narrative continued to evolve along with immigration policy. In 1965, the very tiny quotas limiting immigrants from non-European countries was lifted. Thus, non-White immigrants, and immigration in general, grew as a significant focus for White supremacist groups.

Hate Groups, Speech, and Crimes

The rise of the current phase of White supremacist movement is a result of many factors. At the top of that list is the explosion of social media and presidential politics of the past decade and some, including backlash against the election and presidency of Barack Obama (2008–2016) and the emboldening of White supremacy by the election of Donald Trump in 2016. The Southern Poverty Law Center tracked the proliferation of hate groups (only a small number of which are not White supremacist) in recent years:

- 2000: 555 identified hate groups

- 2018: 1,020 identified hate groups (Southern Poverty Law Center 2019)

This movement consists of a wide range of groups that may go by different names (alt-right, boogaloo movement, militias, Proud Boys, etc.). The varied organized groups lumped together under this label share the common historical narrative that White people:

- are inherently superior

- should be running the nation

- must protect themselves from threats to their power and privilege

They continue to focus on non-White immigrants, especially those coming across the Southern border, as a threat to White people's well-being. A relatively new villain is the Muslim, another addition to the list of threats to the White race. All Muslims are depicted as terrorists, despite the fact that the vast majority of domestic terrorism is carried out by men with connections to White supremacist groups and/or ideology.

In the last four years, and from the highest levels of our government, vocal attacks as well as policy changes are rolling back rights and threatening the safety of many oppressed groups, including women, transgender people, the disabled, immigrants, people of color, and anyone falling under the queer umbrella.

There has been a dramatic rise in hate speech in schools and on college campuses (Bauer-Wolf 2019), much of it instigated by the alt-right. The alt-right has targeted college campuses in various ways, including leafleting, posting hate-filled flyers and posters, funding alt-right speakers, and creating alt-right student clubs.

In the one-month period following the 2016 presidential election, over 1,000 hate crimes were reported. The greatest number of incidents targeted immigrants, followed by Blacks, and then Muslims. In 2016, hate crimes reached a five-year high. The FBI reported that 2017 saw a 17% increase above 2016 (U.S. Department of Justice 2019; Southern Poverty Law Center 2019).

The language of White supremacy can complicate and distort the extent to which we are a White supremacist nation. The United States was established as a White republic built on slavery, and threats to slavery were seen as threats to White supremacy. Whenever it appears non-Whites are gaining any economic success or access to power, this is perceived as an attack on White supremacy, and movement activism heats up.

However, labeling these activist movements "White supremacist" has served to redefine the meaning of White supremacy. Its use has been tied, almost completely, to references to these organizations, and the country itself has been defined as the home of equal opportunity. Defining groups like racist skinheads and the boogaloo militia as White supremacist extremists serves to obscure the White supremacy ingrained into our nation and its institutions, and the norm has been imagined as non-racist. The reality is that the organized White supremacist movement is the tip of the iceberg of White supremacy, and it is the body of systemic White supremacy that looms beneath the surface and holds it all up (Ferber 1989, 2020, 2021).

Critical Thinking

1. Have you ever joined a social movement? If so, what was your experience? If not, why not?

2. Why do you think the Black Lives Matter movement has become so visible and so central to the contemporary discussion? How would our society (world?) look now *if* Black lives, Black experiences, Black stories, etc., had mattered all along?

3. The White supremacist narrative has remained largely unchanged throughout its history. What are the dimensions of this narrative? Why do you think it has stayed relatively the same?

RACE IS EVERYONE'S "PROBLEM"

Many of you may have started this course with the assumption that its focus would be limited to people of color. Frequently White students, and White people in general, think of race and racism as irrelevant to their own lives. As long as White people see themselves as non-racist and free of prejudice, they often believe they are not contributing to the problem. Of course, that is the trouble with an individual approach.

We hope that this text has changed your frame of reference. Emerging/transforming stories about race show that inequity is everyone's problem. The matrix framework we have embraced lays the foundation for emerging/transformative stories that narrate race as a part of everyone's lives, and deeply ingrained in our history and institutions. And we see that race cannot be examined in a vacuum; the way race shapes our life opportunities and experiences is also shaped by our gender, sexuality, class, nationality, religion, ability, and more.

We have highlighted the resistance of people of color working for change in their daily lives, resisting and organizing in workplaces and other institutions, and in social movements like Black Lives Matter. Middle-class African Americans must deal with ongoing diversions of their time and energy just to be seen and heard in their place of work. Faculty members at institutions of higher education are challenged to prove that they are scholars to be taken seriously, by students as well as colleagues and administration (Porter 2019). For many people of color, struggling to make it through each day, to live to see their families again, are forms of resistance in the context of the White supremacist systems and foundations established to deny them basic human rights. Fighting racism on the individual, cultural, institutional, and movement levels leads to "racial stress" (Szymanski and Lewis 2015). Some choose to engage centrally in the fight for racial justice, despite the stress of doing so, and to seek avenues for activism.

Activism

In his interviews with longtime racial justice activists, race scholar Paul C. Gorski describes them as "people who identify racial justice activism as their central life passion." Following Szymanski's (2012) work on racial justice engagement, **activism** refers to purposeful action to cultivate social or political change. While some of the research participants Gorski interviewed worked in social justice organizations, many did not. No matter what field of employment they were in, they still identified themselves as activists, and saw this work as a meaningful part of who they are (Gorski 2019).

Research on African Americans has consistently found that the more racial discrimination and resulting stress they have experienced, the stronger their activism and involvement in organizations working for social and political justice (Gorski 2019; Mattis et al., 2004 ; Szymanski 2012). Activists face the threat of violence, harassment, and stigma; White activists are significantly less likely to be targeted. In working to end racism, White people's privilege protects them from the greater consequences faced by people of color (Gorski 2019).

Important research has examined how White people have committed, and can and do continue to commit, to dismantling White supremacy. For example, scholar Mark Warren asks, "How can white Americans come to care enough about racism to take action against it?" (2010, 8). In order to answer this question, he conducted 50 in-depth exploratory interviews with White racial justice activists to provide insight into how White people move from mere concern to commitment.

Warren's book *Fire in the Heart* finds that activism is an ongoing process, a journey that must be sustained over time and requires commitment. He found that activists frequently go through stages, often beginning with a moral shock or seminal experience, which challenges their assumptions about race and racism in the U.S. and throws into question their moral compass. It is the conflict these individuals see between the values they have been taught to believe in and deeply embrace, and the reality of racism, that is so jarring, and often leads to anger. They feel what Warren describes as a "moral impulse to act" (2010, 213).

The lives of the 50 activists Warren interviewed provide further insight here. It is through ongoing relationships with people of color that White activists remain committed and continue to learn and understand racism at a deeper level. Rather than remaining an abstract moral problem, they come to see its real impact on the lives of people they care about. Building relationships with others committed to racial justice, and especially interracial relationships, nurtures an ongoing commitment. In relationship and community with others, the subjects he interviewed came to develop a sense that they were in this struggle not just out of altruism, but felt a personal sense of investment in the struggle, and saw themselves as part of a community working toward a moral and political vision of a more just future.

Working for racial justice means challenging stock stories and the racial status quo. The result is that these activists often face backlash and resistance from friends and family. Activists go through a redefinition of their own identity and must find and build new communities of belonging. Relationships grow into collaborative and collective action, and the development of a moral vision. Ultimately, these individuals find great meaning in working to create a society that works for all, including themselves.

Based on his findings, Warren identifies a model of activism:

- Head (knowledge, interests)

- Hand (building relationships, taking action)

- Heart (values, emotions)

A family preparing to join the 2018 Women's March in San Francisco, CA.

Shelly Rivoli/Alamy

Each impacts the other in a circular fashion, with no end point. Commitment to racial justice—indeed to social justice for all humans—is a fluid and dynamic process and a lifelong journey of learning, growing, and acting. Each one of us has the ability to change over our lifetimes, and to make conscious choices about how we want to change. First, we need to figure out where we are.

Allyship

You do not have to join a social movement to contribute to dismantling White supremacy. We all spend our lives embedded in the many institutions we have examined, where we take part in reproducing the status quo. Each one of us can question and challenge the operations of racism and other inequities in our own daily lives where we are already situated. In fact, real change will require all of our contributions.

The problems, pain, and depth of inequality we have examined throughout this text can feel overwhelming, and in very different ways depending on who you are. Nevertheless, keep in mind the words of Anne Frank: "How wonderful it is that nobody need wait a single moment before starting to improve the world." There are opportunities all around us. Each one of us can make a difference starting now.

Many authors have written about the concept of allyship. Some prefer the term co-conspirator, which nuances the meaning; others offer other terminology. Allyship is used most often. How individuals create an identity and actions as an "ally" to people of color and/or movements for racial justice is not yet fully understood, and, indeed, may be quite complex (Sumerau et al., 2020). Popular conceptions of an ally (and therefore allyship) suggests that an ally is an individual, usually White, who understands their limited knowledge about the experiences of people of color, and is willing to actively work to educate themselves and speak up among their White community members to challenge privilege and systemic racism.

Allyship, the process whereby allies work to combat racial injustice, is important because "we need people who face *less* risks to take on *more* risks to disrupt harm" (Kim 2019). Unfortunately, when oppressed groups speak out about social change and inequity, they are often seen as biased, angry, and only looking out for themselves. Research has found that this is not the case for White men (Kim 2019). This pattern has also been found in a large body of scholarship on students' evaluations of faculty. People of color, as well as White women, consistently receive lower ratings and more personal attacks than White men (Peterson et al., 2019).

With allyship, we ask people with privileges to take on the burden of challenging the status quo, so those without aren't the only ones fighting the battle.

Being an Ally versus Catering

There is a difference between allyship and catering to the audience. The former is focusing on what is right, while the latter is appearing to be right. Allyship is about being in the trenches, dodging bullets, and taking chances. Catering is about using the movement for personal gain, looking for photo ops, promoting personal agendas, and, in general, what scholars call "virtue siganling."

In 2020, joining the bandwagon of companies making public statements declaring their outrage with racism, the Band-Aid brand announced that it would begin selling bandages that

Ice cream company Ben and Jerry's provides one model of long-term anti-racism and social justice support; they have been educating people about White supremacy on their website and donating portions of sales to nonprofits ever since their founding. Here, co-founder Jerry Greenfield celebrates the launch of "Bob Marley's One Love" flavor with Ziggy Marley.

Jerritt Clark/Getty Images

match black and brown skin tones. The concealed story, however, is that in response to demand and criticism, they sold this line of bandages in 2005, but stopped making them because they did not sell well enough. Some critics have applauded this move, while also critiquing the commitment that now looks like an attempt to demonstrate their support for antiracism work in a public way. We can ask why it took 100 years to decide to sell these products, even if they may not bring in as much profit. To what extent is this an act of co-optation, using the current movement to express the support they have refused to provide in the past, while also getting a lot of free publicity for making such a change? (Milling 2020).

If you want to demonstrate authenticity in the struggle, go to your job or place of business and begin to identify and dismantle racist barriers. Take some risks, make some individual and collective sacrifices by funding some scholarships, providing skills training, opening up pathways to occupations and crafts. Then you will demonstrate that you are indeed an ally.

There are many organizations committed to bringing White people into the work at international, national, regional, and local levels. There are endless resources, websites, workshops, and conferences available, such as the Annual White Privilege Conference which "strives to empower and equip individuals to work for equity and justice through self and social transformation" (Kivel 2002; Tochluk 2008). There are hundreds of books that examine the history of racism, specific targeted groups, and other systems of oppression. There are even many children's books available.

Taking the First Step

Starting with the matrix framework as a foundation, we offer the following suggestions. While many of these points speak to antiracism work, keep in mind we all have some form of privilege and therefore can support and act in concert with others waging battles against sexism, transphobia, homophobia, ableism, and ageism. Research and best practice models developed by critical scholars (Boom 2018; Cabrera, Watson and Franklin, 2016; Wijeyesinghe, Griffin, and Love 1997; Kivel 2002; Ferber 2010; Stewart 2020) have identified many things that one can do, in addition to the many things we have learned that one can do within the matrix across the chapters of this textbook. These include, but are certainly not limited to:

- Take responsibility for continuing to learn about how oppression and privilege works, and teach others. Do not expect marginalized people to teach you.

- Follow the lead of people of color: Listen more and speak less.

- Search for concealed stories. We have seen that inequities exist across all institutions; assume that concealed stories are all around us, and seek them out.

- Think intersectionally. How are individual experiences as well as institutional arrangements and systems of privilege and oppression interconnected? How do they rationalize or justify one another?

- Speak out! Take a stand against injustice. Take risks and be willing to act in spite of your own fear and the resistance you face from others.

- Listen to, respect, and support the leadership, perspectives, experiences, and resistance of members of oppressed groups.

- Seek out, support, contribute to, create, and share emerging and transforming narratives advancing social change and justice.

- Do not wallow in guilt, shame, or other emotions. It does not help anyone. Let go and get to work now.

- Do not be passive—believing in the values of diversity, inclusion, and equity is great, but it is not enough to just believe. You must actively live those values through concrete actions and behaviors.

- It is not allyship if we fail to prioritize marginalized people's needs.

Allyship is about action and it is not self-claimed. Whatever action we take, the communities we seek to be in solidarity with must recognize our actions as acts of allyship. Only they get to decide which actions qualify as "allyship." Because of this, it is vital that we always seek out information that validates the best way for us to support the communities we seek to ally ourselves with.

During a New York City protest against police brutality, a White protester wearing a mask holds up a home-made sign.

Ira L. Black/Corbis via Getty Images

Your Story: Sometimes One Person Is All it Takes

Our realities are a composite of the multiplicity of stories. These stories are layered, nuanced, and rehearsed. Our stories, reflecting the many lived stories of place and space, time and distance, perception and experience, are constantly being produced and reproduced.

Novelist Chimamanda Ngozi Adichie (2009) warns of what happens when all we hear is a single story, about a single people, country, or group—we make critical mistakes as we stereotype, marginalize, and delegitimize others. When, on the one hand, we have thousands upon thousands of stories that rehearse the wonders of White culture, while those of the Asian, African, and Middle Eastern cultures come to life only during clashes with Europeans (often where they are being subjugated), we are essentially reifying Whiteness at the expense of others. The problem comes in not knowing these other stories.

When we begin the story of our country with the arrival of the Spanish, French, and English, and ignore the rich history of Native Americans and Africans before they encountered Europeans, we end up with one story. But if we start with the Native Americans before Columbus, the African civilizations that preceded and perhaps seeded the European contentment, then we have a totally different story (Adichie 2009).

Our task has been to try to tell these other stories. Stories are about power—whose stories get told, who gets to tell them, and from which vantage point. Who listens? Which stories matter? The number, variety, and richness of stories are also about power, as dominance is associated with not only quantity but also quality. Whose story is considered to be the norm, and whose story is marginalized from that norm, also speaks of power.

Earlier, we asked you to assess where you stood as an ally. Now, we return to the same questions:

- Where do you see yourself on this action continuum?

- Has your positioning changed at all?

- Now that you have gained a deeper understanding of the history and reality of racism, where would you like to be on this continuum?

- What can you do to get there?

FIGURE 12.1 ■ Action Continuum

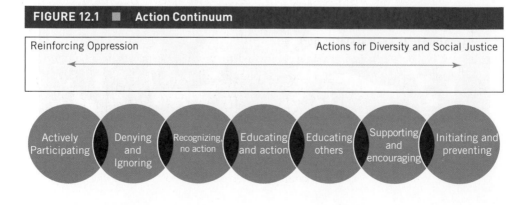

Reinforcing Oppression   Actions for Diversity and Social Justice

Actively Participating · Denying and Ignoring · Recognizing, no action · Educating and action · Educating others · Supporting and encouraging · Initiating and preventing

Think about the immediate and realistic next steps you can take to assess where you are now on the action continuum (Figure 12.1).

Critical Thinking

1. Commitment to racial justice is a fluid and dynamic process—a lifelong journey. Where do you currently fall in your journey? How do you wish to change? Why? How can you begin to make those changes?

2. Are you an ally? If so, what kind? If not, why not?

3. Which three of the allyship suggestions can you commit to this coming year? What do you see as the challenges of such a commitment? What do you see as some of the celebrations?

CHAPTER SUMMARY

12.1 Explore the connections between the past and the present, the global and the local, and the individual and collective action.

Emerging/transforming stories are all around us; we must learn how to recognize them, acknowledge them, and celebrate as well as amplify them. Doing so will help remake the matrix of race to one that is more inclusive and validating for everyone. Recognizing that some stories serve the status quo—that the stock stories often are only so because they are repeated the most, ingrained within our dominant institutions, and, therefore, wrapped up with power and privilege—is crucial to building a new future. Understanding the past and its stories, both those dominant ones and those concealed ones, will help us move forward in strength as a society. This also involves recognizing the connections between the global, the regional, the national, and the local. NGOs are working to give voice to those whose stories have been silenced and excluded, in order to weave a new matrix for all. Connections between the past and the present, the global and the local, and individual and collective action, will help us transform the matrix—stories are fundamental to this process.

12.2 Compare social movements that are organized for racial justice and those designed to maintain the racial status quo.

When people band together in common desire to effect change, to fight for rights, to amplify and raise their experiences, their stories, and their hopes and dreams in a society that has squashed and made them invisible, these are social movements for social justice. People can also band together to attempt to reclaim their oppression over others, pass legislation that supports only a small echelon of society (e.g., White men), and otherwise push against those crying out for social justice—these are social movements of backlash, designed to further bolster structures of oppression and power. The Black Lives Movement is an excellent example of a movement for social justice; the White

Supremacist movement, in all its various guises, is a good example of a movement against social justice. It is important to understand the power of social movements and compare those organized for racial justice and those designed to maintain the racial status quo in order to work to transform the matrix.

12.3 Identify the differences between activism and allyship and evaluate your own engagement in transforming the matrix of race.

Transforming the matrix where the dizzying variations of experience can come together to create a society that works for all involves recognizing that we are all implicated in the matrix of race: It connects (and works to separate) all of us, and it affects each and every one of our lives, identities, communities, and opportunities. As such, we all have a part to play in understanding and then working to change the matrix of race. Activism for racial justice and the involvement of allies in the fight for racial justice are crucial. It is equally crucial to understand the differences between activism and allyship and evaluate your own engagement in transforming the matrix of race. We are all in this together and each of us must work to change the matrix.

KEY TERMS

activism

allyship

globalization

nongovernmental organizations

REFERENCES

Adichie, C.N., 2009. Chimamanda Adichie: The danger of a single story. TED.

Aguilera, Jasmine. 2020. "One Year After Mass Shooting, El Paso Residents Grapple With White Supremacy: 'It Was There the Whole Time'" Time. Accessed online January 22, 2021. https://time.com/5874088/el-paso-shooting-racism/

Aptheker, H., 1992. Anti-racism in US history: The first two hundred years (Vol. 143). Greenwood Publishing Group.

Balsamo, Michael. Nov. 16, 2020. "Hate Crimes in U.S. reach Highest level in More than a Decade." Accessed January 22, 2021. https://apnews.com/article/hate-crimes-rise-fbi-data-ebbcadca8458aba96575da905650120d

Bauer-Wolf, J., 2019. Hate incidents on campus still rising. February, 25.

Bell, L.A., 2010. Storytelling for social justice: Connecting narrative and the arts in antiracist teaching. Routledge.

Blacklivesmatter.com https://blacklivesmatter.com/about/. Accessed January 17, 2021

Blee, K.M., 2008. Women of the Klan: Racism and Gender in the 1920s. Univ of California Press.

Bonnett, A., 2000. *Anti-racism*. Psychology Press.

Boom, Kesiana. 2018 "100 Ways White People Can Make Life Less Frustrating For People of Color." Vice. Accessed January 17, 2021. https://www.vice.com/en_us/article/ne95dm/how-to-be-a-white-ally-to-people-of-color

Brown, L.D., S., Khagram, M.H. and Moore, P., Frumkin, 2000. Globalization, NGOs and multi-sectoral relations. Hauser Center for Nonprofit Org. Working Paper, (1).

Cabrera, N.L., Watson, J.S. and Franklin, J.D., 2016. Racial arrested development: A critical whiteness analysis of the campus ecology. Journal of College Student Development, 57(2), pp. 119–134.

Du Bois 2017. Black Reconstruction in the United States.

Feagin, J., 2013. Systemic racism: A theory of oppression. Routledge.

Ferber, Abby L. "The white supremacist movement in the US through the lens of the matrix of race." *Routledge International Handbook of Contemporary Racisms* NY: Routledge, 2020.

Ferber, A.L., 1998. White man falling: Race, gender, and white supremacy. Rowman & Littlefield Publishers.

Ferber, A.L., 2010. Unlearning Privilege and Becoming and Ally: It Is Never Too Young to Start. *Reflections: Narratives of Professional Helping*, 16(1), pp. 133–139.

Gorski, P.C., 2019. Racial battle fatigue and activist burnout in racial justice activists of color at predominately white colleges and universities. Race ethnicity and education, 22(1), pp. 1–20.

Heintz, S., 2006, January. The role of NGOs in modern societies and an increasingly interdependent world. In Annual Conference of the Institute for Civil Society (pp. 1–14).

Holt, T.C., 1977. Black over white: Negro political leadership in South Carolina during Reconstruction (Vol. 82). University of Illinois Press.

Kendi, I.X., 2017. Stamped from the beginning: The definitive history of racist ideas in America. Random House.

Kim, Michelle. Nov. 10, 2019. "Allyship" Medium

Kivel, P., 2002. Uprooting Racism: How White people can work for racial justice, Vol. 1.

Mattis, J.S., Beckham, W.P., Saunders, B.A., Williams, J.E., Myers, V., Knight, D., Rencher, D. and Dixon, C., 2004. Who will volunteer? Religiosity, everyday racism, and social participation among African American men. *Journal of Adult Development*, 11(4), pp. 261–272.

Milling, Marla. Jun 15, 2020. "Johnson & Johnson Announces New Band-Aids, But That Can't Fix Racial Inequality." Accessed January 17, 2021. https://www.forbes.com/sites/marlamilling/2020/06/15/johnson--johnson-announces-new-band-aids-but-that-cant-fix-racial-inequality/#5ed1ca746e7d

Olson, Wendy K. 2004. "Triangulation in Social Research: Qualitative and Quantitative Methods Can Really Be Mixed." pp. 103–121 in *Developments in Sociology: An Annual Review*, edited by M. Holborn. Ormskirk, UK: Causeway Press.

Peterson, D.A., Biederman, L.A., Andersen, D., Ditonto, T.M. and Roe, K., 2019. Mitigating gender bias in student evaluations of teaching. *PloS one*, 14(5), p. e0216241.

Porter, Lavelle. *The Blackademic Life: Academic Fiction, Higher Education, and the Black Intellectual*. Northwestern University Press, 2019.

Solomon, A. (2014, Sept. 5). "Get on the bus: Inside the Black Life Matters 'Freedom Ride' to Ferguson." *Colorlines*. https://www.colorlines.com/articles/get-bus-inside-black-life-matters-freedom-ride-ferguson

Southern Poverty Law Center."In 2019, We Tracked 940 hate groups across the U.S." Accessed January 22, 2021. https://www.splcenter.org/hate-map

Stewart, Emily. June 2, 2020. How to be a Good White Ally, According to Activists. Vox. Accessed January 17, 2021. https://www.vox.com/2020/6/2/21278123/being-an-ally-racism-george-floyd-protests-white-people?fbclid=IwAR2FgVTWuxzBdVBou8h0-7RZ8meXZL038igVVGqGUF-G2tgZsxzr--3LWMo

Sue, Derald Wing. 2017."The challenges of becoming a White ally." *The Counseling Psychologist* 45, no. 5 (2017): 706-716.

Sumerau, J.E., T.D., Forbes, E.A. and Grollman, L.A., Mathers, 2020. Constructing Allyship and the Persistence of Inequality. Social Problems.

Szymanski, Dawn M., and Jioni A. Lewis. "Race-related stress and racial identity as predictors of African American activism." *Journal of Black Psychology* 41, no. 2 (2015): 170–191.

Szymanski, D.M. 2012. "Racist Events and individual coping styles as predictors of African American activism" Journal of Black Psychology,

This American Life. 2017. Accessed January 2021. https://www.thisamericanlife.org/623/we-are-in-the-future-2017/act-three-2

Tochluk, S., 2008. Witnessing Whiteness: First Steps toward an Antiracist Practice and Culture. Rowman & Littlefield Education. Blue Ridge Summit, PA.

U.S. Department of Justice 2019. 2019 Hate crime Statistics. Accessed January 22, 2021. https://www.justice.gov/hatecrimes/hate-crime-statistics

Warren, M.R., 2010. Fire in the heart: How white activists embrace racial justice. Oxford University Press.

Wellington, Elizabeth, and Raishad Hardnett. Feb. 26, 2020. "Afrofuturism is all around us and we don't even know it." The Philadelphia Inquirer. Accessed January 17, 2021.https://www.inquirer.com/columnists/afrofuturism-future-the-black-tribbles-black-panther-octavia-butler-20200226.html

Wijeyesinghe, C.L., Griffin, P. and Love, B., 1997. Racism curriculum design. Teaching for diversity and social justice: A sourcebook, pp. 82–109.

GLOSSARY

affirmative action. Programs, begun under the administration of President Richard Nixon, requiring employers receiving federal funding to take affirmative steps to eliminate discrimination based on race, ethnicity, national origin, or gender in the hiring and treatment of employees.

agency. The ability to effect change, to act independently, and to exercise free choices.

American Medical Association. A formal organization established by physicians as a way of defining themselves as the only authentic and legitimate practitioners of medicine.

ancestry. An individual's point of origin, lineage, or descent.

apprenticeship model of education. A form of education in which skills are transferred from a master/teacher to an apprentice/student and the skills needed to perform a job are learned on the job.

assimilation. The process through which people gradually accept and adapt to the dominant culture after immigrating to a new society. The stages of assimilation generally begin with adoption of the dominant language and cultural patterns and then advance to increased interaction between newcomers and dominant group members, reduced levels of prejudice and discrimination, intermarriage, and eventually full integration and acceptance.

Atlanta Compromise. An agreement articulated by Booker T. Washington in 1895 to pacify White business owners; it suggested that Blacks and Whites could work together to play their economic roles while remaining socially separate.

Bacon's Rebellion of 1676. A revolt in which Black, Irish, Scottish, and English bond servants fought against the planter elite in Virginia.

Battle of New Orleans. The final major battle of the War of 1812, in which the British army was defeated and prevented from seizing New Orleans and subsequently all the lands associated with the Louisiana Purchase.

binary constructs. In relation to identity groups, the representation of two groups in opposition (such as White/Black, male/female); such constructs normalize and legitimate racial and gender hierarchies at the expense of other outsiders, such as other racial minorities (Jews, Hispanics, Italians) and gender groups (LGBT).

biological determinism. The concept that an individual's behavior is innately related to components of his or her physiology, such as body type and brain size.

Black civil rights movement. A movement orchestrated by southern Blacks—in partnership with northern allies, both White and Black—in the period 1955–68 that not only challenged but also effectively nullified the intimidation and segregation of the Old South.

Black Code. France's Colonial Ordinance of 1685, which legislated the life, death, purchase, marriage, and religion of slaves, as well as the treatment of slaves by their masters.

boycotts. Voluntary acts of protest in which individuals or groups seek to punish or coerce corporations, nations, or persons by refusing to purchase their products, invest in them, or otherwise interact with them.

Bracero Program. Guest worker program established in 1942 because of labor shortages caused by World War II; allowed Mexican contract laborers to enter the United States to work in agriculture and on railroads.

broken windows theory. A theory of crime that asserts that a relationship exists between urban disorder and vandalism, such that if vandalism can be stopped, serious crime will decrease.

Brown v. Board of Education of Topeka. The landmark 1954 U.S. Supreme Court case that struck down the 1896 decision in *Plessy v. Ferguson,* making the racial segregation of public accommodations, including public schools, illegal.

capitalism. A type of economy in which the means of production are held and controlled by private owners, not the government, and in which prices are set by the forces of supply and demand with minimal government interference.

chattel slavery. Slavery in which the enslaved persons are considered personal property, owned by their masters for life, and their children are the owners' property as well.

citizenship. A status reflecting the legal process countries use to regulate national identity, membership, and rights.

class. A person's location in the social stratification, which encompasses particular levels of access to and control over resources for survival.

class approach. An approach to issues of power, politics, and identity that assumes that power is derived from having control over specific economic structures within society.

club movement. A late 19th-century movement in the United States through which lower-status White ethnics sought to gain elite status through the establishment of exclusive sport groups.

coalitional politics. Politics characterized by alliances of various identity groups whose shared purpose is to establish a specific political agenda.

coercive force. Force that involves the use of intimidation to obtain compliance.

colonialism. A set of hierarchical relationships in which groups are defined culturally, ethnically, and/or racially and in which these relationships serve to guarantee the political, social, and economic interests of the dominant group.

colonization of the mind. From the work of Frantz Fanon, the concept that our cognitions, our ideologies, and our worldviews are often those of those in power.

color blindness. The view (or assertion) that one does not see race or ethnicity, only humans.

color-blind racism. An ideology with four components: *abstract liberalism,* which encompasses abstract concepts of equal opportunity, rationality, free choice, and individualism and is used to argue that discrimination is no longer a problem, and any individual who works hard can succeed; *naturalization,* in which ongoing inequality is reframed as the result of natural processes rather than social relations; *cultural racism,* in which inherent cultural differences are used to separate racialized groups; and *minimization of racism,* or the argument that we now have a fairly level playing field, everyone has equal opportunities to succeed, and racism is no longer a real problem.

communal experience. Shared knowledge across group members occupying the same spaces.

concealed stories. Narratives consisting of the data and voices that stock stories ignore; these stories often convey a very different understanding of identity and inequity.

conversion therapy. Treatment programs that purport to change the sexual orientations of gays and lesbians.

crime. A form of deviance that violates moral and ethical standards and is generally defined as such by law.

critical pedagogy. Strategies of education that seek to create structures of liberation rather than reproduce the status quo.

critical race theory. A theoretical approach that represents an attempt by scholars and activists to transform the relationships among race, racism, and power.

cultural capital. The resources that individuals have, from their social networks, that enable them to interact in certain social situations and move up the socioeconomic ladder through the adoption of particular styles, tastes, and dispositions.

cultural values. Sets of beliefs and interpretations that are shared across group members.

culture of poverty. An approach to crime and deviance that associates self-perpetuating cycles of dependency with poor families, specifically poor families of color.

curandero/as. Traditional or native healers in Latino/a cultures.

Dawes Act. Law passed by the U.S. Congress in 1887 that required Native American nations to divide their communal reservations into individual plots of 160 acres, with each assigned to a family head. The remaining land was given to White homesteaders and various corporations, such as railroads and ranching companies.

de facto political practices. Extralegal processes and methods that restrict political and other rights.

de jure political practices. Legal enactments and processes that restrict political and other rights.

democratic equilibrium. A dynamic working balance between and among various groups.

deviance. Actions and behaviors that defy social norms, from crimes to failures to meet social expectations.

differential association theory. A theory that proposes that differences in criminal involvement among groups result from the groups' different definitions of criminality.

differential labeling. The systematic singling out of individuals for labeling as deviant by virtue of their membership in particular groups.

discrimination. The differential allocation of goods, resources, and services, and the limitation of access to full participation in society, based on an individual's membership in a particular social category.

disenfranchisement. Revocation of the right to vote.

drapetomania. A "mental illness" invented to explain why slaves tried to escape slavery.

dysfunctional. Disruptive to social structures, increasing stress and violating norms and rules of engagement.

economic restructuring. The shift from a manufacturing- to a service-based economy in urban areas.

epidemiology. The study of the causes and distribution of diseases and injuries in a population.

ethnicity. Identity that encompasses cultural aspects of an individual's life, including religion, tradition, language, ancestry, nation, geography, history, belief, and practice.

eugenics. A science concerned with improving genetic quality or desired characteristics of a population through practices of breeding and/or extermination.

Fair Deal. A series of federal programs initiated in the late 1940s and early 1950s by President Harry Truman to protect workers from unfair employment practices, raise the minimum wage, and provide housing assistance, among other goals.

formal or overt racism. Discriminatory practices and behaviors that are sanctioned by official rules, codes, or laws of an organization, institution, or society.

frontiers. Contested spaces or borders, such as those between the Spanish, French, and English colonies in the Americas.

functionalist approach to the military. The theory that the military, war, and terrorism serve specific and important tasks, or functions, within society, including socialization, integration, and reduction of conflict.

functionalist theory of sport. A theory that argues that sport fulfills a multitude of societal needs, such as shared values, acquisition of life skills, conflict management, and social mobility.

general strain theory. A theory that proposes that racism produces stressful events and environments, which in turn lead to emotional reactions (such as anger, fear, depression, and rage) that indirectly or directly lead to acts of crime.

genocide. The large-scale, systematic destruction of a people or nation.

gestational surrogacy. The practice of a woman carrying an implanted embryo, not her own, to full term for the biological parent(s).

GI Bill of Rights. The Servicemen's Readjustment Act, passed in 1944 to support veterans. The law included provisions for low-cost guaranteed loans for college degrees, new homes, and businesses; job training; and unemployment benefits.

grandfather clauses. Legal provisions used in the South to restrict voting rights; such clauses granted the right to vote to anyone whose grandfather qualified to vote prior to the Civil War.

Great Compromise of 1787. Compromise reached during the Constitutional Convention, under which the Congress would be composed of two governing bodies, one in which population would determine the number of seats each state would hold (the House of Representatives), and one in which each state would have two members (the Senate). It was further decided that each slave would be counted as three-fifths of a person in population counts determining numbers of representatives as well as presidential electors, and for purposes of taxation.

Great Migration. The movement, from 1916 to 1970, of more than 6 million African Americans out of the rural South to the urban areas of the North, Midwest, and West, in search of greater safety and higher-paying, industrial jobs.

hate strikes. A series of White supremacist wildcat strikes that took place throughout World War II, targeting Black workers competing with White labor.

human capital. The resources that individuals have from their education and training that can be traded for status in an occupational market.

Human Genome Project. An international research collaboration (begun in 1990, completed in 2003) that mapped all human genes.

identity politics. A political process/structure that relies on people of specific religions, racial and ethnic groups, or social backgrounds to form exclusive political alliances.

ideology of domesticity. An ideology in which the home and family became defined as women's realm, and women were not expected to work for pay outside the home. This ideal was generally attainable only by well-off White families.

income. The sum of earnings from work, profit from items sold, and returns on investments.

indentured servants. Persons who are legally bound to work for their masters for a set number of years.

informal or covert racism. Discriminatory practices and behaviors that are not formally sanctioned but rather are often assumed to be the natural, legitimate, and normal workings of society and its institutions.

insider groups. Those groups that hold the bulk of the power in society.

instrumentalism. Derived from the class approach to issues of power, politics, and identity, assumes that the state is dominated by an elite class that controls both the political and economic spheres.

internalized racism. The acceptance by members of minority groups of White society's negative beliefs about, actions toward, and characterizations of them.

intersectional theories. Theories that argue that race and gender (as well as other salient social identities) are intertwined and inseparable, and no individual social identity can be fully comprehended on its own.

interstate forms of war. Conflicts involving national states, such as World Wars I or II; considered to be legitimate wars.

intrastate forms of war. Conflicts that exist or occur within the boundaries of particular states; considered to be less legitimate than interstate wars.

Islamophobia. Intense fear and paranoia regarding Muslims and Arabs, both those living in the United States and those abroad.

Jim Crow laws. Laws designed to preserve Whiteness by criminalizing and sanctioning Blacks, Native Americans, and other racial and ethnic minorities; such laws were widespread across the United States from the 1880s to the 1960s.

Jim Crow racism. Racism supported by the laws and practices that originated in the American South to enforce racial segregation.

left-handed marriages. Temporary alliances between men and women equivalent to common-law marriages, particularly common in the French colonies in the Americas. These unions often resulted in children who served as interpreters and mediators.

legacy of slavery thesis. A theoretical approach that argues that Black family structures are the result of the long history of structural inequality faced by Blacks since slavery.

literacy tests. De jure enactments employed in the South to disadvantage Blacks by restricting the access to vote to those who could read and interpret sections of the state constitution.

marriage promotion programs. State and federal programs that teach relationship and communication skills to women in poverty, with the aim of increasing their chances of marriage, as marriage is assumed to be a solution to poverty for single mothers. No research evidence exists to support the ideas on which such programs are based.

marriage squeeze. A change in demographic patterns leading to fewer marriages and fewer suitable partners for Black women.

Marxist theories. Social theories concerning the impacts of economic change on class relations and conditions, as examined in the work of Karl Marx.

matrix. The surrounding environment in which something (e.g., values, cells, humans) originates, develops, and grows. The concept of a matrix captures the basic sociological understanding that contexts—social, cultural, economic, historical, and otherwise—matter.

Medal of Honor. The highest military honor awarded in the United States for combat heroism; often called the Congressional Medal of Honor because it is awarded in the name of Congress.

medical sociology. The sociological study of the field and practice of medicine and their social effects.

Mendez et al. v. Westminster School District of Orange County. The 1946 U.S. Supreme Court case in which the segregation of Mexicans and non-Mexicans in public schools was found to be unconstitutional.

Mexican-American War. Conflict (1846–48) primarily associated with the U.S. government's desire to annex Texas, California, and other Mexican territories.

microaggressions. Intentional or unintentional brief insults to a person or group; these may be verbal, nonverbal, or behavioral.

military-industrial complex. The informal alliance between the U.S. military and major industries that produce arms and other military materials and seek to influence public policy.

military sociology. The sociological study of armed forces and war.

millennials. People in the generation born roughly from 1980 to 2000.

miscegenation. The mixing of different racial groups.

monopoly and materialist perspectives. Perspectives on the military that posit that military organizations must maintain a legitimate monopoly on the use of force, and the use of this force is uniquely tied to the material instruments of war.

morbidity rates. Rates of disease.

mortality rates. Rates of death.

national origins formula. A formula instituted under the 1921 Emergency Quota Act to set annual limits on the numbers of immigrants admitted to the United States from individual countries; quotas were calculated at 3% of the total number of foreign-born persons from particular countries as recorded in the 1910 U.S. census.

nature perspective. A view of sport that posits that biological differences between genders and among racial, cultural, and national groups account for variations in athletic ability, performance, and success.

neoliberal theory. A social theory that embraces individualism, free markets, free trade, and limited government intervention or regulation. Also known as *market fundamentalism*.

New Deal. A series of programs initiated in the mid-1930s by President Franklin Roosevelt in response to the Great Depression, with the aim of providing economic relief and instituting banking reform.

new immigrants. Immigrants to the United States from Ireland, Switzerland, Poland, Germany, and other Southern European countries between 1886 and 1920.

nonstate actors. Individuals and organizations with economic, political, or social power that allows them to influence both national and international events, typically with violence.

nuclear family. A family consisting of a mother, a father, and their children (biological or adopted), living together. The idea of the "ideal" and "traditional" nuclear family usually assumes a working father and stay-at-home mother.

nurture perspective. A view of sport that sees gender, racial, cultural, and national group differences in athleticism as products of socialization and environment.

old immigrants. Immigrants to the United States from England, Scotland, and Wales.

one-drop rule. The rule, based on a definition in the 1924 Racial Integrity Act, that a person was to be considered Black if he or she had any Black or Native American ancestry at all (i.e., "one drop" of Black blood).

oppression. The systematic devaluing, undermining, marginalizing, and disadvantaging of certain social identity groups in contrast to a privileged norm.

organized crime. Crime involving groups of people participating in highly centralized criminal enterprises.

outsider groups. Those groups within a society that are marginalized and have limited power.

panethnicity. The placing of various regional groups into one large ethnic category.

pedagogy of liberation. From the work of Paulo Freire, an empowering approach to education in which the pedagogical process goes both ways—teachers becoming students, students becoming teachers—leading to altered social structures of liberation and equality.

phenotypical traits. Physical traits such as skin color, hair texture, and facial features typically used to characterize people into racial groups.

pigmentocracies. Governments and other social structures that grant political power based on a hierarchy defined by skin tone, regardless of race or social status.

plaçage. The name given to the social arrangement of left-handed marriages by free people of color in the colonial era. A woman involved in such an arrangement had a status lower than that of a wife but higher than that of a concubine.

Plessy v. Ferguson. The landmark 1896 case in which the U.S. Supreme Court declared the doctrine of separate but equal to be constitutional and the law of the land, leading to Jim Crow segregation in all public facilities.

pluralism. An approach to the issue of power within society that posits that power is decentralized, widely shared, diffuse, and fragmented.

political activism. Actions of political involvement that go beyond voting; includes posting opinions online and participating in letter-writing campaigns, boycotts, protests, and demonstrations.

political identities. Political positions based on the interests and perspectives of social groups with which people identify.

political sociology. The study of government, political behaviors, institutions, and processes that occur between the state and its society and citizens.

politics. All of the processes, activities, and institutions having to do with governance.

poll taxes. Taxes a person must pay to qualify to vote; before the practice of levying such taxes was prohibited, southern states enacted poll tax laws as a way of restricting voting by Blacks.

power. The ability to acquire scarce resources.

power elite model. A model of the distribution of power in society that posits that power is concentrated among discrete elites of relatively equal power; these elites control the resources of significant social institutions.

prejudice. A judgment of an individual or group, often based on race, ethnicity, religion, gender, class, and other social identities.

prison-industrial complex. The system resulting from policies of aggressive policing targeting specific groups, which have greatly expanded the U.S. inmate population. In this system, government and industry uses of surveillance, policing, and imprisonment have been merged in an effort to solve economic, social, and political problems.

privilege. The systemic favoring, valuing, validating, and including of certain social identities over others.

quadroon. A person who is one-fourth Black by descent.

quinceañera. The custom in many Latino cultures of celebrating a girl's transformation from a child to an adult at age 15.

race. A social and cultural system by which people are categorized based on presumed biological differences.

racial caste system. A hierarchical social system based on race that is considered to be permanent.

racial categorizations. Categorizations of people according to race that employ reputed differences in behaviors, skill sets, and inherent intelligence; such categorizations are uniquely social creations that have been purposefully constructed.

racial consciousness. The awareness of race shared by members of a racial group and the wider society.

racial frames. The ideological justifications, processes, procedures, and institutions that define and structure society.

racial profiling. The targeting of particular racial and ethnic groups by law enforcement and private security agencies.

racial violence. Violence in which one racial group is pitted against another.

racism. A system of oppression by which those groups with relatively more social power subordinate members of targeted racial groups who have relatively little social power.

redlining. A practice of evaluating mortgage lending potential for designated areas that typically discriminated against racial and ethnic minorities.

relational aspects of race. A concept that encompasses the defining of categories of race in opposition to each other (e.g., to be White means one is not Black, Asian, Hispanic, or Native American) and according to where they fall along the continuum of hierarchy.

reproductive justice. A concept involving the right to have or not have children, and to parent children in safe and healthy environments.

resistance stories. Narratives that directly challenge stock stories by speaking of defying domination and actively struggling for racial justice and social change.

resocialization. A process whereby an individual is taught new norms and is expected to act accordingly in order to fulfill institutional and social obligations.

restrictive covenants. Rules inserted into real estate contracts that specify which racial groups may purchase the land.

revisionist thesis. A theoretical approach, developed in direct response to stereotypes and the legacy of slavery thesis, involving research that redirects attention to the strength and resilience of Black families.

Seminole Wars. Three conflicts (circa 1817–98) that took place in Florida between the U.S. military and the Seminole, who allied with African escaped slaves and Black Seminoles.

separate spheres. The concept that men's area of influence, or sphere, is the world outside the home, and women's sphere is the home and domesticity. The ideology of separate spheres for men and women developed along with industrialization and created a public/private dichotomy.

settler colonies. Colonies created by external, imperialist nations in which those nations control political, economic, social, and cultural mechanisms through a colonial elite.

silent generation. People born from 1925–45.

slave patrols. Organized groups of White men with police powers who systematically enforced the slave codes in the pre-Civil War South.

social cohesion. A sense of togetherness in a social structure.

social construction of race. The concept that the outcomes of the systematic distribution of rewards, privileges, and sanctions across populations through time have produced and reproduced social hierarchies that reflect society's racial categorizations.

social Darwinism. An ideology that attempts to apply Charles Darwin's theory of natural selection to people at the individual or group level over a few generations, based on a misguided and incorrect interpretation of Darwin's work.

social disorganization. A theory that links crime to neighborhood ecological patterns.

social institutions. Patterned and structured sets of roles and behaviors centered on the performance of important social tasks within any given society.

socialization. The process through which individuals are taught the norms and expectations of their societies.

split labor market. A labor market in which higher-paid workers, largely White, try to protect their jobs and wages (often through unions) by excluding new groups (often minorities) entering the labor market from the higher-paying jobs.

sport. A range of activities that involve physical exertion and skill. These activities are organized around sets of rules and can be played at either the individual or the team level.

stereotypes. Assumptions or generalizations applied to an entire group.

stock stories. The narratives of the dominant group, often embraced by those whose oppression these stories reinforce. Such stories are shaped by the White racial frame, and they inform and organize the practices of social institutions and are encoded in law, public policy, public space, history, and culture.

structural inequities. Institutional processes that deferentially distribute rewards such as status, privilege, compensation and access according to membership in specific categories or group membership.

structuralism. Derived from the class approach to issues of power, politics, and identity, assumes that the state and all political institutions exist relatively independent of each other and are essentially by-products of conflict between and within class groups.

symbolic interaction perspective on sport. An approach that posits that sports are created and maintained by shared meanings and social interaction.

symbolic interactionist approach to the military. A theoretical approach concerned with how people attach meaning to things (flags and memorials), events (wars), and other representations (heroes and patriotism) in support of war, terrorism, and the military.

systemic nature of racial oppression. The manifestation of core racist realities, values, and ideologies in all of the major institutions within society.

terrorism. The unlawful use of force, particularly against civilians, in pursuit of political, economic, or social aims.

Title IX. Legislation enacted in 1972 that declared that "no person in the United States shall, on the basis of sex, be excluded from participation in, be denied the benefits of, or be subjected to discrimination under any program or activity receiving federal financial assistance."

traditional medicine. Physical, mental, and spiritual healing that makes use of indigenous knowledge, skills, and practices that have been passed down over generations.

Trail of Tears. Name given by Native Americans to the forced relocation, 1838–39, of tribal groups from their traditional lands to Indian Territory, west of the Mississippi River; during this relocation, thousands died of exposure and disease.

transforming stories. Narratives that demonstrate how change and social justice come about.

transmigrants. People who live their lives crossing national borders, for whom participating in more than one nation is central to their lives.

triple glass ceiling. Limits placed on women because of threefold discrimination based on race, gender, and class.

Turner thesis. The theory, developed by historian Frederick J. Turner in the late 19th century, that the American identity—including democratic governance, rugged individualism, innovative thinking, and egalitarian viewpoints—was forged in the nation's frontier experience.

war. The use of organized force; a state of armed conflict between nations, states, or groups within a nation or state.

War of 1812. A military conflict between the United States and Great Britain that began because of British violations of U.S. maritime and trading rights with Europe and quickly became a war pitting the United States against Native Americans, who forged alliances with Britain and France.

war on terrorism. A series of military and legislative campaigns that began after the September 11, 2001, attacks on the United States.

wealth. The market value of all assets owned (such as homes, cars, artwork, jewelry, businesses, and savings and retirement accounts) minus any debts owed (such as credit card debts, mortgages, and college loans).

welfare. Policies and programs designed to support people in great financial need. Examples of forms of welfare are food stamps, Social Security benefits, Medicare, and Medicaid.

welfare fraud. The illegal use of deception to collect more funds than allowed from state welfare systems.

White flight. The movement of Whites from urban areas to suburbs in response to Black civil rights activism.

White normative structures. Norms and institutions that obscure the racial intent of laws, practices, and behaviors that preserve and (re)create societal benefits for White people, creating the illusion that White privilege is natural and normal.

White privilege. The advantage that White people have (over Blacks, Native Americans, Asians, Hispanics, and others) as the result of laws, practices, and behaviors that preserve and (re)create societal benefits for them.

white-collar crime. Crime, typically nonviolent, committed by business or government professionals; the motivation for such crime is often financial.

Whiteness studies. An interdisciplinary subfield of scholarship examining Whiteness and White privilege that includes contributions by literary theorists, legal scholars, anthropologists, historians, psychologists, and sociologists.

World War II. A major worldwide conflict (U.S. involvement 1941–45) that spanned Europe, Africa, Asia, and the Middle East.

INDEX